Essentials of
CORPORATE FINANCIAL
MANAGEMENT

Visit the *Essentials of Corporate Financial Management* Companion Website with Grade Tracker at **www.pearsoned.co.uk/arnold** to find valuable **student** learning material including:

- **Pre-** and **Post-tests**, with instant feedback and results, designed to help you track your progress and diagnose your strengths and weaknesses through the use of an online gradebook
- Regularly updated **Podcasts** on topical issues in Corporate Finance, easily downloadable to your PC or iPod/MP3 player for you to review at your own leisure
- A wide selection of **FT articles**, additional to those found in the book, to provide real-world examples of financial decision-making in practice
- **Excel spreadsheet examples** of many of the problems in the book demonstrating the calculations necessary to answer a problem successfully
- Interactive online **Flashcards** that will enable you to revise key terms and definitions
- **Weblinks** to relevant, specific Internet resources to facilitate in-depth independent research
- A searchable online **Glossary**

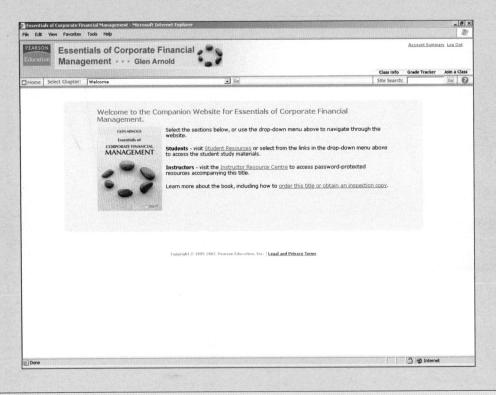

GLEN ARNOLD

BSc (Econ), PhD
University of Salford

Essentials of
CORPORATE FINANCIAL
MANAGEMENT

FT Prentice Hall
FINANCIAL TIMES

An imprint of **Pearson Education**
Harlow, England • London • New York • Boston • San Francisco • Toronto
Sydney • Tokyo • Singapore • Hong Kong • Seoul • Taipei • New Delhi
Cape Town • Madrid • Mexico City • Amsterdam • Munich • Paris • Milan

Pearson Education Limited
Edinburgh Gate
Harlow
Essex CM20 2JE
England

and Associated Companies throughout the world

Visit us on the World Wide Web at:
www.pearsoned.co.uk/arnold

First published 2007

ISBN-13: 978-0-273-70508-6
ISBN-10: 0-273-70508-3

British Library Cataloguing-in-Publication Data
A catalogue record for this book is available from the British Library

Library of Congress Cataloging-in-Publication Data
A catalog record for this book is available from the Library of Congress

10 9 8 7 6 5 4 3 2 1
11 10 09 08 07

Typeset in 9.5/11 Sabon by 30
Printed and bound by Mateu Cromo Artes Graficas, Spain

The publisher's policy is to use paper manufactured from sustainable forests.

To Terry Lucey, who encouraged and inspired me to write books

Brief contents

Contents

Supporting resources
Visit **www.pearsoned.co.uk/arnold** to find valuable online resources

Companion Website with Grade Tracker for students
- **Pre-** and **Post-tests**, with instant feedback and results, designed to help you track your progress and diagnose your strengths and weaknesses through the use of an online gradebook
- Regularly updated **Podcasts** on topical issues in Corporate Finance, easily downloadable to your PC or iPod/MP3 player for you to review at your own leisure
- A wide selection of **FT articles**, additional to those found in the book, to provide real-world examples of financial decision-making in practice
- **Excel spreadsheet examples** of many of the problems in the book demonstrating the calculations necessary to answer a problem successfully
- Interactive online **Flashcards** that will enable you to revise key terms and definitions
- **Weblinks** to relevant, specific Internet resources to facilitate in-depth independent research
- A searchable online **Glossary**

For instructors
- A downloadable **Lecturer's Guide** including answers to all the questions not already provided in the book as well as extra additional questions
- **Excel spreadsheet examples** of some of the problems in the book with answers in the Lecturer's Guide demonstrating the calculations necessary to answer a problem successfully
- Fully customisable and animated **PowerPoint slides** including a class test feature, developed to enliven presentations
- **TestGen testbank** software containing hundreds of questions for use in formal assessment both online and as paper tests

Also: The regularly maintained Companion Website provides the following features:

- Search tool to help locate specific items of content
- Online help and support to assist with website usage and troubleshooting

For more information please contact your local Pearson Education sales representative or visit **www.pearsoned.co.uk/arnold**

Preface

I am surprised, as well as grateful, for the way in which my textbook *Corporate Financial Management* has taken off. Despite its remarkable success it has become increasingly apparent that there is need for another book, one that supports a university course designed to cover the core topics of finance in 15 to 30 hours of lectures. Many courses in finance are only one semester long, and much of the content of *Corporate Financial Management*, now running to well over 1000 pages, cannot be covered in this space of time.

When starting this project I had a clear vision – the forming of which was helped by the comments made in a survey by over 70 corporate finance lecturers. This new book has to be different from the competition. Rather than skimming the surface of dozens of financial subjects I felt that the best approach would be to select the core topics and key concepts and deliver them with some depth. This allows the student to gain an understanding of lively debates within the field, where disagreements, alternative perspectives or placement of emphasis lead to discussion, rather than dulled acceptance.

It is important not to present a set of theories as though they are *the* truth, and there is only one way of running a business. Real life is too nuanced for that – and able MBA and under-graduates know it. Often there is a need for the assimilation of arguments from two sides of a debate, thinking them through, and arriving at one's own conclusions. Room for debate occurs across the field of finance: from whether to employ beta in risk adjustment, to the advantage of using payback as well as net present value for assessing investment projects; from whether dividend policy is irrelevant to shareholder wealth, to the practical usefulness of shareholder value analysis.

Despite assuming no prior knowledge of finance I hope the readers of the book will be empowered to enter into discussion about vital practical issues about the firm drawing on the frameworks of finance. It is designed to achieve this by building knowledge in a series of easily surmountable steps, to lead the student as painlessly as possible to a high level of competence. There is heavy emphasis relating the concepts to real business, with plenty of up-to-date examples, mostly drawn from extracts taken from the *Financial Times*.

As well as appealing to students studying a one-off course in finance within a more general business studies degree this book will, I hope, provide the foundation elements needed by those students who choose to go on to study more advanced finance.

Glen Arnold, September 2006

Guided Tour

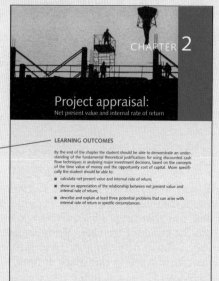

Learning outcomes introduce topics covered and summarise what you should have learnt by the end of the chapter.

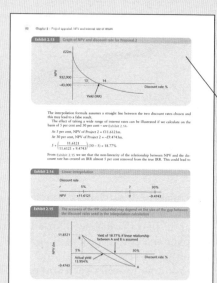

Exhibits provide explanations and demonstrations of mathematical concepts and techniques.

Articles from *Financial Times* feature throughout the book to illustrate the practical application of theoretical material.

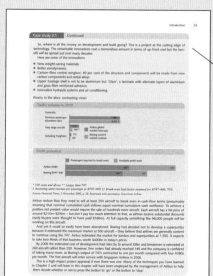

Case Studies from a variety of sources are used to demonstrate arguments in the chapter and provide a different dimension to an issue.

Further reading and websites sections point you to resources you can use to expand your knowledge.

Concluding comments round up the chapter themes.

Key points and concepts are at the end of each chapter and give an outline of the essential concepts covered. New concepts, jargon and equations are summarised for easy reference.

Self-review questions allow you to test your understanding and apply your knowledge. Answers to the questions can be found in Appendix VII at the end of the book.

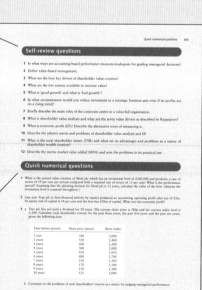

Quick numerical questions appear at the end of some chapter – again the answers appear in Appendix VII.

Questions and problems vary in difficulty. Some answers are provided in Appendix VII, others are reserved for the Lecturer's Guide thus allowing you to be assessed.

Assignments Are projects requiring you to investigate real-world practice in a firm and relate this to the concepts and techniques learnt in the chapter.

Acknowlegements

My thanks to the following for their help in the preparation of this book:

The international panel of reviewers for the major contribution they made to providing realism, balance and accuracy:

Heather Tarbert, Glasgow Caledonian University
Arif Khurshed, Manchester Business School, Manchester University
Morten Helbak, Nord-Trøndelag University College, Norway
Ronald Huisman, RSM Erasmus University Rotterdam
Gary Shea, St Andrews University
Poul Wolffsen, Roskilde University, Denmark
Javed Hussain, UCE Birmingham
Kadom Shubber, University of Westminster

The 96 finance directors who responded to a financial survey in 1997, for contributing to our understanding of modern financial practice.

The publishing team at Pearson Education, particularly Tim Parker, Stephanie Poulter, Julian Partridge, Justinia Seaman, Sylvia Edvinsson, Pauline Gillett, Kevin Ancient, Andrea Bannuscher, Kay Holman, Stephen Pepper, Lorna Cullen and Jane Ashley for their patience, professionalism and faith.

The *Financial Times*, *Investors Chronicle*, the London Stock Exchange and all those organisations and individuals acknowledged in the text, for allowing the use of their material.

We are grateful to the following to reproduce copyright material:

Cadbury Schweppes for an extract from 'Cadbury Schweppes 2003 Report and Accounts and Form 20F'; Exhibit 5.39 appeared in an article, which is reprinted with permission from Institutional Investor, Inc. It originally appeared in the Fall issue of the Journal of

Portfolio Management. It is illegal to make unauthorised copies of this Exhibit. For more details please visit www.iijournals.com. All rights Reserved. Chapter 10 Exhibit 10.2 and 10.6 from *The Financial Times Limited*, 10/11 October 2005, © 2006 Reuters. Reprinted with permission from Reuters. Reuters content is the intellectual property of Reuters or its third party content providers. Any copying, republication or redistribution of Reuters content is expressly prohibited without the prior written consent of Reuters. Reuters shall not be liable for any errors or delays in content, or for any actions taken in reliance thereon. Reuters and the Reuters Sphere Logo are registered trademarks of the Reuters group of companies around the world. For additional information about Reuters content and services, please visit Reuters website at www.reuters.com." License # REU-GC7544;

We are grateful to the Financial Times Limited for permission to reprint the following material:

Chapter 6 Exhibit 6.17 © *Financial Times*, 9 August 2005; Chapter 7 Exhibit 7.18 © *Financial Times*, 10 January 2006: Chapter 7 Exhibit 7.19 © *Financial Times*, 11/12 September 2004; Chapter 6 Exhibit 6.16 © *Financial Times*, 6 and 9 January 2006; Chapter 1 Profits fall 39% on scheduled flights, © *Financial Times*, 5 April 2000; Chapter 1 United airlines: The experiment that fell to earth © *Financial Times*, 18 March 2003; Chapter 1 Investors warn drugs industry of backlash over health crises, © *Financial Times*, 24 March 2003; Chapter 1 Forget how the crow flies, © *Financial Times*, 17 January 2004; Chapter 1 Milton Friedman – The long view, © *Financial Times*, 7 June 2003; Chapter 1 Homestyle Quantifies Deferral, © *Financial Times*, 14 March 2002; Chapter 1 Under-fire companies might find it's good to talk, © *Financial Times*, 17–18 January 2004; Chapter 1 Returns become new status symbol, © *Financial Times*, 8 March 2002; Chapter 2 Tesco to raise £1.7bn for further growth, © *Financial Times*, 14 January 2004; Chapter 6 Professional expenses prove a deterrent to maintaining stock market exposure, © *Financial Times*, 31 August 1999; Chapter 6 Corus Raises £300m for revival, © *Financial Times*, 13 November 2003; Chapter 6 Beware little devils hidden among the business angels, © *Financial Times*, 27 January 2004; Chapter 6 Banks replace management at Unipoly, ©*Financial Times*, 12 June 2001; Chapter 6 West Midlands to set up £60m enterprise fund, © *Financial Times*, 12 February 2004; Chapter 7 Photobition cautions on covenants, © *Financial Times*, 28 February 2001; Chapter 7 Natwest deletes overdraft clause, © *Financial Times*, 21 November 2000; Chapter 7 Branson wins £17m loan facility increase, © *Financial Times*, 12 June 2001; Chapter 7 Companies and regulators go on offensive in the global ratings game, © *Financial Times*, 5 July 2003; Chapter 7 Vital factor in surviving a slump, © *Financial Times*, 24 January 2002; Chapter 9 Big feet shrinking values, surreal numbers, © *Financial Times*, 2 June 2003; Chapter 9 Lex Column: Return and investment, © *Financial Times*, 7 May 1996; Chapter 9 Investment community piles on pressure for better returns, © *Financial Times*, 10 December 1999; Chapter 9 Shell all but withdraws from Angola, © *Financial Times*, 10 April 2004; Chapter 10 Hanson cuts asset value by £3.2bn, © *Financial Times*, 9 July 1996; Chapter 10 Canary Wharf reflects change of sentiment to unloved sector, © *Financial Times*, 26 March 2004; Chapter 10 Jefferson Smurfit, © *Financial Times*, 24 August 1995; Chapter 10 Paper groups see few signs of upturn, © *Financial Times*, 24 October 2003; Chapter 10 Why policymakers should take note, © *Financial Times*, 5 February 1996; Chapter 11 Goodbye Gearing, © *Financial Times*, 9 October 1995; Chapter 11 Glas Cymru launches bond campaign, © *Financial Times*, 9 April 2001; Chapter 11 Ntl lost 73,400 customers during rescue talks, © *Financial Times*, 12 June 2002; Chapter 11 Companies go back to basics in search for cash, © *Financial Times*, 1 October 2002; Chapter 12 Arc agrees to hand back £50m, © *Financial Times*, 23-24 November 2002; Chapter 12 Higher pay-out welcomed at Hanson, © *Financial Times*, 21 February 2003; Chapter 12 Lurid acquisitions lose their edge as the retro dividend makes a comeback, © *Financial Times*, 15 September 2004; Chapter 12 The dilemma of how best to share the wealth, © *Financial Times*, 17-18 July 2004; Chapter 12 The 'Quasi-Dividend' of a buy-back programme, © *Financial Times*, 2 October 2004; Case Study 1.1, © *Financial Times*, 18-19 June 2005; Exhibit 1.13, © *Financial Times*, 23 February 2005; Exhibit 6.2, © *Financial Times*, 20 July 2005; Exhibit 7.6, © *Financial Times*, 8 June 2005; Exhibit 7.15, © *Financial Times*, 8 February 2005; Exhibit 11.13, © *Financial Times*, 21 March 2005; Exhibit 12.4, © *Financial Times*, 2 May 2005; Exhibit 12.3, © *Financial Times*, 19 January 2005; Exhibit 12.9, © *Financial Times*, 3 March 2005;

In some instances we have been unable to trace the owners of copyright material, and we would appreciate any information that would enable us to do so.

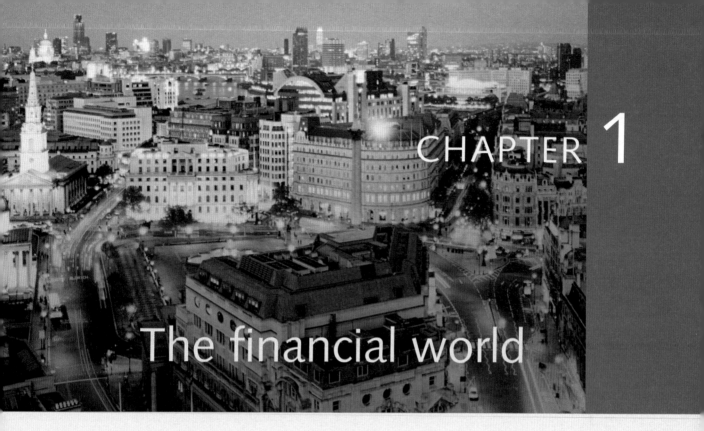

CHAPTER 1

The financial world

LEARNING OUTCOMES

At the end of this chapter the reader will have a balanced view of the purpose and value of the finance function, at both the corporate and the national level. More specifically, the reader should be able to:

- explain the role of the financial manager;

- detail the value of financial intermediaries;

- show an appreciation of the function of the major financial institutions and markets;

- describe alternative views on the purpose of the business and show the importance to any organisation of clarity on this point;

- describe the impact of the divorce of corporate ownership from day-to-day managerial control.

Introduction

Managers, at all levels, very quickly discover the need for a good working knowledge of finance. Those with ambitions to climb the corporate ladder find that the further they advance the more they need to understand the concepts and jargon of finance, both for internal decision making and external interaction with investors, bankers and the City. This message is not directed just at those who specialise in accounting or finance. Too many marketing directors and production directors have found themselves unable to follow boardroom (or even divisional) discussions because they are unfamiliar with financial language and the central ideas of corporate finance. It is clear that the imperatives of day-to-day management and the forming of sound long-term plans mean that all middle and senior managers must have a firm grasp of fundamental financial issues. Discussion throughout the modern organisation is mostly couched in financial terms: e.g. would we achieve a sufficient rate of return on an investment in that proposed new factory? What proportion of annual profits should we pay out as dividends? Should we take the risk of borrowing more money? How do you sell more shares in the company to allow it to expand? Finance is about hundreds of questions like this.

Because the language of modern business is largely financial, managers need to understand that language if they want to know what is going on, and to advance in their careers. Simply being able to read the *Financial Times* and other financial papers intelligently makes it worthwhile studying corporate finance, let alone the benefit of appreciating the workings of the corporate environment in which you may find yourself.

Before getting carried away with specific financial issues and technical detail, it is important to gain a broad perspective by looking at the fundamental questions and the place of finance in the overall scheme of things. Conveying this broad perspective is the main aim of this chapter.

What is corporate finance?

So, what are the key aspects of corporate finance you need to know? To illustrate the scope of the subject we can make use of a mini-case study drawn from a *Financial Times* article about Inmarsat, which, in the summer of 2005, floated on the London Stock Exchange (*see* **Case study 1.1**).

Case study 1.1   INMARSAT

Financial knowledge is crucial for Inmarsat's success

Shares in Inmarsat rose 18 per cent after the mobile satellite operator debuted on the London Stock Exchange, raising £354.6m in the UK's largest flotation this year that valued the company at £1.12bn.

The company, whose controlling shareholders are Apax Partners and Permira, the private equity groups, will use the funds to reduce its net debt from $1.5bn to $860m (£475m) and to expand its core data and voice services markets.

The offering of 150m new shares represents 33 per cent of the 456.7m shares in issue. The offer price of 245p was at the top end of the price range of 215p to 245p and the offer was 10 times oversubscribed.

None of the shareholders is selling their stake in the company at its market debut.

John Hyman, head of European equity capital markets at Morgan Stanley, one of the joint investment banks to have managed the sale, said: "It demonstrated that investors felt this company had a unique set of attributes – long-term growth, a visible revenue stream, high free cash flow and good management. You have to go back three to four years to find an IPO in London that has been as successful."

In June, the company said it would return at least half its free annual cash flow as dividends.

Last year, Inmarsat had revenue of $480.7m and operating profit of $159.1m.

More than half of its revenues derive from providing customers at sea with phone, fax and internet services. Customers include the British Ministry of Defence, the BBC, CNN, British Airways and Shell.

JPMorgan, Cazenove, Lehman Brothers, Merrill Lynch and Morgan Stanley have managed the sale.

The shares closed 43p higher at 288p yesterday.

Source: Malini Guha, *Financial Times*, 18/19 June 2005. Reprinted with permission.

There are four vital financial issues facing management:

What type of finance should we raise?

In the past the Inmarsat business has been supported by money injected by private equity investors, such as Apax Partners and Permira. These are organisations that invest in the shares of non-stock-market-listed companies. Now Inmarsat has turned to the London Stock Exchange (LSE), where it has already raised £354.6m by selling new shares. Also, being listed on the LSE will enhance its ability to raise more capital in the future, because of the additional credibility that flows from being on the exchange. The modern financial world provides a wide range of options for companies when it comes to raising finance to allow growth. The array of choice can be dizzying so Chapters 6 and 7 provide some sort of order, describing the characteristics of the main forms of finance and their relative advantages and drawbacks. Chapter 6 guides the reader through the various ways in which a company can raise finance by selling shares. Chapter 7 discusses the benefits and dangers of a variety of forms of debt finance, including using bank loans and overdrafts and bond markets.

In what projects are we going to invest our shareholders' money?

The directors of Inmarsat believe they have a fantastic investment opportunity in supplying telecommunication services to customers who cannot access normal mobile phone networks. It uses a system of Earth-orbiting satellites to provide phone, fax and internet services for those in out-of-the-way places, e.g. soldiers in war zones are given regular contact with their families, the International Red Cross can coordinate its activities and sailors can stay in touch. It intends to invest heavily in the next generation of satellites to keep one step ahead of the competition by providing ever more valuable services to customers. It has raised £354.6m to fulfil its ambitions. This money has come from people and institutions purchasing newly created shares in Inmarsat. Sound financial techniques are needed to make a judgement on whether it is worth committing the large sums required to build up its coverage and technical capability. Furthermore, financial tools will be needed to decide such questions as whether it is best for Inmarsat to build the satellites in-house or to purchase them from another company. There are dozens of investment choices to be made, e.g. is it better to spend hundreds of millions creating a marketing and customer service organisation to supply the end-user directly, or continue supplying via its current 440 independent service providers, leaving Inmarsat to concentrate on providing a 'wholesale' service? Three chapters of this book are devoted to describing proven approaches adopted by all leading corporations in deciding where to concentrate the firm's financial resources (Chapters 2, 3 and 4). This class of decision is sometimes referred to as capital expenditure, 'capex' for short, and the process is referred to as capital budgeting.

How do we create and measure shareholder value?

Value creation by a corporation, or by individual business units within a large firm, is about much more than deciding whether to invest in specific projects. Inmarsat will need to consider a number of strategic implications of its actions, such as: what is the current and likely future return on capital in the industries that it may choose to enter? Will Inmarsat have a competitive edge over its rivals in those industries? Value-based management brings together a number of disciplines, such as strategy and resource management, and draws on the analytical techniques developed in the finance field to help judge the extent of value creation from current operations, or from new strategic and tactical moves (covered in Chapter 9). At the centre of value-based management is recognition of the need to produce a return on capital devoted to an activity commensurate with the risk. Establishing the minimum required return is the 'cost of capital' issue – the logic behind this calculation is discussed in Chapter 8. Being able to value business units, companies and shares is a very useful skill. Possessors of this skill can avoid overpaying when buying an established business. They also have insight into how stock market investors value the manager's company. Inmarsat, when preparing for its stock market flotation, employed individuals with knowledge of how to price its shares, which was crucial in establishing a healthy market for them. Chapter 10 covers the main valuation approaches used today.

A further key value decision is how much of the annual profit to keep in the business to support investment and how much to pay out to shareholders. Is a 50:50 split about right? Or, how about keeping just 30 per cent in the company and paying the other 70 per cent in dividends? This is not an easy decision, but someone has to make it. Chapter 12 outlines the key considerations.

How do we manage risk?

Inmarsat is faced with many operational risks. Perhaps it will fail to achieve the rise in mobile phone or internet customers it projects. Perhaps its new satellites will be superseded by cheaper, faster systems developed by competitors a couple of years down the line. There are some risks that firms have to accept, including these operational risks. However, there are many others that can be reduced by taking a few simple steps. For example, the risk of a rise in interest rates increasing the cost of borrowings, thus wiping out profits, can be reduced/eliminated in various ways, for example, by choosing a less risky capital structure. That is, the proportion of finance raised from debt is lowered while that from share owners is raised. Chapter 11 discusses this issue alongside a number of other factors to be taken into account when considering how much debt to take on.

I hope I have convinced you that the finance function is a vital one, both within an individual organisation and for society as a whole. It is also a fascinating area of study, especially given that the ever-dynamic financial markets are constantly innovating. They are also subject to sudden shocks. Almost every day the television news reports a dramatic financial story, whether it is in the stock market, loan markets or a corporate collapse due to a poor financial structure. To give some idea of the importance of finance in the UK it is worth reflecting on the fact that the financial services industry now accounts for a larger proportion of employees and national output than the whole of the manufacturing industry.

We now move on to look in more detail at the role and value of the finance function. This will be followed by a brief description of the different financial markets, from money markets to currency markets. Finally, this chapter considers the most fundamental question facing anyone trying to make decisions within an organisation – what is the objective of the business? This must be addressed before we can use the financial tools provided in the rest of the book.

A simple model of the interactions between the financial manager and the capital markets

To be able to carry on a business a company needs real assets. These real assets may be tangible, such as buildings, plant, machinery, vehicles and so on. Alternatively a firm may invest in intangible real assets, for example patents, expertise, licensing rights, etc. To obtain these real assets corporations sell financial claims to raise money; to lenders a bundle of rights are sold within a loan contract, to shareholders rights over the ownership of a company are sold as well as the right to receive a proportion of profits produced. The financial manager has the task of both raising finance by selling financial claims and advising on the use of those funds within the business. This is illustrated in Exhibit 1.1.

In order to raise finance, knowledge is needed of the financial markets and the way in which they operate. To raise share (equity) capital, awareness of the rigours and processes involved in 'taking a new company to market' might be useful. For instance, what is the role of an issuing house? What services do brokers, accountants, solicitors, etc. provide to a company wishing to float? Once a company is quoted on a stock market it will be useful to know about ways of raising additional equity capital.

If the firm does not wish to have its shares quoted on an exchange perhaps an investigation needs to be made into the possibility of raising money through the private equity industry, where finance is available for those companies where the owner(s) is willing to sell a portion of the company's shares to outsiders who might bring managerial expertise as well as money.

| Exhibit 1.1 | The flow of cash between capital markets and the firm's operations |

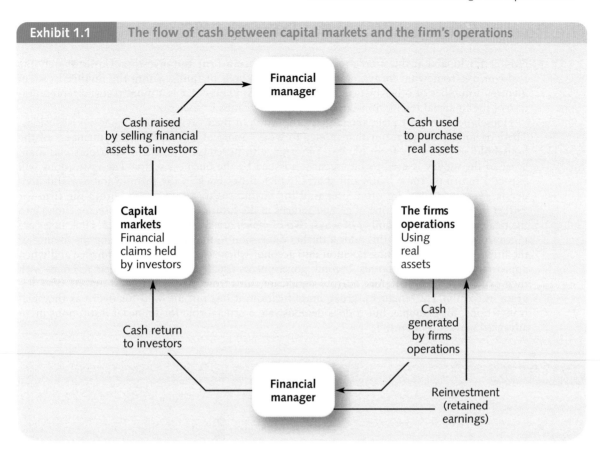

Understanding how shares are priced and what it is that shareholders are looking for when sacrificing present consumption to make an investment could help the firm to tailor its strategy, operations and financing decisions to suit its owners. These, and dozens of other equity finance questions, are part of the remit of the finance expert within the firm (all other managers need a working knowledge of these issues too).

Another major source of finance comes from banks. Understanding the operation of banks and what concerns them when lending to a firm may enable you to present your case better, to negotiate improved terms and obtain finance which fits the cash flow patterns of the firm. Then there are ways of borrowing which bypass banks. Bonds could be issued either domestically or internationally. Medium-term notes, commercial paper, leasing, hire purchase and factoring are other possibilities (all described in Chapter 7).

Once a knowledge has been gained of each of these alternative financial instruments and of the operation of their respective financial markets, then the financial manager has to consider the issue of the correct balance between the different types. What proportion of debt to equity? What proportion of short-term finance to long-term finance and so on?

Perhaps you can already appreciate that the finance function is far from a boring 'bean-counting' role. It is a dynamic function with a constant need for up-to-date and relevant knowledge. The success or failure of the entire business may rest on the quality of the interaction between the firm and the financial markets. The financial manager stands at the interface between the two.

Decisions also need to be made concerning how much to invest in real assets and which specific projects to undertake. Managers need knowledge of both analytical techniques to aid these sorts of decisions and the influence of a wide variety of factors that might have some impact on the wisdom of proceeding with a particular investment. These range from corporate strategy and budgeting restrictions to culture and the commitment of individuals likely to be called upon to support an activity.

The flow of funds and financial intermediation

Exhibit 1.1 looked at the simple relationship between a firm and investors. Unfortunately the real world is somewhat more complicated and the flow of funds within the financial system involves a number of other institutions and agencies. Exhibit 1.2 is a more realistic representation of the financial interactions between different groups in society.

Households generally place the largest proportion of their savings with financial institutions. These organisations then put that money to work. Some of it is lent back to members of the household sector in the form of, say, a mortgage to purchase a house, or as a personal loan. Some of the money is used to buy securities issued by the business sector. The institutions will expect a return on these loans and shares, which flows back in the form of interest and dividends. However, they are often prepared for businesses to retain profit within the firm for further investment in the hope of greater returns in the future. The government sector enters into the financial system in a number of ways, two of which are shown in Exhibit 1.2. First, taxes are taken from businesses and this adds a further dimension to the choices concerning the finance of the firm – for example, taking taxation into account when selecting sources of finance and when approving investment proposals. Second, governments usually fail to match their revenues with their expenditure and therefore borrow significant sums from the financial institutions. The diagram in Exhibit 1.2 remains a gross simplification; it has not allowed for overseas financial transactions, for example, but it does demonstrate a crucial role for financial institutions in an advanced market economy.

| Exhibit 1.2 | The flow of funds and financial intermediation |

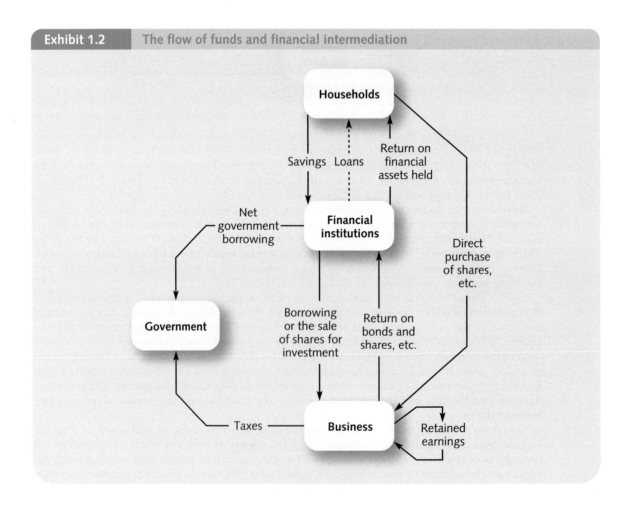

Primary investors

Typically the household sector is in financial surplus. This sector contains the savers of society. It is these individuals who become the main providers of funds used for investment in the business sector. Primary investors tend to prefer to exchange their cash for financial assets which (a) allow them to get their money back quickly should they need to (with low transaction cost of doing so) and (b) have a high degree of certainty over the amount they will receive back. That is, primary investors like high liquidity and low risk. Lending directly to a firm with a project proposal to build a North Sea oil platform which will not be sold until five years have passed is not a high-liquidity and low-risk investment. However, putting money into a sock under the bed is high-liquidity and low-risk (if we exclude the possibility of the risk of sock theft).

Ultimate borrowers

In our simplified model the ultimate borrowers are in the business sector. These firms are trying to maximise the wealth generated by their activities. To do this companies need to invest in real buildings, equipment and other assets, often for long periods of time. The firms, in order to serve their social function, need to attract funds for use over many years. Also, these funds are to be put at risk, sometimes very high risk. (Here we are using the term 'borrower' broadly to include all forms of finance, even 'borrowing' by selling shares.)

Conflict of preferences

We have a conflict of preferences between the primary investors wanting low-cost liquidity and certainty, and the ultimate borrowers wanting long-term risk-bearing capital. A further complicating factor is that savers usually save on a small scale, £100 here or £200 there, whereas businesses are likely to need large sums of money. Imagine some of the problems that would occur in a society that did not have any financial intermediaries. Here, lending and share buying will occur only as a result of direct contact and negotiation between two parties. If there were no organised market where financial securities could be sold on to other investors, the fund provider, once committed, would be trapped in an illiquid investment. Also, the costs that the two parties might incur in searching to find each other in the first place might be considerable. Following contact a thorough agreement would need to be drawn up to safeguard the investor, and additional expense would be incurred obtaining information to monitor the firm and its progress. In sum, the obstacles to putting saved funds to productive use would lead many to give up and to retain their cash. Those that do persevere will demand exceptionally high rates of return from the borrowers to compensate them for poor liquidity, risk, search costs, agreement costs and monitoring costs. This will mean that few firms will be able to justify investments because they cannot obtain those high levels of return when the funds are invested in real assets. As a result few investments take place and the wealth of society fails to grow. Exhibit 1.3 shows (by the top arrow) little money flowing from saving into investment.

The introduction of financial intermediaries

The problem of under-investment can be alleviated greatly by the introduction of financial institutions (e.g. banks) and financial markets (e.g. a stock exchange). Their role is to facilitate the flow of funds from primary investors to ultimate borrowers at a low cost. They do this by solving the conflict of preferences. There are two types of financial intermediation: the first is an agency or brokerage-type operation which brings together lenders and firms; the second is an asset-transforming-type of intermediation, in which the conflict is resolved by creating intermediate securities which have the risk, liquidity and volume characteristics that the investors prefer. The financial institution raises money by offering these securities, and then uses the acquired funds to purchase primary securities issued by firms.

Exhibit 1.3   Savings into investment in an economy without financial intermediaries

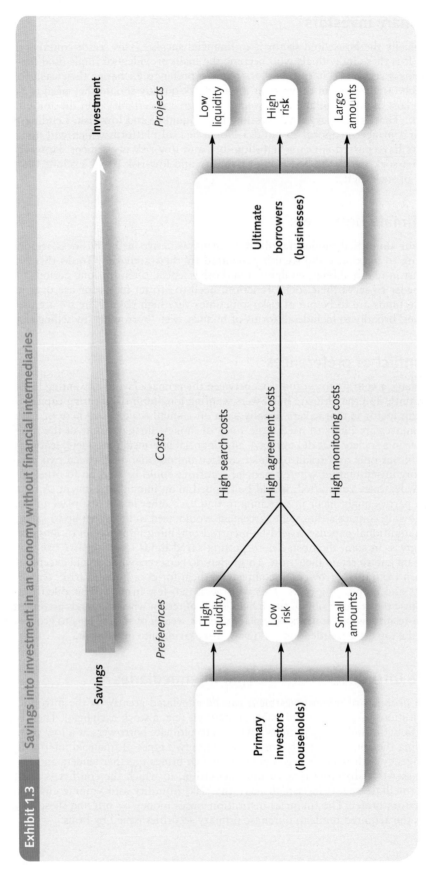

Brokers

At its simplest an intermediary is a 'go-between', someone who matches up a provider of finance with a user of funds. This type of intermediary is particularly useful for reducing the search costs for both parties. Stockbrokers, for example, make it easy for investors wanting to buy shares in a newly floated company. Brokers may also have some skill at collecting information on a firm and monitoring its activities, saving the investor time. They also act as middlemen when an investor wishes to sell to another, thus enhancing the liquidity of the fund providers. Another example is the Post Office, which enables individuals to lend to the UK government in a convenient and cheap manner by buying National Savings certificates or Premium Bonds.

Asset transformers

Intermediaries, by creating a completely new security, the intermediate security, increase the opportunities available to savers, encouraging them to invest and thus reducing the cost of finance for the productive sector. The transformation function can act in a number of different ways.

Risk transformation

For example, instead of an individual lending directly to a business with a great idea, such as digging a tunnel under the English Channel, a bank creates a deposit account or current account with relatively low risk for the investor's savings. Lending directly to the firm, the saver would demand compensation for the probability of default on the loan and therefore the business would have to pay a very high rate of interest, which would inhibit investment. The bank acting as an intermediary creates a special kind of security called a bank account agreement. The intermediary then uses the funds attracted by the new financial asset to buy a security issued by the tunnel owner (the primary security) when it obtains long-term debt capital. Because of the extra security that a lender has by holding a bank account as a financial asset rather than by making a loan direct to a firm, the lender is prepared to accept a lower rate of interest and the ultimate borrower obtains funds at a relatively low cost. The bank is able to reduce its risk exposure to any one project by diversifying its loan portfolio among a number of firms. It can also reduce risk by building up expertise in assessing and monitoring firms and their associated risk. Another example of risk transformation is when unit or investment trusts (see later in this chapter) take savers' funds and spread these over a wide range of company shares.

Maturity (liquidity) transformation

The fact that a bank lends long term for a risky venture does not mean that the primary lender is subjected to illiquidity. Liquidity is not a problem because banks maintain sufficient cash funds to meet their liabilities when they arise. You can walk into a bank and take the money from your account at short notice because the bank, given its size, exploits economies of scale and anticipates that only a small fraction of its customers will withdraw their money on any one day. Banks and building societies play an important role in borrowing 'short' and lending 'long'.

Volume transformation

Many institutions gather small amounts of money from numerous savers and repackage these sums into larger bundles for investment in the business sector. Apart from the banks and building societies, unit trusts are important here. It is uneconomic for an investor with, say, £50 per month, who wants to invest in shares, to buy small quantities periodically. Unit trusts gather together hundreds of individuals' monthly savings and invest them in a broad range of shares, thereby exploiting economies in transaction costs.

Intermediaries' economies of scale

The intermediary is able to accept lending to (and investing in shares of) companies at a relatively low rate of return because of the economies of scale enjoyed compared with the primary investor. These economies of scale include:

(a) *Efficiencies in gathering information* on the risk of lending to a particular firm. Individuals do not have access to the same data sources or expert analysis.

(b) *Risk spreading* Intermediaries are able to spread funds across a large number of borrowers and thereby reduce overall risk. Individual investors may be unable to do this.

(c) *Transaction costs* They are able to reduce the search, agreement and monitoring costs that would be incurred by savers and borrowers in a direct transaction. Banks, for example, are convenient, safe locations with standardised types of securities. Savers do not have to spend time examining the contract they are entering upon when, say, they open a bank account. How many of us read the small print when we opened a bank account?

The reduced information costs, convenience and passed-on benefits from the economies of operating on a large scale mean that primary investors are motivated to place their savings with intermediaries.

Financial markets

A financial market, such as a stock exchange, has two aspects; there is the *primary market* where funds are raised from investors by the firm, and there is the *secondary market* in which investors buy and sell shares, bonds, etc. between each other. The securities sold into the primary market are generally done so on the understanding that repayment will not be made for many years, if ever. This would mean that the holder is trapped in that investment if it were not for the existence of the secondary market; it is highly beneficial for the original buyer to be able to sell on to other investors. In this way the firm achieves its objective of raising finance that will stay in the firm for a lengthy period and the investor has retained the ability to liquidate (turn into cash) a holding by selling to another investor. In addition a well-regulated exchange encourages investment by reducing search, agreement and monitoring costs – see Exhibit 1.4.

The financial system

To assist with orientating the reader within the financial system and to carry out more jargon busting, a brief outline of the main financial services sectors and markets is given here.

The institutions

The banking sector

Retail banks

Put at its simplest, the retail banks take (small) deposits from the public which are repackaged and lent to businesses and households. This is generally high-volume and low-value business that contrasts with wholesale banking which is low volume but each transaction is for high value. The distinction between retail and wholesale banks has become blurred over recent years as the large institutions have diversified their operations. The retail banks operate nationwide branch networks and a subset of banks provide a cheque clearance system (transferring money from one account to another) – these are the *clearing* banks. The five largest UK clearing banks are Barclays, Lloyds TSB, Royal Bank of Scotland (including NatWest), HSBC and HBOS group (including Bank of Scotland and Halifax). Loans, overdrafts and mortgages are the main forms of retail bank lending. The trend has been for retail banks to

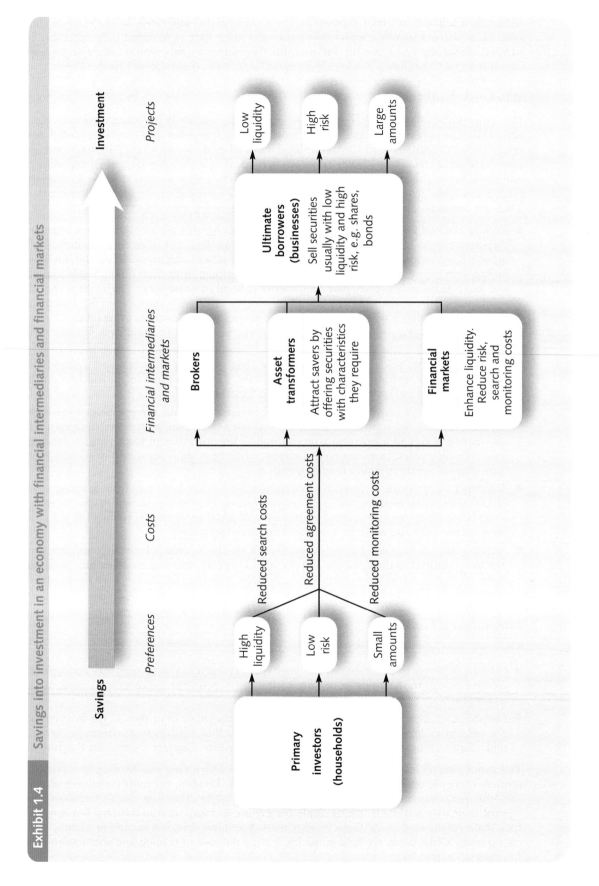

Exhibit 1.4 Savings into investment in an economy with financial intermediaries and financial markets

reduce their reliance on retail deposits and raise more wholesale funds from the money markets. They also get together with other banks if a large loan is required by a borrower (say £150m) rather than provide the full amount themselves as this would create an excessive exposure to one customer – this is called a syndicated loan, discussed in Chapter 7.

Wholesale banks

The terms wholesale bank, merchant bank and investment bank are often used interchangeably. There are subtle differences but for most practical purposes they can be regarded as the same. These institutions tend to deal in large sums of money – at least £250,000 – although some have set up retail arms. They concentrate on dealing with other large organisations, corporations, institutional investors and governments. While they undertake some lending their main focus is on generating commission income by providing advice and facilitating deals. There are five main areas of activity:

- *Raising external finance for companies* These banks provide advice and arrange finance for corporate clients. Sometimes they provide loans themselves, but often they assist the setting up of a bank syndicate or make arrangements with other institutions. They will advise and assist a firm issuing a bond, they have expertise in helping firms float on the Stock Exchange and make rights issues. They may 'underwrite' a bond or share issue. (This means that they will buy any part of the issue not taken up by other investors – *see* Chapter 6.) This assures the corporation that it will receive the funds it needs for its investment programme.

- *Broking and dealing* They act as agents for the buying and selling of securities on the financial markets, including shares, bonds and Eurobonds. Some also have market-making arms, which quote prices at which they are willing to buy or sell from, say, a shareholder, thus assisting the operation of secondary markets. They also trade in the markets on their own account and assist companies with export finance.

- *Fund management (asset management)* The investment banks offer services to rich individuals who lack the time or expertise to deal with their own investment strategies. They also manage unit and investment trusts as well as the portfolios of some pension funds and insurance companies. In addition corporations often have short-term cash flows which need managing efficiently (treasury management).

- *Assistance in corporate restructuring* Merchant banks earn large fees from advising acquirers on mergers and assisting with the merger process. They also gain by helping target firms avoid being taken over too cheaply. Corporate disposal programmes (selling off a division, for example) may also need the services of an investment bank.

- *Assisting risk management using derivatives* Risk can be reduced through hedging strategies using futures, options, swaps and the like. However, this is a complex area with large room for error and terrible penalties if a mistake is made. The banks may have specialist knowledge to offer in this area.

International banks

There are two types of international banking:

- *Foreign banking* transactions in the host country currency with overseas residents and companies, e.g. transactions in sterling with non-UK residents (lending/borrowing, etc.) by UK banks.

- *Eurocurrency banking* for transactions in a currency other than that of the host country, e.g. yen transactions in Canada. Thus for UK banks this involves transactions in currencies other than sterling with both residents and non-residents (Chapter 7 considers this further).

The major part of international banking these days is borrowing and lending in foreign currencies. There are over 470 non-UK banks operating in London, the most prominent of which are American, German, Swiss and Japanese. Their initial function was mainly to provide services for their own nationals, for example for export and import transactions, but nowadays their main emphasis is in the Eurocurrency market and international securities (shares, bonds, etc.) trading. Often funds are held in the UK for the purpose of trading and speculation on the foreign exchange market.

Building societies

Building societies collect funds from millions of savers by enticing them to put their money in interest-bearing accounts. The vast majority of that deposited money is then lent to people wishing to buy a home – in the form of a mortgage. Thus, they take in short-term deposits and they lend money for long periods, usually for 25 years. More recently building societies have diversified their sources of finance (e.g. using the wholesale financial markets) and increased the range of services they offer.

Finance houses[1]

Finance houses are responsible for the financing of hire purchase agreements and other instalment credit, for example, leasing. If you buy a large durable good such as a car or a washing machine you often find that the sales assistant also tries to get you interested in taking the item on credit, so you pay for it over a period of, say, three years. It is usually not the retailer that provides the finance for the credit. The retailer usually works in conjunction with a finance house, which pays the retailer the full purchase price of the good and therefore becomes the owner. You, the customer, get to use the good, but in return you have to make regular payments to the finance house, including interest. Under a **hire purchase** agreement, when you have made enough payments you will become the owner. Under **leasing**, the finance house retains ownership (for more detail see Chapter 7). Finance houses also provide **factoring** services – providing cash to firms in return for receiving income from the firms' debtors when they pay up. Most of the large finance houses are subsidiaries of the major conglomerate banks. The size of the market is in the region of £25bn (new finance provided by Finance and Leasing Association members to companies each year).

Long-term savings institutions

Pension funds

Pension funds are set up to provide pensions for members. For example, the University Superannuation Scheme (USS), to which university lecturers belong, takes about 6.35 per cent of working members' salaries each month and puts it into the fund. In addition the employing organisation pays money into the scheme. When a member retires the USS will pay a pension. Between the time of making a contribution and retirement, which may be decades, the pension trustees oversee the management of the fund. They may place some or all of the fund with specialist investment managers. This is a particularly attractive form of saving because of the generous tax relief provided. The long time horizon of the pension business means that large sums are built up and available for investment – currently around £800bn in the UK funds. A typical allocation of a fund is:

- 30–40 per cent in UK shares;
- 20–30 per cent in overseas company shares;
- 10–15 per cent lending to the UK government by buying bonds and bills;
- 10 per cent in index-linked government bonds (gilts);
- 5–15 per cent other (e.g. property, cash and overseas bonds).

Insurance funds

Insurance companies engage in two types of activity:

- *General insurance* This is insurance against specific contingencies such as fire, theft, accident, generally for a one-year period. The money collected in premiums is mostly held in financial assets which are relatively short term and liquid so that short-term commitments can be met.

[1] The term finance house is also used for broadly based financial-service companies carring out a wide variety of financial activities from share brokerage to corporate lending. However, we will confine the term to instalment credit and related services.

- *Life assurance* With *term assurance*, your life is assured for a specified period. If you die, your beneficiaries get a payout. If you live, you get nothing at the end of the period. With *whole-of-life policies*, the insurance company pays a capital sum upon death whenever this occurs. *Endowment* policies are more interesting from a financial systems perspective because they act as a savings vehicle as well as cover against death. The premium will be larger but after a number of years have passed the insurance company pays a substantial sum of money even if you are still alive. The life company has to take the premiums paid over, say, 10 or 25 years, and invest them wisely to satisfy its commitment to the policy holder. Millions of UK house buyers purchase with an endowment mortgage. They simply pay interest to the lender (e.g. a building society) while also placing premiums into an endowment fund. The hope is that after 25 years or so the value of the accumulated fund will equal or be greater than the capital value of the loan.

Life assurance companies also provide *annuities*. Here a policy holder pays an initial lump sum and in return receives regular payments in subsequent years. They have also moved into personal pensions.

Life assurance companies have over £900bn under management. A typical fund allocation is:

- 30–50 per cent UK shares;
- 20 per cent lending to the UK government;
- 10 per cent property;
- 10–15 per cent overseas securities;
- 5–10 per cent other.

The risk spreaders

These institutions allow small savers a stake in a large diversified portfolio.

Unit trusts

Unit trusts are 'open-ended' funds, so the size of the fund and the number of units depends on the amount of money investors wish to put into the fund. If a fund of one million units suddenly doubled in size because of an inflow of investor funds it would become a fund of two million units through the creation and selling of more units. The buying and selling prices of the units are determined by the value of the fund. So if a two-million unit fund is invested in £2m worth of shares in the UK stock market, the value of each unit will be £1. If, over a period, the value of the shares rises to £3m, the units will be worth £1.50 each. Unit holders sell units back to the managers of the unit trust if they want to liquidate their holding. The manager would then either sell the units to another investor or sell some of the underlying investments to raise cash to pay the unit holder. The units are usually quoted at two prices depending on whether you are buying (higher) or selling. There is also usually an initial charge and an ongoing management charge for running the fund. Trustees supervise the funds to safeguard the interests of unit holders but employ managers to make the investment decisions.

There is a wide choice of unit trusts (over 1,000) specialising in different types of investments ranging from Japanese shares to privatised European companies. Of the £250bn invested in unit trusts and their cousins, OEICs, 50–60 per cent is devoted to UK company securities, with the remainder mostly devoted to overseas company securities. Instruments similar to unit trusts are called mutual funds in other countries.

Investment trusts

Investment trusts differ from unit trusts by virtue of the fact that they are companies (rather than trusts!) able to issue shares and other securities. Investors can purchase these securities when the investment trust is first launched or purchase shares in the secondary market from other investors. These are known as closed-end funds because the company itself is closed to new investors – if you wished to invest your money you would go to an existing investor (via a broker) and not buy from the company. Investment trusts usually spread the investors' funds across a range of other companies' shares. They are also more inclined to invest in a broader range of assets than unit trusts – even property and shares not listed on a stock market. Approximately one-half of the money devoted to UK investment trusts (£60bn) is put into UK securities, with the remainder placed in overseas securities. The managers of these funds are able to borrow in order to invest. This has the effect of increasing returns to shareholders when things go well. Correspondingly, if the value of the underlying investments falls, the return to shareholders falls even more, because of the obligation to meet interest charges.

Open-ended investment companies (OEICs)

Open-ended investment companies are hybrid risk-spreading instruments which allow an investment in an open-ended fund. Designed to be more flexible and transparent than either investment or unit trusts, OEICs have just one price. However, as with unit trusts, OEICs can issue more shares, in line with demand from investors, and they can borrow.[2]

The markets

The money markets

The money markets are wholesale markets (usually involving transactions of £500,000 or more) which enable borrowing on a short-term basis (less than one year). The banks are particularly active in this market – both as lenders and as borrowers. Large corporations, local government bodies and non-banking financial institutions also lend when they have surplus cash and borrow when short of money.

The bond markets

A bond is merely a document that sets out the borrower's promise to pay sums of money in the future – usually regular interest plus a capital amount upon the maturity of the bond. These are long-dated securities (in excess of one year) issued by a variety of organisations including governments and corporations. The UK bond markets are over three centuries old and during that time they have developed very large and sophisticated primary and secondary sub-markets encompassing gilts (UK government bonds), corporate bonds, local authority bonds and Eurobonds, among others. Bonds as a source of finance for firms will be examined in Chapter 7.

The foreign exchange markets (Forex or FX)

The foreign exchange markets are the markets in which one currency is exchanged for another. They include the spot market, where currencies are bought and sold for 'immediate' delivery (in reality, one or two days later) and the *forward* markets, where the deal is agreed now to exchange currencies at some fixed point in the future. Also currency *futures* and *options* and other Forex derivatives are employed to hedge risk and to speculate.

The share markets

All major economies now have share markets. For UK companies and for hundreds of overseas companies the London Stock Exchange is an important potential source of long-term equity (ownership) capital. Firms can raise finance in the primary market by a new issue, a rights issue, open offer, etc., either in the main London market (the Official List), or on the Alternative Investment Market. Subsequently investors are able to buy and sell to each other on the very active secondary market. Chapter 6 examines stock markets and the raising of equity capital.

---

[2] There is much more on unit trusts, investment trusts and OEICs in G.C. Arnold (2004), *The Financial Times Guide to Investing* (Harlow: FT Prentice Hall).

The derivative markets

A derivative is a financial instrument derived from other financial securities or some other underlying asset. For example, a future is the right to buy something (e.g. currency, shares, bond) at some date in the future at an agreed price. This *right* becomes a saleable derived financial instrument. The performance of the derivative depends on the behaviour of the underlying asset. Companies can use these markets for the management and transfer of risk. They can be used to reduce risk (hedging) or to speculate. Euronext.liffe trades options and futures in shares, bonds and interest rates. This used to be the only one of the markets listed here to have a trading floor where face-to-face dealing took place on an open outcry system (traders shouting and signalling to each other, face to face in a trading pit, the price at which they are willing to buy and sell). Now all the financial markets (money, bond, Forex, derivative and share markets) are conducted using computers (and telephones) from isolated trading rooms located in the major financial institutions. In the derivative markets a high proportion of trades take place on what is called the over-the-counter (OTC) market rather than on a regulated exchange. The OTC market flexibility allows the creation of tailor-made derivatives to suit a client's risk situation.

The objective of the firm

Cadbury Schweppes, widely regarded as one of the best-managed companies in the world, has a clear statement of its objective in the 2005 Report and Accounts – *see* **Case study 1.2**. Notice that there is not a confusion of objectives (as there is in many companies) with no one knowing which of a long list of desirable outcomes is the dominant purpose of the firm. Cadbury Schweppes does not confuse the objective with the strategy to be employed to achieve the objective. Many managerial teams believe that it is their objective to operate within a particular market or take particular actions. They seem unable to distinguish market positions or actions from the ultimate purpose for the existence of the organisation. This will lead not only to poor strategic decisions but frequently makes intelligent financial decisions impossible.

This book is all about practical decision making in the real world. When people have to make choices in the harsh environment in which modern businesses have to operate, it is necessary to be clear about the purpose of the organisation; to be clear about what objective is set for management to achieve. A multitude of small decisions are made every day; more importantly, every now and then major strategic commitments of resources are made. It is imperative that the management teams are aware of, respect and contribute to the fundamen-

---

Case study 1.2	Cadbury Schweppes

The first goal and overarching objective is to deliver superior shareowner returns.

2004–7 Goals

1 Deliver superior shareowner performance
2 Profitably and significantly increase global confectionery share
3 Profitably secure and grow regional beverages share
4 Ensure our capabilities are best in class
5 Reinforce reputation with employees and society

Our overarching objective of superior shareholder performance is supported by continued execution of these goals.

Value Based Management remains fundamental to our strategic and operational processes. It enables us to identify the generators of economic profit, and thus sustainable long-term value growth, within our business. (Value based management is explained in Chapter 8.)

Source: Cadbury Schweppes Reports and Accounts 2005. Reprinted with permission.

tal objective of the firm in all these large and small decisions. Imagine the chaos and confusion that could result from the opposite situation where there is no clear, accepted objective. The outcome of each decision, and the direction of the firm, will become random and rudderless. One manager on one occasion will decide to grant long holidays and a shorter working week, believing that the purpose of the institution's existence is to benefit employees, while on another occasion a different manager sacks 'surplus' staff and imposes lower wages, seeing the need to look after the owner's interests as a first priority. So, before we can make decisions in the field of finance we need to establish what it is we are trying to achieve.

You have probably encountered elsewhere the question, 'In whose interests is the firm run?' This is a political and philosophical as well as an economic question and many books have been written on the subject. Here we will provide a brief overview of the debate because of its central importance to making choices in finance. The list of interested parties in Exhibit 1.5 could be extended, but no doubt you can accept the point from this shortened version that there are a number of claimants on a firm.

Sound financial management is necessary for the survival of the firm and for its growth. Therefore, all of these stakeholders, to some extent, have an interest in seeing sensible financial decisions being taken. Many business decisions do not involve a conflict between the objectives of each of the stakeholders. However, there are occasions when someone has to decide which claimants are to have their objectives maximised, and which are merely to be satisfied – that is, given just enough of a return to induce them to make their contributions.

There are some strong views held on this subject. The pro-capitalist economists, such as Friedrich Hayek and Milton Friedman, believe that making shareholders' interests the paramount objective will benefit both the firm and society at large. This approach is not quite as extreme as it sounds because these thinkers generally accept that unbridled pursuit of shareholder returns, to the point of widespread pollution, murder and extortion, will not be in society's best interest and so add the proviso that maximising shareholder wealth is the desired objective provided that firms remain within 'the rules of the game'. This includes obeying the laws and conventions of society, behaving ethically and honestly.

At the opposite end of the political or philosophical spectrum are the left-wing advocates of the primacy of workers' rights and rewards. The belief here is that labour should have its rewards maximised. The employees should have all that is left over, after the other parties have been satisfied. Shareholders are given just enough of a return to provide capital; suppliers are given just enough to supply raw materials and so on.

Standing somewhere in the middle are those keen on a balanced stakeholder approach. Here the (often conflicting) interests of each of the claimants is somehow maximised but within the constraints set by the necessity to compromise in order to provide a fair return to the other stakeholders.

Exhibit 1.5	A company has responsibilities to a number of interested parties

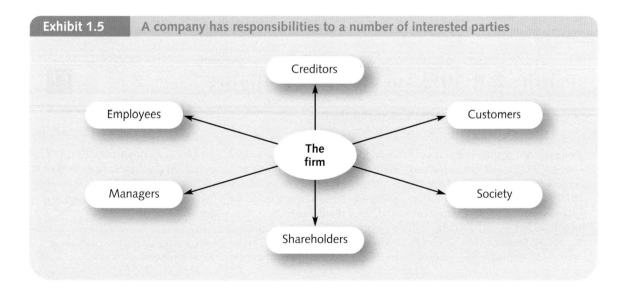

Some possible objectives

A firm can choose from an infinitely long list of possible objectives. Some of these will appear noble and easily justified; others remain hidden, implicit, embarrassing, even subconscious. The following represent some of the most frequently encountered.

● *Achieving a target market share* In some industrial sectors, to achieve a high share of the market gives high rewards. These may be in the form of improved profitability, survival chances or status. Quite often the winning of a particular market share is set as an objective because it acts as a proxy for other, more profound objectives, such as generating the maximum returns to shareholders. On other occasions matters can get out of hand and there is an obsessive pursuit of market share with only a thin veneer of shareholder wealth espousement – *see* Exhibit 1.6.

● *Keeping employee agitation to a minimum* Here, return to the organisation's owners is kept to a minimum necessary level. All surplus resources are directed to mollifying employees. Managers would be very reluctant to admit publicly that they place a high priority on reducing workplace tension, encouraging peace by appeasement and thereby, it is hoped, reducing their own stress levels, but actions tend to speak louder than words. An example of this kind of prioritisation was evident in a number of state-owned UK industries in the 1960s and 1970s. Unemployment levels were low, workers were in a strong bargaining position and there were, generally, state funds available to bail out a loss-making firm. In these circumstances it was easier to buy peace by acquiescing to union demands than to fight on the picket lines. Some companies have tried to reduce workplace tension by giving workers a large proportion of the shares, i.e. making them part-owners. But, as the example of United Airlines shows, 'differences in expectations' can destroy the business. UA ended up with ever more extreme demands from the unions, followed by bankruptcy – *see* Exhibit 1.7.

● *Survival* There are circumstances where the overriding objective becomes the survival of the firm. Severe economic or market shock may force managers to focus purely on short-term issues to ensure the continuance of the business. In firefighting they end up paying little attention to long-term growth and return to owners. However, this focus is clearly inadequate in the long run – there must be other goals. If survival were the only objective then putting all the firm's cash reserves into a bank savings account might be the best option. When managers say that their objective is survival what they generally mean is the avoidance of large risks which endanger the firm's future. This may lead to a greater aversion to risk, and a rejection of activities that shareholders might wish the firm to undertake. Shareholders are in a position to diversify their investments: if one firm goes bankrupt they may be disappointed but they have other companies' shares to fall back on. However, the managers of that one firm may have the majority of their income, prestige and security linked to the continuing existence of that firm. These managers may deliberately avoid high-risk/high-return investments and therefore deprive the owners of the possibility of large gains.

Exhibit 1.6

Profits fall 39% on scheduled flights

FT

By Kevin Done, Aerospace Correspondent

International airlines last year suffered a 39 per cent fall in the net profits of their scheduled services to $1.9bn, the lowest level for five years, according to the International Air Transport Association (Iata).

Pierre Jeanniot, Iata director-general, warned that airlines should 'stop chasing the chimera of endless traffic growth at any price'.

'If governments are no longer going to subsidise such folly,' he said, 'why should we?'

Mr Jeanniot warned that most airline strategies continued to be based on market growth and on increasing market share instead of being driven by profits. Airline shareholders should be moved 'to the top of the priority list for rewards'.

Source: Financial Times, 5 April 2000, p. 13. Reprinted with permission.

Exhibit 1.7

United Airlines: the experiment that fell to earth

The carrier's bankruptcy has raised serious doubts about the viability of workers controlling the companies they work for

write Caroline Daniel and Simon London

. . . Three months ago the world's second largest airline filed for bankruptcy amid spiralling losses. Last week, after nine years of 55 per cent employee ownership, workers at last dumped enough stock to push their stake below 20 per cent, triggering so-called 'sunset clauses'. The experiment was finally declared dead. . . .

Differences in expectations emerged quickly, says one former employee. 'The silliest of all was when John Edwardson [then number two] had a meeting with the pilots' union early on and the union said: "Now we are owners, we have the right to fire one officer every year" and John just looked at him and understood it wasn't a joke. It was a tense moment. And he replied: "I suppose then that officers can fire one pilots' union leader every year." Then the light went on.'

Moreover, it was hard to get employees to think like owners. Middle managers in particular were uneasy about giving up precious power. 'We started to say:

"We are all owners now, instead of just bosses and employees, so bosses needed to learn quickly how to supervise as coaches, cajolers, advisers – but not with a whip. But some supervisors didn't get it and said: "If I criticise one of my people, and they write to the chief executive, I'll be in trouble."' . . .

Along with restrictions over which aircraft would fly certain routes, the absurdity of some of the arcane work rules was underscored by the fact that the pilots' contract included a promise that the company would pick up the tab if a pilot moved city and his piano needed re-tuning, according to one employee. . . Employees were given just three out of 12 board seats. But they were also granted the ability to veto chief executives and strategic decisions, such as acquisitions.

Wielding that power required enlightened union leaders. Instead, unions exploited it, denying Mr Edwardson the chief executive's post and later ousting Jim Goodwin, their own appointee,

when he warned United would perish without wage cuts. . .

In 2000 pilots' wages soared an immediate 29 per cent, with 4.5 per cent rises scheduled to follow. Mr Dubinsky, then head of United's pilots' union, gloated that he intended to choke the golden goose 'by its neck until it gives us every last egg'. . . A senior pilot recalls: 'From 2000 to 2002, labour costs rose $1.4bn (£886m) but at the same time revenues fell $5.5bn.'

The pilot continues: 'The problem was that United was employee-owned but union-controlled. Union leaders needed to satisfy their members who were concerned about work rules and wages, rather than valuation issues. There was a corrupting influence of politics on decision-making . . . the equity culture never caught on.' . . .

The implications of union control over time led to the bleeding of management talent . . .

Source: Financial Times, 18 March 2003, p. 15. Reprinted with permission.

- *Creating an ever-expanding empire* This is an objective that is rarely openly discussed, but it seems reasonable to propose that some managers drive a firm forward, via organic growth or mergers, because of a desire to run an ever-larger enterprise. Often these motives become clearer with hindsight; when, for instance, a firm meets a calamitous end the post-mortem often reveals that profit and efficiency were given second place to growth. The volume of sales, number of employees or overall stock market value of the firm have a much closer correlation with senior executive salaries, perks and status than do returns to shareholder funds. This may motivate some individuals to promote growth.

- *Maximisation of profit* This is a much more acceptable objective, although not everyone would agree that maximisation of profit should be the firm's purpose.

- *Maximisation of long-term shareholder wealth* While many commentators concentrate on profit maximisation, finance experts are aware of a number of drawbacks of profit. The maximisation of the returns to shareholders in the long term is considered to be a superior goal. We look at the differences between profit maximisation and wealth maximisation later.

This list of possible objectives can easily be extended but it is not possible within the scope of this book to examine each of them. Suffice it to say, there can be an enormous variety of objectives and a large potential for conflict and confusion. We have to introduce some sort of order.

The assumed objective for finance

The *company should make investment and financing decisions with the aim of maximising long-term shareholder wealth*. Throughout the remainder of this book we will assume that the firm gives primacy of purpose to the wealth of shareholders. This assumption is made mainly on practical grounds, but there are respectable theoretical justifications too.

The practical reason

If one may assume that the decision-making agents of the firm (managers) are acting in the best interests of shareholders then decisions on such matters as which investment projects to undertake, or which method of financing to use, can be made much more simply. If the firm has a multiplicity of objectives, imagine the difficulty in deciding whether to introduce a new, more efficient machine to produce the firm's widgets, where the new machine both will be more labour efficient (thereby creating redundancies) and will eliminate the need to buy from one half of the firm's suppliers. If one focuses solely on the benefits to shareholders, a clear decision can be made. This entire book is about decision-making tools to aid those choices. These range from whether to produce a component in-house, to whether to buy another company. If for each decision scenario we have to contemplate a number of different objectives or some vague balance of stakeholder interests, the task is going to be much more complex. Once the basic decision-making frameworks are understood within the tight confines of shareholder wealth maximisation, we can allow for complications caused by the modification of this assumption. For instance, shareholder wealth maximisation is clearly not the only consideration motivating actions of organisations such as Body Shop or the Co-operative Bank, each with publicly stated ethical principles. Drugs companies are coming under pressure from shareholders to be more generous to AIDS victims – *see* Exhibit 1.8. Just how generous should they be and still be shareholder wealth maximisers? Real-world decision making can be agonisingly hard.

Exhibit 1.8

Investors warn drugs industry of backlash over health crises

By Geoff Dyer

The pharmaceuticals industry could suffer serious damage to its profitability and end up with a reputation similar to that of the tobacco industry if it does not do more to resolve health crises in poor countries, a group of Europe's leading investors will warn today.

The institutional investors will take the unusual step of issuing a statement on how companies should respond to events such as the Aids pandemic. They fear a popular backlash could limit the prices the industry is able to charge in wealthy countries.

The group of investors, which together have £600bn of funds under management, also caution that failure to reach a deal on drug patents in the developing world could harm the industry's reputation.

The statement, sent to 20 leading companies, makes a number of recommendations. It urges them to provide more scope to poorer countries to override drug patents. It also asks them to set prices in different countries that take into account what they can afford and to make more information available to purchasers. . .

Source: *Financial Times*, 24 March 2003, p. 25. Reprinted with permission.

The theoretical reasons

The 'contractual theory' views the firm as a network of contracts, actual and implicit, which specify the roles to be played by various participants in the organisation. For instance, the workers make both an explicit (employment contract) and an implicit (show initiative, reliability, etc.) deal with the firm to provide their services in return for salary and other benefits, and suppliers deliver necessary inputs in return for a known payment. Each party has well-defined rights and pay-offs. Most of the participants bargain for a limited risk and a fixed pay-off. Banks, for example, when they lend to a firm, often strenuously try to reduce risk by making sure that the firm is generating sufficient cash flow to repay, and that there are assets that can be seized if the loan is not repaid and so on. The bankers' bargain, like that of many of the parties, is a low-risk one and so, the argument goes, they should be rewarded with just the bare minimum for them to provide their service to the firm. Shareholders, on the other hand, are asked to put money into the business at high risk. The deal here is, 'You give us your £10,000 nest egg that you need for your retirement and we, the directors of the firm, do not promise that you will receive a dividend or even see your capital again. We will try our hardest to produce a return on your money but we cannot give any guarantees. Sorry.' Thus the firm's owners are exposed to the possibilities that the firm may go bankrupt and all will be lost. Because of this unfair balance of risk between the different potential claimants on a firm's resources it seems reasonable that the owners should be entitled to any surplus returns which result after all the other parties have been satisfied.

Another theoretical reason hinges on the practicalities of operating in a free market system. In such a capitalist system, it is argued, if a firm chooses to reduce returns to shareholders because, say, it wishes to direct more of the firm's surplus to the workers, then this firm will find it difficult to survive. Some shareholders will sell their shares and invest in other firms more orientated towards their benefit. (United Airlines perhaps, where even the workers sold their shares?) In the long run those individuals who do retain their shares may be amenable to a takeover bid from a firm that does concentrate on shareholder wealth creation. The acquirer will anticipate being able to cut costs, not least by lowering the returns to labour. In the absence of a takeover the company would be unable to raise more finance from shareholders and this might result in slow growth and liquidity problems and possibly corporate death, throwing all employees out of work.

For over 200 years it has been argued that society is best served by businesses focusing on returns to the owner. Adam Smith (1776) expressed the argument very effectively:

> The businessman by directing . . . industry in such a manner as its produce may be of the greatest value, intends only his own gain, and he is in this, as in many other cases, led by an invisible hand to promote an end which was no part of his intention. Nor is it always the worse for society that it was no part of it. By pursuing his own interest he frequently promotes that of the society more effectually than when he really intends to promote it. I have never known much good done by those who affected to trade for the public good. It is an affectation, indeed, not very common among merchants.
>
> *Source*: Adam Smith, *The Wealth of Nations*, 1776, p. 400.

Adam Smith's objection to businessmen affecting to trade for the public good is echoed in Michael Jensen's writings in which he attacks the stakeholder approach (and its derivative, the Balanced Scorecard of Kaplan and Norton (1996)). His main worry is the confusion that results from having a multiplicity of targets to aim for, but he also takes a sideswipe at managers who are able to use the smokescreen of the stakeholder approach to cloak their actions in pursuit of benefits for themselves, or their pet 'socially beneficial' goals:

> Stakeholder theory effectively leaves managers and directors unaccountable for their stewardship of the firm's resources . . . [it] plays into the hands of managers by allowing them to pursue their own interests at the expense of the firm's financial claimants and society at large. It allows managers and directors to devote the firm's resources to their own favorite causes – the environment, arts, cities, medical research – without being held accountable . . . it is not surprising that stakeholder theory receives substantial support from them.
>
> (Jensen 2001).

However, Jensen goes on to say that companies cannot create shareholder value if they ignore important constituencies. They must have good relationships with customers, employees, suppliers, government and so on. This is a form of corporate social responsibility (CSR), within an overall framework of shareholder wealth maximisation. (Some of the CSR officers, consultants and departments go too far in balancing all the stakeholder interests in Jensen's view.) Also, to simply tell people to maximise shareholder value is not enough to motivate them to deliver value. They must be turned on by a vision or a strategy, e.g. to put a PC on every desk, to produce a drug to cure AIDs, or to build a state-of-the-art aeroplane. Shareholder value can measure how successful you are, but it does not create superior vision or strategy – you need additional (but subsidiary) goals and measures, which may be identified and supported through a Balanced Scorecard approach, because it allows a greater understanding of what creates value.

John Kay also points out that firms going directly for 'shareholder value' may actually do less well for shareholders than those that focus on vision and excellence first and find themselves shareholder wealth maximisers in an oblique way. He argues that Boeing, in the 1990s, sacrificed its vision of being a company always on the cutting edge of commercial plane design, breaking through technological and marketplace barriers. This reduced the vibrancy of the pioneering spirit of the organisation, as it refocused on short-term financial performance measures – *see* Exhibit 1.9. However, it is possible to argue that Boeing's managers in the 1990s were not, in fact, shareholder wealth maximisers because they forgot the crucial 'long-term' focus. Being daring and at the cutting edge may be risky, but it often leads to the highest long-term shareholder wealth. Concentrating on short-term financial goals and presenting these as shareholder wealth-maximising actions can lead to slow pace and market irrelevance. So, being too fastidious in requiring immediately visible and quantifiable returns in an uncertain world can result in the rejection of extremely valuable projects that require a leap into the unknown by a team of enthusiasts. Where would Microsoft be today if in the 1970s it required a positive number popping out of a rigorous financial analysis of the prospects for its operating systems, when sales of PCs numbered in hundreds?

Exhibit 1.9

Forget how the crow flies

If you want to go in one direction, the best route may involve going in the other. Paradoxical as it sounds, goals are more likely to be achieved when pursued indirectly. So the most profitable companies are not the most profit-oriented, and the happiest people are not those who make happiness their main aim. The name of this idea? Obliquity

. . . I once said that Boeing's grip on the world civil aviation market made it the most powerful market leader in world business. Bill Allen was chief executive from 1945 to 1968, as the company created its dominant position. He said that his spirit and that of his colleagues was to eat, breathe, and sleep the world of aeronautics. 'The greatest pleasure life has to offer is the satisfaction that flows from participating in a difficult and constructive undertaking', he explained. . .

The company's largest and riskiest project was the development of the 747 jumbo jet. When a non-executive director asked about the expected return on investment, he was brushed off: there had been some studies, he was told, but the manager concerned couldn't remember the results.

It took only 10 years for Boeing to prove me wrong in asserting that its market position in civil aviation was impregnable. The decisive shift in corporate culture followed the acquisition of its principal US rival, McDonnell Douglas, in 1997. The transformation was exemplified by the CEO, Phil Condit. The company's previous preoccupation with meeting 'technological challenges of supreme magnitude' would, he told Business Week, now have to change. 'We are going into a

Exhibit 1.9 continued

value-based environment where unit cost, return on investment and shareholder return are the measures by which you'll be judged. That's a big shift.'

The company's senior executives agreed to move from Seattle, where the main production facilities were located, to Chicago. More importantly, the more focused business reviewed risky investments in new civil projects with much greater scepticism. The strategic decision was to redirect resources towards projects for the US military that involved low financial risk. Chicago had the advantage of being nearer to Washington, where government funds were dispensed.

So Boeing's civil orderbook today lags behind that of Airbus, the European consortium whose aims were not initially commercial but which has, almost by chance, become a profitable business. . . And what was the market's verdict on the company's performance in terms of unit cost, return on investment and shareholder return? Boeing stock, $48 when Condit took over, rose to $70 as he

affirmed the commitment to shareholder value; by the time of his enforced resignation in December 2003 it had fallen to $38. . .

At Boeing, the attempt to focus on simple, well defined objectives proved less successful than management with a broader, more comprehensive conception of objectives. . .

Obliquity gives rise to the profit-seeking paradox: the most profitable companies are not the most profit-oriented. Boeing illustrate how a greater focus on shareholder returns was self-defeating in its own narrow terms. . .

Collins and Porras compared the philosophy of George Merck ('We try never to forget that medicine is for the people. It is not for the profits. The profits follow, and if we have remembered that, they have never failed to appear. The better we have remembered it, the larger they have been') with that of John McKeen of Pfizer ('So far as humanly possible, we aim to get profit out of everything we do').

The individuals who are most successful at making money are

not those who are most interested in making money. This is not surprising. The principal route to great wealth is the creation of a successful business, and building a successful business demands exceptional talents and hard work. There is no reason to think these characteristics are associated with greed and materialism: rather the opposite. People who are obsessively interested in money are drawn to get-rich-quick schemes rather than to business opportunities, and when these schemes come off, as occasionally they do, they retire to their villas in the sun. . .

Although we crave time for passive leisure, people engaged in watching television reported low levels of contentment. Csikszentmihalyi's systematic finding is that the activities that yield the highest for satisfaction with life require the successful performance of challenging tasks.

John Kay is the author of *The Truth About Markets* (Allen Lane).

Source: John Kay, *Financial Times Magazine*, 17 January 2004, pp. 17–21. Reproduced with kind permission of the *Financial Times*.

In an interview in 2003 Milton Friedman focused on the main benefit of encouraging businesses to pursue high returns for owners. He said that this results in the best allocation of investment capital among competing industries and product lines. This is good for society because consumers end up with more of what they want because scarce investment money is directed to the best uses, producing the optimum mix of goods and services. 'The self-interest of employees in retaining their jobs will often conflict with this overriding objective.' He went on:

> the best system of corporate governance is one that provides the best incentives to use capital efficiently . . . You want control . . . in the hands of those who are residual recipients [i.e. shareholders bear the residual risk when a company fails] because they are the ones with the direct interest in using the capital of the firm efficiently.

Source: Simon London, *Financial Times Magazine*, 'Milton Friedman – The Long View' 7 June 2003, p. 13.

One final and powerful reason for advancing shareholders' interests above all others (subject to the rules of the game) is very simple: they own the firm and therefore deserve any surplus it produces. The views of an opponent to shareholder wealth maximisation are presented in Exhibit 1.10.

Exhibit 1.10

It is time to knock shareholder value

FT

Michael Skapinker

Are business schools destroying business? A growing number of business school professors believe they are. Now one of their best-liked colleagues has added his voice, posthumously. Sumantra Ghoshal of London Business School died last year, aged 55, while he was still developing his critique of management educators and the damage they had wrought.

His paper, "Bad Management Theories are Destroying Good Management Practices", is among many pieces of Ghoshal's work that will resonate after his premature death.

"Much of the worst excesses of recent management practices have their roots in a set of ideas that have emerged from the business school academics over the past 30 years," Ghoshal wrote. Many of those bad ideas, he said, had their origins in the dismal influence of economists, and one economist in particular – Milton Friedman, who declared that managers' sole responsibility was to make money for shareholders.

The attraction of shareholder value, in its supporters' view, was that it set a standard against which managers could be judged. Asking managers to aim at anything else – the good of the wider community, for example – was a distraction from the central task. Other goals were too imprecise: how would you measure whether managers had succeeded or failed?

Having decided that managers' sole task was to make money for shareholders, the economists promptly declared they could not be trusted to do so. What was to stop managers pursuing their own interests, rather than those of

shareholders? There were several attempts to solve this "agency problem". Giving managers share options to align their interests with shareholders' was the first. When that failed, amid the managerial excesses and fraud of the past few years, governments and regulators turned to controlling managers through independent directors. But, Ghoshal said, there was no evidence that corporate governance reform improved corporate performance.

Managerial malpractice, Ghoshal argued, was not the result of insufficient independent directors. It was the consequence of believing that shareholder return was all that mattered and that managers should battle their way through any obstacle to achieve it, free "from any sense of moral or ethical responsibility for their actions". It was also the result of assuming managers could not be trusted. Treated as untrustworthy, that is what they became.

Business schools, he wrote, had been at the forefront of propagating shareholder value, agency theory and the rest, with all the baleful consequences of recent years. Ghoshal quoted Keynes: "The ideas of economists and political philosophers, both when they are right and when they are wrong, are more powerful than is commonly understood . . . Practical men, who believe themselves to be quite exempt from any intellectual influences, are usually the slaves of some defunct economist."

What should we make of this? First, like Jeffrey Pfeffer of Stanford who endorses his views in the same journal, Ghoshal overstated business schools' importance. As Rosabeth Moss

Kanter of Harvard Business School says in her response to Ghoshal, the business schools' ideas "have hardly been foisted on innocent capitalists".

It was not just that business schools propounded shareholder value: managers were all too ready to practise it. "Why has there been such a receptive audience?" Prof Kanter asks. First, because what preceded it was so unattractive, a "cosy managerialism" in which US business leaders ignored the threat, for example, from Japanese manufacturing. Nor, as Donald Hambrick, another contributor, points out, were old-fashioned managers caring paternalists. They feathered their nests too, building company golf courses, among other things.

Prof Kanter adds that the rise of shareholder value coincided with capitalism's victory over communism. "American theories and theorists had disproportionate influence. One-sided shareholder capitalism was in vogue," Prof Kanter says. "Valuing all stakeholders, being socially responsible and caring about people sounded a little 'pinko' to business managers, when the world had so roundly rejected socialism in any form. Greed was legitimated as producing a better society, not just better companies."

The second objection to Ghoshal's argument was that Enron, Tyco, WorldCom and the others did not happen because managers put shareholders first. They happened because managers put themselves first. Shareholders suffered from their behaviour, along with employees. Share options and independent directors might not be the answer to

Exhibit 1.10 continued

the agency problem, but the corporate scandals demonstrated that there undoubtedly was an agency problem.

Third, while the shareholder value philosophy had its unattractive side, it had its successes too. For all the scandals, US companies remained the world's most innovative.

This is not to say we have to accept the system as it is.

Disillusionment with modern capitalism is widespread. We see it in opinion polls showing great mistrust of corporate leaders. We see it, as customers, in employees' alienated, could-not-care-less attitudes. It is fortunate for free-market capitalism that there is, at present, no workable alternative. If there were, it would have millions of takers.

This is the final problem with Ghoshal's argument: having set

out to demolish shareholder value, he proposed nothing in its place. He acknowledged this weakness: "Thomas Kuhn [the philosopher of scientific revolutions] was right in arguing that mere disconfirmation or challenge never dislodges a dominant paradigm; only a better alternative does."

Source: michael.skapinker@ft.com, 23 February 2005. Reprinted with permission.

This is not the place to advocate one philosophical approach or another which is applicable to all organisations at all times. Many organisations are clearly not shareholder wealth maximisers and are quite comfortable with that. Charities, government departments and other non-profit organisations are fully justified in emphasising a different set of values from those espoused by the commercial firm. The reader is asked to be prepared for two levels of thought when using this book. While it focuses on corporate shareholder wealth decision making, it may be necessary to make small or large modifications to be able to apply the same frameworks and theories to organisations with different goals. However, beware of organisations that try to balance a number of objectives. Take, for example, football clubs that have floated on the stock market. They have at least two parties to satisfy: (i) shareholders looking for good return on their savings, and (ii) fans looking for more spending on players and lower ticket prices. It is very difficult to satisfy both – hence the dramatic tensions and suspicions at so many clubs.

What is shareholder wealth?

Maximising wealth can be defined as maximising purchasing power. The way in which an enterprise enables its owners to indulge in the pleasures of purchasing and consumption is by paying them a dividend. The promise of a flow of cash in the form of dividends is what prompts investors to sacrifice immediate consumption and hand over their savings to a management team through the purchase of shares. Shareholders are interested in a flow of dividends over a long time horizon and not necessarily in a quick payback. Take the electronics giant Philips: it could raise vast sums for short-term dividend payouts by ceasing all research and development (R&D) and selling off the R&D laboratories. But this would not maximise shareholder wealth because, by retaining funds within the business, it is believed that new products and ideas, springing from the R&D programme, will produce much higher dividends in the future. Maximising shareholder wealth means maximising the flow of dividends to shareholders *through time* – there is a long-term perspective.

Profit maximisation is not the same as shareholder wealth maximisation

Profit is a concept developed by accountants to aid decision making, one decision being to judge the quality of stewardship shown over the owner's funds. The accountant has to take what is a continuous process, a business activity stretching over many years, and split this into accounting periods of, say, a year, or six months. To some extent this exercise is bound to be artificial and fraught with problems. There are many reasons why accounting profit may not be a good proxy for shareholder wealth. Here are five of them:

● *Prospects* Imagine that there are two firms that have reported identical profits but one firm is, with good reason, more highly valued by its shareholders than the other. One possible explanation for this is that recent profit figures fail to reflect the relative potential of the two firms. The stock market will give a higher share value to the company that shows the greater future growth outlook. Perhaps one set of managers chose a short-term approach and raised their profits in the near term but have sacrificed long-term prospects. One way of achieving this is to raise prices and slash marketing spend – over the subsequent year profits might be boosted as customers are unable to switch suppliers immediately. Over the long term, however, competitors will respond and profits will fall.

● *Risk* Two firms could report identical historical profit figures, and have future prospects indicating the same average annual returns. However, one firm's returns are subject to much greater variability and so there will be years of losses and, in a particularly bad year, the possibility of bankruptcy. **Exhibit 1.11** shows two firms which have identical average profit but Volatile Joe's profit is subject to much greater risk than that of Steady Eddie. Shareholders are likely to value the firm with stable income flows more highly than one with high risk.

● *Accounting problems* Drawing up a set of accounts is not as scientific and objective as some people try to make out. There is plenty of scope for judgement, guesswork or even cynical manipulation. Imagine the difficulty facing the company accountant and auditors of a clothes retailer when trying to value a dress that has been on sale for six months. Let us suppose the dress cost the firm £50. Perhaps this should go into the balance sheet and then the profit and loss account will not be affected. But what if the store manager says that he can only sell that dress if it is reduced to £30, and contradicting him the managing director says that if a little more effort was made £40 could be achieved? Which figure is the person who drafts the financial accounts going to take? Profits can vary significantly depending on a multitude of small judgements like this. Another difficult accounting issue is demonstrated in **Exhibit 1.12** – just when does a sale add to profits?

● *Communication* Investors realise and accept that buying a share is risky. However, they like to reduce their uncertainty and nervousness by finding out as much as they can about the firm. If the firm is reluctant to tell shareholders about such matters as the origin of reported profits, then investors generally will tend to avoid those shares. Fears are likely to arise in the minds of poorly informed investors: did the profits come from the most risky activities and might they therefore disappear next year? Is the company being used to run guns to unsavoury regimes abroad? The senior executives of large quoted firms spend a great deal of time explaining their strategies, sources of income and future investment plans to the large institutional shareholders to make sure that these investors are aware of the quality of

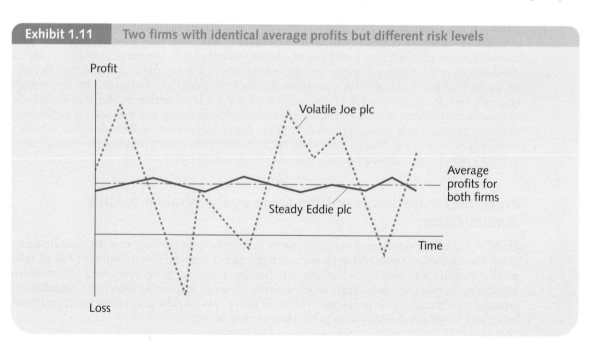

Exhibit 1.11   Two firms with identical average profits but different risk levels

Exhibit 1.12

Homestyle quantifies deferral

By Maggie Urry

Homestyle, the discount retailer specialising in furniture, beds and soft furnishings, yesterday put a figure of £4.5m on the profit that it said in January would be deferred because of an accounting change. . .The accounting change affects the timing of profit recognition on furniture sales from the Harveys chain, which was acquired in August 2000.

Previously, profits were booked on order date; that has been changed to delivery date, delaying recognition by several weeks. . .

Since furniture sales peak in the post-Christmas period, the group's current year-end meant these peak deliveries would come into the 2003 year instead. The group now plans to change the financial year-end to April, which it said would be 'more appropriate' to the business. . .

Source: Financial Times, 14 March 2002. Reprinted with permission.

the firm and its prospects. Firms that ignore the importance of communication and image in the investment community may be doing their shareholders a disservice as the share price might fall. The London Stock Exchange encourages companies to improve their communication with shareholders – *see* **Exhibit 1.13**.

● *Additional capital* Profits can be increased simply by making use of more shareholders' money. If shareholders inject more money into the company or the firm merely retains profits (which belong to shareholders), their future profits can rise, but the *return* on shareholders' money may fall to less than what is available elsewhere for the same level of risk. This is shareholder wealth destructive. For more on this, see Chapter 9.

Exhibit 1.13

Under-fire companies might find it's good to talk **FT**

Deborah Hargreaves

Communication matters to markets. Anyone who doubts this should look no further than the 7 per cent drop in Shell's shares last Friday after the disastrous announcement of a 20 per cent reduction in its estimate of proven crude reserves.

The change in classification of oilfields to represent fewer reserves than expected was enough of a shock on its own. But what really sent shareholders into a lather was the fact that no executive board members were available to explain the move. They wanted Sir Philip Watts,

chief executive, who had been running the exploration business when these fields were first booked as reserves, to answer their queries. The absence of top directors from Friday's conference call has also fuelled traders' much-loved conspiracy theories. Maybe Sir Philip and Judy Boynton, finance director, know something even more damaging and did not want to be subjected to public scrutiny, the tattle runs.

This is why companies should try to offer credible explanations of material factors affecting them, if they want to avoid the market

filling the void with rumours and gossip. . .

It is hard to quantify the benefits of a good communications strategy, but so often an open chief executive reflects a wider company culture. This is, of course, not just about who tells investors what. But the benefits of a clearly outlined strategy and a communicative chief executive should not be underestimated. One of the most important things that companies can lose is their reputation.

Source: Financial Times, 17–18 January 2004, p. M21. Reprinted with permission.

Ownership and control

The problem

In theory, the shareholders, being the owners of the firm, control its activities. In practice, the large modern corporation has a very diffuse and fragmented set of shareholders and control often lies in the hands of directors. It is extremely difficult to marshall thousands of shareholders, each with a small stake in the business, to push for change. Thus in many firms we have what is called a separation, or a divorce, of ownership and control. In times past the directors would usually be the same individuals as the owners. Today, however, less than 1 per cent of the shares of most of the UK's 100 largest firms are owned by the directors.

The separation of ownership and control raises worries that the management team may pursue objectives attractive to them, but which are not necessarily beneficial to the shareholders – this is termed 'managerialism' or 'managementism'. This conflict is an example of the principal–agent problem. The principals (the shareholders) have to find ways of ensuring that their agents (the managers) act in their interests. This means incurring costs, 'agency costs', to (a) monitor managers' behaviour, and (b) create incentive schemes and controls for managers to encourage the pursuit of shareholders' wealth maximisation. These costs arise in addition to the agency cost of the loss of wealth caused by the extent to which prevention measures do not work and managers continue to pursue non-shareholder wealth goals.

Some solutions?

Various methods have been used to try to align the actions of senior management with the interests of shareholders, that is, to achieve 'goal congruence'.

- *Linking rewards to shareholder wealth improvements* A technique widely employed in industry is to grant directors and other senior managers share options. These permit managers to purchase shares at some date in the future at a price which is fixed now. If the share price rises significantly between the date when the option was granted and the date when the shares can be bought the manager can make a fortune by buying at the pre-arranged price and then selling in the marketplace. For example in 2007 managers might be granted the right to buy shares in 2012 at a price of £1.50. If the market price moves to say £2.30 in 2012 the managers can buy and then sell the shares, making a gain of 80p. The managers under such a scheme have a clear interest in achieving a rise in share price and thus congruence comes about to some extent. An alternative method is to allot shares to managers if they achieve certain performance targets, for example, growth in earnings per share or return on assets.

- *Sackings* The threat of being sacked with the accompanying humiliation and financial loss may encourage directors/managers not to diverge too far from the shareholders' wealth path. However, this method is employed in extreme circumstances only. It is sometimes difficult to implement because of difficulties of making a coordinated shareholder effort. However, if the majority of the directors on the board are independent of the executive directors (not full-time employees, but on the board to look after shareholders' interests) then the threat of removal becomes more credible.

- *Selling shares and the takeover threat* Over 60 per cent of the shares of the typical company quoted on the London stock market are owned by financial institutions such as pension and insurance funds. These organisations generally are not prepared to put large resources into monitoring and controlling all the hundreds of firms of which they own a part. Quite often their first response, if they observe that management is not acting in what they regard as their best interest, is to sell the share rather than intervene. This will result in a lower share price, making the raising of funds more difficult. If this process continues the firm may become vulnerable to a merger bid by another group of managers, resulting in a loss of top management posts. Fear of being taken over can establish some sort of backstop position to prevent shareholder wealth considerations being totally ignored.

- *Corporate governance regulations* There is a considerable range of legislation and other regulatory pressures designed to encourage directors to act in shareholders' interests. The Companies Acts require certain minimum standards of behaviour, as does the Stock

Exchange. There is the back-up of the Serious Fraud Office (SFO) and the financial industry regulators. Following a number of financial scandals, guidelines of best practice in corporate governance were issued by the Cadbury, Greenbury, Hampel and Hicks committees, now consolidated in the Combined Code of Corporate Governance, which is backed by the London Stock Exchange. Directors have to state in the accounts how the principles of the code have been applied. If a principle has not been followed they have to state why. The principles include: transparency on directors' remuneration requiring a remuneration committee consisting mainly of non-executive directors; directors retiring by rotation at least every three years; the chairman should not also be the chief executive officer to avoid domination by one person (in exceptional circumstances this may be ignored, if a written justification is presented to shareholders); the audit committee (responsible for validating financial figures, e.g. by appointing effective external auditors) should consist mainly of independent[3] non-executive directors and not by executive directors, otherwise the committee would not be able to act as a check and balance to the executive directors; at least half the members of the board, excluding the chairman, should be independent non-executive directors; the accounts must contain a statement by the directors that the company is a going concern, i.e. it will continue for at least one year.

● *Information flow* The accounting profession, the Stock Exchange and the investing institutions have conducted a continuous battle to encourage or force firms to release more accurate, timely and detailed information concerning their operations. The quality of corporate accounts and annual reports has generally improved, as has the availability of other forms of information flowing to investors and analysts, such as company briefings and press announcements. All this helps to monitor firms, and identify any wealth-destroying actions by wayward managers early, but, as a number of recent scandals have shown, matters are still far from perfect.

Asian companies became notorious for growing in size and prestige rather than producing wealth for shareholders in the 1980s and 1990s. However, there are indications that investment returns are now being given the highest priority – *see* Exhibit 1.14.

Concluding comments

We now have a clear guiding principle set as our objective for the myriad financial decisions discussed later in this book: maximise shareholder wealth. Whether we are considering a major investment programme, or trying to decide on the best kind of finance to use, the criterion of creating value for shareholders over the long run will be paramount. A single objective is set primarily for practical reasons to aid exposition in this text; however, many of the techniques described in later chapters will be applicable to organisations with other purposes as they stand, while others will need slight modification.

There is an old joke about financial service firms: they just shovel money from one place to another making sure that some of it sticks to the shovel. The implication is that they contribute little to the well-being of society. Extremists even go so far as to regard these firms as parasites on the 'really productive' parts of the economies. And yet very few people avoid extensive use of financial services. Most have bank and building society accounts, pay insurance premiums and contribute to pension schemes. People do not put their money into a bank account unless they get something in return. Likewise building societies, insurance companies, pension funds, unit trusts, investment banks and so on can only survive if they offer a service people find beneficial and are willing to pay for. Describing the mobilisation and employment of money in the service of productive investment as pointless or merely 'shovelling it around the system' is as logical as saying that the transport firms which bring goods to the high street do not provide a valuable service because there is an absence of a tangible 'thing' created by their activities.

---

[3] To be independent the non-executive director should not, for example, be a customer, ex-employee, supplier, or a friend of the founding family or the chief executive.

Exhibit 1.14

Returns become new status symbol

The state of the balance sheet is of greater concern since the financial crisis than the height of an HQ

writes Joe Leahy

In Asia, corporate success used to be measured more in terms of the height of a company's office tower, its number of workers or even the size of its boardroom rather than the health of its balance sheet.

'I remember Indonesian boardrooms were always the biggest', says one Hong Kong-based fund manager.

For the tycoons running the region's leading companies, usually conglomerates, size and status were more important than profits in securing government contracts and attracting local and foreign investors.

Today, evidence is emerging of a shift in the way many regional

companies run their businesses. Starved of capital for five years following the Asian financial crisis, the region's corporate survivors are increasingly focusing on improving investment returns.

This in turn is set to reshape the region's economies and benefit stock market valuations.

'The over-investment bubble has now reversed itself and when that happens the returns from investment rise', said Ajay Kapur, regional equities strategist with Morgan Stanley in Hong Kong.

Mr Kapur forecasts average Asian returns on equity will reach 12 per cent this year, surpassing the US where ROEs have fallen to about 10 per cent. . .

Better capital allocation by more discerning markets and lenders has curbed the excesses of companies splurging easy money on petrochemical plants, tollroads and luxury apartments no one needs or can afford.

Instead, they are being forced to make themselves more attractive to markets by focusing on profits.

In the absence of sales growth, neutered by the economic slump, many have been vigorously cutting costs, reducing headcount and other expenses to boost returns. 'People haven't gone on a repeated orgy of new capex for the past five years', Mr Kapur said.

Source: Financial Times, 8 March 2002, p. 31. Reprinted with permission.

Key points and concepts

- **Financial institutions and markets** encourage growth and progress by **mobilising savings** and encouraging investment.

- Financial managers contribute to firms' success primarily through **investment and finance decisions**. Their knowledge of financial markets, investment appraisal methods, cash management, value management and risk management techniques are vital for company growth and stability.

- Financial institutions encourage the flow of saving into investment by acting as **brokers** and **asset transformers**, thus alleviating the **conflict of preferences** between the **primary investors** (households) and the **ultimate borrowers** (firms).

- **Asset transformation** is the creation of an intermediate security with characteristics appealing to the primary investor to attract funds, which are then made available to the ultimate borrower in a form appropriate to them. Types of asset transformation: risk transformation; maturity transformation; volume transformation.

- Intermediaries are able to transform assets and encourage the flow of funds because of their **economies of scale** *vis-à-vis* the individual investor: (i) efficiencies in gathering information; (ii) risk spreading; (iii) transaction costs.

● The **secondary markets** in financial securities encourage investment by enabling investor liquidity (being able to sell quickly and cheaply to another investor) while providing the firm with long-term funds.

● **Banking sector:**

  – **Retail banks** – high-volume and low-value business.
  – **Wholesale banks** – low-volume and high-value business. Mostly fee based.
  – **International banks** – mostly Eurocurrency transactions.
  – **Building societies** – still primarily small deposits aggregated for mortgage lending.
  – **Finance houses** – hire purchase, leasing, factoring.

● **Long-term savings institutions:**

  – **Pension funds** – major investors in financial assets.
  – **Insurance funds** – life assurance and endowment policies provide large investment funds.

● **The risk spreaders:**

  – **Unit trusts** – genuine trusts which are open-ended investment vehicles.
  – **Investment trusts** – companies which invest in other companies' financial securities.
  – **Open-ended investment companies** (OEICs) – a hybrid between unit and investment trusts.

● **The markets:**

  – **The money markets** are short-term wholesale lending and/or borrowing markets.
  – **The bond markets** deal in long-term bond debt issued by corporations, governments, etc.
  – **The foreign exchange market** – one currency is exchanged for another.
  – **The share market** – primary and secondary trading in companies' shares takes place.
  – **The derivatives market** – Euronext.liffe dominates the 'exchange-traded' derivatives market in options and futures. There is a flourishing over-the-counter market.

● Firms should clearly define the **objective** of the enterprise to provide a focus for decision making.

● **Sound financial management** is necessary for the achievement of all **stakeholder** goals.

● Some stakeholders will have their returns **satisficed** – given just enough to make their contribution worthwhile. One (or more) group(s) will have their returns maximised.

● The assumed objective of the firm for finance is to **maximise shareholder wealth**. Reasons include: the practical necessity of a single objective leading to clearer decisions; the **contractual theory; survival** in a competitive world; it is better for **society**; counters the tendency of managers to pursue goals for their own benefit; they **own** the firm.

● **Maximising shareholder wealth is maximising purchasing power** or **maximising the flow of discounted cash flow** to shareholders over a long time horizon.

● **Profit maximisation** is not the same as shareholder wealth maximisation. Some things a profit comparison does not allow for: future prospects; risk; accounting problems; communication; additional capital.

● Large corporations usually have a **separation of ownership and control**. This may lead to **managerialism** where the agents (the managers) take decisions primarily with their interests in mind rather than those of the principals (the shareholders). This is a **principal–agent problem**. Solutions include: link managerial rewards to shareholder wealth improvement; sackings; selling shares and the takeover threat; corporate governance regulation; improve information flow.

Further reading

Students of finance, or any managerial discipline, should get into the habit of reading the *Financial Times* and *The Economist* to (a) reinforce knowledge gained from a course, and (b) appreciate the wider business environment.

For more on the financial system and instruments see Arnold, G.C. (2004), Blake, D. (2000), Howells, P. and K. Bain (2004), Levinson, M. (2002), Roberts, R. (2004) and Valdez, S. and J. Wood (2003).

Corporate governance is discussed in 'The Cadbury Report' (1992), 'The Greenbury Report' (1995), 'The Hampel Report' (1998) and 'The Higgs Report' (2003).

The objective of the firm is discussed by Donaldson G. (1963), who provides a clear discussion of the conflict of interest between managers and shareholders, and Doyle, P. (1994), who argues that western firms are over-focused on short-term financial goals (profit, ROI). Reconciling the interests of stakeholders should not be difficult as they are 'satisficers' rather than maximisers: Friedman, M. (1970) places shareholder wealth first (also interviewed in London, S. (2003)); Galbraith, J. (1967) observes that survival, sales and expansion of the 'technostructure' are emphasised; Hayek, F.A. (1969) argues that the objective should be long-run return on owners' capital subject to restraint by general legal and moral rules. Kaplan, R. and Norton, D.P. (1996) present the managerial equivalent of stakeholder theory in which multiple measures are used to evaluate performance – the Balanced Scorecard. Kay, J. (2004) suggests that obliquity is the way to go. Simon, H.A. (1959) challenges traditional economic theories, drawing on psychology. Discusses the goals of the firm: satisficing vs. maximising. Smith, A. (1776) is an early advocate of shareholder supremacy within the rules of the game.

Agency theory is set out in Jensen, M.C. and Meckling, W.H. (1976). It was applied to the use to which managers put business cash inflows in Jensen, M.C. (1986). Jensen, M.C. (2001) cogently argues against simple stakeholder balancing or a Balanced Scorecard approach to directing a company because of the violation of the proposition that a single-valued objective is a prerequisite for purposeful or rational behaviour by any organisation, thus politicising the corporation and leaving managers empowered to exercise their own preferences. Williamson, O. (1963) argues that managerial security, power, prestige, etc. are powerful motivating forces. These goals may lead to less than profit-maximising behaviour.

Websites

Association of British Insurers www.abi.org.uk
Association of Investment Trust Companies www.aitc.co.uk
Bank for International Settlement www.bis.org
Bank of England www.bankofengland.co.uk
British Bankers Association www.bankfacts.org.uk or www.bba.org.uk
British Venture Capital Association www.bvca.co.uk
Building Societies Association www.bsa.org.uk
Chartered Institute of Bankers www.cib.org.uk
Combined Code of Corporate Governance www.fsa.gov.uk/pub/ukla
Companies House www.companieshouse.gov.uk
Finance and Leasing Association www.fla.org.uk
Financial Times www.FT.com
Investment Management Association www.investment.org.uk
National Association of Pension Funds www.napf.co.uk
London International Financial Futures and Options Exchange www.liffe.com
London Stock Exchange www.londonstockexchange.com

Self-review questions

1 What are the economies of scale of intermediaries?

2 Distinguish between a primary market and a secondary market. How does the secondary market aid the effectiveness of the primary market?

3 Illustrate the flow of funds between primary investors and ultimate borrowers in a modern economy. Give examples of intermediary activity.

4 List as many financial intermediaries as you can. Describe the nature of their intermediation and explain the intermediate securities they create.

5 Briefly describe the main types of financial decisions a firm has to deal with.

6 Briefly explain the role of the following:

   a The money markets
   b The bond markets
   c The foreign exchange markets
   d The share markets
   e The derivatives market.

7 Why is it important to specify a goal for the corporation?

8 What is the 'contractual theory'? Do you regard it as a strong argument?

9 What is the principal–agent problem?

10 How can 'goal congruence' for managers and shareholders be achieved?

11 What difficulties might arise in state-owned industries in making financial decisions?

Questions and problems

1 Explain the rationale for selecting shareholder wealth maximisation as the objective of the firm. Include a consideration of profit maximisation as an alternative goal.

2 What benefits are derived from the financial services sector which have led to its growth over recent years in terms of employment and share of GDP?

3 What is managerialism and how might it be incompatible with shareholder interests?

4 Why has an increasing share of household savings been channelled through financial intermediaries?

5 Firm A has a stock market value of £20m (number of shares in issue × share price), while firm B is valued at £15m. The firms have similar profit histories:

	Firm A	Firm B
2002	1.5	1.8
2003	1.6	1.0
2004	1.7	2.3
2005	1.8	1.5
2006	2.0	2.0

Provide reasons why, despite the same total profit over the last five years, shareholders regard firm A as being worth £5m more (extend your thoughts beyond the numbers in the table).

6 The chief executive of Geight plc receives a salary of £80,000 plus 4 per cent of sales. Will this encourage the adoption of decisions that are shareholder wealth enhancing? How might you change matters to persuade the chief executive to focus on shareholder wealth in all decision making?

Assignments

1 Consider the organisations where you have worked in the past and the people you have come into contact with. List as many objectives as you can, explicit or implicit, that have been revealed to, or suspected by, you. To what extent was goal congruence between different stakeholders achieved? How might the efforts of all individuals be channelled more effectively?

2 Review all the financial services you or your firm purchase. Try to establish a rough estimate of the cost of using each financial intermediary and write a balanced report considering whether you or your firm should continue to pay for that service.

Visit www.pearsoned.co.uk/arnold to get access to Gradetracker diagnostic tests, Podcasts, Excel Spreadsheet Solutions, FT articles, a Flashcard revision tool, Weblinks, a searchable Glossary and more.

CHAPTER 2

Project appraisal:
Net present value and internal rate of return

LEARNING OUTCOMES

By the end of the chapter the student should be able to demonstrate an understanding of the fundamental theoretical justifications for using discounted cash flow techniques in analysing major investment decisions, based on the concepts of the time value of money and the opportunity cost of capital. More specifically the student should be able to:

■ calculate net present value and internal rate of return;

■ show an appreciation of the relationship between net present value and internal rate of return;

■ describe and explain at least three potential problems that can arise with internal rate of return in specific circumstances.

Introduction

Shareholders supply funds to a firm for a reason. That reason, generally, is to receive a return on their precious resources. The return is generated by management using the finance provided to invest in real assets. It is vital for the health of the firm and the economic welfare of the finance providers that management employ the best techniques available when analysing which of all the possible investment opportunities will give the best return.

Someone (or a group) within the organisation may have to take the bold decision on whether it is better to build a new factory or extend the old; whether it is wiser to use an empty piece of land for a multi-storey car park or to invest a larger sum and build a shopping centre; whether shareholders would be better off if the firm returned their money in the form of dividends because shareholders can obtain a better return elsewhere, or whether the firm should pursue its expansion plan and invest in that new chain of hotels, or that large car show-room, or the new football stand.

These sorts of decisions require not only brave people, but informed people; individuals of the required calibre need to be informed about a range of issues: for example, the market environment and level of demand for the proposed activity, the internal environment, culture and capabilities of the firm, the types and levels of cost elements in the proposed area of activity, and, of course, an understanding of the risk and uncertainty appertaining to the project.

Tesco presumably considered all these factors before making its multi-million pound investments – *see* Exhibit 2.1.

Exhibit 2.1

Tesco to raise £1.7bn for further growth

By Susanna Voyle, Retail Correspondent

Tesco has turned up the heat on its rivals with surprise plans to invest an extra £1.7bn in the supermarket business, the majority to be spent strengthening its dominant position at home. Sir Terry Leahy, chief executive, said yesterday he wanted to build more hypermarkets to allow for a jump in sales of non-food items, expand his convenience chain and services such as banking. He challenged international rivals with plans for extra invest-ment in overseas expansion and a change of strategy by promising to add convenience stores and smaller superstores to its hypermarket operations.

Source: *Financial Times*, 14 January 2004, p. 1. Reprinted with permission.

Bravery, information, knowledge and a sense of proportion are all essential ingredients when undertaking the onerous task of investing other people's money, but there is another element which is also of crucial importance, that is, the employment of an investment appraisal technique which leads to the 'correct' decision, a technique which takes into account the fundamental considerations.

This chapter examines two approaches to evaluating investments within the firm. Both emphasise the central importance of the concept of the time value of money and are thus described as discounted cash flow (DCF) techniques. Net present value (NPV) and internal rate of return (IRR) are in common usage in most large commercial organisations and are regarded as more complete than the traditional techniques of payback and accounting rate of return (e.g. return on capital employed – ROCE). The relative merits and demerits of these alternative methods are discussed in Chapter 3 alongside a consideration of some of the practical issues of project implementation. In this chapter we concentrate on gaining an understanding of how net present value and internal rate of return are calculated, as well as their theoretical underpinnings.

Value creation and corporate investment

If we accept that the objective of investment within the firm is to create value for its owners then the purpose of allocating money to a particular division or project is to generate cash inflows in the future significantly greater than the amount invested. Put most simply, the project appraisal decision is one involving the comparison of the amount of cash put into an investment with the amount of cash returned. The key phrase and the tricky issue is 'significantly greater than'. For instance, would you, as part-owner of a firm, be content if that firm asked you to swap £10,000 of your hard-earned money for some new shares so that the management team could invest it in order to hand back to you, in five years, the £10,000 plus £1,000? Is this a significant return? Would you feel that your wealth had been enhanced if you were aware that by investing the £10,000 yourself, by, for instance, lending to the government, you could have received a 5 per cent return per year? Or that you could obtain a return of 10 per cent per annum by investing in other shares on the stock market? Naturally, you would feel let down by a management team that offered a return of less than 2 per cent per year when you had alternative courses of action that would have produced much more.

This line of thought is leading us to a central concept in finance and, indeed, in business generally – the time value of money. Investors have alternative uses for their funds and they therefore have an opportunity cost if money is invested in a corporate project. The *investor's opportunity cost* is the sacrifice of the return available on the best forgone alternative.

Investments must generate at least enough cash for all investors to obtain their required returns. If they produce less than the investor's opportunity cost then the wealth of shareholders will decline.

Exhibit 2.2 summarises the process of good investment appraisal. The achievement of value or wealth creation is determined not only by the future cash flows to be derived from a project but also by the timing of those cash flows and by making an allowance for the fact that time has value.

The time value of money

When people undertake to set aside money for investment something has to be given up now. For instance, if someone buys shares in a firm or lends to a business there is a sacrifice of consumption. One of the incentives to save is the possibility of gaining a higher level of future

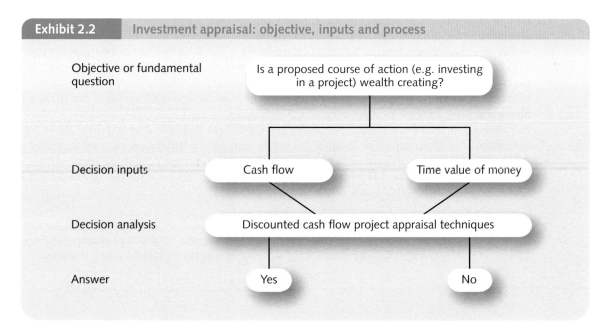

Exhibit 2.2   Investment appraisal: objective, inputs and process

Objective or fundamental question — Is a proposed course of action (e.g. investing in a project) wealth creating?

Decision inputs — Cash flow — Time value of money

Decision analysis — Discounted cash flow project appraisal techniques

Answer — Yes — No

consumption by sacrificing some present consumption. Therefore, it is apparent that compensation is required to induce people to make a consumption sacrifice. Compensation will be required for at least three things:

- *Impatience to consume* Individuals generally prefer to have £1.00 today than £1.00 in five years' time. To put this formally: the utility of £1.00 now is greater than £1.00 received five years hence. Individuals are predisposed towards *impatience to consume*, thus they need an appropriate reward to begin the saving process. The rate of exchange between certain future consumption and certain current consumption is the *pure rate of interest* – this occurs even in a world of no inflation and no risk. If you lived in such a world you might be willing to sacrifice £100 of consumption now if you were compensated with £102 to be received in one year. This would mean that your pure rate of interest is 2 per cent.

- *Inflation* The price of time (or the discount rate needed to compensate for time preference) exists even when there is no inflation, simply because people generally prefer consumption now to consumption later. If there is inflation then the providers of finance will have to be compensated for that loss in purchasing power as well as for time.

- *Risk* The promise of the receipt of a sum of money some years hence generally carries with it an element of **risk**; the payout may not take place or the amount may be less than expected. Risk simply means that the future return has a variety of possible values. Thus, the issuer of a security, whether it be a share, a bond or a bank account, must be prepared to compensate the investor for impatience to consume, inflation and risk involved, otherwise no one will be willing to buy the security.

Take the case of Mrs Ann Investor who is considering a £1,000 one-year investment and requires compensation for three elements of time value. First, a return of 2 per cent is required for the pure time value of money. Second, inflation is anticipated to be 3 per cent over the year. At time zero (t_0) £1,000 buys one basket of goods and services. To buy the same basket of goods and services at time t_1 (one year later) £1,030 is needed. To compensate the investor for impatience to consume and inflation the investment needs to generate a return of 5.06 per cent, that is:

$$(1 + 0.02)(1 + 0.03) - 1 = 0.0506$$

The figure of 5.06 per cent may be regarded here as the **risk-free return (RFR)**, the interest rate that is sufficient to induce investment assuming no uncertainty about cash flows. Investors tend to view lending to reputable governments through the purchase of bonds or bills as the nearest they are going to get to risk-free investing, because these institutions have unlimited ability to raise income from taxes or to create money. The RFR forms the bedrock for time value of money calculations as the pure time value and the expected inflation rate affect all investments equally. Whether the investment is in property, bonds, shares or a factory, if expected inflation rises from 3 per cent to 5 per cent then the investor's required return on all investments will increase by 2 per cent.

However, different investment categories carry different degrees of uncertainty about the outcome of the investment. For instance, an investment on the Russian stock market, with its high volatility, may be regarded as more risky than the purchase of a share in BP with its steady growth prospects. Investors require different **risk premiums** on top of the RFR to reflect the perceived level of extra risk. Thus:

Required return (Time value of money) = RFR + Risk premium

In the case of Mrs Ann Investor, the risk premium pushes up the total return required to, say, 10 per cent, thus giving full compensation for all three elements of the time value of money.

Discounted cash flow

The net present value and internal rate of return techniques, both being discounted cash flow methods, take into account the time value of money. Exhibit 2.3, which presents Project Alpha, suggests that, on a straightforward analysis, Project Alpha generates more cash inflows than outflows. An outlay of £2,000 produces £2,400.

Exhibit 2.3	Project Alpha, simple cash flow	
Points in time (yearly intervals)		**Cash flows (£)**
0 Now		−2,000
1 (1 year from now)		+600
2		+600
3		+600
4		+600

However, we may be foolish to accept Project Alpha on the basis of this crude methodology. The £600 cash flows occur at different times and are therefore worth different amounts to a person standing at time zero. Quite naturally, such an individual would value the £600 received after one year more highly than the £600 received after four years. In other words, the present value of the pounds (at time zero) depends on when they are received.

It would be useful to convert all these different 'qualities' of pounds to a common currency, to some sort of common denominator. The conversion process is achieved by discounting all future cash flows by the time value of money, thereby expressing them as an equivalent amount received at time zero. The process of discounting relies on a variant of the compounding formula:

$$F = P (1 + i)^n$$

where F = future value P = present value
        i = interest rate n = number of years over which compounding takes place

If a saver deposited £100 in a bank account paying interest at 8 per cent per annum, after three years the account will contain £125.97:

$$F = 100 (1 + 0.08)^3 = £125.97$$

This formula can be changed so that we can answer the following question: 'How much must I deposit in the bank now to receive £125.97 in three years? We need to rearrange the formula so that we are calculating for present value, P:

$$P = \frac{F}{(1 + i)^n} \text{ or } F \times \frac{1}{(1 + i)^n}$$

$$P = \frac{125.97}{(1 + 0.08)^3} = 100$$

In this second case we have discounted the £125.97 back to a present value of £100. If this technique is now applied to Project Alpha to convert all the money cash flows of future years into their present value equivalents the result is as follows (assuming that the time value of money is 10 per cent) – *see* Exhibit 2.4.

We can see that, when these future pounds are converted to a common denominator, this investment involves a larger outflow (£2,000) than inflow (£1,901.92). In other words the return on the £2,000 is less than 10 per cent.

Exhibit 2.4	Project Alpha, discounted cash flow	
Points in time (yearly intervals)	**Cash flows (£)**	**Discounted cash flows (£)**
0	−2,000	−2,000.00
1	+600	$\dfrac{600}{(1 + 0.1)}$ = +545.45
2	+600	$\dfrac{600}{(1 + 0.1)^2}$ = +495.87
3	+600	$\dfrac{600}{(1 + 0.1)^3}$ = +450.79
4	+600	$\dfrac{600}{(1 + 0.1)^4}$ = +409.81

Technical aside

If your calculator has a 'powers' function (usually represented by x^y or y^x) then compounding and discounting can be accomplished relatively quickly. Alternatively, you may obtain discount factors from the table in Appendix II at the end of the book. If we take the discounting of the fourth year's cash flow for Alpha as an illustration:

$$\frac{1}{(1 + 0.10)^4} \times 600$$

Calculator: Input 1.10
Press y^x (or x^y)
Input 4
Press =
Display 1.4641
Press $^1/_x$
Display 0.6830
Multiply by 600
Answer 409.81.

Using Appendix II, look down the column 10% and along the row 4 years to find discount factor of 0.683:   0.683 × £600 = £409.81

(Some calculators do not use x^y or y^x – check the instructions)

Net present value and internal rate of return

Net present value: examples and definitions

The conceptual justification for, and the mathematics of, the net present value and internal rate of return methods of project appraisal will be illustrated through an imaginary but realistic decision-making process at the firm of Hard Decisions plc. This example, in addition to describing techniques, demonstrates the centrality of some key concepts such as opportunity cost and time value of money and shows the wealth-destroying effect of ignoring these issues.

Imagine you are the finance director of a large publicly quoted company called Hard Decisions plc. The board of directors agrees that the objective of the firm should be shareholder wealth maximisation. Recently, the board appointed a new director, Mr Brightspark, as an 'ideas' man. He has a reputation as someone who can see opportunities where others see only problems. He has been hired especially to seek out new avenues for expansion and make better use of existing assets. In the past few weeks Mr Brightspark has been looking at some land that the company owns near the centre of Birmingham. This is a ten-acre site on which the flagship factory of the firm once stood; but that was 30 years ago and the site is now derelict. Mr Brightspark announces to a board meeting that he has three alternative proposals concerning the ten-acre site.

Mr Brightspark stands up to speak: Proposal 1 is to spend £5m clearing the site, cleaning it up, and decontaminating it. [The factory that stood on the site was used for chemical production.] It would then be possible to sell the ten acres to property developers for a sum of £12m in one year's time. Thus, we will make a profit of £7m over a one-year period.

Proposal 1: Clean up and sell – Mr Brightspark's figures

Clearing the site plus decontamination, payable t_0	–£5m
Sell the site in one year, t_1	£12m
Profit	£7m

The chairman of the board stops Mr Brightspark at that point and turns to you, in your capacity as the financial expert on the board, to ask what you think of the first proposal. Because you have studied assiduously on your financial management course you are able to make the following observations:

Point 1

This company is valued by the stock market at £100m because our investors are content that the rate of return they receive from us is consistent with the going rate for our risk class of shares; that is, 15 per cent per annum. In other words, the opportunity cost for our shareholders of buying shares in this firm is 15 per cent. (Hard Decisions is an all-equity firm; no debt capital has been raised.) The alternative to investing their money with us is to invest it in another firm with similar risk characteristics yielding 15 per cent per annum. Thus, we may take this *opportunity cost of capital* as our minimum required return from any project (of the same risk) we undertake. This idea of opportunity cost can perhaps be better explained by the use of a diagram (*see* Exhibit 2.5).

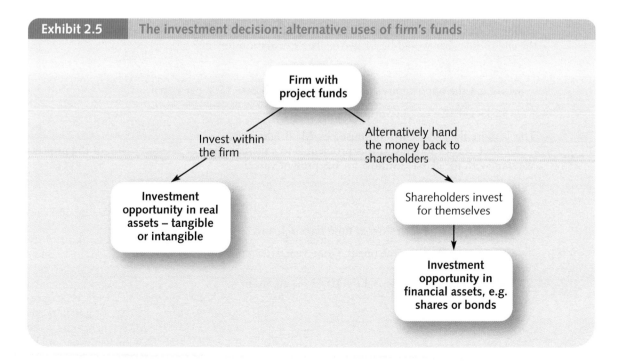

Exhibit 2.5 The investment decision: alternative uses of firm's funds

If we give a return of less than 15 per cent then shareholders will lose out because they can obtain 15 per cent elsewhere and will, thus, suffer an opportunity cost. We, as managers of shareholders' money, need to use a discount rate of 15 per cent for any project of the same risk class that we analyse. The discount rate is the opportunity cost of investing in the project rather than the capital markets, for example, buying shares in other firms giving a 15 per cent return. Instead of accepting this project the firm can always give the cash to the shareholders and let them invest it in financial assets.

Point 2

I believe I am right in saying that we have received numerous offers for the ten-acre site over the past year. A reasonable estimate of its immediate sale value would be £6m. That is, I could call up one of the firms keen to get its hands on the site and squeeze out a price of about £6m. This £6m is an opportunity cost of the project, in that it is the value of the best alternative course of action. Thus, we should add to Mr Brightspark's £5m of clean-up costs the £6m of opportunity cost because we are truly sacrificing £11m to put this proposal into operation. If we did not go ahead with Mr Brightspark's proposal, but sold the site as it is, we could raise our bank balance by £6m, plus the £5m saved by not paying clean-up costs.

Proposal 1: Clean up and sell – sacrifice at t_0

Immediate sale value (opportunity cost)	£6m
Clean-up, etc.	£5m
Total sacrifice at t_0	£11m

Finally

I can accept Mr Brightspark's final sale price of £12m as being valid in the sense that he has, I know, employed some high-quality experts to derive the figure, but I do have a problem with comparing the initial outlay *directly* with the final cash flow on a simple *nominal* sum basis. The £12m is to be received in one year's time, whereas the £5m is to be handed over to the clean-up firm immediately, and the £6m opportunity cost sacrifice, by not selling the site, is being made immediately.

   If we were to take the £11m initial cost of the project and invest it in financial assets of the same risk class as this firm, giving a return of 15 per cent, then the value of that investment at the end of one year would be £12.65m. The calculation for this:

$$F = P (1 + k)$$

where k = the opportunity cost of capital (in this case 15% per year):

$$11 (1 + 0.15) = £12.65m$$

This is more than the return promised by Mr Brightspark.

   Another way of looking at this problem is to calculate the net present value of the project. We start with the classic formula for net present value:

$$NPV = CF_0 + \frac{CF_1}{(1 + k)^n}$$

where CF_0 = cash flow at time zero (t_0), and

   CF_1 = cash flow at time one (t_1), one year after time zero:

$$NPV = -11 + \frac{12}{1 + 0.15} = -11 + 10.435 = -0.565m$$

All cash flows are expressed in the common currency of pounds at time zero. Thus, everything is in present value terms. When the positives and negatives are netted out we have the net present value. The decision rules for net present value are:

NPV ≥ 0   Accept

NPV < 0   Reject

Project proposal 1's negative NPV indicates that a return of less than 15 per cent per annum will be achieved.

An investment proposal's net present value is derived by discounting the future net cash receipts at a rate which reflects the value of the alternative use of the funds, summing them over the life of the proposal and deducting the initial outlay.

In conclusion, Ladies and Gentlemen, given the choice between:

(a) selling the site immediately, raising £6m and saving £5m of expenditure – a total of £11m, or

(b) developing the site along the lines of Mr Brightspark's proposal,

I would choose to sell it immediately, because £11m would get a better return elsewhere. The chairman thanks you and asks Mr Brightspark to explain Project proposal 2.

Proposal 2: Office complex – Mr Brightspark's figures

Mr Brightspark: Proposal 2 consists of paying £5m immediately for a clean-up. Then, over the next two years, spending another £14m building an office complex. Tenants would not be found immediately on completion of the building. The office units would be let gradually over the following three years. Finally, when the office complex is fully let, in six years' time, it would be sold to an institution, such as a pension fund, for the sum of £40m (*see* Exhibit 2.6).

Exhibit 2.6   Cash flows for office project

Points in time (yearly intervals)	Cash flows (£m)	Event	
0 (now)	–5	Clean-up costs	
0 (now)	–6	Opportunity cost	
1	–4	Building cost	
2	–10	Building cost	
3	+1	Net rental income, $\frac{1}{4}$ of offices let	
4	+2	Net rental income, $\frac{1}{2}$ of offices let	
5	+4	Net rental income, all offices let	
6	+40	Office complex sold	
Total	+22	Inflow	£47m
		Outflow	£25m
Profit	22		

Note: Mr Brightspark has accepted the validity of your argument about the opportunity cost of the alternative 'project' of selling the land immediately and has quickly added this –£6m to the figures.

Mr Brightspark claims an almost doubling of the money invested (£25m invested over the first two years leads to an inflow of £47m).

The chairman turns to you and asks: Is this project really so beneficial to our shareholders?

You reply: The message rammed home to me by my finance textbook was that the best method of assessing whether a project is shareholder wealth enhancing is to discount all its cash flows at the opportunity cost of capital. This will enable a calculation of the net present value of those cash flows.

$$\text{NPV} = CF_0 + \frac{CF_1}{1+k} + \frac{CF_2}{(1+k)^2} + \frac{CF_3}{(1+k)^3} \cdots + \frac{CF_n}{(1+k)^n}$$

So, given that Mr Brightspark's figures are true cash flows, I can calculate the NPV of Proposal 2 – *see* **Exhibit 2.7**. Note that we again use a discount rate of 15 per cent, which implies that this project is at the same level of risk as Proposal 1 and the average of the existing set of projects of the firm. If it is subject to higher risk, an increased rate of return would be demanded (Chapter 8 discusses the calculation of the required rate of return).

Exhibit 2.7	Office project: discounted cash	
Points in time (yearly intervals)	**Cash flows (£m)**	**Discounted cash flows (£m)**
0	−5	−5
0	−6	−6
1	−4	$\dfrac{-4}{(1+0.15)}$ −3.48
2	−10	$\dfrac{-10}{(1+0.15)^2}$ −7.56
3	1	$\dfrac{1}{(1+0.15)^3}$ 0.66
4	2	$\dfrac{2}{(1+0.15)^4}$ 1.14
5	4	$\dfrac{4}{(1+0.15)^5}$ 1.99
6	40	$\dfrac{40}{(1+0.15)^6}$ 17.29
Net present value		−0.96

AN EXCEL SPREADSHEET VERSION OF THIS CALCULATION IS AVAILABLE AT
www.pearsoned.co.uk/arnold

Because the NPV is less than 0, we would serve our shareholders better by selling the site and saving the money spent on clearing and building and putting that money into financial assets yielding 15 per cent per annum. Shareholders would end up with more in Year 6.

The chairman thanks you and asks Mr Brightspark for his third proposal.

Proposal 3: Worldbeater manufacturing plant

Mr Brightspark: Proposal 3 involves the use of the site for a factory to manufacture the product 'Worldbeater'. We have been producing 'Worldbeater' from our Liverpool factory for the past ten years. Despite its name, we have confined the selling of it to the UK market. I propose the setting up of a second 'Worldbeater' factory that will serve the European market. The figures are as follows (*see* Exhibit 2.8).

Exhibit 2.8	Worldbeater factory cash flow	

Points in time (yearly intervals)	Cash flows (£m)	Event
0	–5	Clean-up
0	–6	Opportunity cost
1	–10	Factory building
2	0	
3 to infinity	+5	Net income from additional sales of 'Worldbeater'.

Note: Revenue is gained in Year 2 from sales but this is exactly offset by the cash flows created by the costs of production and distribution. The figures for Year 3 and all subsequent years are net cash flows, that is, cash outflows are subtracted from cash inflows generated by sales.

The chairman turns to you and asks your advice.

You reply: Worldbeater is a well-established product and has been very successful. I am happy to take the cash flow figures given by Mr Brightspark as the basis for my calculations, which are set out in Exhibit 2.9. Note that the annual cash flow for year 3 of £5m is to be received every year thereafter as well as in year 3, and is therefore a 'perpetuity' (see page 64 for perpetuity calculations).

Exhibit 2.9	Discounted cash flows for Worldbeater	

Points in time (yearly intervals)	Cash flows (£m)		Discounted cash flows (£m)
0	–11		–11
1	–10	$\dfrac{-10}{(1 + 0.15)}$	–8.7
2	0		0.0
3 to infinity	5	Value of perpetuity at time t_2: $$P = \frac{F}{k} = \frac{5}{0.15} = 33.33$$ This has to be discounted back two years: $$\frac{33.33}{(1 + 0.15)^2}$$	=25.20
Net present value			+5.5

AN EXCEL SPREADSHEET VERSION OF THIS CALCULATION IS AVAILABLE AT
www.pearsoned.co.uk/arnold

Note   If these calculations are confusing you, now might be a good time to read the mathematical tool Appendix 2.1 at the end of this chapter. Also try the questions set as 'Mathematical tool exercises'. Answers are given at the back of the book, in Appendix VI.

The perpetuity $\frac{F}{k}$ formula can be used on the assumption that the first payment arises one year from the time at which we are valuing. So, if the first inflow arises at time 3 we are valuing the perpetuity as though we are standing at time 2. The objective of this exercise is not to convert all cash flows to time 2 values, but rather to time 0 value. Therefore, it is necessary to discount the perpetuity value by two years.

This project gives an NPV that is positive and, therefore, is shareholder wealth enhancing. The third project provides a rate of return that is greater than 15 per cent per annum. It produces a return of 15 per cent plus a present value of £5.5m. Based on these figures I would recommend that the board looks into Proposal 3 in more detail.

The chairman thanks you and suggests that this proposal be put to the vote.

Mr Brightspark (interrupts): Just a minute, are we not taking a lot on trust here? Our finance expert has stated that the way to evaluate these proposals is by using the NPV method, but in the firms where I have worked in the past, the internal rate of return (IRR) method of investment appraisal was used. I would like to see how these three proposals shape up when the IRR calculations are done.

The chairman turns to you and asks you to explain the IRR method, and to apply it to the figures provided by Mr Brightspark.

Before continuing this boardroom drama it might be useful at this point to broaden understanding of NPV by considering two worked examples.

Worked example 2.1   Camrat plc

Camrat plc requires a return on investment of at least 10 per cent per annum over the life of any proposed project with the same risk as its existing projects in order to meet the opportunity cost of its shareholders (Camrat is financed entirely by equity). The dynamic and thrusting strategic development team have been examining the possibility of entering the new market area of mosaic floor tiles. This will require an immediate outlay of £1m for factory purchase and tooling-up which will be followed by net (i.e. after all cash outflows, e.g. wages, variable costs, etc.) cash inflows of £0.2m in one year, and £0.3m in two years' time. Thereafter, annual net cash inflows will be £180,000.

Required

Given these cash flows, will this investment provide a 10 per cent return (per annum) over the life of the project? Assume for simplicity that all cash flows arise on anniversary dates and the project has the same risk level as the company's existing set of projects.

Answer

First, lay out the cash flows with precise timing. (Note: the assumption that all cash flows arise on anniversary dates allows us to do this very simply.)

Points in time (yearly intervals)	0	1	2	3 to infinity
Cash flows (£)	−1m	0.2m	0.3m	0.18m

Worked example 2.1   Continued

Second, discount these cash flows to their present value equivalents.

Points in time   0   1   2   3 to infinity

$$CF_0 \qquad \frac{CF_1}{1+k} \qquad \frac{CF_2}{(1+k)^2} \qquad \frac{CF_3}{k} \times \frac{1}{(1+k)^2}$$

$$-1m \qquad \frac{0.2}{1+0.1} \qquad \frac{0.3}{(1+0.1)^2} \qquad \frac{0.18}{0.1}$$

This discounts back two years

$$\frac{0.18/0.1}{(1+0.1)^2}$$

$$-1m \qquad 0.1818 \qquad 0.2479 \qquad \frac{1.8}{(1.1)^2} = 1.4876$$

Third, net out the discounted cash flows to give the net present value.

$$
\begin{array}{r}
-1.0000 \\
+0.1818 \\
+0.2479 \\
+1.4876 \\
\hline
\end{array}
$$

Net present value +0.9173

AN EXCEL SPREADSHEET VERSION OF THIS CALCULATION IS AVAILABLE AT
www.pearsoned.co.uk/arnold

Conclusion

The positive NPV result demonstrates that this project gives not only a return of 10 per cent per annum but a large surplus above and beyond a 10 per cent per annum return. This is an extremely attractive project: on a £1m investment the surplus generated beyond the opportunity cost of the shareholders (their time value of money) is £917,300; thus by accepting this project we would increase shareholder wealth by this amount.

Worked example 2.2   Actarm plc

Actarm plc is examining two projects, A and B. The cash flows are as follows:

	A £	B £
Initial outflow, t_0	240,000	240,000
Cash inflows:		
Time 1 (one year after t_0)	200,000	20,000
Time 2	100,000	120,000
Time 3	20,000	220,000

Worked example 2.2   **Continued**

Using discount rates of 8 per cent, and then 16 per cent, calculate the NPVs and state which project is superior. Why do you get a different preference depending on the discount rate used?

Answer

Using 8 per cent as the discount rate

$$\text{NPV} = CF_0 + \frac{CF_1}{1+k} + \frac{CF_2}{(1+k)^2} + \frac{CF_3}{(1+k)^3}$$

Project A

$$-240,000 + \frac{200,000}{1+0.08} + \frac{100,000}{(1+0.08)^2} + \frac{20,000}{(1+0.08)^3}$$

$-240,000 + 185,185 + 85,734 + 15,877 = £46,796$

Project B

$$-240,000 + \frac{20,000}{1+0.08} + \frac{120,000}{(1+0.08)^2} + \frac{220,000}{(1+0.08)^3}$$

$-240,000 + 18,519 + 102,881 + 174,643 = £56,043$

Using an 8 per cent discount rate both projects produce positive NPVs and therefore would enhance shareholder wealth. However, Project B is superior because it creates more value than Project A. Thus, if the accepting of one project excludes the possibility of accepting the other then B is preferred.

Using 16 per cent as the discount rate

Project A

$$-240,000 + \frac{200,000}{1.16} + \frac{100,000}{(1.16)^2} + \frac{20,000}{(1.16)^3}$$

$-240,000 + 172,414 + 74,316 + 12,813 = + £19,543$

Project B

$$-240,000 + \frac{20,000}{1.16} + \frac{120,000}{(1.16)^2} + \frac{220,000}{(1.16)^3}$$

$-240,000 + 17,241 + 89,180 + 140,945 = + £7,366$

With a 16 per cent discount rate Project A generates more shareholder value and so would be preferred to Project B. This is despite the fact that Project B, in pure undiscounted cash flow terms, produces an additional £40,000.

The different ranking (order of superiority) occurs because Project B has the bulk of its cash flows occurring towards the end of the project's life. These large distant cash flows, when discounted at a high discount rate, become relatively small compared with those of Project A, which has its high cash flows discounted by only one year.

AN EXCEL SPREADSHEET VERSION OF THIS CALCULATION IS AVAILABLE AT
www.pearsoned.co.uk/arnold

Internal rate of return

We now return to Hard Decisions plc. The chairman has asked you to explain internal rate of return (IRR).

You respond: The internal rate of return is a very popular method of project appraisal and it has much to commend it. In particular it takes into account the time value of money. I am not surprised to find that Mr Brightspark has encountered this appraisal technique in his previous employment. Basically, what the IRR tells you is the rate of return you will receive by putting your money into a project. It describes by how much the cash inflows exceed the cash outflows on an annualised percentage basis, taking account of the timing of those cash flows.

The internal rate of return is the rate of return which equates the present value of future cash flows with the outlay:

Outlay = Future cash flows discounted at rate r

Thus:

$$CF_0 = \frac{CF_1}{1+r} + \frac{CF_2}{(1+r)^2} + \frac{CF_3}{(1+r)^3} \cdots \frac{CF_n}{(1+r)^n}$$

IRR is also referred to as the 'yield' of a project.

Alternatively, the internal rate of return, r, is the discount rate at which the net present value is zero. It is the value for r which makes the following equation hold:

$$CF_0 + \frac{CF_1}{1+r} + \frac{CF_2}{(1+r)^2} + \frac{CF_3}{(1+r)^3} \cdots \frac{CF_n}{(1+r)^n} = 0$$

(*Note*: in the first formula CF_0 is expressed as a positive number, whereas in the second it is usually a negative.)

These two equations amount to the same thing. They both require knowledge of the cash flows and their precise timing. The element that is unknown is the rate of return which will make the time-adjusted outflows and inflows equal to each other.

I apologise, Ladies and Gentlemen, if this all sounds like too much jargon. Perhaps it would be helpful if you could see the IRR calculation in action. Let's apply the formula to Mr Brightspark's Proposal 1.

Proposal 1: Internal rate of return

Using the second version of the formula, our objective is to find an r which makes the discounted inflow at time 1 of £12m plus the initial £11m outflow equal to zero:

$$CF_0 + \frac{CF_1}{1+r} = 0$$

$$-11 + \frac{12}{1+r} = 0$$

The method I would recommend for establishing r is trial and error (assuming we do not have the relevant computer program available). So, to start with, simply pick an interest rate and plug it into the formula. Let's try 5 per cent:

$$-11 + \frac{12}{1+0.05} = £0.42857\text{m or } £428,571$$

(You can pick any (reasonable) discount rate to begin with in the trial and error approach.)

A 5 per cent rate is not correct because the discounted cash flows do not total to zero. The surplus of approximately £0.43m suggests that a higher discount rate will be more suitable. This will reduce the present value of the future cash inflow. Let's try 10 per cent:

$$-11 + \frac{12}{1+0.1} = -0.0909 \text{ or } -£90,909$$

Again, we have not hit on the correct discount rate. Let's try 9 per cent:

$$-11 + \frac{12}{1 + 0.09} = 0.009174 \text{ or } +£9,174$$

The last two calculations tell us that the interest rate which causes the discounted future cash flow to equal the initial outflow lies somewhere between 9 per cent and 10 per cent. The precise rate can be found through interpolation.

First, display all the facts so far established (*see* **Exhibit 2.10**).

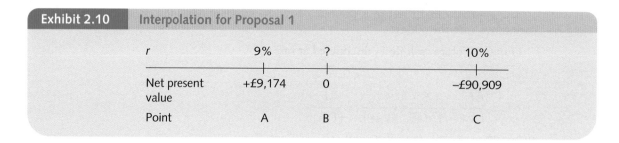

Exhibit 2.10	**Interpolation for Proposal 1**

r	9%	?	10%
Net present value	+£9,174	0	−£90,909
Point	A	B	C

Exhibit 2.10 illustrates that there is a yield rate (r) that lies between 9 per cent and 10 per cent which will produce an NPV of zero. The way to find that rate is to first find the distance between points A and B as a proportion of the entire distance between points A and C.

$$\frac{A \rightarrow B}{A \rightarrow C} = \frac{9,174 - 0}{9,174 + 90,909} = 0.0917$$

Thus the ? lies at a distance of 0.0917 away from the 9 per cent point.

Thus, IRR:

$$= 9 + \frac{9,174}{100,083} \times (10 - 9) = 9.0917 \text{ per cent}$$

To check our result:

$$-11 + \frac{12}{1 + 0.090917} = -11 + 11 = 0$$

Internal rate of return decision rules

The rules for internal rate of return decisions are:

● If $k > r$ **reject** If the opportunity cost of capital (k) is greater than the internal rate of return (r) on a project then the investor is better served by not going ahead with the project and applying the money to the best alternative use.

● If $k \leq r$ **accept** Here, the project under consideration produces the same or a higher yield than investment elsewhere for a similar risk level.

The IRR of Proposal 1 is 9.091 per cent, which is below the 15 per cent opportunity cost of capital used by Hard Decisions plc for projects of this risk class. Therefore, using the IRR method as well as the NPV method, this project should be rejected.

It might be enlightening to consider the relationship between NPV and IRR. **Exhibit 2.11** shows what happens to NPV as the discount rate is varied between zero and 10 per cent for Proposal 1. At a zero discount rate the £12m received in one year is not discounted at all, so the NPV of £1m is simply the difference between the two cash flows. When the discount rate is raised to 10 per cent the present value of the year 1 cash flow becomes less than the current outlay. Where the initial outflow equals the *discounted* future inflows, i.e. when NPV is zero, we can read off the internal rate of return.

Exhibit 2.11	The relationship between NPV and the discount rate (Proposal 1's figures)

Discount rate (%)	NPV
10	−90,909
9.0917	0
9	9,174
8	111,111
7	214,953
6	320,755
5	428,571
4	538,461
3	650,485
2	764,706
1	881,188
0	1,000,000

Proposal 2: IRR

To calculate the IRR for Proposal 2 we first lay out the cash flows in the discount formula:

$$-11 + \frac{-4}{(1+r)} + \frac{-10}{(1+r)^2} + \frac{1}{(1+r)^3} + \frac{2}{(1+r)^4} + \frac{4}{(1+r)^5} + \frac{40}{(1+r)^6} = 0$$

Then we try alternative discount rates to find a rate, r, that gives a zero NPV:

Try 14 per cent: NPV (approx.) = −£0.043m or −£43,000

At 13 per cent: NPV (approx.) = £932,000

Interpolation is required to find an internal rate of return accurate to at least one decimal place (*see* Exhibit 2.12).

Exhibit 2.12	Interpolation for Proposal 2

Discount rate

r	13%		?	14%
NPV	+932,000		0	−43,000

$$13 + \frac{932,000}{975,000} \times (14 - 13) = 13.96\%$$

AN EXCEL SPREADSHEET VERSION OF THIS CALCULATION IS AVAILABLE AT
www.pearsoned.co.uk/arnold

This project produces an IRR (13.96%) which is less than the opportunity cost of shareholders' funds; so it should be rejected under the IRR method. Exhibit 2.13 shows how the NPV of Project 2 changes as the discount rate used is raised. Because the line in Exhibit 2.13 is curved, it is important to have only a small gap in trial and error discount rates prior to interpolation.

Exhibit 2.13	Graph of NPV and discount rate for Proposal 2

The interpolation formula assumes a straight line between the two discount rates chosen and this may lead to a false result.

The effect of taking a wide range of interest rates can be illustrated if we calculate on the basis of 5 per cent and 30 per cent – *see* **Exhibit 2.14**.

At 5 per cent, NPV of Project 2 = £11.6121m.

At 30 per cent, NPV of Project 2 = –£9.4743m.

$$5 + \left(\frac{11.6121}{11.6121 + 9.4743}\right)(30 - 5) = 18.77\%$$

From **Exhibit 2.15** we see that the non-linearity of the relationship between NPV and the discount rate has created an IRR almost 5 per cent removed from the true IRR. This could lead to

Exhibit 2.14	Linear interpolation

Discount rate

r	5%	?	30%
NPV	+11.6121	0	–9.4743

Exhibit 2.15	The accuracy of the IRR calculated may depend on the size of the gap between the discount rates used in the interpolation calculation

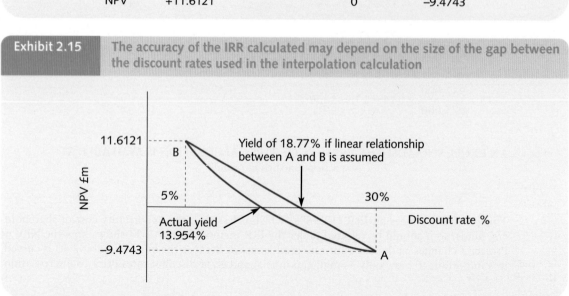

an erroneous acceptance of this project given the company's hurdle rate of 15 per cent. In reality this project yields less than the company could earn by placing its money elsewhere for the same risk level.

Proposal 3: IRR

$$CF_0 + \frac{CF_1}{1 + r} + \frac{CF_3 / r}{(1 + r)^2} = 0$$

Try 19 per cent: $-11 + \dfrac{-10}{1 + 0.19} + \dfrac{5/0.19}{(1 + 0.19)^2} = -£0.82m$

Try 18 per cent: $-11 + \dfrac{-10}{1 + 0.18} + \dfrac{5/0.18}{(1 + 0.18)^2} = -£0.475m$

$18 + \dfrac{475,000}{1,295,000} \times (19 - 18) = 18.37\%$

AN EXCEL SPREADSHEET VERSION OF THIS CALCULATION IS AVAILABLE AT
www.pearsoned.co.uk/arnold

Project 3 produces an internal rate of return of 18.37 per cent which is higher than the opportunity cost of capital and therefore is to be commended.

We temporarily leave the saga of Mr Brightspark and his proposals to reinforce understanding of NPV and IRR through the worked example of Martac plc.

Worked example 2.3	Martac plc

Martac plc is a manufacturer of *Martac-aphro*. Two new automated process machines used in the production of *Martac-aphro* have been introduced to the market, the CAM and the ATR. Both will give cost savings over existing processes:

£000s	CAM	ATR
Initial cost (machine purchase and installation, etc.)	120	250
Cash flow savings:		
At Time 1 (one year after the initial cash outflow)	48	90
At Time 2	48	90
At Time 3	48	90
At Time 4	48	90

All other factors remain constant and the firm has access to large amounts of capital. The required return on projects is 8 per cent.

Required

(a) Calculate the IRR for the CAM project.
(b) Calculate the IRR for the ATR project.
(c) Based on IRR which machine would you purchase?
(d) Calculate the NPV for each project.
(e) Based on NPV which machine would you buy?
(f) Is IRR or NPV the better decision tool?

| Worked example 2.3 | Continued |

Answers

In this problem the total cash flows associated with the alternative projects are not given. Instead the incremental cash flows are provided, for example, the additional savings available over the existing costs of production. This, however, is sufficient for a decision to be made about which machine to purchase.

(a) IRR for CAM

$$CF_0 + \frac{CF_1}{1+r} + \frac{CF_2}{(1+r)^2} + \frac{CF_3}{(1+r)^3} + \frac{CF_4}{(1+r)^4} = 0$$

Try 22 per cent:

−120,000 + 48,000 annuity factor (af) for 4 years @ 22%

(*See* Appendix 2.1 to this chapter for annuity calculations and Appendix III at the end of the book for an annuity table.)

The annuity factor tells us the present value of four lots of £1 received at four annual intervals. This is 2.4936, meaning that the £4 in present value terms is worth just over £2.49.

−120,000 + 48,000 × 2.4936 = −£307.20

Try 21 per cent:

−120,000 + 48,000 × annuity factor (af) for 4 years @ 21%
−120,000 + 48,000 × 2.5404 = +£1,939.20

Discount rate

	21%	?	22%
NPV	1,939.2	0	−307

$$21 + \frac{1939.2}{1939.2 + 307} \times (22 - 21) = 21.86\%$$

(b) IRR for ATR

Try 16 per cent:

−250,000 + 90,000 × 2.7982 = +£1,838

Try 17 per cent:

−250,000 + 90,000 × 2.7432 = −£3,112

r	16%	?	17%
NPV	+1,838	0	−3,112

$$16 + \left(\frac{1,838}{1,838 + 3,112} \right) \times (17 - 16) = 16.37\%$$

(c) Choice of machine on basis of IRR

If IRR is the only decision tool available then as long as the IRRs exceed the discount rate (or cost of capital) the project with the higher IRR might appear to be the preferred choice. In this case CAM ranks higher than ATR.

(d) NPV for machines:

CAM −120,000 + 48,000 × 3.3121 = +£38,981

NPV for ATR

−250,000 + 90,000 × 3.3121 = +£48,089

Worked example 2.3	Continued

(e) Choice of machine on basis of NPV

ATR generates a return which has a present value of £48,089 in addition to the minimum return on capital required. This is larger than for CAM and therefore ATR ranks higher than CAM if NPV is used as the decision tool.

(f) Choice of decision tool

This problem has produced conflicting decision outcomes, which depend on the project appraisal method employed. NPV is the better decision-making technique because it measures in absolute amounts of money. That is, it gives the increase in shareholder wealth available by accepting a project. In contrast IRR expresses its return as a percentage which may result in an inferior low-scale project being preferred to a higher-scale project.

> **AN EXCEL SPREADSHEET VERSION OF THIS CALCULATION IS AVAILABLE AT**
> **www.pearsoned.co.uk/arnold**

Choosing between NPV and IRR

We now return to Hard Decisions plc.

Mr Brightspark: I have noticed your tendency to prefer NPV to any other method. Yet, in the three projects we have been discussing, NPV and IRR give the same decision recommendation. That is, reject Projects 1 and 2 and accept Project 3. So, why not use IRR more often?

You reply: It is true that the NPV and IRR methods of capital investment appraisal are closely related. Both are 'time-adjusted' measures of profitability. The NPV and IRR methods gave the same results in the cases we have considered today because the problems associated with the IRR method are not present in the figures we have been working with. In the appraisal of other projects we may encounter the severe limitations of the IRR method and therefore I prefer to stick to the theoretically superior NPV technique. I will illustrate three of the most important problems – multiple solutions, ranking and confusion between investing-type decisions and financing-type decisions.

Multiple solutions

There may be a number of possible IRRs. This can be explained by examining the problems Mr Flummoxed is having (*see* Worked example 2.4).

The cause of multiple solutions is unconventional cash flows. Conventional cash flows occur when an outflow is followed by a series of inflows or a cash inflow is followed by a series of cash outflows. Unconventional cash flows are a series of cash flows with more than one change in sign. In the case of Project Oscillation the sign changes from negative to positive once, and from positive to negative once. Multiple yields can be adjusted for while still using the IRR method, but the simplest approach is to use the NPV method.

Ranking

The IRR decision rule does not always rank projects in the same way as the NPV method. Sometimes it is important to find out, not only which project gives a positive return, but which one gives the greater positive return. For instance, projects may be mutually exclusive, that is, only one may be undertaken and a choice has to be made. The use of IRR alone sometimes leads to a poor choice (see **Exhibit 2.16**).

Worked example 2.4	Mr Flummoxed

Mr Flummoxed of Deadhead plc has always used the IRR method of project appraisal. He has started to have doubts about its usefulness after examining the proposal 'Project Oscillation'.

Project Oscillation

Points in time (yearly intervals)	0	1	2
Cash flow	−3,000	+15,000	−13,000

Internal rates of return are found at 11.56 per cent *and* 288.4 per cent.

Given that Deadhead plc has a required rate of return of 20 per cent, it is impossible to decide whether to implement Project Oscillation. If there are a number of possible IRRs this means that they are all meaningless.

From Exhibit 2.16, it is clear that the ranking of the projects by their IRRs is constant at 75 per cent and 100 per cent, regardless of the opportunity cost of capital (discount rate). Project A is always better. On the other hand, ranking the projects by the NPV method is not fixed. The NPV ranking depends on the discount rate. Thus, if the discount rate used in the NPV calculation is higher than 50 per cent, the ranking under both IRR and NPV would be the same, i.e. Project A is superior. If the discount rate falls below 50 per cent, Project B is the better choice. One of the major elements leading to the theoretical dominance of NPV is that it takes into account the scale of investment; thus the shareholders are made better off by £20.87m when the opportunity cost of capital is 15 per cent by undertaking Project B because the initial size of the project is larger. NPVs are measured in absolute amounts.

Confusion over investing-type decisions versus financing-type decisions

Hard Decisions plc's Proposal 1 required a cash outflow of £11m at time zero followed by a cash inflow of £12m one year later. This resulted in an IRR of 9.0917 per cent and negative NPV of −£0.565m; thus the project is rejected under both methods given the required rate of return of 15 per cent. This is an investing-type decision, because the initial cash flow is an outflow. Now consider a project that resulted in £11m being *received* at time zero and £12m

Exhibit 2.16	Illustration of the IRR ranking problem

Project		Cash flows £m	IRR	NPV (at 15%) £m
	Time 0	One year later		
A	−20	+40	100%	+14.78m
B	−40	+70	75%	+20.87m

	NPV at different discount rates (£m)	
Discount rate (%)	Project A	Project B
0	20	30
20	13.33	18.33
50	6.67	6.67
75	2.86	0
100	0	−5
125	−2.22	−8.89

flowing out at time 1 (one year later). Here we have a financing-type decision. You need to be careful in interpreting the results of a financing-type decision IRR. The IRR is again 9.0917 and given the opportunity cost of capital there is a danger of automatically rejecting the project if you have it stuck in your mind that the IRR must exceed 15 per cent for the project to be accepted. This would be wrong because you are being offered the chance to receive £11m, which can then be invested at 15 per cent per year at that risk level. This will outweigh the outflow that occurs at time one of £12m. In other words, this project gives a positive NPV and should be accepted.

NPV = £11m – £12m/(1.15) = +£0.565m

This leads us to reverse the IRR rules for a financing-type situation. To avoid confusion use NPV. **Exhibit 2.17** summarises the characteristics of NPV and IRR.

Exhibit 2.17	Summary of the characteristics of NPV and IRR

NPV	IRR
• It recognises that £1 today is worth more than £1 tomorrow.	• Also takes into account the time value of money.
• In conditions where all worthwhile projects can be accepted (i.e. no mutual exclusivity) it maximises shareholder utility. Projects with positive NPVs should be accepted since they increase shareholder wealth, while those with negative NPVs decrease shareholder wealth.	• In situations of non-mutual exclusivity, shareholder wealth is maximised if all projects with a yield higher than the opportunity cost of capital are accepted, while those with a return less than the time value of money are rejected.
• It takes into account investment size – absolute amounts of wealth change.	• Fails to measure in terms of absolute amounts of wealth changes. It measures percentage returns and this may cause ranking problems in conditions of mutual exclusivity, i.e. the wrong project may be rejected.
• It is not as intuitively understandable as a percentage measure.	
• It can handle non-conventional cash flows.	• It is easier to communicate a percentage return than NPV to other managers and employees, who may not be familiar with the details of project appraisal techniques. The appeal of quick recognition and conveyance of understanding should not be belittled or underestimated.
• Can handle both investing-type and financing-type decisions.	
• Additivity is possible: because present values are all measured in today's £s they can be added together. Thus the returns (NPVs) of a group of projects can be calculated.	
• It assumes that cash inflows arising during the life of the project are reinvested at the opportunity cost of capital; which is a reasonable assumption.	• Non-conventional cash flows cause problems, e.g. multiple solutions.
	• Financing-type decisions may result in misinterpretation of IRR results.
	• Additivity is not possible.
	• IRR implicitly assumes that the cash inflows that are received, say, half-way through a project, can be reinvested elsewhere at a rate equal to the IRR until the end of the project's life. This is intuitively unacceptable. In the real world, if a firm invested in a very high-yielding project and some cash was returned after a short period, this firm would be unlikely to be able to deposit this cash elsewhere until the end of the project and reach the same extraordinary high yield. It is more likely that the intra-project cash inflows will be invested at the 'going rate' or the opportunity cost of capital. In other words, the firm's normal discount rate is the better estimate of the reinvestment rate. The effect of this erroneous reinvestment assumption is to inflate the IRR of the project under examination.

Concluding comments

This chapter has provided insight into the key factors for consideration when an organisation is contemplating using financial (or other) resources for investment. The analysis has been based on the assumption that the objective of any such investment is to maximise economic benefits to the owners of the enterprise. To achieve such an objective requires allowance for the opportunity cost of capital or time value of money as well as robust analysis of relevant cash flows. Given that time has a value, the precise timing of cash flows is important for project analysis. The net present value (NPV) and internal rate of return (IRR) methods of project appraisal are both discounted cash flow techniques and therefore allow for the time value of money. However, the IRR method does present problems in a few special circumstances and so the theoretically preferred method is NPV. On the other hand, NPV requires diligent studying and thought in order to be fully understood, and therefore it is not surprising to find in the workplace a bias in favour of communicating a project's viability in terms of percentages. Most large organisations, in fact, use three or four methods of project appraisal, rather than rely on only one for both rigorous analysis and communication – see Chapter 3 for more detail. The fundamental conclusion of this chapter is that the best method for maximising shareholder wealth in assessing investment projects is net present value.

Key points and concepts

- **Time value of money** has three component parts each requiring compensation for a delay in the receipt of cash: (i) the pure time value, or impatience to consume, (ii) inflation, (iii) risk.

- **Opportunity cost of capital** is the yield forgone on the best available investment alternative – the risk level of the alternative being the same as for the project under consideration.

- Taking account of the time value of money and opportunity cost of capital in project appraisal leads to **discounted cash flow analysis** (DCF).

- **Net present value** (NPV) is the present value of the future cash flows after netting out the initial cash flow. Present values are achieved by discounting at the opportunity cost of capital.

$$NPV = CF_0 + \frac{CF_1}{1 + k} + \frac{CF_2}{(1 + k)^2} + \dots \frac{CF_n}{(1 + k)^n}$$

- **The net present value decision rules** are:

    NPV $\geq$ 0 accept   NPV $<$ 0 reject

- **Internal rate of return** (IRR) is the discount rate which, when applied to the cash flows of a project, results in a zero net present value. It is an 'r' which results in the following formula being true:

$$CF_0 + \frac{CF_1}{1 + r} + \frac{CF_2}{(1 + r)^2} + \dots \frac{CF_n}{(1 + r)^n} = 0$$

- **The internal rate of return decision rule** is:

    IRR $\geq$ opportunity cost of capital – accept   IRR $<$ opportunity cost of capital – reject

- IRR is poor at handling situations of unconventional cash flows. **Multiple solutions** can be the result.

- There are circumstances when IRR ranks one project higher than another, whereas NPV ranks the projects in the opposite order. This **ranking problem** becomes an important issue in situations of mutual exclusivity.

- The IRR decision rule is reversed for financing-type decisions.

- NPV measures in **absolute amounts** of money. IRR is a percentage measure.

- IRR assumes that intra-project cash flows can be invested at a rate of return equal to the IRR. This biases the IRR calculation.

Appendix 2.1 Mathematical tools for finance

The purpose of this Appendix is to explain essential mathematical skills that will be needed for this book. The author has no love of mathematics for its own sake and so only those techniques of direct relevance to the subject matter of this textbook will be covered in this section.

Simple and compound interest

When there are time delays between receipts and payments of financial sums we need to make use of the concepts of simple and compound interest.

Simple interest

Interest is paid only on the original principal. No interest is paid on the accumulated interest payments.

Example 1

Suppose that a sum of £10 is deposited in a bank account that pays 12 per cent per annum. At the end of year 1 the investor has £11.20 in the account. That is:

$$F = P(1 + i)$$

$$11.20 = 10(1 + 0.12)$$

where F = Future value, P = Present value, i = Interest rate.

The initial sum, called the principal, is multiplied by the interest rate to give the annual return. At the end of five years:

$$F = P(1 + in)$$

where n = number of years. Thus,

$$16 = 10(1 + 0.12 \times 5)$$

Note from the example that the 12 per cent return is a constant amount each year. Interest is not earned on the interest already accumulated from previous years.

Compound interest

The more usual situation in the real world is for interest to be paid on the sum that accumulates – whether or not that sum comes from the principal or from the interest received in previous periods.

Example 2

An investment of £10 is made at an interest rate of 12 per cent with the interest being compounded. In one year the capital will grow by 12 per cent to £11.20. In the second year the capital will grow by 12 per cent, but this time the growth will be on the accumulated value of £11.20 and thus will amount to an extra £1.34. At the end of two years:

$$F = P(1 + i)(1 + i)$$

$$F = 11.20(1 + i)$$

$$F = 12.54$$

Alternatively,

$$F = P(1 + i)^2$$

Exhibit 2.18 displays the future value of £1 invested at a number of different compound interest rates and for alternative numbers of years. This is extracted from Appendix I at the end of the book.

Exhibit 2.18	The future value of £1				
	Interest rate (per cent per annum)				
Year	**1**	**2**	**5**	**12**	**15**
1	1.0100	1.0200	1.0500	1.1200	1.1500
2	1.0201	1.0404	1.1025	1.2544	1.3225
3	1.0303	1.0612	1.1576	1.4049	1.5209
4	1.0406	1.0824	1.2155	1.5735	1.7490
5	1.0510	1.1041	1.2763	1.7623	2.0114

From the second row of the table in Exhibit 2.18 we can read that £1 invested for two years at 12 per cent amounts to £1.2544. Thus, the investment of £10 provides a future capital sum 1.2544 times the original amount:

$$£10 \times 1.2544 = £12.544$$

Over five years the result is:

$$F = P(1 + i)^n$$

$$17.62 = 10(1 + 0.12)^5$$

The interest on the accumulated interest is therefore the difference between the total arising from simple interest and that from compound interest:

$$17.62 - 16.00 = 1.62$$

Almost all investments pay compound interest and so we will be using compounding throughout the book.

Present values

There are many occasions in financial management when you are given the future sums and need to find out what those future sums are worth in present value terms today. For example, you wish to know how much you would have to put aside today which will accumulate, with compounded interest, to a defined sum in the future; or you are given the choice between receiving £200 in five years or £100 now and wish to know which is the better option, given anticipated interest rates; or a project gives a return of £1m in three years for an outlay of £800,000 now and you need to establish if this is the best use of the £800,000. By the process of discounting, a sum of money to be received in the future is given a monetary value today.

Example 3

If we anticipate the receipt of £17.62 in five years' time we can determine its present value. Rearrangement of the compound formula, and assuming a discount rate of 12 per cent, gives:

$$P = \frac{F}{(1 + i)^n} \text{ or } P = F \times \frac{1}{(1 + i)^n}$$

$$10 = \frac{17.62}{(1 + 0.12)^5}$$

Alternatively, discount factors may be used, as shown in Exhibit 2.19 (this is an extract from Appendix II at the end of the book). The factor needed to discount £1 receivable in five years when the discount rate is 12 per cent is 0.5674.

		Interest rate (per cent per annum)			
Year	**1**	**5**	**10**	**12**	**15**
1	0.9901	0.9524	0.9091	0.8929	0.8696
2	0.9803	0.9070	0.8264	0.7972	0.7561
3	0.9706	0.8638	0.7513	0.7118	0.6575
4	0.9610	0.8227	0.6830	0.6355	0.5718
5	0.9515	0.7835	0.6209	0.5674	0.4972

Exhibit 2.19 The present value of £1

Therefore the present value of £17.62 is:

$$0.5674 \times £17.62 = £10$$

Examining the present value table in Exhibit 2.19 you can see that, as the discount rate increases, the present value goes down. Also, the further into the future the money is to be received, the less valuable it is in today's terms. Distant cash flows discounted at a high rate have a small present value; for instance, £1,000 receivable in 20 years when the discount rate is 17 per cent has a present value of £43.30. Viewed from another angle, if you invested £43.30 for 20 years it would accumulate to £1,000 if interest compounds at 17 per cent.

Determining the rate of interest

Sometimes you wish to calculate the rate of return that a project is earning. For instance, a savings company may offer to pay you £10,000 in five years if you deposit £8,000 now, when interest rates on accounts elsewhere are offering 6 per cent per annum. In order to make a comparison you need to know the annual rate being offered by the savings company. Thus, we need to find i in the discounting equation.

To be able to calculate i it is necessary to rearrange the compounding formula.

$$F = P(1 + i)^n$$

First, divide both sides by P: $F/P = (1 + i)^n$ (The Ps on the right side cancel out.)

Second, take the root to the power n of both sides and subtract 1 from each side:

$$i = \sqrt[n]{[F / P]} - 1 \text{ or } i = [F / P]^{1/n} - 1$$

Example 4

In the case of a five-year investment requiring an outlay of £10 and having a future value of £17.62 the rate of return is:

$$i = \sqrt[5]{\frac{17.62}{10}} - 1 \qquad i = 12\%$$

$$i = [17.62/10]^{1/5} - 1 \qquad i = 12\%$$

Technical aside

You can use the $\sqrt[x]{y}$ or the $\sqrt[y]{x}$ button, depending on the calculator.

Alternatively, use the future value table, an extract of which is shown in Exhibit 2.18. In our example, the return on £1 worth of investment over five years is:

$$\frac{17.62}{10} = 1.762$$

In the body of the future value table look at the year 5 row for a future value of 1.762. Read off the interest rate of 12 per cent.

An interesting application of this technique outside finance is to use it to put into perspective the pronouncements of politicians. For example, in 1994 John Major made a speech to the Conservative Party conference promising to double national income (the total quantity of goods and services produced) within 25 years. This sounds impressive, but let us see how ambitious this is in terms of an annual percentage increase.

$$i = \sqrt[25]{\frac{F}{P}} - 1$$

F, future income, is double P, the present income.

$$i = \sqrt[25]{\frac{2}{1}} - 1 = 0.0281 \text{ or } 2.81\%$$

The result is not too bad compared with the previous 20 years. However, performance in the 1950s and 1960s was better and countries in the Far East have annual rates of growth of between 5 per cent and 10 per cent.

The investment period

Rearranging the standard equation so that we can find n (the number of years of the investment), we create the following equation:

$$F = P(1 + i)^n$$

$$F / P = (1 + i)^n$$

$$\log(F / P) = \log(1 + i)n$$

$$n = \frac{\log(F / P)}{\log(1 + i)}$$

Example 5

How many years does it take for £10 to grow to £17.62 when the interest rate is 12 per cent?

$$n = \frac{\log(17.62/10)}{\log(1 + 0.12)} \quad \text{Therefore } n = 5 \text{ years}$$

An application outside finance How many years will it take for China to double its real national income if growth rates continue at 10 per cent per annum?
Answer:

$$n = \frac{\log(2/1)}{\log(1 + 0.1)} = 7.3 \text{ years (quadrupling in less than 15 years)}$$

Annuities

Quite often there is not just one payment at the end of a certain number of years. There can be a series of identical payments made over a period of years. For instance:

- bonds usually pay a regular rate of interest;
- individuals can buy, from saving plan companies, the right to receive a number of identical payments over a number of years;
- a business might invest in a project which, it is estimated, will give regular cash inflows over a period of years.

An annuity is a series of payments or receipts of equal amounts. We are able to calculate the present value of this set of payments.

Example 6

For a regular payment of £10 per year for five years, when the interest rate is 12 per cent, we can calculate the present value of the annuity by three methods.

Method 1

$$P_{an} = \frac{A}{(1+i)} + \frac{A}{(1+i)^2} + \frac{A}{(1+i)^3} + \frac{A}{(1+i)^4} + \frac{A}{(1+i)^5}$$

where A = the periodic receipt.

$$P_{10,5} = \frac{10}{(1.12)} + \frac{10}{(1.12)^2} + \frac{10}{(1.12)^3} + \frac{10}{(1.12)^4} + \frac{10}{(1.12)^5} = £36.05$$

Method 2

Using the derived formula:

$$P_{an} = \frac{1 - 1(1+i)^n}{i} \times A$$

$$P_{10,5} = \frac{1 - 1/(1+0.12)^5}{0.12} \times 10 = £36.05$$

Method 3

Use the 'present value of an annuity' table. (*See* Exhibit 2.20, an extract from the more complete annuity table at the end of the book in Appendix III.) Here we simply look along the year 5 row and 12 per cent column to find the figure of 3.605 (strictly: 3.6048). This refers to the present value of five annual receipts of £1. Therefore we multiply by £10:

$$3.605 \times £10 = £36.05$$

Exhibit 2.20	The present value of an annuity of £1 per annum				
			Interest rate (per cent per annum)		
Year	1	5	10	12	15
1	0.9901	0.9524	0.9091	0.8929	0.8696
2	1.9704	1.8594	1.7355	1.6901	1.6257
3	2.9410	2.7232	2.4869	2.4018	2.2832
4	3.9020	3.5459	3.1699	3.0373	2.8550
5	4.8535	4.3295	3.7908	3.6048	3.3522

The student is strongly advised against using Method 1. This was presented for conceptual understanding only. For any but the simplest cases, this method can be very time consuming.

Perpetuities

Some contracts run indefinitely and there is no end to the series of payments. Perpetuities are rare in the private sector, but certain government securities do not have an end date; that is, the amount paid when the bond was purchased by the lender will never be repaid, only interest payments are made. For example, the UK government has issued Consolidated Stocks or War Loans, which will never be redeemed. Also, in a number of project appraisals or share valuations it is useful to assume that regular annual payments go on forever. Perpetuities are annuities that continue indefinitely. The value of a perpetuity is simply the annual amount received divided by the interest rate when the latter is expressed as a decimal.

$$P = \frac{A}{i}$$

If £10 is to be received as an indefinite annual payment then the present value, at a discount rate of 12 per cent, is:

$$P = \frac{10}{0.12} = £83.33$$

It is very important to note that in order to use this formula we are assuming that the first payment arises 365 days after the time at which we are standing (the present time or time zero).

Discounting semi-annually, monthly and daily

Sometimes financial transactions take place on the basis that interest will be calculated more frequently than once a year. For instance, if a bank account paid 12 per cent nominal return per year, but credited 6 per cent after half a year, in the second half of the year interest could be earned on the interest credited after the first six months. This will mean that the true annual rate of interest will be greater than 12 per cent. The greater the frequency with which interest is earned, the higher the future value of the deposit.

Example 7

If you put £10 in a bank account earning 12 per cent per annum then your return after one year is

$$10(1 + 0.12) = £11.20$$

If the interest is compounded semi-annually (at a nominal annual rate of 12 per cent):

$$10(1 + [0.12 / 2]) (1 + [0.12 / 2]) = 10(1 + [0.12 / 2])^2 = £11.236$$

In Example 7 the difference between annual compounding and semi-annual compounding is an extra 3.6p. After six months the bank credits the account with 60p in interest so that in the following six months the investor earns 6 per cent on the £10.60.

If the interest is compounded quarterly:

$$10(1 + [0.12 / 4])^4 = £11.255$$

Daily compounding:

$$10(1 + [0.12 / 365])^{365} = £11.2747$$

Example 8

If £10 is deposited in a bank account that compounds interest quarterly and the nominal return per year is 12 per cent, how much will be in the account after eight years?

$$10(1 + [0.12 / 4])^{4 \times 8} = £25.75$$

Continuous compounding

If the compounding frequency is taken to the limit we say that there is continuous compounding. When the number of compounding periods approaches infinity the future value is found by $F = Pe^{in}$ where e is the value of the exponential function. This is set as 2.71828 (to five decimal places, as shown on a scientific calculator). So, the future value of £10 deposited in a bank paying 12 per cent nominal compounded continuously after eight years is:

$$10 \times 2.712828^{0.12 \times 8} = £26.12$$

Converting monthly and daily rates to annual rates

Sometimes you are presented with a monthly or daily rate of interest and wish to know what that is equivalent to in terms of Annual Percentage Rate (APR) (or Effective Annual Rate (EAR)).

If m is the monthly interest or discount rate, then over 12 months:

$$(1 + m)^{12} = 1 + i$$

where i is the annual compound rate.

$$i = (1 + m)^{12} - 1$$

Thus, if a credit card company charges 1.5 per cent per month, the annual percentage rate (APR) is:

$$i = (1 + 0.015)^{12} - 1 = 19.56\%$$

If you want to find the monthly rate when you are given the APR:

$$m = (1 + i)^{1/12} - 1 \text{ or } m = \sqrt[12]{(1 + i)} - 1$$

$$m = (1 + 0.1956)^{1/12} - 1 = 0.015 = 1.5\%$$

Daily rate:

$$(1 + d)^{365} = 1 + i$$

where d is the daily discount rate.

The following exercises will consolidate the knowledge gained by reading through this appendix (answers are provided at the end of the book in Appendix VI).

Mathematical tools exercises

1 What will a £100 investment be worth in three years' time if the rate of interest is 8 per cent, using: (a) simple interest? (b) annual compound interest?

2 You plan to invest £10,000 in the shares of a company.
   a If the value of the shares increases by 5 per cent a year, what will be the value of the shares in 20 years?
   b If the value of the shares increases by 15 per cent a year, what will be the value of the shares in 20 years?

3 How long will it take you to double your money if you invest it at: (a) 5 per cent? (b) 15 per cent?

4 As a winner of a lottery you can choose one of the following prizes:
   a £1,000,000 now.
   b £1,700,000 at the end of five years.
   c £135,000 a year for ever, starting in one year.
   d £200,000 for each of the next 10 years, starting in one year.
      If the time value of money is 9 per cent, which is the most valuable prize?

5 A bank lends a customer £5,000. At the end of 10 years he repays this amount plus interest. The amount he repays is £8,950. What is the rate of interest charged by the bank?

6   The Morbid Memorial Garden company will maintain a garden plot around your grave for a payment of £50 now, followed by annual payments, in perpetuity, of £50. How much would you have to put into an account which was to make these payments if the account guaranteed an interest rate of 8 per cent?

7   If the flat (nominal annual) rate of interest is 14 per cent and compounding takes place monthly, what is the effective annual rate of interest (the Annual Percentage Rate)?

8   What is the present value of £100 to be received in 10 years' time when the interest rate (nominal annual) is 12 per cent and (a) annual discounting is used? (b) semi-annual discounting is used?

9   What sum must be invested now to provide an amount of £18,000 at the end of 15 years if interest is to accumulate at 8 per cent for the first 10 years and 12 per cent thereafter?

10 How much must be invested now to provide an amount of £10,000 in six years' time assuming interest is compounded quarterly at a nominal annual rate of 8 per cent? What is the effective annual rate?

11 Supersalesman offers you an annuity that would pay you £800 per annum for 10 years with the first payment in one year. The price he asks is £4,800. Assuming you could earn 11 per cent on alternative investments would you buy the annuity?

12 Punter buys a car on hire purchase paying five annual instalments of £1,500, the first being an immediate cash deposit. Assuming an interest rate of 8 per cent is being charged by the hire purchase company, how much is the current cash price of the car?

Self-review questions

1   What are the theoretical justifications for the NPV decision rules?

2   Explain what is meant by conventional and unconventional cash flows and what problems they might cause in investment appraisal.

3   Define the time value of money.

4   What is the reinvestment assumption for project cash flows under IRR? Why is this problematical?

5   Rearrange the compounding equation to solve for: (a) the annual interest rate, and (b) the number of years over which compounding takes place.

6   What is the 'yield' of a project?

7   Explain why it is possible to obtain an inaccurate result using the trial and error method of IRR when a wide difference of two discount rates is used for interpolation.

Questions and problems

An asterisk against a question indicates that the answer is only presented in the lecturer's guide, not Appendix VII at the end of the book.

1 Proast plc is considering two investment projects whose cash flows are:

Points in time (yearly intervals)	Project A	Project B
0	–120,000	–120,000
1	60,000	15,000
2	45,000	45,000
3	42,000	55,000
4	18,000	60,000

The company's required rate of return is 15 per cent.

a Advise the company whether to undertake the two projects.
b Indicate the maximum outlay in year 0 for each project before it ceases to be viable.

> **AN EXCEL SPREADSHEET VERSION OF THIS CALCULATION IS AVAILABLE AT**
> www.pearsoned.co.uk/arnold

2 Highflyer plc has two possible projects to consider. It cannot do both – they are mutually exclusive. The cash flows are:

Points in time (yearly intervals)	Project A	Project B
0	–420,000	–100,000
1	150,000	75,000
2	150,000	75,000
3	150,000	0
4	150,000	0

Highflyer's cost of capital is 12 per cent. Assume unlimited funds. These are the only cash flows associated with the projects.

a Calculate the internal rate of return (IRR) for each project.
b Calculate the net present value (NPV) for each project.
c Compare and explain the results in (a) and (b) and indicate which project the company should undertake and why.

> **AN EXCEL SPREADSHEET VERSION OF THIS CALCULATION IS AVAILABLE AT**
> www.pearsoned.co.uk/arnold

3* Mr Baffled, the managing director of Confused plc, has heard that the internal rate of return (IRR) method of investment appraisal is the best modern approach. He is trying to apply the IRR method to two new projects.

Cash flow

Year	0	1	2
Project C	–3,000	+14,950	–12,990
Project D	–3,000	+7,500	–5,000

a Calculate the IRRs of the two projects.
b Explain why Mr Baffled is having difficulties with the IRR method.
c Advise Confused whether to accept either or both projects. (Assume a discount rate of 25 per cent.)

4 Using a 13 per cent discount rate find the NPV of a project with the following cash flows:
   Why would this project be difficult to evaluate using IRR?

Points in time (yearly intervals)	t_0	t_1	t_2	t_3
Cash flow (£)	−300	+260	−200	+600

5* Seddet International is considering four major projects which have either two- or three-year lives. The firm has
   raised all of its capital in the form of equity and has never borrowed money. This is partly due to the success of the
   business in generating income and partly due to an insistence by the dominant managing director that borrowing is
   to be avoided if at all possible. Shareholders in Seddet International regard the firm as relatively risky, given its
   existing portfolio of projects. Other firms' shares in this risk class have generally given a return of 16 per cent per
   annum and this is taken as the opportunity cost of capital for the investment projects. The risk level for the proposed projects is the same as that of the existing range of activities.

Project

	Net cash flows			
Points in time (yearly intervals)	t_0	t_1	t_2	t_3
Project A	−5,266	2,500	2,500	2,500
Project B	−8,000	0	0	10,000
Project C	−2,100	200	2,900	0
Project D	−1,975	1,600	800	0

Ignore taxation and inflation.

a The managing director has been on a one-day intensive course to learn about project appraisal techniques.
   Unfortunately, during the one slot given over to NPV he had to leave the room to deal with a business crisis,
   and therefore does not understand it. He vaguely understands IRR and insists that you use this to calculate
   which of the four projects should be proceeded with, if there are no limitations on the number that can be
   undertaken.
b State which is the best project if they are mutually exclusive (i.e. accepting one excludes the possibility of
   accepting another), using IRR.
c Use the NPV decision rule to rank the projects and explain why, under conditions of mutual exclusivity, the
   selected project differs from that under (b).
d Write a report for the managing director, detailing the value of the net present value method for shareholder
   wealth enhancement and explaining why it may be considered of greater use than IRR.

Assignments

1 Try to discover the extent to which NPV and IRR are used in your organisation. Also try to gauge the
   degree of appreciation of the problems of using IRR.

2 If possible, obtain data on a real project, historical or proposed, and analyse it using the techniques
   learned in this chapter.

Visit www.pearsoned.co.uk/arnold to get access to Gradetracker diagnostic tests, Podcasts, Excel
Spreadsheet Solutions, FT articles, a Flashcard revision tool, Weblinks, a searchable Glossary and more.

CHAPTER 3

Practical project appraisal

LEARNING OUTCOMES

By the end of this chapter the reader will be able to:

■ identify and apply relevant and incremental cash flows in net present value calculations;

■ recognise and deal with sunk costs, incidental costs and allocated overheads;

■ describe and explain the advantages and disadvantages of the traditional investment appraisal techniques of payback and accounting rate of return;

■ describe the capital-allocation planning process in a corporation;

■ explain the rules to follow when investment appraisal is done in an environment of capital rationing, taxation and inflation.

Introduction

The last chapter outlined the basics of project evaluation. This required consideration of the fundamental elements; first, recognition of the fact that time has a value and that money received in the future has to be discounted at the opportunity cost of capital; second, the identification of relevant cash flows that are to be subject to the discounting procedure. This chapter starts by addressing this second issue. The relevant cash flows are not always obvious and easy to obtain and therefore diligent data collection and rigorous analysis are required. Defining and measuring future receipts and outlays accurately is central to successful project appraisal.

An organisation may be viewed simply as a collection of projects, some of which were started a long time ago, some only recently begun, many are major 'strategic' projects and others minor operating-unit-level schemes. It is in the nature of business for change to occur, and through change old activities, profit centres and methods die, to be replaced by the new. Without a continuous process of regeneration firms will cease to progress and be unable to compete in a dynamic environment. It is vital that the processes and systems that lead to the development of new production methods, new markets and products are efficient. That is, both the project appraisal techniques and the entire process of proposal creation and selection lead to the achievement of the objective of the organisation. Poor appraisal technique, set within the framework of an investment process that does not ask the right questions and which provides erroneous conclusions, will destroy the wealth of shareholders. In this chapter we take a closer look at appraisal techniques and the process of proposal creation and project selection.

The payback and accounting rate of return (ARR) methods of evaluating capital investment proposals have historically been, and continue to be, very popular approaches. This is despite the best efforts of a number of writers to denigrate them. It is important to understand the disadvantages of these methods, but it is also useful to be aware of why practical business people still see a great deal of merit in observing the outcome of these calculations.

The employment of project appraisal techniques must be seen as merely one of the stages in the process of the allocation of resources within a firm. The appraisal stage can be reached only after ideas for the use of capital resources have been generated and those ideas have been filtered through a consideration of the strategic, budgetary and business resource capabilities of the firm. Following the appraisal stage are the approval, implementation and post-completion auditing stages.

Any capital allocation system has to be viewed in the light of the complexity of organisational life. This aspect has been ignored in Chapter 2, where mechanical analysis is applied. The balance is corrected in this chapter.

In all the analysis conducted so far in this book, bold simplifying assumptions have been made in order to convey the essential concepts and techniques of project appraisal. First, it was assumed that there are no limits placed on finance available to fund any project the firm thinks viable, that is, there is no capital rationing. Second, it was assumed that individuals and firms do not have to concern themselves with taxation – oh, if only it were so! Third, it was assumed that there is no such thing as inflation to distort cash flow projections and cost of capital calculations. The analysis is made more sophisticated in this chapter by dropping these assumptions and allowing for greater realism.

Investment, as in the case of Airbus's A380 superjumbo (*see* **Case study 3.1**), needs to be thoroughly evaluated. This chapter considers the process of project development, appraisal and post-investment monitoring.

Case study 3.1   Will it fly?

Airbus's superjumbo

Surely one of the biggest investment appraisal decisions ever made was when Airbus decided to go ahead and produce the A380 superjumbo. This is one of those 'bet the company' type investments. A massive £6,500 million was the estimate of the amount needed to create this monster aircraft.

It was touch and go all through 2000 as to whether Airbus would dare to invest so much money. Before they said 'yes let's do it' they had to have firm orders for at least 50 aircraft. Finally, just before Christmas the sixth major buyer signed up, to take the order book to 50 'definites' and 42 on option (the airlines have the right to buy, but not the obligation).

The A380 will be significantly larger than Boeing's highly successful 747. It will carry 555 to 800 passengers (compared with 416). It will also cut direct operating costs for the airlines by 15–20 per cent for carrying one passenger one mile compared with Boeing's B747-400 and will be able to fly 10 per cent further (8,150 nautical miles).

Case study 3.1   Continued

So, where is all the money on development and build going? This is a project at the cutting edge of technology. The remarkable innovations cost a tremendous amount in terms of up-front cost but the benefit will be spread out over many decades.

Here are some of the innovations:

- New weight-saving materials.
- Better aerodynamics.
- Carbon-fibre central wingbox; 40 per cent of the structure and components will be made from new carbon components and metal alloys.
- Upper fuselage shell is not to be aluminium but 'Glare', a laminate with alternate layers of aluminium and glass-fibre reinforced adhesive.
- Innovative hydraulic systems and air conditioning.

Rivalry in the skies: contrasting views

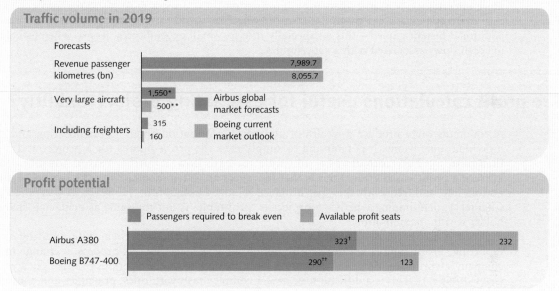

* *500 seats and above* ** *Larger than 747*
† *Assuming same revenue per passenger as B747–400* †† *Break-even load factor assumed for B747–400; 70%*

Source: *Financial Times*, 2 November 2000, p. 28. Reprinted with permission. Data from Airbus.

Airbus reckon that they need to sell at least 250 aircraft to break even in cash-flow terms (presumably meaning that nominal cumulative cash inflows equal nominal cumulative cash outflows). To achieve a positive net present value would require the sale of hundreds more aircraft. Each aircraft has a list price of around $216m–$230m – but don't pay too much attention to that, as airlines receive substantial discounts (early buyers were thought to have paid $160m). At full capacity something like 96,000 people will be working on this aircraft.

And yet it could so easily have been abandoned. Boeing had decided not to develop a superjumbo because it estimated the maximum market at 500 aircraft – they believe that airlines are generally content to continue using the 747. Airbus estimated the market for jumbos and superjumbos at 1,550. It expects to take two-thirds of that business, worth $400bn in today's prices.

By 2005 the estimated cost of development had risen by to around £9bn and breakeven is estimated at 260 aircraft rather than 250. However, firm orders had already reached 149 and the company is confident of taking many more, as Boeing's output of 747s contracted to one per month compared with four A380s per month. The first aircraft will enter service with Singapore Airlines in 2006.

This is a high-impact project appraisal if ever there was one. Many of the techniques you have learned in Chapter 2 and will learn in this chapter will have been employed by the management of Airbus to help them decide whether or not to press the button to 'go' or the button to 'stop'.

Quality of information

Good decisions are born of good information. This principle applies to all types of business decisions but is especially appropriate in the case of capital investment decisions in which a substantial proportion of the firm's assets can be put at risk. Obtaining relevant, complete and accurate information reduces the extent of the risk for the enterprise. Information varies greatly in its reliability, which often depends upon its source. The financial manager or analyst is often dependent on the knowledge and experience of other specialists within the organisation to supply data. For example, the marketing team may be able to provide an estimate of likely demand, while the production team could help establish the costs per unit. Allowance will have to be made for any bias that may creep into the information passed on; for instance, a manager who is particularly keen on encouraging the firm to expand in a particular geographical area might tend to be over-optimistic concerning market demand. For some elements of a project there might be high-quality information, whereas other aspects have a lower quality. Take the case of the investment in a new lorry for a courier firm; the cost of purchase can be estimated with high precision, whereas the reaction of competitor firms is subject to much more uncertainty. Managers gathering information for a project must also take into account that there comes a point when the cost of collecting further information can outweigh the additional benefit gained – this is especially true for small expenditures, less so when estimating cash flows associated with a superjumbo.

Are profit calculations useful for estimating project viability?

Accountants often produce a wealth of numerical information about an organisation and its individual operations. It is tempting to simply take the profit figures for a project and put these into the NPV formula as a substitute for cash flow. A further reason advanced for favouring profit-based evaluations is that managers are often familiar with the notion of 'the bottom line' and frequently their performance is judged using profit. However, as was noted in Chapter 1, determining whether a project is 'profitable' is not the same as achieving shareholder wealth maximisation.

Profit is a concept developed by accountants in order to assist them with auditing and reporting. Profit figures are derived by taking what is a continuous process, a change in a company's worth over time, and allocating these changes to discrete periods of time, say a year (see Exhibit 3.1). This is a difficult task. It is a complex task with rules, principles and conventions in abundance.

Profit uses two carefully defined concepts: income and expenses. Income is not cash inflow, it is the amount earned from business activity whether or not the cash has actually been handed over. So, if a £1,000 sofa has been sold on two years' credit the accountant's income arises in the year of sale despite the fact that cash actually flows in two years later. Expense relates the use of an asset to a particular time period whether or not any cash outflow relating to that item occurs in that period. If a firm pays immediately for a machine that will have a ten-year useful life it does not write off the full cost of the machine against the first year's

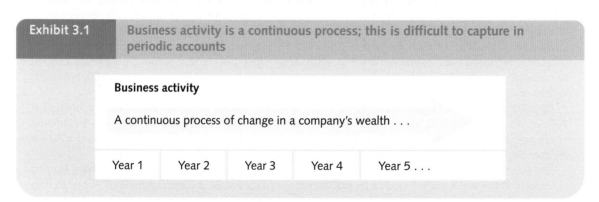

Exhibit 3.1   Business activity is a continuous process; this is difficult to capture in periodic accounts

Business activity

A continuous process of change in a company's wealth . . .

| Year 1 | Year 2 | Year 3 | Year 4 | Year 5 . . . |

profit, but allocates a proportion of the cost to each of the next ten years. The cash outflow occurs in the first year but the expense (use) of the asset occurs over ten years.

Shareholders make current consumption sacrifices, or they give up the return available elsewhere when they choose to invest their money in a firm. They do this in anticipation of receiving more £s in the future than they laid out. Hence, what is of interest to them are the future cash flows and the precise timing of these cash flows. The accountant does a difficult and important job but the profit figures produced are not suitable for project appraisal. Profit is a poor approach for two main reasons: first, depreciation and, second, working capital.

Depreciation

Accounting profit is calculated after deducting depreciation, whereas what we are interested in is net cash inflows for a year. Depreciation should not be deducted to calculate net cash inflows. For example, if a firm buys a machine for £20,000 that is expected to be productive for four years and then have a zero scrap value, the firm's accountant may allocate the depreciation on the machine over the four years to give the profit figures of say, a stable £7,000 per year – *see* Exhibit 3.2. The reason for doing this may be so that the full impact of the £20,000 payout in the first year is not allocated solely to that year's profit and loss account, but is spread over the economic life of the asset. This makes good sense for calculating accounting profit. However, this is not appropriate for project appraisal based on NPV because these figures are not true cash flows. We need to focus on the cash flows at the precise time they occur and should not discount back to time zero the figure of £7,000, but the actual cash flows at the time they occur.

Exhibit 3.2	ABC plc: an example of adjustment to profit and loss account

Machine cost £20,000, at time 0 **Productive life of four years**

			Accountant's figures	
Year	**1**	**2**	**3**	**4**
	£	**£**	**£**	**£**
Profit before depreciation	12,000	12,000	12,000	12,000
Depreciation	5,000	5,000	5,000	5,000
Profit after depreciation	7,000	7,000	7,000	7,000

Cash flow

Point in time (yearly intervals)	**0**	**1**	**2**	**3**	**4**
	£	**£**	**£**	**£**	**£**
Cash outflow	–20,000				
Cash inflow		12,000	12,000	12,000	12,000

Working capital

When a project is accepted and implemented the firm may have to invest in more than the large and obvious depreciable assets such as machines, buildings, vehicles and so forth. Investment in a new project often requires an additional investment in working capital, that is, the difference between short-term assets and liabilities. The main short-term assets are cash, stock (inventories) and debtors. The principal short-term liabilities are creditors.

So, a firm might take on a project that involves an increase in the requirements for one of these types of working capital. Each of these will be taken in turn.

Cash floats

It may be that the proposed project requires the firm to have a much higher amount of cash float. For instance, a firm setting up a betting shop may have to consider not only the cash outflow for building or refurbishment, but also the amount of extra cash float needed to meet minute-by-minute betting payouts. Thus, we have to take into account this additional aspect of cash inputs when evaluating the size of the initial investment. This is despite the fact that the cash float will be recoverable at some date in the future (for instance, when the shop is closed in, e.g., three years' time). The fact that this cash is being used to lubricate day-to-day business and is therefore not available to shareholders means that a sacrifice has been made at a particular point. The owners of that money rightfully expect to receive a suitable return while that money is tied up and unavailable for them to use as they wish.

Stock (inventories)

Examples of stock are raw materials and finished goods. If a project is undertaken which raises the level of inventories then this additional cash outflow has to be allowed for. So, for a retail business opening a number of new shops the additional expenditure on stock is a form of investment. This extra cash being tied up will not be recognised by the profit and loss accounts because all that has happened is that one asset, cash, has been swapped for another, inventory. However, the cash use has to be recognised in any NPV calculation. With some projects there may be a reduction in inventory levels. This may happen in the case of the replacement of an inefficient machine with a new piece of equipment. In this case the stock reduction releases cash and so results in a positive cash flow.

Debtors

Accounting convention dictates that if a sale is made during a year it is brought into the profit and loss account for that year. But in many cases a sale might be made on credit and all the firm has is a promise that cash will be paid in the future, the cash inflow has not materialised in the year the sale was recorded. Also, at the start of the financial year this firm may have had some outstanding debtors, that is, other firms or individuals owing this firm money, and in the early months of the year cash inflow is boosted by those other firms paying off their debt.

If we want to calculate the cash flow for the year then the annual profit figure has to be adjusted to exclude the closing balance of debtors (cash owed by customers at the end of the year but not yet paid over), and include the opening balance of debtors (cash owed by the customers at the beginning of the year which is actually received in this year for sales that took place the previous year).

Creditors

Whether suppliers send input goods and services to this firm for payment on 'cash on delivery terms' or 'credit terms' the accountant, rightly, records the value of these as an expense (if they are used up this year), and deducts this from the profit and loss account, in the year of delivery. The cash flow analyst needs to make an adjustment here because the full amount of the expense may not yet have flowed out in cash. So, if creditor balances increase, we need to recognise that the profit and loss account has a higher figure for outflows than the true outflow of cash. We need then to add back the extent to which the creditor amount outstanding has increased from the beginning of the year to the end to arrive at the cash flow figure.

Thus we may have four working capital adjustments to make to the profit and loss account figures to arrive at cash flow figures. The value of the firm's investment in net working capital, associated with a project, is found by the:

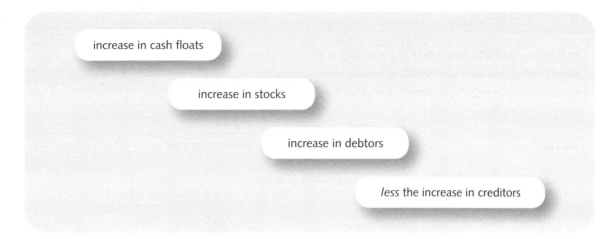

Net operating cash flow

The **net operating cash flow** associated with a new investment is equal to the profit, with depreciation added back plus or minus any change in working capital. If the project results in an increase in working capital then:

$$\begin{array}{ccc} \text{Net operating cash flow} & = & \text{Profit before depreciation} \end{array} - \begin{array}{c} \text{Periodic investment in net working capital} \end{array}$$

An example illustrating the differences between profit and cash flow

We now turn to an example of a firm, ABC plc, carrying out a project appraisal. The manager has been provided with forecast profit and loss accounts and has to adjust these figures to arrive at cash flow (*see* **Exhibit 3.3**). This project will require investment in machinery of £20,000 at the outset. The machinery will have a useful life of four years and a zero scrap value when production ceases at the end of the fourth year.

ABC's business involves dealing with numerous customers and the cash flows within any particular week are unpredictable. It therefore needs to maintain a cash float of £5,000 to be able to pay for day-to-day expenses. (Note: this cash float is not used up, and cannot therefore be regarded as a cost – in some weeks cash outflows are simply greater than cash inflows and to provide adequate liquidity £5,000 is needed for the firm to operate efficiently. The £5,000 will not be needed when output ceases.)

To produce the product it will be necessary to have a stock of raw materials close to hand. The investment in this form of inventory, together with the cash committed to work in progress and finished goods, amounts to £2,000 at the beginning of production. However, more cash (an extra £1,000) is expected to be required for this purpose at the end of the second year. When the new business is begun a large proportion of raw materials will come from suppliers who will grant additional credit. Therefore, the level of creditors will rise by £1,000 over the period of the project.

| Exhibit 3.3 | ABC plc: an example of profit to cash flow conversion |

- Machinery cost £20,000 at time 0, life of four years, zero scrap value
- Extra cash floats required: £5,000, at time 0
- Additional stock: £2,000 at time 0, £3,000 at time 2
- increase in creditors: £1,000

ABC plc		Accounting year			
Point in time (yearly intervals)	0	1	2	3	4
	£	£	£	£	£
Accounting profit		7,000	7,000	7,000	7,000
Add back depreciation		5,000	5,000	5,000	5,000
		12,000	12,000	12,000	12,000
Initial machine cost	−20,000				
Cash float	−5,000				5,000
Stock					
Closing stock	2,000	2,000	3,000	3,000	0
Opening stock		2,000	2,000	3,000	3,000
Net stock adjustment	−2,000	0	−1,000	0	+3,000
(Outflow −tive, Inflow +tive)					
Creditors					
End of year	1,000	1,000	1,000	1,000	0
Start of year		1,000	1,000	1,000	−1,000
Cash flow effect of creditors	+1,000	0	0	0	−1,000
(Outflow −tive, Inflow +tive)					
Net operating cash flow	−26,000	12,000	11,000	12,000	19,000
Point in time (yearly intervals)	0	1	2	3	4
Cash flow	−26,000	12,000	11,000	12,000	19,000
Cost of capital 12%					

$$\text{NPV} = -26,000 + \frac{12,000}{(1+0.12)} + \frac{11,000}{(1+0.12)^2} + \frac{12,000}{(1+0.12)^3} + \frac{19,000}{(1+0.12)^4} = +£14,099$$

This project produces a positive NPV, i.e. it generates a return which is more than the required rate of 12%, and therefore should be accepted.

AN EXCEL SPREADSHEET VERSION OF THIS CALCULATION IS AVAILABLE AT
www.pearsoned.co.uk/arnold

To illustrate some of the differences between profit and cash flow there follows a conversion from projected accounting figures to cash flow. First, it is necessary to add back the depreciation and instead account for the cost of the machine at time 0, the start date for the project when the cash actually left the firm. This is shown in Exhibit 3.3. To capture the cash flow effect of the investment in inventories (stock) we need to see if any additional cash has been required between the beginning of the year and its end. If cash has been invested in inventory then the net stock adjustment to the cash flow calculation is negative. If cash has been released by the running down of inventory the cash flow effect is positive.

Now we turn to creditors. The accounting profit is derived after subtracting the expense of all inputs in a period, whether or not the payment for those inputs has been made in that period. If at the start ABC's suppliers provide goods and services to the value of £1,000 without requiring immediate payment then £1,000 needs to be added to the accountant's figures for true cash flow at that point. If the creditor's adjustment is not made then we are denying that of the £2,000 of stock delivered on the first day of trading half is bought on credit. It is not necessary for ABC to pay £2,000 at the start to suppliers; they pay only £1,000 and thus the creditor adjustment shows a positive cash flow at time 0, offsetting the outflow on stock. (In other examples, later in the book, it may be assumed that all stock is bought on trade credit and therefore there would not be a cash outflow for stock payments at time 0. In these examples all creditor and debtor adjustments are made at the year ends and not at time 0.) In subsequent years the prior year's creditor debts actually paid match the amount outstanding at the year end, thus no net cash flow effect adjustment is necessary.

In this simplified example it is assumed that after exactly four years all production ceases and outstanding creditors and debtors are settled on the last day of the fourth year. Also on the last day of the fourth year the money tied up in cash float and stock is released. Furthermore, the net cash flows from each year's trading all arrive on the last day of the respective year. These assumptions are obviously unrealistic, but to make the example more realistic would add to its complexity.

Strictly speaking we should allow for the fact that a business generally receives and pays cash flows fairly evenly through the year rather than assume that all cash flows occur at the end of the year. So, in theory, we should discount cash flows weekly or even daily (365 discount calculations per year!). The practice of simplifying to one net cash flow per year, followed by most managers, is justified on the grounds of practical necessity to avoiding over-complicated calculations.

Furthermore, by assuming cash comes in at the end of the year, and not any earlier, managers are, if anything, underestimating NPV. This more conservative estimate of project viability encourages greater confidence in the likelihood of project acceptance boosting shareholder wealth. An alternative is to assume cash inflows halfway through the year, in which case the discount factor becomes $1/(1+k)^{0.5}$, $1/(1+k)^{1.5}$, etc.

Incremental cash flows

A fundamental principle in project appraisal is to include only incremental cash flows. These are defined as the cash flows dependent on the project's implementation. Only those cash flows that are induced by the investment at time 0 (and in subsequent years) are regarded as incremental. Some of these cash flows are easy to establish but others are much more difficult to pin down.

Here are some guideposts for finding relevant/incremental cash flows.

Include all opportunity costs

The direct inputs into a project are generally easy to understand and measure. However, quite often a project uses resources that already exist within the firm but which are in short supply and cannot be replaced in the immediate future. That is, the project under consideration may be taking resources away from other projects. The loss of net cash flows from these other projects is termed an opportunity cost. For example, a firm may be considering a project that makes use of a factory that at present is empty. Because it is empty we should not automatically assume that the opportunity cost is zero. Perhaps the firm could engage in the alternative project of renting out the factory to another firm. The forgone rental income is a cost of the project under consideration.

Likewise if a project uses the services of specialist personnel this may be regarded as having an opportunity cost. The loss of these people to other parts of the organisation may reduce cash flows on other projects. If they cannot be replaced with equally able individuals then the opportunity cost will be the lost net cash flows. If equally able hired replacements are found then the extra cost imposed, by the additional salaries etc., on other projects should be regarded as an opportunity cost of the new project under consideration.

For a third example of opportunity cost, imagine your firm bought, when the price was low, a stock of platinum to use as a raw material. The total cost was £1m. It would be illogical to sell the final manufactured product at a price based on the old platinum value if the same quantity would now cost £3m. An alternative course of action would be to sell the platinum in its existing state, rather than to produce the manufactured product. The current market value of the raw platinum (£3m) is then the opportunity cost.

Include all incidental effects

It is possible for a new project to either increase or reduce sales of other products of the company. Take the case of an airline company trying to decide whether to go ahead with a project to fly between the USA and Japan. The direct cash flows of selling tickets, etc. on these flights may not give a positive NPV. However, it could be that the new service generates additional net revenue not only for USA–Japan flights but also on existing routes as customers switch to this airline because it now offers a more complete worldwide service. If this additional net cash flow is included the project may be viable.

On the other hand, if a clothes retailer opens a second or a third outlet in the same town, it is likely to find custom is reduced at the original store. This loss elsewhere in the organisation becomes a relevant cash flow in the appraisal of the *new* project, that is, the new shop.

In the soft drink business the introduction of a new brand can reduce the sales of the older brands. This is not to say that a company should never risk any cannibalisation, only that if a new product is to be launched it should not be viewed in isolation. All incremental effects have to be allowed for, including those effects not directly associated with the new product or service.

Ignore sunk costs

Do not include sunk costs. For example, the project to build Concorde involved an enormous expenditure in design and manufacture. At the point where it had to be decided whether to put the aeroplane into service, the costs of development became irrelevant to the decision. Only incremental costs and inflows should be considered. The development costs are in the past and are bygones; they should be ignored. The money spent on development is irrecoverable, whatever the decision on whether to fly the plane. Similarly with Eurotunnel, the fact that the overspend runs into billions of pounds and the tunnel service is unlikely to make a profit does not mean that the incremental cost of using some electricity to power the trains and the cost of employing some train drivers should not be incurred. The £9bn+ already spent is irrelevant to the decision on whether to transport passengers and freight between France and the UK. So long as incremental costs are less than incremental benefits (cash flows when discounted) then the service should operate.

A common mistake in this area is to regard pre-project survey work already carried out or committed to (market demand screening, scientific study, geological survey, etc.) as a relevant cost. After all, the cost would not have been incurred but for the *possibility* of going ahead with the project. However, at the point of decision on whether to proceed, the survey cost is sunk – it will be incurred whether or not implementation takes place, and it therefore is not incremental. Sunk costs can be either costs for intangibles (such as research and development expenses), or costs for tangibles that may not be used for other purposes (such as the cost of the Eurotunnel). When dealing with sunk costs it is sometimes necessary to be resolute in the face of comments such as 'good money is being thrown after bad', but always remember the 'bad' money outflow happened in the past and is no longer an input factor into a rigorous decision-making process.

Be careful with overheads

Overheads consist of such items as managerial salaries, rent, light, heat, etc. These are costs that are not directly associated with any one part of the firm or one item produced. An accountant often allocates these overhead costs among the various projects a firm is involved in. When trying to assess the viability of a project we should only include the incremental or extra expenses that would be incurred by going ahead with a project. Many of the general overhead expenses may be incurred regardless of whether the project takes place.

There are two types of overhead. The first type is truly incremental costs resulting from a project. For example, extra electricity, rental and administrative staff costs may be incurred by going ahead rather than abstaining. The second type of overhead consists of such items as head office managerial salaries, legal expertise, public relations, research and development and even the corporate jet. These costs are not directly associated with any one part of the firm or one project and will be incurred regardless of whether the project under consideration is embarked upon. The accountant generally charges a proportion of this overhead to particular divisions and projects. When trying to assess the viability of a project only the incremental costs incurred by going ahead are relevant. Those costs that are unaffected are irrelevant.

Dealing with interest

Interest on funds borrowed to invest in a project does represent a cash outflow. However, it is wrong to include this element in the cash flow calculations. **To repeat, interest should not be deducted from the net cash flows.** This is because if it were subtracted this would amount to double counting because the opportunity cost of capital used to discount the cash flows already incorporates a cost of these funds. The net cash flows are reduced to a present value by allowing for the weighted average cost of finance to give a return to shareholders and lenders. If the un-discounted cash flows also had interest deducted there would be a serious understatement of NPV. For more details, see Chapter 8 on the calculation of the firm's discount rate (cost of capital).

Worked example 3.1	Tamcar plc

The accountants at Tamcar plc, manufacturers of hairpieces, are trying to analyse the viability of a proposed new division, 'Baldies heaven'. They estimate that this project will have a life of four years before the market is blown away by the lifting of the present EU import ban on hairpieces. The estimated sales, made on three months' credit, are as follows:

Year	Sales (£)	
20X1	1.5m	There are no bad debts.
20X2	2.0m	
20X3	2.5m	Costs of production can be assumed to be paid
20X4	3.0m	for on the last day of the year. There are no creditors.

Year	Cost of production (£)	
20X1	0.75m	At the start of the project an investment of £1m will be
20X2	1.00m	required in buildings, plant and machinery. These items
20X3	1.25m	will have a net worth of zero at the end of this project.
20X4	1.50m	The accountants depreciate the plant and machinery at
		25 per cent per annum on a straight line basis.

▶

Worked example 3.1   **Continued**

A cash float of £0.5m will be required at the start. Also stocks will increase by £0.3m. These are both recoverable at the end of the project's life.

A £1m invoice for last year's scientific study of 'Baldies heaven' hairpiece technology (e.g. wind resistance and combability) has yet to be paid.

The head office always allocates a proportion of central expenses to all divisions and projects. The share to be borne by 'Baldies heaven' is £500,000 per annum. The head office costs are unaffected by the new project.

The accountants have produced the following profit and loss accounts:

Year	20X1	20X2	20X3	20X4
	£m	£m	£m	£m
Sales	1.50	2.00	2.50	3.00
Costs of production	0.75	1.00	1.25	1.50
Depreciation	0.25	0.25	0.25	0.25
Scientific survey	0.25	0.25	0.25	0.25
Head office	0.50	0.50	0.50	0.50
Profit/loss	–0.25	0	0.25	0.50

Accountants' summary

Investment: £2m, Return: £0.5m over 4 years

$$\text{Average return on investment (ROI)} = \frac{\text{Average profit}}{\text{Investment}} = \frac{0.5 \div 4}{2} = 0.0.65 \text{ or } 6.25\%$$

Recommendation: do not proceed with this project as 6.25% is a poor return.

Required

Calculate the Net Present Value and recommend whether to accept this project or invest elsewhere.

Assume

- No tax.
- The return required on projects of this risk class is 11%.
- Start date of the project is 1.1.20X1.

Answer

- Depreciation is not a cash flow and should be excluded.
- The scientific survey is a sunk cost. This will not alter whether Tamcar chooses to go ahead or refuses to invest – it is irrelevant to the NPV calculation.
- Head office costs will be constant regardless of the decision to accept or reject the project, they are not incremental.

The sales figures shown in the first line of the table below are not the true cash receipts for each of those years because three months' credit is granted. Thus, in year 1 only three-quarters of £1.5m is actually received. An adjustment for debtors shows that one-quarter of the first year's sales are deducted. Thus £375,000 is received in the second year and therefore this is added to time 2's cash flow. However, one-quarter of the £2m of time 2's sales is subtracted because this is not received until the following year.

An assumption has been made concerning the receipt of debtor payments after production and distribution has ceased. The 20X4 sales still outstanding on credit at the end of the year are all paid for three months after the year-end at time 4.25.

Worked example 3.1	Continued

Tamcar cash flows

Time (annual intervals)	0	1	2	3	4	4.25
	start	end	end	end	end	
Years	20X1	20X1	20X2	20X3	20X4	20X5
Sales		+1.5	+2.0	+2.5	+3.0	
Buildings, plant, machinery	−1.0					
Cash float	−0.5				+0.5	
Stocks	−0.3				+0.3	
Costs of production		−0.75	−1.00	−1.25	−1.50	
Adjustment for debtors:						
Opening debtors	*0*	*0*	*0.375*	*0.500*	*0.625*	*0.75*
Closing debtors	*0*	*0.375*	*0.500*	*0.625*	*0.750*	*0*
Cash flow adjustment for debtors		−0.375	−0.125	−0.125	−0.125	+0.75
Cash flow	−1.8	+0.375	+0.875	+1.125	+2.175	+0.75

$$\text{Net present value} \quad -1.8 + \frac{0.375}{(1.11)} + \frac{0.875}{(1.11)^2} + \frac{1.125}{(1.111)^3} + \frac{2.175}{(1.11)^4} + \frac{0.75}{(1.11)^{4.25}}$$

	−1.8	+0.338	+0.710	+0.823	+1.433	+0.481

NPV = +£1.985m

This is a project that adds significantly to shareholder wealth, producing £1.985m more than the minimum rate of return of 11 per cent required by the firm's finance providers.

AN EXCEL SPREADSHEET VERSION OF THIS CALCULATION IS AVAILABLE AT www.pearsoned.co.uk/arnold

Worked example 3.2	The International Seed Company (TISC)

As the newly appointed financial manager of TISC you are about to analyse a proposal for the marketing and distribution of a range of genetically engineered vegetable seeds which have been developed by a bio-technology firm. This firm will supply the seeds and permit TISC to market and distribute them under a licence.

Market research, costing £100,000, has already been carried out to establish the likely demand. After three years TISC will withdraw from the market because it anticipates that these products will be superseded by further bio-technological developments.

The annual payment to the bio-technology firm will be £1m for the licence; this will be payable at the end of each accounting year.

Also £500,000 will be needed initially to buy a fleet of vehicles for distribution. These vehicles will be sold at the end of the third year for £200,000.

There will be a need for a packaging and administrative facility. TISC is large and has a suitable factory with offices, which at present are empty. Head office has stated that they will let this space to your project at a reduced rent of £200,000 per annum payable at the end of the accounting year (the open market rental value is £1m p.a.).

Worked example 3.2   Continued

The project would start on 1.1.20X1 and would not be subject to any taxation because of its special status as a growth industry. A relatively junior and inexperienced accountant has prepared forecast profit and loss accounts for the project as shown in the following table.

Year	20X1	20X2	20X3
	£m	£m	£m
Sales	5	6	6
Costs			
Market research	0.1		
Raw material (seeds)	2.0	2.4	2.4
Licence	1.0	1.0	1.0
Vehicle fleet depreciation	0.1	0.1	0.1
Direct wages	0.5	0.5	0.5
Rent	0.2	0.2	0.2
Overhead	0.5	0.5	0.5
Variable transport costs	0.5	0.5	0.5
Profit	0.1	0.8	0.8

By expanding its product range with these new seeds the firm expects to attract a great deal of publicity which will improve the market position, and thus the profitability, of its other products. The benefit is estimated at £100,000 for each of the three years.

Head office normally allocates a proportion of its costs to any new project as part of its budgeting/costing process. This will be £100,000 for this project and has been included in the figures calculated for overhead by the accountant. The remainder of the overhead is directly related to the project.

The direct wages, seed purchases, overhead and variable transport costs can be assumed to be paid at the end of each year. Most of the sales revenue may be assumed to be received at the end of each year. However, the firm will grant two months' credit to its customers which means that for some of the sales recorded by the accountant for a year the actual cash is received in the following year. An initial cash float of £1m will be needed. This will be returned at the end of the third year.

Assume no inflation. An appropriate discount rate is 15 per cent.

Required

Assess the viability of the proposed project using the discounted cash flow technique you feel to be most appropriate.

Suggestion

Try to answer this question before reading the model answer.

Answer

Notes
- Market research cost is non-incremental.
- Opportunity cost of factory is £1m per annum.
- Vehicle depreciation does not belong in a cash flow calculation.
- The effect on TISC's other products is an incidental benefit.
- Head office cost apportionment should be excluded.

Worked example 3.2   **Continued**

	£m	20X1 start	20X1 end	20X2 end	20X3 end	20X3 end	20X4 2 months
				Cash flows			
Inflows							
Sales			5.0	6.0	6.0		
Benefit to divisions			0.1	0.1	0.1		
Cash at end						1.0	
Vehicles						0.2	
Total inflows		0	5.1	6.1	6.1	1.2	0
Outflows							
Licence			1.0	1.0	1.0		
Vehicles		0.5					
Property rent (opportunity cost)			1.0	1.0	1.0		
Raw matcrials			2.0	2.4	2.4		
Direct wages			0.5	0.5	0.5		
Overheads			0.4	0.4	0.4		
Variable transport			0.5	0.5	0.5		
Initial cash		1.0					
Cash flows after outflows		−1.5	−0.3	0.3	0.3	1.2	0
Adjustment for debtors							
Debtor: start			0	0.833	1.00		1.0
end			0.833	1.000	1.00		0
Cash flow effect of debtors			−0.833	−0.167	0	0	+1.0
Cash flows		**−1.5**	**−1.133**	**+0.133**	**+0.3**	**+1.2**	**+1.0**
Net present value							

NPV =

$$-1.5 \; + \; \frac{-1.133}{(1.15)} \; + \; \frac{0.133}{(1.15)^2} \; + \; \frac{0.3}{(1.15)^3}$$

$$+ \; \frac{1.2}{(1.15)^3} \; + \; \frac{1.00}{(1.15)^{3.167}}$$

NPV = −1.5 − 0.985 + 0.101 + 0.197 + 0.789 + 0.642 = −£0.756m

Conclusion

Do not proceed with the project as it returns less than 15 per cent.

AN EXCEL SPREADSHEET VERSION OF THIS CALCULATION IS AVAILABLE AT
www.pearsoned.co.uk/arnold

Evidence on the employment of appraisal techniques

A number of surveys enquiring into the appraisal methods used in practice have been conducted over the past 20 years. The results from surveys conducted by Pike and by the author jointly with Panos Hatzopoulos are displayed in **Exhibit 3.4**. Some striking features emerge from these and other studies. Payback remains in wide use, despite the increasing application of discounted cash flow techniques. Internal rate of return is at least as popular as net present value. However, NPV is gaining rapid acceptance. Accounting rate of return continues to be the laggard, but is still used in over 50 per cent of large firms. One observation that is emphasised in many studies is the tendency for decision makers to use more than one method. In the 1997 study 67 per cent of firms use three or four of these techniques. These methods are regarded as being complementary rather than competitors.

Exhibit 3.4	Appraisal techniques used

	Proportion of companies using technique							
	Pike surveys[a]				Arnold and Hatzopoulos survey[b]			
	1975 %	1980 %	1986 %	1992 %	1997			
					Small %	Medium %	Large %	Total %
Payback	73	81	92	94	71	75	66	70
Accounting rate of return	51	49	56	50	62	50	55	56
Internal rate of return	44	57	75	81	76	83	84	81
Net present value	32	39	68	74	62	79	97	80

Capital budget (per year) for companies in Arnold and Hatzopoulos study approx. Small: £1–50m. Medium: £51–100m. Large: £100m+

(a) *Pike's studies focus on 100 large UK firms.*
(b) *In the Arnold and Hatzopoulos study (2000), 300 finance directors of UK companies taken from The Times 1000 (London: Times Books), ranked according to capital employed (excluding investment trusts), were asked dozens of questions about project appraisal techniques, sources of finance and performance measurement. The first 100 (Large size) of the sample are the top 100; another 100 are in the rankings at 250–400 (Medium size); the final 100 are ranked 820–1,000 (Small size). The capital employed ranges between £1.3bn and £24bn for the large firms, £207m and £400m for the medium-sized firms, and £40m and £60m for the small companies. Ninety-six usable replies were received: 38 large, 24 medium and 34 small.*

Sources: Pike (1988 and 1996) and Arnold and Hatzopoulos (2000).

There is an indication in the literature that, while some methods have superior theoretical justification, other, simpler methods are used for purposes such as communicating project viability and gaining commitment throughout an organisation. It is also suggested that those who sponsor and advance projects within organisations like to have the option of presenting their case in an alternative form which shows the proposal in the best light. Another clear observation from the literature is that small and medium-sized firms use the sophisticated formal procedures less than their larger brethren.

Payback

The payback period for a capital investment is the length of time before the cumulated stream of forecasted cash flows equals the initial investment. The decision rule is that if a project's payback period is less than or equal to a predetermined threshold figure it is acceptable. Consider the case of Tradfirm's three mutually exclusive proposed investments (*see* **Exhibit 3.5**).

Exhibit 3.5   Tradfirm

Cash flows (£m)

Points in time (yearly intervals)	0	1	2	3	4	5	6
Project A	−10	6	2	1	1	2	2
Project B	−10	1	1	2	6	2	2
Project C	−10	3	2	2	2	15	10

Note: Production ceases after six years, and all cash flows occur on anniversary dates.

There is a boardroom battle in Tradfirm, with older members preferring the payback rule. They set four years as the decision benchmark. For both A and B the £10m initial outflow is recouped after four years. In the case of C it takes five years for the cash inflows to cumulate to £10m. Thus payback for the three projects is as follows:

Project A: 4 years

Project B: 4 years

Project C: 5 years

If the payback rule is rigidly applied, the older members of the board will reject the third project, and they are left with a degree of indecisiveness over whether to accept A or B. The younger members prefer the NPV rule and are thus able to offer a clear decision.

Exhibit 3.6   Tradfirm: Net Present Values (£m)

$$\text{Project A}\quad -10 + \frac{6}{1.1} + \frac{2}{(1.1)^2} + \frac{1}{(1.1)^3} + \frac{1}{(1.1)^4} + \frac{2}{(1.1)^5} + \frac{2}{(1.1)^6} = \text{£0.913m}$$

$$\text{Project B}\quad -10 + \frac{1}{1.1} + \frac{1}{(1.1)^2} + \frac{2}{(1.1)^3} + \frac{6}{(1.1)^4} + \frac{2}{(1.1)^5} + \frac{2}{(1.1)^6} = -\text{£0.293m}$$

$$\text{Project C}\quad -10 + \frac{3}{1.1} + \frac{2}{(1.1)^2} + \frac{2}{(1.1)^3} + \frac{2}{(1.1)^4} + \frac{15}{(1.1)^5} + \frac{10}{(1.1)^6} = \text{£12.207m}$$

Note: The discount rate is 10 per cent.

As **Exhibit 3.6** shows, Project A has a positive NPV and is therefore shareholder wealth enhancing. Project B has a negative NPV; the firm would be better served by investing the £10m in the alternative that offers a 10 per cent return. Project C has the largest positive NPV and is therefore the one that creates most shareholder wealth.

Drawbacks of payback

The first drawback of payback is that it makes no allowance for the time value of money. It ignores the need to compare future cash flows with the initial investment after they have been discounted to their present values. The second drawback is that receipts beyond the payback period are ignored. This problem is particularly obvious in the case of Project C. A third disadvantage is the arbitrary selection of the cut-off point. There is no theoretical basis for setting the appropriate time period and so guesswork, whim and manipulation take over.

Discounted payback

With discounted payback the future cash flows are discounted prior to calculating the payback period. This is an improvement on the simple payback method in that it takes into account the time value of money. In **Exhibit 3.7** the *discounted* cash inflows are added together to calculate payback. In the case of Project B the discounted cash inflows never reach the level of the cash outflow.

This modification tackles the first drawback of the simple payback method but it is still necessary to make an arbitrary decision about the cut-off date and it ignores cash flows beyond that date.

Exhibit 3.7	Discounted payback: Tradfirm plc (£m)							
Points in time (yearly intervals)	0	1	2	3	4	5	6	Discounted payback
Project A								
Undiscounted cash flow	–10	6	2	1	1	2	2	
Discounted cash flow	–10	5.45	1.65	0.75	0.68	1.24	1.13	Year 6
Project B								
Undiscounted cash flow	–10	1	1	2	6	2	2	Outflow –10m
Discounted cash flow	–10	0.909	0.826	1.5	4.1	1.24	1.13	Inflow +£9.7m
Project C								
Undiscounted cash flow	–10	3	2	2	2	15	10	
Discounted cash flow	–10	2.72	1.65	1.5	1.37	9.3	5.64	Year 5

Note: The discount rate is 10 per cent.

Reasons for the continuing popularity of payback

Payback remains a widely used project appraisal method despite its drawbacks. This requires some explanation. The first fact to note is that payback is rarely used as the primary investment technique, but rather as a secondary method which supplements the more sophisticated methods. Although it appears irrational to employ payback when the issue is examined in isolation, we may begin to see the logic behind its use if we take into account the organisational context and the complementary nature of alternative techniques. For example, payback may be used at an early stage to filter out projects which have clearly unacceptable risk and return characteristics. Identifying those projects at a preliminary stage avoids the need for more detailed evaluation through a discounted cash flow method, thus increasing the efficiency of the appraisal process. This early sifting has to be carefully implemented so as to avoid premature rejection.

Payback also has one extraordinarily endearing quality to busy managers and hard-pressed students alike – it is simple and easy to use. Executives often admit that the payback rule, used indiscriminately, does not always give the best decisions, but it is the simplest way to communicate an idea of project profitability. NPV is difficult to understand and so it is useful to have an alternative measure that all managers can follow. In the workplace a project's success often relies on the gaining of widespread employee commitment. Discussion, negotiation and communication of ideas often need to be carried out in a simple form so that non-quantitative managers can make their contribution and, eventually, their commitment. Communication in terms of the sophisticated models may lead to alienation and exclusion and, ultimately, project failure.

Another argument advanced by practitioners is that projects which return their outlay quickly reduce the exposure of the firm to risk. In the world beyond the simplifications needed in academic exercises, as described in Chapter 2, there is frequently a great deal of uncertainty about future cash flows. Managers often distrust forecasts for more distant years. Payback has an implicit assumption that the risk of cash flows is directly related to the time distance from project implementation date. By focusing on near-term returns this approach uses only those data in which management have greatest faith. Take the case of the Web-based music provider industry. Here, competitive forces and technology are changing so rapidly that it is difficult to forecast for eight months ahead, let alone for eight years. Thus, managers may choose to ignore cash flow projections beyond a certain number of years. Those who advocate NPV counter this approach by saying that risk is accounted for in a better way in the NPV model than is done by simply excluding data. This is examined in the next chapter.

There is some evidence that payback is more popular in companies who measure and reward executive performance through accounting profit numbers. Payback tends to be high when there are high near-term cash flows/profits.

A further advantage of payback, as perceived by many managers, is its use in situations of capital shortage. If funds are limited, there is an advantage in receiving a return on projects earlier rather than later, as this permits investment in other profitable opportunities. Theoretically, this factor can be allowed for in a more satisfactory way with the NPV method; capital rationing is discussed later in this chapter.

This section is not meant to promote the use of payback. It remains a theoretically inferior method to the discounted cash flow approaches. Payback has a number of valuable attributes, but the primary method of project appraisal in most organisations should take into account all of the relevant cash flows and then discount them.

Accounting rate of return

The accounting rate of return (ARR) method may be known to readers by other names such as the return on capital employed (ROCE) or return on investment (ROI). The ARR is a ratio of the accounting profit to the investment in the project, expressed as a percentage.

The *decision rule* is that if the ARR is greater than, or equal to, a hurdle rate then accept the project.

This ratio can be calculated in a number of ways but the most popular approach is to take profit after the deduction of depreciation. For the investment figure we regard any increases in working capital as adding to the investment required. Three alternative versions of ARR are calculated for Timewarp plc; each gives markedly different results (*see* Worked example 3.3). Note: these are just three of all the possible ways of calculating ARR – there are many more.

Worked example 3.3	Timewarp plc

Timewarp is to invest £30,000 in machinery for a project which has a life of three years. The machinery will have a zero scrap value and will be depreciated on a straight-line basis.

Accounting rate of return, version 1 (annual basis)

$$ARR = \frac{\text{Profit for the year}}{\text{Asset book value at start of year}} \times 100$$

▶

Worked example 3.3	Continued				

Time (year)	1	2	3
	£	£	£
Profit before depreciation	15,000	15,000	15,000
Less depreciation	10,000	10,000	10,000
Profit after depreciation	5,000	5,000	5,000
Value of asset (book value)			
Start of year	30,000	20,000	10,000
End of year	20,000	10,000	0

$$\text{Accounting rate of return} \qquad \frac{5{,}000}{30{,}000} = 16.67\% \qquad \frac{5{,}000}{20{,}000} = 25\% \qquad \frac{5{,}000}{10{,}000} = 50\%$$

On average the ARR is: $1/3 \times (16.67 + 25 + 50)\% = 30.55\%$.

Note the illusion of an annual rise in profitability despite profits remaining constant year on year.

Accounting rate of return, version 2 (total investment basis)

$$ARR = \frac{\text{Average annual profit}}{\text{Initial capital invested}} \times 100$$

$$ARR = \frac{(5{,}000 + 5{,}000 + 5{,}000)/3}{30{,}000} \times 100 = 16.67\%$$

Accounting rate of return, version 3 (average investment basis)

$$ARR = \frac{\text{Average annual profit}}{\text{Average capital invested}} \times 100$$

$$\text{Average capital invested:} \quad \frac{30{,}000}{2} = 15{,}000$$

(At time 0 the machinery has a value of £30,000, three years later it has a value of zero. If we assume constant devaluation then the average value of the machinery is £15,000.)

$$ARR = \frac{(5{,}000 + 5{,}000 + 5{,}000)/3}{15{,}000} \times 100 = 33.33\%$$

Drawbacks of accounting rate of return

- The number of alternative ARR calculations can be continued beyond the three possibilities described in Worked example 3.3. Each alternative would be a legitimate variant and would find favour with some managers and accountants. The almost wide-open field for selecting profit and asset definitions is a major weakness of ARR. This flexibility may tempt decision makers to abuse the technique to suit their purposes.

- Second, the inflow and outflow of cash should be the focus of investment analysis appraisals. Profit figures are very poor substitutes for cash flow.

- The most important criticism of accounting rate of return is that it fails to take account of the time value of money. There is no allowance for the fact that cash received in year 1 is more valuable than an identical sum received in year 3.

- There is a high degree of arbitrariness in defining the cut-off or hurdle rate. There is no sound logical reason for selecting 10, 15 or 20 per cent as the acceptable ARR. This arbitrariness contrasts with NPV, which has a firm logical base to the discount rate used by the company for a project. It is the opportunity cost of the suppliers of capital. We examine this calculation in Chapter 8.

- Accounting rate of return can lead to some perverse decisions. For example, suppose that Timewarp use the second version, the total investment ARR, with a hurdle rate of 15 per cent, and the appraisal team discover that the machinery will in fact generate an additional profit of £1,000 in a fourth year for no extra cost. Common sense suggests that if all other factors remain constant this new situation is better than the old one, and yet the ARR declines to below the threshold level because the profits are averaged over four years rather than three and the project is therefore rejected.

The original situation is:

$$ARR = \frac{(5,000 + 5,000 + 5,000)/3}{30,000} = 16.67\%. \text{ Accepted}$$

The new situation is:

$$ARR = \frac{(5,000 + 5,000 + 5,000 + 1,000)/4}{30,000} = 13.33\%. \text{ Rejected}$$

An alternative way of viewing this problem is to think of two projects that are identical except that one offers the additional £1,000. If only one project can be accepted, which will the managers go for? If they are motivated by ARR (e.g. by bonuses related to ARR achieved) they may be inclined to accept the project that offers the higher ARR even if this means sacrificing £1,000 of shareholders' money.

Reasons for the continued use of accounting rate of returns

Exhibit 3.4 shows that over one-half of large firms calculate ARR when appraising projects and so the conclusion must be that, in the practical world of business, some merit is seen in this technique. One possible explanation is that managers are familiar with this ancient and extensively used profitability measure. The financial press regularly report accounting rates of return. Divisional performance is often judged on a profit-to-assets employed ratio. Indeed, the entire firm is often analysed and management evaluated on this ratio. Because performance is measured in this way, managers have a natural bias towards using it in appraising future projects. Conflicting signals are sometimes sent to managers controlling a division. They are expected to use a discounted cash flow approach for investment decisions, but find that their performance is being monitored on a profit-to-investment ratio basis. This dichotomy may produce a resistance to proposed projects which produce low returns in the early years and thus report a low ARR to head office. This may result in excellent long-term opportunities being missed.

Internal rate of return: reasons for continued popularity

Exhibit 3.4 shows that firms use IRR as much as the theoretically superior NPV. Given the problems associated with IRR described in Chapter 2, this may seem strange. It is all the more perplexing if one considers that IRR is often more difficult to calculate manually than NPV (although, with modern computer programs, the computational difficulties virtually disappear). Some possible explanations follow.

- *Psychological* Managers are familiar with expressing financial data in the form of a percentage. It is intuitively easier to grasp what is meant by an IRR of 15 per cent than, say, an NPV of £2,000.

● *IRR can be calculated without knowledge of the required rate of return* Making a decision using the IRR involves two separate stages. Stage 1 involves gathering data and then computing the IRR. Stage 2 requires comparing this with the cut-off rate. By contrast, it is not possible to calculate NPV without knowing the required rate of return. The proposal has to be analysed in one stage only. In a large company it is possible for senior managers to request that profit centres and divisions appraise projects on the basis of their IRRs, while refusing to communicate in advance the rate of return required. This has at least two potential advantages. First, the required rate may change over time and it becomes a simple matter of changing the cut-off comparison rate at head office once the IRR computations are received from lower down the organisation. With NPV, each project's cash flows would need to be calculated again at the new discount rate. Second, managers are only human and there is a tendency to bias information passed upwards so as to achieve their personal goals. For instance, it has been known for ambitious managers to be excessively optimistic concerning the prospects for projects that would lead to an expansion of their domain. If they are provided with a cut-off rate prior to evaluating projects you can be sure that all projects they sponsor will have cash flows 'forecasted' to produce a return greater than the target. If the head office team choose not to communicate a cut-off rate, this leaves them free to adjust the required return to allow for factors such as overoptimism. They may also adjust the minimum rate of return for perceived risk associated with particular projects or divisions.

● *Ranking* Some managers are not familiar with the drawbacks of IRR and believe that ranking projects to select between them is most accurately and most easily carried out using the percentage-based IRR method. This was, in Chapter 2, shown not to be the case.

The managerial art of investment appraisal

This book places strong emphasis on the formal methods of project appraisal, so a word of warning is necessary at this point. Mathematical technique is merely one element needed for successful project appraisal. The quantitative analysis is only the starting point for decision making. In most real-world situations there are many qualitative factors that need to be taken into account. The techniques described in Chapter 2 cannot be used in a mechanical fashion. Management is largely an art form with a few useful quantitative techniques to improve the quality of the art. For instance, in generating and evaluating major investments the firm has to take into account:

● *Strategy* The relationship between the proposed project and the strategic direction of the firm is very important. A business-unit investment isolated from the main thrust of the firm may be a distraction in terms of managerial attention and financial resources. A project that looks good at divisional level may not be appropriate when examined from the whole-firm perspective. It may even be contradictory to the firm's goals. For example, luxury goods companies are sometimes enticed to produce lower-priced items for the mass market or to stretch the brand into unrelated areas. The project, when judged on its own, appears to have a very high NPV. But there is the danger of losing the premium brand (expensive and exclusive) strategic position in the existing product ranges by association with something that does not quite fit the image the firm has nurtured.

● *Social context* The effect on individuals is a crucial consideration. Projects require people to implement them. Their enthusiasm and commitment will be of central importance. Neglecting this factor may lead to resentment and even sabotage. Discussion and consensus on major project proposals may matter more than selecting the mathematically correct option. In many cases, quantitative techniques are avoided because they are precise. It is safer to sponsor a project in a non-quantified or judgemental way at an early stage in its development. If, as a result of discussion with colleagues and superiors, the idea becomes more generally accepted and it fits into the pervading view on the firm's policy and strategy, the figures are presented in a report. Note here the order of actions. First, general acceptance. Second, quantification. A proposal is usually discussed at progressively higher levels of management before it is 'firmed up' into a project report. One reason for this is that continuing commitment and support from many people will be needed if the project is to succeed. In order to engender support and to improve the final report it is necessary to start the process in a rather vague way, making room for modifications in the light of suggestions. Some of these suggestions will be motivated by shareholder wealth considerations; others will be motivated by goals closer to the hearts of key individuals. Allowing adaptability in project development also means that if circumstances change, say, in the competitive environment, the final formal appraisal takes account of this. The sponsor or promoter of a capital investment has to be aware of, and to adjust for, social subsystems within the organisation.

- *Expense* Sophisticated project evaluation can cost a considerable amount of money. The financial experts' input is costly enough, but the firm also has to consider the time and trouble managers throughout the organisation might have to devote to provide good-quality data and make their contribution to the debate. In a firm of limited resources it may be more efficient to search for projects at an informal or judgement level, thus generating a multitude of alternative avenues for growth, rather than to analyse a few in greater quantitative depth.

- *Stifling the entrepreneurial spirit* Excessive emphasis on formal evaluatory systems may be demotivating to individuals who thrive on free thinking, fast decision making and action. The relative weights given to formal approaches and entrepreneurialism will depend on the context, such as the pace of change in the marketplace.

- *Intangible benefits* Frequently, many of the most important benefits that flow from an investment are difficult to measure in money terms. Improving customer satisfaction through better service, quality or image may lead to enhanced revenues, but it is often difficult to state precisely the quantity of the increased revenue flow. For example, new technology often provides a number of intangible benefits, such as reduced time needed to switch machine tools to the production of other products, thereby reducing risk in fluctuating markets, or a quicker response to customer choice. These non-quantifiable benefits can amount to a higher value than the more obvious tangible benefits. An example of how intangible benefits could be allowed for in project appraisal is shown through the example of Crowther Precision plc.

Worked example 3.4	Crowther Precision plc

Crowther Precision plc produces metal parts for the car industry, with machinery that is now more than 20 years old. With appropriate maintenance these machines could continue producing indefinitely. However, developments in the machine tool industry have led to the creation of computer-controlled multi-use machines. Crowther is considering the purchase of the Z200 which would provide both quantifiable and non-quantifiable benefits over the old machine. The Z200 costs £1.2m but would be expected to last indefinitely if maintenance expenditure were increased by £20,000 every year forever.

The quantifiable benefits are:

(a) Reduced raw material requirements, due to lower wastage, amounting to £35,000 in each future year.
(b) Labour cost savings of £80,000 in each future year.

These quantifiable benefits are analysed using the NPV method (on page 92).

Examining the quantifiable elements in isolation will lead to a rejection of the project to buy the Z200. However, the non-quantifiable benefits are:

- Reduced time required to switch the machine from producing one version of the car component to one of the other three versions Crowther presently produces.
- The ability to switch the machine over to completely new products in response to changed industry demands, or to take up, as yet unseen, market opportunities in the future.
- Improved quality of output leading to greater customer satisfaction.

▶

Worked example 3.4   Continued

Incremental net present value analysis of Z200

		Present value £
Purchase of machine		−1,200,000
Present value of raw material saving	$\dfrac{35,000}{0.1}$	+350,000
Present value of labour saving	$\dfrac{80,000}{0.1}$	+800,000
Less present value of increased maintenance costs	$\dfrac{20,000}{0.1}$	−200,000
Net present value		−250,000

Note: Assume discount rate of 10 per cent, all cash flows arise at the year ends, zero scrap value of old machine.

It is true that the discounted cash flow analysis has failed to take into account all the relevant factors, but this should not lead to its complete rejection. In cases where non-quantifiable elements are present, the problem needs to be separated into two stages.

1 Analyse those elements that are quantifiable using NPV.
2 If the NPV from Stage 1 is negative, then managerial judgement will be needed to subjectively assess the non-quantifiable benefits. If these are judged to be greater than the 'loss' signalled in Stage 1 then the project is viable. For Crowther, if the management team consider that the intangible benefits are worth more than £250,000 they should proceed with the purchase of the Z200.

This line of thought is continued in Chapter 4, where operational and strategic decisions with options (real options) are considered.

The investment process

There is a great deal more to a successful investment programme than simply project appraisal. As **Exhibit 3.8** demonstrates, project appraisal is one of a number of stages in the investment process. The emphasis in the academic world on ever more sophistication in appraisal could be seriously misplaced. Attention paid to the evolution of investment ideas, their development and sifting may produce more practical returns. Marrying the evaluation of projects once screened with strategic, resource and human considerations may lead to avoidance of damaging decisions. Following through the implementation with a review of what went right, what went wrong, and why, may enable better decision making in the future.

Investment by a firm is a process often involving large numbers of individuals up and down an organisational hierarchy. It is a complex and infinitely adaptable process, which is likely to differ from one organisation to another. However, we can identify some common threads.

Generation of ideas

A firm is more likely to founder because of a shortage of good investment ideas than because of poor methods of appraisal. A good investment planning process requires a continuous flow of ideas to regenerate the organisation through the exploitation of new opportunities. Thought needs to be given to the development of a system for the encouragement of idea gen-

Exhibit 3.8	The investment process

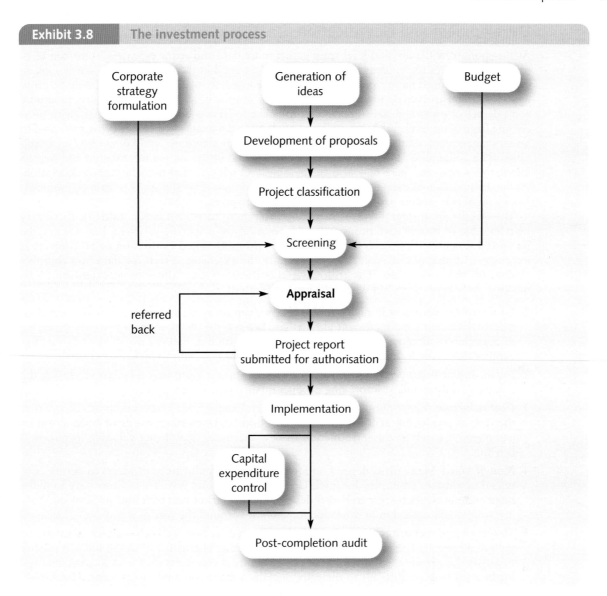

eration and subsequent communication through the firm. Indeed, one of the central tasks of senior management is to nurture a culture of search for and sponsorship of ideas. In the absence of a well-functioning system, the danger remains that investment proposals only arise in a reactive manner. For example, a firm examines new product possibilities only when it is realised that the old product is becoming, or has become, obsolete. Or else the latest technology is installed in reaction to its adoption by a competitor. A system and culture is needed to help the firm 'get ahead of the game' and be proactive rather than reactive.

One of the main inputs into a more systematic search for ideas is likely to be an environment-scanning process. It is also helpful if all potential idea-generators are made aware of the general strategic direction of the firm and the constraints under which it operates. Idea-generators often become sponsors of their proposals within the organisation. These individuals, in a poorly operating system, can see themselves taking a high risk for very little reward. Their reputation and career prospects can be intimately associated with a project. If it goes badly then they may find themselves blamed for that failure. In a system with such poor incentives the natural response of most people would be to hold back from suggesting ideas and pushing them through, and concentrate on day-to-day management. This defensive attitude could be bad for the organisation and it is therefore incumbent on senior management to develop reward systems that do not penalise project idea-generators and sponsors.

Development and classification

As the sponsor or the division-level team gather more data and refine estimates, some degree of early filtering takes place. Ideas that may have looked good in theory do not necessarily look so good when examined more closely. In a well-functioning system, idea generation should be propagated in an unstructured, almost random manner, but the development phase starts to impose some degree of order and structure. Many firms like to have a bottom-up approach, with ideas coming from plant level and being reviewed by divisional management before being presented to senior management. At the development stage the sponsor elaborates and hones ideas in consultation with colleagues. The divisional managers may add ideas, ask for information and suggest alternative scenarios. There may also be division-level projects that need further consideration. As the discussions and data gathering progress the proposal generally starts to gain commitment from a number of people who become drawn in and involved.

The classification stage involves matching projects to identified needs. Initially, there may be a long list of imaginative project ideas or solutions to a specific problem, but this may be narrowed down in these early stages to two or three. Detailed evaluation of all projects is expensive. Some types of project do not require the extensive search for data and complex evaluation that others do. The following classification may allow more attention to be directed at the type of project where the need is greatest:

1 *Equipment replacement* Equipment obsolescence can occur because of technological developments which create more efficient alternatives, because the old equipment becomes expensive to maintain or because of a change in the cost of inputs, making an alternative method cheaper (for example, if the oil price doubles, taxi firms may shift to fuel-efficient cars).

2 *Expansion or improvement of existing products* These investments relate to increasing the volume of output and/or improving product quality and market position.

3 *Cost reduction* A continuous process of search and analysis may be necessary to ensure that the firm is producing at lowest cost. Small modifications to methods of production or equipment, as well as the introduction of new machines, may bring valuable incremental benefits.

4 *New products* Many firms depend on a regular flow of innovatory products to permit continued expansion. Examples are Intel, GlaxoSmithKline and 3M. These firms have to make huge commitments to research and development, market research and promotion. Vast investments are needed in new production facilities around the world.

5 *Statutory and welfare* Investments may be required by law for such matters as safety, or pollution control. These do not, generally, give a financial return and so the focus is usually to satisfy the requirement at minimum cost. Welfare investments may lead to some intangible benefits that are difficult to quantify, such as a more contented workforce. The Arnold and Hatzopoulos (2000) survey showed that 78 per cent of the firms undertook non-economic projects directed at health and safety issues; 74 per cent accepted projects motivated by legislation; and 54 per cent had paid for uneconomic projects for social and environmental reasons.

The management team need to weigh up the value of a more comprehensive analysis against the cost of evaluation. Regular equipment replacement, cost reduction and existing product expansion decisions are likely to require less documentation than a major strategic investment in a new product area. Also, the information needs are likely to rise in proportion to the size of the investment. A £100m investment in a new pharmaceutical plant is likely to be treated differently to a £10,000 investment in a new delivery vehicle.

Screening

At this stage, each proposal will be assessed to establish whether it is sufficiently attractive to receive further attention through the application of sophisticated analysis. Screening decisions should be made with an awareness of the strategic direction of the firm and the limitations imposed by the financial, human and other resources available. There should also be a check on the technical feasibility of the proposal and some preliminary assessment of risk.

Strategy

Capital allocation is a pivotal part of the overall strategic process. A good investment appraisal system must mesh with the firm's long-term plan. The managers at plant or division level may not be able to see opportunities at a strategic level, such as the benefits of combining two divisions, or the necessity for business-unit divestment. Thus, the bottom-up flow of ideas for investment at plant level should complement the top-down strategic planning from the centre. Each vantage point has a valuable contribution to make.

Budget

Most large firms prepare capital budgets stretching over many years. Often a detailed budget for capital expenditure in the forthcoming year is set within the framework of an outline plan for the next five years. Individual projects are required to conform to the corporate budget. However, the budget itself, at least in the long run, is heavily influenced by the availability of project proposals. The Arnold and Hatzopoulos (2000) survey shows the use of budgets by UK firms – *see* Exhibit 3.9.

Exhibit 3.9	Capital expenditure budgets for UK firms		
	Small firms %	**Medium-sized firms %**	**Large firms %**
Outline capital expenditure budgets are prepared for:			
1 year ahead	18	8	–
2 years ahead	18	25	13
3 years ahead	35	50	18
4 years ahead	9	–	5
More than 4 years ahead	21	13	61
Blank	–	4	3
Detailed capital expenditure budgets are prepared for:			
1 year ahead	70	79	55
2 years ahead	21	13	21
3 years ahead	9	4	8
4 years ahead	–	–	5
More than 4 years ahead	–	4	11

Note: 96 firms completed the survey questionnaire.

Source: Arnold and Hatzopoulos (2000).

Appraisal

It is at the appraisal stage that detailed cash flow forecasts are required as inputs to the more sophisticated evaluation methods, such as net present value. Manuals provide detailed check-lists that help the project sponsor to ensure that all relevant costs and other factors have been considered. These manuals may explain how to calculate NPV and IRR and may also supply the firm's opportunity cost of capital. (If risk adjustment is made through the discount rate there may be more than one cost of capital and the sponsor then has to classify the project into, say, high-, medium- or low-risk categories – see Chapter 4.) The project promoter may seek the aid of specialists, such as engineers, accountants and economists, in the preparation of the formal analysis.

Report and authorisation

Many firms require that project proposals are presented in a specific manner through the use of capital appropriation request forms. Such forms will detail the nature of the project and the amount of finance needed, together with the forecasted cash inflows and the NPV, IRR, ARR and/or payback. Some analysis of risk and a consideration of alternatives to the proposed course of action may also be required.

Expenditure below a threshold, say £100,000, will gain authorisation at division level, while that above the threshold will need approval at corporate level. At head office a committee consisting of the most senior officers (chairman, chief executive, finance director, etc.) will meet on a regular basis to consider major capital projects. Very few investment proposals are turned down by this committee, mainly because these project ideas will have already been through a number of stages of review and informal discussion up and down the organisation, and the obviously non-viable will have been eliminated. Also, even marginally profitable projects may get approval to give a vote of confidence to the sponsoring management team. The alternative of refusal may damage motivation and may cause loss of commitment to developing other projects. If the senior management had had doubts about a proposal they would have influenced the sponsoring division(s) long before the proposal reached the final report stage. In most cases there is a long period of consultation between head office and division managers, and informal pressures to modify or drop proposals can be both more efficient and politically astute ways of proceeding than refusal at the last hurdle.

Implementation

Capital expenditure controls

Firms must keep track of investment projects so as to be quickly aware of delays and cost differences compared with the plan. When a project is authorised there is usually a specified schedule of expenditure, and the accountants and senior management will keep a watchful eye on cash outflows. During the installation, purchasing and construction phases, comparisons with original estimates will be made on a periodic basis. Divisions may be permitted to overspend by, say, 10 per cent before a formal request for more funds is required. A careful watch is also kept on any changes to the projected start and completion dates. Deviations from projected cash flows can be caused by one of two factors:

a inaccuracy in the original estimate, that is, the proposal report did not reflect reality perfectly;

b poor control of costs.

It is often difficult to isolate each of these elements. However, deviations need to be identified and explained as the project progresses. This may permit corrective action to be taken to avoid further overspending and may, in extreme circumstances, lead to the cancellation of the project.

Post-completion audit

Post-completion auditing is the monitoring and evaluation of the progress of a capital investment project through a comparison of the actual cash flows and other costs and benefits with those forecasted at the time of authorisation. Companies need a follow-up procedure that examines the performance of projects over a long time-span, stretching over many years. It is necessary to isolate and explain deviations from estimated values. **Exhibit 3.10** shows the extent of the use of post-competition audits by UK companies.

There are three main reasons for carrying out a post-completion audit:

1 *Financial control mechanism* This monitoring process helps to identify problems and errors evident in a particular project. A comparison with the original projections establishes whether the benefits claimed prior to approval actually materialise. If a problem is encountered then modifications or abandonment may be possible before it is too late.

Exhibit 3.10	Replies to the question: 'Does your company conduct post-audits of major capital expenditure?'			
	Small %	Medium-sized %	Large %	Composite %
Always	41	17	24	28
Sometimes/on major projects	41	67	71	59
Rarely	12	17	5	10
Never	6	–	–	2

Note: 96 companies responded to the survey.

Source: Arnold and Hatzopoulos (2000).

2 *Insight gained may be useful for future capital investment decisions* One benefit of auditing existing projects is that it might lead to the identification of failings in the capital investment process generally. It may be discovered that data collection systems are inadequate or that appraisal methods are poor. Regular post-completion auditing helps to develop better decision making. For instance, past appraisals may have paid scant regard to likely competitor reaction; once recognised this omission will be corrected for in all future evaluations.

3 *The psychological effect* If potential project sponsors are aware that implemented proposals are monitored and reviewed they may be encouraged to increase their forecasting accuracy. They may also be dissuaded from playing 'numbers games' with their project submission, designed to draw more resources to their divisions or pet schemes unjustifiably. In addition, they may take a keener interest in the implementation phase.

Senior management must conduct a careful balancing act because the post-completion audit may encourage another sort of non-optimal behaviour. For instance, if managers are judged on the extent to which project outcomes exceed original estimates, there will be a tendency to deliberately understate the forecast. Also, if the audit is too inquisitorial, or if it too forcefully apportions blame for results that are only partially under the control of managers, then they may be inclined to suggest only relatively safe projects with predictable outcomes. This may result in a loss of opportunities. Ideally, regular post-completion reviews are needed, but many firms settle for an audit one year after the asset has been put in place. This may be inadequate for projects producing returns over many years. Some firms do manage an annual review of progress, and some even go as far as monthly monitoring during the first year followed by annual reviews thereafter. On the other hand, many projects involve only minor commitment of resources and are routine in nature. The need for post-completion auditing is not as pressing for these as it would be for strategic projects requiring major organisational resource commitment. Given the costs involved in the auditing process, many firms feel justified in being highly selective and auditing only a small proportion. Another reason for not carrying out a post-completion audit in all cases is the difficulty of disentangling the costs and benefits of a specific project in a context of widespread project interaction and interdependence.

Capital rationing

Our discussion, until now, has rested on the assumption that if a project had a positive net present value then it both *should* be undertaken, and *could* be undertaken. The wealth of shareholders is highest if the firm accepts every project that has a positive NPV. But to undertake every possible project assumes that the firm has sufficient funds available. Quite often, in the practical world of business, there are limits placed on the availability of project finance and a choice has to be made between a number of positive NPV projects. This is the capital rationing problem.

Capital rationing occurs when funds are not available to finance all wealth-enhancing projects. There are two types of capital rationing: soft rationing and hard rationing.

Soft rationing

Soft capital rationing is internal management-imposed limits on investment expenditure. Such limits may be linked to the firm's financial control policy. Senior management may try to retain financial control over divisions by placing limits on the amount any particular division can spend on a set of projects. Some ambitious managers may be tempted to overstate the extent of investment opportunities within their sector of responsibility. To sort out the good projects from the bad, head office could examine each individually, but this would be bureaucratic and time consuming. The alternative is to impose a limit on the amount a division may invest in projects within a particular time frame. It is then the division's responsibility to decide which projects rank higher than others.

Some firms operate in very dynamic sectors and have a large number of potentially profitable expansion opportunities. To undertake all of them would put intolerable strains on the management and the organisation because of the excessive growth this might imply. For example, Microsoft's thousands of technically able employees might generate dozens or even hundreds of ideas for significant new businesses, ranging from new software and multimedia to links with television broadcasters and book publishers. Over-rapid expansion may lead to difficulties in planning and control. Intangible stresses and strains are difficult to quantify and therefore the rationing of capital is used to place some limits to growth. Capital rationing acts as a proxy for other types of resources in short supply, such as managerial talent or time, technical expertise or even equipment.

Firms may aim to avoid exceeding certain values for key financial ratios. One of the most important ratios examined is the relationship between borrowing and asset levels. Management may be fearful of the increasing risk associated with extensive borrowing and become reluctant to enter into the capital markets to borrow. Unwillingness to borrow more money has elements of soft and hard capital rationing. It is a form of self-imposed rationing, but it may have been prompted by signals from the capital markets that borrowing would be difficult or would be available only with onerous strings attached. Another limit on the availability of finance can be created because the existing owner-manager or family shareholders do not wish to lose control by permitting the firm to raise equity finance by selling new shares to outsiders.

Hard rationing

Hard capital rationing relates to capital from external sources. Agencies external to the firm will not supply unlimited amounts of investment capital, even though positive NPV projects are identified. In a perfect capital market hard rationing should never occur, because if a firm has positive NPV projects it will be able to raise any finance it needs. Hard rationing, therefore, implies market imperfections. This is a problem that has been evident since business activity first started. It is a particular problem for smaller, less profitable and more high-risk firms. Numerous governments have tried to improve the availability of funds to firms. Also, stock exchanges, over recent years, have encouraged the development of equity markets specifically targeted at small firms trying to raise finance. In addition, a venture capital market has been developed by institutions to provide for start-up and early stage development. (Sources of equity capital are examined in Chapter 6.) Despite all these advances companies still complain regularly in the press about the gap between the amount of capital firms would like to use and that which is made available.

One-period capital rationing

The simplest and most straightforward form of rationing occurs when limits are placed on finance availability for only one year; for all the other years funds are unlimited. There are two possibilities within this one-period rationing situation.

1 *Divisible projects* The nature of the proposed projects is such that it is possible to undertake a fraction of a total project. For instance, if a project is established to expand a retail group by opening a further 100 shops, it would be possible to take only 30 per cent (that is 30 shops) or any other fraction of the overall project. To make the mathematical calculations less complicated, and to make conceptual understanding easier, it is often assumed that all cash flows change in proportion to the fraction of the project implemented.

2 *Indivisible projects* With some projects it is impossible to take a fraction. The choice is between undertaking the whole of the investment or none of it (for instance, a project to build a ship, or a bridge or an oil platform).

Divisible projects

A stylised example of a one-period constraint problem with divisible projects is Bigtasks plc, a subsidiary of a major manufacturing group.

Worked example 3.5   Bigtasks plc

Bigtasks has four positive NPV projects to consider. Capital at time zero has been rationed to £4.5m because of head office planning and control policies, and because the holding company has been subtly warned that another major round of fresh borrowing this year would not be welcomed by the financial institutions in the City of London. However, funds are likely to be effectively unlimited in future years. The four projects under consideration can each be undertaken once only and the acceptance of one of the projects does not exclude the possibility of accepting another one. The cash flows are as follows:

Point in time (yearly intervals)	0 £m	1 £m	2 £m	NPV at 10% £m
Project A	–2	6	1	4.281
Project B	–1	1	4	3.215
Project C	–1	1	3	2.388
Project D	–3	10	10	14.355

All these projects have positive net present values and would therefore all be accepted in the absence of capital rationing. We need to determine the optimal combination of projects which will require a total investment the same as, or less than, the capital constraint. Ranking projects by the absolute NPV will usually give an incorrect result. Such an approach will be biased towards the selection of large projects. It may be better to invest in a number of smaller projects with lower individual NPVs. If we do select according to the highest absolute NPV, the total NPV produced is £17.566m, because we would allocate £3m first to Project D, and then the remaining £1.5m would be invested in three-quarters of Project A because this has the next highest absolute NPV.

Ranking according to absolute NPV

	Initial outlay	NPV (£m)
All of Project D	3	14.355
3/4 of Project A	1.5	3.211
	4.5	Total NPV 17.566

To achieve an optimum allocation of the £4.5m we need to make use of either the profitability index (PI) or the benefit–cost ratio.[1]

---

[1] The use of these terms is often muddled and they may be used interchangeably in the literature and in practice, so you should ensure that it is clearly understood how the ratio used in a particular situation is calculated.

Worked example 3.5   **Continued**

$$\text{Profitability index} = \frac{\text{Gross present value}}{\text{Initial outlay}}$$

$$\text{Benefit–cost ratio} = \frac{\text{Net present value}}{\text{Initial outlay}}$$

The gross present value is the total present value of all the cash flows excluding the initial investment. Both ratios provide a measure of profitability per £ invested. For example, in **Exhibit 3.11**, for every £1 invested in Project A, £3.14 is returned in future cash flows when discounted. The benefit–cost ratio is, of course, closely related to the profitability index and for Project A shows that £1 committed at time zero will produce a net present value of £2.14.

Exhibit 3.11   Bigtasks plc: Profitability indices and benefit–cost ratios

Project	NPV (@ 10%)	GPV (@ 10%)	Profitability index	Benefit–cost ratio
A	4.281	6.281	$\frac{6.281}{2} = 3.14$	$\frac{4.281}{2} = 2.14$
B	3.215	4.215	$\frac{4.215}{1} = 4.215$	$\frac{3.215}{1} = 3.215$
C	2.388	3.388	$\frac{3.388}{1} = 3.388$	$\frac{2.388}{1} = 2.388$
D	14.355	17.355	$\frac{17.355}{3} = 5.785$	$\frac{14.355}{3} = 4.785$

The use of profitability indices or benefit–cost ratios is a matter of personal choice. Whichever is used, the next stage is to arrange the projects in order of the highest profitability index or benefit–cost ratio. Then work down the list until the capital limit is reached. Here, the profitability index (PI) will be used (*see* **Exhibit 3.12**).

Exhibit 3.12   Bigtasks plc: Ranking according to the highest profitability index

Profit	Profitability index	Initial outlay £m	NPV £m
D	5.785	3	14.355
B	4.215	1	3.215
1/2 of C	3.388	0.5	1.194
Nothing of A	3.14	0	0
Total investment		4.5	18.764

With the profitability index, Project D gives the highest return and so is the best project in terms of return per £ of outlay. However, Project A no longer ranks second because this provides the lowest return per unit of initial investment. The smaller projects, B and C, give a higher PI.

The overall result for Bigtasks is that an extra £1.198m (£18.764 – £17.566m) is created for shareholders by selecting projects through one of the ratios rather than sticking rigidly to NPV.

Indivisible projects

In practice, few projects are divisible and so the profitability index is inappropriate. Now, assume that it is not possible to take a fraction of Bigtask's projects and that the capital limit at time zero is £3m. In these circumstances the easiest approach is to examine the total NPV values of all the feasible alternative combinations of whole projects, in other words, trial and error. (*See* **Exhibit 3.13**.)

Exhibit 3.13	Individual project with capital constraint of £3m

Feasible combination 1	**NPV (£m)**
£2m invested in Project A	4.281
£1m invested in Project B	3.215
Total NPV	7.496

Feasible combination 2	**NPV (£m)**
£2m invested in Project A	4.281
£1m invested in Project C	2.388
Total NPV	6.669

Feasible combination 3	**NPV (£m)**
£1m invested in Project B	3.215
£1m invested in Project C	2.388
Total NPV	5.603

Feasible combination 4	**NPV (£m)**
£3m invested in Project D Total NPV	14.355

Taxation and investment appraisal

Taxation can have an important impact on project viability. If management are implementing decisions that are shareholder wealth enhancing, they will focus on the cash flows generated which are available for shareholders. Therefore, they will evaluate the after-tax cash flows of a project. There are two rules to follow in investment appraisal in a world with taxation:

- **Rule 1** If acceptance of a project changes the tax liabilities of the firm then incremental tax effects need to be accommodated in the analysis.
- **Rule 2** Get the timing right. Incorporate the cash outflow of tax into the analysis at the correct time. For example, it is often the case that tax is paid up to one year after the receipt of the related cash flows.

In the UK the HM Revenue and Customs collect corporation tax based on the taxable income of companies. Specific projects are not taxed separately, but if a project produces additional profits in a year, then this will generally increase the tax bill. If losses are made on a project, then the overall tax bill will generally be reduced. Taxable income is rarely the same as the profit reported in the annual reports and accounts because some of the expenses deducted to produce the reported profit are not permitted by HM Revenue and Customs when calculating taxable income. For example, depreciation is not an allowable cost. The HM Revenue and Customs permit a 'writing-down' allowance rather than depreciation. So for most plant and machinery in the UK, a writing-down allowance of 25 per cent on a declining balance is permitted. In a firm's accounts, such equipment may be depreciated by only, say, 10 per cent a year, whereas the tax authorities permit the taxable income to be reduced by 25 per cent of the equipment value. Thus, reported profit will often be higher than taxable income. Other types of long-lived assets, such as industrial buildings, have different percentage writing-down allowances – some assets carry a 100 per cent writing-down allowance in the year of purchase.

If we are deducting tax from the cash flow figures for a project then we should be using a discount rate that allows for tax, i.e. the required rate of return after tax is less than the required rate of return before tax is deducted from the returns required to be paid to the finance providers – see Chapter 8.

Inflation

Annual inflation in the UK has varied from 1 per cent to 26 per cent since 1945. It is important to adapt investment appraisal methods to cope with the phenomenon of price movements. Future rates of inflation are unlikely to be precisely forecasted; nevertheless, we will assume in the analysis that follows that we can anticipate inflation with reasonable accuracy. **Case study 3.2** shows the importance of allowing for inflation.

Case study 3.2	Eurotunnel's inflation allowance

Peter Puplett, writing in the *Investors Chronicle*, pointed out some of the forecasting errors made in Eurotunnel's pathfinder prospectus issued in November 1987, one of which was to do with inflation:

> The total cost of the project was stated as £4,874m in the prospectus, as shown in the table. The uplift directors made for inflation was less than 14%, even though they knew the project would take at least six years to complete.

General inflation in the UK was far higher than 14 per cent over this period. The projected costs, therefore, were too low.

1987 Eurotunnel costs

	£m
Construction @ 1987 prices	2,788
Corporate costs @ 1987 prices	642
	3,430
Plus:	
Provision for inflation	469
Building cost	3,899
Net financing costs	975
Total project cost	4,874

Source: Based on *Investors Chronicle*, 19 April 1996, p. 20.

Two types of inflation can be distinguished. *Specific inflation* refers to the price changes of an individual good or service. *General inflation* is the reduced purchasing power of money and is measured by an overall price index, which follows the price changes of a 'basket' of goods and services through time.

Inflation creates two problems for project appraisal. First, the estimation of future cash flows is made more troublesome. The project appraiser will have to estimate the degree to which future cash flows will be inflated. Second, the rate of return required by the firm's security holders, such as shareholders, will rise if inflation rises. Thus, inflation has an impact on the discount rate used in investment evaluation. We will look at the second problem in more detail first.

'Real' and 'money' rates of return

A point was made in Chapter 2 of demonstrating that the rate of return represented by the discount rate usually takes account of three types of compensation:

- the pure time value of money, or impatience to consume;
- risk;
- inflation.

Thus, the interest rates quoted in the financial markets are sufficiently high to compensate for all three elements. A 10-year loan to a reputable government (such as the purchase of a bond) may pay an interest rate of 9 per cent per annum. Some of this is compensation for time preference and a little for risk, but the majority of that interest is likely to be compensation for future inflation. It is the same for the cost of capital for a business. When it issues financial securities, the returns offered include a large element of inflation compensation.

To illustrate: even in a situation of no inflation, given the choice between receiving goods and services now or receiving them some time in the future, shareholders would rather receive them now. If these pure time and risk preferences were valued, the value might turn out to be 8 per cent per annum. That is, in a world without inflation, investors are indifferent as to whether they receive a given basket of commodities today or receive a basket of commodities which is 8 per cent larger in one year's time.

The *real rate of return* is defined as the rate of return that would be required in the absence of inflation – in this case 8 per cent.

If we change the assumption so that prices do rise then investors will demand compensation for general inflation. They will require a larger monetary amount at Time 1 to buy 1.08 baskets. If inflation is 4 per cent then the money value of the commodities at Time 1, which would leave the investor indifferent when comparing it with one basket at Time 0, is:

$$1.08 \times 1.04 = 1.1232$$

That is, investors will be indifferent as to whether they hold £1,000 now or receive £1,123.20 one year hence. Since the money cash flow of £1,123.20 at Time 1 is financially equivalent to £1,000 now, the money rate of return is 12.32 per cent. The *money rate of return* includes a return to compensate for inflation.

The generalised relationship between real rates of return and money (or market, or nominal) rates of return and inflation is expressed in Fisher's (1930) equation:

(1 + money rate of return) = (1 + real rate of return) $\times$ (1 + anticipated rate of inflation)

$(1 + m) = (1 + h) \times (1 + i)$

$(1 + 0.1232) = (1 + 0.08) \times (1 + 0.04)$

'Money' cash flows and 'real' cash flows

We have now established two possible discount rates, the money discount rate and the real discount rate. There are two alternative ways of adjusting for the effect of future inflation on cash flows. The first is to estimate the likely specific inflation rates for each of the inflows and outflows of cash and calculate the actual monetary amount paid or received in the year that the flow occurs. This is the money cash flow or the nominal cash flow. With a *money cash flow*, all future cash flows are expressed in the prices expected to rule when the cash flow occurs.

The other possibility is to measure the cash flows in terms of real prices. That is, all future cash flows are expressed in terms of, say, Time 0's prices. With *real cash flows*, future cash flows are expressed in terms of constant purchasing power.

Adjusting for inflation

There are two correct methods of adjusting for inflation when calculating net present value. They will lead to the same answer:

● *Approach 1* Estimate the cash flows in money terms and use a money discount rate.

● *Approach 2* Estimate the cash flows in real terms and use a real discount rate.

For now we will leave discussion of conversion to real prices and focus on the calculations using money cash flow. This will be done through the examination of an appraisal for Amplify plc.

Worked example 3.6   Amplify plc

Cash flow in money terms and money discount rate

Amplify plc is considering a project which would require an outlay of £2.4m at the outset. The money cash flows receivable from sales will depend on the specific inflation rate for Amplify's product. This is anticipated to be 6 per cent per annum. Cash outflows consist of three elements: labour, materials and overheads. Labour costs are expected to increase at 9 per cent per year, materials by 12 per cent and overheads by 8 per cent. The discount rate of 12.32 per cent that Amplify uses is a money discount rate, including an allowance for inflation. One of the key rules of project appraisal is now followed: if the discount rate is stated in money terms, then consistency requires that the cash flows be estimated in money terms. (It is surprising how often this rule is broken.)

$$NPV = M_0 + \frac{M_1}{1 + m} + \frac{M_2}{(1 + m)^2} + \frac{M_n}{(1 + m)^n}$$

where M = actual or money cash flow
m = actual or money rate of return

Annual cash flows in present (Time 0) prices are as follows:

	£m	Inflation
Sales	2	6%
Labour costs	0.3	9%
Material costs	0.6	12%
Overhead	0.06	8%

All cash flows occur at year ends except for the initial outflow.

The first stage is to calculate the money cash flows. We need to restate the inflows and outflows for each of the years at the amount actually changing hands in nominal terms. (*See* **Exhibit 3.14**.) Then we discount at the money rate of return (*see* **Exhibit 3.15**). This project produces a positive NPV and is therefore to be recommended.

Worked example 3.6   **Continued**

Exhibit 3.14   Amplify plc: Money cash flow

Point in time (yearly intervals)	Cash flow before allowing for price rises £m	Inflation adjustment	Money cash flow £m
0 Initial outflow	−2.4	1	−2.4
1 Sales	2	1.06	2.12
Labour	−0.3	1.09	−0.327
Materials	−0.6	1.12	−0.672
Overheads	−0.06	1.08	−0.065
Net money cash flow for Year 1			+1.056
2 Sales	2	$(1.06)^2$	2.247
Labour	−0.3	$(1.09)^2$	−0.356
Materials	−0.6	$(1.12)^2$	−0.753
Overheads	−0.06	$(1.08)^2$	−0.070
Net money cash flow for Year 2			+1.068
3 Sales	2	$(1.06)^3$	2.382
Labour	−0.3	$(1.09)^3$	−0.389
Materials	−0.6	$(1.12)^3$	−0.843
Overheads	−0.06	$(1.08)^3$	−0.076
Net money cash flow for Year 3			+1.074

Exhibit 3.15   Amplify plc: Money cash flow discounted at the money discount rate

Point in time (yearly intervals)	0 £m	1 £m	2 £m	3 £m
Undiscounted cash flows	−2.4	1.056	1.068	1.074
Discounting calculation	−2.4	$\dfrac{1.056}{1 + 0.1232}$	$\dfrac{1.068}{(1 + 0.1232)^2}$	$\dfrac{1.074}{(1 + 0.1232)^3}$
Discounted cash flows	−2.4	0.9402	0.8466	0.7579

Net present value = +£0.1447 million.

> **AN EXCEL SPREADSHEET VERSION OF THIS CALCULATION IS AVAILABLE AT**
> www.pearsoned.co.uk/arnold

Cash flow in real terms and real discount rate

The second approach is to calculate the net present value by discounting real cash flow by the real discount rate. A real cash flow is obtainable by discounting the money cash flow by the general rate of inflation, thereby converting it to its current purchasing power equivalent.

Worked example 3.6   Continued

The general inflation rate is derived from Fisher's equation:

$$(1 + m) = (1 + h) \times (1 + i)$$

where m = money rate of return; h = real rate of return; i = inflation rate.

m is given as 0.1232, h as 0.08, i as 0.04.

$$i = \frac{(1 + m)}{(1 + h)} - 1 = \frac{1 + 0.1232}{1 + 0.08} - 1 = 0.04$$

Under this method net present value becomes:

$$NPV = R_0 + \frac{R_1}{1 + h} + \frac{R_2}{(1 + h)^2} + \frac{R_3}{(1 + h)^3} + \dots$$

The net present value is equal to the sum of the real cash flows R_t discounted at a real rate of interest, h. The first stage is to discount money cash flows by the general inflation rate to establish real cash flows (Exhibit 3.16).

Exhibit 3.16   Amplify plc: Discounting money cash flows by the general inflation rate

Points in time (yearly intervals)	Cash flow £m	Calculation	Real cash flow £m
0	−2.4	–	−2.4
1	1.056	$\dfrac{1.056}{1 + 0.04}$	1.0154
2	1.068	$\dfrac{1.068}{(1 + 0.04)^2}$	0.9874
3	1.074	$\dfrac{1.074}{(1 + 0.04)^3}$	0.9548

The second task is to discount real cash flows at the real discount rate (Exhibit 3.17).

Exhibit 3.17   Amplify plc: Real cash flows discounted at the real discount rate

Point in time (yearly intervals)	0 £m	1 £m	2 £m	3 £m
Real cash flow	−2.4	1.0154	0.9874	0.9548
Discounting calculation	−2.4	$\dfrac{1.0154}{1 + 0.08}$	$\dfrac{0.9874}{(1 + 0.08)^2}$	$\dfrac{0.9548}{(1 + 0.08)^3}$
Discounted cash flow	−2.4	0.9402	0.8465	0.7580

Net present value = +£0.1447 million.

Worked example 3.6   Continued

Note that the net present value is the same as before. To discount at the general inflation rate, i, followed by discounting at the real rate of return, h, is arithmetically the same as discounting money cash flows at the money rate, m. Often, in practice, to calculate future cash flows the analyst, instead of allowing for specific inflation rates, will make the simplifying assumption that all prices will stay the same, at Time 0's prices. This could lead to errors if a cost item (e.g. oil) is a major component and is subject to a very high specific inflation. However, in most cases reasonably accurate results can be obtained.

Also note that the money cash flows are deflated by the general rate of inflation, not by the specific rates. This is because the ultimate beneficiaries of this project are interested in their ability to purchase a basket of goods generally and not their ability to buy any one good, and therefore the link between the real cost of capital and the money cost of capital is the general inflation rate.

The two methods for adjusting for inflation produce the same result and therefore it does not matter which method is used. The first method, using money discount rates, has the virtue of requiring only one stage of discounting.

A warning

Never do either of the following:

1 Discount money cash flows with the real discount rate. This gives an apparent NPV much larger than the true NPV and so will result in erroneous decisions to accept projects which are not shareholder wealth enhancing.

2 Discount real cash flows with the money discount rate. This will reduce the NPV from its true value which causes the rejection of projects which will be shareholder wealth enhancing.

The treatment of inflation in practice

Exhibit 3.18 shows that UK companies generally either specify cash flow in constant prices and apply a real rate of return or express cash flows in inflated price terms and discount at the market rate of return.

Exhibit 3.18   Inflation adjustment methods used for investment appraisal by UK firms

	Small %	Medium-sized %	Large %	Composite %
Specify cash flow in constant prices and apply a real rate of return	47	29	45	42
All cash flows expressed in inflated price terms and discounted at the market rate of return	18	42	55	39
Considered at risk analysis or sensitivity stage	21	13	16	17
No adjustment	18	21	3	13
Other	0	0	3	1

Source: Arnold and Hatzopoulos (2000).

Concluding comments

The key point I would like to emphasise from this chapter is that the typical student of finance will spend a great deal of time trying to cope with problems presented in a mathematical form. This is necessary because these are often the most difficult aspects of the subject to absorb. However, readers should not be misled into thinking that complex computations are at the centre of project investment in the practical world of business. Managers are often either ignorant of the principles behind discounted cash flow techniques or choose to stress more traditional rule-of-thumb techniques, such as payback and accounting rate of return, because of their communicatory or other perceived advantages. These managers recognise that good investment decision making and implementation require attention to be paid to the social and psychological factors at work within an organisation. They also know that formal technical appraisal takes place only after a long process of idea creation and development in a suitably nurturing environment. There is also a long period of discussion and commitment-forming, and continuous re-examination and refinement. The real art of management is in the process of project creation and selection and not in the technical appraisal stage.

Key points and concepts

- **Raw data** have to be checked for accuracy, reliability, timeliness, expense of collection, etc.

- **Profit** is a poor substitute for cash flow. For example, **working capital adjustments** may be needed to modify the profit figures for NPV analysis, **depreciation** is not a cash flow and should be excluded.

- Analyse on the basis of **incremental cash flows**. That is the difference between the cash flows arising if the project is implemented and the cash flows if the project is not implemented. Take into account **opportunity costs** associated with, say, using an asset which has an alternative employment; **incidental effects**, that is, cash flow effects throughout the organisation, should be considered along with the obvious direct effects; **sunk costs** – costs which will not change regardless of the decision to proceed – are clearly irrelevant; **allocated overhead** is a non-incremental cost and is irrelevant; **interest** should not be double counted by both including interest as a cash flow and including it as an element in the discount rate.

- **Payback and ARR** are widely used methods of project appraisal, but discounted cash flow methods are the most popular. However, most large firms use **more than one appraisal method**.

- **Payback** is the length of time for cumulated future cash inflows to equal an initial outflow. Projects are accepted if this time is below an agreed cut-off point. It has a **few drawbacks**: no allowance for the time value of money; cash flows after the cut-off are ignored; arbitrary selection of cut-off date. **Discounted payback** takes account of the time value of money.

- **Payback's attractions**: it complements more sophisticated methods; simple, and easy to use; good for communication with non-specialists; makes allowance for increased risk of more distant cash flows; projects returning cash sooner are ranked higher; thought to be useful when capital is in short supply.

- **Accounting rate of return** is the ratio of accounting profit to investment, expressed as a percentage. It has **a few drawbacks**: it can be calculated in a wide variety of ways; profit is a poor substitute for cash flow; no allowance for the time value of money; arbitrary cut-off rate; some perverse decisions can be made.

- **Accounting rate of return attractions**: familiarity, ease of understanding and communication; managers' performances are often judged using ARR and therefore they wish to select projects on the same basis.

- **Internal rate of return** is used more than NPV: psychological preference for a percentage; can be calculated without cost of capital; thought (wrongly) to give a better ranking.

- **Mathematical technique is only one element** needed for successful project appraisal. Other factors to be taken into account are: strategy; social context; expense; entrepreneurial spirit; intangible benefits.

- **The investment process** is more than appraisal. **It has many stages:** generation of ideas; development and classification; screening; appraisal; report and authorisation; implementation; post-completion auditing.

- **Soft capital rationing** – internal management-imposed limits on investment expenditure despite the availability of positive NPV projects.

- **Hard capital rationing** – externally imposed limits on investment expenditure in the presence of positive NPV projects.

- For **divisible one-period capital rationing problems**, focus on the returns per £ of outlay:

$$\text{Profitability index} = \frac{\text{Gross present value}}{\text{Initial outlay}}$$

$$\text{Benefit–cost ratio} = \frac{\text{Net present value}}{\text{Initial outlay}}$$

- For **indivisible one-period capital rationing problems**, examine all the feasible alternative combinations.

- The two rules for **allowing for taxation** in project appraisal: (i) include incremental tax effects of a project as a cash outflow; (ii) get the timing right.

- **Taxable profits are not the same as accounting profits**. For example, depreciation is not allowed for in the taxable profit calculation, but writing-down allowances are permitted.

- **Specific inflation** means price changes of an individual good or service over a period of time.

- **General inflation** – the reduced purchasing power of money.

- General inflation affects the rate of return required on projects: **real rate of return** – the return required in the absence of inflation; **money rate of return** – includes a return to compensate for inflation.

- **Fisher's equation**

  (1 + money rate of return) = (1 + real rate of return) $\times$ (1 + anticipated rate of inflation)
  $(1 + m) = (1 + h) \times (1 + i)$

- Inflation affects future cash flows: **money cash flows** – all future cash flows are expressed in the prices expected to rule when the cash flow occurs; **real cash flows** – future cash flows are expressed in constant purchasing power.

- **Adjusting for inflation in project appraisal:**

  - Approach 1 – Estimate the cash flows in money terms and use a money discount rate.

  - Approach 2 – Estimate the cash flows in real terms and use a real discount rate.

Further reading

The following provide survey evidence on corporate use of the techniques discussed in this chapter: Arnold, G.C. and Hatzopoulos, P.D. (2000), Carsberg, B.V. and Hope, A. (1976), Coulthurst, N.J. (1986), Graham, J.R. and Harvey, C.R. (2001) (US evidence), Ho, S.M. and Pike, R.H. (1991), McIntyre, A.D. and Coulthurst, N.J. (1986), Pike, R.H. (1982), Pike, R.H. (1983), Pike, R.H. (1988), Pike, R.H. (1996), Pike, R.H. and Wolfe, M. (1988), Sangster, A. (1993).

Self-review questions

1 'Those business school graduates don't know what they are talking about. We have to allocate overheads to every department and activity. If we simply excluded this cost there would be a big lump of costs not written off. All projects must bear some central overhead.' Discuss this statement in the context of project appriasal.

2 Arcmat plc owns a factory which at present is empty. Mrs Hambicious, a business strategist, has been working on a proposal for using the factory for doll manufacture. This will require complete modernisation. Mrs Hambicious is a little confused about project appraisal and has asked your advice about which of the following are relevant and incremental cash flows.

a The future cost of modernising the factory.
b The £100,000 spent two months ago on a market survey investigating the demand for these plastic dolls.
c Machines to produce the dolls – cost £10m payable on delivery.
d Depreciation on the machines.
e Arcmat's other product lines are expected to be more popular due to the complementary nature of the new doll range with these existing products – the net cash flow effect is anticipated at £1m.
f Three senior managers will be drafted in from other divisions for a period of a year.
g A proportion of the US head office costs.
h The tax saving due to the plant investment being offset against taxable income.
i The £1m of additional raw material stock required at the start of production.
j The interest that will be charged on the £20m bank loan needed to initiate this project.
k The cost of the utility services installed last year.

3 Payback is dismissed as unsound. Discuss. Describe discounted payback.

4 Define accounting rate of return and compare it with net present value.

5 Do you believe the arguments for using IRR are strong enough to justify relying on this technique alone?

6 Why is investment project generation, selection and implementation closer to an art form than a science?

7 How would you appraise a project with a high proportion of non-quantifiable benefits?

8 If you were chief executive of a large corporation, how would you encourage project idea generation, communication and sponsorship?

9 Why is project screening necessary?

10 When do capital expenditure controls and post-completion audits become an excessive burden, and when are they very important?

11 Explain why hard and soft rationing occur. Why not simply rank projects on the basis of the highest NPV in conditions of capital rationing?

12 Explain the alternative methods of dealing with inflation in project appraisal.

Quick numerical questions

1 The Tenby-Saundersfoot Dock company is considering the reopening of one of its mothballed loading docks. Repairs and new equipment will cost £250,000 payable immediately. To operate the new dock will require additional dockside employees, costing £70,000 per year. There will also be a need for additional administrative staff and other overheads such as extra stationery, insurance and telephone costs amounting to £85,000 per year. Electricity and other energy used on the dock is anticipated to cost £40,000 per year. The London head office will allocate £50,000 of its (unchanged) costs to this project. Other docks will experience a reduction in receipts of about £20,000 per year due to some degree of cannibalisation. Annual fees expected from the new dock are £255,000 per year.

Assume

- all cash flows arise at the year ends except the initial repair and equipment costs which are incurred at the outset;
- no tax or inflation;
- no sales are made on credit.
a   Lay out the net annual cash flow calculations. Explain your reasoning.
b   Assume an infinite life for the project and a cost of capital of 17 per cent. What is the net present value?

2 The senior management team at Railcam, a supplier to the railway industry, is trying to prepare a cash flow forecast for the years 20X2–20X4. The estimated sales are:

Year	20X1	20X2	20X3	20X4	20X5
Sales (£)	20m	22m	24m	21m	25m

These sales will be made on three months' credit and there will be no bad debts.

There are only three cost elements. First, wages amounting to £6m p.a. Second, raw materials costing one-half of sales for the year. Raw material suppliers grant three months of credit. Third, direct overhead (only incurred if the project is undertaken) at £5m per year. Start date: 1.1.20X1.

Calculate the net operating cash flow for the years 20X2–20X4.

3 For the following projects, calculate the payback and the discounted payback.

Point in time (yearly intervals)	Cash flows							
	0	1	2	3	4	5	6	7
	£	£	£	£	£	£	£	£
A	−3,000	500	500	500	500	500	500	500
B	−10,000	2,000	5,000	3,000	2,000	–	–	–
C	−15,000	5,000	4,000	4,000	5,000	10,000	–	–
D	−4,000	1,000	1,000	1,000	1,000	7,000	7,000	7,000
E	−8,000	500	500	500	2,000	5,000	10,000	–

The cost of capital is 12 per cent.

4   A project has a £10,000 initial investment and cash inflows of £3,334 per year over six years. What is the payback period? What will be the payback period if the receipts of £3,334 per year occur for only three years? Explain the significance of your answer.

5   If the general rate of inflation is 5 per cent and the market rate of interest is 9 per cent, what is the real interest rate?

6   The business insurance premiums of £20,000 for the next year have just been paid. What will these premiums be in three years' time, if the specific rate of inflation for insurance premiums is 8 per cent per annum? If the money rate of return is 17 per cent and the general inflation rate is anticipated to average 9 per cent over three years, what is the present value of the insurance premiums payable at Time 3?

Questions and problems

*An asterisk * indicates that the answers are provided in the lecturer's guide only.*

1   *(Examination level)* Pine Ltd have spent £20,000 researching the prospects for a new range of products. If it were decided that production is to go ahead, an investment of £240,000 in capital equipment on 1 January 20X1 would be required.

   The accounts department has produced budgeted profit and loss statements for each of the next five years for the project. At the end of the fifth year the capital equipment will be sold and production will cease. The capital equipment is expected to be sold for scrap on 31.12.20X5 for £40,000.

£000s	Year end 31.12.20X1	Year end 31.12.20X2	Year end 31.12.20X3	Year end 31.12.20X4	Year end 31.12.20X5
Sales	400	400	400	320	200
Materials	240	240	240	192	120
Other variable costs	40	40	40	32	20
Overheads	20	20	24	24	24
Depreciation	40	40	40	40	40
Net profit/(loss)	60	60	56	32	(4)

(All figures in £000s)

When production is started it will be necessary to raise material stock levels by £30,000 and other working capital by £20,000.

   Both the additional stock and other working capital increases will be released at the end of the project.

   Customers receive one year's credit from the firm.

   The overhead figures in the budgeted accounts have two elements – 60 per cent is due to a reallocation of existing overheads, 40 per cent is directly incurred because of the take-up of the project.

   For the purposes of this appraisal you may regard all receipts and payments as occurring at the year end to which they relate, unless otherwise stated. The company's cost of capital is 12 per cent.

   Assume no inflation or tax.

Required

a   Use the net present value method of project appraisal to advise the company on whether to go ahead with the proposed project.

b   Explain to a management team unfamiliar with discounted cash flow appraisal techniques the significance and value of the NPV method.

IN ADDITION TO THE SOLUTION GIVEN IN APPENDIX VII THERE IS AN EXCEL SPREADSHEET SOLUTION AVAILABLE AT www.pearsoned.co.uk/arnold

2* *(Examination level)* Mercia plc owns two acres of derelict land near to the centre of a major UK city. The firm has received an invoice for £50,000 from consultants who were given the task of analysis, investigation and design of some project proposals for using the land. The consultants outline the two best proposals to a meeting of the board of Mercia.

Proposal 1 is to spend £150,000 levelling the site and then constructing a six-level car park at an additional cost of £1,600,000. The earthmoving firm will be paid £150,000 on the start date and the construction firm will be paid £1.4m on the start date, with the balance payable 24 months later.

It is expected that the car park will be fully operational as from the completion date (365 days after the earthmovers first begin).

The annual income from ticket sales will be £600,000 to an infinite horizon. Operational costs (attendants, security, power, etc.) will be £100,000 per annum. The consultants have also apportioned £60,000 of Mercia's central overhead costs (created by the London-based head office and the executive jet) to this project.

The consultants present their analysis in terms of a commonly used measure of project viability, that of payback.

This investment idea is not original; Mercia investigated a similar project two years ago and discovered that there are some costs which have been ignored by the consultants. First, the local council will require a payment of £100,000 one year after the completion of the construction for its inspection services and a trading and environmental impact licence. Second, senior management will have to leave aside work on other projects, resulting in delays and reduced income from these projects amounting to £50,000 per year once the car park is operational. Also, the proposal is subject to depreciation of one-fiftieth (1/50) of the earthmoving and construction costs each year.

Proposal 2 is for a health club. An experienced company will, for a total cost of £9m payable at the start of the project, design and construct the buildings and supply all the equipment. It will be ready for Mercia's use one year after construction begins. Revenue from customers will be £5m per annum and operating costs will be £4m per annum. The consultants allocate £70,000 of central general head office overhead costs for each year from the start. After two years of operating the health club Mercia will sell it for a total of £11m.

Information not considered by the consultants for Proposal 2
The £9m investment includes £5m in buildings not subject to depreciation. It also includes £4m in equipment, 10 per cent of which has to be replaced each year. This has not been included in the operating costs.

A new executive will be needed to oversee the project from the start of the project – costing £100,000 per annum.

The consultants recommend that the board of Mercia accept the second proposal and reject the first.

Assume

- If the site was sold with no further work carried out it would fetch £100,000.
- No inflation or tax.
- The cost of capital for Mercia is 10 per cent (this is the relevant rate for this project).
- It can be assumed, for simplicity of analysis, that all cash flows occur at year ends except those occurring at the start of the project.

Required

a Calculate the net present value of each proposal. State whether you would recommend Proposal 1 or 2.
b Calculate the internal rate of return for each proposed project.

IN ADDITION TO THE SOLUTION GIVEN IN THE LECTURER'S GUIDE THERE IS AN EXCEL SPREADSHEET SOLUTION AVAILABLE AT www.pearsoned.co.uk/arnold (Lecturer's Guide)

3* *(Examination level)* Mines International plc

The Albanian government is auctioning the rights to mine copper in the east of the country. Mines International plc (MI) is considering the amount they would be prepared to pay as a lump sum for the five-year licence. The auction is to take place very soon and the cash will have to be paid immediately following the auction.

In addition to the lump sum the Albanian government will expect annual payments of £500,000 to cover 'administration'. If MI wins the licence, production would not start until one year later because it will take a year to prepare the site and buy in equipment. To begin production MI would have to commission the manufacture of specialist engineering equipment costing £9.5m, half of which is payable immediately, with the remainder due in one year.

MI has already conducted a survey of the site which showed a potential productive life of four years with its new machine. The survey cost £300,000 and is payable immediately.

The accounts department produced the following projected profit and loss accounts.

			Year		
Projected profit and loss (£m)	1	2	3	4	5
Sales	0	8	9	9	7
Less expenses					
Materials and consumables	0.6	0.4	0.5	0.5	0.4
Wages	0.3	0.7	0.7	0.7	0.7
Overheads	0.4	0.5	0.6	0.6	0.5
Depreciation of equipment	0	2.0	2.0	2.0	2.0
Albanian govt payments	0.5	0.5	0.5	0.5	0.5
Survey costs written off	0.3				
Profit (loss) excluding licence fee	(2.1)	3.9	4.7	4.7	2.9

The following additional information is available:

a Payments and receipts arise at the year ends unless otherwise stated.
b The initial lump sum payment has been excluded from the projected accounts as this is unknown at the outset.
c The customers of MI demand and receive a credit period of three months.
d The suppliers of materials and consumables grant a credit period of three months.
e The overheads contain an annual charge of £200,000 which represents an apportionment of head office costs. This is an expense that would be incurred whether or not the project proceeds. The remainder of the overheads relate directly to the project.
f The new equipment will have a resale value at the end of the fifth year of £1.5m.
g During the whole of Year 3 a specialised item of machinery will be needed, which is currently being used by another division of MI. This division will therefore incur hire costs of £100,000 for the period the machinery is on loan.
h The project will require additional cash reserves of £1m to be held in Albania throughout the project for operational purposes. These are recoverable at the end of the project.
i The Albanian government will make a one-off refund of 'administration' charges one and a half months after the end of the fifth year of £200,000.

The company's cost of capital is 12 per cent. Ignore taxation, inflation and exchange rate movements and controls.

Required

a Calculate the maximum amount MI should bid in the auction.
b What would be the internal rate of return on the project if MI did not have to pay for the licence?
c The board of directors have never been on a finance course and do not understand any of the finance jargon. However, they have asked you to persuade them that the appraisal method you have used in (a) above can be relied on. Prepare a presentation for the board of directors explaining the reasoning and justification for using your chosen project appraisal technique and your treatment of specific items in the accounts. You will need to explain concepts such as the time value of money, opportunity cost and sunk cost in plain English.

4* (Examination level) Oakland plc is considering a major investment project. The initial outlay of £900,000 will, in subsequent years, be followed by positive cash flows, as shown below. (These occur on the anniversary dates.)

Year	1	2	3	4	5
Cash flow (£)	+50,000	+120,000	+350,000	+80,000	+800,000

After the end of the fifth year this business activity will cease and no more cash flows will be produced.

The initial £900,000 investment in plant and machinery is to be depreciated over the five-year life of the project using the straight-line method. These assets will have no value after Year 5.

The management judge that the cash inflows shown above are also an accurate estimation of the profit before depreciation for each of the years. They also believe that the appropriate discount rate to use for the firm's projects is 10 per cent per annum.

The board of directors are used to evaluating project proposals on the basis of a payback rule, which requires that all investments achieve payback in four years.

As the newly appointed executive responsible for project appraisal you have been asked to assess this project using a number of different methods and to advise the board on the advantages and disadvantages of each. Do this in the following sequence.

(i) a Calculate the payback period.
    b Calculate the discounted payback period.
    c Calculate an accounting rate of return.
    d Calculate the internal rate of return.
    e Calculate the net present value.
(ii) Compare the relative theoretical and practical merits and demerits of each of the methods used.

Assume: No tax or inflation.

5* A firm is considering investing in a project with the following cash flows:

Year	1	2	3	4	5	6	7	8
Net cash flow (£)	1,000	1,500	2,000	1,750	1,500	1,000	500	500

The initial investment is £6,250. The firm has a required rate of return of 10 per cent. Calculate:

a the payback period;
b the discounted payback;
c the net present value.

What are the main objections to the use of payback? Why does it remain a very popular method?

6 Maple plc is considering which of two mutually exclusive projects to accept, each with a five-year life. Project A requires an initial expenditure of £2,300,000 and is forecast to generate annual cash flows before depreciation of £800,000. The equipment purchased at time zero has an estimated residual value after five years of £300,000. Project B costs £660,000 for equipment at the start. This has a residual value of £60,000 after five years. Cash inflows before depreciation of £250,000 per annum are anticipated. The company has a straight-line depreciation policy and a cost of capital of 15 per cent (relevant for projects of this risk class). You can assume that the cash flows are also equal to the profits before depreciation. Calculate:

a an accounting rate of return;
b the net present value.

What are the disadvantages of using ARR?

7 Camelia plc has been run in an autocratic style by the chief executive and main shareholder, Mr Linedraw, during its 40-year history. The company is now too large for Mr Linedraw to continue being involved in all decisions. As part of its reforms the firm intends to set up a structured programme of capital investment. You have been asked to compile a report which will guide management. This will detail the investment process and will not be confined to appraisal techniques.

8 'The making of good investment decisions is as much about understanding human psychology as it is about mathematics.' Explain this statement.

9 Explain how each of the following can lead to a sub-optimal investment process:

    a relying on top-down idea generation;
    b managers being judged solely on accounting rate of return;
    c a requirement that projects have a quick payback;
    d post-auditing once only, one year after completion;
    e post-auditing conducted by managers from 'rival' divisions;
    f overoptimism of project sponsors.

10 The washer division of Plumber plc is permitted to spend £5m on investment projects at Time 0. The cash flows for five proposed projects are:

	Points in time (yearly intervals)				
Project	*0*	*1*	*2*	*3*	*4*
	£m	*£m*	*£m*	*£m*	*£m*
A	−1.5	0.5	0.5	1.0	1.0
B	−2.0	0	0	0	4.0
C	−1.8	0	0	1.2	1.2
D	−3.0	1.2	1.2	1.2	1.2
E	−0.5	0.3	0.3	0.3	0.3

The cost of capital for all projects is 12 per cent, all projects are divisible and none may be repeated. The projects are not mutually exclusive.

    a Which projects should be undertaken to maximise NPV in the presence of the capital constraint?
    b If the division was able to undertake all positive NPV projects, what level of NPV could be achieved?
    c If you now assume that these projects are indivisible, how would you allocate the available £5m?

11* (*Examination level*) Wishbone plc is considering two mutually exclusive projects. Project X requires an immediate cash outflow of £2.5m and Project Y requires £2m. If there was no inflation then the cash flows for the three-year life of each of the projects would be:

Annual cash flows	Project X		Project Y	
	£	£	£	£
Inflow from sales		2,100,000		1,900,000
Cash outflows:				
Materials	800,000		200,000	
Labour	300,000		700,000	
Overheads	100,000		50,000	
		(1,200,000)		(950,000)
Net cash flow		900,000		950,000

These cash flows can be assumed to arise at the year ends of each of the three years. Specific annual inflation rates have been estimated for each of the cash flow elements.

Sales	5%
Materials	4%
Labour	10%
Overheads	7%

The money cost of capital is 17 per cent per annum.

a Use the money cash flows and money cost of capital to calculate the NPV of the two projects and recommend the most appropriate course of action.

b Now assume that the general inflation rate is anticipated to be 8 per cent per annum. Calculate the real cash flows and the real cost of capital and use these to calculate the NPVs.

IN ADDITION TO THE SOLUTION GIVEN IN THE LECTURER'S GUIDE THERE IS AN EXCEL SPREADSHEET SOLUTION AVAILABLE AT www.pearsoned.co.uk/arnold (Lecturer's Guide)

12* (*Examination level*) Clipper plc is considering five project proposals. They are summarised below:

Project	Initial investment (£000)	Annual revenue (£000)	Annual fixed costs (cash outflows) (£000)	Life of project (years)
A	10	20	5	3
B	30	30	10	5
C	15	18	6	4
D	12	17	8	10
E	18	8	2	15

Variable costs (cash outflows) are 40 per cent of annual revenue. Projects D and E are mutually exclusive. Each project can only be undertaken once and each is divisible.

Assume

– The cash flows are confined to within the lifetime of each project.
– The cost of capital is 10 per cent.
– No inflation.
– No tax.
– All cash flows occur on anniversary dates.

a If the firm has a limit of £40,000 for investment in projects at Time 0, what is the optimal allocation of this sum among these projects, and what is the maximum net present value obtainable?

b Distinguish between 'soft' and 'hard' capital rationing and explain why these forms of rationing occur.

Assignments

1 Obtain budgeted profit and loss accounts for a proposed project and by combining these with other data produce cash flow estimates for the project. Calculate the NPV and contrast your conclusions on the viability of the project with that suggested by the profit and loss projections.

2 Investigate the capital investment process in a firm you know well. Relate the stages and methods used to the process outlined in this chapter. Consider areas for improvement.

3 Investigate the capital rationing constraints placed on a firm you are familiar with. Are these primarily soft or hard forms of rationing? Are they justified? What are the economic costs of this rationing? What actions do you suggest to circumvent irrational constraints?

4 Write a report on how inflation and tax are allowed for in project appraisal within a firm you know well. To what extent are the rules advocated in this chapter obeyed?

Visit www.pearsoned.co.uk/arnold to get access to Gradetracker diagnostic tests, Podcasts, Excel Spreadsheet Solutions, FT articles, a Flashcard revision tool, Weblinks, a searchable Glossary and more.

CHAPTER 4

Risk and project appraisal

LEARNING OUTCOMES

The reader is expected to be able to present a more realistic and rounded view of a project's prospects by incorporating risk in an appraisal. This enables more informed decision making. Specifically the reader should be able to:

■ adjust for risk by varying the discount rate;

■ present a sensitivity graph and discuss break-even NPV;

■ undertake scenario analysis;

■ make use of probability analysis to describe the extent of risk facing a project and thus make more enlightened choices;

■ explain the nature of real options and the advantages in recognising value in them;

■ discuss the limitations, explain the appropriate use and make an accurate interpretation of the results of the risk techniques described in this chapter.

Introduction

Businesses operate in an environment of uncertainty. The 3G investment and Camelot examples in **Case study 4.1** show that managers can never be sure about what will happen in the future. There is the upside possibility of events turning out to be better than anticipated and the downside possibility of everything going wrong. Implementing an investment project requires acceptance of the distinct possibility that the managers have got it wrong; that the project or enterprise will result in failure. However, to avoid any chance of failure means the adoption of a 'play-safe' or 'do-nothing' strategy. This may itself constitute a worse business sin, that of inertia, and will result in greater failure. There has to be an acceptance of risk and of the potential for getting decisions wrong, but this does not mean that risk cannot by analysed and action taken to minimise its impact.

Case study 4.1   Two risky ventures . . .

One that will (probably) not pay off . . .

The £200 billion gamble – wireless telecommunications

In 2000 the telecommunication companies of Europe committed themselves to what may prove to be one of the biggest gambles ever. They agreed to pay £80–£100 billion to purchase 3G (third-generation) licences from various European governments. As a result they are now able to offer internet access, video calls, emails and film clips from mobile phones.

The 'winners' of the auctions for licences are, in addition to handing over thousands of millions of pounds to government, investing another £100 billion building the infrastructure needed to deliver the service to the customer supposedly hungry for internet-enabled phones. As quickly as the middle of 2001, so great was the outflow of cash that major telecommunication companies had become burdened with extraordinary amounts of debt. For example, over the three years to 2001 BT's debts rose from £1 billion to over £20 billion, and serious concern was expressed in the City of London about the excessive debt. Over the same period France Telecom's debt rocketed to over €63 billion and Deutsche Telekom's went to €60 billion. Shares tumbled as shareholders worried that too much was being paid for projects based on a high degree of optimism. Nobody knows whether consumers really want to surf the internet with their phones – however, by 2005 things were not looking too hopeful as less than 10 per cent of UK households, for example, used 3G (The licences cost £22.5bn in the UK and the industry spent around the same again on setting up the networks, over £760 per UK citizen). Furthermore, the level of competition is likely to be so intense that the companies may lose money even with millions of customers.

Perhaps, as the new technology develops, an application will be discovered that is very attractive to consumers ('a killer application') and the investment projects turn out to be very rewarding for shareholders. Perhaps the 3G projects will be superseded by new technology (WiMAX?) before they are properly up and running. The truth is that we will not know for many years. Such is the fun and excitement of real-world business decisions!

and one that did . . .

Camelot

Camelot bid for, and won, the right to create the UK's national lottery. They invested in a vast computer network linking 30,000 retail outlets and paid for three hundred man-years to develop specialised software. Camelot also had to train 91,000 staff to operate the system, which can handle over 30,000 transactions a minute, and spend large amounts on marketing. The gamble seems to have paid off. In 2004 Camelot produced a pre-tax profit of £45.5m. The owners of Camelot – Cadbury Schweppes, De La Rue, Fujitsu, Thales Electronics and Royal Mail Enterprises – have a political battle on their hands trying to persuade the public and authorities that they took a risk and things happened to turn out well. It could have been so different; they could have made a multi-million-pound investment followed by public indifference and enormous losses.

Source: 3G – numerous *Financial Times articles*; Camelot – based on *Financial Times*, 5 June 1996 and Camelot's annual report, 2004.

What is risk?

A key feature of project appraisal is its orientation to the future. Management rarely have precise forecasts regarding the future return to be earned from an investment. Usually the best that can be done is to make an estimate of the range of the possible future inflows and outflows. There are two types of expectations individuals may have about the future: certainty and uncertainty.

1 *Certainty* Under expectations of certainty future outcomes can be expected to have only one value. That is, there is not a variety of possible future eventualities – only one will occur. Such situations are rare, but there are some investments which are a reasonable approximation to certainty, for instance, lending to a reputable government by purchasing three-month treasury bills. Unless you are very pessimistic and expect catastrophic change over the next three months, such as revolution, war or major earthquake, then you can be certain of receiving your original capital plus interest. Thus a firm could undertake a project that had almost complete certainty by investing its funds in treasury bills, and receiving a return of, say, 5 per cent per year. Shareholders may not, however, be very pleased with such a low return.

2 *Risk and uncertainty* The terms *risk* and *uncertainty* are used interchangeably in the subsequent analysis. Strictly speaking, risk occurs when specific probabilities can be estimated for the possible outcomes. Uncertainty applies in cases when it is not possible to assign probabilities (or even identify all the possible outcomes). Risk describes a situation where there is not just one possible outcome, but an array of potential returns. The range and distribution of these possible outcomes may be estimated on the basis of either objective probabilities or subjective probabilities (or a combination of the two).

Objective probabilities

An objective probability can be established mathematically or from historical data. The mathematical probability of a tossed coin showing a head is 0.5. The probability of taking the Ace of Hearts from a pack of 52 cards is 0.0192 (or 1/52). A probability of 0 indicates nil likelihood of outcome. A probability of 1 denotes that there is absolute certainty that this outcome will occur. A probability of 0.3 indicates that in three times out of ten this will occur. The probabilities for all possible outcomes must sum to 1. We will now examine an example of an objective probability assessment based on historical data for the supermarket retailer Safeburys. If the firm is considering a project that is similar to numerous projects undertaken in the past it may be able to obtain probabilities for future profitability. For instance, the Safeburys supermarket chain is examining the proposal to build and operate a new supermarket in Birmingham. Because the firm has opened and operated 100 other supermarkets in the past, and has been able to observe their profitability, it is able to assign probabilities to the performance of the supermarket it is proposing to build (*see* Exhibits 4.1 and 4.2).

Exhibit 4.1	Safebury's profitability frequency distribution of existing 100 supermarkets	
Profitability range (£m)	**Frequency (Number of stores)**	**Probability**
−30 to −20.01	1	0.01
−20 to −10.01	3	0.03
−10 to −0.01	11	0.11
0 to 9.99	19	0.19
10 to 19.99	30	0.30
20 to 29.99	20	0.20
30 to 39.99	10	0.10
40 to 49.99	6	0.06
TOTAL	100	1.00

| Exhibit 4.2 | Frequency distribution of supermarket profitability |

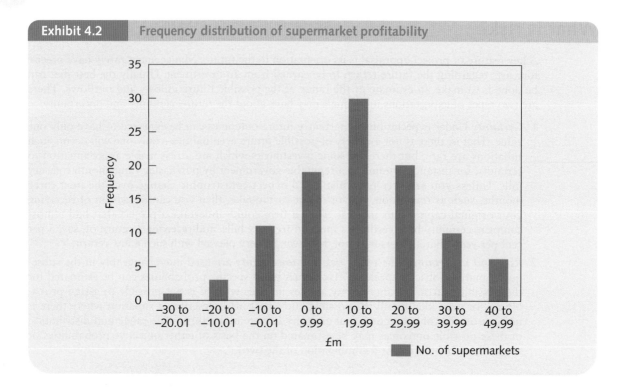

The examination of this sort of historical record may be a useful first step in the process of making a decision. However, it must be borne in mind that the probabilities may have to be modified to take into account the particular circumstances surrounding the site in Birmingham. For instance demographic trends, road connections and competitor activity may influence the probabilities for profit or loss. Even with large quantities of historical data there is often still a lot of room for subjective assessment in judging the range of possible outcomes.

Subjective probabilities

In many project assessments there is a complete absence of any past record to help in the creation of the distribution of probabilities profile. For instance, the product may be completely new, or a foreign market is to be entered. In situations like these, subjective probabilities are likely to dominate, that is, personal judgement of the range of outcomes along with the likelihood of their occurrence. Managers, individually or collectively, must assign probability numbers to a range of outcomes.

It must be acknowledged that the probabilities assigned to particular eventualities are unlikely to be entirely accurate and thus the decision making that follows may be subject to some margin of error. But consider the alternative of merely stating the most likely outcomes. This can lead to less well-informed decisions and greater errors. For example, a firm might be considering two mutually exclusive projects, A and B (*see* **Exhibit 4.3**). Both projects are expected to be shareholder wealth enhancing, based on the estimate of the most likely outcome. The most likely outcome for A is for it to be shareholder wealth enhancing, with an estimated 95 per cent chance of occurrence. Similarly the most likely outcome for B is a shareholder wealth enhancing return, with an estimated 55 per cent chance of occurrence.

By using probabilities, a more informed decision is made. The project appraiser has been forced to consider the degree of confidence in the estimate of expected viability. It is clear that Project A is unlikely to fail, whereas Project B has a fairly high likelihood of failure. We will examine in detail the use of probability distribution for considering risk later in the chapter. We now turn to more pragmatic, rule-of-thumb and intuitively easier methods for dealing with project risk.

Exhibit 4.3	Probability outcome for two projects	
Outcome	Project A probability	Project B probability
Shareholder wealth enhancing	0.95	0.55
Not shareholder wealth enhancing	0.05	0.45

Adjusting for risk through the discount rate

A traditional and still popular method of allowing for risk in project appraisal is the risk premium approach. The logic behind this is simple: investors require a greater reward for accepting a higher risk, thus the more risky the project the higher is the minimum acceptable rate of return. In this approach a number of percentage points (the premium) are added to the risk-free discount rate. (The risk-free rate of return is usually taken from the rate available on government bonds.) The risk-adjusted discount rate is then used to calculate net present value in the normal manner.

An example is provided by Sunflower plc, which adjusts for risk through the discount rate by adding various risk premiums to the risk-free rate depending on whether the proposed project is judged to be low, medium or high risk (*see* Exhibit 4.4).

Exhibit 4.4	Adjusting for risk – Sunflower plc		
Level of risk	Risk-free rate (%)	Risk premium (%)	Risk-adjusted rate (%)
Low	9	+3	12
Medium	9	+6	15
High	9	+10	19

The project currently being considered has the following cash flows:

Point in time (yearly intervals)	0	1	2
Cash flow (£)	−100	55	70

If the project is judged to be low risk:

$$NPV = -100 + \frac{55}{1 + 0.12} + \frac{70}{(1 + 0.12)^2} = +£4.91 \text{ Accept}$$

If the project is judged to be medium risk:

$$NPV = -100 + \frac{55}{1 + 0.15} + \frac{70}{(1 + 0.15)^2} = +£0.76 \text{ Accept}$$

If the project is judged to be high risk:

$$NPV = -100 + \frac{55}{1 + 0.19} + \frac{70}{(1 + 0.19)^2} = -£4.35 \text{ Reject}$$

This is an easy approach to understand and adopt, which explains its continued popularity.

Drawbacks of the risk-adjusted discount rate method

The risk-adjusted discount rate method relies on an accurate assessment of the riskiness of a project. Risk perception and judgement are bound to be, to some extent, susceptible to personal bias. There may also be a high degree of arbitrariness in the selection of risk premiums. In reality it is extremely difficult to allocate projects to risk classes and identify appropriate risk premiums as personal analysis and casual observation can easily dominate.

Sensitivity analysis

The net present values calculated in previous chapters gave a static picture of the likely future outcome of an investment project. In many business situations it is desirable to generate a more complete and realistic impression of what may happen to NPV in conditions of uncertainty. Net present value calculations rely on the appraiser making assumptions about some crucial variables: for example the sale price of the product, the cost of labour and the amount of initial investment are all set at single values for input into the formula. It might be enlightening to examine the degree to which the viability of the project changes, as measured by NPV, as the assumed values of these key variables are altered. An interesting question to ask might be: if the sale price is raised by 10 per cent, by what percentage would NPV increase? In other words, it would be useful to know how sensitive NPV is to changes in component values. Sensitivity analysis is essentially a 'what-if' analysis, for example what if labour costs are 5 per cent lower? or, what if the raw materials double in price? By carrying out a series of calculations it is possible to build up a picture of the nature of the risks facing the project and their impact on project profitability. Sensitivity analysis can identify the extent to which variables may change before a negative NPV is produced. A series of 'what-if' questions are examined in the example of Acmart plc.

Worked example 4.1   **Acmart plc**

Acmart plc has developed a new product line called Marts. The marketing department in partnership with senior managers from other disciplines have estimated the likely demand for Marts at 1,000,000 per year, at a price of £1, for the four-year life of the project. (Marts are used in mobile telecommunications relay stations and the market is expected to cease to exist or be technologically superseded after four years.)

If we can assume perfect certainty about the future then the cash flows associated with Marts are as set out in Exhibit 4.5:

Exhibit 4.5   Cash flows of Marts

		£
Initial investment	£800,000	
Cash flow per unit		£
Sale price		1.00
Costs		
Labour	0.20	
Materials	0.40	
Relevant overhead	0.10	
		0.70
Cash flow per unit		0.30

Worked example 4.1   Continued

The finance department have estimated that the appropriate required rate of return on a project of this risk class is 15 per cent. They have also calculated the expected net present value.

Annual cash flow = 30p × 1,000,000 = £300,000.
Present value of annual cash flows = 300,000 annuity factor for 4 years @ 15%

		£
	= 300,000 × 2.855	= 856,500
Less initial investment		−800,000
Net present value		+56,500

The finance department are aware that when the proposal is placed before the capital investment committee they will want to know how the project NPV changes if certain key assumptions are altered. As part of the report the finance team ask some 'what-if' questions and draw a sensitivity graph.

● What if the price achieved is only 95p (5 per cent below the expected £1) for sales of 1m units (all other factors remaining constant)?
Annual cash flow = 25p × 1m = £250,000.

	£
250,000 × 2.855	713,750
Less initial investment	800,000
Net present value	−86,250

● What if the price rose by 1 per cent?
Annual cash flow = 31p × 1m = £310,000.

	£
310,000 × 2.855	885,050
Less initial investment	800,000
Net present value	+85,050

● What if the quantity demanded is 5 per cent more than anticipated?
Annual cash flow = 30p × 1.05m = £315,000.

	£
315,000 × 2.855	899,325
Less initial investment	800,000
Net present value	+99,325

● What if the quantity demanded is 10 per cent less than expected?
Annual cash flow = 30p × 900,000 = £270,000.

	£
270,000 × 2.855	770,850
Less initial investment	800,000
Net present value	−29,150

▶

Worked example 4.1   Continued

- What if the appropriate discount rate is 20 per cent higher than originally assumed (that is, it is 18 per cent rather than 15 per cent)?
  300,000 × annuity factor for 4 years @ 18%.

	£
300,000 × 2.6901	807,030
Less initial investment	800,000
	+7,030

- What if the discount rate is 10 per cent lower than assumed (that is, it becomes 13.5 per cent)?
  300,000 × annuity factor for 4 years @ 13.5%.

	£
300,000 × 2.9438	883,140
Less initial investment	800,000
	+83,140

These findings can be summarised more clearly in a sensitivity graph (*see* **Exhibit 4.6**).

Exhibit 4.6   Sensitivity graph for Marts

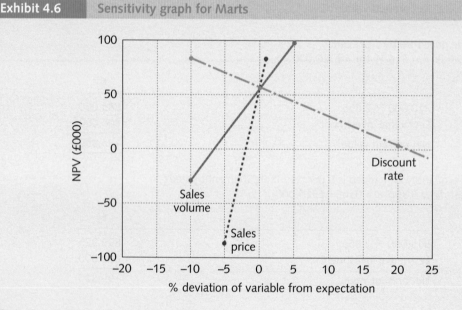

An examination of the sensitivity graph in Exhibit 4.6 gives a clear indication of those variables to which NPV is most responsive. This sort of technique can then be extended to consider the key factors that might cause a project to become unviable. This allows the management team to concentrate their analysis, by examining in detail the probability of actual events occurring which would alter the most critical variables. They may also look for ways of controlling the factors to which NPV is most sensitive in any future project implementation. For example, if a small change in material costs has a large impact, the managers may investigate ways of fixing the price of material inputs.

Worked example 4.1	Continued

The break-even NPV

The break-even point, where NPV is zero, is a key concern of management. If the NPV is below zero the project is rejected; if it is above zero it is accepted.

The finance team at Acmart now calculate the extent to which some of the variables can change before the decision to accept switches to a decision to reject. (We will not go through all the possible variables.)

Initial investment

A rise of £56,500 will leave NPV at zero. A percentage increase of:

$$\frac{£56,500}{£800,000} \times 100 = 7.06\%$$

Sales price

The cash flow per unit (after costs), c, can fall to 28 pence before break-even is reached:

$$800,000 = c \times 1,000,000 \times 2.855$$

$$c = \frac{800,000}{2.855 \times 1,000,000} = 0.2802$$

Thus the price can decline by only 2 per cent from the original price of £1. An alternative approach is to look up the point at which the sales price line crosses the NPV axis in the sensitivity graph.

Material cost

If the cash flow per unit can fall to 28 pence before break-even is reached, 2 pence can be added to the price of materials before the project produces a negative net present value (assuming all other factors remain constant). In percentage terms the material cost can rise by 5 per cent (($2 \div 40$) $\times$ 100) before break-even is reached.

Discount rate

One approach is to calculate the annuity factor that will lead to the four annual inflows of £300,000 equalling the initial outflow of £800,000 after discounting.

$$300,000 \times \text{annuity factor} = 800,000$$

$$\text{Annuity factor (four-year annuity)} = \frac{800,000}{300,000} = 2.667$$

The interest rate corresponding to a four-year annuity factor of 2.667 is approximately 18.5 per cent. This is a percentage rise of 23.3 per cent.

$$\frac{18.5 - 15}{15} \times 100 = 23.3$$

This project is relatively insensitive to a change in the discount rate but highly responsive to a change in the sales price. This observation may lead the managers to request further work to improve the level of confidence in the sales projections.

Advantages of using sensitivity analysis

- *Information for decision making* At the very least it allows the decision makers to be more informed about project sensitivities, to know the room they have for judgemental error and to decide whether they are prepared to accept the risks.

- *To direct search* It may lead to an indication of where further investigation might be worthwhile. Data collection can be time consuming and expensive; if sensitivity analysis points to some variables being more crucial than others, then search time and money can be concentrated.

- *To make contingency plans* During the implementation phase of the investment process the original sensitivity analysis can be used to highlight those factors that have the greatest impact on NPV. Then these parameters can be monitored for deviation from projected values. The management team can draw on contingency plans if the key parameters differ significantly from the estimates. For example, a project may be highly sensitive to the price of a bought-in component. The management team, after recognising this from the sensitivity analysis, prepare contingency plans to: (a) buy the component from an alternative supplier, should the present one increase prices excessively, (b) produce the component in-house, or (c) modify the product so that a substitute component can be used. Which of the three is implemented, if any, will be decided as events unfold.

Drawbacks of sensitivity analysis

The absence of any formal assignment of probabilities to the variations of the parameters is a potential limitation of sensitivity analysis. For Marts the discount rate can change by 23.3 per cent before break-even NPV is reached, whereas the price can only change by 2 per cent. Thus, at first glance, you would conclude that NPV is more vulnerable to the price changes than to variability in the discount rate. However, if you are now told that the market price for Marts is controlled by government regulations and therefore there is a very low probability of the price changing, whereas the probability of the discount rate rising by more than 23.3 per cent is high, you might change your assessment of the nature of the relative risks. This is another example where following the strict mathematical formula is a poor substitute for judgement. At the decision-making stage the formal sensitivity analysis must be read in the light of subjective or objective probabilities of the parameter changing.

The second major criticism of sensitivity analysis is that each variable is changed in isolation while all other factors remain constant. In the real world it is perfectly conceivable that a number of factors will change simultaneously. For example, if inflation is higher then both anticipated selling prices and input prices are likely to be raised. The next section presents a partial solution to this problem.

Scenario analysis

With sensitivity analysis we change one variable at a time and look at the result. Managers may be especially concerned about situations where a number of factors change. They are often interested in establishing a worst-case and a best-case scenario. That is, what NPV will result if all the assumptions made initially turned out to be too optimistic? And what would be the result if, in the event, matters went extremely well on all fronts?

Exhibit 4.7 describes only a worst-case and a best-case scenario for Marts, but management may like to try alternative scenarios.

Exhibit 4.7	Acmart plc: Project proposal for the production of Marts – worst-case and best-case scenarios

Worst-case scenario

Sales	900,000 units
Price	90p
Initial investment	£850,000
Project life	3 years
Discount rate	17%
Labour costs	22p
Material costs	45p
Overheads	11p

Cash flow per unit		**£**
Sale price		0.90
Costs		
Labour	0.22	
Material	0.45	
Overhead	0.11	
		0.78
Cash flow per unit		0.12

Annual cash flow = 0.12 × 900,000 = £108,000

	£
Present value of cash flows 108,000 × 2.2096 =	238,637
Less initial investment	–850,000
Net present value	–611,363

Best-case scenario

Sales	1,200,000 units
Price	120p
Initial investment	£770,000
Project life	4 years
Discount rate	14%
Labour costs	19p
Material costs	38p
Overhead	9p

Cash flow per unit		**£**
Sale price		1.20
Costs		
Labour	0.19	
Material	0.38	
Overhead	0.09	
		0.66
Cash flow per unit		0.54

Annual cash flow – 0.54 × 1,200,000 = £648,000

	£
Present value of cash flows 648,000 × 2.9137 =	1,888,078
Less initial investment	–770,000
Net present value	1,118,078

Having carried out sensitivity, break-even NPV and scenario analysis the management team have a more complete picture of the project. They then need to apply the vital element of judgement to make a sound decision.

Probability analysis

A further technique to assist the evaluation of the risk associated with a project is to use probability analysis. If management have obtained, through a mixture of objective and subjective methods, the probabilities of various outcomes this will help them to decide whether to go ahead with a project or to abandon the idea. We will look at this sort of decision making for the firm Pentagon plc, a company trying to decide between five mutually exclusive one-year projects (*see* Exhibit 4.8).

Exhibit 4.8	Pentagon plc: Use of probability analysis		
		Return	**Probability of return occurring**
Project 1		16	1.0
Project 2		20	1.0
Project 3			
	Recession	−16	0.25
	Growth	36	0.50
	Boom	48	0.25
Project 4			
	Recession	−8	0.25
	Growth	16	0.50
	Boom	24	0.25
Project 5			
	Recession	−40	0.10
	Growth	0	0.60
	Boom	100	0.30

Projects 1 and 2 represent perfectly certain outcomes. For both projects the chance of not receiving the returns is so small as to be regarded as zero. These securities carry no risk. However, Project 2 has a higher return and is therefore the obvious preferred choice. (These projects, with different returns for zero risk, only exist in an inefficient market environment because you should find increased return is only available for accepting increased risk; market efficiency is discussed in Chapter 6.)

In comparing Project 2 with Projects 3, 4 and 5 we have a problem: which of the possible outcomes should we compare with Project 2's outcome of 20? Take Project 3 as an example. If the outcome is −16 then clearly Project 2 is preferred. However, if the outcome is 36, or even better, 48, then Project 3 is preferred to Project 2.

Expected return

A tool that will help Pentagon choose between these projects is the expected return.

The *expected return* is the mean or average outcome calculated by weighting each of the possible outcomes by the probability of occurrence and then summing the result (*see* Exhibit 4.9).

Algebraically:

$$\bar{x} = x_1 p_1 + x_2 p_2 + \ldots x_n p_n \qquad \text{or} \qquad \bar{x} = \sum_{i=1}^{i=n}(x_i p_i)$$

where $\bar{x}$ = the expected return,
         i = each of the possible outcomes (outcome 1 to outcome n)
         p = probability of outcome i occurring
         n = the number of possible outcomes

$\sum_{i=1}^{i=n}$ means add together the results for each of the possible outcomes i from the first to the nth outcome.

Exhibit 4.9	Pentagon plc: Expected returns	

Pentagon plc		Expected return
Project 1	16 × 1	16
Project 2	20 × 1	20
Project 3	−16 × 0.25 = −4	
	36 × 0.50 = 18	
	48 × 0.25 = 12	
		26
Project 4	−8 × 0.25 = −2	
	16 × 0.50 = 8	
	24 × 0.25 = 6	
		12
Project 5	−40 × 0.1 = −4	
	0 × 0.6 = 0	
	100 × 0.3 = 30	
		26

The preparation of probability distributions gives the management team some impression of likely outcomes. The additional calculation of expected returns adds a further dimension to the informed vision of the decision maker. Looking at expected returns is more enlightening than simply examining the single most likely outcome, which is significantly different from the expected return of 26. For Project 5 the most likely outcome of 0 is not very informative and does not take into account the range of potential outcomes.

It is important to appreciate what these statistics are telling you. The expected return represents the outcome expected if the project is undertaken many times. If Project 4 is undertaken 1,000 times then on average the return would be 12. If the project is undertaken only once, as is the case in most business situations, there would be no guarantee that the actual outcome would equal the expected outcome.

The projects with the highest expected returns turn out to be Projects 3 and 5, each with an expected return of 26. However, we cannot get any further in our decision making by using just the expected return formula. This is because the formula fails to take account of risk. Risk is concerned with the likelihood that the actual performance might diverge from what is expected. Note that risk in this context has both positive and negative possibilities of diverging from the mean, whereas in everyday speech 'risk' usually has only negative connotations. If we plot the possible outcomes for Projects 3 and 5 against their probabilities of occurrence we get an impression that the outcome of Project 5 is more uncertain than the outcome of Project 3 (see Exhibit 4.10).

The range of possible outcomes is relatively narrow for Project 3 and therefore presents an impression of lower risk. This is only a general indication. We need a more precise measurement of the dispersion of possible outcomes. This is provided by the standard deviation.

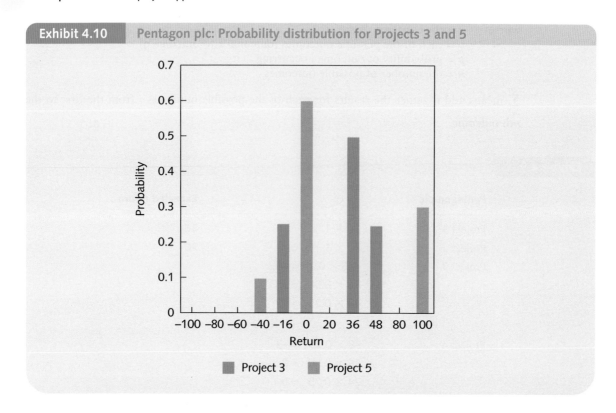

Exhibit 4.10   Pentagon plc: Probability distribution for Projects 3 and 5

Standard deviation

The standard deviation, σ, is a statistical measure of the dispersion around the expected value. The standard deviation is the square root of the variance, σ^2.

Variance of $x = \sigma_x^2 = (x_1 - \bar{x})^2 p_1 + (x_2 - \bar{x})^2 p_2 + \ldots (x_n - \bar{x})^2 p_n$

or $\sigma_x^2 = \sum\limits_{i=1}^{i=n} \{(x_i - \bar{x})^2 p_i\}$

Standard deviation

$$\sigma_x = \sqrt{\sigma_x^2} \quad \text{or} \quad \sqrt{\sum\limits_{i=1}^{i=n} \{(x_i - \bar{x})^2 p_i\}}$$

Calculating the variance is straightforward if you take it in stages:

- **Stage 1.** First obtain the deviation of each potential outcome from the expected outcome $(x_i - \bar{x})$. So, in the case of Project 3 the first outcome is –16 (this is our x_i) and the expected outcome ($\bar{x}$) is 26. So, subtracting the second number from the first we have –42.

- **Stage 2.** Square the result from Stage 1 for each of the outcomes $(x_i - \bar{x})^2$. So, for the first outcome of Project 3 we take the –42 and multiply it by itself: –42 × –42 = 1,764.

- **Stage 3.** Multiply the number generated in Stage 2 by the probability of that outcome occurring. In the case of the first outcome of Project 3 we multiply 1,764 by 0.25 = 441. That is, $(x_i - \bar{x})^2 p_i$.

- **Stage 4.** Finally, add together the results of all these calculations for that particular project. So, for Project 3 we add 441 to 50 to 121, which gives a variance of 612 – see Exhibit 4.11.

Note that the variances are very large numbers compared with the original potential outcomes. For Project 3 these are –16, 36 and 48 whereas the variance is over 600. This is because the variance measures are in pounds squared or returns squared, etc. The next stage is to obtain the standard deviation σ, by taking the square root of the variance. This measures variability around the expected value in straightforward pound or return terms. The standard deviation provides a common yardstick to use when comparing the dispersions of possible outcomes for a number of projects. So, for Project 3, the standard deviation is $\sqrt{612} = 24.7$.

Exhibit 4.11		Pentagon plc: Calculating the standard deviations for the five projects				
	Outcome (return)	Probability	Expected return	Deviation	Deviation squared	Deviation squared times probability
Project	x_i	p_i	$\bar{x}$	$x_i - \bar{x}$	$(x_i - \bar{x})^2$	$(x_i - \bar{x})^2 p_i$
1	16	1.0	16	0	0	0
2	20	1.0	20	0	0	0
3	−16	0.25	26	−42	1,764	441
	36	0.5	26	10	100	50
	48	0.25	26	22	484	121
					Variance =	612
					Standard deviation =	24.7
4	−8	0.25	12	−20	400	100
	16	0.5	12	4	16	8
	24	0.25	12	12	144	36
					Variance =	144
					Standard deviation =	12
5	−40	0.1	26	−66	4,356	436
	0	0.6	26	−26	676	406
	100	0.3	26	74	5,476	1,643
					Variance =	2,485
					Standard deviation =	49.8

**AN EXCEL SPREADSHEET VERSION OF THESE CALCULATIONS IS AVAILABLE AT
www.pearsoned.co.uk/arnold**

If we now put together the two sets of measurements about the five projects, as shown in Exhibit 4.12, we might be able to make a decision on which one should be selected.

Exhibit 4.12	Pentagon plc: Expected return and standard deviation	
	Expected return $\bar{x}$	Standard deviation σ_x
Project 1	16	0
Project 2	20	0
Project 3	26	24.7
Project 4	12	12
Project 5	26	49.8

Project 1 would not, presumably, be chosen by anyone. Also, Project 4 is obviously inferior to Project 2 because it has both a lower expected return and a higher standard deviation. That leaves us with Projects 2, 3 and 5. To choose between these we need to introduce a little utility theory in order to appreciate the significance of the standard deviation figures.

Risk and utility

Utility theory recognises that money in itself is unimportant to human beings. What is important is the well-being, satisfaction or utility to be derived from money. For most people a doubling of annual income will not double annual well-being. Money is used to buy goods and services. The first £8,000 of income will buy the most essential items – food, clothing, shelter, etc. Thus an individual going from an income of zero to one of £8,000 will experience a large increase in utility. If income is increased by a further £8,000 then utility will increase again, but the size of the increase will be less than for the first £8,000, because the goods and services bought with the second £8,000 provide less additional satisfaction. If the process of adding incremental amounts to annual income is continued then, when the individual has an income of, say, £150,000, the additional utility derived from a further £8,000 becomes very small. For most people the additional utility from consumption diminishes as consumption increases. This is the concept of *diminishing marginal utility*. Now consider the case of an individual who must choose between two alternative investments, A and B (*see* **Exhibit 4.13**).

Both investments give an expected return of £4,000, but the outcomes of B are more widely dispersed. In other words, Investment B is more risky than Investment A. Suppose the individual has invested in A but is considering shifting all her money to B. As a result, in a poor year she will receive £2,000 less on Investment B than she would have received if she had stayed with A. In a good year Investment B will provide £2,000 more than if she had left her money in A. So the question is: is it worthwhile to shift from Investment A to Investment B? The answer hinges on the concept of diminishing marginal utility. While Investments A and B have the same expected returns they have different utilities. The extra utility associated with B in a good year is small compared with the loss of utility in a bad year when returns fall by an extra £2,000. Investment A is preferred because utility is higher for the first £2,000 of return than for the last £2,000 of return (increasing return from £6,000 to £8,000 by switching from A to B). Investors whose preferences are characterised by diminishing marginal utility are called risk averters.

Exhibit 4.13	Returns and utility			
	Investment A		**Investment B**	
	Return	**Probability**	**Return**	**Probability**
Poor economic conditions	2,000	0.5	0	0.5
Good economic conditions	6,000	0.5	8,000	0.5
Expected return	4,000		4,000	

A *risk averter* prefers a more certain return to an alternative with an equal but more risky expected outcome. The alternative to being a risk averter is to be a risk lover (risk seeker). These investors are highly optimistic and have a preference rather than an aversion for risk. For these people the marginal utility of each £ increases. A *risk lover* prefers a more uncertain alternative to an alternative with an equal but less risky expected outcome. These are rare individuals and it is usually assumed that shareholders are risk averters. When faced with two investments, each with the same expected return, they will select the one with the lower standard deviation or variance. This brings us to the mean-variance rule.

Mean-variance rule

Project X will be preferred to Project Y if at least one of the following conditions apply:

1 The expected return of X is at least equal to the expected return of Y, and the variance is less than that of Y.

2 The expected return of X exceeds that of Y and the variance is equal to or less than that of Y.

So, returning to Pentagon plc, we can see from **Exhibit 4.14** that Project 5 can be eliminated from any further consideration using the mean-variance rule because it has the same expected return as Project 3 but a wider dispersion of possible outcomes.

Exhibit 4.14	**Pentagon plc: Expected returns and standard deviations**

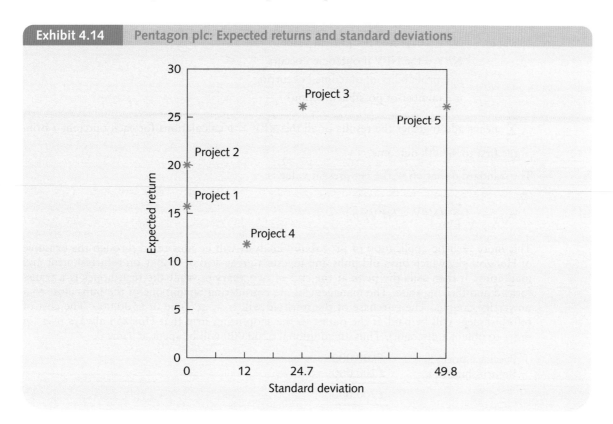

Projects 1, 4 and 5 are recognisably inferior, leaving a choice between Projects 2 and 3. From this point on there is no simple answer. The solution depends on the risk-return utility attitude of the decision maker. This is fundamentally a matter for subjective judgement and different management teams will make different choices. When the author has put the choice between Projects 2 and 3 to MBA classes of middle and senior managers approximately one-half take the safe option of Project 2. However, others in the class say that for the sake of a little more risk Project 3 gives a significantly higher return and so should be accepted. The board of directors of Pentagon need to weigh up the risk preferences of the owners of the company and choose one project or the other. In doing so they may like to consider how this new project fits with the rest of the company's projects. If the firm already has other projects (operations, strategic business units, product lines, etc.) and many of these projects tend to do well in circumstances when Project 3 does badly, and vice versa, they may consider the benefits of diversification incline them to accept this investment.

Another factor in the decision equation is that variability (standard deviation) may not be a worry if the project forms a small part of the firm's assets. If, however, choosing either Project 2 or Project 3 would entail the commitment of most of the company's assets, the directors may take the safer option.

Expected net present values and standard deviation

In the example of Pentagon plc we have simply taken the potential returns of the projects as given. Now we will look at a project under circumstances of risk when you are not handed the *returns*, but have to calculate the NPV and the standard deviation of NPV using the cash flows associated with the investment. In addition, these cash flows will occur over a number of years and so the analysis becomes both more sophisticated and more challenging. First, the notation of the statistical formulae needs to be changed.

The expected net present value is:

$$\overline{NPV} = \sum_{i=1}^{i=n} (NPV_i p_i)$$

where $\overline{NPV}$ = expected net present value

NPV_i = the NPV if outcome i occurs

p_i = probability of outcome i occurring

n = number of possible outcomes

$\sum_{i=1}^{i=n}$ means add together the results of all the $NPV \times p$ calculations for each outcome *i* from the first to the nth outcome.

The standard deviation of the net present value is:

$$\sigma_{NPV} = \sqrt{\sum_{i=1}^{i=n}\left\{(NPV_i - \overline{NPV})^2 p_i\right\}}$$

This more realistic application of probability analysis will be illustrated through the example of Horizon plc, which buys old pubs and invests a great deal of money on refurbishment and marketing. It then sells the pubs at the end of two years in what the firm hopes is a transformed and thriving state. The management are considering buying one of the pubs close to a university campus. The purchase of the freehold will cost, at Time 0, £500,000. The cost of refurbishment will be paid at the outset to the shopfitting firm that Horizon always uses (in order to obtain a discount). Thus an additional £200,000 will be spent at Time 0.

Purchase price, t_0	£500,000
Refurbishment, t_0	£200,000
	£700,000

Experience has taught the management team of Horizon that pub retailing is a very unpredictable game. Customers are fickle and the slightest change in fashion or trend and the level of customers drops dramatically. Through a mixture of objective historical data analysis and subjective 'expert' judgement the managers have concluded that there is a 60 per cent probability that the pub will become a trendy place to be seen in and meet people. There is a 40 per cent chance that potential customers will not switch to this revamped hostelry within the first year.

The Year 1 cash flows are as follows:

	Probability	Cash flow at end of Year 1
Good customer response	0.6	£100,000
Poor customer response	0.4	£10,000

Note: For simplicity it is assumed that all cash flows arise at the year ends.

If the response of customers is good in the first year there are three possibilities for the second year.

1 Customer flow will increase further and the pub can be sold at the end of the second year for a large sum. The total of the net operating cash flows for the second year and the sale proceeds will be £2m. This eventuality has a probability of 0.1 or 10 per cent.

2 Customer levels will be the same as in the first year and at the end of the second year the total cash flows will be £1.6m. The probability of this is 0.7 or 70 per cent.

3 Many customers will abandon the pub. This may happen because of competitor action; for example other pubs in the area are relaunched, or perhaps the fashion changes. The result will be that the pub will have a net cash outflow on trading, and will have a much lower selling price. The result will be a cash inflow for the year of only £800,000. This has a 20 per cent chance of occurring.

If, however, the response in the first year is poor then one of two eventualities may occur in the second year:

1 Matters continue to deteriorate and sales fall further. At the end of the second year the cash flows from trading and the sale of the pub total only £700,000. This has a probability of 0.5, or a 50:50 chance.

2 In the second year sales rise, resulting in a total t_2 cash flow of £1.2m. Probability: 0.5.

The conditional probabilities (conditional on what happens in the first year) for the second year are as follows:

If the first year elicits a *good response* then:

	Probability	Cash flow at end of Year 2
1 Sales increase in second year	0.1	£2m
or		
2 Sales are constant	0.7	£1.6m
or		
3 Sales decrease	0.2	£0.8m

If the first year elicits a *poor response* then:

	Probability	Cash flow at end of Year 2
1 Sales fall further	0.5	£0.7m
or		
2 Sales rise slightly	0.5	£1.2m

Note: All figures include net trading cash flow plus sale of pub.

To be able to calculate the expected return and standard deviation for a project of this nature, we first need to establish the probability of each of the possible outcomes. This is shown in **Exhibit 4.15**. This shows that there are five possible outcomes. The probability that the initial expenditure is followed by a cash inflow of £100,000 after one year, and £2m after two years (that is, outcome *a*) is very low. This is as we might expect given that this is an extreme, positive outcome. The overall probability of this path being followed is the first year's probability (0.6) multiplied by the second year's probability (0.1) to give 0.06 or a 6 per cent chance of occurrence. The most likely outcome is for the first year to be successful (£100,000) followed by a continuation of the same sales level resulting in Year 2 cash flow of £1.6m (outcome b) with a probability of 0.42.

The second stage is to calculate the expected return making use of the probabilities calculated in Exhibit 4.15 – *see* **Exhibit 4.16**.

Exhibit 4.15   An event tree showing the probabilities of the possible returns for Horizon plc

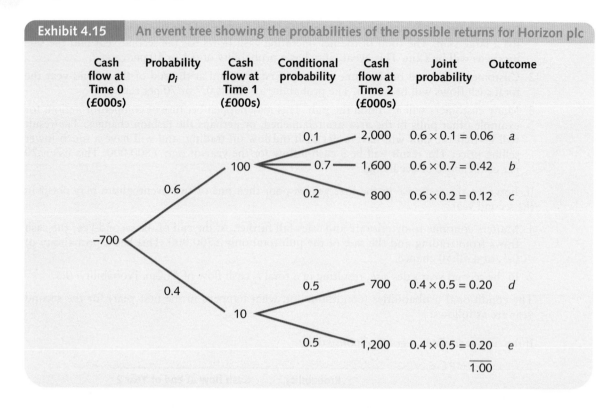

Cash flow at Time 0 (£000s)	Probability p_i	Cash flow at Time 1 (£000s)	Conditional probability	Cash flow at Time 2 (£000s)	Joint probability	Outcome

Exhibit 4.16   Expected net present value, Horizon plc

Outcome	Net present values (£000s)		NPV × Probability	
a	$-700 + \dfrac{100}{1.1} + \dfrac{2{,}000}{(1.1)^2}$	= 1,044	1,044 × 0.06	= 63
b	$-700 + \dfrac{100}{1.1} + \dfrac{1{,}600}{(1.1)^2}$	= 713	713 × 0.42	= 300
c	$-700 + \dfrac{100}{1.1} + \dfrac{800}{(1.1)^2}$	= 52	52 × 0.12	= 6
d	$-700 + \dfrac{10}{1.1} + \dfrac{700}{(1.1)^2}$	= −112	−112 × 0.20	= −22
e	$-700 + \dfrac{10}{1.1} + \dfrac{1{,}200}{(1.1)^2}$	= 301	301 × 0.20	= 60
Expected net present value				407
				or £407,000

Note: Assuming a 10% opportunity cost of capital.

AN EXCEL SPREADSHEET VERSION OF THIS CALCULATION IS AVAILABLE AT
www.pearsoned.co.uk/arnold

Then the standard deviation for this pub project can be calculated – *see* **Exhibit 4.17**.

Exhibit 4.17	Standard deviation for Horizon plc				
Outcome £000s NPV_i	Probability p_i	Expected NPV $\overline{NPV}$	Deviation $NPV_i - \overline{NPV}$	Deviation squared $(NPV_i - \overline{NPV})^2$	Deviation squared times probability $(NPV_i - \overline{NPV})^2 p_i$
a	1,044	0.06	407	637	405,769	24,346
b	713	0.42	407	306	93,636	39,327
c	52	0.12	407	−355	126,025	15,123
d	−112	0.20	407	−519	269,361	53,872
e	301	0.20	407	−106	11,236	2,247

Variance = 134,915

Standard deviation = $\sqrt{134{,}915}$ = 367

Or £367,000

AN EXCEL SPREADSHEET VERSION OF THIS CALCULATION IS AVAILABLE AT
www.pearsoned.co.uk/arnold

Now that the management team have a calculated expected NPV of £407,000 and a standard deviation of £367,000 they are in a position to make a more informed decision. The probability analysis can be taken on to further stages; for example, an additional dimension that may affect their judgement of the worth of the project is the probability of certain extreme eventualities occurring, such as the project outcome being so bad as to lead to the insolvency of the company. This technique is described in the next section.

The risk of insolvency

On occasions a project may be so large relative to the size of the firm that if the worst-case scenario occurred the firm would be made bankrupt. It is sometimes of interest to managers to know the probability that a project will have a sufficiently poor outcome as to threaten the survival of the company. We can estimate this probability if we know the shape of the probability distribution. We usually assume that the probability distribution of a project's potential return is 'normal, bell-shaped'. The distribution of possible outcomes is symmetrical about the expected return μ. This means that the probability of an outcome, X, occurring between the expected return and one standard deviation away from the expected return is 34.13 per cent (one half of 68.26 per cent). That is, the chance of the outcome landing in the shaded area of **Exhibit 4.18** is 34.13 per cent.

The probability of the outcome being between the expected value and two standard deviations from the expected value is 47.72 per cent (one-half of 95.44 per cent). To find the probability that the outcome will be between two particular values we first need to obtain the Z statistic. This simply shows the number of standard deviations from the mean to the value that interests you.

$$Z = \frac{X - \mu}{\sigma}$$

where   Z is the number of standard deviations from the mean
         X is the outcome that you are concerned about
         μ is the mean of the possible outcomes
         σ is the standard deviation of the outcome distribution

We also need to use the standard normal distribution table. This is in Appendix V at the end of the book but an extract is presented in Exhibit 4.19.

Exhibit 4.18	Probability of outcome being between expected return and one standard deviation from expected return

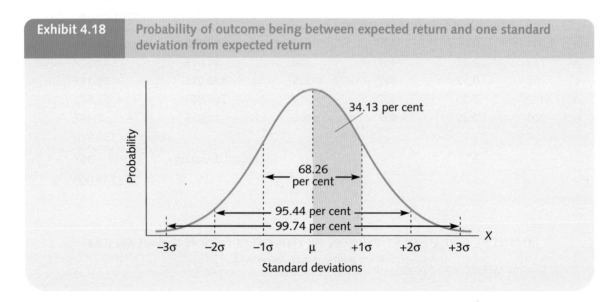

Exhibit 4.19	The standard normal distribution

Value of the Z statistic	Probability that X lies within Z standard deviations above (or below) the expected value (%)
0.0	0.00
0.2	7.93
0.4	15.54
0.6	22.57
0.8	28.81
1.0	34.13
1.4	41.92
2.0	47.72
3.0	49.87

The use of the standard normal distribution table will be illustrated by the example of Roulette plc in Worked example 4.2.

Worked example 4.2	Roulette plc

Roulette plc is considering undertaking a very large project and if the economy fails to grow there is a risk that the losses on this project will cause the liquidation of the firm. It can take a maximum loss of £5m (negative NPV of £5m) and still keep the rest of the business afloat. But if the loss is more than £5m the firm will become bankrupt. The managers are keen to know the percentage probability that more than £5m will be lost.

The expected NPV has already been calculated at £8m but there is a wide variety of possible outcomes. If the economy booms the firm will make a fortune. If it is reasonably strong it will make a respectable return and if there is zero or negative growth large sums will be lost. These NPVs are judged to be normally distributed, that is, a bell-shaped distribution. The standard deviation is £6.5m.

To calculate the probability of insolvency we first calculate the Z statistic, when the X in which we are interested is at a value of –5.

$$Z = \frac{X - \mu}{\sigma}$$

$$Z = \frac{-5 - 8}{6.5} = -2$$

The value of –2 means that the distance between the expected outcome and the point of bankruptcy is two standard deviations. From the standardised normal distribution table (Appendix V) we can see that the probability that the return will lie between the mean and two standard deviations below the mean is 47.72 per cent (see Exhibit 4.20).

Exhibit 4.20	Probability of outcome between μ and 2σ from μ

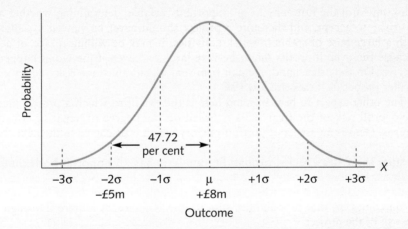

The probability distribution is symmetrical about the mean; therefore, the probability that the return will be above the mean (£8m) is 50 per cent. Thus, the probability of the firm achieving an NPV greater than a loss of £5m is 97.72 per cent (47.72 per cent plus 50 per cent). To make the final decision on whether to proceed with this project we need to consider the owners' and the managers' attitude to this particular level of risk of insolvency. This is likely to vary from one company to another. In some situations shareholders and managers will have well-diversified interests and so are reasonably sanguine about this risk. Other decision makers will not even take a 2.28 per cent (100 per cent – 97.72 per cent) chance of insolvency.

Problems in using probability analysis

Too much faith can be placed in quantified subjective probabilities

When dealing with events occurring in the future, managers can usually only make informed guesses as to likely outcomes and their probabilities of occurrence. A danger lies in placing too much emphasis on analysis of these subjective estimates once they are converted to numerical form. It is all too easy to carry out detailed computations with accuracy to the nth degree, forgetting that the fundamental data usually have a small objective base. Again, mathematical purity is no substitute for thoughtful judgement.

The alternative to the assignment of probabilities, that of using only the most likely outcome estimate in the decision-making process, is both more restricted in vision and equally subjective. At least probability analysis forces the decision maker to explicitly recognise a range of outcomes and the basis on which they are estimated, and to express the degree of confidence in the estimates.

Too complicated

Investment decision making and subsequent implementation often require the understanding and commitment of large numbers of individuals. Probability analysis can be a poor communicating tool if important employees do not understand what the numbers mean. Perhaps here there is a need for education combined with good presentation.

Projects may be viewed in isolation

The context of the firm may be an important variable, determining whether a single project is too risky to accept, and therefore a project should never be viewed in isolation. Take a firm with a large base of stable low-risk activities. It may be willing to accept a high-risk project because the overall profits might be very large and even if the worst happened the firm will survive. On the other hand, a small firm that already has one risky activity may only accept further proposals if they are low risk.

The other aspect to bear in mind here is the extent to which a project increases or reduces the overall risk of the firm. This is based on the degree of negative covariance of project returns. (This is an aspect of portfolio theory which is discussed in the next chapter.)

Despite these drawbacks, probability analysis has an important advantage over scenario analysis. In scenario analysis the focus is on a few highly probable scenarios. In probability analysis consideration must be given to all possible outcomes (or at least an approximation of all outcomes) so that probabilities sum to one. This forces a more thorough consideration of the risk of the project.

Evidence of risk analysis in practice

Exhibit 4.21 summarises the risk analysis techniques used by UK firms.

UK firms have increased the extent of risk analysis in project appraisal over the past 20 years (evident from surveys conducted by Pike (1988, 1996) and Ho and Pike (1991)). This trend has been encouraged by a greater awareness of the techniques and aided by the availability of computing software. Sensitivity and scenario analysis remain the most widely adopted approaches. Probability analysis is now used more widely than in the past but few smaller firms use it on a regular basis. Beta analysis, based on the capital-asset pricing model (discussed in Chapter 5) is rarely used. Simple, rule-of-thumb approaches have not been replaced by the more complex methods. Firms tend to be pragmatic and to use a multiplicity of techniques in a complementary fashion.

Exhibit 4.21	Risk analysis techniques used in UK firms			
	Small %	**Medium %**	**Large %**	**Total %**
Sensitivity/Scenario analysis	82	83	89	85
Reduced payback period	15	42	11	20
Risk-adjusted discount rate	42	71	50	52
Probability analysis	27	21	42	31
Beta analysis	3	0	5	3
Subjective assessment	44	33	55	46

Source: Arnold and Hatzopoulos (2000) sample of 96 firms: 34 small, 24 medium, 38 large. Survey date July 1997.

Real options (managerial options)

Traditional project appraisal, based on the calculation of NPV, generally implicitly assumes that the investment being analysed is a straightforward go-now-or-don't-go-ever decision, and that you either accept the project in its entirety at the outset or forget about the whole idea. So, if a company is considering a project with cash flow spread over, say, eight years it would estimate the expected cash flows and discount all eight of them (usually following a probability analysis to allow for uncertainty). Under this view of decision making there is only the initial decision to accept or reject; and if accepted the project is persisted with for the full term analysed (say, eight years).

Some business decisions are like this. For example, if the project is to build a bridge for a government, then once you have signed the contract, regardless of what happens in the future, you are obligated to deliver a bridge. You cannot delay the start date, nor can you abandon the project halfway through if new information is received indicating that the worst-case scenario is now likely to happen (say, building costs double).

However, with most projects the managers are not making all-or-nothing decisions at the outset. They are able to respond to changing circumstances as they unfold over the life of the project. For example, if events turn out badly they can react by abandoning the project. So, a company that goes ahead with wind power electricity machinery production on the basis of a positive NPV given the government's current support for subsidising renewable energy may abandon the project if government policy changes two years later. The option to abandon rather than be forced to persist has value. This value is usually ignored in traditional NPV analysis.

Sometimes it is the option to expand if events turn out well that is extremely valuable. On other occasions the decision to go ahead or not to go ahead is not now-or-never but to consider a range of dates for going ahead; this year, next year or the year after. That is, the company has the option to defer the project, e.g. developing a copper mine only when the world market price of copper rises sufficiently. Going ahead now would destroy value at current low copper prices (a negative NPV) but the option to develop has value. The ability to abandon, expand or defer a project can add considerable value compared with a project without one of these flexibilities.

The real options perspective takes account of future managerial flexibility whereas the traditional NPV framework tends to assume away such flexibility.

Real options give the right, but not the obligation, to take an action in the future. They give value by presenting managers with the opportunity to exploit an uncertain future in which conditions change unpredictably, making one decision choice better than the other(s). By holding a real option we have the right to select whatever decision suits us best at the time. They differ from financial options traded in the market in that their value does not depend on the movement of a financial security or instrument, such as a share, or currency rate, but on the cash flows of real investment projects within the firm.

Some examples of valuable real options

Firms sometimes undertake projects which apparently have negative NPVs. They do so because an option is thereby created to expand, should this be seen to be desirable. The value of the option outweighs the loss of value on the project. For example, many Western firms have set up offices, marketing and production operations in China which run up losses. This has not led to a pull-out because of the long-term attraction to expand within the world's largest market. If they withdrew they would find it very difficult to re-enter, and would therefore sacrifice the option to expand. This option is considered to be so valuable that some firms are prepared to pay the price of many years of losses.

Another example would be where a firm has to decide whether to enter a new technological area. If it does it may make losses but at least it has opened up the choices available to the firm. To have refused to enter at all on the basis of a crude NPV calculation could close off important future avenues for expansion. Microsoft is thought to have lost $4 billion on the original X-box. However, three assets were created (options to expand): a prominent market position, some strong franchises (e.g. 'Halo' series of games) and the online-gaming service. The introduction of the X-box 360 exercises these options to grow. The pharmaceutical giants run dozens of research programmes showing apparent negative NPVs: they do so for what is often described as 'strategic reasons'. We might alternatively call this intuitive option analysis. Perhaps the drugs a company is currently developing in a field of medicine, say, for the treatment of Alzheimer's disease, show negative NPVs when taken in isolation. However, by undertaking this activity the firm builds capabilities within this specialism, allowing the firm to stay in the game and participate in future generations of drugs which may have very high payoffs.

If a property developer purchases a prime site near a town centre there is, in the time it takes to draw up plans and gain planning permission, the alternative option of selling the land (abandonment option). Flexibility could also be incorporated in the construction process itself – for example, perhaps alternative materials can be used if the price of the first choice increases. Also, the buildings could be designed in such a way that they could be quickly and cheaply switched from one use to another (switching option), for example from offices to flats, or from hotel to shops. At each stage there is an option to abandon plan A and switch to plan B. Having plan B available has value. To have plan A only leaves the firm vulnerable to changing circumstances.

Perhaps in the example of the property developer it may be possible to create more options by creating conditions that do not compel the firm to undertake investment at particular points in time. If there was an option to wait a year, or two years, then the prospects for rapid rental growth for office space *vis-à-vis* hotels, flats and shops could be more accurately assessed (deferral option or timing option). Thus a more informed, and in the long run more value-creating, decision can be made.

True NPV

Thus we need to raise the sophistication of NPV analysis by allowing for the value of flexibility during the life of the project. A project in which there is the ability to take further action after uncertainty has been resolved or reduced significantly is more valuable than one that is rigid.

True NPV	=	Crude NPV	+	NPV of expansion option	+	NPV of the option to abandon	+	NPV of timing option	+	NPV of other option possibilities

Note: some of these options may be mutually exclusive, e.g. the option to expand and the option to abandon.

An example of option use – the option to abandon

Imagine you are the chief executive of a company that designs, creates and sells computer games. A film studio is about to start shooting a major action thriller film. It will reach the box office in one year from now. The film company have contacted you offering you the right to develop and market a game based on the film (with film clips and voice-overs from the principal actors). You would have to pay £10m now for this. From previous experience you estimate that there is a 50 : 50 chance of the film being a success or a box office flop. If it is a success the present value of all the future cash flows for the game will amount to £50m. If, however, it is a flop, the high costs of development and promotion will mean a present value of all the future cash flows associated with the game will be negative £50m.

Should you pay £10m now for the game rights?

Conventional NPV analysis is likely to mislead you in this decision. You would set out the cash flows and their probabilities and calculate an expected NPV from them, which will be –£10m (*see* Exhibit 4.22). Hence you would reject the project.

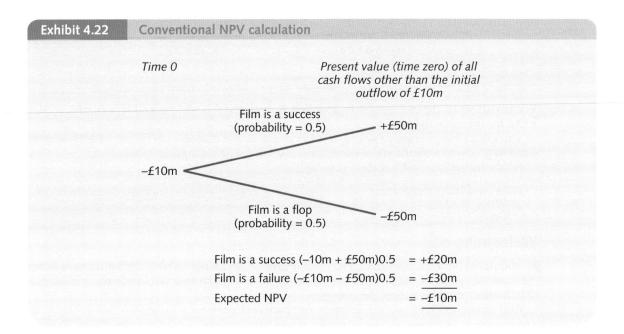

| Exhibit 4.22 | Conventional NPV calculation |

The fact that you would be purchasing merely an option to develop the game, without the obligation to do so, is very significant in the valuation of this project. You can abandon the whole plan in one year's time when you have some vital information: how the film performs at the box office after release. If it is a success then continue. If it is a failure then do not invest any more than the original £10m and save yourself £50m.

With this flexibility built in, your cash flows in the future are +£50m if the film is well received, and zero if it is hammered by the critics and audiences stay away. Each of these has a 50 per cent chance of occurring (*see* Exhibit 4.23).

The important point is that we don't view the project as a take-it-now-in-its-entirety-or-forget-it deal, but rather consider the possibility of future managerial choices. In other words managers are not passive, but active over the life of the project. There are contingent future decisions which can boost NPV. We need to allow for these possibilities now, when deciding whether to buy the game rights.

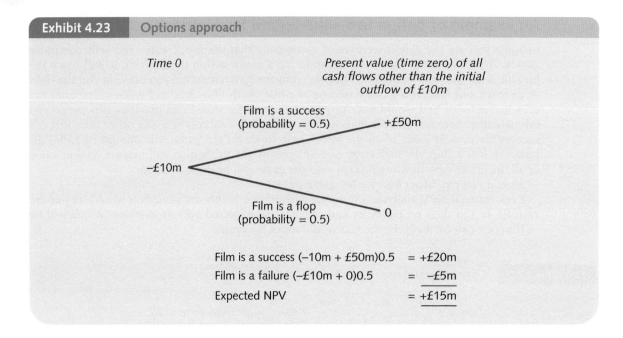

Exhibit 4.23   Options approach

The payoff when the real option to abandon is considered is +£15m and it is correct to pay £10m for the game rights now.

The value of the option to abandon is calculated as the difference between the NPV if obligated to go ahead with the entire project and the NPV with the option to abandon.

NPV with option – NPV if there is no option

+£15 – (–£10m) = £25m

Welcoming risk

In traditional NPV analysis the greater the degree of uncertainty about the future cash flows the lower the value of the project. The higher standard deviation is offputting to a risk-averse shareholder, and their agents, the managers.

Real option analysis takes a different perspective. Uncertainty provides value because the opportunity to exercise the option to take action later becomes all the more precious. To illustrate, let us double the range of the present value of the cash flows after the initial payment. So there is now a 50 per cent chance of +£100m and a 50 per cent chance of –£100m. The expected NPV under traditional analysis of this remains at –£10m but the range of outcomes has increased, i.e. risk has risen.

Film is a success	(–£10m + £100m)0.5	=	+£45m
Film is a failure	(–£10m – £100m)0.5	=	–£55m
Crude NPV		=	–£10m

This project is even more unattractive under traditional NPV analysis than the original situation because of the higher risk for the same return.

The options perspective shows the more volatile cash flow project to be more valuable than the less volatile one because managers can avoid the downside risk by simply abandoning the project if the news turns out to be bad in one year's time. Risk is no longer symmetrical, that is, with equal probabilities of negative outcomes and positive outcomes around the expected return. It is asymmetrical: you benefit if things go well and do not lose if things go badly (at least you lose no more than you put down as a 'premium' to purchase the option in the first place).

Film is a success	(−£10m + £100m)0.5	=	£45m
Film is a failure	(−£10m + 0)0.5	=	−£5m
Option perspective NPV		=	£40m

Uncertainty can therefore be a good thing, if you hold an option to exploit the change in circumstances as time goes on. If you do not have flexibility to respond then uncertainty is a bad thing and reduces value. Traditional NPV analysis assumes away the possibility of response to contingencies, resulting in a symmetric risk profile. Thus traditional NPV can seriously underestimate the true NPV of many capital investments.

Difficulties with real option analysis

- *Complexity of the valuation process* This book has explained real options using very simple mathematical examples. Analysts in this field often make use of complex option pricing models. This complexity means that most managers are unable to participate in the valuation process in an informed manner without extensive training. The danger is that untrained managers treat the exercise as black box decision making: supplying some inputs, e.g. standard deviation of key cost or revenue components, then handing the numbers over to the financial wizards who put them into the model and out pops the answer. The managers are totally unable critically to assess the machinations within the black box. It may be necessary to question the assumptions behind the calculations but the key managers are not empowered to do so. This could lead to poor decision making because the quality of inputs is often poor (see next point) and to cynicism about the real options approach throughout the organisation.

- *Measuring uncertainty* There is a practical constraint of not being able to measure the degree of uncertainty, and therefore the value of an option. Historic data is usually used (where available), e.g. historic volatility of oil prices for an oil exploration and development project. A leap of faith is then made in assuming that future standard deviations will be like those in the past. In many cases the option valuer clutches at straws to provide inputs to the calculations – giving the impression of scientific rigour, when the foundations are in fact very weak. Standard deviation numbers are often derived from a source only tangentially related to the project, e.g. average standard deviation of technology company share price movements may be used as a proxy for the standard deviation of outcomes for a new project initiated by a new company in a new technological field.

- *Over optimism* In circumstances of very high uncertainty, e.g. when there is brand new technology such as the internet in the 1990s, there is a tendency to be overoptimistic about the value of expanding. In 1999 new 'dotcom' companies joined the stock market proclaiming that once their model was established the potential for scaling up was almost limitless. The market was so huge, they said, that even if the company had an 80 per cent chance of complete failure it was still worth backing as it might be the one left standing with options to expand to control the industry standard (the one most visited by travellers, pet owners, book buyers, etc.). These companies presented 'analysis' from 'independent' experts on the growth of internet connections (usually exponential) and the revenues in this field (again exponentially rising). Sadly too many people believed the hype. Similar hype can be exhibited by junior and middle managers about a growth area they are particularly enthusiastic about. Senior managers need to view the high ranges of likely outcomes presented to them with scepticism. In particular they should ask whether the firm's competitors are really going to do nothing while they take all this market for themselves.

- *What is the life of an option?* It may not be clear how long the option value will be available to the firm. For example, a pharmaceutical company may have invested considerably in cardiovascular drug R&D, providing it with potential competitive advantages for many years to come through its options to expand to new generations of drugs. But it is impossible to be precise on how many years the option to develop more drugs in this field will be valuable: is it three years, five or twenty years? The life of the option depends on so many variables, e.g. developments in surgery or competitors' actions.

Concluding comments

This chapter, and the previous one, have dealt with some of the more sophisticated aspects of project analysis. They have, it is hoped, encouraged the reader to consider a wider range of factors when embarking on investment appraisal. Taking into account more real-world influences such as inflation, rationing, tax and risk will enable the appraiser and the decision maker to obtain a clearer picture of the nature of the proposal being discussed. Greater realism and more information clear away some of the fog which envelops many capital investment decision-making processes.

However, this chapter has focused primarily on the technical/mathematical aspects of the appraisal stage of the investment process sequence. While these aspects should not be belittled, as we ought to improve the analysis wherever we can, it should be noted that a successful programme of investment usually rests far more on quality management of other stages in the process. Issues of human communication, enthusiasm and commitment are as vital to investment returns as, for example, assessing risk correctly.

Key points and concepts

- **Risk** – more than one possible outcome. **Objective probability** – likelihood of outcomes established mathematically or from historical data. **Subjective probability** – personal judgement of the likely range of outcomes along with the likelihood of their occurrence.

- Risk can be allowed for by **raising or lowering the discount rate**: Advantages: (i) easy to adopt and understand; (ii) some theoretical support. Drawbacks: susceptible to subjectivity in risk premium and risk class allocation.

- **Sensitivity analysis** views a project's NPV under alternative assumed values of variables, changed one at a time. It permits a broader picture to be presented, enables search resources to be more efficiently directed and allows contingency plans to be made. Drawbacks of sensitivity analysis: (i) does not assign probabilities and these may need to be added for a fuller picture; (ii) each variable is changed in isolation.

- **Scenario analysis** permits a number of factors to be changed simultaneously. Allows best- and worst-case scenarios.

- **Probability analysis** allows for more precision in judging project viability.

- **Expected return** – the mean or average outcome is calculated by weighting each of the possible outcomes by the probability of occurrence and then summing the result:

$$\bar{x} = \sum_{i=1}^{i=n}(x_i p_i)$$

- **Standard deviation** – a measure of dispersion around the expected value:

$$\sigma_x = \sqrt{\sigma_x^2} \quad \text{or} \quad \sqrt{\sum_{i=1}^{i=n}\{(x_i - \bar{x})^2\, p_i\}}$$

- It is assumed that most people are **risk averters** who demonstrate **diminishing marginal utility**, preferring less risk to more risk.

- **Mean-variance rule**: Project X will be preferred to Project Y if at least one of the following conditions applies: the expected return of X is at least equal to the expected return of Y, and the variance is less than that of Y or the expected return of X exceeds that of Y and the variance is equal to or less than that of Y.

- If a normal, bell-shaped distribution of possible outcomes can be assumed, the probabilities of various events, for example insolvency, can be calculated using the **Z statistic**.

$$Z = \frac{X - \mu}{\sigma}$$

- **Problems with probability analysis:** (i) undue faith can be placed in quantified results; (ii) can be too complicated for general understanding and communication; (iii) projects may be viewed in isolation rather than as part of the firm's mixture of projects.

- Sensitivity analysis and scenario analysis are the most popular methods of allowing for project risk.

- The **real options** perspective takes account of future managerial flexibility whereas the traditional NPV framework tends to assume away such flexibility. Real options give the right, but not the obligation, to take an action in the future.

Further reading

Real options are discussed in the following: Amran, M. and Kulatilaka, N. (1999), Brennan, M.J. and Schwartz, E.S. (1985), Brennan, M.J. and Trigeorgis, L. (eds) (2000), Childs, P.D., Ott, S.M. and Triantis, A.J. (1998), Copeland, T. and Antikarov, V. (2001), Copeland, T. and P. Tufano (2004), Dixit, A. and Pindyck, R. (1994), Dixit, A.K. and Pindyck, R.S. (1995), Hertz, D.B. (1964), Hertz, D.B and Thomas, H. (1984), Howell, S., Stark, A., Newton, D., Paxson, D., Cavus, M. and Pereira, J. (2001), Luehrman, T. A. (1998a), Luehrman, T. A. (1998b), Merton, R.C. (1998), Moel, A. and Tufano, P. (2002), Pike, R.H. (1988), Pike, R.H. (1996), Quigg, L. (1993), Schwartz, E.S. and Trigeorgis, L. (eds) (2001), Triantis, A.J. and Hodder, J.E. (1990), Trigeorgis (1996), Van Putten, A. B. and I. C. MacMillan (2004).

The following show surveys of practical use of the techniques discussed in the chapter: Arnold, G.C. and Hatzopoulos, P.D. (2000), Graham, J.R. and Harvey, C.R. (2001), Hertz, D.B and Thomas, H. (1984), Ho, S. and Pike, R.H. (1991), Pike, R.H. (1988), Pike, R.H. (1996).

Self-review questions

1 Explain, with reference to probability and sensitivity analysis, why the examination of the most likely outcome of an investment in isolation can both be limiting and give a false impression.

2 What do you understand by the following?
   (i) Risk-lover.
   (ii) Diminishing marginal utility.
   (iii) Standard deviation.

3 Discuss the consequences of the quantification of personal judgements about future eventualities. Are we right to undertake precise analysis on this sort of basis?

4 Explain the attraction of using more than one method to examine risk in project appraisal.

5 Why has the development of powerful computers helped the more widespread adoption of scenario analysis?

6 Suggest reasons why probability analysis is used so infrequently by major international corporations.

7 'The flatter the line on the sensitivity graph, the less attention we have to pay to that variable.' Is the executive who made this statement correct in all cases?

Quick numerical questions

1 Calculate the NPV of the following project with a discount rate of 9 per cent.

Point in time (yearly intervals)	0	1	2	3	4
Cash flow (£000s)	−800	300	250	400	500

Now examine the impact on NPV of raising the discount rate by the following risk premiums:
a 3 percentage points;
b 6 percentage points.

2 Project W may yield a return of £2m with a probability of 0.3, or a return of £4m with a probability of 0.7. Project X may earn a negative return of £2m with a probability of 0.3 or a positive return of £8m with a probability of 0.7. Project Y yields a return of £2m, which is certain. Compare the expected return and risk of the projects.

3 The returns from a project are normally distributed with a mean of £220,000 and a standard deviation of £160,000. If the project loses more than £80,000 the company will be made insolvent. What is the probability of insolvency?

4 A project with an initial outlay of £1m has a 0.2 probability of producing a return of £800,000 in Year 1 and a 0.8 probability of delivering a return of £500,000 in Year 1. If the £800,000 result occurs then the second year could return either £700,000 (probability of 0.5) or £300,000 (probability of 0.5). If the £500,000 result for Year 1 occurs then either £600,000 (probability 0.7) or £400,000 (probability 0.3) could be received in the second year. All cash flows occur on anniversary dates. The discount rate is 12 per cent.

Calculate the expected return and standard deviation.

> **AN EXCEL SPREADSHEET VERSION OF THIS CALCULATION IS AVAILABLE AT**
> **www.pearsoned.co.uk/arnold**

Questions and problems

Answers for those questions marked with an asterisk * are reserved for the lecturer's guide

1* (*Examination level*) Cashion International are considering a project that is susceptible to risk. An initial investment of £90,000 will be followed by three years with the following 'most likely' cash flows (there is no inflation or tax):

	£	£
Annual sales (volume of 100,000 units multiplied by estimated sales price of £2)	200,000	
Annual costs		
Labour	100,000	
Materials	40,000	
Other	10,000	
	150,000	(150,000)
		50,000

The initial investment consists of £70,000 in machines, which have a zero scrap value at the end of the three-year life of the project, and £20,000 in additional working capital, which is recoverable at the end. The discount rate is 10 per cent.

Required

a Draw a sensitivity graph showing the sensitivity of NPV to changes in the following:
   sales price; labour costs; material costs; discount rate.
b For the four variables considered in (a) state the break-even point and the percentage deviation from 'most likely' levels before break-even NPV is reached (assuming all other variables remain constant).

> AN EXCEL SPREADSHEET VERSION OF THESE CALCULATIONS IS AVAILABLE IN THE LECTURERS-ONLY SECTION AT www.pearsoned.co.uk/arnold

2* Use the data in question 2 to calculate the NPV in two alternative scenarios:

Worst-case scenario		Best-case scenario	
Sales volume	90,000	Sales volume	110,000
Sales price	£1.90	Sales price	£2.15
Labour costs	£110,000	Labour costs	£95,000
Material costs	£44,000	Material costs	£39,000
Other costs	£13,000	Other costs	£9,000
Project life	3 years	Project life	3 years
Discount rate	13%	Discount rate	10%
Initial investment	£90,000	Initial investment	£90,000

3 (*Examination level*) A company is trying to decide whether to make a £400,000 investment in a new product area. The project will last 10 years and the £400,000 of machinery will have a zero scrap value. Other best estimate forecasts are:
   – sales volume of 22,000 units per year;
   – sales price £21 per unit;
   – variable direct costs £16 per unit.

There are no other costs and inflation and tax are not relevant.
a The senior management team have asked you to calculate the internal rate of return (IRR) of this project based on these estimates.
b To gain a broader picture they also want you to recalculate IRR on the assumption that each of the following variables changes adversely by 5 per cent in turn: sales volume; sales price; variable direct costs.
c Explain to the management team how this analysis can help to direct attention and further work to improve the likelihood of a successful project implementation.

> IN ADDITION TO THE SOLUTION IN APPENDIX VII AN EXCEL SPREADSHEET VERSION OF THESE CALCUATIONS IS AVAILABLE AT www.pearsoned.co.uk/arnold

4 A project requires an immediate outflow of cash of £400,000 in return for the following probable cash flows:

State of economy	Probability	End of Year 1 (£)	End of Year 2 (£)
Recession	0.3	100,000	150,000
Growth	0.5	300,000	350,000
Boom	0.2	500,000	550,000

Assume that the state of the economy will be the same in the second year as in the first. The required rate of return is 8 per cent. There is no tax or inflation.

a Calculate the expected NPV.
b Calculate the standard deviation of NPV.

5* (*Examination level*) The UK manufacturer of footwear, Willow plc, is considering a major investment in a new product area, novelty umbrellas. It hopes that these products will become fashion icons. The following information has been collected:

a   The project will have a limited life of 11 years.
b   The initial investment in plant and machinery will be £1m and a marketing budget of £200,000 will be allocated to the first year.
c   The net cash flows before depreciation of plant and machinery and before marketing expenditure for each umbrella will be £1.
d   The products will be introduced both in the UK and in France.
e   The marketing costs in Years 2 to 11 will be £50,000 per annum.
f   If the product catches the imagination of the consumer in both countries then sales in the first year are anticipated at 1m umbrellas.
g   If the fashion press ignore the new products in one country but become enthusiastic in the other, the sales will be 700,000 umbrellas in Year 1.
h   If the marketing launch is unsuccessful in both countries, first year sales will be 200,000 umbrellas.

The probability of each of these events occurring is: 1m sales: 0.3; 0.7m sales: 0.4; 0.2m sales: 0.3.

If the first year is a success in both countries then two possibilities are envisaged:
a   Sales levels are maintained at 1m units per annum for the next 10 years – probability 0.3.
b   The product is seen as a temporary fad and sales fall to 100,000 units for the remaining 10 years – probability 0.7.

If success is achieved in only one country in the first year then for the remaining 10 years there is:
a   a 0.4 probability of maintaining the annual sales at 700,000 units; and
b   a 0.6 probability of sales immediately falling to 50,000 units per year.

If the marketing launch is unsuccessful in both countries then production will cease after the first year.

The plant and machinery will have no alternative use once installed and will have no scrap value. The annual cash flows and marketing costs will be payable at each year end.

Assume: Cost of capital: 10 per cent; no inflation or taxation; no exchange rate changes.

Required

a   Calculate the expected net present value for the project.
b   Calculate the standard deviation for the project.
c   If the project produces a net present value less than minus £1m the directors fear that the company will be vulnerable to bankruptcy. Calculate the probability of the firm avoiding bankruptcy. Assume a normal distribution.

> **AN EXCEL SPREADSHEET VERSION OF THESE CALCUATIONS IS AVAILABLE IN THE LECTURERS-ONLY SECTION AT www.pearsoned.co.uk/arnold**

Assignments

1   Gather together sufficient data on a recent or forthcoming investment in a firm you know well to be able to carry out the following forms of risk analysis: sensitivity analysis; scenario analysis; risk-adjusted return analysis; probability analysis (expected return, standard deviation, probabilities of various eventualities). Write a report giving as full a picture of the project as possible.

2   Comment on the quality of risk assessment for major investments within your firm. Provide implications and recommendations sections in your report.

Visit www.pearsoned.co.uk/arnold to get access to Gradetracker diagnostic tests, Podcasts, Excel Spreadsheet Solutions, FT articles, a Flashcard revision tool, Weblinks, a searchable Glossary and more.

CHAPTER 5

Portfolio theory and the capital asset pricing model

LEARNING OUTCOMES

This chapter should enable the student to understand, describe and explain in a formal way the interactions between investments and the risk-reducing properties of portfolios. The student will also be able to explain the ideas, frameworks and theories surrounding the relationship between the returns on a security, such as a share, and its risk. By the end of this chapter the reader should be able to:

- calculate two-asset portfolio expected returns and standard deviations;

- estimate measures of the extent of interaction – covariance and correlation coefficients;

- describe the fundamental features of the Capital Asset Pricing Model (CAPM);

- show an awareness of the empirical evidence relating to the CAPM;

- express a reasoned and balanced judgement of the risk-return relationship in financial markets.

Introduction

The principles discussed in this chapter are as old as the hills. If you are facing a future that is uncertain, as most of us do, you will be vulnerable to negative shocks if you rely on a single source of income. It is less risky to have diverse sources of income or, to put it another way, to hold a portfolio of assets or investments. You do not need to study high-level portfolio theory to be aware of the common sense behind the adage 'don't put all your eggs in one basket'.

Here we examine the extent of risk reduction when an investor switches from complete commitment to one asset, for example shares in one company or one project, to the position where resources are split between two or more assets. By doing so it is possible to maintain returns while reducing risk. In this chapter we will focus on the use of portfolio theory, particularly in the context of investment in financial securities, for instance shares in companies. The reader needs to be aware, however, that the fundamental techniques have much wider application – for example, observing the risk-reducing effect of having a diversity of projects within the firm.

The basis of portfolio theory was first developed in 1952 by Harry Markowitz. Following on from the work of Markowitz was the development of a financial theory that has dominated the academic literature and influenced greatly the practical world of finance and business for over four decades since it was first expounded by William Sharpe and other theoreticians.[1] This is the Capital Asset Pricing Model (CAPM). At its heart the CAPM (pronounced cap-em) has an old and common observation – the returns on a financial asset increase with risk. The 'breakthrough' in the 1960s was to define risk in a very precise way. It was no longer enough to rely on standard deviation after the work of Markowitz and others had shown the benefits of diversification. The argument goes that it is illogical to be less than fully diversified so investors tend to create large portfolios. When a portfolio is formed one type of risk factor is eliminated – that which is specifically associated with the fortunes and misfortunes of particular companies. This is called unsystematic risk or unique risk. Once this is taken from the scene the investor merely has to concentrate on risks that cannot be eliminated by holding ever larger portfolios. This is systematic risk, an element of risk common to all firms to a greater or lesser extent.

A central tenet of the CAPM is that systematic risk, as measured by beta, is the only factor affecting the level of return required on a share for a completely diversified investor. For practical use this risk factor is considered to be the extent to which a particular share's returns move when the stock market as a whole moves. Furthermore, the relationship between this beta factor and returns is described by a straight line (it is linear). This neat and, at first sight, apparently complete model changed the way people viewed the world of finance and influenced their actions.

Its far-reaching consequences changed the way in which portfolios were constructed for many pension and insurance funds of millions of people. It contributed to the strengthening of the notion of stock market efficiency – the idea that the stock market 'correctly' prices shares (see Chapter 6). It has affected the investment philosophies of large numbers of investors. It has influenced the calculation of the cost of capital for a firm, or to express it another way, the required rate of return on projects. By providing a target figure of the return required by shareholders the CAPM has enabled management to vary the discount rate by which project cash flows were discounted, depending on the perceived level of systematic risk as defined by beta. Thus countless investment proposals have been accepted or rejected on the strength of what the CAPM has to say about the minimum return demanded by shareholders. In the view of many this is regrettable. Some see the CAPM as artificially restricting the investment opportunities undertaken by firms in national economies and has led to charges of under-investment, economic backwardness and short-termism.

Far more damning criticism was to come for the CAPM in the 1980s and 1990s when researchers looked at the relationship between the CAPM's systematic risk measure, beta, and the returns on shares over the period since the mid-1960s. They discovered either that there was absolutely no relationship at all or that beta had only a weak influence on the return shares produced. They commented that there were other factors determining the returns on shares. This opened up a raging debate within the academic community, with some saying beta was dead, some saying that it was only wounded, and some saying it was alive and well.

The irony is that just as the academic community is having serious doubts about the model, in the outside world the CAPM is reaching new heights of popularity. Hundreds of thousands, if not millions, have studied the CAPM in universities over the past three decades and are now placed in important positions around the world ready to make key decisions often under the subliminal influence of the CAPM. Indeed, a new industry has been built selling data and information that can be plugged into CAPM-based decision-making frameworks in the workplace.

---

[1] Sharpe (1964), Lintner (1965), Mossin (1966), Treynor (1965) and Black (1972).

Partly in response to the empirical evidence, and partly because of theoretical doubts about the CAPM, academics began exploring models that were based on a number of explanatory factors influencing the returns on shares rather than the one solitary variable considered in the CAPM. But wait! We are running ahead of the story. First we have to understand portfolio theory, the workings of the CAPM, and the various items of jargon that have grown up within this area of finance. Only then will a full appreciation of the limitations of these approaches be possible, along with a consideration of alternative risk-return approaches.

Holding period returns

To invest in a share is to become part owner of a business. If the business performs well then high returns will be earned. If the business does less well the holders of other types of securities, for instance the lenders, have the right to demand their contractual return before the ordinary shareholders receive anything. This can result in the share investor receiving little or nothing. The return earned on a share is defined by the holding period returns: R. For one year this is:

$$\text{Return} = \frac{\text{Dividends received} + (\text{Share price at end of period} - \text{Purchase price})}{\text{Purchase price}}$$

$$R = \frac{D_1 + P_1 - P_0}{P_0}$$

The return is the money received less the cost, where P_0 is the purchase price, P_1 the security's value at the end of the holding period and D_1 the dividend paid during the period (usually assumed to occur at the end, for ease of calculations). Thus the return on a share consists of two parts: first, a dividend; and, second, a capital gain (or loss), $P_1 - P_0$. For example if a share was bought for £2, and paid a dividend after one year of 10p and the share was sold for £2.20 after one year the return was:

$$\frac{0.10 + 2.20 - 2.00}{2} = 0.15 \text{ or } 15\%$$

If another share produced a holding period return of, say, 10 per cent over a six-month period we cannot make a direct comparison between the two investments. However, a one-year return and a six-month return are related through the formula:

$$(1 + s)^2 = 1 + R$$

where: s = semi-annual rate R = annual rate[2]

Thus if the semi-annual return is converted to an annual rate we have a true comparison (*see* Exhibit 5.1).

Exhibit 5.1	Comparison of returns	
First investment		**Second investment**
		$(1 + 0.1)^2 = 1 + R$
		$R = (1 + 0.1)^2 - 1$
Return = 0.15 or 15%		Return = 0.21 or 21%

---

[2] See Appendix 2.1 for mathematical tools.

For a three-year holding period, with dividends received at Time 1, 2 and 3 (yearly intervals) the annual rate of return is obtained by solving for R in the following formula:

$$P_0 = \frac{D_1}{1 + R} + \frac{D_2}{(1 + R)^2} + \frac{D_3}{(1 + R)^3} + \frac{P_3}{(1 + R)^3}$$

So, for example if the initial share price was £1 and the share price three years later (P_3) was £1.20 and a dividend of 6p was paid at the end of Year 1 (D_1), 7p was paid at the end of Year 2 (D_2) and 8p was paid at the end of Year 3 (D_3), the annual rate of return can be found by trial and error:[3]

Try 13%

	Pence	Discounted
D_1	6	5.31
D_2	7	5.48
D_3	8	5.54
P_3	120	83.17
		99.50

Try 12%

	Pence	Discounted
D_1	6	5.36
D_2	7	5.58
D_3	8	5.69
P_3	120	85.41
		102.04

$$12 + \frac{2.04}{(102.04 - 99.50)} (13 - 12) = 12.8\%$$

If the annual rate of return was 12.8 per cent then the three-year holding period return was (assuming dividend income was reinvested at the internal rate of return):

$$(1 + 0.128)^3 - 1 = 43.5\%$$

or

$$P(1 + i)^n = F$$

$$£100(1 + 0.128)^3 = £143.52$$

AN EXCEL SPREADSHEET VERSION OF THIS CALCULATION IS AVAILABLE AT
www.pearsoned.co.uk/arnold

The analysis so far has been backward looking, as it focused on the certain returns that have already been received. Given perfect hindsight it is easy to make a choice between investments. When making investment decisions we are concerned with the future. The only certain fact the

---

[3] As demonstrated in the IRR calculations in Chapter 2. Alternatively, it can be found by the goal seek function in Excel – see www.pearsoned.co.uk/arnold

investor has is the price P_0 to be paid. The uncertainty over the future dividend has to be taken into account and, in addition, the even more difficult task of estimating the market value of the share at the end of the period has to be undertaken. Pearson, the owner of the *Financial Times* and *FT Prentice Hall*, has steadily raised its dividend year on year and therefore the estimation of the dividend one year hence can be predicted with a reasonable amount of confidence. However, forecasting the future share price is formidable. This is subject to a number of influences ranging from the talent of the editorial team to the general sentiment in the stock market about macroeconomic matters.

So when dealing with the future we have to talk about expected returns. An expected return is derived by considering a variety of possibilities and weighting the possible outcomes by the estimated probability of occurrence. The list of possible outcomes along with their probability of occurrence is called the frequency function.

Expected return and standard deviation for shares

A frequency function or probability distribution for shares in Ace plc is described in **Exhibit 5.2**. If the economy booms over the next year then the return will be 20 per cent. If normal growth occurs the return will be 5 per cent. A recession will produce a negative return, losing an investor 10 per cent of the original investment.

Exhibit 5.2   Ace plc

A share costs 100p to purchase now and the estimates of returns for the next year are as follows.

Event	Estimated selling price, P_1	Estimated dividend, D_1	Return R_i	Probability
Economic boom	114p	6p	+20%	0.2
Normal growth	100p	5p	+5%	0.6
Recession	86p	4p	−10%	0.2
				1.0

The example shown in Exhibit 5.2 lists only three possibilities. This small number was chosen in order to simplify the analysis, but it is possible to imagine that in reality there would be a number of intermediate outcomes, such as a return of 6 per cent or −2 per cent. Each potential outcome would have a defined probability of occurrence but the probability of all the outcomes would sum to 1.0. This more sophisticated approach to probability distribution is illustrated in **Exhibit 5.3** where the distribution is assumed to be normal, symmetrical and bell-shaped.

We could add to the three possible events shown in Exhibit 5.2, for example slow growth, bad recession, moderate recession and so on, and thereby draw up a more complete representation of the distribution of the probabilities of eventualities. However, to represent all the possibilities would be an enormous task and the table would become unwieldy. Furthermore, the data we are dealing with, namely, future events, do not form a suitable base for such precision. We are better off representing the possible outcomes in terms of two summary statistics, the expected return and standard deviation.

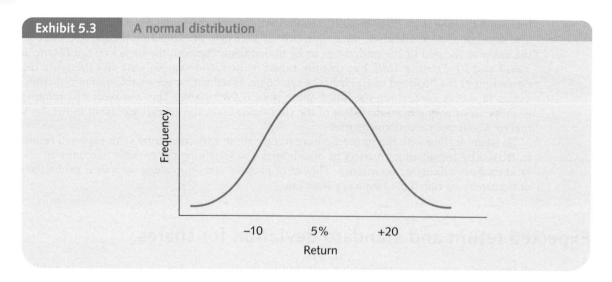

Exhibit 5.3   A normal distribution

The expected return

The expected return is represented by the following formula:

$$\bar{R} = \sum_{i=1}^{n} R_i p_i$$

where:

$\bar{R}$ = expected return
R_i = return if event i occurs
p_i = probability of event i occurring
n = number of events

In the case of Ace plc the expected return is as set out in **Exhibit 5.4.**

Exhibit 5.4   Expected return, Ace plc

Event	Probability of event p_i	Return R_i	$R_i \times p_i$	
Boom	0.2	+20	4	
Growth	0.6	+5	3	
Recession	0.2	−10	−2	
		Expected return	5	or 5%

Standard deviation

The standard deviation gives a measure of the extent to which outcomes vary around the expected return, as set out in the following formula:

$$\sigma = \sqrt{\sum_{i=1}^{n} (R_i - \bar{R_i})^2 \, p_i}$$

For Ace plc, the standard deviation calculation is displayed in **Exhibit 5.5.**

| Exhibit 5.5 | | Standard deviation, Ace plc | | |

Probability p_i	Return R_i	Expected return $\bar{R}_i$	Deviation $R_i - \bar{R}_i$	Deviation squared × probability $(R_i - \bar{R}_i)^2 p_i$
0.2	20%	5%	15	45
0.6	5%	5%	0	0
0.2	−10%	5%	−15	45
			Variance σ^2	90
			Standard deviation σ	9.49%

Comparing shares

If we contrast the expected return and standard deviation of Ace with that for a share in a second company, Bravo, then, using the mean-variance rule described in the previous chapter, we would establish a preference for Ace (*see* **Exhibits 5.6** and **5.7**).

| Exhibit 5.6 | | Returns for a share in Bravo plc | |

Event	Return R_i	Probability p_i
Boom	−15%	0.2
Growth	+5%	0.6
Recession	+25%	0.2
		1.0

Thus, using the numbers in Exhibit 5.6, the expected return on Bravo is:

$(-15 \times 0.2) + (5 \times 0.6) + (25 \times 0.2) = 5$ per cent

The standard deviation for Bravo is as set out in Exhibit 5.7.

If we had to choose between these two shares then we would say that Ace is preferable to Bravo for a risk-averse investor because both shares have an expected return of 5 per cent but the standard deviation for Ace is lower at 9.49.

| Exhibit 5.7 | | Standard deviation, Bravo plc | | |

Probability p_i	Return R_i	Expected return $\bar{R}_i$	Deviation $R_i - \bar{R}_i$	Deviation squared × probability $(R_i - \bar{R}_i)^2 p_i$
0.2	−15%	5%	−20	80
0.6	+5%	5%	0	0
0.2	+25%	5%	+20	80
1.0			Variance σ^2	160
			Standard deviation σ	12.65%

Combinations of investments

In the last section we confined our choice to two options – either invest all the money in Ace, or, alternatively, invest everything in Bravo. If the option were taken to invest in Ace then over a few years the returns might turn out to be as shown in **Exhibit 5.8**.

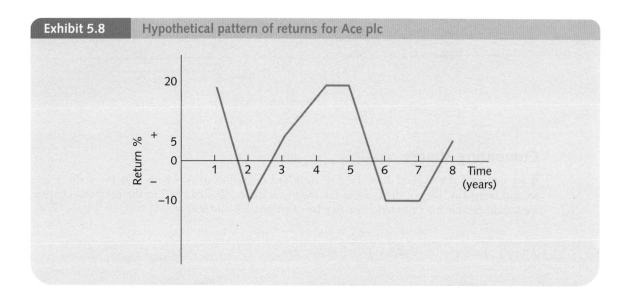

Exhibit 5.8 **Hypothetical pattern of returns for Ace plc**

Note, in Exhibit 5.8, the large variability from one year to the next. The returns on Ace are high when the economy is doing well but fall dramatically when recession strikes. There are numerous industries that seem to follow this sort of pattern. For example, the luxury car market is vulnerable to the ups and downs of the economy, as are the hotel and consumer goods sectors.

If all funds were invested in Bravo in isolation then the patterns of future returns might turn out as shown in **Exhibit 5.9**.

Bravo is in the sort of industry that performs best in recession years; for example, it could be an insolvency practice. Again, note the large swings in returns from year to year.

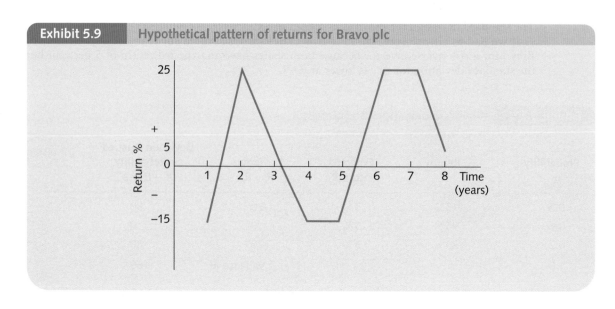

Exhibit 5.9 **Hypothetical pattern of returns for Bravo plc**

Now assume that the investor is not confined to a pure investment in either Ace's shares or Bravo's shares. Another possibility is to buy a portfolio, in other words, to split the fund between the two companies. We will examine the effect on return and risk of placing £571 of a fund totalling £1,000 into Ace, and £429 into Bravo (*see* **Exhibits 5.10** and **5.11**).

Exhibit 5.10	Returns over one year from placing £571 in Ace and £429 in Bravo			
Event	Returns Ace £	Returns Bravo £	Overall returns on £1,000	Percentage returns
Boom	571(1.2) = 685	429 − 429(0.15) = 365	1,050	5%
Growth	571(1.05) = 600	429(1.05) = 450	1,050	5%
Recession	571 − 571(0.1) = 514	429(1.25) = 536	1,050	5%

Exhibit 5.11	Hypothetical pattern of returns for Ace, Bravo and the two-asset portfolio

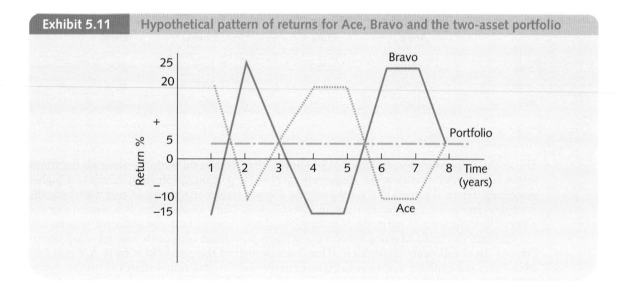

By spreading the investment between these two companies we have achieved complete certainty. Year after year a constant return of 5 per cent is assured rather than the fluctuations experienced if only one share is chosen. Risk has been reduced to zero but average return has remained the same. This is a rare case of receiving something for nothing: without needing to sacrifice any gain we eliminate a 'bad', that is, variability in return.

Perfect negative correlation

So, we have a dramatic demonstration of how the risk (degree of deviation from the expected value) on a portfolio can be less than the risk of the individual constituents. The risk becomes zero because the returns on Bravo are highest in circumstances when the returns on Ace are at their lowest, and vice versa. The co-movement of the returns on Ace and Bravo is such that they exactly offset one another. That is, they exhibit *perfect negative correlation*.

Perfect positive correlation

By contrast to the relationship of perfect negative correlation between Ace and Bravo, **Exhibit 5.12** shows that the returns on Ace and Clara move exactly in step. This is called *perfect positive correlation*.

Exhibit 5.12	Annual returns on Ace and Clara		
Event i	Probability p_i	Returns on Ace %	Returns on Clara %
Boom	0.2	+20	+50
Growth	0.6	+5	+15
Recession	0.2	−10	−20

If a portfolio is constructed from equal investments of Ace and Clara the result is as shown in **Exhibit 5.13**.

Exhibit 5.13	Returns over a one-year period from placing £500 in Ace and £500 in Clara			
Event i	Outcome for Ace £	Outcome for Clara £	Overall outcome on £1,000 investment	Percentage return
Boom	600	750	1,350	35%
Growth	525	575	1,100	10%
Recession	450	400	850	−15%

The situation portrayed in Exhibit 5.13 indicates that, compared with investing all the funds in Ace, the portfolio has a wider dispersion of possible percentage return outcomes. A higher percentage return is earned in a good year and a lower return in a recession year. However, the portfolio returns are less volatile than an investment in Clara alone. There is a general rule for a portfolio consisting of perfectly positively correlated returns: both the expected returns and the standard deviation of the portfolio are weighted averages of returns and standard deviations of the constituents respectively. Thus because half of the portfolio is from Ace and half from Clara the expected return is halfway between the two individual shares. Also the degree of oscillation is halfway between the small variability of Ace and the large variability of Clara. Perfectly positively correlated investments are at the opposite extreme to perfectly negatively correlated investments. In the former case risk is not reduced through diversification, it is merely averaged. In the latter case risk can be completely eliminated by selecting the appropriate proportions of each investment.

A typical pattern of returns over an eight-year period might be as shown in **Exhibit 5.14** for Ace and Clara and a 50:50 portfolio.

Independent investments

A third possibility is that the returns on shares in two firms are completely unrelated. Within a portfolio of two statistically independent shares we find that when one firm gives a high return the other one may give a high return or it may give a low return: that is, we are unable to state any correlation between the returns. The example of X and Y in **Exhibits 5.15–5.18** shows the effect on risk of this kind of zero correlation situation when two shares are brought together in a portfolio. Shares in X have a 0.5 probability of producing a return of 35 per cent and a 0.5 probability of producing a return of negative 25 per cent. Shares in Y have exactly the same returns and probabilities but which of the two outcomes will occur is totally independent of the outcome for X.

Exhibit 5.14 Hypothetical pattern of returns for Ace and Clara

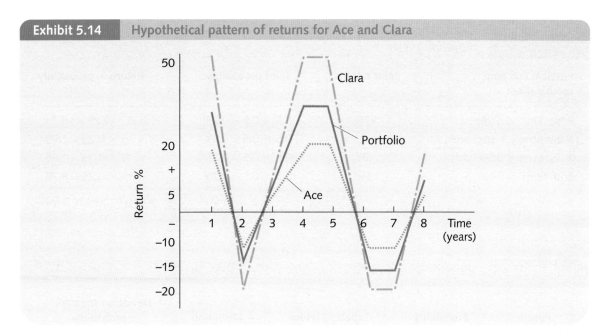

Exhibit 5.15 Expected returns for shares in X and shares in Y

Expected return for shares in X	Expected returns for shares in Y
Return × Probability	Return × Probability
−25 × 0.5 = −12.5	−25 × 0.5 = −12.5
35 × 0.5 = 17.5	5 × 0.5 = 17.5
5.0%	5.0%

Exhibit 5.16 Standard deviations for X or Y as single investments

Return R_i	Probability p_i	Expected return $\bar{R}_i$	Deviation $R_i - \bar{R}_i$	Deviation squared × probability $(R_i - \bar{R}_i)^2 p_i$
−25%	0.5	5%	−30	450
35%	0.5	5%	30	450
			Variance σ^2	900
			Standard deviation σ	30%

If a 50:50 portfolio is created we see that the expected returns remain at 5 per cent, but the standard deviation is reduced (*see* Exhibits 5.17 and 5.18).

Exhibit 5.17	A mixed portfolio: 50 per cent of the fund invested in X and 50 per cent in Y, expected return

Possible outcome combinations	Joint returns	Joint probability	Return × probability
Both firms do badly	−25	0.5 × 0.5 = 0.25	−25 × 0.25 = −6.25
X does badly Y does well	5	0.5 × 0.5 = 0.25	5 × 0.25 = 1.25
X does well Y does badly	5	0.5 × 0.5 = 0.25	5 × 0.25 = 1.25
Both firms do well	35	0.5 × 0.5 = 0.25	35 × 0.25 = 8.75
		1.00	Expected return 5.00%

Exhibit 5.18	Standard deviation, mixed portfolio of X and Y

Return R_i	Probability P_i	Expected return $\bar{R}_i$	Deviation $R_i - \bar{R}_i$	Deviation squared × probability $(R_i - \bar{R}_i)^2 \, p_i$
−25	0.25	5	−30	225
5	0.50	5	0	0
35	0.25	5	30	225
			Variance σ^2	450
			Standard deviation σ	21.21%

The reason for the reduction in risk from a standard deviation of 30 (as shown in Exhibit 5.16) to one of 21.21 (as shown in Exhibit 5.18), is that there is now a third possible outcome. Previously the only outcomes were −25 and +35. Now it is possible that one investment will give a positive result and one will give a negative result. The overall effect is that there is a 50 per cent chance of an outcome being +5. The diversified portfolio reduces the dispersion of the outcomes, and the chance of suffering a major loss of 25 per cent is lowered from a probability of 0.5 to only 0.25 for the mixed portfolio.

A correlation scale

We have examined three extreme positions which will provide the foundation for more detailed consideration of portfolios. The case of Ace and Bravo demonstrated that, when investments produce good or bad outcomes that vary in exact opposition to each other, risk can be eliminated. This relationship, described as perfect negative correlation, can be assigned the number −1 on a correlation scale which ranges from −1 to +1. The second example, of Ace and Clara, showed a situation where returns on both shares were affected by the same events and these returns moved in lock-step with one another. This sort of perfect positive correlation can be assigned a value of +1 on a correlation scale. The third case, of X and Y where returns are independent, showed that risk is not entirely eliminated but it can be reduced. (Extreme outcomes are still possible, but they are less likely.) Independent investments are assigned a value of zero on the correlation scale (*see* Exhibit 5.19).

Exhibit 5.19   Correlation scale

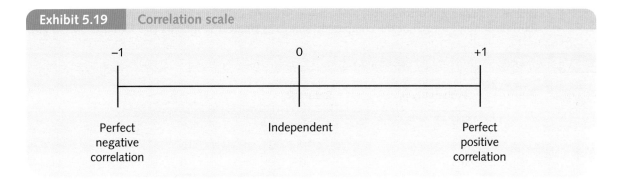

This leads to an important conclusion from portfolio theory:

So long as the returns of constituent assets of a portfolio are not perfectly positively correlated, diversification can reduce risk. The degree of risk reduction depends on:

(a) **the extent of statistical interdependence between the returns of the different investments: the more negative the better; and**

(b) **the number of securities over which to spread the risk: the greater the number, the lower the risk.**

This is an amazing conclusion because it is only in the very extreme and rare situation of perfect positive correlation that risk is not reduced.

It is all very well focusing on these three unusual types of relationships but what about the majority of investments in shares, projects or whatever? Real-world assets tend to have returns which have some degree of correlation with other assets but this is neither perfect nor zero. It is to this slightly more complex situation we now turn.

Initially the mathematics of portfolio theory may seem daunting but they do break down into manageable components. The algebra and theory are necessary to gain a true appreciation of the uses of portfolio theory, but the technical aspects are kept to a minimum.

The effects of diversification when security returns are not perfectly correlated

We will now look at the risk-reducing effects of diversification when two financial securities, two shares, have only a small degree of interrelatedness between their returns. Suppose that an investor has a chance of either investing all funds in one company, A or B, or investing a fraction in one with the remainder purchasing shares in the other. The returns on these companies respond differently to the general activity within the economy. Company A does particularly well when the economy is booming. Company B does best when there is normal growth in the economy. Both do badly in a recession. There is some degree of 'togetherness' or correlation of the movement of the returns, but not much (*see* Exhibit 5.20).

Exhibit 5.20   Returns on shares A and B for alternative economic states

Event i State of the economy	Probability p_i	Return on A R_A	Return on B R_B
Boom	0.3	20%	3%
Growth	0.4	10%	35%
Recession	0.3	0%	−5%

Before examining portfolio risk and returns we first calculate the expected return and standard deviation for each of the companies' shares as single investments (*see* Exhibits 5.21–5.25).

Exhibit 5.21   Company A: Expected return

Probability p_i	Return R_A	$R_A \times p_i$
0.3	20	6
0.4	10	4
0.3	0	0
		10%

Exhibit 5.22   Company A: Standard deviation

Probability p_i	Return R_i	Expected return $\bar{R}_A$	Deviation $R_A - \bar{R}_A$	Deviation squared × probability $(R_A - \bar{R}_A)^2 p_i$
0.3	20	10	10	30
0.4	10	10	0	0
0.3	0	10	−10	30
			Variance σ^2	60
			Standard deviation σ	7.75%

Exhibit 5.23   Company B: Expected return

Probability p_i	Return R_B	$R_B \times p_i$
0.3	3	0.9
0.4	35	14.0
0.3	−5	−1.5
		13.4%

Exhibit 5.24   Company B: Standard deviation

Probability p_i	Return R_B	Expected return $\bar{R}_B$	Deviation $(R_B - \bar{R}_B)$	Deviation squared × probability $(R_B - \bar{R}_B)^2 p_i$
0.3	3	13.4	10.4	32.45
0.4	35	13.4	21.6	186.62
0.3	−5	13.4	−18.4	101.57
			Variance σ^2	320.64
			Standard deviation σ	17.91%

Exhibit 5.25	Summary table: Expected returns and standard deviations for Companies A and B	

	Expected return	Standard deviation
Company A	10%	7.75%
Company B	13.4%	17.91%

Compared with A, Company B is expected to give a higher return but also has a higher level of risk. If the results are plotted on a diagram we can give an impression of the relative risk-return profiles (*see* **Exhibit 5.26**).

Exhibit 5.26	Return and standard deviation for shares in companies A and B

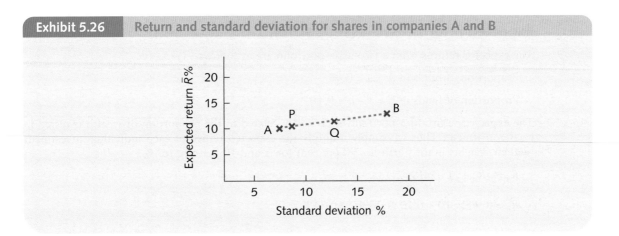

From a first glance at Exhibit 5.26 it might be thought that it is possible to invest in different proportions of A and B and obtain a risk-return combination somewhere along the dotted line. That is, a two-asset portfolio of A and B has an expected return which is a weighted average of the expected returns on the individual investments *and* the standard deviation is a weighted average of the risk of A and B depending on the proportions of the portfolio devoted to A and B. So if point Q represented a 50 : 50 split of capital between A and B the expected return, following this logic, would be:

$$(10 \times 0.5) + (13.4 \times 0.5) = 11.7\%$$

and the standard deviation would be:

$$(7.75 \times 0.5) + (17.91 \times 0.5) = 12.83\%$$

Point P represents 90 per cent of the fund in A and 10 per cent in B. If this portfolio was on the dotted line the expected return would be:

$$(10 \times 0.9) + (13.4 \times 0.1) = 10.34\%$$

and the standard deviation would be:

$$(7.75 \times 0.9) + (17.91 \times 0.1) = 8.766\%$$

However, this would be **wrong** because the risk of any portfolio of A and B is less than the weighted average of the two individual standard deviations. You can, in fact, reduce risk at each level of return by investing in a portfolio of A and B. This brings us to a general rule in portfolio theory:

Portfolio returns are a weighted average of the expected returns on the individual investments ...

BUT ...

Portfolio standard deviation is less than the weighted average risk of the individual investments, except for perfectly positively correlated investments.

Portfolio expected return and standard deviation

The rule stated above will now be illustrated by calculating the expected return and standard deviation when 90 per cent of the portfolio funds are placed in A and 10 per cent are placed in B.

Expected returns, two-asset portfolio

The expected returns from a two-asset portfolio are as follows.

Proportion of funds in A = a = 0.90

Proportion of funds in B = $1 - a$ = 0.10

The expected return of a portfolio R_p is solely related to the proportion of wealth invested in each constituent. Thus we simply multiply the expected return of each individual investment by their weights in the portfolio, 90 per cent for A and 10 per cent for B.

$$\bar{R}_p = a\bar{R}_A + (1 - a)\bar{R}_B$$

$$\bar{R}_p = 0.90 \times 10 + 0.10 \times 13.4 = 10.34\%$$

Standard deviation, two-asset portfolio

Now comes the formula that for decades has made the hearts of students sink when first seen – the formula for the standard deviation of a two-asset portfolio. This is:

$$\sigma_p = \sqrt{a^2\sigma_A^2 + (1 - a)^2\,\sigma_B^2 + 2a(1 - a)\text{cov}(R_A, R_B)}$$

where:

σ_p = portfolio standard deviation

σ_A^2 = variance of return on investment A

σ_B^2 = variance of return on investment B

$\text{cov}(R_A, R_B)$ = covariance of A and B

The formula for the standard deviation of a two-asset portfolio may seem daunting at first. However, the component parts are fairly straightforward. To make the formula easier to understand it is useful to break it down to three terms:

1 The first term, $a^2\sigma_A^2$, is the variance for A multiplied by the square of its weight – in the example $a^2 = 0.90^2$.

2 The second term, $(1 - a)^2\,\sigma_B^2$, is the variance for the second investment B multiplied by the square of its weight in the portfolio, 0.10^2.

3 The third term, $2a(1 - a)\,\text{cov}(R_A, R_B)$, focuses on the covariance of the returns of A and B, which is examined below.

When the results of all three calculations are added together the square root is taken to give the standard deviation of the portfolio. The only piece of information not yet available is the covariance. This is considered next.

Covariance

The covariance measures the extent to which the returns on two investments 'co-vary' or 'co-move'. If the returns tend to go up together and go down together then the covariance will be a positive number. If, however, the returns on one investment move in the opposite direction to the returns on another when a particular event occurs then these securities will exhibit negative covariance. If there is no co-movement at all, that is, the returns are independent of each other, covariance will be zero. This positive–zero–negative scale should sound familiar, as covariance and the correlation coefficient are closely related. However, the correlation coefficient scale has a strictly limited range from −1 to +1 whereas the covariance can be any positive or negative value. The covariance formula is:

$$\text{cov}(R_A, R_B) = \sum_{i=1}^{n} [(R_A - \bar{R}_A)\ (R_B - \bar{R}_B)\ p_i]$$

To calculate covariance take each of the possible events that could occur in turn and calculate the extent to which the returns on investment A differ from expected return $(R_A - \bar{R}_A)$ – and note whether this is a positive or negative deviation. Follow this with a similar deviation calculation for an investment in B if those particular circumstances (that is, boom, recession, etc.) prevail $(R_B - \bar{R}_B)$. Then multiply the deviation of A by the deviation of B and the probability of that event occurring, p_i. (Note that if the deviations are both in a positive direction away from the mean, that is, a higher return than average, or both negative, then the overall calculation will be positive. If one of the deviations is negative while the other is positive the overall result is negative.) Finally, the results from all the potential events are added together to give the covariance.

Applying the formula to A and B will help to clarify matters (*see* **Exhibit 5.27**).

Exhibit 5.27		Covariance							

Event and probability of event p_i		Returns		Expected returns		Deviations		Deviation of A × deviation of B × probability
		R_A	R_B	$\bar{R}_A$	$\bar{R}_B$	$(R_A - \bar{R}_A)$	$(R_B - \bar{R}_B)$	$(R_A - \bar{R}_A)(R_B - \bar{R}_B)\ p_i$
Boom	0.3	20	3	10	13.4	10	−10.4	10 × −10.4 × 0.3 = −31.2
Growth	0.4	10	35	10	13.4	0	21.6	0 × 21.6 × 0.4 = 0
Recession	0.3	0	−5	10	13.4	−10	−18.4	−10 × −18.4 × 0.3 = 55.2
							Covariance of A and B, cov (R_A, R_B) =	+24

**AN EXCEL SPREADSHEET SHOWING THESE COVARIANCE CALCULATIONS
IS AVAILABLE AT www.pearsoned.co.uk/arnold**

It is worth spending a little time dwelling on the covariance and seeing how a positive or negative covariance comes about. In the calculation for A and B the 'Boom' eventuality contributed a negative 31.2 to the overall covariance. This is because A does particularly well in boom conditions and the returns are well above expected returns, but B does badly compared with its expected return of 13.4 and therefore the co-movement of returns is a negative one. In a recession both firms experience poor returns compared with their expected values, thus the contribution to the overall covariance is positive because they move together. This second element of co-movement outweighs that of the boom possibility and so the total covariance is positive 24.

Now that we have the final piece of information to plug into the standard deviation formula we can work out the risk resulting from splitting the fund, with 90 per cent invested in A and 10 per cent in B.

$$\sigma_p = \sqrt{a^2 \sigma_A^2 + (1-a)^2 \sigma_B^2 + 2a(1-a)\mathrm{cov}(R_A, R_B)}$$

$$\sigma_p = \sqrt{0.90^2 \times 60 + 0.10^2 \times 320.64 + 2 \times 0.90 \times 0.10 \times 24}$$

$$\sigma_p = \sqrt{48.6 + 3.206 + 4.32}$$

$$\sigma_p = \quad 7.49\%$$

A 90:10 portfolio gives both a higher return and a lower standard deviation than a simple investment in A alone (*see* **Exhibit 5.28**).

Exhibit 5.28	Summary table: expected return and standard deviation	
	Expected return (%)	**Standard deviation (%)**
All invested in Company A	10	7.75
All invested in Company B	13.4	17.91
Invested in a portfolio (90% in A, 10% in B)	10.34	7.49

AN EXCEL SPREADSHEET SHOWING ALL THE CALCULATIONS FOR A and B IS AVAILABLE AT www.pearsoned.co.uk/arnold

Diversification

The fundamental point about portfolio theory is that if an investor has one company's shares in his 'portfolio' then risk is likely to be very high. Adding a second reduces risk (except in the rare cases of perfect positive correlation). If we had taken the mathematics of portfolio theory further we would have demonstrated that risk could be reduced again by the addition of a third, and then a fourth share. This sort of effect is demonstrated in **Exhibit 5.29**. The reason for the risk reduction is that security returns generally do not vary with perfect positive correlation. At any one time the good news about one share is offset to some extent by bad news about another.

Generally within a portfolio of shares, if one is shooting up, others are stable, going down or rising. Each share movement depends mostly on the news emanating from the company. News is generally particular to companies and so we should not expect them each to report good (or bad) news on the same day. So, if on a day one share in the portfolio reports the resignation of a brilliant chief executive we might expect that share to fall. But, because the portfolio owner is diversified the return on the portfolio will not move dramatically downward. Other companies are reporting marketing coups, big new contracts, etc., pushing up their share prices. Others (the majority) are not reporting any news and their share prices do not move much at all. The point is by not having all your eggs in one basket you reduce the chance of the collective value of your investments falling off a cliff.

So, despite the fact that returns on individual shares can vary dramatically, a portfolio will be relatively stable. The type of risk that is being reduced through diversification is referred to as unique or unsystematic risk (or idiosyncratic or specific risk – you wouldn't expect financial economists to make things easy by having one word for it, would you?). This element of variability in a share's return is due to the particular circumstances of the individual firm. In a portfolio these individual ups and downs tend to cancel out – at least, to some extent. Another piece of jargon applied to this type of risk is that it is 'diversifiable'. That is, it can be eliminated simply by holding a sufficiently large portfolio.

| Exhibit 5.29 | Systematic and unsystematic risk |

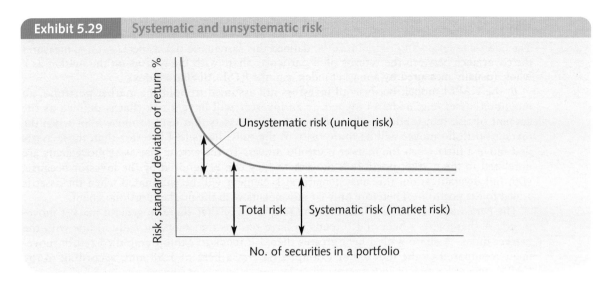

Systematic risk

However, no matter how many shares are held, there will always be an element of risk that cannot be cancelled out by broadening the portfolio. This is called systematic or market risk. There are some risk factors that are common to all firms to a greater or lesser extent. These include macro-economic movements such as economic growth, inflation and exchange rate changes. No firm is entirely immune from these factors. For example, a deceleration in gross domestic product (GDP) growth or a rise in tax rates is likely to impact on the returns of all firms within an economy.

Note, however, that while all shares respond to these system-wide risk factors they do not all respond equally. Some shares will exhibit a greater sensitivity to these systematic risk elements than others. The revenues of the luxury goods sectors, for example, are particularly sensitive to the ups and downs of the economy. Spending on electrical goods and sports cars rises when the economy is in a strong growth phase but falls off significantly in recession. On the other hand, some sectors experience limited variations in demand as the economy booms and shrinks; the food-producing and food-retailing sector are prime examples here. People do not cut down significantly on food bought for home consumption even when their incomes fall.

It is assumed, quite reasonably, that investors do not like risk. If this is the case, then the logical course of action is going to be to eliminate as much unsystematic risk as possible by diversifying. Most of the shares in UK companies are held by highly diversified institutional investors such as pension funds, insurance funds, unit trusts and investment trusts. While it is true that many small investors are not fully diversified, it is equally true that the market, and more importantly market returns, are dominated by the actions of fully diversified investors. These investors ensure that the market does not reward investors for bearing some unsystematic risk.

To understand this, imagine that by some freak accident a share offered a return of, say, 50 per cent per annum which includes compensation for both unsystematic and systematic risk. There would be a mad scramble to buy these shares, especially by the major diversified funds, which are not concerned about the unsystematic risk on this share – they have other share returns to offset the oscillations of this new one. The buying pressure would result in a rise in the share price. This process would continue until the share offered the same return as other shares offering that level of systematic risk. Let us assume that the price doubles and therefore the return falls to 25 per cent. Undiversified investors will be dismayed that they can no longer find any share which will compensate for what they perceive as the relevant risk for them, consisting of both unsystematic and systematic elements.

In the financial markets the risk that matters is the degree to which a particular share tends to move when the market as a whole moves. This is the only issue of concern to investors that are fully diversified, because ups and downs due to specific company events do not affect the return on the portfolio – only market-wide events affect the portfolio's return.

This is leading to a new way of measuring risk. For the diversified investor, the relevant measure of risk is no longer standard deviation, it is systematic risk.

Beta

The Capital asset pricing model (CAPM) defined this systematic risk as beta. Beta, β, measures the covariance between the returns on a particular share with the returns on the market as a whole (usually measured by a market index, e.g. the FTSE All Share index).

In the CAPM model, because all investors are assumed to hold the market portfolio, an individual asset (e.g. a share) owned by an investor will have a risk that is defined as the amount of risk that it adds to the market portfolio. Assets that tend to move a lot when the market portfolio moves will be more risky to the fully diversified investor than those assets that move a little when the market portfolio moves. To the extent that asset movements are unrelated to the market portfolio's movement they can be ignored by the investor because, with full diversification, this unsystematic risk element will be eliminated when the asset is added to the portfolio. Therefore only co-movements with the market portfolio count.

The beta value for a share indicates the sensitivity of that share to general market movements. A share with a beta of 1.0 tends to have returns that move broadly in line with the market index. A share with a beta greater than 1.0 tends to exhibit amplified return movements compared to the index. For example, BT has a beta of 1.58 and, according to the CAPM, when the market index return rises by, say, 10 per cent, the returns on BT shares will tend to rise by 15.8 per cent. Conversely, if the market falls by 10 per cent, the returns on BTs shares will tend to fall by 15.8 per cent.

Shares with a beta of less than 1.0, such as Marks & Spencer with a beta of 0.48, will vary less than the market as a whole. So, if the market is rising, shares in M&S will not enjoy the same level of upswing. However, should the market ever suffer a downward movement, for every 10 per cent decline in shares generally, M&S will, according to CAPM theory, give a return decline of only 4.8 per cent. Note that these co-movements are to be taken as statistical expectations rather than precise predictions. Thus, over a large sample of return movements M&S's returns will move by 4.8 per cent for a 10 per cent market movement if beta is a correct measure of company to market returns. On any single occasion the co-movements may not have this relationship. Exhibit 5.30 displays the betas for some large UK companies.

Exhibit 5.30	Betas as measured in 2005		
Share	**Beta**	**Share**	**Beta**
BOC Group	0.88	Barclays Bank	1.01
Sainsbury's (J)	0.93	Marks & Spencer	0.48
Great Universal Stores	1.20	BT	1.58

Source: Thomson Financial Datastream.

The basic features of beta are:

When

$\beta = 1$ A 1 per cent change in the market index return generally leads to a 1 per cent change in the return on a specific share.

$0 < \beta < 1$ A 1 per cent change in the market index return generally leads to a less than 1 per cent change in the returns on a specific share.

$\beta > 1$ A 1 per cent change in market index return generally leads to a greater return than 1 per cent on a specific company's share.

The Security Market Line (SML)

In Chapter 2 it was explained that investors require a risk premium (extra return) on top of what they can receive on a risk-free investment r_f to induce them to invest in something risky like a share. Thus the return expected on a share J is $r_j = r_f + RP$, where RP is the risk premium. To calculate the expected return on an average share (or whole share market return) we need two figures: (i) the current risk-free rate of return available to investors, and (ii) the RP for the average share. However, this is not enough information when we are examining shares that are not in the same risk category as the market as a whole. So, we must adjust (up or down) the RP for the averagely risky share to calculate the required return on a specific share.

Risk has been redefined for a fully diversified investor in an efficient market as systematic risk because this is the risk that cannot be diversified away and so a higher return is required if an investor is to bear it. In the CAPM the relationship between risk as measured by beta and expected return is shown by the security market line as in **Exhibit 5.31**. Shares perfectly correlated with the market return (r_m) will have a beta of 1.0 and are expected to produce an annual return of 11 per cent in the circumstances of a risk-free rate of return at 6 per cent and the risk premium on the market portfolio of shares over safe securities at 5 per cent (point M). Shares which are twice as risky, with a beta of 2.0, will have an expected return of 16 per cent; shares which vary half as much as the market index are expected to produce a return of 8.5 per cent in this *particular hypothetical* risk-return line.

Exhibit 5.31   A hypothetical Security Market Line (SML)

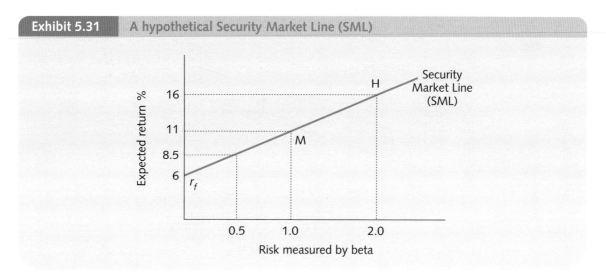

To find the level of return expected for a given level of beta risk along the SML the following equation can be used:

Expected return = risk-free rate + beta × The average risk premium for shares (expected return on the market minus the risk-free rate),

or $r_j = r_f + \beta (r_m - r_f)$

Thus for a share with a beta of 1.31 the expected return will be:

$$r_j = 6 + 1.31 (11 - 6) = 12.55\%$$

The better way of presenting this is to place the risk premium (RP) in the brackets rather than r_m and r_f separately because this reminds us that what is important is the required extra return over the risk-free rate as revealed by investors over many years – not the current risk-free rate. It is amazing how often financial journalists get this wrong and fixate on the current r_m and r_f rather than the long-term historical difference between the two. The market risk premium ($r_m - r_f$) is fairly stable over time as it is taken from a long-term historical relationship. Indeed, taking a short period to estimate this would result in wild fluctuations from year to year (e.g. shares lost value 2000–2003). None of these fluctuations would reflect the premiums investors demand for holding a risky portfolio of shares compared with a risk-free security. It is only over long periods that we can get a clearer view of returns required by shareholders as an acceptable premium.

At any one time the position of the SML depends primarily on the risk-free rate of return. If the interest rate on government securities rises by, say, four percentage points, the SML lifts upwards by 4 per cent (*see* **Exhibit 5.32**). Note that the slope of the SML does not change even though the r_f in ($r_m - r_f$) changes because $r_m - r_f$ is the *long-term* historical risk premium for shares over the risk-free rate.

Exhibit 5.32	Shifts in the SML: a 4 percentage point rise in the risk-free rate

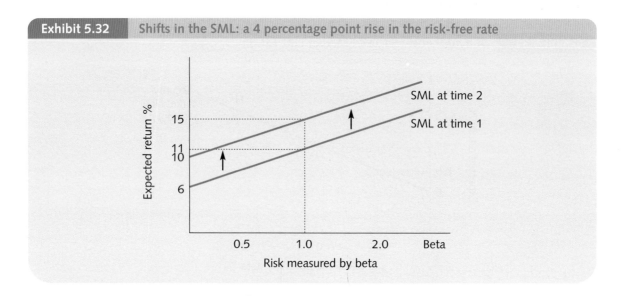

Risk premiums across the world

Exhibit 5.33 shows estimates of the extra annual return received by investors for holding a portfolio of shares compared with government bonds over various time periods. The extra return over periods as short as 1 year can give a distorted picture – we cannot possibly assume that the negative return on UK shares in 2002 (down 29 per cent) represents the normal 'additional' return demand by investors above a risk-free investment. Notice that the risk premium received for holding shares rather than government bonds has generally been in the range of 3 per cent to 6 per cent for the 16 countries listed. This gives us a strong indication of the likely future-focused risk premium demanded by investors today. Therefore using a risk premium in this range for cost of equity capital calculation could be defended on these grounds. But note the assumption you would be making: that the returns investors actually received after the event (e.g. over the twentieth century) reflect the return they would have been demanding before the event (e.g. start of the twentieth century) for investing in shares rather than bonds.

Exhibit 5.33	Equity risk premiums	
		% per annum
UK		
101 years 1900–2000		4.4
51 years 1950–2000		6.8
31 years 1970–2000		3.5
Other countries		
Australia 101 years 1900–2000		6.3
Belgium 101 years 1900–2000		2.9
Canada 101 years 1900–2000		4.5
Denmark 101 years 1900–2000		2.0
France 101 years 1900–2000		4.9
Germany 99 years 1900–2000[4]		6.7
Ireland 101 years 1900–2000		3.2
Italy 101 years 1900–2000		5.0
Japan 101 years 1900–2000		6.2
N'lands101 years 1900–2000		4.7
South Africa 101 years 1900–2000		5.4
Spain 101 years 1900–2000		2.3
Sweden 101 years 1900–2000		5.2
Switz 90 years 1911–2000		2.7
US 101 years 1900–2000		5.0
World 101 years 1900–2000		4.6

Source: Elroy Dimson, Paul Marsh and Mike Staunton, *Triumph of the Optimists: 101 Years of Global Investment Returns*, Princeton, NJ: Princeton University Press, 2002.

Estimating some expected returns

To calculate the returns investors require from particular shares you need to obtain three numbers using the CAPM: (i) the risk-free rate of return, r_f, (ii) the risk premium for the market portfolio, $(r_m - r_f)$, and (iii) the beta of the share. In 2006 the returns on UK government securities are about 4–5 per cent. For practical use we will take a risk premium of 5 per cent. We have to acknowledge our imprecision at this point (even though some consultants will give a cost of equity capital to a tenth of a percentage point). Looking at the figures in Exhibit 5.33 we could go for a risk premium of, say, 6.8 per cent to reflect the fact that shares returned a much higher premium to UK investors in the last 51 years of the twentieth century. On the other hand, we could plump for a much lower figure if we accept the argument that investors were surprised by the size of the premium they actually received; they weren't demanding it *a priori*, it was just that the optimists (share investors) were lucky and got it anyway – see Shiller (2000) and Dimson, Marsh and Staunton (2002) for this view – in future they will get a smaller return above the government bond rate. **Exhibit 5.34** calculates the returns required on shares of some leading UK firms using beta as the only risk variable influencing returns, a risk-free rate of 4.5 per cent and a risk premium of 5 per cent.

---

[4] For Germany the years 1922–23 are excluded.

Exhibit 5.34	Returns required by investors based on the capital asset pricing model

Share	Beta (β)	Required returns $r_f + \beta\,(r_m - r_f)$
BOC	0.88	4.5 + 0.88(5) = 8.9
BT	1.58	4.5 + 1.58(5) = 12.4
Sainsbury's (J)	0.93	4.5 + 0.93(5) = 9.2
GUS	1.20	4.5 + 1.20(5) = 10.5
Barclays Bank	1.01	4.5 + 1.01(5) = 9.5
Marks & Spencer	0.48	4.5 + 0.48(5) = 6.9

Calculating beta

To make the capital asset pricing model workable for making decisions concerning the future it is necessary to calculate the *future* beta. That is, how much more or less volatile is a particular share going to be relative to the market. Investors want extra compensation for relative volatility over the period when they hold the share – i.e. time yet to come. Obviously, the future cannot be foreseen, and so it is difficult to obtain an estimate of the likely co-movements of the returns on a share and the market portfolio. One approach is to substitute subjective probability beliefs, but this has obvious drawbacks. The most popular method is to observe the historical relationship between returns and to assume that this covariance will persist into the future. This is called *ex post* analysis because it takes place after the event.

Exhibit 5.35 shows a simplified and idealised version of this sort of analysis. Here are shown twelve monthly observations for, say, 2005 (commercially supplied beta calculations are often based on at least 60 monthly observations stretching back over five years). Each plot point expresses the return on the market index portfolio r_m for a particular month and the return on the specific shares r_j being examined in that same month.

In an analysis such as that presented in Exhibit 5.35 the market portfolio will be represented by some broad index containing many hundreds of shares. In this highly idealised example the relative returns plot along a straight line is referred to as the *characteristic line*. Exhibit 5.35 shows a perfect statistical relationship in that there is no statistical 'noise' causing the plot points to be placed off the line.

Exhibit 5.35	The characteristic line; no unsystematic risk

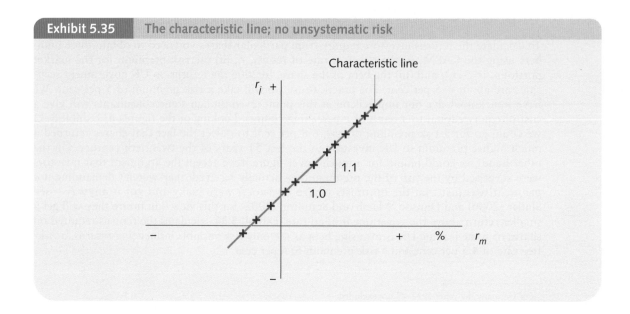

The slope of the characteristic line is the beta for share j. That is:

$$\frac{\text{Change in } r_j}{\text{Change in } r_m} = \frac{\Delta r_j}{\Delta r_m} = \beta$$

In this case the slope is 1.1 and therefore $\beta = 1.1$.

A more realistic representation of the relationship between the monthly returns on the market and the returns on a specific share is shown in Exhibit 5.36. Here very few of the plot points fall on the fitted regression line (the line of best fit). The reason for this scatter of points is that the unsystematic risk effects in any one month may cause the returns on a specific share to rise or fall by a larger or smaller amount than they would if the returns on the market were the only influence.

To gain an appreciation of what the model presented in Exhibit 5.36 reveals, we will examine two of the plot points. Take point A: this represents the returns for the market and for share j in the month of, say, August. Part of the movement of j is explained by the general market changes – this is the distance UV. However, a large element of j's returns in that month is attributable to unsystematic risk factors – this is represented by the distance AU. Now consider point B for the month of November. If systematic risk is the only influence on the return of a single share then we would expect the change in j's return to be XW. However, unsystematic risk influences have reduced the extent of variation to only BX. The distance AU and WB make up part of the error term e in the market model formula.

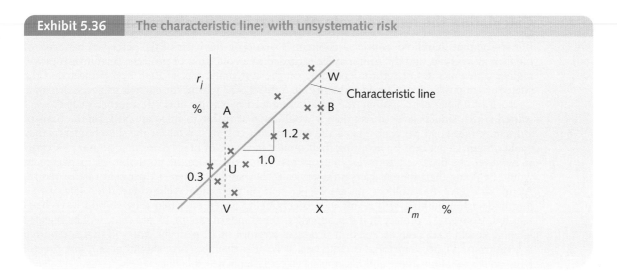

Exhibit 5.36   The characteristic line; with unsystematic risk

Applications of the CAPM

Investment in the financial markets

Portfolio selection

The beta metric has been used to construct different types of portfolio. For highly risk-averse investors a portfolio consisting of low beta securities may be chosen. If the average beta of the shares comprising the portfolio is 0.7 then for every 1 per cent change in the index the portfolio is expected to change by only 0.7 per cent. Similarly, a high-risk portfolio could be created which consisted of high beta stocks and this will be expected to outperform the market in an upswing but underperform in a market correction.

Mispriced shares

Investors have used beta estimates to identify shares with anomalous risk-return characteristics. A share with an unusually attractive expected return for its beta level would be a 'buy' opportunity and one with an unusually low anticipated return a 'sell'. Getting this analysis correct is easier said than done, even if the CAPM worked perfectly.

Measuring portfolio performance

If a fund manager produces a high annual return of, say, 15 per cent, how do you judge if this is due to good share selection? Well, one of the elements to consider is the systematic risk of the fund. If the 15 per cent return has been achieved because particularly risky shares were selected then perhaps you would hesitate to congratulate the manager. For example, if the beta risk is 1.7, the risk-free rate of return is 8 per cent and the historical risk premium for the market index over the risk-free investment $(r_m - r_f)$ has been 5 per cent then you would expect a return of 16.5 per cent:

$$r_j = r_f + \beta\,(r_m - r_f) = 8 + 1.7(5) = 16.5\%$$

On the other hand, if the beta of the portfolio is only 0.8 you might be willing to agree to that promotion the fund manager has been pushing for (expected return on the fund would be 8 + 0.8(5) = 12%).

Calculating the required rate of return on a firm's investment projects

If it is true that shareholders price a company's shares on the basis of the perceived beta risk of the firm as a whole, and the firm may be regarded as a collection of projects, then investors will require different rates of return depending on the systematic risk of each new project that the company embarks upon. Consider the firm in **Exhibit 5.37** which, for current projects, demands a return of 15 per cent (assume the firm is financed by equity only). If another project were started with a similar level of risk then it would be reasonable to calculate NPV on the basis of a discount rate of 15 per cent. This is the opportunity cost of capital for the shareholders – they could obtain 15 per cent by investing their money in shares of other firms in a similar risk class. If, however, the firm were to invest in project A with a risk twice the normal level, management would be doing their shareholders a disservice if they sought a mere 15 per cent rate of return. At this risk level shareholders can get 24 per cent on their money elsewhere. This sort of economic decision making will result in projects being accepted when they should have been rejected. Conversely, project B, if discounted at the standard rate of 15 per cent, will be rejected when it should have been accepted. It produces a return of 13 per cent when all that is required is a return of 11 per cent for this risk class. It is clear that this firm should accept any project lying above the sloping line and reject any project lying below this line.

Exhibit 5.37	Rates of return for projects of different systematic risk levels

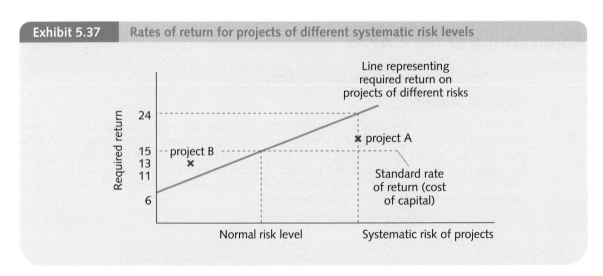

The rule taught in Chapter 2 that a firm should accept any project that gives a return greater than the firm's opportunity cost of capital now has to be refined. This rule can only be applied if the marginal project has the same risk level as the existing set of projects. Projects with different risk levels require different levels of return.

Accepted theory and controversial theory

This is a good point at which to recap, and to point out those issues that are generally accepted and those that are controversial.

- Shareholders demand a higher return for riskier assets – **uncontroversial**.
- Risk-averters are wise to diversify – **uncontroversial**.
- The risk of securities (for example shares) has two elements: (a) unsystematic risk factors specific to firms which can be diversified away; and (b) systematic risk caused by risk factors common to all firms – **uncontroversial**.
- Investors will not be rewarded for bearing unsystematic risk – **uncontroversial**.
- Different shares have different degrees of sensitivity to the systematic risk elements – **uncontroversial**.
- Systematic risk is measured by beta which, in practice, is calculated as the degree of co-movement of a security's return with a market index return – **highly controversial**. As we will see later, some researchers believe beta has no effect on the level of returns earned on shares (that is, there is no relationship, and the SML does not exist); others believe that beta is one of a number of systematic risk factors influencing share returns.
- Beta, as calculated by examining past returns, is valid for decision making concerned with the future – **controversial**.

Technical problems with the CAPM

There are two issues that need to be addressed if the CAPM is to be a valid and useful tool in the commercial world. First, the CAPM has to be workable from the technical point of view. Second, the users have to be reassured that the CAPM, through its emphasis on beta, does accurately describe the returns witnessed on shares and securities. This second issue has been examined in scores of marketplace studies. The results of some of them are discussed in the next section; here we concentrate on the technical problems.

Measuring beta

The mathematics involved in obtaining a historic beta are straightforward enough; however, it is not clear whether it is more appropriate to use weekly or monthly data, or whether the observation period should be three, five or ten years. (Some people observe market and share returns over a mere 30 days!) Each is likely to provide a different estimate of beta. Even if this issue is resolved, the difficulty of using a historical measure for estimating a future relationship is very doubtful. Betas tend to be unstable over time. This was discovered as long ago as the early 1970s. For a more recent example take Marks & Spencer; in 1997 its beta was 0.95. A mere three years later Datastream calculated (based on the five years to 2000) its value at less than half that, at 0.44. In 2005 the same organization calculated M&S's beta at 0.48. For Sainsbury's the change is even more dramatic: 0.60 in 1997, 0.19 in 2000, 0.93 in 2005.

Ex ante theory with *ex post* testing

Applications of the CAPM tend to be focused on the future, for example deciding whether a share will provide a sufficiently high return to compensate for its risk level. Thus, it is investors' *expectations* that drive share prices. The CAPM follows this *ex ante* (before the event) line of reasoning; it describes *expected* returns and *future* beta. However, when it comes to testing the theory, we observe what has already occurred – these are *ex post* observations. There is usually a large difference between investors' expectations and the outcome. Therefore when we obtain, say, the risk premium for the market from historical data (*ex post*) we may be making an error in assuming that this is the appropriate rate today for calculating the required rate of return for an input to our *ex ante* (forward looking) analysis of say an investment project.

The market portfolio is unobtainable

In theory the market portfolio consists of a portion of all the potential assets in the world weighted in proportion to their respective market values. In practice, just identifying, let alone obtaining, the market portfolio is pretty well impossible. Consider what you would need to do. It would be necessary to identify all possible assets: that is, all the securities issued by firms in every country of the world, as well as all government debt, buildings and other property, cash and metals. Other possibilities for inclusion would be consumer durables and what is called human capital – the skills and knowledge of people. The value of these assets is clearly very difficult to assess. Because of these difficulties practitioners of the CAPM use market portfolio proxies such as broad share indices. Richard Roll (1977) has put forward the argument that the impossibility of obtaining or even identifying the market portfolio means that the CAPM is untestable. Using proxies can lead to conflicting results and the CAPM is not being properly employed.

One-period model

Investments usually involve a commitment for many years, whether the investment is made by a firm in real assets or by investors purchasing financial assets. However, the CAPM is based on parameters measured at one point in time. Key variables such as the risk-free rate of return might, in reality, change. A strict interpretation of the CAPM would insist on the use of the 3-month Treasury bill rate of return sold by a reputable government to investors (lending to a (reputable) government for three months is as safe as you are going to get). In 2003, for example, US Treasury bill rates fell to as low as 1 per cent. If this is used for r_f the required rate of return for an average risk-level share is about 5–6 per cent. For shares or projects within firms with a beta of 0.4 some analysts (and, it would seem, some textbook writers) would ask for a return of less than 4 per cent (less than individuals can get on savings accounts put at very low risk). This is odd given that many of these firms are investing in projects with 5–15-year lives, not three months. Furthermore, this was at a time when lending to the government could gain you return of 4.5 per cent, if you lent for five years or more. The practical solution is to use long-term government bond rates for r_f – more on this in Chapter 8.

Unrealistic assumptions

The CAPM is created on the foundation of a number of assumptions about the behaviour of investors and the operation of capital markets. Here are some of them:

- Investors are rational and risk averse.
- Investors are able to assess returns and standard deviations. Indeed, they all have the same forecasts of returns and risk because of the free availability of information.
- There are no taxes or transaction costs.
- All investors can borrow or lend at the risk-free rate of interest.
- All assets are traded and it is possible to buy a fraction of a unit of an asset.

Clearly some of these assumptions do not reflect reality. But then, that is the way of economic modelling – it is necessary to simplify in order to explain real-world behaviour. In a sense it is not of crucial importance whether the assumptions are realistic. The important consideration is whether the model describes market behaviour. If it has some degree of predictive power about real-world relationships then it would be reasonable to overlook some of its technical problems and absurd assumptions.

Does the CAPM work in practice?

Researchers have sidestepped or ignored the technical and theoretical problems to try to see if taking on higher risk, as measured by beta, is rewarded by higher return, as described by the CAPM. More significantly, they have tried to establish if beta is the *only* factor influencing returns.

Empirical research carried out in the twenty years or so following the development of the CAPM tended to support the model. Work by Black *et al.* (1972) and Fama and MacBeth (1973), among dozens of others, demonstrated that risk when measured by beta did have an influence on return. Eugene Fama and James MacBeth, for instance, allocated all the shares listed on the New York Stock Exchange between 1935 and 1966 to 20 portfolios. Over five-year periods monthly returns on specific shares and the market index were observed to calculate each share's beta. The shares were then allocated to portfolios. Portfolio 1 contained the 5 per cent of shares with the lowest betas. Portfolio 2 consisted of the second-lowest 5 per cent of shares as measured by their betas, and so on. Then a comparison was made for each subsequent four-year period between the calculated betas and the rate of return earned on each portfolio. If beta explained returns completely then the expectation is that the graphical plot points of beta and returns would be described by a straight line. The results did not show a perfect relationship. However, the plot points were generally placed around a Security Market Line and Fama and MacBeth felt able to conclude that 'there seems to be a positive trade-off between returns and risk'.

While the early empirical work helped to spread the acceptance of the CAPM, a few nagging doubts remained because, in general, the results gave only limited support to the notion that beta completely explains returns. An overview of these studies (presented in diagram form in Exhibit 5.38) gives the following conclusions. First, the intercept value for the Security Market Line (SML) tends to be higher than the risk-free rate of return, r_f. Perhaps this indicates other risk factors at play, or perhaps investors expected to be compensated for accepting unsystematic risk. Second, the slope of the SML is much flatter than theory would imply – that is, low-risk shares tend to show rates of return higher than theory would suggest and high beta shares show lower returns than the CAPM predicts. Third, when individual shares are examined, the R^2 (coefficient of determination) of the characteristic line is low, suggesting that systematic risk as measured by beta is only a very small part of the explanation of the overall variability in share returns. Unsystematic risk and other types of systematic risk have far more significant effects on returns.

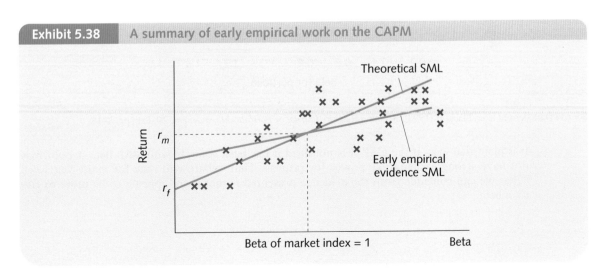

Exhibit 5.38   A summary of early empirical work on the CAPM

Work carried out in more recent years has generally caused more problems for the CAPM. For example Fischer Black (1993) discovered major differences in the strength of the beta-return relationship in the period 1931–65 compared with the period 1966–91. Ironically, up until the time of the development of the CAPM in the mid-1960s, the model seems to work reasonably well; but following its development and subsequent implementation the relationship breaks down. In his paper published in 1993 Black simulates a portfolio strategy that investors might adopt. The shares of quoted US companies (on the New York Stock Exchange) are allocated on an annual basis to 10 categories of different beta levels. Each year the betas are recalculated from the returns over the previous 60 months. The first investment portfolio is constructed by hypothetically purchasing all those shares within the top 10 per cent of beta values. As each year goes by the betas are recalculated and shares that are no longer in the top 10 per cent are sold and replaced by shares which now have the highest levels of beta. The second portfolio consists of the 10 per cent of shares with the next highest betas and this is reconstituted each year.

If ten portfolios with different levels of beta are created it should be possible to observe the extent to which beta risk is related to return in the period after portfolio formation. The pre-1965 data confirm a risk-return relationship roughly corresponding to the CAPM but with a flatter line. However, the post-1965 data (in **Exhibit 5.39**) show a complete absence of a relationship. Both the high-beta portfolio and the low-beta portfolio show average annual returns over the risk-free rate of 6 per cent. A further blow to the CAPM came with the publication of Eugene Fama and Kenneth French's (1992) empirical study of US share returns over the period 1963–90. They found 'no reliable relation between β, and average return'. In the last fifteen years there has been an avalanche of research casting doubt on whether investors are demanding higher returns for higher betas

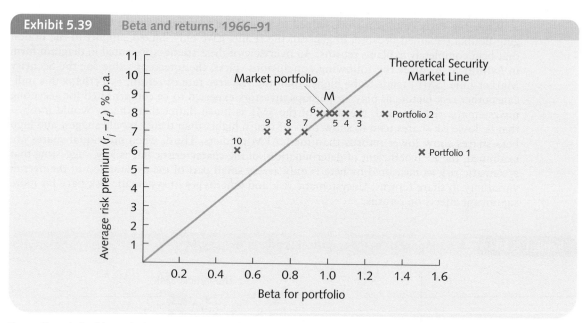

Exhibit 5.39   Beta and returns, 1966–91

Source: Data derived from Black, F. (1993) 'Beta and Return', *Journal of Portfolio Management*, 20, Fall, pp. 8–18.

It is plain that even if the CAPM is not dead it has been severely wounded. Beta may or may not have strong explanatory power for returns. That debate will rage for many years yet. What we can conclude from the evidence presented is that there appears to be more to risk than beta.

Factor models

The capital asset pricing model assumes that there is a single factor influencing returns on securities. This view has been difficult to sustain over recent years given the empirical evidence and theoretical doubts. It also seems to defy common sense; for example, it seems reasonable, and is observed in practice, that the returns on a share respond to industry or sector changes as well as to the general market changes.

Multi-factor models are based on the notion that a security's return may be sensitive to a variety of factors. Using these models the analyst attempts, first, to identify the important influences within the business and financial environment and, second, measure the degree of sensitivity of particular securities to these factors. The most discussed models are the Arbitrage Pricing Theory developed by Stephen Ross and the three-factor model developed by Eugene Fama and Kenneth French. While this line of enquiry is interesting, multi-factor model building and usage is beset with its own problems and we still do not have a universally accepted and employed model.

Concluding comments

Selecting shares (or other types of securities, projects or assets) on the basis of expected returns alone is inadequate. The additional dimensions of risk and the ability to reduce risk through diversification must be taken into account. In trying to achieve a low standard deviation it is not enough to invest in a large number of securities. The fundamental requirement is to construct a portfolio in which the securities have low covariance between them. Thus, to invest in the shares of 100 different engineering firms will not bring about as many benefits of diversification as the same sized portfolio spread between the sectors of paper manufacturers, retailers, media companies, telecommunications operators, computer software producers, etc. Returns on firms in the same industry are likely to respond in similar ways to economic and other events, to greater or lesser degrees, and so may all do badly at the same time. Firms in different industries are likely to have lower covariances than firms within an industry.

On asset pricing models, it is clear that we are far from the end of the road of discovery. We have not yet reached *the* answer. However, the theoretical and empirical work has helped to clarify some important matters. The distinction between systematic and unsystematic risk is an important one. It seems reasonable to focus on the former when describing the relationship between risk and return. It also seems reasonable to assume that one of the systematic risk factors is the general movement of the securities market.

Investors' buying and selling actions have given us two benchmarks by which to judge returns; if the investment is without systematic risk then the risk-free rate of return, approximated by the returns on government-issued securities, gives us the marker at the lower end of risk spectrum; we also have a revealed demand for a risk premium of around 5 per cent for investors accepting a risk level equivalent to that on the average ordinary share. The problem is that we cannot unequivocally, given the recent empirical evidence, draw a straight line between these two plot points with beta values placed on the x-axis. The relationship appears to be far more complex – the 'x-axis' probably consists of numerous risk factors. Nevertheless a finding of sorts emerges: higher risk, however defined, requires higher return. Therefore, for a company trying to estimate the rate of return a shareholder will require from a project, it is right that the estimate is calculated after taking account of some measure of systematic risk. If the project has a systematic risk which is lower than that on the average share then it would seem sensible that the returns attributable to shareholders on this project should be somewhere between the risk-free rate and the risk-free rate plus, say, 5 per cent. If the project has a systematic risk greater than that exhibited by shares generally then the returns required for shareholders will be more than the risk-free rate plus, say, 5 per cent.

The tricky part is calculating the systematic risk level. In the heyday of the CAPM this was simple: beta was all that was necessary. Today we have to allow for a multiplicity of systematic risk factors, and these are not clearly defined in the literature. Not unnaturally, many business people shrug their shoulders at the prospect of such a burdensome approach and fall back on their 'judgement' to adjust for the risk of a project. In practice it is extremely difficult to state precisely the riskiness of a project – we are dealing with future uncertainties about cash flows from day-to-day business operations subject to sudden and unforeseen shocks. The pragmatic approach is to avoid precision and simply place each proposed project into one of three risk categories: low, medium or high. This neatly bypasses the complexities laid on by the theorists and also accurately reflects the fact that decisions made in the real world are made with less than complete knowledge. Mechanical decision making within the firm based on oversimplistic academic models is often a poor substitute for judgement recognising the imperfections of reality.

Having been so critical of the theoretical models we have to be careful not to 'throw out the baby with the bathwater'. The academic debate has enabled us to ask the right questions and to focus on the key issues when enquiring what it is we should be doing to enhance share-holder value. It has also enabled a greater understanding of price setting in the financial markets and insight into the behaviour of investors.

The road is long and winding but the vistas revealed along the way provide enlightenment, if only of the kind captured in the following phrase: 'The fool says he is knowledgeable and has the answers; the wise man says he has much to learn.'

Key points and concepts

- The one-year holding period return: $R = \dfrac{D_1 + P_1 - P_0}{P_0}$ Use IRR-type calculation for multi-period returns.

- With **perfect negative correlation** the risk on a portfolio can fall to zero if an appropriate allocation of funds is made. With **perfect positive correlations** between the returns on investments, both the expected returns and the standard deviations of portfolios are weighted averages of the expected returns and standard deviations, respectively, of the constituent investments.

- The **correlation coefficient** ranges from –1 to +1. Perfect negative correlation has a correlation coefficient of –1. Perfect positive correlation has a correlation coefficient of +1.

- **The degree of risk reduction** for a portfolio depends on: (a) the extent of statistical interdependency between the returns on different investments; and (b) the number of securities in the portfolio.

- **Portfolio expected returns** are a weighted average of the expected returns on the constituent investments: $R_P = aR_A + (1 - a) R_B$

- **Portfolio standard deviation** is less than the weighted average of the standard deviation of the constituent investments (except for perfectly positively correlated investments):

$$\sigma_P = \sqrt{a^2\sigma_A^2 + (1 - a)^2\, \sigma_B^2 + 2a(1 - a)\mathrm{cov}(R_A, R_B)}$$

- **Covariance** means the extent to which the returns on two investments move together:

$$\mathrm{cov}(R_A, R_B) = \sum_{i=1}^{n} \{(R_A - \bar{R}_A)\,(R_B - \bar{R}_B)\,p_i\}$$

- **Covariance and the correlation coefficient** are related. Covariance can take on any positive or negative value. The correlation coefficient is confined to the range –1 to +1.

- **Total risk** consists of two elements: (a) **systematic risk** (or market risk, or non-diversifiable risk) – risk factors common to all firms; (b) **unsystematic risk** (or specific risk, or diversifiable risk).

- **Unsystematic risk can be eliminated by diversification**. An efficient market will not reward unsystematic risk.

Key points and concepts continued

● **Beta** measures the covariance between the returns on a particular share with the returns on the market as a whole.

● The **Security Market Line (SML)** shows the relationship between risk as measured by beta and expected returns.

● The equation for the **capital asset pricing model** is: $r_i = r_f + \beta (r_m - r_f)$

● **Some examples of the CAPM's application:** (a) portfolio selection; (b) identifying mispriced shares; (c) measuring portfolio performance; (d) rate of return on firm's projects.

● **Technical problems with the CAPM:** (a) measuring beta; (b) *ex ante* theory but *ex post* testing and analysis; (c) unobtainability of the market portfolio; (c) one-period model; (d) unrealistic assumptions.

● **Early research** seemed to confirm the **validity of beta** as the measure of risk influencing returns. **Later work cast serious doubt** on this. Some researchers say beta has no influence on returns.

● **Beta is not the only determinant of return. Multi-factor models** allow for a variety of influences on share returns, but the validity and usefulness of these models is doubted by many.

Further reading

Publications with data on share and bond returns include: Barclays Capital annual *Equity Gilt Studies*, Dimson, E., Marsh, P. and Staunton, M. (2002).

Books with more technical/theoretical detail: Blake, D. (2000), Cochrane, J.H. (2001), Damodaran, A. (1999), Elton, E.J., Gruber, M.J., Brown, S.J. and Goetzmann, W.N. (2003), Fama, E.F. and Miller, M.H. (1972), Haugen, R.A. (2001), McKinsey: Koller, Goedhart and Wessels (2005), Ross, S.A., Westerfield, R.W. and Jaffe, J. (2002), Sharpe, W.F., Alexander, G.J. and Bailey, J.V. (1999), Solnik, B.H. and McLeavey, D. (2003).

For views on risk and return of market practitioners see: Buffett, W. (1993 letter to shareholders), Dreman, D. (1998), Graham, B. (1973, 2003), Lowenstein, L. (1991), Malkiel, B.G. (1990), Montier, J. (2002).

Academic papers advancing the theories/models: Black, F. (1972), Fama, E.F. and French, K.R. (1993), Friend, I. and Blume, M. (1970), Frost, P.A. and Savarino, J.E. (1986), Lewis, K. (1996), Lintner, J. (1965), Markowitz, H.M. (1952), Markowitz, H.M. (1959), Markowitz, H.M. (1991), Mossin, J. (1966), Roll, R. (1977), Ross, S.A. (1974), Ross, S.A. (1976), Sharpe, W.F. (1963), Sharpe, W.F. (1964), Tobin, J. (1958), Treynor, J. (1965).

Academic papers showing empirical evidence on portfolio theory or asset pricing: Adedeji, A. (1997), Arnott, R. and Bernstein, P. (2002), Barry, C.B., Peavy J.W. (III) and Rodriguez, M. (1998), Black, F. (1993), Black, F., Jensen, M.C. and Scholes, M. (1972), Blume, M.E. (1971), Blume, M.E. (1975), Blume, M. and Friend, I. (1973), Chan, A. and Chui, A.P.L. (1996), Chan, L.K.C. and Lakonishok, J. (1993), Chi-Hsiou Hung, D., Shackleton, M. and Xu, X. (2004), Cooper, I. and Kaplanis, E. (1994), Corhay, A., Hawawini, G. and Michel, P. (1987), Divecha, A.B., Drach, J. and Stefek, D. (1992), Fama, G. and French, K. (1992), Fama, E.F. and French, K.R. (1995), Fama, E.F. and French, K.R. (1996), Fama E.F. and French, K.R. (2002), Fama, E.F. and MacBeth, J. (1973), Friend, I., Westerfield, R. and Granito, M. (1978), Fuller, R.J. and Wong, G.W. (1988), Hsia, C-C, Fuller, B.R. and Chen, B.Y.J. (2000), Hung, D. C-H., Shackleton, M. and Xu, X. (2004), Jorion, P. (1992), Kaplanis, E. and Schaefer, S. (1991), Lakonishok, J. and Shapiro, A.C. (1984), Lakonishok, J. and Shapiro, A.C. (1986), Levy, H. (1978), Levy, R.A. (1971), Mehra, R. (2003), Mehra, R. and Prescott, E.C. (1985), Michaud, R.O. (1989), Michaud, R.O., Bergstorm, G.L., Frashure, R.D. and Wolahan, B.K. (1996), Miles, D. and Timmermann, A. (1996), Reinganum, M.R. (1982), Roll, R. and Ross, S.A. (1980), Rosenberg, B. and Rudd, A. (1986), Rouwenhorst, K.G. (1999), Rouwenhorst, K.G., Heston, S. and Wessels, R.E. (1999), Solnik, B.H. (1974), Spiedell, L.S. and Sappenfield, R. (1992), Strong, N. and Xu, X.G. (1997), Wagner, W.H. and Lau, S. (1971).

Self-review questions

1 How are holding-period returns calculated?

2 How do you calculate the risk on a two-asset portfolio?

3 Show how the covariance and correlation coefficient are related.

4 Explain the necessary conditions for the standard deviation on a portfolio to be zero.

5 A risk-averse investor currently holds low-risk shares in one company only. In what circumstances would it be wise to split the fund by purchasing shares in a high-risk and high-return share?

6 'The objective of portfolio investment is to minimise risk.' Do you agree?

7 Why is the standard deviation on a portfolio not a weighted average of the standard deviations of the constituent securities?

8 Outline the difference between systematic and unsystematic risk.

9 State the equation for the Security Market Line.

10 What problems are caused to the usefulness of the CAPM if betas are not stable over time?

11 What influences the beta level for a particular share?

12 List the theoretical and practical problems of the CAPM.

13 In 2000, 2001 and 2002 the return on UK shares was less than the return on UK Government bonds. Why don't we take the most recent returns for $r_m - r_f$ in the CAPM rather than the long-term historical average $r_m - r_f$?

Quick numerical questions

1 What is the holding-period return for a share which cost £2.50, was held for a year and then sold for £3.20, and which paid a dividend at the end of the holding period of 10p?

2 Calculate the percentage holding-period return for a share that is held for three months and sold for £5. The purchase price was £4.80 and no dividend is payable.

3 Shares in Whitchat plc can be purchased today for £1.20. The expected dividend in one year is 5p. This is expected to be followed by annual dividends of 6p and 7p respectively in the following two years. The shares are expected to be sold for £2 in three years. What is the average annual rate of return? What is the three-year holding-period return?

4 Company X has a beta value of 1.3, the risk-free rate of return is 8 per cent and the historical risk premium for shares over the risk-free rate of return has been 5 per cent. Calculate the return expected on shares in X assuming the CAPM applies.

5 The risk-free return is 9 per cent, Company J has a beta of 1.5 and an expected return of 20 per cent. Calculate the risk premium for the share index over the risk-free rate assuming J is on the Security Market Line.

Questions and problems

An asterisk* indicates that the answers are reserved for the Lecturer's Guide.

1 The returns on shares S and T vary depending on the state of economic growth.

State of economy	Probability of economic state occurring	Returns on S if economic state occurs (%)	Returns on T if economic state occurs (%)
Boom	0.15	45	18
Growth	0.70	20	17
Recession	0.15	–10	16

Required

a Calculate the expected return and standard deviation for share S.
b Calculate the expected return and standard deviation for share T.
c What is the covariance between returns on S and returns on T?
d Determine a portfolio expected return and standard deviation if two-thirds of a fund are devoted to S and one-third devoted to T.

> **AN EXCEL SPREADSHEET SHOWING THESE CALCULATIONS IS AVAILABLE AT**
> www.pearsoned.co.uk/arnold

2* (*Examination level if combined with Question 3*) The probability of a hot summer is 0.2. The probability of a moderately warm summer is 0.6, whereas the probability of a wet and cold summer is 0.2. If a hot summer occurs then the return on shares in the Ice Cream Manufacturing Company will be 30 per cent. If moderately warm the return will be 15 per cent, and if cold 2 per cent. What is the expected return and the standard deviation?

3* Splash plc owns a swimming pool near to a major seaside resort town. Holidaymakers boost the turnover of this firm when they are unable to use the beach on cold and wet days. Thus Splash's returns are best when the weather is poor. The returns on the shares are shown in the table below, together with the probability of when a particular weather 'event' may occur.

Event	Probability	Returns on shares in Splash plc (%)
Hot weather	0.2	5
Modestly warm	0.6	15
Cold weather	0.2	20
	1.0	

a Calculate the expected return and the standard deviation of a share in Splash plc.
b Given the data on the Ice Cream Manufacturing Company (ICMC) in Question 2 and Splash plc, now calculate the expected returns and standard deviation of the following portfolios:

Portfolio	Proportion of funds invested in ICMC	Proportion of funds invested in Splash
A	0.80	0.20
B	0.50	0.50
C	0.25	0.75

c Describe the circumstances in which diversification can and cannot reduce standard deviation.

> AN EXCEL SPREADSHEET SHOWING THESE CALCULATIONS IS AVAILABLE IN THE
> LECTURERS-ONLY SECTION AT www.pearsoned.co.uk/arnold

4   (*Examination level*) Suppose that Mrs Qureshi can invest all her savings in shares of Ihser plc, or all her savings in Resque plc. Alternatively she could diversify her investment between these two. There are three possible states of the economy, boom, growth or recession, and the returns on Ihser and Resque depend on which state will occur.

State of the economy	Probability of state of the economy occurring	Ihser return (%)	Resque return (%)
Boom	0.3	40	10
Growth	0.4	30	15
Recession	0.3	−10	20

Required

a   Calculate the expected return, variance and standard deviation for each share.
b   Calculate the expected return, variance and standard deviation for the following diversifying allocations of Mrs Qureshi's savings:
  i   50% in Ihser, 50% in Resque;
  ii   10% in Ihser, 90% in Resque.
c   Explain the relationship between risk reduction and the correlation between individual financial security returns.
d   Share A has a beta of 2, share B has a beta of 0.5 and C a beta of 1. The riskless rate of interest is 7 per cent and the risk premium for the market index has been 5 per cent. Calculate the expected returns on A, B and C (assuming the CAPM applies).
e   Describe and explain the characteristic line

5   'Last year I bought some shares. The returns have not been as predicted by the CAPM.' Is this sufficient evidence to reject the CAPM?

6   Shares in M and N lie on the Security Market Line.

	Share M	Share N
Expected return	18%	22%
Beta	1	1.5
(assume the CAPM holds)		

a   What is the riskless rate of return and the risk premium on the market index portfolio?
b   Share P has an expected return of 30 per cent and a beta of 1.7. What is likely to happen to the price and return on shares in P given the Security Market Line in (a)?
c   Share Q has an expected return of 10 per cent and a beta of 0.8. What is likely to happen to the price and returns on a share in Q given the Security Market Line in (a)?

7   Explain from first principles the CAPM and how it may be used in financial markets and within a firm for determining the discount used in project appraisal. Why might you have doubts about actually using the model?

8   The directors of Frane plc are considering a project with an expected annual return of 23 per cent, a beta coefficient of 1.4 and a standard deviation of 40 per cent. The risk-free rate of return is 10 per cent and the risk premium for shares generally has been 5 per cent. (Assume the CAPM applies.)

a   Explain whether the directors should focus on beta or the standard deviation given that the shareholders are fully diversified.
b   Is the project attractive to those shareholders? Explain to the directors unfamiliar with the jargon of the CAPM the factors you are taking into account in your recommendation.

9   True or false?

   a A £1,000 investment in the market portfolio combined with a £500 investment in the risk-free security will
      have a beta of 2.
   b The risk premium on the market portfolio of shares has always been 5 per cent.
   c The CAPM states that systematic risk is the only factor influencing returns in a diversified portfolio.
   d Beta has proved to be an excellent predictor of share returns over the past thirty years.
   e Investors expect compensation for risk factors other than beta such as macroeconomic changes.

Assignments

1 If you have access to the estimated probability distribution of returns for some projects within the
   firm, consider the impact of accepting these projects on the overall risk-return profile of the firm. For
   instance, are they positively or negatively correlated with the existing set of activities?

2 (a) Find out your firm's beta from published sources and calculate the rate of return expected from
   your firm's shares on the assumption that the CAPM holds. (b) Investigate how systematic risk factors
   are taken into account when setting discount rates for projects of different risk levels for your firm.
   Write a report detailing how this process might be improved.

Visit www.pearsoned.co.uk/arnold to get access to Gradetracker diagnostic tests, Podcasts, Excel
Spreadsheet Solutions, FT articles, a Flashcard revision tool, Weblinks, a searchable Glossary and more.

CHAPTER **6**

Equity capital

LEARNING OUTCOMES

By the end of this chapter the reader will have a firm grasp of the variety of methods of raising finance by selling shares and understand a number of the technical issues involved. More specifically the reader should be able to:

■ contrast equity finance with debt and preference shares;

■ give an account of the stock markets available to UK firms;

■ explain the admission requirements and process for joining the Official List of the London Stock Exchange and for the Alternative Investment Market;

■ describe the nature and practicalities of rights issues, vendor placings and open offers;

■ give an account of the options open to an unquoted firm wishing to raise external equity finance;

■ explain why some firms become disillusioned with quotation, and present balanced arguments describing the pros and cons of quotation;

■ discuss the meaning of the efficient markets hypothesis and comment on the implications of the evidence for efficiency for investors and corporate management;

■ understand many of the financial terms expressed in the broadsheet newspapers (particularly the *Financial Times*).

Introduction

There are many ways of raising money by selling shares. This chapter looks at the most important. It considers the processes that a firm would have to go through to gain a quotation on the Official List (OL) and raise fresh equity finance. We will examine the tasks and responsibilities of the various advisers and other professionals who assist a company like Oxford BioMedica (Case study 6.1) to present itself to investors in a suitable fashion.

A firm wishing to become quoted may, in preference to the OL, choose to raise finance on the Alternative Investment Market (AIM), also run by the London Stock Exchange, where the regulations and the costs are lower.

In addition to, or as an alternative to, a 'new issue' on a stock market, which usually involves raising finance by selling shares to a new group of shareholders, a company may make a rights issue, in which existing shareholders are invited to pay for new shares in proportion to their present holdings. This chapter explains the mechanics and technicalities of rights issues as well as some other methods, such as placings and open offers.

It is necessary to broaden our perspective beyond stock markets, to consider the equity finance-raising possibilities for firms that are not quoted on an exchange. There are over one million limited liability companies in the UK and only 0.2 per cent of them have shares traded on the recognised exchanges. For decades there has been a perceived financing gap for small and medium-sized firms which has to a large extent been filled by the rapidly growing venture capital/private equity industry, which have supplied share and debt capital to thousands of companies on fast-growth trajectories, such as the company established by Professor Young (Case study 6.1).

Many, if not most, companies are content to grow without the aid of either stock markets or venture capital. For example J.C. Bamford (JCB), which manufactures earth-moving machines, has built a large, export award winning company, without needing to bring in outside shareholders. This contentedness and absence of a burning desire to be quoted is reinforced by the stories which have emerged of companies which became disillusioned with being quoted. The pressures and strains of being quoted are considered by some (for example Philip Green, owner of Arcadia and BHS, and bidder for Marks & Spencer) to be an excessively high price to pay for access to equity finance. We examine some of the arguments advanced against gaining a quotation and contrast these with the arguments a growing company might make for joining a market.

Then, there is the question of whether the stock market prices shares correctly, or is it inefficient in doing so. The answer to this question has important implications way beyond those for managers wishing to raise equity capital. For example, investors are keen to know if particular categories of shares are regularly under- or over-priced. We round off the chapter with a look at share price tables in the *Financial Times*, explaining some of the technical jargon such price-earning ratio and dividend yield.

Case study 6.1   To float or not to float?

Some firms are keen to float on the London Stock Exchange . . .

Alan and Sue Kingsman started an Oxford University-backed company called Oxford BioMedica in 1995. This company develops technologies to treat diseases including cancer, cystic fibrosis, Parkinson's disease and AIDS using gene therapy. The aim is to replace faulty genes.

Alan and Sue are biochemistry academics who lacked the finance needed for future research and development. They raised seed finance in June 1996 (small amounts of start-up money) and then sought several millions by floating on the Alternative Investment Market in December 1996.

Oxford BioMedica was upgraded to the Official List of the London Stock Exchange in April 2001 following a successful £35.5 million fund-raising. In 2003 a further £20.4 million was raised through a rights issue (selling more shares to existing shareholders) to give the company enough cash to see it through to 2007. The company has a number of products in trial. TroVax is an anti-cancer vaccine. MetXia is a gene therapy for breast cancer. It also has gene therapy approaches to Parkinson's disease (ProSavin) and loss of eyesight (RetinoStat). It is even testing a way of treating spinal injuries through gene therapy. The company has never made a profit, but shareholders are willing to wait. The potential rewards are huge, running into billions of pounds if successful treatments are created. The rewards to patients could be beyond price.

Case study 6.1	Continued

Some firms are desperate to leave the London Stock Exchange . . .

Bernard Matthews, **Richard Branson**, **Alan Sugar**, **Andrew Lloyd Webber** and **Anita and Gordon Roddick** have demonstrated deep dissatisfaction with their companies' quotation. Sir Richard Branson floated the Virgin Group in 1986, then bought it back in 1988. Lord Lloyd Webber bought back his Really Useful Theatre Group in 1990 four years after floating. Alan Sugar had made plain his dislike of the City and its ways, and was particularly annoyed when investors rejected his 1992 offer to buy the Amstrad group for £175m. Bernard Matthews concluded that his turkey business was paying too high a price for a quotation and so he bought back the company in 2000. Anita Roddick, co-founder of Body Shop which floated in 1984, for many years made no secret of her desire to free herself of the misunderstanding and constraints imposed by City Folk, who she once described as 'pin-striped dinosaurs'.

And some firms are content to raise equity finance without being quoted on an exchange . . .

Professor Steve Young, a specialist in information engineering at Cambridge University, became a millionaire by commercialising speech recognition software in the early 1990s. His project proceeded very nicely without a stock market quotation.

Initially his invention was licensed to a US company by Cambridge University. In 1995 the business was further developed by the creation of a UK company, half of which was owned by the US company. The other half was jointly held by the university, Professor Young and fellow academic Phil Woodland.

To grow further they needed 'venture money'. First, the US and UK companies combined and then the merged group took $3m from Amadeus Capital Partners (venture capitalists). By 1999, with 60 staff, the company, Entropic, was in need of more equity capital. Venture capitalists offered $20m, but here the story takes a strange twist. Young thought that it would be wise to have some of the shares bought by corporate investors. Microsoft was approached; they said they were not interested in making small corporate investments. A few weeks later, however, Microsoft telephoned and offered to buy the whole company instead. The deal is secret, but is thought to be worth tens of millions of pounds. Professor Young has returned to full-time academia a richer man and grateful for the existence of venture capital funds.

What is equity capital?

Ordinary shares

Ordinary shares represent the equity share capital of the firm. The holders of these securities share in the rising prosperity of a company. These investors, as owners of the firm, have the right to exercise control over the company. They can vote at shareholder meetings to determine such crucial matters as the composition of the team of directors. They can also approve or disapprove of major strategic and policy issues such as the type of activities that the firm might engage in, or the decision to merge with another firm. These ordinary shareholders have a right to receive a share of dividends distributed as well as, if the worst came to the worst, a right to share in the proceeds of a liquidation sale of the firm's assets. To exercise effective control over the firm the shareholders will need information; and while management are reluctant to put large amounts of commercially sensitive information which might be useful to competitors into the public domain, they are required to make available to each shareholder a copy of the annual report.

There is no agreement between ordinary shareholders and the company that the investor will receive back the original capital invested. What ordinary shareholders receive depends on how well the company is managed. To regain invested funds an equity investor must either sell the shares to another investor (or, in rare circumstances, to the company – firms are now allowed to repurchase their own shares under strict conditions) or force the company into liquidation, in which case all assets are sold and the proceeds distributed. Both courses of action may leave the investor with less than originally invested. There is a high degree of discretion left to the directors in proposing an annual or semi-annual dividend, and individual shareholders are often effectively powerless to influence the income from a share – not only because of the risk attached to the trading profits which generate the resources for a dividend, but also because of the relative power of directors in a firm with a disparate or divided shareholder body.

Ordinary shareholders are the last in the queue to have their claims met. When the income for the year is being distributed others, such as debenture holders and preference shareholders, get paid first. If there is a surplus after that, then ordinary shareholders may receive a dividend. Also when a company is wound up, employees, tax authorities, trade creditors and lenders all come before ordinary shareholders. Given these disadvantages there must be a very attractive feature to ordinary shares to induce individuals to purchase and keep them. The attraction is that if the company does well there are no limits to the size of the claim equity shareholders have on profit. There have been numerous instances of investors placing modest sums into the shares of young firms who find themselves millionaires. For example, if you had bought £1,000 shares in Racal in 1961, your holding would now be worth millions (Vodafone is one of Racal's creations).

Contrasting equity with debt capital

● **Control**. Debt is very different from equity finance. Usually the lenders to the firm have no official control; they are unable to vote at general meetings and therefore cannot choose directors and determine major strategic issues. However, there are circumstances in which lenders have significant influence. For instance, they may insist that the company does not exceed certain liquidity or solvency ratio levels (*see* negative covenants in Chapter 7, p. 244), or they may take a charge over a particular building as security for a loan, thus restricting the directors' freedom of action over the use and disposal of that building. Entrepreneurs sometimes have a difficult choice to make – they need additional equity finance for the business and are unable to borrow any more, but dislike the notion of inviting external equity investors to buy shares. The choice is sometimes between slow/no growth or dilution of the entrepreneurs' control. External equity providers may impose conditions such as veto rights over important business decisions and the right to appoint a number of directors. In many instances, founders take the decision to forgo expansion in order to retain control.

● **Cost.** Debt finance is less expensive than equity (ordinary share) finance, not only because the costs of raising external funds in this form (for example arrangement fees with a bank or the issue costs of a bond) are lower, but because the annual return required to attract investors is less than for equity. This is because investors recognise that investing in a firm via debt finance is less risky than investing via shares. It is less risky because interest is paid out before dividends are paid even if that means there is nothing left to pay the shareholders a dividend. Thus there is greater certainty of receiving a return than there would be for equity holders. Also, if the firm goes into liquidation, the holders of a debt type of financial security are paid back before shareholders receive anything. Thus, we say that debt holders 'rank' higher than equity holders for annual payouts and liquidation proceeds.

● **Extraordinary profits.** Offsetting the plus-points for debt (from the debt holder's point of view) is the fact that lenders do not, generally, share in the value created by an extraordinarily successful business. They usually receive the contractual minimum and no more, whereas shareholders can gain much more than the minimum required because they are the recipients of any surplus the firm generates.

● **Shock absorption.** With debt the firm is usually committed to regular cash outlays in the form of interest and the repayment of the capital sum through good times and bad, or face the possibility of the lenders taking action to recover their dues by forcing the sale of assets or liquidation. High debt levels therefore pose a risk to the existence of the company – a poor performance over a few years can wipe out shareholders' wealth as the firm digs into the equity base to pay debt obligations. The fact that shares carry no right to pay a dividend or ever repay the capital allows them to act as shock absorbers for the company. When losses are made the company does not have the problem of finding money for a dividend.

- **Dividends cannot be used to reduce taxable profit**. Dividends are paid out of after-tax earnings, whereas interest payments on loans are tax deductible. This affects the relative costs to the company of financing by issuing interest-based securities or financing through ordinary shares. The effect of tax deductibility of interest is shown later in this chapter (in the section on preference shares). When a company pays interest the tax authorities regard this as a cost of doing business and therefore it can be used to reduce the profit subject to tax. This lowers the effective cost to the firm of servicing the debt. Thus, to the attractions of the low required return on debt we must add the benefit of tax deductibility.

Authorised, issued and par values

When a firm is created the original shareholders will decide the number of shares to be *authorised* (the *authorised capital*).[1] This is the maximum amount of share capital that the company can issue (unless shareholders vote to change the limit). In many cases firms do not issue up to the amount specified. For example, Green plc has authorised capital of £5m, split between £1m of preference shares and £4m of ordinary shares. The company has issued all of the preference shares (at par) but the issued ordinary share capital is only £2.5m, leaving £1.5m as *authorised but unissued ordinary share capital*. This allows the directors to issue the remaining £1.5m of capital without being required to ask shareholders for further permission (subject to the rights issue or placing rules – see later in chapter).

Shares have a stated par value, say 25p or 5p. This nominal value usually bears no relation to the price at which the shares could be sold or their subsequent value on the stock market. So let us assume Green has 10 million ordinary shares issued, each with a par value of 25p (£2.5m total nominal value divided by the nominal price per share, 25p = 10m shares); these were originally sold for £2 each, raising £20m, and the present market value is £3.80 per share.

The par value has no real significance[2] and for the most part can be ignored. However, a point of confusion can arise when one examines company accounts because issued share capital appears on the balance sheet at par value and so often seems pathetically small. This item has to be read in conjunction with the *share premium account*, which represents the difference between the price received by the company for the shares and the par value of those shares. Thus, in the case of Green the premium on each share was 200p – 25p = 175p. The total share premium in the balance sheet will be £17.5m.

Limited companies, plcs and listed companies

Limited liability means that the ordinary shareholders are only liable up to the amount they have invested or have promised to invest in purchasing shares. Lenders and other creditors are not able to turn to the ordinary shareholder should they find on a liquidation that the company, as a separate legal 'person', has insufficient assets to repay them in full. This contrasts with the position for a partner in a partnership who will be liable for all the debts of the business to the point where personal assets such as houses and cars can be seized to be sold to pay creditors.

Private companies, with the suffix 'Limited' or 'Ltd', are the most common form of company (over 95 per cent of all companies). The less numerous, but more influential, form of company is a public limited company (or just public companies). These firms must display the suffix 'plc'. The private company has no minimum amount of share capital and there are restrictions on the type of purchaser who can be offered shares in the enterprise, whereas the plc has to have a minimum share capital of £50,000 but is able to offer shares to a wide range of potential investors. Not all public companies are quoted on a stock market. This can be particularly confusing when the press talks about a firm 'going public' – it may have been a

---

[1] Note that not all businesses are incorporated (that is, set up as a separate legal 'person' with its own constitution – memorandum and articles of association), limited liability and issuing shares. Many businesses are set up in an unincorporated fashion, e.g. sole trader or partnership, in which one, two or more people share risks and profits. Each partner is liable for the debts and business actions of the others, to the full extent of his/her resources.

[2] Except that it shows proportional voting and income rights.

public limited company for years and has merely decided to 'come to the market' to obtain a quotation. Strictly speaking, the term 'listed' should only be applied to those firms on the Official List but the term is used rather loosely and shares on the Alternative Investment Market (AIM) are often referred to as being quoted or listed.

Preference shares

Preference shares usually offer their owners a fixed rate of dividend each year, unlike ordinary shares which offer no regular dividend. However, if the firm has insufficient profits the amount paid would be reduced, sometimes to zero. Thus, there is no guarantee that an annual income will be received, unlike with debt capital. The dividend on preference shares is paid before anything is paid out to ordinary shareholders – indeed, after the preference dividend obligation has been met there may be nothing left for ordinary shareholders. Preference shares are attractive to some investors because they offer a regular income at a higher rate of return than that available on fixed interest securities, e.g. bonds. However, this higher return also comes with higher risk, as the preference dividend ranks after bond interest, and upon liquidation preference holders are further back in the queue as recipients of the proceeds of asset sell-offs.

Preference shares are part of shareholders' funds but are not equity share capital. The holders are not usually able to benefit from any extraordinarily good performance of the firm – any profits above expectations go to the ordinary shareholders. Also preference shares usually carry no voting rights, except if the dividend is in arrears or in the case of a liquidation.

Advantages to the firm of preference share capital

Preference share capital has the following advantages to the firm.

1 *Dividend 'optional'* Preference dividends can be omitted for one or more years. This can give the directors more flexibility and a greater chance of surviving a downturn in trading. Although there may be no legal obligation to pay a dividend every year the financial community is likely to take a dim view of a firm which missed a dividend – this may have a deleterious effect on the ordinary share price as investors become nervous and sell (dividends cannot be paid to ordinary shareholders before preference dividend arrears are cleared).

2 *Influence over management* Preference shares are an additional source of capital which, because they do not (usually) confer voting rights, do not dilute the influence of the ordinary shareholders on the firm's direction.

3 *Extraordinary profits* The limits placed on the return to preference shareholders mean that the ordinary shareholders receive all the extraordinary profits when the firm is doing well (unless the preference shares are 'participating' – *see* below).

4 *Financial gearing considerations* There are limits to safe levels of borrowing. Preference shares are an alternative, if less effective, shock absorber to ordinary shares because of the possibility of avoiding the annual cash outflow due on dividends. In some circumstances a firm may be prevented from raising finance by borrowing as this increases the risk of financial distress (*see* Chapter 11), and the shareholders may be unwilling to provide more equity risk capital. If this firm is determined to grow by raising external finance, preference shares are one option.

Disadvantages to the firm of preference share capital

Preference share capital also has disadvantages to the firm.

1 *High cost of capital* The higher risk attached to the annual returns and capital cause preference shareholders to demand a higher level of return than debt holders.

2 *Dividends are not tax deductible* Because preference shares are regarded as part of share-holders' funds the dividend is regarded as an appropriation of profits. Tax is payable on the firm's profit before the deduction of the preference dividend. In contrast, lenders are not regarded as having any ownership rights and interest has to be paid whether or not a profit is made. This cost is regarded as a legitimate expense reducing the profit subject to tax. In recent years preference shares have become a relatively unpopular method of raising finance because bonds and bank loans, rival types of long-term finance, have this tax advantage. This is illustrated by the example of companies A and B. Both firms have raised £1m, but Company A sold bonds yielding 8 per cent, Company B sold preference shares offering a dividend yield of 8 per cent. (Here we assume the returns are identical for illustration pur-poses – in reality the return on preference shares might be a few percentage points higher than that on bonds.) *See* Exhibit 6.1.

Exhibit 6.1	Preference shares versus bonds	
	Company A	**Company B**
Profits before tax, dividends and interest	200,000	200,000
Interest payable on bonds	80,000	0
Taxable profit	120,000	200,000
Tax payable @ 30% of taxable profit	36,000	60,000
	84,000	140,000
Preference dividend	0	80,000
Available for ordinary shareholders	84,000	60,000

Company A has a lower tax bill because its bond interest is used to reduce taxable profit, result-ing in an extra £24,000 (£84,000 – £60,000) being available for the ordinary shareholders.

Types of preference shares

There are a number of variations on the theme of preference shares. Here are some features that can be added:

- *Cumulative* If dividends are missed in any year the right to eventually receive a dividend is carried forward. These prior-year dividends have to be paid before any payout to ordinary shareholders.

- *Participating* As well as the fixed payment, the dividend may be increased if the company has high profits. (Usually the additional payment is a proportion of any ordinary dividend declared.)

- *Redeemable* These have a finite life, at the end of which the initial capital investment will be repaid. Irredeemables have no fixed redemption date.

- *Convertibles* These can be converted at the holder's request into ordinary shares at specific dates and on pre-set terms (for example, one ordinary share for every two preference shares). These shares often carry a lower yield (dividend as a proportion of share price) since there is the attraction of a potentially large capital gain.

- *Variable rate* A variable dividend is paid. The rate may be linked to general interest rates, e.g. LIBOR (*see* Chapter 7) or to some other variable factor.

The London Stock Exchange

Large sums of money flow from the savers in society via the London Stock Exchange (LSE) to firms wanting to invest and grow. In 2006 there were over 1,200 UK companies on the Official List and 145 UK companies on the techMARK (also run by the London Stock Exchange). There were also over 1,450 companies on the Exchange's market for smaller and younger companies, the Alternative Investment Market (AIM) – in recent years hundreds of companies have joined AIM each year.

During 2005, UK-listed firms raised new share capital amounting to over £5 billion by coming to the Official List for the first time – a 'new issue' or IPO, initial public offering. Companies already quoted on the Official List sold a further £7 billion of shares through events such as rights issues. AIM companies sold over £6 billion of shares. UK companies also raised money by selling bonds and preference shares.

The LSE is clearly an important source of new finance for UK corporations. However, it is not the most significant source. The most important source of funds is generally from within the firm itself (internal finance). This is the accumulated profits retained within the firm and not distributed as dividends. In an average year retained profits account for about one-half of the new funds for UK firms. These retained earnings are also equity capital because this is money that belongs to shareholders – they have merely allowed companies to use it within the business rather than paying it out to the owners. Thus the amount of equity capital devoted to a firm can grow to be worth millions of pounds largely through the retention of profits, despite the fact that it might have raised only a few thousands by selling shares to investors at its start. The sale of ordinary shares rarely accounts for a significant proportion of capital raised (it is usually less than 15 per cent of funds raised). Following retained earnings, bank loans are often very important for companies, but this does vary significantly. The sale of bonds and preference shares combined generally accounts for less than 5 per cent of new capital put into UK companies.

Floating on the Official List

The Official List (OL) is the main market on the LSE. Companies wishing to be listed have to sign a Listing Agreement, which commits directors to certain high standards of behaviour and levels of reporting to shareholders. This is a market for medium and large established firms with a reasonably long trading history. The costs of launching even a modest new issue runs into hundreds of thousands of pounds and therefore small companies are unable to justify a full main market listing.

To 'go public' and become a listed company is a major step for a firm. The substantial sums of money involved can lead to a new, accelerated phase of business growth. Obtaining a quotation is not a step to be taken lightly; it is a major legal undertaking. The United Kingdom Listing Authority, UKLA (part of the Financial Services Authority),[3] rigorously enforces a set of demanding rules and the directors will be put under the strain of new and greater responsibilities both at the time of flotation and in subsequent years. As the example of RHM shows (*see* Exhibit 6.2), new issues can produce a greater availability of equity finance to fund expansion and development programmes. It may also allow existing shareholders to sell a proportion of their investment and for employees to be rewarded through share option schemes. Not only do shareholders like to know that they can sell when they want to, they may simply appreciate knowing the market price of their holdings even if they have no intention of selling. By contrast, an unquoted firm's shareholders often find it difficult to assess the value of their holding. In addition a floatation can 'raise the profile' of a company both in the financial world and in its product markets, which may give it a competitive edge. A float may also make mergers easier. This is especially true if the payment for the target shares is shares in the acquirer; a quoted share has a valuation placed on it by the market, whereas shares in unquoted companies are less attractive because of the greater doubt about the value.

---

[3] Responsibility for governing admission to listing, the continuing obligations of issuers, the enforcement of those obligations and suspension and cancellation of listing was transferred from the LSE to the UKLA in 2000. However, companies also need to be admitted to trading by the Exchange.

Exhibit 6.2

Flotation price of 275p set for RHM

By Maggie Urry

The flotation price of RHM, the food group whose brands include Hovis, Mr Kipling, Sharwoods and Bisto, was set at 275p yesterday.

The closing price valued the company at slightly more than £1bn.

The offer raised £475m gross for RHM and £118m for Doughty Hanson, the private equity group.

Ian McMahon, chief executive, sold 500,000 shares in the offer and is set to receive £1.38m while retaining 2m shares worth £5.85m at yesterday's close. Andrew Allner,

finance director, sold 200,000 shares for £550,000 and has kept 800,000, worth £2.34m. Paul Wilkinson, who retired as chief executive early in 2003, sold his entire 1.88m shareholding in the sale, worth £5.16.

Source: Financial Times, 20 July 2005, p. 22. Reprinted with permission.

Prospectus

To create a stable market and encourage investors to place their money with companies the UKLA tries to minimise the risk of investing by ensuring that the firms which obtain a quotation abide by high standards and conform to strict rules. For example, the directors are required to prepare a detailed prospectus ('listing particulars') to inform potential shareholders about the company. This may contain far more information about the firm than it has previously dared to put into the public domain. Even without the stringent conditions laid down by the UKLA the firm has an interest in producing a stylish and informative prospectus. A successful flotation can depend on the prospectus acting as a marketing tool as the firm attempts to persuade investors to apply for shares.

The content and accuracy of this vital document is the responsibility of the directors. Contained within it must be three years of audited accounts, details of indebtedness and a statement as to the adequacy of working capital. Statements by experts are often required: valuers may be needed to confirm the current value of property, engineers may be needed to state the viability of processes or machinery and accountants may be needed to comment on the profit figures. All major contracts entered into in the past two years will have to be detailed and a description of the risks facing the firm provided. Any persons with a shareholding of more than 3 per cent have to be named. A mass of operational data is required, ranging from an analysis of sales by geographic area and category of activity, to information on research and development and significant investments in other companies.

The Listing Rules state that the expected market value of the company's shares is to be at least £700,000 to allow for sufficient dealings to take place. However, this is an absurdly small figure in this day and age. Given that the cost of advisers and underwriters to the new issue will be at least £500,000 it is rarely worth floating on the OL unless the market capitalisation is at least £10m.

Conditions and responsibilities imposed

All companies obtaining a full listing must ensure that at least 25 per cent of their share capital is in public hands, to ensure that the shares are capable of being traded actively on the market. If a reasonably active secondary market is not established, trading may become stultified and the shares may become illiquid. 'Public' means people or organisations not associated with the directors or major shareholders.

Directors may find their room for discretion restricted when it comes to paying dividends. Stock market investors, particularly the major institutions, tend to demand regular dividends. Not only do they usually favour consistent cash flow, they also use dividend policy as a kind of barometer of corporate health (*see* Chapter 12). This can lead to pressure to maintain a growing dividend flow, which the unquoted firm may not experience.

There is also a loss of some privacy and autonomy, e.g. greater disclosure of directors' remuneration, responding to the demands of a wider range of shareholders.

There are strict rules concerning the buying and selling of the company's shares by its own directors. The Criminal Justice Act 1993 and the Model Code for Director Dealings have to be followed. Directors are prevented from dealing for a minimum period (normally two months) prior to an announcement of regularly recurring information such as annual results. They are also forbidden to deal before the announcement of matters of an exceptional nature involving unpublished information which is potentially price sensitive. These rules apply to any employee in possession of such information. When directors do buy or sell shares in their company they are required to disclose these dealings publicly.

Suitability

The UKLA tries to ensure that the 'quality of the company' is sufficiently high to appeal to the investment community. The management team must have the necessary range and depth, and there must be a high degree of continuity and stability of management over recent years. Investors do not like to be over-reliant on the talents of one individual and so will expect a team of able directors and managers, and – preferably – a separation of the roles of chief executive and chairman. They also expect to see an appropriately qualified finance director.

The UKLA usually insists that a company has a track record (in the form of accounting figures) stretching back at least three years. However, this requirement has been relaxed since 1993 for scientific research-based companies and companies undertaking major capital projects. In the case of scientific research-based companies there is the requirement that they have been conducting their activity for three years even if no revenue was produced. Some major project companies, for example Eurotunnel, have been allowed to join the market despite an absence of a trading activity or a profit record.

Companies can be admitted to the techMARK, the part of the OL especially reserved for technology-led companies, with only one year of accounts so long as they have a market capitalisation of at least £50m and are selling at least £20m of new or existing shares when floating.

Another suitability factor is the timing of the flotation. Investors often desire stability, a reasonable spread of activities and evidence of potential growth in the core business. If the underlying product market served by the firm is going through a turbulent period it may be wise to delay the flotation until investors can be reassured about the long-run viability.

Other suitability factors are a healthy balance sheet, sufficient working capital, good financial control mechanisms and clear accounting policies.

The issuing process

The issuing process involves a number of specialist advisers (discussed below). The process is summarised in Exhibit 6.3.

The sponsor

Given the vast range of matters that directors have to consider in order to gain a place on the OL it is clear that experts are going to be required to guide firms through the complexities. The key adviser in a flotation is the sponsor. This may be an investment bank, stockbroker or other professional adviser. Directors, particularly of small companies, often first seek advice from their existing professional advisers, for example accountants and lawyers. These may have the necessary expertise (and approval of the UKLA – see www.fsa.gov.uk/ukla for a list of approved sponsors) themselves to act for the company in the flotation or may be able to recommend a more suitable sponsor. Sponsors have to be chosen with care as the relationship is likely to be one that continues long after the flotation. For large or particularly complex issues investment banks are employed, although experienced stockbrokers have been used. The UKLA requires sponsors to certify that a company has complied with all the regulatory requirements and to ensure that all necessary documentation is filed on time.

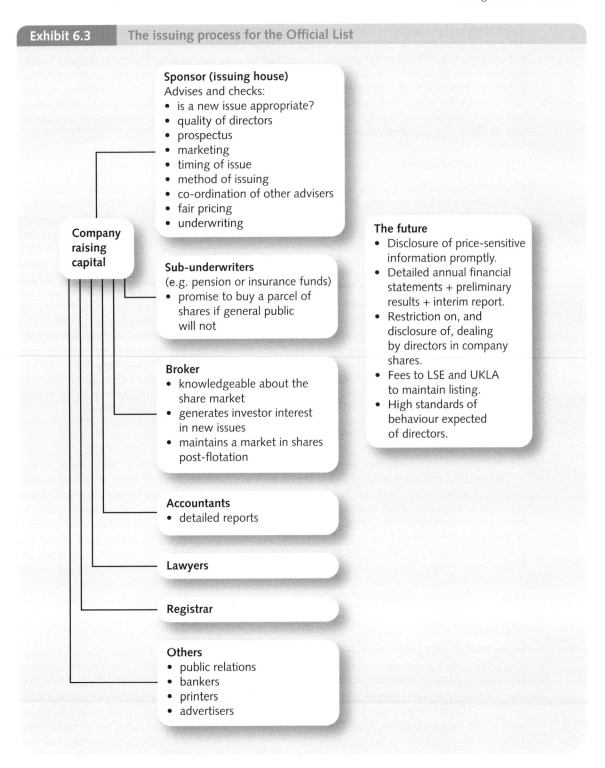

Exhibit 6.3   The issuing process for the Official List

Company raising capital

Sponsor (issuing house)
Advises and checks:
- is a new issue appropriate?
- quality of directors
- prospectus
- marketing
- timing of issue
- method of issuing
- co-ordination of other advisers
- fair pricing
- underwriting

Sub-underwriters
(e.g. pension or insurance funds)
- promise to buy a parcel of shares if general public will not

Broker
- knowledgeable about the share market
- generates investor interest in new issues
- maintains a market in shares post-flotation

Accountants
- detailed reports

Lawyers

Registrar

Others
- public relations
- bankers
- printers
- advertisers

The future
- Disclosure of price-sensitive information promptly.
- Detailed annual financial statements + preliminary results + interim report.
- Restriction on, and disclosure of, dealing by directors in company shares.
- Fees to LSE and UKLA to maintain listing.
- High standards of behaviour expected of directors.

The sponsor (sometimes called the issuing house) will first examine the company and the aspirations of the management team to assess whether flotation is an appropriate corporate objective by taking into account its structure, strategy and capital needs. The sponsor will also comment on the composition of the board and the calibre of the directors. The sponsor may even recommend supplementation with additional directors if the existing team do not come up to the quality expected. Sponsors can be quite forceful in this because they do not want to damage their reputation by bringing a poorly managed company to market. The sponsor will draw up a timetable, which can be lengthy – sometimes the planning period for a successful flotation may extend over two years. There are various methods of floating, ranging from a placing to an offer for sale, and the sponsor will advise on the most appropriate. Another important function is to help draft the prospectus and provide input to the marketing strategy. Throughout the process of flotation there will be many other professional advisers involved and it is vital that their activities mesh into a coherent whole. It is the sponsor's responsibility to coordinate the activities of all the other professional advisers.

Paying underwriters

Shortly before the flotation the sponsor will have the task of advising on the best price to ask for the shares and, at the time of flotation, the sponsor will usually underwrite the issue. Most new issues are underwritten, because the correct pricing of a new issue of shares is extremely difficult. If the price is set too high, demand will be less than supply and not all the shares will be bought. The company is usually keen to have certainty that it will receive money from the issue so that it can plan ahead. To make sure it sells the shares it buys a kind of insurance called underwriting. In return for a fee the underwriter guarantees to buy the proportion of the issue not taken up by the market. An investment bank sponsoring the issue will usually charge a fee of 2 per cent of the issue proceeds and then pays part of that fee, say 1.25 per cent of the issue proceeds, to sub-underwriters (usually large financial institutions such as pension funds and banks) who each agree to buy a certain number of shares if called on to do so. In most cases the underwriters do not have to purchase any shares because the general public are keen to take them up. However, occasionally they receive a shock and have to buy large quantities. As well as coordinating the UKLA's listing process the sponsor will apply to the Exchange to have the company's securities admitted to trading on its markets. The LSE has its own set of admission and disclosure standards that are designed to sit alongside the UKLA's Listing Rules.

The corporate broker

When a broker is employed as a sponsor the two roles can be combined. If the sponsor is, say, an investment bank the UKLA requires that a broker is also appointed. However, most investment banks also have corporate broking arms and so can take on both roles. Brokers play a vital role in advising on share market conditions and the likely demand from investors for the company's shares. They also represent the company to investors to try to generate interest. When debating issues such as the method to be employed, the marketing strategy, the size of the issue, the timing or the pricing of the shares, the company may value the market knowledge the broker has to offer. Brokers can also organise sub-underwriting and in the years following the flotation may work with the company to maintain a liquid and properly informed market in its shares. They may also help raise additional money through rights issues, for example.

Accountant

The reporting accountant in a flotation has to be different from the company's existing auditors, but can be a separate team in the same firm. The accountant will be asked by the sponsor to prepare a detailed report on the firm's financial controls, track record, financing and forecasts (the 'long form' report). Not all of this information will be included in the prospectus but it does serve to reassure the sponsor that the company is suitable for flotation. Accountants may also have a role in tax planning from both the company's viewpoint and that of its shareholders. They also investigate working capital requirements. The UKLA insists that companies show that they have enough working capital for current needs and for at least the next 12 months.

Lawyers

All legal requirements in the flotation preparation and in the information displayed in the prospectus must be complied with. Examples of other legal issues are directors' contracts, changes to the articles of association, re-registering the company as a plc, underwriting agreements and share option schemes.

Lawyers also prepare the 'verification' questions that are used to confirm that every statement in the prospectus can be justified as fact. Directors bear the ultimate responsibility for the truthfulness of the documents.

Registrar

The record on the ownership of shares is maintained by the registrar as shares are bought and sold. They keep the company's register and issue certificates. There are about two dozen major registrars linked up to CREST through which they are required to electronically adjust records of ownership of company shares within two hours of a trade.

After flotation

The UKLA insists on listed companies having 'continuing obligations'. One of these is that all price-sensitive information is given to the market as soon as possible and that there is 'full and accurate disclosure' to all investors at the same time. Information is price sensitive if it might influence the share price or the trading in the shares. Investors need to be sure that they are not disadvantaged by market distortions caused by some participants having the benefit of superior information. Public announcements will be required in a number of instances, for example: the development of major new products; the signing of major contracts; details of an acquisition; a sale of large assets; a change in directors or a decision to pay a dividend. The website www.uk-wire.com and many other financial websites show all major announcements made by companies going back many years.

Listed companies are also required to provide detailed financial statements within six months of the year-end. Firms usually choose to make preliminary profit announcements based on unaudited results for the year a few weeks before the audited results are published. Interim reports for the first half of each accounting year are also required (within four months of the end of the half-year). The penalty for non-compliance is suspension from the Exchange.

Other ongoing obligations include the need to inform the market about director dealings in the company's shares. The UKLA and the Exchange also encourage high standards of corporate governance as set out in the Combined Code on Corporate Governance (see Chapter 1, p. 29). While these standards of behaviour are encouraged they are not required by the UKLA. However, if a company does not comply, it must explain why not in the annual reports.

Methods of issue

The sponsor will look at the motives for wanting a quotation, at the amount of money that is to be raised, at the history and reputation of the firm and will then advise on the best method of issuing the shares. There are various methods, ranging from a full-scale offer for sale to a relatively simple introduction. The final choice often rests on the costs of issue, which can vary considerably. Here are the main options.

Offer for sale

The company sponsor offers shares to the public by inviting subscriptions from institutional and individual investors. Sometimes newspapers carry a notice and an application form. However, most investors will need to contact the sponsor or the broker to obtain an application form. Publications such as *Investors Chronicle* show the telephone numbers to call for each company floating. Also details of forthcoming flotations are available at www.london-stockexchange.com. and on many other financial websites. Normally the shares are offered at a fixed price determined by the company's directors and their financial advisers. A variation of this method is an *offer for sale* by *tender*. Here investors are invited to state a price at which they are willing to buy (above a minimum reserve price). The sponsor gathers the applications and then selects a price that will dispose of all the shares – the strike price. Investors bidding a price above this will be allocated shares at the strike price – not at the price of their bid. Those who bid below the strike price will not receive any shares. This method is useful in situations where it is very difficult to value a company, for instance, where there is no comparable company already listed or where the level of demand is difficult to assess.

Introduction

Introductions do not raise any new money for the company. If the company's shares are already quoted on another stock exchange or there is a wide spread of shareholders, with more than 25 per cent of the shares in public hands, the Exchange permits a company to be 'introduced' to the market. This method may allow companies trading on AIM to move up to the Official List or for foreign corporations to gain a London listing. This is the cheapest method of flotation since there are no underwriting costs and relatively small advertising expenditures. When Carlton and Granada came together to form ITV plc in 2003 they were permitted to float the new company by way of an introduction as both component companies already had a wide spread of investors and these people merely swapped their old shares for shares issued by ITV plc.

Offer for subscription

An offer for subscription is similar to an offer for sale, but it is only partially underwritten. This method is used by new companies that state at the outset that if the share issue does not raise a certain minimum the offer will be aborted. This is a particularly popular method for new investment trusts – if the fund managers do not raise enough to create a large investment company that will be able to pay them large ongoing management fees, then they abandon the whole idea (*see* Chapter 1 for a description of investment trusts).

Placing

In a placing, shares are offered to the public but the term 'public' is narrowly defined. Instead of engaging in advertising to the population at large, the sponsor or broker handling the issue sells the shares to institutions it is in contact with, such as pension and insurance funds. The costs of this method are considerably lower than those of an offer for sale. There are lower publicity costs and legal costs. A drawback of this method is that the spread of shareholders is going to be more limited. To alleviate this problem the Stock Exchange does insist on a large number of placees holding shares after the new issue.

In the 1980s the most frequently used method of new issue was the offer for sale. This ensured a wide spread of share ownership and thus a more liquid secondary market. It also permitted all investors to participate in new issues. Placings were only permitted for small offerings (< £15m) when the costs of an offer for sale would have been prohibitive. Today any size of new issue can be placed. As this method is much cheaper and easier than an offer for sale, companies have naturally switched to placings so there are now few offers for sale.

Intermediaries offer

Another method, which is often combined with a placing, is an intermediaries offer. Here the shares are offered for sale to financial institutions such as stockbrokers. Clients of these intermediaries can then apply to buy shares from them.

Reverse takeover

Sometimes a larger unquoted company makes a deal with a smaller quoted company whereby the smaller company 'takes over' the larger firm by swapping newly created shares in itself for the shares in the unquoted firm currently held by its owners. Because the quoted firm creates and issues more new shares in itself than it had to start with the unquoted firm's shareholders end up with the majority of the shares in the newly merged entity. They therefore now control a quoted company. The only task remaining is to decide on a name for the company – frequently the name of the previously unquoted company is chosen.

Book-building

Selling new issues of shares through book-building is a popular technique in the USA. It is starting to catch on in Europe. Under this method the financial advisers to an issue contact major institutional investors to get from them bids for the shares over a period of eight to ten working days. The investors' orders are sorted according to price, quantity and other factors such as 'firmness' of bid (e.g. a 'strike bid' means the investor will buy a given number of shares within the initial price range, leaving it to others to set the price. A 'limit bid' means the investor would buy a particular quantity at a particular price). These data may then be used to establish a price for the issue and the allocation of shares. Virgin Mobile's sponsors used book-building to place the shares – see next section.

Timetable for a new offer

The various stages of a new share issue will be explained using the example of the flotation of Virgin Mobile on the OL. This timetable is set out in Exhibit 6.4.

Virgin Mobile
Pre-launch publicity

Sir Richard Branson shunned the OL of the London Stock Exchange for many years after buying back Virgin Group in 1988. However, in 2004 he returned. This time, instead of floating a large conglomerate company comprising many businesses, he planned to sell shares in separate companies, each focused on a particular activity. He had already floated Victory Corp, the clothing and cosmetics business, on AIM in 1996; Virgin Express, the Brussels-based and listed airline, in 1997 and, in 2003, Virgin Blue, the Australian airline. To follow the 2004 Virgin Mobile float he was already lining up Virgin Entertainment (retail and cinema), Virgin Atlantic (airline), Trainline.com (rail booking portal), Virgin Active (health clubs), Virgin Rail and Virgin Money for flotation between 2005 and 2010.

The financial markets welcomed him back, understanding that he needed additional funds (£2bn or more) to fund new ventures, such as a mobile phone business and a budget airline in the USA.

For many years before the flotation Virgin Mobile raised its profile with the public with exciting news stories and extensive advertising. Of course, Richard Branson himself is a constant source of publicity for the Virgin companies. Virgin Mobile portrayed itself as an innovative 'virtual' operator (no network infrastructure) with a loyal customer base, particularly with the young. By 2004 it had four million users, an annual turnover of more than £400m and £75m in profits before interest and tax.

Technicalitics

JP Morgan and Morgan Stanley acted as joint bookrunners and as underwriters with co-lead manager Investec Securities. They aimed to raise at least £230m with the sale of between 37 and 43 per cent of the company's shares. However, £50m of the proceeds would have to be paid to T-Mobile. The German company gave up its 50 per cent stake in Virgin Mobile in January 2004, partly in return for receiving a proportion of the proceeds from the flotation. Thus, by July 2004 Virgin Group owned all of the shares in Virgin Mobile.

To strengthen the management team Charles Gurassa, a former British Airways executive, joined the board as chairman. Three other distinguished non-executive directors were also appointed to do the key things that non-execs do: help with strategy and to oversee the quality of stewardship of the executive directors.

Exhibit 6.4	Timetable of an offer for sale and a placing							
Time relative to Impact Day	*1–2 years*	*Several weeks (usually 12–24 weeks)*	*A few days*	*IMPACT DAY*		*A few days*	*2 days to 2 weeks for offer for sale*	*2 weeks or so for an offer for sale*
Stage	Pre-launch publicity.	Sponsor and other advisers consider details such as drawing up accountants report, price and method of issue. Also obtain underwriting, etc.	Pathfinder prospectus • to Press; • to major investors. No firm price	Prospectus published. Price announced in a fixed-price sale offer or placing.	Investors apply and send payments.	Offer closes.	Allotment.	Admission to the Exchange and dealing begins.
Dates for Virgin Mobile (placing)	2002 to 2004	Early 2004	7 July: price range of 235p to 285p is announced.	21 July: a price is given: 200p.				26 July: first dealings.

In the first three weeks of July the directors went on a 'roadshow' – they made presentations to institutional investors at various locations. Roadshows are important not just for marketing the issue, but because they allow sponsors to gather information from investors, such as their opinions of the company and its valuation.

Pathfinder prospectus

On 7 July the Pathfinder prospectus was published and the price range was set at 235p to 285p, valuing the group at £588m to £713m. This is not a firm expectation of the sale price, but a 'test the water' type of price announcement. The institutions responded badly to being asked to pay so much relative to its earnings (profits) per share. After all, Vodafone and MMO_2 traded on lower price-to-earnings ratios. As a result of this feedback the price range was reduced to 200p to 220p on 19 July. There was also a cut in the number of shares to be sold so that only 25 per cent would be in a free float. The need to keep a good reputation in the financial markets, given that he has bigger companies to float over the next few years, may have encouraged Sir Richard to be cautious about the risk of over-pricing.

Impact day

The full prospectus is published on impact day, together with the price. For Virgin Mobile on 21 July the price was set at 200p, valuing the company at £500m. A total of 62.5 million shares were sold by Virgin Group at 200p each, far less than originally hoped for.

Offer closes

In an offer for sale, up to two weeks is needed for investors to consider the offer price and send in payments. There is a fixed cut-off date for applications. In the case of a placing the time needed is much shorter as the share buyers have already indicated to the sponsors and managers their interest and transactions can be expedited between City institutions. In the case of Virgin Mobile the price was announced five days before formal admission to the Exchange, allowing the first proper trading to take place. During those five days 'conditional trading' took place in the 'grey market' (that is, the selling of shares that you *expect* to receive but do not actually hold yet).

Allotment

More than twice as many shares were applied for than were available. The shares are allocated by the sponsors in a placing/book-building depending on commitments made in the book-building process. In an offer for sale allocation can be achieved in a number of different ways. A ballot means that only some investors receive shares (recipients are selected at random). In a scaledown applicants generally receive some shares, but fewer than they applied for. A cut-off point might be used in which applicants for large quantities are excluded.

Dealing begins

Formal dealing in the shares through the Stock Exchange started at 8 a.m. on 26 July. Formal dealing means on the Exchange after the shares have been allocated. The shares traded above the placing price, at 203p, giving investors an immediate profit. However, by the end of the week they were trading 4 per cent less than the placing price.

The Virgin Group managed to take £400m from the float in pre-float dividends and sales of the shares and is still left with 75 per cent of the company.

The Alternative Investment Market (AIM)

There is a long-recognised need for equity capital by small, young companies that are unable to afford the costs of full Official listing. Many stock exchanges have alternative equity markets that set less stringent rules and regulations for joining or remaining quoted (often called second-tier markets).

Lightly regulated or unregulated markets have a continuing dilemma. If the regulation is too lax, scandals of fraud or incompetence will arise, damaging the image and credibility of the market, and thus reducing the flow of investor funds to companies. (This happened to the German market for small companies, Neuer Markt, which had to close in 2002 because of the loss in investor confidence.) On the other hand, if the market is too tightly regulated, with more company investigations, more information disclosure and a requirement for longer trading track records prior to flotation, the associated costs and inconvenience will deter many companies from seeking a quotation.

The driving philosophy behind AIM is to offer young and developing companies access to new sources of finance, while providing investors with the opportunity to buy and sell shares in a trading environment run, regulated and marketed by the LSE. Efforts are made to keep the costs down and make the rules as simple as possible. In contrast to the OL there is no requirement for AIM companies to be a minimum size, to have traded for a minimum period of three years or for a set proportion of their shares to be in public hands – if they wish to sell a mere 1 per cent or 5 per cent of the shares to outsiders then that is acceptable. They do not have to ensure that 25 per cent of the shares are in public hands (that is, not in the hands of dominant shareholders or connected persons).

Investors are reassured about the quality of companies coming to the market by the requirement that the floating firms have to appoint, and retain at all times, a nominated adviser and nominated broker. The nominated adviser ('nomad') is selected by the corporation from a Stock Exchange approved register. These advisers have demonstrated to the Exchange that they have sufficient experience and qualifications to act as a 'quality controller', confirming to the LSE that the company has complied with the rules. Unlike with OL companies there is no pre-vetting of admission documents by the UKLA (or the Exchange) as a lot of weight is placed on the nominated advisers' investigations and informed opinion about the company.

Nominated brokers have an important role to play in bringing buyers and sellers of shares together. Investors in the company are reassured that at least one broker is ready to trade or do its best to match up buyers and sellers. The adviser and broker are to be retained throughout the company's life on AIM. They have high reputations and it is regarded as a very bad sign if either of them abruptly refuses further association with a firm.

Upon flotation an 'AIM admission document' is required – this is similar to a prospectus, but less detailed. AIM companies are also expected to comply with strict rules regarding the publication of price-sensitive information and the quality of annual and interim reports.

When the cost of the nominated adviser's and broker's time is added to those of the Stock Exchange fees, accountants, lawyers, printers and so on, the (administrative) cost of raising capital can be as much as 10–12 per cent of the amount being raised. This, as a proportion, is comparable with the main market but the sums of money raised are usually much less on AIM and so the absolute cost is lower. AIM was designed so that the minimum cost of joining was in the region of £40,000–£50,000, but it has now risen so that frequently more than £300,000 is paid. Most of the additional cost arises on raising funds by selling shares rather than just joining AIM, which costs about £100,000 to £200,000. Nominated advisers' fees have risen because they now incur more investigatory costs due to increasing emphasis put on their policing role by the Stock Exchange.

The real cost savings of floating on AIM rather than the OL come in the continuing annual expense of managing the quotation. For example AIM companies do not have to disclose as much information as companies on the OL. Price-sensitive information will have to be published but normally this will require only an electronic message from the adviser to the Exchange rather than a circular to shareholders. The LSE charges companies an annual fee of over £4,000 to maintain quotation on AIM. If to this is added the cost of financial advisers (nomads are paid an annual fee of £20,000 to £40,000) and of management time spent communicating with institutions and investors, the annual cost of being quoted on AIM runs into many tens of thousands of pounds. This can be a deterrent for some companies. There is an additional incentive for a flotation on AIM rather than the OL: there are tax advantages for shareholders investing in AIM companies via venture capital trusts (see later in this chapter) as well as a lower level of capital gains tax for private (individual investors).

Offsetting the cost advantages AIM has over the OL is the fact that the higher level of regulation and related enhanced image, prestige and security of OL companies means that equity capital can usually be raised at a lower required rate of return (the shares can be sold for more per unit of projected profit).

AIM is not just a stepping-stone for companies planning to graduate to the OL. It has many attractive features in its own right – it has attracted far more companies in recent years than the OL.

techMARK

At the end of 1999, at the height of high technology fever, the London Stock Exchange launched a 'market-within-a-market' called techMARK. This is part of the OL and is therefore technically not a separate market. It is a grouping of technology companies on the OL. One of the reasons for its creation was that many companies lacking the minimum three-year account history required to join the OL had relatively high market values and desired the advantages of being on a prestigious market. The LSE relaxed its rule and permitted a listing if only one year of accounts is available for techMARK companies. This allowed investors to invest through a well-regulated exchange in companies at an early stage of development, such as Freeserve and lastminute.com. At least 25 per cent of their shares must have a free float (in public hands) and they must publish quarterly reports of the company's activities, including financial and non-financial (e.g. number of visitors to the company website for dot.com companies) operating data.

PLUS-quoted shares

Companies that do not want to pay the costs of a flotation on one of the markets run by the LSE and the ongoing annual costs could go for a 'secondary market trading facility' on PLUS. By having their shares quoted on PLUS companies provide a service to their shareholders, allowing them to buy and sell shares at reasonable cost. It also allows the company to gain access to capital, for example by selling more shares in a placing, without submitting to the rigour and expense of a quotation on LSE.

PLUS (originally called OFEX) was set up by broker J.P. Jenkins in 1995 and is now owned by PLUS-Markets Group. It is a dealing facility with few of the rules that apply to the OL or AIM. However, there is an annual fee of a few thousand pounds. When companies join the market there are also advisers' fees of around £20,000. If new capital is raised charges by financial institutions can raise costs above £100,000. PLUS companies are generally very small and often brand new, but there are some long-established and well-known firms also trading on PLUS, such as Shepherd Neame and Arsenal Football Club.

Jenkins makes a market in a company's shares by giving two prices to brokers who enquire about a share: the price at which it is willing to buy (bid price) and a price at which it is willing to sell (offer price). The spread between these prices is normally a maximum of around 5 per cent. Five other institutions have recently decided to act as market makers. Having competing market makers should improve the position for investors considerably, leading (hopefully) to greater liquidity and tighter bid–offer spreads.

PLUS is not a Recognised Investment Exchange (RIE) under the law, therefore securities traded on PLUS are defined as unlisted and unquoted and are not traded on-exchange. PLUS has now been formally separated from J.P. Jenkins so it can be regulated by the FSA. While it is termed 'a regulated exchange' market, investors must note that the companies on PLUS are not subject to the same rigorous rules as those of the Official List or AIM. PLUS is described as a 'prescribed' market, which means that companies have to adhere to its code of conduct; for example, insider trading by directors is prohibited; companies raising fresh capital on PLUS must have a corporate adviser (e.g. a stockbroker, accountant or lawyer); PLUS insists on seeing a prospectus produced to raise funds for companies and expects this to comply with certain minimum standards as laid down in law.

There are 162 companies with a combined market capitalisation of around £2,000m paying for a PLUS dealing facility. A note of warning is in order here: the criteria for companies gaining admission do not include compliance with the strict rules applying to LSE companies, so investors have far fewer quality assurances about these companies. Also, the secondary market can be relatively illiquid, so shareholders need to be wary, but it is better than no secondary market at all (PLUS-Markets also provide an alternatve trading facility for over 640 companies quoted on AIM).

The formal exchanges are far from being the only or even the most desirable places for companies to raise equity finance. The OL in particular is expensive on an annual basis, and listed companies are often frustrated in the lack of attention given to them by the financial institutions – *see* **Exhibit 6.5**. (Management buy-outs and public-to-private deals are discussed later in the chapter.)

Exhibit 6.5

Professional expenses prove a deterrent to maintaining stock market exposure

But costs of public-to-private deals can also be considerable

Bertrand Benoit reports

Ask Richard Johnson, chief executive of Wyko, what the industrial distribution and maintenance group gained in 10 years on the stock market and the answer is likely to be short.

Launched with a market value of about £50m in 1989, the group was performing honorably until investors began to pull out from the small company sector last year.

In less than six months, its shares fell from 190p to 64p. 'This happened as we were considering a £60m acquisition,' Mr Johnson says. 'But with a p/e of 5, we had suddenly become vulnerable to a takeover.'

Unable to expand in a market where size increasingly mattered, Wyko put an end to its turbulent relationship with the Stock Exchange last week by going private in a management buy-out valuing it at £92.2m, a 30 per cent discount to its peak price.

This is not an isolated case. So far this year, nearly 40 companies have pulled out of the exchange, against 25 last year...some are no longer prepared to bear the cost and bother maintaining a listing.

Although linked to the size of the company, the expense typically amounts to £250,000 a year. Businesses meeting the minimum requirements imposed by the exchange pay a lot less. However, Roy Hill, chief executive of Liberfabrica, the book manufacturer bought by a trade buyer this month, claims his company will save up to £400,000 a year in City-associated costs.

These include fees paid to stockbroker, registrars, lawyers, merchant banker and financial PR company, as well as the exchange fee and the auditing, printing and distribution of accounts.

Another problem has been the low rating experienced by some of the smaller companies that have virtually disappeared from investors' radar screens. As institutions have grown increasingly reluctant to invest in small caps, brokers have stopped following many of them, thus hastening share price declines. 'Some institutions have stopped investing in companies with a market capitalisation below £100m,' says Penny Freer, head of smaller companies research at Crédit Lyonnais in London. 'Some smaller companies that deliver good results may end up with a single digit p/e.'

Exhibit 6.5 continued

For Tony Fry, partner at KPMG Transaction Services, 'being on the stock market is all about getting access to funding, if you are barred from such access, then the attraction disappears'.

In addition to the venture capital funding that can facilitate acquisitions, managers have been lured into public-to-private deals by the chance of raising their stake in the business. In a typical MBO backed by a private equity house, managers can end up owning up to 20 per cent of the bidding vehicle. One banker calculates that the value of such a stake can grow 10 times if the company is later sold for twice the price of the buy-out.

But because MBOs are highly geared operations, the risks involved are equally considerable. The same managers could lose all their investment if the company were sold below the original offer price.

Nor are the financial costs associated with a public-to-private transaction negligible. According to Richard Grainger, managing director at Close Brothers, the advisory firm, fees paid to bankers, registrars, venture capital funds and PR firms, can amount to 4 or 5 per cent of the purchase price.

The time spent in putting transactions together can also be consuming. 'The negotiations are so absorbing and involve so many parties that it can be very easy for management to take their eyes off the ball, especially if they do not have first class advisers,' says

Mr Johnson, whose MBO of Wyko was concluded after seven months of talks.

In some instances, these efforts prove fruitless, as at Liberfabrica, whose management team was outbid by a trade buyer. Mr Hill reckons that £500,000 in fees was wasted in the exercise.

Source: Financial Times, 31 August 1999, p. 18. Reprinted with permission.

The cost of listing
Estimated annual cost of listing for a company with a market capitalisation of around £100m

Stockbroker	£20,000 to £25,000
Financial PR	£20,000 to £25,000
Financial reports and accounts	around £30,000
Registrars	£5,000 to £25,000
High profile merchant bank	around £50,000
Solicitors	around £50,000
Other costs	around £50,000
Total (per year)	£250,000 to £350,000

Private
Estimated cost of going private for a company with a purchase price of around £100m

Advisors to the bidders	around 1% of purchase price
Lawyers to the bidders	£100,000 to £200,000
Due diligence account	£100,000 to £400,000
Market report due diligence	£30,000 to £50,000
Stamp duty	around 0.5% of purchase price
Printers	£15,000 to £20,000
Receiving banks	£10,000 to £15,000
Takeover panel fee	around £25,000
Funders fee	2 % to 3% of purchase price
Total	£3,780,000 to £5,210,000

Source: Industry estimate

The ownership of UK quoted shares

There has been a transformation in the pattern of share ownership in Britain over the last four decades (*see* **Exhibit 6.6**). The tax-favoured status of pension funds made them a very attractive vehicle for savings, resulting in billions of pounds being put into them each year. Most of this money used to be invested in equities, making pension funds the most influential investing group on the stock market. However, in the last five years pension funds have been taking

Exhibit 6.6	Share ownership in Britain, distribution by sector (quoted shares) (%)				
Sector	**1963**	**1975**	**1989**	**1997**	**2005**
Individuals	54.0	37.5	20.6	16.5	14.1
Pension funds	6.4	16.8	30.6	22.1	15.7
Insurance companies	10.0	15.9	18.6	23.5	17.2
Rest of the world	7.0	5.6	12.8	24.0	32.6
Unit trusts and investment trusts	–	–	7.5	8.6	5.2
Others – banks, public sector, charities (+ unit and inv. Trusts prior to 1989)	22.6	24.2	9.9	5.3	15.2

Source: Office for National Statistics, *Share Ownership, 2005*. Reproduced by permission of the Controller of HMSO and the Office for National Statistics. www.statistics.gov.uk.

money out of quoted shares and placing it in other investments such as bonds and venture capital. Insurance companies similarly rose in significance, doubling their share of quoted equities from 10 per cent to about 20 per cent by the early 1990s. The group which decreased in importance is ordinary individuals holding shares directly. They used to dominate the market, with 54 per cent of quoted shares in 1963. By the late 1980s this had declined to about 20 per cent. Investors tended to switch from direct investment to collective investment vehicles. They gain benefits of diversification and skilled management by putting their savings into unit and investment trusts or into endowment and other savings schemes offered by the insurance companies. The most remarkable trend over the last thirty years has been the increasing share of equities held by overseas investors: only 5.6 per cent in 1975, but over 32 per cent at the beginning of 2005. This increase partly reflects international mergers where the new company is listed in the UK. Also foreign companies sometimes float their UK subsidiaries but hold on to a large shareholding. It also reflects an increasing tendency of investors to buy shares in overseas markets.

Although the mode of investment has changed from direct to indirect, Britain remains a society with a deep interest in the stock market. Very few people are immune from the performance of the Exchange. The vast majority have a pension plan or endowment savings scheme, an individual savings account (ISA) or a unit trust investment. Some have all four.

In 1980 only 3 million individuals held shares. After the privatisation programme, which included British Gas, British Telecom and TSB, the figure rose to 9 million by 1988. By 1991 the flotations of Abbey National, the water companies and regional electricity companies had taken the numbers to 11 million. The stampede of building societies to market in 1997 produced a record 16 million individual shareholders.

Rights issues

A rights issue is an invitation to existing shareholders to purchase additional shares in the company. This is a very popular method of raising new funds. It is easy and relatively cheap (compared with new issues). Directors are not required to seek the prior consent of shareholders, and the London Stock Exchange will only intervene in larger issues (to adjust the timing so that the market does not suffer from too many issues in one period). The UK has particularly strong traditions and laws concerning *pre-emption rights*. These require that a company raising new equity capital by selling shares first offers those shares to the existing shareholders. The owners of the company are entitled to subscribe for the new shares in proportion to their existing holding. This will enable them to maintain the existing percentage ownership of the company – the only difference is that each slice of the company cake is bigger because it has more financial resources under its control.

The shares are usually offered at a significantly discounted price from the market value of the current shares – typically 10–25 per cent. Shareholders can either buy these shares themselves or sell the 'right' to buy to another investor. For further reassurance that the firm will raise the anticipated finance, rights issues are usually underwritten by institutions.

An example

Take the case of the imaginary listed company Swell plc with 100 million shares in issue. It wants to raise £25m for expansion but does not want to borrow it. Given that its existing shares are quoted on the stock market at 120p, the new rights shares will have to be issued at a lower price to appeal to shareholders because there is a risk of the market share price falling in the period between the announcement and the purchasing of new shares. (The offer must remain open for at least three weeks.) Swell has decided that the £25m will be obtained by issuing 25 million shares at 100p each. Thus the ratio of new shares to old is 25:100. In other words, this issue is a 'one-for-four' rights issue. Each shareholder will be offered one new share for every four already held. The discount on these new shares is 20p or 16.7 per cent. The market price of Swell shares will not be able to stay at 120p after the rights issue is complete. The *ex-rights price* is the price at which the shares should theoretically sell after the issue. This is calculated as follows:

Four existing shares at a price of 120p	480p
One new share for cash at 100p	100p
Value of five shares	580p
Value of one share ex-rights 580p/5	116p

An alternative way of viewing this is to focus on the worth of the firm before and after the rights. Prior to the issue the total capitalisation of the firm was £120m (£1.20 × 100 million shares). The rights issue put another £25m into the company but also created 25 million additional shares. A company that was previously valued at £120m which then adds £25m of value to itself in the form of cash should be worth £145m. This company now has 125 million shares; therefore each share is worth £1.16 (disregarding stock market fluctuations and revaluations of the company):

$$\frac{\text{Total market capitalisation}}{\text{Total shares available}} = \frac{£145m}{125m} = £1.16$$

The shareholders have experienced a decline in the price of their old shares from 120p to 116p. A fall of this magnitude necessarily follows from the introduction of new shares at a discounted price. However, the loss is exactly offset by the gain in share value on the new rights issue shares. They cost 100p but have a market price of 116p. This can be illustrated through the example of Sid, who owned 100 shares worth £120 prior to the rights announcement. Sid loses £4 on the old shares – their value is now £116. However he makes a gain of £4 on the new shares:

Cost of rights shares (25 × £1)	£25
Ex-rights value (25 × £1.16)	£29
Gain	£4

What if a shareholder does not want to take up the rights?

As owners of the firm all shareholders must be treated in the same way. To make sure that some shareholders do not lose out because they are unwilling or unable to buy more shares the law requires that shareholders have a third choice, other than to buy or not buy the new shares. This is to sell the rights on to someone else on the stock market (selling the rights nil paid). Take the case of impoverished Sid, who is unable to find the necessary £25. He could sell the rights to subscribe for the shares to another investor and not have to go through the process of taking up any of the shares himself. Indeed, so deeply enshrined are pre-emption rights that even if the shareholder does nothing the company will sell his rights to the new shares on his behalf and send the proceeds to him.[4] Thus, Sid would benefit to the extent of 16p per share or a total of £4 (if the market price stays constant), which adequately compensates for the loss on the 100 shares he holds. But the extent of his control over the company has been reduced – his percentage share of the votes has decreased.

The value of a right on one new share is:

Theoretical market value of share ex-rights – subscription price = 116p – 100p = 16p

The value of a right on one old share in Swell is:

$$\frac{\text{Theoretical market value of share ex-rights – subscription price}}{\text{No. of old shares required to purchase one new share}}$$

$$= \frac{116 - 100}{4} = 4\text{p}$$

Ex-rights and cum-rights

Shares bought in the stock market designated cum-rights carry with them to the new owner the right to subscribe for the new shares in the rights issue. After a cut-off date the shares go ex-rights, which means that any purchaser of old shares will not have the right to the new shares; they remain with the former shareholder.

The price discount decision

It does not matter greatly whether Swell raises £25m on a one-for-four basis at 100p or on a one-for-three basis at 75p per share, or on some other basis (see **Exhibit 6.7**).

Exhibit 6.7	Comparison of different rights bases		
Rights basis	**Number of new shares (m)**	**Price of new shares (p)**	**Total raised (£m)**
1 for 4	25	100	25
1 for 3	33.3	75	25
1 for 2	50	50	25
1 for 1	100	25	25

As Exhibit 6.7 shows, whatever the basis of the rights issue, the company will receive £25m and the shareholders will see the price of their old shares decrease, but this will be exactly offset by the value of the rights on the new shares. However, the ex-rights price will change. For a one-for-three basis it will be £108.75:

Three shares at 120p	360p
One share at 75p	75p
Value of four shares	435p
Value of one share (435/4)	108.75p

---

[4] For companies whose shares are not quoted on a recognised stock exchange it may be difficult to sell the rights to another investor.

If Swell chose the one-for-one basis this would be regarded as a *deep-discounted rights issue*. With an issue of this sort there is only a minute probability that the market price will fall below the rights offer price and therefore there is almost complete certainty that the offer will be taken up. It seems reasonable to suggest that the underwriting service provided by the institutions is largely redundant here and that the firm can make a significant saving. Yet 95 per cent of all rights issues are underwritten,[5] usually involving between 100 and 400 sub-underwriters. The underwriting fees used to be a flat 2 per cent of the offer. Of this the issuing house received 0.5 per cent, the broker received 0.25 per cent and the sub-underwriter 1.25 per cent (the same distribution as in a new issue). However, fees have fallen recently and can now be as little as 0.75 per cent for low-risk deep-discounted issues.

When the press talks glibly of a rights offer being 'very attractively priced for shareholders' they are generally talking nonsense. Whatever the size of the discount, the same value will be removed from the old shares to leave the shareholder no worse or better off. Logically value cannot be handed over to the shareholders from the size of the discount decision. Shareholders own all the company's shares before and after the rights issue – they can't hand value to themselves without also taking value from themselves. Of course, if the prospects for the company's profits rise because it can now make brilliant capital expenditures, which lead to dominant market positions, then the value of shares will rise – for both the old and the new shares. But this is value creation that has nothing to do with the level of the discount.

Case study 6.2   **Cookson: a very troubled rights issue**

The industrial material manufacturer Cookson announced on 19 July 2002 that it intended to raise £277.5m from a rights issue. The company needed the money to pay off its rapidly accumulating debt (a *rescue rights issue*). It was to be an 8 for 5 issue, that is, 8 new shares would be sold at 25 pence for every 5 shares currently held. Prior to the announcement the shares traded at 52p and Cookson took the bold decision not to underwrite the issue, saving about £4m; at 25p it was deeply discounted.

If the old shares remained at 52p then the theoretical ex-rights price is 35p:

5 old shares at 52p	260p
8 new shares at 25p	200p
	460p
Theoretical ex-rights price: 460p/13	= 35p

However, the shares did not remain at 52p. On the announcement, they immediately fell to 33p as investors took the issue to be a sign of great problems at Cookson. Worse was to come a week later when the price of the old shares moved to 20p.

Shareholders were now being asked to pay 25p for new shares when the company's shares can be bought on the Exchange for less. Obviously no one would want to support the issue in these circumstances. If the issue had been underwritten then the underwriter would have been obliged to buy the new shares at 25 pence and Cookson would have been guaranteed the money it so badly needed. The next few weeks were a tense time for the managers.

Fortunately, by the time the offer closed in late August the shares had risen to 29.75p. Almost 92 per cent of the shares on offer were taken up by existing shareholders; the remainder were placed with institutions.

---

[5] It has also been suggested that when sponsors are underwriters they have an additional incentive to price the shares cheaply as this reduces the risk of being required to buy the shares. If they do buy them, they then obtain them at a good price.

Other equity issues

Some companies argue that the lengthy procedures and expense associated with rights issues (for example, a minimum three-week offer period) frustrate directors' efforts to take advantage of opportunities in a timely fashion. Firms in the USA have much more freedom to bypass pre-emption rights. They are able to sell blocks of shares to securities houses for distribution elsewhere in the market. This is fast and has low transaction costs. If this were permitted in the UK there would be a concern for existing shareholders: that is, they could experience a dilution of their voting power and/or the share could be sold at such a low price that a portion of the firm is handed over to new shareholders too cheaply.

The UK authorities have produced a compromise. Here firms must obtain shareholders' approval through a special resolution (a majority of 75 per cent of those voting) at the company's annual general meeting or at an extraordinary general meeting to waive the pre-emption right. Even then the shares must not be sold to outside investors at more than a 5 per cent discount to the share price (except in an issue with a 'clawback' provision – see next section). This is an important condition. It does not make any difference to existing shareholders if new shares are offered at a deep discount to the market price as long as they are offered to them. If external investors get a discount there is a transfer of value from the current shareholders to the new.

Placings and open offers

In placings, new shares from companies already quoted on the stock market are sold directly to a narrow group of external investors. The institutions, wearing their hat of existing shareholders, have produced guidelines to prevent abuse, which normally only allow a placing of a small proportion of the company's capital (a maximum of 5 per cent in a single year and no more than 7.5 per cent is to be added to the company's equity capital over a rolling three-year period) in the absence of a clawback. Under clawback existing shareholders have the right to reclaim the shares as though they were entitled to them under a rights issue. They can buy them at the price they were offered to the external investors. With a clawback the issue becomes an 'open offer'. The major difference compared with a rights issue is that if they do not exercise this clawback right they receive no compensation for a reduction in the price of their existing shares – there are no nil-paid rights to sell. Exhibit 6.8 describes a placing/open offer.

Exhibit 6.8

Corus raises £300m for revival

Troubled Anglo-Dutch steel group says share issue will help it to compete in Europe and plans more cost cuts

By Rebecca Bream

Corus, the Anglo-Dutch steel-maker, raised £307m yesterday through a well-received share issue . . .

Shares in the company rose 6p to 32p following the equity placement, which is designed to strengthen Corus's balance sheet and provide funding for its UK restructuring plan and further productivity initiatives . . .

Corus issued more than 1.3bn new shares – five for 12 – at 23.5p, a discount of 9.6 per cent on Monday's closing price. Analysts said that most buyers were existing investors but, because Corus chose an open share offer instead of a rights issue, it offered a relatively slim discount.

Cazenove and Lazard were joint sponsors and Hoare Govett was joint broker . . .

Source: Financial Times, 13 November 2003, p. 25. Reprinted with permission.

Acquisition for shares

Shares are often issued to purchase businesses or assets. This is usually subject to shareholder approval.

Vendor placing

If a company wishes to pay for an asset such as a subsidiary of another firm or an entire company with newly issued shares, but the vendor does not want to hold the shares, the purchaser could arrange for the new shares to be bought by institutional investors for cash. In this way the buyer gets the asset, the vendors (for example shareholders in the target company in a merger or takeover) receive cash and the institutional investor makes an investment.

There is usually a clawback arrangement for a vendor placing (if the issue is more than 10 per cent of market capitalisation of the acquirer). Again, the price discount can be no more than 5 per cent of the current share price.

Bought deal

Instead of selling shares to investors companies are sometimes able to make an arrangement with a securities house whereby it buys all the shares being offered for cash. The securities house then sells the shares on to investors included in its distribution network, hoping to make a profit on the deal. Securities houses often compete to buy a package of shares from the company, with the highest bidder winning. The securities house takes the risk of being unable to sell the shares for at least the amount that they paid. Given that some of these bought deals are for over £100m, these securities houses need substantial capital backing. Bought deals are limited by the 5 per cent pre-emption rules.

Equity finance for unquoted firms

We have looked at some of the details of raising money on the Stock Exchange. In the commercial world there are thousands of companies which do not have access to the Exchange. We now consider a few of the ways that unquoted firms can raise equity capital.

The financing gap

Small companies usually rely on retained earnings, capital injections from the founder family and bank borrowing for growth. More mature companies can turn to the stock market to raise debt or equity capital. In between these two, it is suggested, lies a financing gap. The intermediate businesses are too large or too fast growing to ask the individual shareholders for more funds or to obtain sufficient bank finance, and they are not ready to launch on the stock market.

These companies may be frustrated in their plans to exploit market opportunities by a lack of available funds. To help fill this gap there has been the rapid development of the private equity finance industry over the past 20 years. Today over £10bn per year is supplied by formal venture capital suppliers to unquoted UK firms. Currently there are 10,000 UK companies with 3 million employees (one in six of the non-government workforce) financed by private equity money. The tremendous growth of private equity capital has to a large extent plugged the financing gap which so vexed politicians and business people alike in the 1970s and 1980s.

Business angels (informal venture capitalists)

Business angels are wealthy individuals, generally with substantial business and entrepreneurial experience, who usually invest between £10,000 and £250,000 primarily in start-up, early-stage or expanding firms. About three-quarters of business angel investments are for sums of less than £100,000 and the average investment is £25,000–£30,000. The majority of investments are in the form of equity finance but they do purchase debt instruments and preference shares.

These companies will be years away from obtaining a quotation or being advanced enough for a sale to other companies or investors, so in becoming a business angel the investor accepts that it may be difficult to dispose of their shares, even if the company is progressing nicely. They also accept a high degree of risk of complete failure – which happens in about one in three cases.

They usually do not have a controlling shareholding and they are willing to invest at an earlier stage than most formal venture capitalists. (They often dislike the term business angel, preferring the title informal venture capitalist.) They are generally looking for entrepreneurial companies that have high aspirations and potential for growth. A typical business angel makes one or two investments in a three-year period, often in an investment syndicate (with an 'archangel' leading the group). They generally invest in companies within a reasonable travelling distance from their homes because most like to be 'hands-on' investors, playing a significant role in strategy and management – on average angels allocate 10 hours a week to their investments. Most angels take a seat on the board.[6] Business angels are patient investors willing to hold their investment for at least a five-year period.

The main way in which firms and angels find each other is through friends and business associates, although there are a number of formal networks. *See* British Venture Capital Association at www.bvca.co.uk for a list of networks.[7]

Angel network events are organised where entrepreneurs can make a pitch to potential investors, who, if they like what they hear in response to their questions, may put in tens of thousands of pounds. Prior to the event the network organisers (or a member) generally screen the business opportunities to avoid time wasting by the no-hopers. To be a member of a network investors are expected either to earn at least £100,000 per year or to have a net worth of at least £250,000 (excluding main residence). If an investor has a specialist skill to offer, for example he/she is an experienced company director or chartered accountant, membership may be permitted despite a lower income or net worth.

Entrepreneurs need to be aware that obtaining money from informal venture capitalists is no easy task as **Exhibit 6.9** makes clear – the rejection rate runs at over 90 per cent; but following rejection the determined entrepreneur has many other angel networks to try.

Many business angel deals are structured to take advantage of tax breaks such as those through enterprise investment schemes (EIS) which offer income tax relief and capital gains tax deferral (see later in this chapter). Even outside EIS the investments often qualify as business assets and for business property relief. This can reduce capital gains tax to 10 per cent after two years and removes the asset from the individual's estate for inheritance tax after two years.

Venture capital

Venture capital (VC) funds provide finance for unquoted firms with high growth potential. Venture capital is a medium- to long-term investment and can consist of a package of debt and equity finance. Venture capitalists take high risks by investing in the equity of young companies often with a limited (or no) track record. Many of their investments are into little more than a management team with a good idea – which may not have started selling a product or even developed a prototype. It is believed, as a rule of thumb in the venture capital industry, that out of ten investments two will fail completely, two will perform excellently and the remaining six will range from poor to very good.

High risk goes with high return. Venture capitalists therefore expect to get a return of between five and ten times their initial equity investment in about five to seven years. This means that the firms receiving equity finance are expected to produce annual returns of at least 26 per cent. Alongside the usual drawbacks of equity capital from the investors' viewpoint (last in the queue for income and on liquidation, etc.), investors in small unquoted

---

[6] Nevertheless, many business angels (generally those with investments of £10,000–£20,000) have infrequent contact with the company.

[7] Other useful contacts: National Business Angels Network (NBAN), www.nban.com; Angel Bourse, www.angelbourse.com; Fisma, www.fisma.org; Venture Capital Report, www.ver1978.com; Katalyst Ventures, www.katalystventures.com; Hotbed, www.hotbed.uk.com; Beer & Partners, www.beerandpartners.com; Entrust, www.entrust.co.uk; Cavendish Management Resources, www.cmrworld.com; Development Capital Exchange, www.dexworld.com; Equity Link, www.equitylink.exemplas.com; Department of Trade and Industry, www.dti.gov.uk.

Exhibit 6.9

Beware little devils hidden among the business angels

Jonathan Guthrie

Entrepreneurs who pitch for the cash of wealthy private investors can face an experience similar to appearing on *The Gong Show*. This 1970s television programme featured roller-dancing housewives, wisecracking pensioners and yodelling infants, all competing for a brief shot of air time before being driven off stage by a compère banging a gong.

Robert Miller, a drug development entrepreneur, still bears the mental scars of his own 'gonging off'. His tale is instructive for any entrepreneur seeking capital from the wealthy investment hobbyists known as business angels. Mr Miller paid a stiff £3,000 to a large accountancy firm for the privilege of pitching to the business angels on its books.

The beauty parade at which he performed was, he says, 'awful' and 'distressing'. 'There was a time limit of 10 minutes and they practically pulled me off stage during my last slide,' he says.

Mr Miller was then surrounded by a knot of men eagerly pressing business cards into his hand. Surely these were angels, keen to back his plans to turn herbal remedies into modern medicines? Not a bit of it. They were consultants. They wanted Mr Miller to give them money, not the other way round. I imagine them clutching at his garments, like zombies in a horror flick.

Steve Tokataian never got as far as a beauty parade. Mr Tokataian is the inventor of Line-Dive, a kind of buoy filled with compressed air and sprouting breathing tubes. Its applications include swimming-pool safety and leisure diving. But he needs more than £250,000 to start production and marketing. Mr Tokataian was dumbstruck when the intermediary he approached demanded £3,500 to prepare a document promoting the venture, a 5 per cent cut of any financing and an option on 4 per cent of the shares.

'It was a lot for writing a document that would have been extracted from the detailed business plan I had already produced,' says Mr Tokataian. He is now advertising his enterprise to angels on DCX World, a web-based newswire on private investment, for the modest sum of $75 (£41)...

So seeking angel investment is a waste of time and the intermediaries who promote it are charlatans? Not at all. This is a useful financing route for some entrepreneurs but they need to pursue it as pragmatically as any aspect of their business.

The sales-driven enterprise operating in a market where entry costs are low has little need of the equity capital that business angels provide. It should be able to grow on the back of rising cash flow. Similarly, entrepreneurs who need capital to pursue an opportunity reasonably certain to create a jump in cash flow – such as a big new contract – should probably hang on to their shares and take out a loan.

But a small proportion of entrepreneurs need money to make step changes whose paybacks are hard to predict, in either scale or timing. For example, Mr Miller is working on a drug that might cure liver disease. He needs to conduct expensive clinical trials to find out whether it does. Mr Tokataian, for his part, must put his invention into production to discover whether swimming-pools and holiday resorts will order it en masse.

This is where business angels can come in, particularly when so many venture capitalists have abandoned the little league of private equity investment.

Angels are generally middle-aged or elderly men who have made six- or seven-figure sums selling their businesses. They want to risk some of that capital – typically in slugs of £10,000 to £250,000 – in pursuit of internal rates of return of 50 per cent or more. They are rarely gauche amateurs.

Doug Allan, an angel in the process of investing £300,000, says: 'I do as much due diligence as when I was considering acquisitions as a chief executive.'

If you can find an angel among your relatives or on the golf course, good luck to you. Websites such as DCX World could be another way of dodging a 5 per cent financing fee. But investments are generally sold rather than bought and there are many good intermediaries, as well as bad ones.

Some, such as London Business Angels and Advantage Business Angels in the West Midlands, even provide match financing from public sources and subsidised help writing business plans. Bestmatch, meanwhile, is to be switched off by NBAN, itself in the throes of reform.

I conclude with our protagonist Mr Miller riding heroically into the sunset, instead of being ignominiously gonged off stage. Swallowing his disappointment, he pitched at other, better-run beauty parades. A fortnight ago, an angel with useful industry expertise bought 10 per cent of Phynova's shares for £250,000. Last Thursday, two more angels subscribed £100,000 between them. Phynova can now afford to set up a trial for its liver disease drug. Mr Tokataian, however, is still waiting for his money.

Source: *Financial Times*, 27 January 2004, p. 13. Reprinted with permission.

companies also suffer from a lack of liquidity because the shares are not quoted on a public exchange. There are a number of different types of venture capital (although these days the last three will often be separated from VC and grouped under the title private equity – see later in this chapter):

- *Seedcorn* This is financing to allow the development of a business concept. This may also involve expenditure on the production of prototypes and additional research.

- *Start-up* A product or idea is further developed and/or initial marketing is carried out. Companies are very young and have not yet sold their product commercially.

- *Other early-stage* Funds for initial commercial manufacturing and sales. Many companies at this stage will remain unprofitable.

- *Expansion (Development or Growth)* Companies at this stage are on to a fast-growth track and need capital to fund increased production capacity, working capital and for the further development of the product or market. Professor Steve Young's company Entropic (see Case study 6.1 at the beginning of the chapter) provides an example of this.

- *Management buy-outs (MBO)* Here a team of managers make an offer to their employers to buy a whole business, a subsidiary or a section so that they own and run it for themselves. Large companies are often willing to sell to these teams, particularly if the business is underperforming and does not fit with the strategic core business. Usually the management team have limited funds of their own and so call on venture capitalists to provide the bulk of the finance.

- *Management buy-ins (MBI)* A new team of managers from outside an existing business buy a stake, usually backed by a venture capital fund.

- *Public-to-private (PTP)* The management of a company currently quoted on a stock exchange may return it to unquoted status with the assistance of venture capital finance being used to buy the shares.

Venture capital firms are less keen on financing seedcorn, start-ups and other early-stage companies than expansions, MBOs, MBIs and PTPs. This is largely due to the very high risk associated with early-stage ventures and the disproportionate time and costs of financing smaller deals. To make it worthwhile for a VC organisation to consider a company the investment must be at least £100,000 – the average investment is about £5m.

Because of the greater risks associated with the youngest companies, the VC funds may require returns of the order of 50–80 per cent per annum. For well-established companies with a proven product and battle-hardened and respected management the returns required may drop to the high 20s. These returns may seem exorbitant, especially to the managers set the task of achieving them, but they have to be viewed in the light of the fact that many VC investments will turn out to be failures and so the overall performance of the VC funds is significantly less than these figures suggest. In fact the British Venture Capital Association which represents 'every major source of venture capital in the UK' reports that returns on funds are not excessively high. The overall long-term net returns to investors for funds raised between 1980 and 1999 measured to the end of 2003 stood at 13.6 per cent.[8] (*See* **Exhibit 6.10.**)

There are a number of different types of VC providers, although the boundaries are increasingly blurred as a number of funds now raise money from a variety of sources. The *independents* can be firms, partnerships, funds or investment trusts, either quoted or private, which have raised their capital from more than one source. The main sources are pension and insurance funds, but banks, corporate investors and private individuals also put money into these VC funds. *Captives* are funds managed on behalf of a parent institution (banks, pension funds, etc.). *Semi-captives* invest funds on behalf of a parent and also manage independently raised funds.

For the larger investments, particularly MBOs and MBIs, the venture capitalist may provide only a fraction of the total funds required. Thus, in a £50m buy-out the venture capitalist might supply (individually or in a syndicate with other VC funds), say, £15m in the form of share capital (ordinary and preference shares). Another £20m may come from a group of banks in the form of debt finance. The remainder may be supplied as mezzanine debt – high-

---

[8] British Venture Capital Association, www.bvca.co.uk.

Exhibit 6.10	Returns of funds raised from external investors for investment in venture capital, 1980–2003

Internal rates of return to investors, net of costs and fees since the inception of the fund

	Return to Dec. 2003 (% per annum)
Early stage	4.7
Development	9.8
Mid-MBO	9.7
Large MBO	16.4
Generalist fund	13.8
Total	13.6
Comparators	
FTSE All-Share (over 10 years)	6.2
Property (over 10 years)	10.5
Overseas equities (over 10 years)	4.2

Note: Excluding venture and development capital investment trusts and venture capital trusts.

Source: *British Venture Capital Association Performance Measurement Survey 2003*, conducted by PricewaterhouseCoopers and Westport Private Equity Limited. See www.bvca.co.uk.

return and high-risk debt which usually has some rights to share in equity values should the company perform well (*see* Chapter 7). In the case of UniPoly (*see* **Exhibit 6.11**), of the £620m that was needed to buy this company and provide it with capital for expansion, 28 per cent was equity, 64 per cent bank debt (28 banks) and 8 per cent mezzanine finance (eight lenders).

Venture capitalists generally like to have a clear target set as the eventual 'exit' (or 'take-out') date. This is the point at which the VC can recoup some or all of the investment. Many exits are achieved by a sale of the company to another firm ('corporate acquisition' or 'trade sale'), but a popular method is a flotation on a stock market. Alternative exit routes are for the company to repurchase its shares (often accompanied by a general recapitalisation of the firm – more debt taken on) or for the venture capitalist to sell the holding to an institution such as an investment trust or to another private equity group ('a secondary buy-out').

Exhibit 6.11

Banks replace management at UniPoly

The banks that backed the £620m management buy-out of UniPoly in 1997 have brought in a new management to improve the performance of the engineering business . . .

The 28 banks and eight mezzanine lenders in the syndicate have promised to support the business after 'a recent period of uncertainty', said Mr Teacher . . .

Unipoly makes industrial belting, fluid handling equipment and owns Schlegel, the US-based shielding equipment maker. It was sold by BTR, since renamed Invensys, in December 1997. At the time, UniPoly's diverse product range included water beds for cows and Wellington boots.

The original plan was that the business would be floated, or broken up and sold, within three to five years . . .

BTR received £515m for the company, which also raised a further £105m of capital for expansion.

Legal and General Ventures led the investors who put in £175m of equity and £50m of mezzanine finance, while Fuji Bank led the £395m debt finance.

Source: Maggie Urry, *Financial Times*, 12 June 2001, p. 30. Reprinted with permission.

Venture capital funds are rarely looking for a controlling shareholding in a company and are often content with a 20 or 30 per cent share. They may also supply funds by the purchase of convertible preference shares which give them rights to convert to ordinary shares – which will boost their equity holding and increase the return if the firm performs well. They may also insist, in an initial investment agreement, on some widespread powers. For instance, the company may need to gain the venture capitalist's approval for the issue of further securities, and there may be a veto over acquisition of other companies. Even though their equity holding is generally less than 50 per cent the VC funds frequently have special rights to appoint a number of directors. If specific negative events happen, such as a poor performance, they may have the right to appoint most of the board of directors and therefore take effective control. More than once the founding entrepreneur has been aggrieved to find him/herself removed from power. (Despite the loss of power, they often have a large shareholding in what has grown to be a multi-million pound company.) They are often sufficiently upset to refer to the fund which separated them from their creation as 'vulture capitalist'. But this is to focus on the dark side. When everything goes well, we have, as they say in the business jargon, 'a win-win-win situation': the company receives vital capital to grow fast, the venture capitalist receives a high return and society gains new products and economic progress.

The venture capitalist can help a company with more than money. Venture capitalists usually have a wealth of experience and talented people able to assist the budding entrepreneur. Many of the UK's most noteworthy companies were helped by the VC industry, for example FocusWickes, Halfords, Waterstones bookshops, Oxford Instruments (and in America: Apple Computers, Sun Microsystems, Netscape, Lotus and Compaq).

Private equity

As share investment outside stock markets has grown it has become differentiated. The main categories are shown in **Exhibit 6.12**. The title overarching all these activities is private equity. Private equity is defined as medium- to long-term finance provided in return for an equity stake in potentially high-growth unquoted companies. In this more differentiated setting the term venture capital is generally confined to describing the building of companies from the ground floor, or at least from a very low base. Management buy-outs and buy-ins of established businesses (already off the ground floor) have become specialist tasks, with a number of dedicated funds. Many of these funds are formed as private partnerships by wealthy individuals, a high proportion of which are American owned. However, there are funds that small investors can buy shares in, such as 3i, that still conduct traditional VC business and MBOs and MBIs. They are frequently classified as venture and development capital investment trusts (VDCITs).[9] The disadvantage of VDCITs is the absence of tax benefits. This is where the

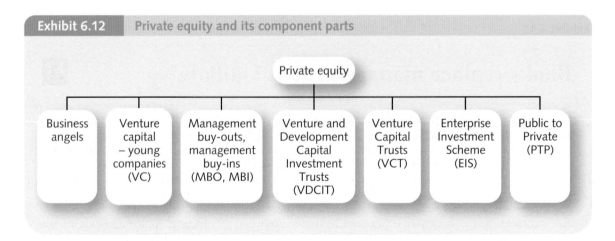

| Exhibit 6.12 | Private equity and its component parts |

---

[9]   More details on these are available from www.bvca.co.uk and www.aitc.co.uk.

Venture Capital Trusts (VCTs) and the Enterprise Investment Scheme (EIS) come in. They both offer significant tax breaks to investors in small unquoted companies – see next section. Finally, some funds have specialised in providing financial and professional support to quoted companies that wish to leave the stock market – public-to-private deals.

Venture Capital Trusts (VCTs)

It is important to distinguish between venture capital trusts, an investment vehicle introduced in 1995 to encourage investment in small and fast-growing companies which have important tax breaks, and two other types of venture capital organisations: venture and development capital investment trusts (VDCITs), which are standard investment trusts with a focus on more risky developing companies, and venture capital funds (described above).

The tax breaks for investors putting money into VCTs include an immediate relief on their current year's income at 30 per cent (by putting £10,000 into a VCT a taxpaying investor will pay £3,000 less tax, so the effective cost is only £7,000). The returns (income and capital gains) on a VCT are free of tax. Investors can place up to £200,000 each per year into VCTs. These benefits are only available to investors buying new VCT shares who hold the investment for five years. The VCT managers can only invest in companies with gross assets less than £7m and the maximum amount a VCT is allowed to put into each unquoted company's shares is limited to £1m per year. ('Unquoted' for VCT is used rather loosely and includes AIM companies.) A maximum of 15 per cent of the VCT fund can be invested in any one company. Purchases of shares in the primary market, i.e. when companies are raising fresh equity capital, are required – not secondary market purchases from other investors. Up to half of the fund's investment in qualifying companies can be in the form of loans. VCTs are quoted on the London Stock Exchange.

Enterprise Investment Scheme (EIS)

Another government initiative to encourage the flow of risk capital to smaller companies is the Enterprise Investment Scheme. Income tax relief at 20 per cent is available for investments made directly (no need for a fund manager as with VCTs) into qualifying company shares. There is also capital gains tax relief, and losses within EISs are allowable against income tax. Investment under EIS means investing when the company issues shares, not the purchase of shares in the secondary market. The tax benefits are lost if the investments are held for less than three years. To raise money from this source the firm must have been carrying out a 'qualifying activity' for three years – this generally excludes financial investment and property companies. The company must not be quoted on the Official List and the most it can raise under the EIS in any one year is usually £1m. The company must not have gross assets worth more than £7m. Funds which invest in a range of EIS companies are springing up to help investors spread risk.

Corporate venturing and incubators

Larger companies sometimes foster the development of smaller enterprises. This can take numerous forms, from joint product development work to an injection of equity finance. The small firm can thereby retain its independence and yet contribute to the large firm: perhaps its greater freedom to innovate will generate new products which the larger firm can exploit to the benefit of both. Intel uses corporate venturing to increase demand for its technology by, for example, investing in start-up companies in China. Shell uses it to promote innovation. BT established a venture unit to harvest value from its 14,000 patents and 2,500 unique inventions.

Incubators are places where a start-up company not only will gain access to finance, but will be able to receive support in many forms. This may include all humdrum operational managerial tasks being taken care of (e.g. accounting, legal, human resources), business plan-ning, the supply of managers for various stages of the company's development, property management, etc. As a result the entrepreneurial team can concentrate on innovation and grow the business, even if they have no prior managerial experience.

Government sources

Some local authorities have set up VC-type funds in order to attract and encourage industry. Large organisations with similar aims include the Scottish Development Agency and the Welsh Development Agency. Equity, debt and grant finance may be available from these sources. **Exhibit 6.13** shows that substantial sums are available from government agencies.

Exhibit 6.13

West Midlands to set up £60m enterprise fund

By Jonathan Guthrie

Businesses in the West Midlands will be able to finance their growth with money from a £60m publicly-backed venture capital fund before floating on a regional stock exchange, under plans drawn up by the development agency for the region.

The innovations combine with existing state-sponsored seed capi-tal funds in the region to allow businesses to complete three key equity funding stages: start-up, growth and flotation.

The moves highlight a wide-spread belief among government officials and business leaders in the regions that the City of London has proved a mediocre provider of

small-scale finance. This has been embraced by the Treasury and Department of Trade and Industry, which believe there is a 'market failure' in finance for smaller com-panies. The seamless financing system that Advantage West Midlands is creating is being closely watched in other parts of the country, which are likely to follow suit if it is successful.

The most ambitious element is the 'advantage enterprise and innovation fund'. At a proposed £60m it is small by the standards of private sector venture capital, but is one of the largest funds a regional development agency has ever attempted to raise. About

£40m of the money comes from the European Union and the gov-ernment. The agency has so far attracted £8.5m in private capital and needs another £11.5m from this source before closing the fund this summer.

The fund will provide money in chunks of £250,000 to £2m. It will work in conjunction with four earlier stage funds backed by Advantage West Midland.

The development agency will today announce the board of the regional stock exchange, which it expects will begin trading before the end of the year.

Source: Financial Times, 12 February 2004, p. 7. Reprinted with permission.

Disillusionment and dissatisfaction with quotation

Many companies are either dissatisfied with being quoted on a stock exchange or have never been quoted and feel no need to join. **Exhibit 6.14** provides a summary of the comments reported in the financial press made by managers arguing for either joining a stock market, leaving the Exchange or for having no intention of floating.[10]

---

[10] The three editions of *Corporate Financial Management* (Arnold, 1998, 2001, 2005) have dozens of FT articles (in Chapter 10) presenting company announcements and managerial thoughts on this issue.

Exhibit 6.14	Arguments for and against joining a stock exchange

For	Against
● Access to new capital for growth. ● Liquidity for existing shareholders. ● Discipline on management to perform. ● Able to use equity to buy businesses. ● Allows founders to diversify. ● Borrow more easily or cheaply. ● Can attract better management. ● Forces managers to articulate strategy clearly and persuasively. ● Succession planning may be made easier – professional managers rather than family. ● Increased customer recognition. ● Allow local people to buy shares. ● Share incentive schemes are more meaningful.	● Dealing with 'City' folk is time consuming and/or boring. ● City is short-termist. ● City does not understand entrepreneurs. ● Stifles creativity. ● Focus excessively on return on capital. ● Empire building through acquisitions on a stock exchange – growth for its own sake (or for directors) can be the result of a quote. ● The stock market undervalues entrepreneur's shares in the entrepreneur's eyes. ● Loss of control for founding shareholders. ● Strong family-held companies in Germany, Italy and Asia where stock markets are used less. ● Examples of good strong unquoted companies in UK: J.C. Bamford, Rothschilds, Littlewoods. ● Press scrutiny is irritating. ● Market share building (and short-term low profit margins) are more possible off exchange. ● The temptation of over-rapid expansion is avoided off exchange. ● By remaining unquoted, the owners, if they do not wish to put shareholder wealth at the centre of the firm's purpose, don't have to (environment or ethical issues may dominate). ● Costs of maintaining a quote, e.g. SE fees, extra disclosure costs, management time.

The efficient market hypothesis

The question of whether the stock market is efficient in pricing shares and other securities has fascinated academics, investors and businessmen for a long time. This is hardly surprising: even academics are attracted by the thought that by studying in this area they might be able to discover a stock market inefficiency which is sufficiently exploitable to make them very rich, or, at least, to make their name in the academic community. In an efficient market systematic undervaluing or overvaluing of shares does not occur, and therefore it is not possible to develop trading rules which will 'beat the market' by, say, buying identifiable underpriced shares, except by chance. However, if the market is inefficient it regularly prices shares incorrectly, allowing a perceptive investor to identify profitable trading opportunities.[11]

---

[11] Even though this discussion of the efficient markets hypothesis is set within the context of the equity markets in this chapter it must be noted that the efficient pricing of financial and real assets is discussed in many contexts; from whether currencies are efficiently priced vis-à-vis each other to the pricing of bonds, property and derivative instruments.

What is meant by efficiency?

In an efficient capital market, security (for example shares) prices rationally reflect available information.

The efficient market hypothesis (EMH) implies that, if new information is revealed about a firm, it will be incorporated into the share price rapidly and rationally, with respect to the direction of the share price movement and the size of that movement. In an efficient market no trader will be presented with an opportunity for making a return on a share (or other security) that is greater than a fair return for the risk associated with that share, except by chance. The absence of abnormal profit possibilities arises because current and past information is immediately reflected in current prices. It is only new information that causes prices to change. News is by definition unforecastable and therefore future price changes are unforecastable. Stock market efficiency does not mean that investors have perfect powers of prediction; all it means is that the current share price level is an unbiased estimate of its true economic value based on the information revealed.

Market efficiency does not mean that share prices are equal to true value at every point in time. It means that the errors that are made in pricing shares are unbiased; price deviations from true value are random. Fifty per cent of efficiently priced shares turn out to perform better than the market as a whole and 50 per cent perform worse; the efficient price is unbiased in the statistical sense. So if Marks & Spencer's shares are currently priced at £3 it could be, over the next five years, that we discover they were grossly overpriced at £3, or that events show them to be underpriced at £3. Efficiency merely means that there is an equal chance of our being too pessimistic at £3 as being too optimistic. The same logic applies to shares on high or low price-earnings ratios (PERs). That is, shares with low PERs should be no more likely to be overvalued or undervalued than shares with high PERs. Both groups have an equal chance of being wrongly priced given future economic events on both the upside and the downside.

In the major stock markets of the world prices are set by the forces of supply and demand. There are hundreds of analysts and thousands of traders, each receiving new information on a company through electronic and paper media. This may, for example, concern a technological breakthrough, a marketing success or a labour dispute. The individuals who follow the market are interested in making money and it seems reasonable to suppose that they will try to exploit quickly any potentially profitable opportunity. In an efficient market the moment an unexpected, positive piece of information leaks out investors will act and prices will rise rapidly to a level which gives no opportunity to make further profit.

Imagine that BMW announces to the market that it has a prototype electric car that will cost £10,000, has the performance of a petrol-driven car and will run for 500 miles before needing a low-cost recharge. This is something motorists and environmentalists have been demanding for many years. The profit-motivated investor will try to assess the value of a share in BMW to see if it is currently underpriced given the new information. The probability that BMW will be able successfully to turn a prototype into a mass-market production model will come into the equation. Also the potential reaction of competitors, the state of overall car market demand and a host of other factors have to be weighed up to judge the potential of the electric car and the future returns on a BMW share. No analyst or shareholder is able to anticipate perfectly the commercial viability of BMW's technological breakthrough but they are required to think in terms of probabilities and attempt to make a judgement.

If one assumes that the announcement is made on Monday at 10 a.m. and the overwhelming weight of investor opinion is that the electric car will greatly improve BMW's returns, in an efficient market the share price will move to a higher level within seconds. The new higher price at 10.01 a.m. is efficient but incorporates a different set of information from that incorporated in the price prevailing at 10 a.m. Investors should not be able to buy BMW shares at 10.01 a.m. and make abnormal profits except by chance.

Most investors are too late

Efficiency requires that new information is rapidly assimilated into share prices. In the sophisticated financial markets of today the speedy dissemination of data and information by cheap electronic communication means that there are large numbers of informed investors and advisers. These individuals are often highly intelligent and capable of fast analysis and quick action, and therefore there is reason to believe many stock markets are efficient at pricing securities. However, this belief is far from universal. Thousands of highly paid analysts and advisers maintain that they can analyse better and act more quickly than the rest of the pack and so make abnormally high returns for their clients. There is a well-known story which is used to mock the efficient market theoreticians:

A lecturer was walking along a busy corridor with a student on his way to lecture on the efficient market hypothesis. The student noticed a £20 note lying on the floor and stooped to pick it up. The lecturer stopped him, saying, 'If it was really there, someone would have picked it up by now.'

With such reasoning the arch-advocates of the EMH dismiss any trading system which an investor may believe he has discovered to pick winning shares. If this system truly worked, they say, someone would have exploited it before and the price would have already moved to its efficient level.

This position is opposed by professional analysts: giving investment advice and managing collective funds is a multi-billion-pound industry and those employed in it do not like being told that most of them do not beat the market. However, a *few* stock pickers do seem to perform extraordinarily well on a consistent basis over a long period of time. There is strong anecdotal evidence that some people are able to exploit inefficiencies.

What efficiency does not mean

To provide more clarity on what efficiency is, we need to deal with a few misunderstandings held by people with a little knowledge (a dangerous thing):

- **Efficiency means that prices do not depart from true economic value** This is false. At any one time we would expect most shares to deviate from true value, largely because value depends on the future, which is very uncertain. However, under the EMH we would expect the deviations to be random.

- **You will not come across an investor beating the market in any single time period** This is false because you would expect, in an efficient market, that approximately one-half of shares bought subsequently outperform. So, many investors, unless they buy such a broad range of shares that their portfolio tracks the market, would outperform. Note that, under the EMH, this is not due to skill, but simply caused by the randomness of price deviations from true economic value.

- **No investor following a particular investment strategy will beat the market in the long term** This is false simply because there are millions of investors. In a completely efficient market, with prices deviating in a random fashion from true value, it is likely that you could find a few investors who have outperformed the market over many years. This can happen because of the laws of probability; even if the probability of your investment approach beating the market is very small, the fact that there are millions of investors means that, purely by chance, a few will beat the market. Unfortunately, it is very difficult to investigate whether a long-term outperformance is luck or evidence against the EMH. Someone who has consistently outperformed for more than forty years is Warren Buffett. Some people believe his success is due to luck in an efficient market; others put it down to superior share-picking.

The black line in **Exhibit 6.15** shows an efficient market response to BMW's (fictional) announcement of an electric car. The share price instantaneously adjusts to the new level. However, there are four other possibilities if we relax the efficiency assumption. First, the market could take a long time to absorb this information (under-reaction) and it could be only after the tenth day that the share price approaches the new efficient level. This is shown in Line 1. Second, the market could anticipate the news announcement – perhaps there have been leaks to the press, or senior BMW management has been dropping hints to analysts for the past two weeks. In this case the share price starts to rise before the announcement (Line 2). It is only the unexpected element of the announcement that causes the price to rise further on the announcement day (from point A to point B). A third possibility is that the market overreacts to the new information (Line 3); the 'bubble' deflates over the next few days. Finally, the market may fail to get the pricing right at all and the shares may continue to be underpriced for a considerable period (Line 4).

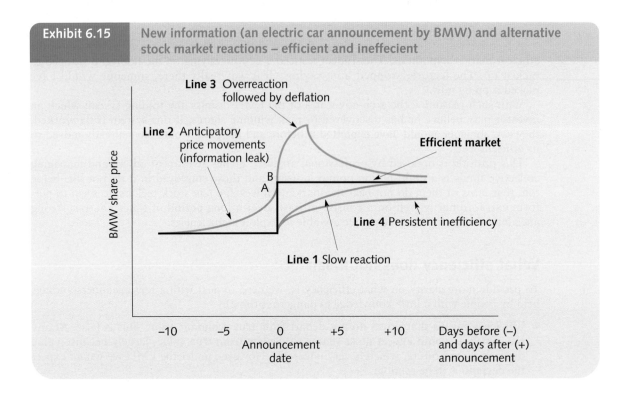

Exhibit 6.15	New information (an electric car announcement by BMW) and alternative stock market reactions – efficient and ineffecient

The value of an efficient market

It is important that share markets are efficient for at least three reasons.

1 *To encourage share buying* Accurate pricing is required if individuals are going to be encouraged to invest in private enterprise. If shares are incorrectly priced many savers will refuse to invest because of a fear that when they come to sell the price may be perverse and may not represent the fundamental attractions of the firm. This will seriously reduce the availability of funds to companies and inhibit growth. Investors need to know they are paying a fair price and that they will be able to sell at a fair price – that the market is a 'fair game'.

2 *To give correct signals to company managers* In Chapter 1 it was stated, for the purposes of this book, that the objective of the firm was the maximisation of shareholder wealth. This can be represented by the share price in an efficient market. Sound financial decision making therefore relies on the correct pricing of the company's shares. In implementing a shareholder wealth-enhancing decision the manager will need to be assured that the implication of the decision is accurately signalled to shareholders and to management through a rise in the share price. It is important that managers receive feedback on their decisions from the share market so that they are encouraged to pursue shareholder wealth strategies. If the share market continually gets the pricing wrong, even the most shareholder-orientated manager will find it difficult to know just what is required to raise the wealth of the owners.

In addition, share prices signal the rate of return investors demand on securities of a particular risk class. If the market is inefficient the risk-return relationship will be unreliable. Managers need to know the rate of return they are expected to obtain on projects they undertake. If shares are wrongly priced there is a likelihood that in some cases projects will be wrongly rejected because an excessively high cost of capital (discount rate) is used in project appraisal. In other circumstances, if the share prices are higher than they should be the cost of capital signalled will be lower than it should be and projects will be accepted when they should have been rejected.

Correct pricing is not just a function of the quality of the analysis and speed of reaction of the investment community. There is also an onus placed on managers to disclose information. Shares can only be priced efficiently if all relevant information has been communicated to the market. Managers neglect this issue at their peril.

3 **To help allocate resources** Deciding what goods and services are produced by a society by the allocation of capital to some industries while withdrawing it from others is described as allocation of resources. Efficient allocation in a market-based system requires both financial market operating efficiency (cost, speed and reliability of transactions in securities on the exchange) and pricing efficiency. If a poorly run company in a declining industry has highly valued shares because the stock market is not pricing correctly then this firm will be able to issue new shares, and thus attract more of society's savings for use within its business. This would be wrong for society as the funds would be better used elsewhere.

The three levels of efficiency

Economists have defined different levels of efficiency according to the type of information which is reflected in prices. Fama (1970) produced a three-level grading system to define the extent to which markets were efficient. These were based on different types of investment approaches which were supposedly designed to produce abnormal returns.

1 **Weak-form efficiency** Share prices fully reflect all information contained in past price movements. It is pointless basing trading rules on share price history as the future cannot be predicted in this way. *Evidence*: mostly in support, but there are some important exceptions.

2 **Semi-strong form efficiency** Share prices fully reflect all the relevant publicly available information. This includes not only past price movements but also earnings and dividend announcements, rights issues, technological breakthroughs, resignations of directors, and so on. The semi-strong form of efficiency implies that there is no advantage in analysing publicly available information after it has been released, because the market has already absorbed it into the price. *Evidence*: substantially in support but there are some exceptions.

3 **Strong-form efficiency** All relevant information, including that which is privately held, is reflected in the share price. Here the focus is on insider dealing, in which a few privileged individuals (for example directors) are able to trade in shares, as they know more than the normal investor in the market. In a strong-form efficient market even insiders are unable to make abnormal profits. The market is acknowledged as being inefficient at this level of definition.

Implications of the EMH for investors

If the market is efficient there are a number of implications for investors. Even if it is merely efficient most of the time, for most participants a sensible working assumption is that pricing is based on fundamental values and the following implications apply.

1 **For the vast majority of people public information cannot be used to earn abnormal returns.** (This refers to returns above the normal level for that systematic risk class.) The implications are that fundamental analysis is a waste of money and that so long as efficiency is maintained the average investor should simply select a suitably diversified portfolio, thereby avoiding costs of analysis and transaction. This message has struck a chord with millions of investors and thousands of billions of pounds have been placed with fund managers who merely replicate a stock market index (index funds) rather than try to pick winners in an actively managed fund. About 25 per cent of UK financial assets managed by professional investors (e.g. unit trusts) is in indexed funds. For the USA the figure is 35 per cent.

2 **Investors need to press for a greater volume of timely information.** Semi-strong efficiency depends on the quality and quantity of publicly available information, and so companies should be encouraged by investor pressure, accounting bodies, government rulings and stock market regulation to provide as much as is compatible with the necessity for some secrecy to prevent competitors gaining useful knowledge.

3 **The perception of a fair game market could be improved by more constraints and deterrents placed on insider dealers.** Strong-form efficiency does not exist and so insiders can gain an unfair advantage.

Implications of the EMH for companies

The efficient market hypothesis also has a number of implications for companies.

1 **Focus on substance, not on short-term appearance.** Some managers behave as though they believe they can fool shareholders. For example, creative accounting is used to show a more impressive performance than is justified. Most of the time these tricks are transparent to investors, who are able to interpret the real position, and security prices do not rise artificially.

There are some circumstances when the drive for short-term boosts to reported earnings can be positively harmful to shareholders. For example, one firm might tend to overvalue its inventory to boost short-term profitability; another might not write off bad debts. These actions will result in additional, or at least earlier, taxation payments which will be harmful to shareholder wealth. Managers, aware that analysts often pay a great deal of attention to accounting rate of return, may, when facing a choice between a project with a higher NPV but a poor short-term ARR, or one with a lower NPV but higher short-term ARR, choose the latter. This principle of short-termism can be extended into areas such as research and development or marketing spend. These can be cut to boost profits in the short term but only at a long-term cost to shareholders. One way to alleviate the short-term/long-term dilemma is for managers to explain why longer-term prospects are better than the current figures suggest. This requires a diligent communications effort.

2 **The timing of security issues does not have to be fine-tuned.** Consider a team of managers contemplating a share issue who feel that their shares are currently underpriced because the market is 'low'. They opt to delay the sale, hoping that the market will rise to a more 'normal level'. This defies the logic of the EMH – if the market is efficient the shares are already correctly (unbiasedly) priced and the next move in prices is just as likely to be down as up. The past price movements have nothing to say about future movements.

The situation is somewhat different if the managers have private information that they know is not yet priced into the shares. In this case if the directors have good news then they would be wise to wait until after an announcement and subsequent adjustment to the share price before selling the new shares. Bad news announcements are more tricky – to sell the shares to new investors while withholding bad news will benefit existing shareholders, but will result in loss for the new shareholders. There are rules against withholding price-sensitive information.

3 **Large quantities of new shares can be sold without moving the price.** A firm wishing to raise equity capital by selling a block of shares may hesitate to price near to the existing share price. Managers may believe that the increase in supply will depress the price of the shares. This is generally not the case. In empirical studies if the market is sufficiently large (for example the London, Euronext or New York Stock Exchange) and investors are satisfied that the new money will generate a return at least as high as the return on existing funds, the price does not fall. This is as we would expect in an efficient market: investors buy the new shares because of the return offered on them for their level of risk. The fact that some old shares of the same company already exist and that therefore supply has risen does not come into the equation. The key question is: what will the new shares produce for their holders? If they produce as much as an old share they should be priced the same as an old share. If they are not, then someone will spot that they can gain an abnormal return by purchasing these shares (which will push up the price).

4 **Signals from price movements should be taken seriously.** If, for instance, the directors announce that the company is to take over another firm and its share price falls dramatically on the day of the announcement this is a clear indication that the merger will be wealth destroying for shareholders – as the majority of mergers are. Managers cannot ignore this collective condemnation of their actions. An exception might be allowed if shareholders are dumping the shares in ignorance because the managers have special knowledge of the benefits to be derived from the merger – but then shouldn't the directors explain themselves properly?

So, are stock markets efficient?

While modern, large and sophisticated stock markets exhibit inefficiencies in some areas, particularly at the strong-form level, it is reasonable to conclude that they are substantially efficient and it is rare that a non-insider can outperform the market. However, there is growing evidence of some indications of important areas of inefficiency, e.g. low price-earnings ratio shares outperforming. Much of this empirical literature has been linked to the influence of psychology on stock market pricing. (For a discussion on efficiency evidence, *see* Arnold 2005.)

The London Stock Exchange is good at pricing shares; however, the person with superior analytical ability, knowledge, dedication and creativity can be rewarded with abnormally high returns.

Understanding the figures in the financial pages

Financial managers and investors need to be aware of what is happening on the financial markets, how their shares are affected and which measures are used as key yardsticks in evaluating a company. The financial pages of the broadsheet newspapers, particularly the *Financial Times*, provide some important statistics on company share price performance and valuation ratios. These enable comparisons to be made between companies within the same sector and across sectors. **Exhibit 6.16** shows extracts from two issues of the *Financial Times* from the same week. The information provided in the Monday edition is different from that provided on the other days of the week.

Indices

Information on individual companies in isolation is less useful than information set in the context of the firm's peer group, or in comparison with quoted companies generally. For example, if ICI shares fall by 1 per cent on a particular day, an investor might be keen to learn whether the market as a whole rose or fell on that day, and by how much. The *Financial Times* (FT) joined forces with the Stock Exchange (SE) to create FTSE International in November 1995, which has taken over the calculation (in conjunction with the Faculty and Institute of Actuaries) of a number of equity indices. These indicate the state of the market as a whole or selected sectors of the market and consist of 'baskets' of shares so that the value of that basket can be compared at different times. Senior managers are often highly sensitive to the relative performance of their company's share price. One reason for this is that their compensation package may be linked to the share price and in extreme circumstances managers are dismissed if they do not generate sufficiently high relative returns.

To calculate the indices shown in **Exhibit 6.17** each component share contributes to the index level. However, the shares do not have an equal weight in calculating the average. Rather, the average is derived by weighting each share by the size of the company, by its market capitalisation. Thus a 2 per cent movement in the share price of a large company has a greater effect on an index than a 2 per cent change in a small company's share price.[12] The characteristics of some of these indices are as follows.

---

[12] The weighting for some shares is reduced if a high proportion of the shares are held not in a free float but in the hands of people closely connected with the business, e.g. directors, major shareholders.

Exhibit 6.16 London Share Service extracts: Aerospace and Defence

FT

FRIDAY JANUARY 6 2006

	Notes	Price	Chng	52 week high	52 week low	Yld	P/E	Vol '000s
AEROSPACE & DEFENCE								
BAE SYS	...♱♣†	393½	−2½	395¾	224½	2.5	51.7	27,954
7¾pCvPf	....	190½	+¼	190¾	124¼	4.1	–	–
Chemring	.......†	757	+33	757	411½	1.2	20.9	112
Cobham	....♣†P	172	−3¼	175¼	123¾	1.9	–	5,057
Hampson	....	146	+1½	150	103¾	–	69.2	457
Meggitt	.......♣†	362	−5½	367½	252	2.0	20.9	4,266
Rolls-Ryc	v	439½	−2	441½	238¼	1.9	27.6	13,692
Smiths	....	1016½	−5	1052	813	2.9	20.8	4,439
Thales€	.........♣	£26 31/32	+7/16	£26 31/32	£21 3/16	1.9	32.1	633
UltraElc	......♣†	992	−16	1008	690½	1.5	22.0	332
UMECO	.....♣†	475½	+2½	530¼	375¾	2.9	15.9	775
VT	................†	438½xd	+3½	438½	298½	2.3	21.3	1,529

MONDAY JANUARY 9 2006

	Notes	Price	W'K% Chng	Div	Div cov.	MCap £m	Last xd	City line
AEROSPACE & DEFENCE								
BAE SYS	...♱♣†	408½	7.0	9.8	0.8	13,123	19.10	1890
7¾pCvPf	....	196½	5.4	7.75	–	523.3	23.11	5174
Chemring	.......†	875	19.2	9.4	3.9	255.3	7.9	2116
Cobham	....♣†P	173¼	2.2	3.19	0.3	1,943	9.11	2627
Hampson	....	145	2.8	–	–	126.8	1'2	2817
Meggitt	.......♣†	361¼	−2	7.2	2.4	1,564	12.10	3331
Rolls-Ryc	v	443	3.6	8.34	1.9	7,836	12.10	3853
Smiths	....	1023	−2.2	29.0	1.7	5,775	19.10	4050
Thales€	.........♣	£26⅞	1.3	75c	1.6	4,619	–	–
UltraElc	......♣†	993	0.1	14.4	3.1	665.9	24.8	1363
UMECO	.....♣†	480½	1.9	13.75	2.2	225.9	16.11	4929
VT	................†	436xd	2.8	10.0	2.1	755.1	23.11	4874

Market price: This is the mid-price (midway between the best buying and selling prices) quoted by market makers at 4.30 p.m. on the previous day.

Change in closing price on Thursday compared with previous trading day.

The highest and lowest prices during the previous 52 weeks.

Dividend yield: The dividend divided by the current share price expressed as a percentage:

$$\frac{\text{dividend per share}}{\text{current share price}} \times 100$$

Volume of trade in those shares that day.

Market capitalisation is calculated by multiplying the number of shares issued by their market price.

Ex-dividend date is the last date on which the share went ex-dividend (new buyers of the shares will not receive the recently announced dividend after this date).

City line: up-to-the-second share prices available by telephone (call 0906 843 000 then 4-digit code).

Price/earnings ratio (PER): Share price divided by the company's earnings (profits after tax) per share in the latest twelve-month period. A much examined and talked about measure (see Chapter 10):

$$\text{PER} = \frac{\text{share price}}{\text{earnings per share}}$$

Share price change over the previous week.

The dividend paid in the company's last full year – it is the cash payment in pence per share.

Dividend cover: Profit after tax divided by the dividend payment, or earnings per share divided by dividend per share:

$$\text{Dividend cover} = \frac{\text{earnings per share}}{\text{dividend per share}}$$

Exhibit 6.17

FTSE Actuaries Share Indices

Produced in conjunction with the Faculty and Institute of Actuaries
UK series

	£ Stlg Aug 8	Day's chge%	Euro Index	£ Stlg Aug 5	£ Stlg Aug 4	Year ago	Actual yield%	Cover	P/E ratio	Xd adj. ytd	Total Return
FTSE 100	5344.3	+0.6	6021.5	5314.7	5315.5	4314.4	3.18	2.11	14.87	112.80	2869.57
FTSE 250	7673.9	−0.1	8646.3	7680.5	7685.6	5834.4	2.50	2.26	17.69	120.06	4020.90
FTSE 250 ex Inv Co	7950.6	−0.1	8958.0	7957.2	7962.6	6079.4	2.58	2.37	16.31	127.08	4210.87
FTSE 350	2722.6	+0.5	3067.6	2709.9	2710.4	2179.7	3.09	2.13	15.19	55.36	2985.53
FTSE 350 ex Inv Co	2718.4	+0.5	3062.8	2705.4	2705.9	2179.9	3.11	2.14	15.01	55.65	1530.79
FTSE 350 Higher Yield	3439.1	+0.6	3874.9	3418.7	3423.1	2766.7	3.73	1.84	14.58	85.73	3440.55
FTSE Lower Yield	1986.2	+0.3	2237.9	1979.9	1977.8	1579.6	2.31	2.71	16.01	29.71	1653.06
FTSE SmallCap	3075.94	+0.2	3465.71	3069.02	3066.15	2435.97	2.00	1.23	40.56	38.25	3216.48
FTSE SmallCap ex Inv Co	3019.43	+0.3	3402.04	3011.13	3005.74	2453.79	2.14	1.29	36.22	39.09	3221.98
FTSE All-Share	2675.08	+0.5	3014.06	2662.74	2663.22	2140.91	3.05	2.11	15.50	53.67	2975.23
FTSE All-Share ex Inv Co	2668.86	+0.5	3007.04	2656.20	2656.60	2140.97	3.09	2.13	15.23	54.11	1529.67
FTSE All-Share ex Multinational	936.94	+0.1	874.95	935.63	934.75	762.63	3.25	2.04	15.07	19.89	1124.77
FTSE Fledgling	3452.73	+0.2	3890.25	3446.97	3439.13	2729.24	2.11	‡	‡	43.37	4700.93
FTSE Fledgling ex Inv Co	4369.00	+0.2	4922.63	4360.72	4343.62	3623.02	2.01	‡	‡	49.41	5874.93
FTSE All-Small	2043.03	+0.2	2301.91	2038.60	2036.30	1616.53	2.01	0.77	64.89	25.46	2739.22
FTSE All-Small ex Inv Co	2128.19	+0.3	2397.87	2122.55	2118.22	1732.09	2.12	0.71	66.67	27.14	2885.73
FTSE AIM All-Share	1068.2	−0.2	1203.6	1070.1	1070.7	854.6	0.49	0.07	80.00†	3.61	1029.73
FTSE Actuaries Industry Sectors											
RESOURCES(30)	7358.65	+1.3	8291.11	7266.30	7274.68	5430.77	2.74	2.28	15.99	132.61	4159.01
Mining (11)	9844.30	+1.3	11091.74	9714.51	9668.05	6657.20	2.24	3.51	12.70	124.76	3883.17
Oil & Gas(19)	7508.81	+1.3	8460.31	7415.82	7435.71	5663.45	2.87	2.03	17.13	146.58	4366.29
BASIC INDUSTRIES(47)	3339.39	−0.7	3762.55	3363.55	3387.45	2485.51	2.76	3.35	10.81	59.71	2528.50
Chemicals(9)	2482.30	−0.2	2796.85	2486.85	2512.06	1947.51	3.10	1.91	16.84	62.44	1667.65
Construction & Bld Matls(36)	3710.58	−1.0	4180.78	3747.21	3772.17	2672.11	2.75	3.58	10.17	61.45	2618.40
Forestry & Paper(1)	8663.31	−0.2	9761.90	8677.02	8635.89	8328.03	5.32	1.55	12.14	142.56	5636.38
Steel & Other Metals(1)	1125.37	+0.5	1267.98	1119.36	1119.36	1005.01	0.00	–	5.09	0.00	794.69
GENERAL INDUSTRIES(46)	2013.69	+0.8	2268.86	1998.46	1998.83	1466.45	2.74	1.84	19.89	27.65	1518.39
Aerospace and Defence(9)	2499.92	+1.1	2816.70	2472.01	2464.25	1719.59	2.71	1.85	19.91	29.24	2032.79
Electronic amd Elect Equip(16)	1747.01	......	1968.38	1746.47	1753.27	1518.67	2.21	1.32	34.34	22.67	1187.71

Source: Financial Times, 9 August 2005. Reprinted with permission.

FTSE 100 The 'Footsie™' index is based on the 100 largest companies (generally over £2bn market capitalisation). Large and relatively safe companies are referred to as 'blue chips'. This index has risen fivefold since it was introduced at the beginning of 1984 at a value of 1,000. This is the measure most watched by investors. It is calculated in real time (every 15 seconds) and so changes can be observed throughout the day. The other international benchmarks are: for the USA, the Dow Jones Industrial Average (DJIA) (30 share) index, the Standard and Poors 500 index and the NASDAQ Comp; for the Japanese market the Nikkei 225 index; for France the CAC-40; for Hong Kong the Hang Seng index and for Germany the Xetra Dax. For Europe as a whole there is FTSEurofirst300 and for the world FTSE Global All-cap.

- *FTSE All-Share* This index is the most representative in that it reflects the average movements of nearly 700 shares representing 98 per cent of the value of the London market. This index is broken down into a number of industrial and commercial sectors, so that investors and companies can use sector-specific yardsticks, such as those for mining or chemicals. Companies in the FTSE All-Share index have market capitalisations above about £45m. It is an aggregation of the FTSE 100, FTSE 250 and the FTSE SmallCap.

- *FTSE 250* This index is based on 250 firms which are in the next size range after the top 100. Capitalisations are generally between £200 million and £2bn. (It is also calculated with investment trusts excluded.)

- *FTSE 350* This index is based on the largest 350 quoted companies. It combines the FTSE 100 and the FTSE 250. This cohort of shares is also split into two to give high and low dividend yield groups. A second 350 index excludes investment trusts.

- *FTSE SmallCap* This index covers companies included in the FTSE All-Share but excluded from the FTSE 350, with a market capitalisation of about £45 million to £200 million.

- *FTSE Fledgling* This includes hundreds of companies too small to be in the FTSE All-Share Index. This index is a mixture of Ordinary List and AIM shares.

- *FTSE AIM All-Share* Index of all AIM companies (except those with low share turnover).

- *FTSE All-small* Combines companies in FTSE SmallCap with those in the FTSE Fledgling.

The indices in the first column in Exhibit 6.17 are price indices only (share price movements only are reflected in the indices). The final column, 'Total return', shows the overall performance with both share price rises and dividends reinvested in the portfolio.

Concluding comments

There are a number of alternative ways of raising finance by selling shares. The advantages and problems associated with each method and type mean that careful thought has to be given to establishing the wisest course of action for a firm, given its specific circumstances. Failure here could mean an unnecessary loss of control, an unbalanced capital structure, an excessive cost of raising funds or some other destructive outcome. But getting the share question right is only one of the key issues involved in financing a firm. The next chapter examines another, that of long-term debt finance.

Key points and concepts

- **Ordinary shareholders** own the company. They have the rights of control, voting, receiving annual reports, etc. They have no rights to income or capital but receive a residual after other claimants have been satisfied. This residual can be very attractive. **Debt capital holders** have no formal control but they do have a right to receive interest and capital.

- **Equity** as a way of financing the firm:

Advantages	*Disadvantages*
1 No obligation to pay dividends 'shock absorber'.	1 High cost: a issue costs; b required rate of return.
2 Capital does not have to be repaid.	2 Loss of control. 3 Dividends not tax deductible.

- **Authorised share** capital is the maximum amount permitted by shareholders to be issued. **Issued share** capital is the amount issued (sold) expressed at par value. **Share premium** is the difference between the sale price and par value of shares.

- **Preference shares** offer a fixed rate of return, but without a guarantee. They are part of shareholders' funds but not part of the equity capital.

Advantages to the firm	*Disadvantages to the firm*
1 Dividend 'optional'.	1 High cost of capital relative to debt.
2 Usually no influence over management.	2 Dividends are not tax deductible.
3 Extraordinary profits go to ordinary shareholders.	
4 Financial gearing considerations.	

Types of preference share: cumulative, participating, redeemable, convertible.

- The **London Stock Exchange** regulates the trading of **equities** (domestic and international) and **debt instruments** (e.g. gilts, corporate bonds and Eurobonds, etc.) and **other financial instruments** (e.g. preference shares). The **primary market** is where firms can raise finance by selling shares (or other securities) to investors. The **secondary market** is where existing securities are sold by one investor to another.

- **Internal funds** are generally the most important source of long-term capital for firms. **Bank borrowing** varies greatly and **new share or bond issues** account for a minority of the funds needed for corporate growth.

- The **Official List (OL)** is the most heavily regulated UK exchange. The **Alternative Investment Market (AIM)** is the lightly regulated exchange designed for small, young companies. **techMARK** is the sector of the Official List focused on technology-led companies. **PLUS** is an unregulated market.

- **To float on the Official List** of the London Stock Exchange the following are required: (i) a prospectus; (ii) an acceptance of new responsibilities; (iii) 25 per cent of share capital in public hands; (iv) that the company is suitable; (v) usually three years of accounts; (vi) competent and broadly based management team; (vii) appropriate timing for flotation; (viii) a sponsor; (ix) a corporate broker; (x) underwriters (usually); (xi) accountants' reports; (xii) lawyers; (xiii) registrar.

- **Following flotation on the OL:** companies need greater disclosure of information; there are restrictions on director share dealings; annual fees to LSE and costs of advisers etc.; high standards of behaviour.

- **Methods of flotation:** (i) offer for sale; (ii) offer for sale by tender; (iii) introduction; (iv) offer for sale by subscription; (v) placing; (vi) intermediaries' offer; (vii) reverse takeover.

- **Book-building** Investors make bids for shares. Issuers decide price and allocation in light of bids.

- **Stages in a flotation:** (i) pre-launch publicity; (ii) decide technicalities, e.g. method, price, underwriting; (iii) pathfinder prospectus; (iv) launch of public offer – prospectus and price; (v) close of offer; (vi) allotment of shares; (vii) admission to Exchange and first trading.

- The **Alternative Investment Market (AIM) differs from the OL in:** (i) nominated advisers, not sponsors; (ii) lower costs; (iii) no minimum capitalisation, trading history or percentage of shares in public hands needed; (iv) lower ongoing costs.

- **Rights issues** are an invitation to existing shareholders to purchase additional shares.

- The **theoretical ex-rights price** is a weighted average of the price of the existing shares and the new shares. **Value of a right on a new share:**

  Theoretical market value of share ex-rights – Subscription price

- **Value of a right on an old share:**

$$\frac{\text{Theoretical market value of share ex-rights} - \text{Subscription price}}{\text{Number of old shares required to purchase one new share}}$$

- The **pre-emption right** can be bypassed in the UK under strict conditions.

- **Placings** New shares sold directly to a group of external investors. If there is a *clawback* provision, so that existing shareholders can buy the shares at the same price instead, the issue is termed an **open offer**.

- **Acquisition for shares** Shares are created and given in exchange for a business.

- **Vendor placing** Shares are given in exchange for a business. The shares can be immediately sold by the business vendors to institutional investors.

Key points and concepts continued

- **Business angels** Wealthy individuals investing £10,000 to £250,000 in shares and debt of small, young companies with high growth prospects. Also offer knowledge and skills.

- **Venture capital (VC)** Finance for high-growth-potential unquoted firms. Sums: £100,000 minimum, average £5m.

- **Exit** ('take-out') is the term used by venture capitalists to mean the availability of a method of selling a holding. Popular methods are trade sale to another organisation, stock market flotation, own-share repurchase and sale to an institution.

- Venture capitalists often strike **agreements** with entrepreneurs to give the venture capitalists **extraordinary powers** if specific negative events occur, e.g. poor performance.

- **Private equity** is a term increasingly used for a range of sources of medium- to long-term finance provided in return for an equity stake in potentially high-growth unquoted companies, including business angel finance, MBOs and the more traditional type of venture capital provided to start-ups or small expanding firms.

- **Venture Capital Trusts (VCTs)** are special tax-efficient vehicles for investing in small unquoted firms through a pooled investment. With the **Enterprise Investment Scheme (EIS)** tax benefits are available to investors in small unquoted firms willing to hold the investment for three years.

- **Corporate venturing** Large firms can sometimes be a source of equity finance for small firms. **Incubators** provide finance and business services.

- **Government agencies** can be approached for equity finance.

- **Being quoted has significant disadvantages**, ranging from consumption of senior management time to lack of understanding between the City and directors and the stifling of creativity.

- **In an efficient market, security prices rationally reflect available information** New information is (a) rapidly and (b) rationally incorporated into share prices.

- **The benefits of an efficient market are:** (i) encourages share buying; (ii) gives correct signals to company managers; (iii) helps to allocate resources.

- **Weak-form efficiency** Share prices fully reflect all information contained in past price movements. *Evidence*: mostly in support, but there are some important exceptions.

- **Semi-strong form efficiency** Share prices fully reflect all the relevant, publicly available information. *Evidence*: substantially in support but there are some exceptions.

- **Strong-form efficiency** All relevant information, including that which is privately held, is reflected in the share price. *Evidence*: stock markets are strong-form inefficient.

- **Insider dealing** is trading on privileged information. It is profitable and illegal.

- **Implications of the EMH for investors:** (i) for the vast majority of people public information cannot be used to earn abnormal returns; (ii) investors need to press for a greater volume of timely information; (iii) the perception of a fair game market could be improved by more constraints and deterrents placed on insider dealers.

- **Implications of the EMH for companies:** (i) focus on substance, not on short-term appearances; (ii) the timing of security issues does not have to be fine-tuned; (iii) large quantities of new shares can be sold without moving the price; (iv) signals from price movements should be taken seriously.

- Dividend yield: $\dfrac{\text{Dividend per share}}{\text{Share price}} \times 100$ Price-earnings ratio (PER): $\dfrac{\text{Share price}}{\text{Earnings per share}}$

- Dividend cover: $\dfrac{\text{Earnings per share}}{\text{Dividend per share}}$

Further reading

For more detail on stockmarkets and other financial markets consult Arnold, G. (2005) Chapter 9, Arnold, G. (2004), Brett, M. (2000), Buckle, M. and Thompson, J. (2004), Roberts, R. (2004), Vaitilingam, R. (2001), Valdez, S. and Wood, J. (2003).

For flotation consult: London Stock Exchange (2004), *A Practical Guide to Listing on the London Stock Exchange*. Available at www.londonstockexchange.com.

For private equity consult publications by British Venture Capital Association, London (www.bvca.co.uk). Also Campbell, K. (2003), Zider, B. (1998), Roberts, M. J. and L. Barley (2004).

For information on the new issue market consult Jenkinson, T. and Ljungquist, A. (2001). For rights issues see Armitage, S. (2000).

For a summary of evidence on EMH consult Arnold, G. (2005) Chapter 14, Lofthouse, S. (2001), Montier, J. (2003), Shefrin, H. (2000), Shleifer, A. (2000), Thaler, R. H. (1993), Thaler, R. H. (2005).

Websites

Angel Bourse www.angelbourse.com
Beer & Partners www.beerandpartners.com
British Venture Capital Association www.bvca.co.uk
Business Links www.businesslinks.co.uk
Cavendish Management Resources www.cmrworld.com
Companies House www.companieshouse.gov.uk
CREST www.crestco.co.uk
Department of Trade and Industry www.dti.gov.uk
Development Capital Exchange www.dcxworld.com
Enterprise zone www.enterprisezone.org.uk
Entrust www.entrust.co.uk
Equity Link www.equitylink.exemplas.com
European Private Equity and Venture Capital Associations www.evca.com
Financial Express Company Announcements www.uk-wire.com
Financial Services Authority www.fsa.gov.uk
Financial Times www.ft.com
Fisma www.fisma.org
FTSE International www.ftse.com
Hemmington Scott www.hemscot.net
Hotbed www.hotbed.uk.com
International Federation of Stock Exchanges www.fibv.com
Investors Chronicle www.investorschronicle.co.uk
London Clearing House, LCH.Clearnet www.lchclearnet.com
Issues Direct www.issuesdirect.com
Katalyst Ventures www.katalystventures.com
London Stock Exchange www.londonstockexchange.com
National Business Angels Network (NBAN) www.nban.com
Office of National Statistics www.statistics.gov.uk
Proshare www.proshare.org
United Kingdom Listing Authority www.fsa.gov.uk/ukla
Venture Capital Report www.vcr1978.com

Self-review questions

1 What is equity capital? Explain the advantages to the firm of raising capital this way. What are the disadvantages?

2 What is the most important source of long-term finance for companies generally?

3 Distinguish between authorised and issued share capital.

4 What is a preference share and why might a company favour this form of finance?

5 Why has it been necessary to have more share exchanges than simply the Official List in the UK?

6 Why is a nominated adviser appointed to a firm wishing to join AIM?

7 Why might you be more cautious about investing in a company listed on PLUS than a company on the Official List of the London Stock Exchange?

8 Why does the United Kingdom Listing Authority impose stringent rules on companies floating on the Official List?

9 Outline the contents of a prospectus in a new issue on the Official List.

10 How might the working lives of directors change as a result of their company gaining a quotation?

11 What does a sponsor have to do to help a company float?

12 What are, and why do the UK authorities insist upon, pre-emption rights?

13 Why are placings subject to strict rules concerning the extent of price discount?

14 What do business angels bring to a firm?

15 What are the following: MBO, MBI, PTP, a venture capital fund, seedcorn?

16 What is meant by the Efficient Markets Hypothesis?

17 What are the implications of the EMH for investors and for managers?

Questions and problems

For questions marked with an asterisk* answers are given in the lecturer's guide and the lecturer's part of the website, www.pearsoned.co.uk/arnold

1 (*Examination level*) Bluelamp plc has grown from a company with £10,000 turnover to one with a £17m turnover and £1.8m profit in the last five years. The existing owners have put all their financial resources into the firm to enable it to grow. The directors wish to take advantage of a very exciting market opportunity but would need to find £20m of new equity capital as the balance sheet is already over-geared (i.e. has high debt). The options being discussed, in a rather uninformed way, are flotation on the Official List of the London Stock Exchange, a flotation on the Alternative Investment Market and venture capital. Write a report to enlighten the board on the merits and disadvantages of each of these three possibilities.

2 Checkers plc is considering a flotation on the Official List of the London Stock Exchange. Outline a timetable of events likely to be encountered which will assist management planning.

3 Discuss the merits and problems of the pre-emption right for UK companies.

4 There are a number of different methods of floating a company on the new issue market of the London Stock Exchange Official List (e.g. offer for sale). Describe these and comment on the ability of small investors to buy newly issued shares.

5* Mahogany plc has an ordinary share price of £3 and is quoted on the Alternative Investment Market. It intends to raise £20m through a one-for-three rights issue priced at £2.

   a What will the ex-rights price be?
   b How many old ordinary shares were in circulation prior to the rights issue?
   c Patrick owns 9,000 shares and is unable to find the cash necessary to buy the rights shares. Reassure Patrick that he will not lose value. How much might he receive from the company?
   d What is the value of a right on one old share?
   e What do the terms cum-rights and ex-rights mean?
   f Advise Mahogany on the virtues of a deep-discounted rights issue.

6 Venture capital funds made an internal rate of return of 13.6 per cent on investments up to the end of 2003. Describe the role of venture capitalists in the UK economy and comment on the rates of return they generally intend to achieve.

7 The shareholders of Yellowhammer plc are to offer a one-for-four rights issue at £1.50 when its shares are trading at £1.90. What is the theoretical ex-rights price and the value of a right per old share?

8 What are the main advantages and disadvantages of raising finance through selling (a) ordinary shares, and (b) preference shares?

9 Manchester United plc, the quoted football and leisure group, wins the cup and therefore can anticipate greater revenues and profits. Before the win in the final the share price was 640p.

   a What will happen to the share price following the final whistle of the winning game?
   b Which of the following suggests the market is efficient? (Assume that the market as a whole does not move and that the only news is the football match win.)
      (i)   The share price rises slowly over a period of two weeks to reach 700p.
      (ii) The share price jumps to 750p on the day of the win and then falls back to 700p one week later.
      (iii) The share price moves immediately to 700p and does not move further relative to the market.

Assignments

Consider the equity base of your company, or one you are familiar with. Write a report outlining the options available should the firm need to raise further equity funds. Also consider if preference share capital should be employed.

Visit www.pearsoned.co.uk/arnold to get access to Gradetracker diagnostic tests, Podcasts, Excel Spreadsheet Solutions, FT articles, a Flashcard revision tool, Weblinks, a searchable Glossary and more.

CHAPTER 7

Debt finance

LEARNING OUTCOMES

An understanding of the key characteristics of the main categories of debt finance is essential to anyone considering the financing decisions of the firm. At the end of this chapter the reader will be able to:

■ explain the nature and the main types of bonds, their pricing and their valuation;

■ describe the main considerations for a firm when borrowing from banks;

■ give a considered view of the role of mezzanine and high-yield bond financing as well as convertible bonds;

■ show awareness of the central importance of trade credit;

■ explain the different services offered by a factoring firm;

■ consider the relative merits of hire purchase and leasing;

■ demonstrate an understanding of the value of the international debt markets;

■ explain the term structure of interest rates and the reasons for its existence;

■ explain the main considerations when trying to decide between borrowing on a short-term rather than a long-term basis.

Introduction

The concept of borrowing money to invest in real assets within a business is a straightforward one, yet in the sophisticated capital markets of today with their wide variety of financial instruments and forms of debt, the borrowing decision can be bewildering. Should the firm tap the domestic bond market or the Eurobond market? Would bank borrowing be best? If so, on what terms, fixed or floating rate interest, a term loan or a mortgage? And what about syndicated lending, mezzanine finance and high-yield bonds? The variety of methods of borrowing long-term finance is infinite. This chapter will outline the major categories and illustrate some of the fundamental issues a firm may consider when selecting its finance mix.

Some fundamental features of debt finance

Put at its simplest, debt is something that has to be repaid. Corporate debt repayments have taken the form of interest and capital payments as well as more exotic compensations such as commodities and shares. The usual method is a combination of a regular interest, with capital (principal) repayments either spread over a period or given as a lump sum at the end of the borrowing. As explained in Chapter 6, debt finance is less expensive than equity finance, due to the lower rate of return required by finance providers, lower transaction costs of raising the funds and the tax deductibility of interest.

There are dangers associated with raising funds through debt instruments. Creditors are often able to claim some or all of the assets of the firm in the event of non-compliance with the terms of the loan. This may result in liquidation. Institutions which provide debt finance often try to minimise the risk of not receiving interest and their original capital. They do this by first of all looking to the earning ability of the firm, that is, the pre-interest profits in the years over the period of the loan. As a back-up they often require that the loan be secured against assets owned by the business, so that if the firm is unable to pay interest and capital from profits the lender can force the sale of the assets to receive their legal entitlement. The matter of security has to be thought about carefully before a firm borrows capital. It could be very inconvenient for the firm to grant a bank a fixed charge on a specific asset – say a particular building – because the firm is then limiting its future flexibility to use its assets as it wishes. For instance, it will not be able to sell that building, or even rent it without the consent of the bank or the bondholders.

Bonds

A bond is a long-term contract in which the bondholders lend money to a company. In return the company (usually) promises to pay the bond owners a series of interest payments, known as coupons, until the bond matures. At maturity the bondholder receives a specified principal sum called the par (face or nominal) value of the bond. This is usually £100 in the UK and $1,000 in the USA. The time to maturity is generally between 7 and 30 years although a number of firms, for example Disney, IBM and Reliance of India, have issued 100-year bonds.

Bonds may be regarded as merely IOUs (I owe you) with pages of legal clauses expressing the promises made. Some corporate bonds are sufficiently liquid (many transactions, so able to sell at low cost without moving the price) to trade on the London Stock Exchange, but the majority of trading occurs in the over-the-counter (OTC) market directly between an investor and a bond dealer. Access to a secondary market means that the investor who originally provided the firm with money does not have to hold on to the bond until the maturity date (the redemption date). However, because so many investors buy and then hold to maturity, rather than trade in and out, bonds generally have very thin secondary markets compared with shares. The amount the investor receives in the secondary market might be more or less than what he/she paid. For instance, imagine an investor paid £99.80 for a bond that promised to pay a coupon of 9 per cent per year on a par value of £100 and to repay the par value in seven years. If one year after issue interest rates on similar bonds are 20 per cent per annum no one will pay £99.80 for a bond agreement offering £9 per year for a further six years plus £100 on the redemption date. We will look at a method for calculating exactly how much they might be willing to pay later in the chapter.

These negotiable (that is, tradable in a secondary market) instruments come in a variety of forms. The most common is the type described above with regular (usually semi-annual) fixed coupons and a specified redemption date. These are known as straight, plain vanilla or bullet bonds. Other bonds are a variation on this. Some pay coupons every three months, some pay no coupons at all (called zero coupon bonds – these are sold at a large discount to the par value and the investor makes a capital gain by holding the bond), some bonds do not pay a fixed coupon but one which varies depending on the level of short-term interest rates (floating-rate or variable-rate bonds), some have interest rates linked to the rate of inflation. In fact, the potential for variety and innovation is almost infinite. Bonds issued in the last few years have linked the interest rates paid or the principal payments to a wide variety of economic events, such as the price of silver, exchange-rate movements, stock market indices, the price of oil, gold, copper – even to the occurrence of an earthquake. These bonds were generally designed to let companies adjust their interest payments to manageable levels in the event of the firm being adversely affected by some economic variable changing. For example, a copper miner pays lower interest on its finance if the copper price falls. In 1999 Sampdoria, the Italian football club, issued a €3.5m bond that paid a higher rate of return if the club won promotion to the 'Serie A' division (2.5 per cent if it stayed in Serie B, 7 per cent if it moved to Serie A). If the club rose to the top four in Serie A the coupon would rise to 14 per cent.

Debentures and loan stocks

The most secured type of bond is called a debenture. They are usually secured by either a fixed or a floating charge against the firm's assets. A fixed charge means that specific assets are used as security that, in the event of default, can be sold at the insistence of the debenture bondholder and the proceeds used to repay them. Debentures secured on property may be referred to as mortgage debentures. A floating charge means that the loan is secured by a general charge on all the assets of the corporation. In this case the company has a high degree of freedom to use its assets as it wishes, such as sell them or rent them out, until it commits a default which 'crystallises' the floating charge. If this happens a receiver will be appointed with powers to dispose of assets and to distribute the proceeds to the creditors. Even though floating-charge debenture holders can force a liquidation, fixed-charge debenture holders rank above floating-charge debenture holders in the payout after insolvency.

The terms bond, debenture and loan stock are often used interchangeably and the dividing line between debentures and loan stock is a fuzzy one. As a general rule debentures are secured and loan stock is unsecured but there are examples which do not fit this classification. If liquidation occurs the unsecured loan stockholders rank beneath the debenture holders and some other categories of creditors such as the tax authorities. In the USA the definitions are somewhat different and this can be confusing. There a debenture is an unsecured bond and so the holders become general creditors who can only claim assets not otherwise pledged. In the USA the secured form of bond is referred to as a mortgage bond and unsecured shorter-dated issues (less than 15 years) are called notes.

Bonds are often referred to collectively as fixed-interest securities. While this is an accurate description for many bonds, others do not offer *regular* interest payments that are *fixed* amounts. Nevertheless they are all lumped together as fixed interest to contrast these types of loan instrument with equities that do not carry a promise of a return.

Trust deeds and covenants

Bond investors are willing to lower the interest they demand if they can be reassured that their money will not be exposed to a high risk. This reassurance is conveyed by placing risk-reducing restrictions on the firm. A trust deed sets out the terms of the contract between bondholders and the company. The trustees ensure compliance with the contract throughout the life of the bond and have the power to appoint a receiver. The loan agreement will contain a number of affirmative covenants. These usually include the requirements to supply regular financial statements, interest and principal payments. The deed may also state the fees due to the lenders and details of what procedures are to be followed in the event of a technical default, for example non-payment of interest.

In addition to these basic covenants are the negative (restrictive) covenants. These restrict the actions and the rights of the borrower until the debt has been repaid in full. Some examples are:

- *Limits on further debt issuance* If lenders provide finance to a firm they do so on certain assumptions concerning the riskiness of the capital structure. They will want to ensure that the loan does not become more risky due to the firm taking on a much greater debt burden relative to its equity base, so they limit the amount and type of further debt issues – particularly debt which is higher ('senior debt') ranking for interest payments and for a liquidation payment. Subordinated debt – with low ranking on liquidation – is more likely to be acceptable.

- *Dividend level* Lenders are opposed to money being taken into the firm by borrowing at one end, while being taken away by shareholders at the other. An excessive withdrawal of shareholder funds may unbalance the financial structure and weaken future cash flows.

- *Limits on the disposal of assets* The retention of certain assets, for example property and land, may be essential to reduce the lenders' risk.

- *Financial ratios* A typical covenant here concerns the interest cover, for example: 'The annual pre-interest pre-tax profit will remain four times as great as the overall annual interest charge'. Other restrictions might be placed on working capital ratio levels, and the debt to net assets ratio. In the case of Photobition the interest cover threshold is 3.25 – *see* Exhibit 7.1.

Exhibit 7.1

Photobition cautions on covenants

FT

Photobition, the Surrey-based graphics business, admitted yesterday it could breach banking covenants over the level of its interest cover if US advertising spending continued to slow down. The company, which also reported a sharp fall in half-year profits, said net debt has risen to $103.5m (£77.3m) after a number of US acquisitions . . .

Analysts forecast that cover might fall to 2.43 times at the year-end in June, below the required minimum of 3.25.

'If they breach the bank covenants, they will be at the mercy of debt holders,' said one analyst. 'They could have to renegotiate their debt, or make some form of debt-equity conversion. They might also resort to a rights issue.'

Source: Florian Gimbel, *Financial Times*, 28 February 2001, p. 28. Reprinted with permission.

While negative covenants cannot provide completely risk-free lending they can influence the behaviour of the management team so as to reduce the risk of default. The lenders' risk can be further reduced by obtaining guarantees from third parties (for example guaranteed loan stock). The guarantor is typically the parent company of the issuer.

Repayments

The principal on many bonds is paid entirely at maturity. However, there are bonds which can be repaid before the final redemption date. One way of paying for redemption is to set up a sinking fund that receives regular sums from the firm that will be sufficient, with added interest, to redeem the bonds. A common approach is for the company to issue bonds where it has a range of dates for redemption; so a bond dated 2012–2016 would allow a company the flexibility to repay a part of the principal in cash over four years. Another way of redeeming bonds is for the issuing firm to buy the outstanding bonds by offering the holder a sum higher than or equal to the amount originally paid. A firm is also able to purchase bonds on the open market.

Some bonds are described as 'irredeemable' as they have no fixed redemption date. From the investor's viewpoint they may be irredeemable but the firm has the option of repurchase and can effectively redeem the bonds.

Bond variations

Bonds which are sold at well below the par value are called deep discounted bonds, the most extreme form of which is the zero coupon bond. It is easy to calculate the rate of return offered to an investor on this type of bond. For example, if a company issues a bond at a price of £60 redeemable at £100 in eight years the annualised rate of return (r) is:

$$60(1+r)^8 = 100$$

$$r = \sqrt[8]{\frac{100}{60}} - 1 = 0.066 \text{ or } 6.6\%$$

(Mathematical tools of this kind are explained in Appendix 2.1 to Chapter 2.)

These bonds are particularly useful for firms with low cash flows in the near term, for example firms engaged in a major property development which will not mature for many years.

A major market has developed over the past two decades called the floating-rate note (FRN) market (also called the variable-rate note market). Two factors have led to the rapid growth in FRN usage. First, the oscillating and unpredictable inflation of the 1970s and early 1980s caused many investors to make large real-term losses on fixed-rate bonds as the coupon rate fell below the inflation rate. As a result many lenders became reluctant to lend at fixed rates on a long-term basis. This reluctance led to floaters being cheaper for the issuer because it does not need to offer an interest premium to compensate the investor for being locked into a fixed rate. Second, a number of corporations, especially financial institutions, hold assets which give a return that varies with the short-term interest rate level (for example bank loans and overdrafts) and so prefer to have a similar floating-rate liability. These instruments pay an interest that is linked to a benchmark rate – such as the LIBOR (London Inter-Bank Offered Rate – the rate that the safest banks charge each other for borrowed funds). The issuer will pay, say, 70 basis points (0.7 of a percentage point) over six-month LIBOR. The coupon is set for (say) the first six months at the time of issue, after which it is adjusted every six months; so if LIBOR was 5 per cent, the FRN would pay 5.7 per cent for that particular six months. (There are LIBOR rates for various lengths of time, for example lending/borrowing between high reputation banks for a few hours (overnight LIBOR), or three months.)

There are many other variations on the basic vanilla bond, two of which will be examined later – high-yield bonds and convertible bonds. We now turn to another major source of long-term debt capital – bank borrowing.

Bank borrowing

For most companies and individuals banks remain the main source of externally (i.e. not retained earnings) raised finance. In this case a tradable security is not issued. The bank makes the loan from its own resources and over time the borrowing company repays the bank with interest. Borrowing from banks is attractive to companies for the following reasons.

● *Administrative and legal costs are low* Because the loan arises from direct negotiation between borrower and lender there is an avoidance of the marketing, arrangement, regulatory and underwriting expenses involved in a bond issue.

- *Quick* The key provisions of a bank loan can be worked out speedily and the funding facility can be in place within a matter of hours.
- *Flexibility* If the economic circumstances facing the firm should change during the life of the loan banks are generally better equipped – and are more willing – to alter the terms of the lending agreement than bondholders. Negotiating with a single lender in a crisis has distinct advantages. If the firm does better than originally expected a bank overdraft (and some loans) can be repaid without penalty. Contrast this with many bonds with fixed redemption dates, or hire purchase/leasing arrangements with fixed terms.
- *Available to small firms* Bank loans are available to firms of almost any size whereas the bond or money markets is for the big players only.

Factors for a firm to consider

There are a number of issues a firm needs to address when considering bank borrowing.

Costs

The borrower may be required to pay an arrangement fee, say 1 per cent of the loan, at the time of the initial lending, but this is subject to negotiation and may be bargained down[1]. The interest rate can be either fixed or floating. If it is floating then the rate will generally be a certain percentage above the bank's base rate or LIBOR. Because the borrowing corporation is not as safe as a high quality bank borrowing in the interbank market a corporation will pay, say, 1 per cent (or 100 basis points) more if it is in a good bargaining position. In the case of base rate-related lending, the interest payable changes immediately the bank announces a change in its base rate. This moves irregularly in response to financial market conditions, which are heavily influenced by the Bank of England in its attempt to control the economy.

For customers in a poorer bargaining position offering a higher-risk proposal the rate could be 5 per cent or more over the base rate or LIBOR. The interest rate will be determined not only by the riskiness of the undertaking and the bargaining strength of the customer but also by the extent of security for the loan and the size of loan – economies of scale in lending mean that large borrowers pay a lower interest rate.

A generation ago it would have been more normal to negotiate fixed-rate loans but most loans today are 'variable rate'. Floating-rate borrowings have advantages for the firm over fixed-rate borrowings:

- If interest rates fall the cost of the loan falls.
- At the time of arrangement fixed rates are usually above floating rates (to allow for lenders' risk of misforecasting future interest rates).
- Returns on the firm's assets may go up at times of higher interest rates and fall at times of lower interest rates, therefore the risk of higher rates is offset. For example, a bailiff firm may prosper in a high interest rate environment.

However, floating rates have some disadvantages:

- The firm may be caught out by a rise in interest rates if, as with most businesses, its profits do not rise when interest rates rise. Many have failed because of a rise in interest rates at an inopportune time.
- There will be uncertainty about the precise cash outflow impact of the interest. Firms need to plan ahead; in particular, they need to estimate amounts of cash coming in and flowing out, not least so that they can pay bills on time. Fixed rates contribute to greater certainty on cash flows.

---

[1] And indeed the firm should always try, where possible, to negotiate terms each year, or as and when the financial position of the company improves.

Security

When banks are considering the provision of debt finance for a firm they will be concerned about the borrower's competence and honesty. They need to evaluate the proposed project and assess the degree of managerial commitment to its success. The firm will have to explain why the funds are needed and provide detailed cash forecasts covering the period of the loan. Between the bank and the firm stands the classic gulf called 'asymmetric information' in which one party in the negotiation is ignorant of, or cannot observe, some of the information which is essential to the contracting and decision-making process. The bank is unable to assess accurately the ability and determination of the managerial team and will not have a complete understanding of the market environment in which they propose to operate. Companies may overcome bank uncertainty to some degree by providing as much information as possible at the outset and keeping the bank informed of the firm's position as the project progresses.

The finance director and managing director need to consider both the quantity and quality of information flows to the bank. An improved flow of information can lead to a better and more supportive relationship. Firms with significant bank financing requirements to fund growth will be well advised to cultivate and strengthen understanding and rapport with their bank(s). The time to lay the foundations for subsequent borrowing is when the business does not need the money, so that when loans are required there is a reasonable chance of being able to borrow the amount needed on acceptable terms.

Another way for a bank to reduce its risk is to ensure that the firm offers sufficient collateral for the loan. Collateral provides a means of recovering all or the majority of the bank's investment should the firm fail. If the firm is unable to meet its loan obligations then holders of fixed-charge collateral can seize the specific asset used to back the loan. Also, on liquidation, the proceeds of selling assets will go first to the secured loan holders, including floating-charge bank lenders. Collateral can include stocks, debtors and equipment as well as land, buildings and marketable investments such as shares in other companies. In theory banks often have this strong right to seize assets or begin proceedings to liquidate. In practice they are reluctant to use these powers because the realisation of full value from an asset used as security is sometimes difficult and such draconian action can bring adverse publicity. Banks are careful to create a margin for error in the assignment of sufficient collateral to cover the loan because, in the event of default, assigned assets usually command a much lower price than their value to the company as a going concern. A quick sale at auction produces bargains for the buyers of liquidated assets and usually little for the creditors.

Another safety feature applied by banks is the requirement that the firm abide by a number of loan covenants which place restrictions on managerial action in a similar fashion to bond covenants (see section on bonds earlier in this chapter).

Finally, lenders can turn to the directors of the firm to provide additional security. They might be asked to sign personal guarantees that the firm will not default. Personal assets (such as homes) may be used as collateral. This erodes the principle of limited liability status and is likely to inhibit risk-taking productive activity. However for many smaller firms it is the only way of securing a loan and at least it demonstrates the commitment of the director to the success of the enterprise.

Repayment

A firm must carefully consider the period of the loan and the repayment schedules in the light of its future cash flows. It could be disastrous, for instance, for a firm engaging in a capital project which involved large outlays for the next five years followed by cash inflows thereafter to have a bank loan which required significant interest and principal payments in the near term. For situations like these repayment holidays or grace periods may be granted, with the majority of the repayment being made once cash flows are sufficiently positive.

It may be possible for a company to arrange a mortgage-style repayment schedule in which monthly payments from the borrower to the lender are constant throughout the term.

A proportion of the interest and the principal can be repaid monthly or annually and can be varied to correspond with the borrower's cash flows. It is rare for there to be no repayment of the principal during the life of the loan but it is possible to request that the bulk of the principal is paid in the later years. Banks generally prefer self-amortising term loans with a high proportion of the principal paid off each year. This has the advantage of reducing risk by imposing a programme of debt reduction on the borrowing firm.

The repayment schedule agreed between bank and borrower is capable of infinite variety – four possibilities are shown in **Exhibit 7.2**.

Exhibit 7.2	Examples of loan repayment arrangements

£10,000 borrowed, repayable over four years with interest at 10% p.a. (assuming annual payments, not monthly)

		1	2	3	4
(a)	Time period (years)	1	2	3	4
	Payment (£)	3,155	3,155	3,155	3,155
(b)	Time period (years)	1	2	3	4
	Payment (£)	1,000	1,000	1,000	11,000
(c)	Time period (years)	1	2	3	4
	Payment (£)	0	0	0	14,641
(d)	Time period (years)	1	2	3	4
	Payment (£)	0	1,000	6,000	6,831

The retail and investment banks are not the only sources of long-term loans. Insurance companies and other specialist institutions such as 3i will also provide long-term debt finance.

Overdraft

Usually the amount that can be withdrawn from a bank account is limited to the amount put in. However, business and other financial activity often requires some flexibility in this principle, and it is often useful to make an arrangement to take more money out of a bank account than it contains – this is an overdraft.

An overdraft is a permit to overdraw on an account up to a stated limit.

Overdraft facilities are usually arranged for a period of a few months or a year and interest is charged on the excess drawings.

Advantages of overdrafts

Overdrafts have the following advantages.

1 *Flexibility* The borrowing firm is not asked to forecast the precise amount and duration of its borrowing at the outset but has the flexibility to borrow up to a stated limit. Also the borrower is assured that the moment the funds are no longer required they can be quickly and easily repaid without suffering a penalty.

2 *Cheapness* Banks usually charge two to five percentage points over base rate (or LIBOR) depending on the creditworthiness, security offered and bargaining position of the borrower. There may also be an arrangement fee of, say, 1 per cent of the facility. However, many banks have dropped arrangement fees completely to attract borrowers. These charges may seem high but it must be borne in mind that overdrafts are often loans to smaller and riskier firms which would otherwise have to pay much more for their funds. Large and well-established borrowers with low borrowing levels and plenty of collateral can borrow on overdraft at much more advantageous rates. A major saving comes from the fact that the banks charge interest on only the daily outstanding balance. So, if a firm has a large cash inflow one week it can use this to reduce its overdraft, temporarily lowering the interest payable, while retaining the ability to borrow more another week.

Drawbacks

A major drawback to an overdraft is that the bank retains the right to withdraw the facility at short notice. Thus a heavily indebted firm may receive a letter from the bank insisting that its account be brought to balance within a matter of days. This right lowers the risk to the lender because it can quickly get its money out of a troubled company; this allows it to lower the cost of lending. However, it can be devastating for the borrower and so firms are well advised to think through the use to which finance provided by way of an overdraft is put. It is not usually wise to use the money for an asset that cannot be easily liquidated; for example, it could be problematic if an overdraft is used for a bridge-building project which will take three years to come to fruition.

The age-old convention of attaching the right of the bank to withdraw the overdraft facility to a loan agreement was flouted by NatWest in 2000 (*see* **Exhibit 7.3.**).

Exhibit 7.3

NatWest deletes overdraft clause

Campaigners for small companies claimed a victory yesterday after NatWest bank abolished its right to remove a customer's overdraft at a moment's notice.

NatWest said it would turn current industry practice on its head by deleting the 'repayable on demand' clause from its small business overdrafts.

The bank said it would end the uncertainty faced by SMEs by ensuring that a three, six or 12 month overdraft meant exactly that. The conditions will apply to both secured and unsecured overdrafts.

Source: Jim Pickard, *Financial Times*, 21 November 2000, p. 6. Reprinted with permission.

Another major consideration for the overdraft borrower is the issue of security. Banks usually take a fixed charge or a floating charge. When Sir Richard Branson borrowed from Lloyds TSB the bank took shares owned by Sir Richard in Virgin Atlantic as security. Note also that, unusually, a three-year overdraft facility was arranged (*see* **Exhibit 7.4.**).

Exhibit 7.4

Branson wins £17m loan facility increase

Sir Richard Branson can borrow a further £17m from Lloyds TSB under a loan facility backed by Virgin Group's controlling stake in Virgin Atlantic, the prize of his business empire.

Virgin said yesterday it had mortgaged his 51 per cent stake in the Virgin Atlantic in exchange for a £67m three-year facility from Lloyds.

Sir Richard's group has already used £50m of the overdraft facility on new businesses, including US and Australian mobile phone ventures and the acquisition of a chain of South African health clubs.

Source: Francesco Guerrera and Thorold Barker, *Financial Times*, 12 June 2001, p. 26. Reprinted with permission.

Overdrafts are particularly useful for seasonal businesses because the daily debit-balance interest charge and the absence of a penalty for early repayment mean that this form of finance can be cheaper than a loan. Take the case of Fruit Growers plc (*see* Worked example 7.1).

Worked example 7.1	Fruit Growers plc

The management of Fruit Growers plc are trying to decide whether to obtain financing from an overdraft or a loan. The interest on both would be 10 per cent per year or 2.5 per cent per quarter. The cash position for the forthcoming year is represented in **Exhibit 7.5**.

Exhibit 7.5	Monthly cash position for Fruit Growers plc

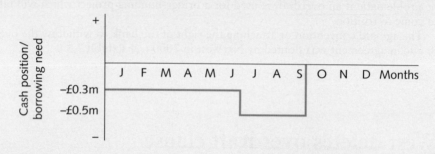

Option 1 A loan for the whole year

A loan for the whole year has the advantage of greater certainty that the lending facility will be in place throughout the year. A total loan of £500,000 will be needed, and this will be repaid at the end of the year with interest. At the beginning of the year Fruit Growers' account is credited with the full £500,000. For the months when the business does not need all the £500,000 the surplus can be invested to receive a return of 2 per cent per quarter.

Cost of a loan for the whole year

Interest charged 500,000 × 10%	= £50,000
Less interest receivable when surplus funds earn 2% per quarter	
January–June 200,000 × 4%	= –£8,000
October–December 500,000 × 2%	= –£10,000
Total cost of borrowing	= £32,000

Option 2 An overdraft facility for £500,000

An overdraft facility for £500,000 has the drawback that the facility might be withdrawn at any time during the year, but it is cheaper:

Costs of an overdraft facility for £500,000

1st quarter (J, F & M) 300,000 × 2.5%	= £7,500
2nd quarter (A, M & J) 300,000 × 2.5%	= £7,500
3rd quarter (J, A & S) 500,000 × 2.5%	= £12,500
4th quarter (O, N & D)	= £0
Total cost of borrowing	= £27,500

Note: We will ignore the complications of compounding intra-year interest.

Term loans

A term loan is a loan of a fixed amount for an agreed time and on specified terms. These loans are normally for a period of between three and seven years, but the period can range from one to twenty years. The specified terms will include provisions regarding the repayment schedule. If the borrower is to apply the funds to a project which will not generate income for perhaps the first three years it may be possible to arrange a grace period during which only the interest is paid, with the capital being paid off once the project has a sufficiently positive cash flow. Other arrangements can be made to reflect the pattern of cash flow of the firm or project: for example a 'balloon' payment structure is one when only a small part of the capital is repaid during the main part of the loan period, with the majority repayable as the maturity date approaches. A 'bullet' repayment arrangement takes this one stage further and provides for all the capital to be repaid at the end of the loan term.

Not all term loans are drawn down in a single lump sum at the time of the agreement. In the case of a construction project which needs to keep adding to its borrowing to pay for the different stages of development, an instalment arrangement might be required with, say, 25 per cent of the money being made available immediately, 25 per cent at foundation stage and so on. This has the added attraction to the lender of not committing large sums secured against an asset not yet created. From the borrower's point of view a drawdown arrangement has an advantage over an overdraft in that the lender is committed to providing the finance if the borrower meets prearranged conditions, whereas with an overdraft the lender can withdraw the arrangement at short notice.

The interest charged on term loans can be at either fixed or floating rates. In addition, the borrower may pay an arrangement fee, which will largely depend on the relative bargaining strength of the two parties.

A term loan often has much more accompanying documentation than an overdraft because of the lengthy bank commitment. This will include a set of obligations imposed on the borrowing firm such as information flows to the bank as well as financial gearing (debt to equity ratio) and liquidity ratio (availability of funds to meet claims) constraints. If these financial ratio limits are breached or interest and capital is not paid on the due date the bank has a right of termination, in which case it could decide not to make any more funds available, or, in extreme cases, insist on the repayment of funds already lent. Even if a firm defaults the bank will often try to reschedule or restructure the finance of the business (e.g. grant a longer period to pay) rather than take tough enforcement action.

Small Firms Loan Guarantee (SFLG)

Many small businesses face difficulty in growing because banks are reluctant to lend when there are few assets in the business to act as collateral for a loan. Fresh equity finance is an alternative, but many owners have put in as much as they can. They may be reluctant to sell ownership capital to outsiders, such as business angels, even if the business is sufficiently well advanced to attract funds from outside the founding family. Thus we have, through lack of finance, the stultification of otherwise vibrant businesses.

The UK government is sufficiently disturbed by this to support a scheme designed to encourage the banks to lend to small businesses less than five years old with a workable business proposal, but lacking security. The SFLG is a joint venture between the Department of Trade and Industry and approved lenders under which 75 per cent of the value of SFLG loans to these companies are guaranteed to be paid from the SFLG fund should the company fail. Note that the banks provide the finance (rather than the SFLG), but receive a guarantee from a government-backed fund that they will get most of their money back should the worst happen to the borrower.

Naturally, companies will fail from time to time and so the SFLG pays out regularly to the banks. The government has chosen not to provide this money from its own coffers, but it requires every business receiving a guarantee to pay an extra 2 per cent interest on SFLG loans outstanding each year into the fund.

The loans can be for any amount, with a minimum of £5,000 and a maximum of £250,000. The loans are for periods of up to 10 years and they are available to sole traders and partnerships as well as limited companies. However, turnover must be below £5.6m. If there are assets in the business then these will be used as security against the loan and will be confiscated first before any drawdown of the guarantee is made. Details on the SFLG are available from www.dti.gov.uk.

Syndicated loans

For large loans a single bank may not be able or willing to lend the whole amount. To do so would be to expose the bank to an unacceptable risk of failure on the part of one of its borrowers. Bankers like to spread their lending to gain the risk-reducing benefits of diversification. They prefer to participate in a number of syndicated loans in which a few banks each contribute a portion of the overall loan. So, for a large multinational company loan of, say, £500m, a single bank may provide £30m, with perhaps 100 other banks contributing the remainder. The bank originating the loan will usually manage the syndicate and is called the lead manager (there might be one or more lead banks). This bank (or these banks) may invite a handful of other banks to co-manage the loan which then persuade other banks to supply much of the funding. That is, they help the process of forming the syndicate group of banks in the general syndication. The managing bank also underwrites much of the loan while inviting other banks to underwrite the rest – that is, guaranteeing to provide the funds if other banks do not step forward. Syndicated loans are available at short notice and can be provided discreetly (helpful if the money is to finance a merger bid, for example). Syndicated loans generally offer lower interest than bonds, but as they rank above most bonds on liquidation payouts there is less risk. The loans carry covenants similar to those on bond agreements. The volume of new international syndicated loans now runs into hundreds of billions of pounds per year.

Exhibit 7.6 provides more on the syndicated loan market (Euribor is the rate at which high reputation banks lend to each other in euros).

Exhibit 7.6

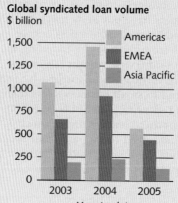

Corporate loans grow ever cheaper

by Gillian Tett

In the past few months, the average cost of a syndicated loan for US and European corporate has declined to levels not seen since 1997, according to data by Dealogic.

Whereas the average spread over Euribor for a high-grade corporate loan in the Europe, Middle East and Africa region was running at 86 basis points months ago, it recently declined to basis points. For the US, the fall has been almost equally marked, with average spreads tumbling from 97bp to 64bp.

This swing has taken several observers aback because the cost of corporate bond issuance, by contrast, has recently risen following the turmoil at Ford and General Motors, particularly for riskier issues.

Bankers attribute the falling syndicated loan prices to several factors. First, banks are awash with cash that they want to invest

Global syndicated loan volume
$ billion

Source: Dealogic

– and they have few more attractive alternative outlets for these funds, particularly in Europe.

"European banks, and to a lesser extent those in the US and Asia, simply don't know what else to do with their money," says one European investment banker.

Second, the supply of these loans is still relatively limited, relative to the soaring demand, partly because cash-rich corporates still appear to have muted willingness to borrow funds.

"With loans this cheap, it is hard to persuade companies to issue bonds on a large scale," says one investment banker.

Source: Financial Times, 8 June 2005, p.4. Reprinted with permission.

Credit rating

Firms often pay to have their bonds and other loans rated by specialist credit-rating organisations. The debt rating depends on the likelihood of payments of interest and/or capital not being paid according to the contract (that is, default) and on the extent to which the lender is protected in the event of a default (an estimate is made of the likelihood of recouping money in the event of insolvency or bankruptcy, the recoverability of the debt). UK government gilts (bonds issued by the UK government to lenders) have an insignificant risk of default whereas unsecured subordinated corporate loan stock has a much higher risk. We would expect that firms in stable industries and with conservative accounting and financing policies and a risk-averse business strategy would have a low risk of default and therefore a high credit rating. Companies with a high total debt burden, a poor cash flow position, in a worsening market environment causing lower and more volatile earnings, will have a high default risk and a low credit rating. The leading organisations providing credit ratings are Moody's, Standard & Poor's (S&P) and Fitch. The highest rating is AAA or Aaa (triple-A rated). Such a rating indicates very high quality. The capacity to repay interest and principal is extremely strong. Single A indicates a strong capacity to pay interest and capital but there is some degree of susceptibility to impairment as economic events unfold. BBB indicates adequate debt service capacity but vulnerability to adverse economic conditions or changing circumstances. B and C rated debt has predominantly speculative characteristics. The lowest is D which indicates the firm is in default. Ratings of BBB– (or Baa3 for Moody's) or above are regarded as 'investment grade' – this is important because many institutional investors are permitted to invest in investment grade bonds only (see **Exhibit 7.7**). Bonds rated below this are called high-yield (or junk) bonds. The specific loan is rated rather than the borrower. If the loan does not have a rating it could be that the borrower has not paid for one, rather than implying anything sinister.

The rating and re-rating of bonds is followed with great interest by borrowers and lenders and can give rise to some heated argument. Credit ratings are of great concern to the borrowing corporation because bonds with lower ratings tend to have higher costs – *see* **Exhibit 7.8**. The exhibit also shows the proportion of bonds in each credit rating category defaulting over

Exhibit 7.7	A comparison of Standard & Poor's, Moody's and Fitch's rating scales			
Standard & Poor's	**Moody's**	**Fitch**	**Grades**	
AAA	Aaa	AAA	Prime, maximum safety	⎫
AA+	Aa1	AA+	High grade, high quality	⎪
AA	Aa2	AA		⎪
AA–	Aa3	AA–		⎪
A+	A1	A+	Upper medium	⎬ Investment grade
A	A2	A		bonds
A–	A3	A–		⎪
BBB+	Baa1	BBB+	Lower medium	⎪
BBB	Baa2	BBB		⎪
BBB–	Baa3	BBB–		⎭
BB+	Ba1	BB+	Speculative	⎫
BB	Ba2	BB		⎪
BB–	Ba3	BB–		⎪
B+	B1	B+	Highly speculative	⎪
B	B2	B		⎬ Non-investment
B–	B3	B–		grade, high-yield
CCC+	Caa1	CCC+	Substantial risk	or 'junk' bonds
CCC	Caa2	CCC	In poor standing	⎪
CCC–	Caa3	CCC–		⎪
CC	Ca	CC	Extremely speculative	⎪
C	C	C	May be in default	⎭
D		D	Default	

Exhibit 7.8

Companies and regulators go on offensive in the global ratings game

Charles Batchelor looks at the fall-out from the down grading of BA, but investors would be lost without the help of Standard & Poor's and other exponents of the credit assessment art

In public, at least, senior executives do not usually take issue with the ratings the credit agencies apply to their debt. But British Airways' reaction to the decision by Standard & Poor's on Tuesday to cut its long term credit rating to junk was an exception.

John Rishton, BA's finance director, expressed 'astonishment' that the agency should downgrade its credit rating at a time when the airline's fortunes appeared to be improving. Mr Rishton is not alone in objecting publicly to a ratings agency downgrade. ThyssenKrupp was furious in February when its debt was downgraded to junk because of the scale of its pension deficit.

The agencies assess confidential and publicly available information on the issuers of debt and assign a rating, which can affect the cost of debt . . .

There can be no denying that the agencies wield enormous power ... Their reach takes in not only corporations but entire countries. Moody's downgraded South Korea's economic outlook in February because of the crisis surrounding North Korea's nuclear weapons programme, sparking sales of the currency and shares. Fitch's downgrade of Japan's banks was accompanied by criticism of the government's economic policies.

Source: Financial Times, 5 July 2003, p. M3. Reprinted with permission.

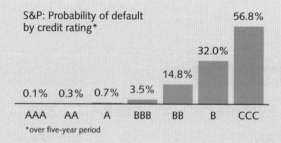

S&P: Probability of default by credit rating*

AAA	AA	A	BBB	BB	B	CCC
0.1%	0.3%	0.7%	3.5%	14.8%	32.0%	56.8%

*over five-year period

a five-year period. Those rated below investment grade have a much higher probability of default. Those rated CCC have a worse than 50:50 chance of default.

When examining data on default rates (as in the bar chart in Exhibit 7.8) it is important to appreciate that default is a wide-ranging term, and could refer to any number of events from a missed payment to liquidation. For some of these events all is lost from the investor's perspective. For other events a very high percentage, if not all, of the interest and principal is recovered. Hickman (1958) observed that defaulted publicly held and traded bonds tended to sell for 40 cents on the dollar. This average recovery rate rule-of-thumb seems to have held reasonably well over time (give or take a few percentage points).

Mezzanine debt and high-yield (junk) bonds

Mezzanine debt is a loan offering a high return with a high risk. It may be either unsecured or secured but ranking behind senior loans for payment of interest and capital. This type of debt generally offers interest rates two to nine percentage points more than that on senior debt and frequently gives the lenders some right to a share in equity values should the firm perform well. It is a kind of hybrid finance ranking for payment below straight debt but above equity – it is thus described alternatively as subordinated, intermediate or low grade. One of the major attractions of this form of finance for the investor is that it often comes with equity warrants [2] or share options attached which can be used to obtain shares in the firm – this is known as an 'equity kicker'. These may be triggered by an event such as the firm joining the stock market.

Mezzanine finance tends to be used when bank borrowing limits are reached and the firm cannot or will not issue more equity. It is more expensive than bank borrowing, but cheaper (in terms of required return) than would be available on the equity market; and it allows the owners of a business to raise large sums of money without sacrificing control. It is a form of finance which permits the firm to move beyond what is normally considered acceptable debt : equity ratios. Crucially, unlike most bank loans, which usually involve annual repayments, mezzanine is often like an interest only mortgage with no capital repayments until the end of the loan. Also mezzanine lenders, which are often specialist funds rather than banks, are usually prepared to lend against the company's prospects in terms of expected cash flows, rather than insisting on security (collateral), as banks tend toward.

Bonds with high-risk and high-return characteristics are called high-yield (junk) bonds. They are rated below investment grade by rating agencies with ratings of Bs and Cs. These may be bonds that started as apparently safe investments but have now become riskier ('fallen angels') or they may be bonds issued specifically to provide higher-risk finance instruments for investors. This latter type began its rise to prominence in the USA in the 1980s, and is now a market with over \$100bn issued per year. The high-yield bond is much more popular in the USA than in Europe because of the aversion (constrained by legislation) to such instruments in many of the major European financial institutions. Nevertheless, billions are raised in Europe each year through the sale of high-yield bonds.

Mezzanine finance/junk bond borrowing usually leads to high debt levels resulting in a high fixed cost imposition on the firm. This can be a dangerous way of financing expansion, and therefore the use of these types of finance has been criticised. On the other hand, some commentators have praised the way in which high gearing and large annual interest payments have focused the minds of managers and engendered extraordinary performance (*see* Chapter 11). Also, without this finance, many takeovers, buy-outs and financial restructurings would not take place.

Convertible bonds

Convertible bonds carry a rate of interest in the same way as vanilla bonds, but they also give the holder the right to exchange the bonds at some stage in the future into ordinary shares (or preference shares) according to some prearranged formula. The owner of these bonds is not obliged to exercise this right of conversion and so the bond may continue until redemption as an interest-bearing instrument. Usually the *conversion price* is 10–30 per cent greater than the existing share price. So if a £100 bond offered the right to convert to 40 ordinary shares the conversion price would be £2.50 (that is, £100/40) which, given the current market price of the shares of, say, £2.20, would be a *conversion premium* of:

$$\frac{2.50\text{-}2.20}{2.20} = 0.136 \text{ or } 13.6\%$$

In a rising stock market it is reasonable to suppose that most convertible bonds issued with a small conversion premium will be converted to shares. However, this is not always the case. Northern Foods issued convertible bonds in February 1993. The issue raised £91.28m. The bonds were to be redeemed in 15 years if they had not been converted before this and were priced at a par value of £100. The coupon was set at 6.75 per cent and the conversion price was at 326p per share. From this information we can calculate the *conversion ratio*:

---

[2] Warrants give the holder the right to subscribe for a specified number of shares at a fixed price during or at the end of a specified time period. If a company has shares currently trading at £3 it might choose to sell warrants (or to attach them to a loan), each of which grants the holder the right to buy a share at, say, £4 over the next five years. If by the fifth year the share price has risen to £6 the warrant holders could exercise their rights and then sell the shares immediately, realising £2 per share, which is likely to be a considerable return on the original warrant price of a few pence. When attached to a mezzanine loan or high yield bond these warrants could give a significant boost to the return on the lending if the firm performs well and the value of the shares rises a lot.

$$\text{Conversion ratio} = \frac{\text{Nominal (par) value of bond}}{\text{Conversion price}} = \frac{£100}{£3.26} = 30.67 \text{ shares}$$

Each bond carries the right to convert to 30.67 shares, which is equivalent to paying 326p for each share at the £100 par value of the bond.

The conversion price was set at a premium of 18.11 per cent over the ordinary share price at the time of pricing which was 276p ((326-276)/276 = 18.11%). At the time of the issue many investors may have looked at the low interest rate on the convertible (for 15-year bonds in 1993 6.75 per cent was low) and said to themselves that although this was greater than the dividend yield on shares (4–5 per cent) it was less than that on conventional bonds, but offsetting this was the prospect of capital gains made by converting the bonds into shares. If the shares rose to, say, £4, each £100 bond could be converted to 30.67 shares worth 30.67 × £4 = £122.68[3]. Unfortunately the share price by 2006 had fallen to about 80p and so the conversion right had not gained any intrinsic value – perhaps by the year 2008 it will be worthwhile exchanging the bonds for shares. In the meantime the investors at least have the comfort of a £6.75 coupon every year.

Advantages to the company of convertible bonds

Convertible bonds have the following advantages to the company.

1 *Lower interest than on a similar debenture* The firm can ask investors to accept a lower interest on these debt instruments because the investor values the conversion right. This was a valuable feature for many dot.com companies in the late 1990s. Companies such as Amazon and AOL could pay 5–6 per cent on convertibles – less than half what they would have paid on straight bonds.

2 *The interest is tax deductible* Because convertible bonds are a form of debt the coupon payment can be regarded as a cost of the business and can therefore be used to reduce taxable profit.

3 *Self-liquidating* When the share price reaches a level at which conversion is worthwhile the bonds will (normally) be exchanged for shares so the company does not have to find cash to pay off the loan principal – it simply issues more shares. This has obvious cash flow benefits. However, the disadvantage is that the other equity holders may experience a reduction in earnings per share and dilution of voting rights.

4 *Fewer restrictive covenants* The directors have greater operating and financial flexibility than they would with a secured debenture. Investors accept that a convertible is a hybrid between debt and equity finance and do not tend to ask for high-level security, impose strong operating restrictions on managerial action or insist on strict financial ratio boundaries. Many Silicon Valley companies with little more than a web-portal and a brand have used convertibles because of the absence of a need to provide collateral or stick to asset:borrowing ratios.

5 *Underpriced shares* A company which wishes to raise equity finance over the medium term but judges that the stock market is temporarily underpricing its shares may turn to convertible bonds. If the firm does perform as the managers expect and the share price rises, the convertible will be exchanged for equity.

6 *Cheap way to issue shares* Graham and Harvey (2001) found that managers favoured convertibles as an inexpensive way to issue 'delayed' equity. Equity capital comes in at a later date without high costs of rights issues etc.

7 *Available finance when straight debt and equity are not available* Some firms locked out of the equity markets (e.g. because of poor recent performance) and the straight debt markets because of high levels of indebtedness may still be able to raise money in the convertible market. Firms use convertible debt 'to attract investors unsure about the riskiness of the company' (Graham and Harvey (2001)).

---

[3] An extra complication was introduced to this convertible bond issue. The trust deed for the bond allowed for the adjustment of the conversion price if the company was split into two. When the dairy business was demerged the conversion price was adjusted to 225p.

Advantages to the investor

The advantages of convertible bonds to the investor are as follows.

1 They are able to wait and see how the share price moves before investing in equity.

2 In the near term there is greater security for their principal compared with equity investment, and the annual coupon is usually higher than the dividend yield.

Valuing bonds

Bonds, particularly those traded in secondary markets such as the London Stock Exchange, are priced according to supply and demand. The main influences on the price of a bond will be the general level of interest rates for securities of that risk level and maturity. If the coupon is less than the current interest rate the bond will trade at less than the par value of £100. Take the case of an irredeemable bond with an annual coupon of 8 per cent. This financial asset offers to any potential purchaser a regular £8 per year forever (i.e. 8 per cent of the par value of £100). When the bond was first issued general interest rates for this risk class may well have been 8 per cent and so the bond may have been sold at £100. However, interest rates change over time. Suppose that the rate demanded by investors is now 10 per cent. Investors will no longer be willing to pay £100 for an instrument that yields £8 per year. The current market value of the bond will fall to £80 (£8/0.10) because this is the maximum amount needed to pay for similar bonds given the current interest rate of 10 per cent. If the coupon is more than the current market interest rate the market price of the bond will be greater than the nominal (par) value. Thus if market rates are 6 per cent the irredeemable bond will be priced at £133.33 (£8/0.06). Note that as interest rates fall the price of the bond rises, and vice versa.

The formula relating the price of an irredeemable bond, the coupon and the market rate of interest is:

$$P_D = \frac{i}{k_D}$$

where
P_D = price of bond
i = nominal annual interest (the coupon rate × nominal (par) value of the bond)
k_D = market discount rate, annual return required on similar bonds

Also:

$$V_D = \frac{I}{k_D}$$

where
V_D = total market value of all of the bonds of this type
I = total annual nominal interest of all the bonds of this type

We may wish to establish the market rate of interest represented by the market price of the bond. For example, if an irredeemable bond offers an annual coupon of 9.5 per cent and is currently trading at £87.50, with the next coupon due in one year, the rate of return is:

$$k_D = \frac{i}{P_D} = \frac{9.5}{87.5} = 0.1086 \text{ or } 10.86\%$$

Redeemable bonds

A purchaser of a redeemable bond buys two types of income promise: first the coupon, second the redemption payment. The amount that an investor will pay depends on the amount these income flows are worth when discounted at the rate of return required on that risk class of debt. The relationships are expressed in the following formulae:

$$P_D = \frac{i_1}{1+k_D} + \frac{i_2}{(1+k_D)^2} + \frac{i_3}{(1+k_D)^3} + \dots + \frac{R_n}{(1+k_D)^n}$$

and:

$$V_D = \frac{I_1}{1+k_D} + \frac{I_2}{(1+k_D)^2} + \frac{I_3}{(1+k_D)^3} + \dots + \frac{R^*_n}{(1+k_D)^n}$$

where i_1, i_2 and i_3 = nominal interest per bond in years 1, 2 and 3 up to n years

I_1, I_2 and I_3 = total nominal interest in years 1, 2 and 3 up to n years

R_n and R^*_n = redemption value of a bond, and total redemption of all bonds in year n, the redemption or maturity date

The worked example of Blackaby illustrates the valuation of a bond when the market interest rate is given.

Worked example 7.2   Blackaby plc

Blackaby plc issued a bond with a par value of £100 in September 2005, redeemable in September 2011 at par. The coupon is 8 per cent payable annually in September – first payment in 2006. The facts available from this are:

● the bond might have a par value of £100 but this may not be what investors will pay for it;
● the annual cash payment will be £8 (8 per cent of par);
● in September 2011, £100 will be handed over to the bondholder.

Question 1

What is the price investors will pay for this bond at the time of issue if the market rate of interest for a security in this risk class is 7 per cent?

Answer

$$P_D = \frac{8}{1 + 0.07} + \frac{8}{(1 + 0.07)^2} + \frac{8}{(1 + 0.07)^3} + \dots + \frac{8}{(1 + 0.07)^6} + \frac{100}{(1 + 0.07)^6}$$

P_D = £8 annuity for 6 years @ 7 per cent = 4.7665 x 8   =   38.132

plus $\dfrac{100}{(1 + 0.07)^6} = 66.364$

	= 66.634
	£104.766

Question 2

What is the bond's value in the secondary market in September 2008 if interest rates rise by 200 basis points (i.e. for this risk class they are 9 per cent) between 2005 and 2008? (Assume the next coupon payment is in one year.)

Answer

P_D = £8 annuity for 3 years @ 9 per cent = 2.5313 × 8   =   20.25

plus $\dfrac{100}{(1+0.09)^3}$

	= 77.22
	= £97.47

Note, again, that as interest rates rise the price of bonds falls.

If we need to calculate the rate of return demanded by investors from a particular bond when we know the market price and the coupon amounts, we compute the internal rate of return. For example, Bluebird plc issued a bond many years ago that is due for redemption at par of £100 in three years. The coupon is 6 per cent and the market price is £91. The rate of return now offered in the market by this bond is found by solving for k_D:

$$P_D = \frac{i_1}{1 + k_D} + \frac{i_2}{(1 + k_D)^2} + \frac{R_n + i_3}{(1 + k_D)^3}$$

$$91 = \frac{6}{1 + k_D} + \frac{6}{(1 + k_D)^2} + \frac{106}{(1 + k_D)^3}$$

To solve this the skills learned in calculating internal rates of return in Chapter 2 are needed. At an interest rate (k_D) of 9 per cent, the right side of the equation amounts to £92.41. At an interest rate of 10 per cent the right-hand side of the equation amounts to £90.05. Using linear interpolation:

Interest rate	9%	?	10%
Value of discounted cash flows	£92.41	£91	£90.05

$$k_D = 9\% + \frac{92.41 - 91}{92.41 - 90.05} \times (10 - 9) = 9.6\%$$

AN EXCEL SPREADSHEET VERSION OF THIS CALCULATION IS AVAILABLE AT
www.pearsoned.co.uk/arnold

The two types of interest yield

There are two types of yield for fixed-interest securities. The *income yield* (also known as the flat yield, interest yield and running yield) is the gross (before tax) interest amount divided by the current market price of the bond expressed as a percentage:

$$\frac{\text{Gross interest (coupon)}}{\text{Market price}} \times 100$$

Thus for a holder of Bluebird's bonds the income yield is:

$$\frac{£6}{£91} \times 100 = 6.59\%$$

This is a gross yield. The after-tax yield will be influenced by the investor's tax position.

Net interest yield = Gross yield $(1 - T)$,
where T = the tax rate applicable to the bondholder

The income yield is not the true rate of return available to the investor should he/she buy it because it fails to take into account the capital gain (or loss) over three years to the expiry of the bond. At a time when interest rates are higher than 6.59 per cent it is obvious that any potential purchaser of Bluebird bonds in the market will be looking for a return other than from the coupon. That additional return comes in the form of a capital gain over three years of £100 – £91 = £9. A rough estimate of this annual gain is (9/91) ÷ 3 = 3.3 per cent per year. When this is added to the income yield we have an approximation to the second type of yield, the yield to maturity (also called the redemption yield). The yield to maturity of a bond is the discount rate such that the present value of all the cash inflows from the bond (interest plus principal) is equal to the bond's current market price. The rough estimate of 9.89 per cent (6.59% + 3.3%) has not taken into account the precise timing of the investor's income flows. When this is adjusted for, the yield to maturity is 9.6 per cent – the internal rate of return calculated above. Thus the yield to maturity includes both coupon payments and the capital gain or loss on maturity.

In the *Financial Times* bond tables the column headed 'bid yield' or GRY (gross redemption yield) is the yield to maturity given the current bid price (traders quote bid and offer prices, the bid is the price at which market makers will buy from investors, the offer price is what an investor would pay to buy from the market maker) – *see* Exhibit 7.18 on page 273 Note in Exhibit 7.18 that for Wal-Mart the yield to redemption (4.83%) is much less than the income yield (6.88/106.63 = 6.45%) due to the capital loss if you bought the bond now (January 2006) and received the par value in August 2009 – this is £106.63 – £100.

Trade credit

Perhaps the simplest and the most important source of short-term finance for many firms is trade credit. This means that when goods or services are delivered to a firm for use in its production they are not paid for immediately. These goods and services can then be used to produce income before the invoice has to be paid.

The writer has been involved with a number of small business enterprises, one of which was a small retail business engaged in the selling of crockery and glassware – Crocks. Reproduced as Exhibit 7.9 is an example of a real invoice (with a few modifications to hide the identity of the supplier). When we first started buying from this supplier we, as a matter of course,

---

Exhibit 7.9	A typical invoice

Supplier XYZ plc
54 West Street, Sussex

Invoice number 501360
Date 29/02/98

Invoice address
Crocks
Melton Mowbray
Leics
LE13 1XH

Branch address
Crocks
Grantham
Lincolnshire

INVOICE

Account TO2251	Customer order No. 81535	Sales order TO1537	Carrier	AEP 090	Despatch No. 000067981	Due date 28/03/98		Page 1

Item	Part code	Description	Unit of Sale	Quantity despatched	Unit price	%	Amount	VAT code
1	1398973	Long glass	each	12	0.84	0.00	10.08	0
2	12810357	Tumbler	each	12	0.84	0.00	10.08	0
3	1395731	Plate	each	60	1.10	0.00	66.00	0
4	1258732	Bowls	each	30	4.23	0.00	126.90	0
5	1310102	Cup	each	1	4.24	0.00	4.24	0
		VAT 0: 217.30 @ 17.5%\						

Note our settlement terms: 2½% discount may be deducted for payment within 14 days of invoice date; otherwise due 30 days strictly nett.		Nett goods	217.30
		Charges	0.00
		VAT	38.03
			255.33

applied for trade credit. We received the usual response, that the supplier requires two references vouching for our trustworthiness from other suppliers that have granted us trade credit in the past, plus a reference from our bankers. Once these confidential references were accepted by the supplier they granted us normal credit terms for retailers of our type of product, that is, 30 days to pay from the date of delivery. One of the things you learn in business is that agreements of this kind are subject to some flexibility. We found that this supplier does not get too upset if you go over the 30 days and pay around day 60: the supplier will still supply to the business on normal credit terms even if you do this on a regular basis.

Each time supplies were delivered by this firm we had to make a decision about when to pay. Option 1 is to pay on the 14th day to receive $2^1/_2$ per cent discount (see note at the bottom of the invoice). Option 2 is to take 60 days to pay. (Note: with Option 1 the $2^1/_2$ per cent deduction is on the 'nett goods' amount, which is the value of the invoice before value added tax (VAT) is added, that is £217.30.)

Option 1

£217.30 × 0.025 = £5.43

So, we could knock £5.43 off the bill if we paid it 14 days after delivery. This looks good but we do not yet know whether it is better than the second option.

Option 2

This business had an overdraft, so if we could avoid taking money from the bank account the interest charge would be less. How much interest could be saved by taking an additional 46 days (60 − 14) to pay this invoice? Assuming the annual percentage rate (APR) charged on the overdraft is 10 per cent the daily interest charge is:

$$(1+d)^{365} = 1+i$$

$$d = \sqrt[365]{(1 + i)} - 1$$

$$= \sqrt[365]{(1 + 0.1)} - 1 = 0.00026116$$

where

d = daily interest, and i = annual interest

Interest charge for 46 days:

$$(1 + 0.00026116)^{46} - 1 = 0.01208 \text{ or } 1.208\%$$

If we go for the early settlement discount and pay on day 14 we would have to borrow £255.33 minus the discount of £5.43 over a 46-day period at 10 per cent per annum interest:

$$(255.33 - 5.43) \times 0.01208 = £3.02$$

Thus £3.02 interest is saved by delaying payment to the sixtieth day, compared with a saving of over £5 on the option of paying early. In this particular case taking extended trade credit is not the cheapest source of finance; it is cheaper to use the overdraft facility.

Many suppliers to our business did not offer a discount for early settlement. This gives the impression that trade credit finance is a free source of funds and therefore the logical course of action is to get as much trade credit as possible. The system is therefore open to abuse. However, the corrective to that abuse is that a supplier will become tired of dealing with a persistent late payer and will refuse to supply, or will only supply on a basis of payment in advance. Another point to be borne in mind is that gaining a bad reputation in the business community may affect relationships with other suppliers.

Advantages of trade credit

Trade credit has the following advantages.

1 *Convenient/informal/cheap* Trade credit has become a normal part of business in most product markets.

2 *Available to companies of any size* Small companies, especially fast growing ones, often have a very limited range of sources of finance to turn to, and banks frequently restrict overdrafts and loans to the asset backing available. It is important to note that trade credit is a vital source of finance for the largest companies in the world as well as the smallest. For example, Wal-Mart UK, which owns Asda, typically has over twice as much owing to suppliers at any one time as the value of all the goods on its shelves – more than £1.6 billion. The suppliers don't just provide food etc.; they supply much of the money needed for the rest of Asda's operations

Factors determining the terms of trade credit:

- **Tradition within the industry** Customs have been established in many industries concerning the granting of trade credit. Individual suppliers may be unwise to step outside these traditions because they may lose sales.

- **Bargaining strength of the two parties** If the supplier has numerous customers, each wanting to purchase the product in a particular region, and the supplier wishes to have only one outlet then it may decide not to supply to those firms which demand extended trade credit. On the other hand, if the supplier is selling into a highly competitive market where the buyer has many alternative sources of supply, credit might be used to give a competitive edge.

- **Product type** Products with a high level of turnover relative to stocks are generally sold on short credit terms (say, 10 days rather than 40 days), for example food. The main reason is that these products usually sell on a low profit margin and the delay in payment can have a large impact on the profits.

Factoring

Factoring (or 'invoice finance') companies provide three services to firms with outstanding debtors, the most important of which, in the context of this chapter, is the immediate transfer of cash. This is provided by the factor on the understanding that when invoices are paid by customers the proceeds will go to them. Factoring is increasingly used by companies of all sizes as a way of meeting cash flow needs induced by rising sales and debtor balances.

1 The provision of finance

At any one time a typical business can have a fifth or more of its annual turnover outstanding in trade debts: a firm with an annual turnover of £5m may have a debtor balance of £1m. These large sums create cash difficulties which can pressurise an otherwise healthy business. Factors step in to provide the cash needed to support stock levels, to pay suppliers and generally aid more profitable trading and growth. The factor will provide an advance payment on the security of outstanding invoices. Normally about 80 per cent of the invoice value can be made available to a firm immediately (with some factors this can be as much as 90 per cent). The remaining 20 per cent is transferred from the factor when the customer finally pays up. Naturally the factor will charge a fee and interest on the money advanced. The cost will vary between clients depending on sales volume, the type of industry and the average value of the invoices. According to HSBC the charge for finance is comparable with overdraft rates (2–3 per cent over base rate). As on an overdraft, the interest is calculated on the daily outstanding balance of the funds that the borrowing firm has transferred to their business account. Added to this is a service charge that varies between 0.2 per cent and 3 per cent of invoiced sales.

This is set at the higher end if there are many small invoices or a lot of customer accounts or the risk is high. **Exhibit 7.10** shows the stages in a typical factoring transaction. First, goods are delivered to the customer and an invoice is sent. Second, the supplier sells the right to receive the invoice amount to a factor in return for, say, 80 per cent of the face value now. Third, some weeks later the customer pays the sum owing, which goes to the factor and, finally, the factor releases the remaining 20 per cent to the supplier less interest and fees.

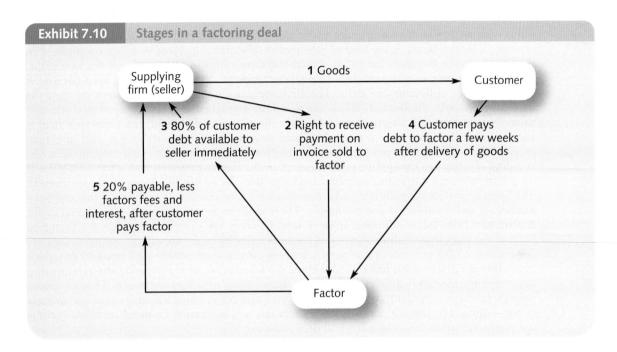

Exhibit 7.10   Stages in a factoring deal

Factors frequently reject clients as unsuitable for their services. The factor looks for 'clean and unencumbered debts' so that it can be reasonably certain of receiving invoice payments. It will also want to understand the company's business and to be satisfied with the competence of its management.

This form of finance has some advantages over bank borrowing. The factor does not impose financial ratio covenants or require fixed asset backing. Also the fear of instant withdrawal of a facility (as with an overdraft) is absent as there is usually a notice period. The disadvantages are the raised cost and the unavailability of factoring to companies with many small-value transactions. Also some businesses say it removes a safety margin. Instead of spending frugally while waiting for customers to pay they may be tempted to splurge the advance.

2 Sales ledger administration

Companies, particularly young and fast-growing ones, often do not want the trouble and expense of setting up a sophisticated system for dealing with the collection of outstanding debts. For a fee (0.5–2.5 per cent of turnover) factors will take over the functions of recording credit sales, checking customers' creditworthiness, sending invoices, chasing late payers and ensuring that debts are paid. The fees might seem high, say £100,000 for a firm with a turnover of £5m, but the company avoids the in-house costs of an administrative team and can concentrate attention on the core business. Moreover, factors are experienced professional payment chasers who know all the tricks of the trade (such as 'the cheque is in the post' excuse) and so can obtain payment earlier. With factoring, sales ledger administration and debt collection generally come as part of the package offered by the finance house, unlike with invoice discounting (*see* below).

3 Credit insurance

The third service available from a factor is the provision of insurance against the possibility that a customer does not pay the amount owed. The charge for this service is generally between 0.3 per cent and 0.5 per cent of the value of the invoices.

Invoice discounting

Firms with an annual turnover under £10m typically use factoring (with sales ledger administration), whereas larger firms tend to use invoice discounting. Here invoices are pledged to the finance house in return for an immediate payment of up to 90 per cent of the face value. The supplying company guarantees to pay the amount represented on the invoices and is responsible for collecting the debt. The customers are generally totally unaware that the invoices have been discounted. When the due date is reached it is to be hoped that the customer has paid in full. Regardless of whether the customer has paid, the supplying firm is committed to handing over the total invoice amount to the finance house and in return receives the remaining 10 per cent less service fees and interest. Note that even invoice discounting is subject to the specific circumstances of the client agreement and is sometimes made on a non-recourse basis (the discounter accepts the risk of non-payment by the customer). The finance provider usually only advances money under invoice discounting if the supplier's business is well established and profitable. There must be an effective and professional credit control and sales ledger administration system. Charges are usually lower than for factoring because the sales ledger administration is the responsibility of the supplying company. Fees are 0.2 per cent to 0.8 per cent of company sales plus interest comparable with business overdraft rates. Invoice discounting has the advantage over factoring of maintaining the relationship between customer and supplier without the intervention of a finance house. Thus customer records are kept confidential, the customer does not get nervous about its supplier using a factor – often seen (usually wrongly) as a desperate act, indicating financial troubles – and is not excessively pressurised by a forceful debt collector.

Exhibit 7.11 illustrates the importance of factoring to a packaging company.

Exhibit 7.11

Vital factor in surviving a slump

Invoice discounting is increasingly used to help survive cashflow problems. But it is not suitable for everyone

says Fergal Byrne

In 1991, as recession took hold, Jitu Shukla, managing director of Shukla Packaging, reached the end of his tether. For months, he had struggled to get customers to pay outstanding invoices. That and a change in the production base of the Watford-based wrapping paper and accessories company, requiring 50 per cent advance payment on international production, meant cashflow was becoming critical.

'I was spending all my time chasing debtors [across England] and I was increasingly stressed,' says Mr Shukla. 'Customers were delaying their payments by 15–20 days on average and we were heading for a cashflow crisis.'

With his bank manager increasingly nervous about the size of the company's overdraft, Mr Shukla opted for full-service factoring plus credit insurance from Lombard, now part of Royal Bank of Scotland Commercial Services. He worried about how his clients might react but it was a risk worth taking because otherwise the business might fail.

While factoring was relatively rare in the UK then, today some 30,000 companies use it in some form. For Mr Shukla, the decision to factor receivables was crucial. '[It] transformed the liquidity position of the company. And it has allowed me to focus my attention where it mattered – building relationships with our customers, vital during a downturn, and on new product development.'

Exhibit 7.11 continued

Factoring is not suitable for every business. It is unlikely to be offered in sectors such as construction and engineering, where payments are made over extended periods.

Factoring is usually more suitable for companies suffering an adverse cash cycle rather than dealing with bad payers – Shukla Packaging suffered both. Unless a company chooses credit insurance – less than 10 per cent do – factoring cannot eliminate bad debts. It may, in some cases, exacerbate the underlying problem, says John Anglin, a business adviser working at Entrust, a local enterprise agency in the north-east of England. 'I have seen companies in serious financial trouble when they have had to pay advances back to the factors – money that had already been spent – when a customer defaulted,' he says.

For Mr Shukla, taking out credit insurance with the factoring saved his business when greetings card company Athena collapsed less than a year later, accounting for almost 40 per cent of his receivables.

Shukla's customers tend to pay the factors quicker than they paid Shukla Packaging but this is not always the case.

The cost of the credit management and bill collection service performed by Royal Bank of Scotland Commercial Services has varied between 1–2 per cent of total invoices, which Mr Shukla says 'is a fraction of the cost of hiring a sales ledger clerk and a credit controller to chase debts throughout the UK, not to mention the possible legal costs'.

The interest rate on the company's factoring advances is lower than the rate on its overdraft, which Mr Shukla attributes to the factoring company's better understanding of the underlying business, helping it make a more accurate risk assessment than the bank. But some companies have seen their working capital position deteriorate when the bank has reduced the overdraft facility dramatically, says Eddy Weatherall, of the Independent Banking Advisory Service.

Both the decision to factor and the choice of factoring company need careful consideration. Mr Savich says his factoring contract was long, with lots of legal detail. 'Many companies simply do not have the expertise or the time to fully assess the nature of the deal,' says Mr Savich. 'And it can be difficult to unwind later.'

Source: Financial Times, 24 January 2002, p. 12. Reprinted with permission.

Hire purchase

With hire purchase the finance company buys the equipment that the borrowing firm needs. The equipment (plant, machinery, vehicles, etc.) belongs to the hire purchase (HP) company. However, the finance house allows the 'hirer' firm to use the equipment in return for a series of regular payments. These payments are sufficient to cover interest and contribute to paying off the principal. While the monthly instalments are still being made the HP company has the satisfaction and security of being the legal owner and so can take repossession if the hirer defaults on the payments. After all payments have been made the hirer becomes the owner, either automatically or on payment of a modest option-to-purchase fee. Nowadays, consumers buying electrical goods or vehicles have become familiar with the attempts of sales assistants to sell an HP agreement also so that the customer pays over an extended period. Sometimes the finance is provided by the same organisation, but more often by a separate finance house. The stages in an HP agreement are as in **Exhibit 7.12**, where the HP company buys the durable good which is made available to the hirer firm for immediate use. A series of regular payments follows until the hirer owns the goods.

There are clearly some significant advantages of this form of finance, given the fact that over £7bn of new agreements are arranged each year for UK small and medium- sized businesses alone. The main advantages are as follows.

1 *Small initial outlay* The firm does not have to find the full purchase price at the outset. A deposit followed by a series of instalments can be less of a cash flow strain. The funds that the company retains by handing over merely a small deposit can be used elsewhere in the business for productive investment. Set against this are the relatively high interest charges and the additional costs of maintenance and insurance.

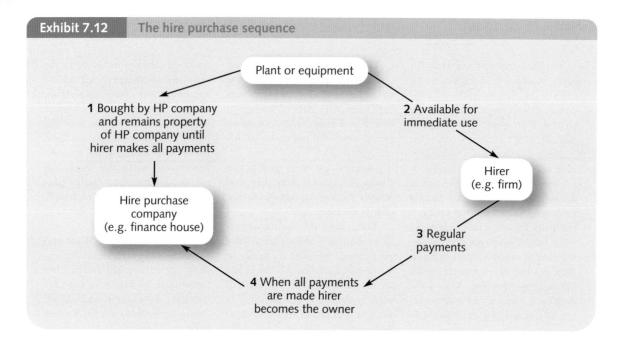

| Exhibit 7.12 | The hire purchase sequence |

2 *Easy and quick to arrange* Usually at point of sale allowing immediate use of the asset.

3 *Certainty* This is a medium-term source of finance which cannot be withdrawn provided contractual payments are made, unlike an overdraft. On the other hand the commitment is made for a number of years and it could be costly to terminate the agreement. There are also budgeting advantages to the certainty of a regular cash outflow.

4 *HP is often available when other sources of finance are not* For some firms the equity markets are unavailable and banks will no longer lend to them, but HP companies will still provide funds as they have the security of the asset to reassure them.

5 *Fixed-rate finance* In most cases the payments are fixed throughout the HP period. While the interest charged will not vary with the general interest rate throughout the life of the agreement the hirer has to be aware that the HP company will quote an interest rate which is significantly different from the true annual percentage rate. The HP company tends to quote the flat rate. So, for example, on a £9,000 loan repayable in equal instalments over 30 months the flat rate might be 12.4 per cent. This is calculated by taking the total payments made over the two and a half years and dividing by the original £9,000. The monthly payments are £401.85 and therefore the total paid over the period is £401.85 × 30 = £12,055.50. The flat interest is:

$$\sqrt[2.5]{(12,055.50 / 9,000)} - 1 = 0.1240 \; or \; 12.4\%$$

This would be the true annual rate if the entire interest and capital were repaid at the end of the thirtieth month. However, a portion of the capital and interest is repaid each month and therefore the annual percentage rate (APR) is much higher than the flat rate. As a rough rule of thumb the APR is about double the flat rate.

6 *Tax relief* The hirer qualifies for tax relief in two ways:

   a The asset can be subject to a writing-down allowance (WDA) on the capital expenditure. For example, if the type of asset is eligible for a 25 per cent WDA and originally cost £10,000 the using firm can reduce its taxable profits by £2,500 in the year of purchase; in the second year taxable profits will be lowered by £7,500 × 0.25 = £1,875. If tax is levied at 30 per cent on taxable profit the tax bill is reduced by £2,500 × 0.30 = £750 in the first year, and £1,875 × 0.3 = £562.50 in the second year. Note that this relief is available despite the hirer company not being the legal owner of the asset.

b Interest payments (an element of the monthly instalment) are deductible when calculating taxable profits.

The tax reliefs are valuable only to profitable companies. Many companies do not make sufficient profit for the WDA to be worth having. This can make HP an expensive form of finance. An alternative form of finance which circumvents this problem (as well as having other advantages) is leasing.

Leasing

Leasing is similar to HP in that an equipment owner (the lessor) conveys the right to use the equipment in return for regular rental payments by the equipment user (the lessee) over an agreed period of time. The essential difference is that the lessee never becomes the owner – the leasing company retains legal title. **Exhibit 7.13** shows that a typical lease transaction involves a firm wanting to make use of an asset approaching a finance house which purchases the asset and rents it to the lessee.

Exhibit 7.13   A leasing transaction

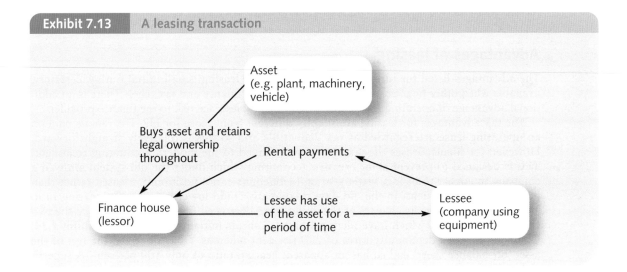

It is important to distinguish between operating leases and finance leases.

Operating lease

Operating leases commit the lessee to only a short-term contract or one that can be terminated at short notice. These are certainly not expected to last for the entire useful life of the asset and so the finance house has the responsibility of finding an alternative use for the asset when the lessee no longer requires it. Perhaps the asset will be sold in the second-hand market, or it might be leased to another client. Either way, the finance house bears the risk of ownership. If the equipment turns out to have become obsolete more quickly than was originally anticipated it is the lessor that loses out. If the equipment is less reliable than expected, the owner (the finance house) will have to pay for repairs. Usually, with an operating lease, the lessor retains the obligation for repairs, maintenance and insurance. It is clear why equipment which is subject to rapid obsolescence and frequent breakdown is often leased out on an operating lease. Photocopiers, for example, used by a university department are far better leased so that if they break down the university staff do not have to deal with the problem. In addition the latest model can be quickly installed in the place of an outdated one. The most common form of operating lease is contract hire. These leases are often used for a fleet of vehicles. The leasing company takes some responsibility for the management and maintenance of the vehicles.

Operating leases are also useful if the business involves a short-term project requiring the use of an asset for a limited period. For example, building firms often use equipment supplied under an operating lease (sometimes called plant hire). Operating leases are not confined to small items of equipment. There is a growing market in leasing aircraft and ships for periods substantially less than the economic life of the asset, thus making these deals operating leases.

Finance lease

Under a finance lease (also called a capital lease or a full payout lease) the finance provider expects to recover the full cost (or almost the full cost) of the equipment, plus interest, over the period of the lease. With this type of lease the lessee usually has no right of cancellation or termination. Despite the absence of legal ownership the lessee will have to bear the risks and rewards that normally go with ownership: the lessee will usually be responsible for maintenance, insurance and repairs and will suffer the frustrations of demand being below expectations or the equipment becoming obsolete more rapidly than anticipated. Most finance leases contain a primary and a secondary period. It is during the primary period that the lessor receives the capital sum plus interest. In the secondary period the lessee pays a very small, 'nominal' rental payment. If the company does not want to continue using the equipment in the secondary period it may be sold second-hand to an unrelated company.

Advantages of leasing

The advantages listed for hire purchase also apply to leasing: small initial outlay, certainty, available when other finance sources are not, fixed-rate finance and tax relief. There is an additional advantage of operating leases: the transfer of obsolescence risk to the finance provider.

The tax advantages for leasing are slightly different from those for HP. The rentals paid on an operating lease are regarded as tax deductible and so this is relatively straightforward. However, for finance leases the tax treatment is linked to the modern accounting treatment. This is designed to prevent some creative accounting which under the old system allowed a company to appear to be in a better gearing (debt/equity ratio) position if it leased rather than purchased its equipment. In the old days a company could lower its apparent gearing ratio and therefore improve its chances of obtaining more borrowed funds by leasing. Take the two companies X and Y, which have identical balance sheets initially, as shown in **Exhibit 7.14**. Company X has a debt/equity ratio of 200 per cent whereas Y has obtained the use of the asset 'off-balance sheet' and so has an apparent gearing ratio of only 100 per cent. A superficial analysis of these two firms by, say, a bank lender may lead to the conclusion that Y is more capable of taking on more debt. However, in reality Y has a high level of fixed cash outflow commitments stretching over a number of years under the lease and is in effect highly

| **Exhibit 7.14** | **Off-balance sheet financing** |

Initial balance sheet for X and Y

Shareholders' funds (net assets)	£1,000,000
Debt capital	£1,000,000
Total assets	£2,000,000

Now if X borrows a further £1m to buy equipment, while Y leases £1m of equipment the balance sheets appear strikingly different under the old accounting rules.

	Company X	Company Y
Shareholders' funds (net assets)	1,000,000	1,000,000
Debt capital	2,000,000	1,000,000
Total assets	3,000,000	2,000,000

geared. Furthermore, Company Y could also show a higher profit to asset ratio despite the fact that the underlying economic position of each firm is almost identical.

Today finance leases have to be 'capitalised' to bring them on to the balance sheet. The asset is stated in the balance sheet and the obligations under the lease agreement are stated as a liability. Over subsequent years the asset is depreciated and, as the capital repayments are made to the lessor, the liability is reduced. The profit and loss account is also affected: the depreciation and interest are both deducted as expenses.

The tax authorities apply similar rules and separate the cost of interest on the asset from the capital cost. The interest rate implicit in the lease contract is tax deductible in the relevant year. The capital cost for each year is calculated by allocating rates of depreciation (capital allowances) to each year of useful life.

These new rules apply only to finance leases and not to operating leases. A finance lease is defined (usually) as one in which the present value of the lease payments is at least 90 per cent of the asset's fair value (usually its cash price). This has led to some bright sparks engineering leasing deals which could be categorised as operating leases and therefore kept off-balance sheets – some are designed so that 89 per cent of the value is paid by the lessee. However, the authorities are fighting back, as **Exhibit 7.15** shows.

Exhibit 7.15

BT may have to review its property lease rules

By Jim Pickard, Property Correspondent

BT Group may have to recognise several hundred million pounds of property leases on its balance sheet under new international accounting rules, it has emerged. The change will be a result of the introduction of standard IAS 17, under which certain leases have to be recategorised.

Many leases that are currently recognised as 'operating leases', where the responsibilities and rewards fall on the landlord, may in fact be 'finance leases' where they are the tenant's responsibility. Typically, this may be where they are very long leases of 30 years or more.

Where a tenant has a finance lease, its payments to the landlord are accounted for as interest rather than rent and it must capi-talise the leases on its balance sheet and record them as an asset and a liability.

While this is seemingly only an accounting technicality, it is likely to have an impact on BT's cost of capital and gearing.

Source: Financial Times, 8 February 2005, p. 22. Reprinted with permission.

International sources of debt finance

Larger and more creditworthy companies have access to a wider array of finance than small firms. These companies can tap the *Euromarkets*, which are informal (unregulated) markets in money held outside its country of origin. For example, there is a large market in *Eurodollars*. These are dollar credits (loans) and deposits managed by a bank not resident in the USA. This has the distinct advantage of transactions not being subject to supervision and regulation by the authorities in the USA. So, for example, an Italian firm can borrow dollars from a Spanish bank in the UK and the US regulatory authorities have no control over the transaction. There is a vast quantity of dollars held outside the USA and this money is put to use by borrowers. The same applies to all the major currencies – the money is lent and borrowed outside its home base and therefore is beyond the reach of the domestic regulators. Today it is not unusual to find an individual holding a dollar account at a UK bank – a *Eurodeposit* account – which pays interest in dollars linked to general dollar rates. This money can be lent to firms wishing to borrow in Eurodollars prepared to pay interest and capital repayments in dollars. There are large markets in Euro Swiss francs, Eurosterling, Euroyen and many other currencies.

The title 'Euro' is misleading as this market is not limited to the European currencies or European banks (and is unconnected with the European single currency, the euro). The title came about because the modern market was started when the former Soviet Union transferred dollars from New York to a French bank at the height of the cold war in 1957. The cable address happened to be EUROBANK. This was long before the currency called the euro was conceived. Nowadays, there is daily Eurosecurities business transacted in all of the major financial centres. To add a little precision: 'Eurocurrency' is short-term (less than one year) deposits and loans outside the jurisdiction of the country in whose currency the deposit/loan is denominated; 'Eurocredit' is used for the market in medium- and long-term loans in the Euromarkets.

The companies which are large enough to use the Eurosecurities markets are able to put themselves at a competitive advantage *vis-à-vis* smaller firms. There are at least four advantages:

- The finance available in these markets can be at a lower cost in both transaction costs and rates of return.

- There are fewer rules and regulations such as needing to obtain official authorisation to issue or needing to queue to issue, leading to speed, innovation and lower costs.

- There may be the ability to hedge foreign currency movements. For example, if a firm has assets denominated in a foreign currency it can be advantageous to also have liabilities in that same currency to reduce the adverse impact of exchange-rate movements.

- National markets are often not able to provide the same volume of finance. The borrowing needs of some firms are simply too large for their domestic markets to supply. To avoid being hampered in expansion plans large firms can turn to the international market in finance.

For these internationally recognised firms there are three sources of debt finance:

(a) the domestic or national market;

(b) the financial markets of other countries which make themselves open to foreign firms – *the foreign debt market*;

(c) the Eurosecurities market which is not based in any one country and is not therefore regulated by any country.

Thus, for example, there are three bond markets available to some firms – as shown in **Exhibit 7.16**.

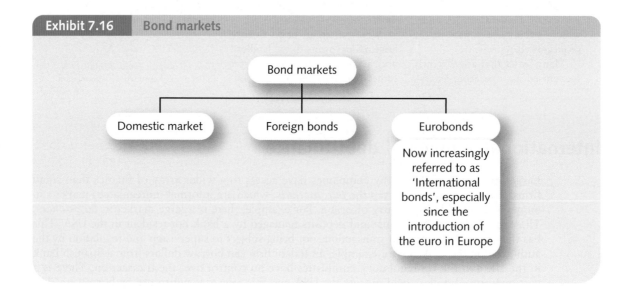

Exhibit 7.16   Bond markets

Foreign bonds

A foreign bond is a bond denominated in the currency of the country where it is issued when the issuer is a non-resident. For example, in Japan bonds issued by non-Japanese companies denominated in yen are foreign bonds. (The interest and capital payments will be in yen.)

Foreign bonds have been given some interesting names: foreign bonds in Tokyo are known as Samurai bonds, foreign bonds issued in New York and London are called Yankees and Bulldogs respectively. Foreign bonds are regulated by the authorities where the bond is issued. These rules can be demanding and an encumbrance to companies needing to act quickly and at low cost. The regulatory authorities have also been criticised for stifling innovation in the financial markets. The growth of the less restricted Eurobond market has put the once dominant foreign bond market in the shade.

Eurobonds (International bonds)

Eurobonds are bonds sold outside the jurisdiction of the country of the currency in which the bond is denominated. So, for example, the UK financial regulators have little influence over the Eurobonds denominated in sterling issued in Luxembourg, even though the transactions (for example interest and capital payments) are in pounds. Bonds issued in US dollars in Paris are outside the jurisdiction of the US authorities. They are medium- to long-term instruments. Eurobonds are not subject to the rules and regulations which are imposed on foreign bonds, such as the requirement to issue a detailed prospectus.[4] More importantly they are not subject to an interest-withholding tax. In the UK most domestic bonds are subject to a withholding tax by which basic rate income tax is deducted before the investor receives interest. Interest on Eurobonds is paid gross without any tax deducted – which has attractions to investors keen on delaying, avoiding or evading tax. Moreover, Eurobonds are bearer bonds, which means that the holders do not have to disclose their identity – all that is required to receive interest and capital is for the holder to have possession of the bond. In contrast, UK domestic bonds are registered, which means that companies and governments are able to identify the owners.

Despite the absence of official regulation, the International Capital Market Association (ICMA) a self-regulatory body, impose some restrictions, rules and standardised procedures on Eurobond issue and trading.

Eurobonds are distinct from euro bonds, which are bonds denominated in euros and issued in the eurozone countries. Increasingly people differentiate between the two by calling old-fashioned Eurobonds 'International bonds', leaving the title 'euro' for the currency introduced in 1999. Of course, there have been euro-denominated bonds issued outside the jurisdiction of the authorities in the euro area. These are euro Eurobonds.

The majority of Eurobonds (more than 80 per cent) are rated AAA or AA although those rated below BBB– are issued. Denominations are usually €1,000, €5,000 or €50,000 (or similar large sums in the currency of issue).

Types of Eurobonds

The Eurobond market has been extraordinarily innovative in producing bonds with all sorts of coupon payment and capital repayment arrangements (for example, the currency of the coupon changes halfway through the life of the bond, or the interest rate switches from fixed to floating rate at some point). We cannot go into detail here on the rich variety but merely categorise the bonds into broad types.

1 *Straight fixed-rate bond* The coupon remains the same over the life of the bond. These are usually paid annually, in contrast to domestic bond semi-annual coupons. The redemption of these bonds is usually made with a 'bullet' repayment at the end of the bond's life.

2 *Equity related* These take two forms:

(a) *Bonds with warrants attached* Warrants are options which give the holder the right to buy some other asset at a given price in the future. An equity warrant, for example, would give the right, but not the obligation, to purchase shares. There are also warrants for commodities such as gold or oil, and for the right to buy additional bonds

---

[4] Although new EU rules mean that a prospectus is required if the bond is marketed at retail (non-professional) investors.

from the same issuer at the same price and yield as the host bond. Warrants are detachable from the host bond and are securities in their own right, unlike convertibles.

(b) *Convertibles* The bondholder has the right (but not the obligation) to convert the bond into ordinary shares at a preset price.

3 *Floating-rate notes (FRNs)* These have a variable coupon reset on a regular basis, usually every three or six months, in relation to a reference rate, such as LIBOR. The size of the spread over LIBOR reflects the perceived risk of the issuer. The typical term for an FRN is about 5 to 12 years.

Exhibit 7.17	Advantages and drawbacks of Eurobonds as a source of finance for corporations

Advantage	Drawback
1 Large loans for long periods are available.	1 Only for the largest companies – minimum realistic issue size is about £50m.
2 Often cheaper than domestic bonds. The finance provider receives the interest without tax deduction and retains anonymity and therefore supplies cheaper finance. Economies of scale also reduce costs.	2 Because interest and capital are paid in a foreign currency there is a risk that exchange-rate movements mean more of the home currency is required to buy the foreign currency than was anticipated.
3 Ability to hedge interest rate and exchange-rate risk.	3 The secondary market can be illiquid.
4 The bonds are usually unsecured. The limitations placed on management are less than those for a secure bond.	
5 The lower level of regulation allows greater innovation and tailor-made financial instruments.	

The *Financial Times* publishes a table showing a selection of secondary market bid prices and yield of actively traded international bonds. This gives the reader some idea of the current market conditions and rates of return demanded for bonds of different maturities, currencies and risk – *see* **Exhibit 7.18**. The FT has another table, showing similar information for high-yield and emerging-market (less financially mature economies, e.g. Argentina) bonds.

Medium-term notes

By issuing a note a company promises to pay the holders a certain sum on the maturity date, and in many cases a coupon interest in the meantime. These instruments are typically unsecured and may carry floating or fixed interest rates. Medium-term notes (MTNs) have been sold with a maturity of as little as nine months and as great as 30 years, so the term is a little deceiving. They can be denominated in the domestic currency of the borrower (MTN) or in a foreign currency (Euro MTN). MTNs normally pay an interest rate above LIBOR, usually varying between 0.2 per cent and 3 per cent over LIBOR.

An MTN programme stretching over many years can be set up with one set of legal documents. Then, numerous notes can be issued under the programme in future years. A programme allows greater certainty that the firm will be able to issue an MTN when it needs the finance and allows issuers to bypass the costly and time-consuming documentation associated with each stand-alone note (bond). The programme can allow for bonds of various qualities, maturities, currencies or type of interest (fixed or floating). Over the years the

Exhibit 7.18

Redemption date:
January 2006

Gross (before
deduction of tax)
redemption yield

Global investment grade   **FT**

Jan 9	Red Date	Coupon	Ratings S*	M*	F*	Bid price	Bid yield	Day's chge yield	Mth's chge yield	Spread vs Govts
US $										
Inter Amer Dev	01/06	5.38	AAA	Aaa	AAA	100.01	4.65	+0.91	+0.57	+0.69
Canada	11/08	5.25	AAA	Aaa	AAA	101.97	4.50	–	–0.12	+0.17
Wal Mart	08/09	6.88	AA	Aa2	AA	106.63	4.83	+0.01	–0.11	+0.51
Du Pont	10/09	6.88	A	A2	A	106.78	4.88	+0.03	–0.08	+0.56
Phillips Petr	05/10	8.75	A–	A1	A–	115.18	4.85	+0.02	–0.24	+0.53
Unilever	11/10	7.13	A+	A1	A+	109.33	4.92	+0.02	–0.11	+0.60
Deutsche Tel	07/13	5.25	A–	A3	A–	100.04	5.24	+0.02	–0.13	+0.87
Daimler Chrysler	01/31	8.50	BBB	A3	BBB+	121.31	6.73	+0.03	–0.20	+2.16
GE Capital	03/32	6.75	AAA	Aaa	AAA	116.95	5.52	+0.04	–0.13	+0.96
Gen Motors	11/31	8.00	BB	Ba1	BB	99.75	8.02	–0.01	–0.40	+3.46
€										
Mannesman Fin	05/09	4.75	A+	A2	A	104.84	3.21	+0.04	–0.03	+0.30
Deutsche Fin	07/09	4.25	AA–	Aa3	AA–	103.98	3.04	+0.03	–0.02	+0.13
Repsol Int Fin	05/10	6.00	BBB+	Baa1	BBB+	110.09	3.44	+0.03	–0.07	+0.43
Elec de France	10/10	5.75	AA–	Aa1	AA–	111.74	3.07	+0.03	–0.08	+0.07
YEN										
Tokyo Elec	11/06	2.80	AA–	Aa3	AA–	102.35	0.13	–	+0.01	–
Toyota Motor	06/08	0.75	AAA	Aaa	n	100.86	0.39	–0.01	+0.02	+0.08
Chubu Elec	07/15	3.40	AA–	Aa3	AA–	116.71	1.41	–	–0.13	–
£										
Daimler Chrysler	12/06	7.50	BBB	A3	BBB+	102.28	4.83	–	–0.16	+0.52
HBOS	04/08	6.38	AA	Aa2	AA+	103.55	4.59	+0.03	–0.16	+0.35
Network Rail	03/09	4.88	AAA	Aaa	AAA	101.15	4.42	+0.02	–0.17	+0.19
Boots	05/09	5.50	BBB+	Baa1	BBB+	101.49	4.94	+0.02	–0.19	+0.71
France Telecom	03/11	7.50	A–	Baa1	A–	111.90	4.87	+0.03	–0.17	+0.67

US $ denominated bonds NY latest; all other London closing. *S - Standard & Poor's, M - Moody's, F - Fitch.

Issuer

Coupon as a
percentage of
the par value

Credit ratings

Bond price
with par value
set at 100

Spread to government bond rate (gilt).
The extent to which the rate of interest
(bid yield or gross redemption yield) is
greater than that on a government
bond of the same length of time to
maturity (in this case 0.71%)

Source: Financial Times, 10 January 2006, p.37. Reprinted with permission.

market can be tapped at short notice in the most suitable form at that time, e.g. US dollars rather than pounds, or redemption in three years rather than in two. It is possible to sell in small denominations, e.g. $5m, and on a continuous basis, regularly dripping bonds into the market. Banks charge a 'commitment fee' (around 10 to 15 basis points) for keeping open the option to borrow under an MTN programme, even if the company chooses not to do so in the end. Management fees will also be payable to the syndication of banks organising the MTN facility.

Commercial paper

The issue and purchase of commercial paper is one means by which the largest commercial organisations can avoid paying the bank intermediary a middleman fee for linking borrower and lender. Commercial paper promises to the holder a sum of money to be paid in a few days. The lender buys these short-term IOUs, with an average life of about 40 days (normal range 30–90 days, but can be up to 270 days), and effectively lends money to the issuer. Normally these instruments are issued at a discount rather than the borrower being required to pay interest – thus the face value (amount paid on redemption) will be higher than the amount paid for the paper at issuance. Large corporations with temporary surpluses of cash are able to put that money to use by lending it directly to other commercial firms at a higher rate of effective interest than they might have received by depositing the funds in a bank.

This source of finance is usually only available to the most respected corporations with the highest credit ratings, as it is usually unsecured lending. Standard & Poor's and Moody's use a different grading system for short-term instruments (e.g. A–1 or P–1 are the highest ratings). The main buyers, such as money market mutual funds (similar to unit trusts), are often restricted to having the bulk of their portfolios in the form of 'tier-one' rated issues – top ratings from credit rating agencies. Tier-two and tier-three issues do exist, but demand is very limited.

While any one issue of commercial paper is short term it is possible to use this market as a medium-term source of finance by 'rolling over' issues. That is, as one issue matures another one is launched. A commercial paper programme (a revolving underwriting facility) can be set up by a bank whereby the bank (or a syndicate of banks) underwrites a specified sum for a period of five to seven years. The borrower then draws on this every few weeks or months by the issue of commercial paper to other lenders. If there are no bids for the paper the under-writing bank(s) buys the paper at a specified price. Eurocommercial paper is issued and placed outside the jurisdiction of the country in whose currency it is denominated.

The term structure of interest rates

Until now we have assumed that the annual interest rate on a debt instrument remained the same regardless of the length of time of the loan. So, if the interest rate on a three-year bond is 7 per cent per year it would be 7 per cent on a five-year bond of the same risk class. However, it is apparent that lenders in the financial markets demand different interest rates on loans of differing lengths of time to maturity – that is, there is a term structure of the interest rates. Three of these relationships are shown in **Exhibit 7.19**. This diagram, taken from a 2004 edition of the *Financial Times*, represents the rate of return that the UK government had to offer on its bonds. It also shows the returns offered on bonds issued by the German and US governments. Note that default risk remains constant along one of the lines; the reason for the different rates is the time to maturity of the bonds. Thus a one-year German government bond has to offer just over 2 per cent whereas a 20-year bond offered by the same borrower offers about 4.5 per cent.

An upward-sloping yield curve occurs in most years but occasionally we have a situation where short-term interest rates (lending for, say, one year) exceed those of long-term interest rates (say, a 20-year bond).

Three main hypotheses have been advanced to explain the shape of the yield curve:

Exhibit 7.19   An approximation to the term structure of interest rates for UK, German and US government securities[5]

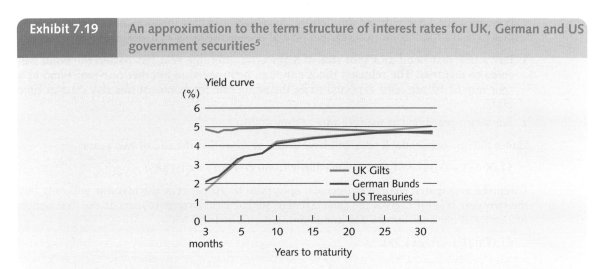

Source: *Financial Times*, 11–12 September 2004, p. 28. Reprinted with permission.

1. The expectation hypothesis

The expectation hypothesis focuses on the changes in interest rates over time. To understand the expectation hypothesis you need to know what is meant by a 'spot rate of interest'. The spot rate is an interest rate fixed today on a loan that is made today. So a corporation, Hype plc, might issue one-year bonds at a spot rate of, say, 8 per cent, two-year bonds at a spot rate of 8.995 per cent and three-year bonds at a spot rate of 9.5 per cent. This yield curve for Hype is shown in Exhibit 7.20. The interest rates payable by Hype are bound to be greater than for the UK government across the yield curve because of the additional default risk on these corporate bonds.

Spot rates change over time. The market may have allowed Hype to issue one-year bonds yielding 8 per cent at time 2006 but a year later (time 2007) the one-year spot rate may have changed to become 10 per cent. If investors expect that one-year spot rates will become 10 per cent at time 2007 they will have a theoretical limit on the yield that they require from a two-

Exhibit 7.20   The term structure of interest rates for Hype plc at time 2006

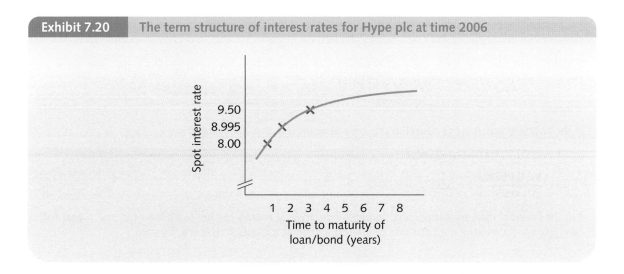

---

[5] Using the benchmark yield curve as an example of term structure of interest rates may offend theoretical purity, but it is a handy approximate measure and helps illustrate this section.

year bond when viewed from time 2006. To understand this imagine an investor (lender) wishes to lend £1,000 for a two-year period and is contemplating two alternative approaches:

1 Buy a one-year bond at a spot rate of 8 per cent; after one year has passed the bond will come to maturity. The released funds can then be invested in another one-year bond at a spot rate of 10 per cent, expected to be the going rate for bonds of this risk class at time 2007.

2 Buy a two-year bond at the spot rate at time 2006.

Under the first option the lender will have a sum of £1,188 at the end of two years:

£1,000 (1 + 0.08) = £1,080 followed by £1,080 (1 + 0.1) = £1,188

Given the anticipated change in one-year spot rates to 10 per cent the investor will only buy the two-year bond if it gives the same average annual yield over two years as the first option of a series of one-year bonds. The annual interest required will be:

$$£1,000 (1 + k)^2 = £1,188$$

$$k = \sqrt{(1,188/1,000)} - 1 = 0.08995 \text{ or } 8.995\%$$

Thus, it is the expectation of spot interest rates changing which determines the shape of the yield curve according to the expectation hypothesis.

Now consider a downward-sloping yield curve where the spot rate on a one-year instrument is 11 per cent and the expectation is that one-year spot rates will fall to 8 per cent the following year. An investor considering a two-year investment will obtain an annual yield of 9.49 per cent by investing in a series of one-year bonds, viz:

£1,000 (1.08) (1.11) = £1,198.80

$$k = \sqrt{(1198.8/1,000)} - 1 = 0.0949 \text{ or } 9.49\% \text{ per year}$$

$$\text{or } \sqrt{(1.08)(1.11)} - 1 = 0.0949$$

With this expectation for movements in one-year spot rates, lenders will demand an annual rate of return of 9.49 per cent from two-year bonds of the same risk class.

Thus in circumstances where short-term spot interest rates are expected to fall, the yield curve will be downward sloping.

Worked example 7.3   Spot rates

If the present spot rate for a one-year bond is 5 per cent and for a two-year bond 6.5 per cent, what is the expected one-year spot rate in a year's time?*

Answer

If the two-year rate is set to equal the rate on a series of one-year spot rates then:

$$(1 + 0.05)(1 + x) = (1 + 0.065)^2$$

$$x = \frac{(1 + 0.065)^2}{1 + 0.05} - 1 = 0.0802 \text{ or } 8.02\%$$

*In the financial markets it is possible to agree now to lend money in one year's time for, say, a year (or two years or six months, etc.) at a rate of interest agreed at the outset. This is a 'forward'.

2. The liquidity-preference hypothesis

The expectation hypothesis does not adequately explain why the most common shape of the yield curve is upward sloping. The liquidity-preference hypothesis helps explain the upward slope by pointing out that investors require an extra return for lending on a long-term basis. Lenders demand a premium return on long-term bonds compared with short-term instruments because of the risk of misjudging future interest rates. Putting your money into a ten-year bond on the anticipation of particular levels of interest exposes you to the possibility that rates will rise above the rate offered on the bond at some point in its long life. Thus, if five years later interest rates double, say because of a rise in inflation expectations, the market price of the bond will fall substantially, leaving the holder with a large capital loss. On the other hand, by investing in a series of one-year bonds, the investor can take advantage of rising interest rates as they occur. The ten-year bond locks in a fixed rate for the full ten years if held to maturity. Investors prefer short-term bonds so that they can benefit from rising rates and so will accept a lower return on short-dated instruments. The liquidity-preference theory focuses on a different type of risk attaching to long-dated debt instruments other than default risk – a risk related to uncertainty over future interest rates. A suggested reinforcing factor to the upward slope is that borrowers usually prefer long-term debt because of the fear of having to repay short-term debt at inappropriate moments. Thus borrowers increase the supply of long-term debt instruments, adding to the tendency for long-term rates to be higher than short-term rates.

Note that the word liquidity in the title is incorrectly used – but it has stuck so we still use it. Liquidity refers to the speed and ease of the sale of an asset. In the case of long-term bonds (especially government bonds) sale in the secondary market is often as quick and easy for short-term bonds. The premium for long bonds is compensation for the extra risk of capital loss; 'term premium' might be a better title for the hypothesis.

3. The market-segmentation hypothesis

The market-segmentation hypothesis argues that the debt market is not one homogeneous whole; that there are, in fact, a number of sub-markets defined by maturity range. The yield curve is therefore created (or at least influenced) by the supply and demand conditions in each of these sub-markets. For example, banks tend to be active in the short-term end of the market and pension funds to be buyers in the long-dated segment. If banks need to borrow large quantities quickly they will sell some of their short-term instruments, increasing the supply on the market and pushing down the price and raising the yield. On the other hand pension funds may be flush with cash and may buy large quantities of 20-year bonds, helping to temporarily move yields downward at the long end of the market. At other times banks, pension funds and the buying and selling pressures of a multitude of other financial institutions will influence the supply and demand position in the opposite direction. The point is that the players in the different parts of the yield curve tend to be different. This hypothesis helps to explain the often lumpy or humped yield curve.

Is it better to borrow long or short?

Once a company has decided to raise funds by borrowing, it then has to decide whether to raise the money through:

(a) short-term debt – a loan which has to be repaid within, say, one year;

(b) medium-term debt; or

(c) long-term debt – where the loan is paid over a 7-, 25- or even 100-year period.

There are a number of factors to be taken into consideration in making a decision of this nature.

- *Maturity structure* A company will usually try to avoid having all of its debts maturing at or near the same date. It could be disastrous if the firm was required to repay loan capital on a number of different instruments all within, say, a six-month period. Even if the firm is profitable the sudden cash outflow could lead to insolvency. A number of major UK retailers came perilously close to this in the early 1990s. In the late 1980s they had experienced a boom in sales and everything the management touched seemed to turn to gold. Buoyed up by overoptimism, they opened up dozens of new branches, funded to a large extent by medium-term finance. By the time these bank loans, bonds, etc. came to maturity in the early 1990s these shop chains were already suffering from a biting recession and an excessive cost base. Negotiations with bankers and others were necessary as loan covenants were broken and bankruptcy loomed. Most of the larger groups survived but they have learnt a hard lesson about the importance of spreading the dates for principal repayment.

- *Costs of issue/arrangement* It is usually cheaper to arrange an overdraft and other one-off short-term finance than long-term debt facilities, but this advantage is sometimes outweighed by the fact that if funds are needed over a number of years short-term debt has to be renewed more often than long-term debt. So over, say, a 20-year period, the issuing and arrangement costs of short-term debt may be much greater than for a 20-year bond.

- *Flexibility* Short-term debt is more flexible than long-term debt. If a business has fluctuations in its needs for borrowed funds, for example if it is a seasonal business, then for some months it does not need any borrowed funds, whereas at other times it needs large loans. A long-term loan may be inefficient because the firm will be paying interest even if it has surplus cash. True, the surplus cash could be invested but the proceeds are unlikely to be as great as the cost of the loan interest. It is cheaper to take out short-term loans or overdrafts when the need arises which can be paid back when the firm has high cash inflows.

- *The uncertainty of getting future finance* If a firm is investing in a long-term project which requires borrowing for many years it would be risky to finance this project using one-year loans. At the end of each year the firm has to renegotiate the loan or issue a new bond. There may come a time when lenders will not supply the new money. There may, for example, be a change in the bank's policy or a reassessment of the borrower's creditworthiness, a crisis of confidence in the financial markets or an imposition of government restrictions on lending. Whatever the reason, the project is halted and the firm loses money.

Thus, to some extent, the type of project or asset that is acquired determines the type of borrowing. If the project or asset is liquid and short term then short-term finance may be favoured. If it is long term then longer-term borrowing gives more certainty about the availability of finance, and (possibly) the interest rate.

- *The term structure of interest rates* It is usual to find interest rates on short-term borrowing which are lower than on long-term debt. This may encourage managers to borrow on a short-term basis. In many circumstances this makes sense. Take the case of Myosotis plc, which requires £10m of borrowed funds for a ten-year project. The corporate treasurer expects long-term interest rates to fall over the next year. It is therefore thought unwise to borrow for the full ten years at the outset. Instead, the firm borrows one-year money at a low interest rate with the expectation of replacing the loan at the end of the year with a nine-year fixed-rate loan at the then reduced rate.

However, there are circumstances where managers find short-term rates deceptively attractive. For example, they might follow a policy of borrowing at short-term rates while the yield curve is still upward sloping, only switching to long-term borrowing when short-term rates rise above long-term rates. Take the case of Rosa plc, which wishes to borrow money for five years and faces the term structure of interest rates shown in the lower line of **Exhibit 7.21**. If it issued one-year bonds the rate of return paid would be 7 per cent. The returns required on four-year and five-year bonds are 8 per cent and 8.3 per cent respectively. The company opts for a one-year bond with the expectation of issuing a four-year bond one year later. However, by the time the financing has to be replaced, 365 days after the initial borrowing, the entire yield curve has shifted upwards due to general macroeconomic changes. Now Rosa has to pay an interest rate of 10 per cent for the remaining four years. This is clearly more expensive than arranging a five-year bond at the outset.

Exhibit 7.21 A shifting yield curve affects the relative cost of long- and short-term borrowing – the example of Rosa plc

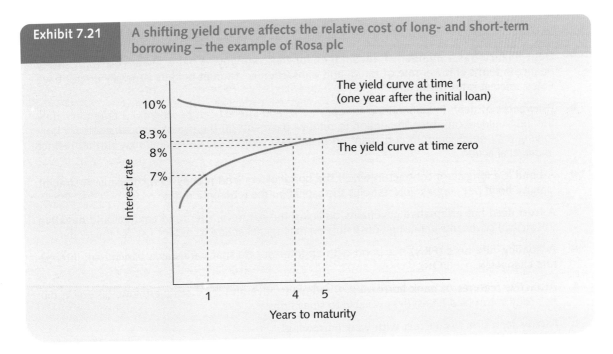

The case of Rosa shows that it can be cheaper to borrow long at low points in the interest rate cycle despite the 'headline' interest charge on long-term debt being greater than on short-term loans.[6]

To 'match' or not to 'match'?

Firms usually come to the conclusion that there is a need for an appropriate mixture of debt finance with regard to length of time to maturity: some short-term borrowing is desirable alongside some long-term borrowing. The major factors which need to be taken into account in achieving the right balance are: (a) cost (interest rate, arrangement fee, etc.) and (b) risk (of not being able to renew borrowings, of the yield curve shifting, of not being able to meet a sudden outflow if the maturity is bunched, etc.). Some firms follow the 'matching' principle, in which the maturity structure of the finance matches the maturity of the project or asset. Here fixed assets and those current assets which are needed on a permanent basis (for example cash, minimum inventory or debtor levels) are financed through long-term sources, while current assets whose financing needs vary throughout the year are financed by short-term borrowings. Examples of the latter type of asset might be stocks of fireworks at certain times of the year, or investment in inventories of chocolate Easter eggs in the spring.

Concluding comments

So far this book has taken a fairly detailed look at a variety of ways of raising money by selling shares and has examined the main methods of raising funds through debt. The decision to raise equity or debt finance is neither simple nor straightforward. Knowledge of these will enable the finance manager or other executives to select and structure the different forms of finance to maximise the firm's potential. Topics covered later in the book draw on the knowledge gained in Chapters 6 and 7 to permit informed discussion of such crucial questions as: What is the appropriate mixture of debt and equity? How is the cost of various forms of finance calculated?

---

[6] There are ways of locking in interest rates in years 2, 3, 4 and 5 through the use of derivatives.

Key points and concepts

- **Debt finance has a number of advantages** for the company: it has a lower cost than equity finance in terms of lower rate of return and transaction costs; debt holders generally do not have votes; interest is tax deductible.

- **Drawbacks of debt:** (i) Committing to repayments and interest can be risky for a firm, ultimately the debt-holders can force liquidation to retrieve payment; (ii) the use of secured assets for borrowing may be an onerous constraint on managerial action; (iii) covenants may further restrict managerial action.

- **A bond** is a long-term contract in which the bondholders lend money to a company. A straight 'vanilla' bond pays regular interest plus the capital on the redemption date.

- **A trust deed** has **affirmative covenants** outlining the nature of the bond contract and **negative** (restrictive) covenants imposing constraints on managerial action to reduce risk for the lenders.

- **A floating-rate note (FRN)** is a bond with an interest rate that varies as a benchmark interest rate changes (e.g. LIBOR).

- **Attractive features of bank borrowing:** (i) administrative and legal costs are low; (ii) quick; (iii) flexibility in troubled times; (iv) available to small firms.

- **Factors for a firm to consider with bank borrowing:**

   Costs: (i) fixed versus floating; (ii) arrangement fees; (iii) bargaining on the rate.
   Security: (i) asymmetric information; (ii) collateral; (iii) covenants; (iv) personal guarantees.
   Repayment arrangements: (i) grace periods; (ii) mortgage style; (iii) term loan.

- **Overdraft** A permit to overdraw on an account up to a stated limit. Advantages: (i) flexibility; (ii) cheap. **Drawbacks:** (i) bank right to withdraw facility quickly; (ii) security is usually required.

- **A bank usually considers the following before lending:** (i) the projected cash flows; (ii) credit-worthiness; (iii) the amount contributed by borrower; (iv) security.

- **Term loan.** A loan of a fixed amount for an agreed time and on specified terms, usually one to seven years. A **syndicated loan** occurs where a number of banks (or other financial institutions) each contribute a portion of a loan.

- **A credit rating** depends on the likelihood of payments of interest and/or capital not being paid (i.e. default); and the extent to which the lender is protected in the event of a default (however, some credit raters provide separate ratings for these factors).

- **Mezzanine debt** and **high-yield bonds** are forms of debt offering a high return with a high risk.

- **Convertible bonds**: issued as debt instruments but also give the holder the right to exchange the bonds at some time in the future into ordinary shares according to some prearranged formula. Advantages: (i) lower interest than on debentures; (ii) interest is tax deductible; (iii) self-liquidating; (iv) few negative covenants; (v) shares might be temporarily underpriced; (vi) cheap way to issue shares; (vii) an available form of finance when straight debt and equity are not.

- A bond is **priced** according to general market interest rates for risk class and maturity:

   Irredeemable:

   $$P_D = \frac{i}{k_D}$$

   Redeemable:

   $$P_D = \frac{i_1}{1 + k_D} + \frac{i_2}{(1 + k_D)^2} + \frac{i_3}{(1 + k_D)^3} + \ldots + \frac{R_n}{(1 + k_D)^n}$$

- The **interest (flat) yield** on a bond is:

$$\frac{\text{Gross interest (coupon)}}{\text{Market price}} \times 100$$

- The **yield to maturity** includes both annual coupon returns and capital gains or losses on maturity.

- **Trade credit**. Goods delivered by suppliers are not paid for immediately. **The early settlement discount** means that taking a long time to pay is not cost free. **Advantages of trade credit:** (i) convenient, informal and cheap; (ii) available to companies of any size.

- **Factoring companies** provide at least three services: (i) providing finance on the security of trade debts; (ii) sales ledger administration; (iii) credit insurance.

- **Invoice discounting** is the obtaining of money on the security of book debts. Usually confidential and with recourse to the supplying firm. The supplying firm manages the sales ledger.

- **Hire purchase** is an agreement to hire goods for a specified period, with an option or an automatic right to purchase the goods at the end for a nominal or zero final payment.

  The main advantages: (i) small initial outlay; (ii) certainty; (iii) available when other sources of finance are not; (iv) fixed-rate finance; (v) tax relief available.

- **Leasing** The legal owner of an asset gives another person or firm (the lessee) the possession of that asset to use in return for specified rental payments. Note that ownership is never transferred to the lessee. **An operating lease** commits the lessee to only a short-term contract, less than the useful life of the asset. **A finance lease** commits the lessee to a contract for the substantial part of the useful life of the asset.

- **Advantages of leasing:** (i) small initial outlay; (ii) certainty; (iii) available when other finance sources are not; (iv) fixed rate of finance; (v) tax relief; (vi) avoid danger of obsolescence with operating lease.

- The **Euromarkets** are informal (unregulated) markets in money held outside the jurisdiction of the country of origin.

- A **foreign bond** is a bond denominated in the currency of the country where it is issued when the issuer is a non-resident.

- A **Eurobond** is a bond sold outside the jurisdiction of the country of the currency in which the bond is denominated.

- The **term structure of interest rates** describes the manner in which the same default risk class of debt securities provides different rates of return depending on the length of time to maturity. There are three hypotheses relating to the term structure of interest rates: (i) the expectations hypothesis; (ii) the liquidity-preference hypothesis; (iii) the market-segmentation hypothesis.

- In deciding **whether to borrow long or short** a company might consider: (i) maturity structure of debt; (ii) cost of issue or arrangement; (iii) flexibility; (iv) the uncertainty of getting future finance; (v) the term structure of interest rates. Firms often strive to **match** the maturity structure of debt with the maturity structure of assets.

Further reading

To keep up to date and reinforce knowledge gained by reading this chapter I can recommend the following publications: *Financial Times, The Economist, Corporate Finance Magazine,* (London: Euromoney), *Bank of England Quarterly Bulletin, Bank for International Settlements Quarterly Review* (www.bis.org), *The Treasurer* (a monthly journal), and The Treasurer's Handbook (by the Association of Corporate Treasurers), *Finance and Leasing Association (FLA) Annual Report* (www.fla.org.uk)

Books describing the financial markets and instruments: Blake, D. (2000), Brett, M. (2000), Buckle, M. and Thompson, J. (2005), Buckley, A. (2004), Eiteman, D.K., Stonehill, A.I. and Moffett, M.H. (2003), Fabozzi, F.J. (2003), Howells, P. and Bain, K. (2004), Valdez, S. and Wood, J. (2003).

For detail on the high yield bond market: Arnold, G. and Smith, M. (1999).

Bond default evidence: Hickman, B.G. (1958).

Liquidity-preference hypothesis: Hicks, J.R. (1946).

Expectations hypothesis: Lutz, F.A. and Lutz, V.C. (1951).

Websites

Association of Corporate Treasurers www.treasurers.org
Bank of England www.bankofengland.co.uk
Bank for International Settlements www.bis.org
Better Payments Practice Group www.payontime.co.uk
British Bankers Association www.bba.org.uk
Department of Trade and Industry www.dti.gov.uk
Economist www.economist.com
Factors and Discounters Association www.factors.org.uk
Federation of Small Businesses www.fsb.org.uk
Finance and Leasing Association www.fla.org.uk
Financial Times www.ft.com
Fitch IBCA www.fitchibca.com
International Capital Market Association www.icma-group.org
Moody's www.moodys.com
Standard & Poor's www.standardandpoors.com

Self-review questions

1 Explain the following (related to bonds):

(a) Par value
(b) Trustee
(c) Debenture
(d) Zero coupon bond
(e) Floating-rate note

2 The inexperienced finance trainee at Mugs-R-Us plc says that he can save the company money on its forthcoming issue of ten-year bonds. 'The rate of return required for bonds of this risk class in the financial markets is 10 per cent and yet I overheard our merchant banking adviser say, "We could issue a bond at a coupon of only 9 per cent." I reckon we could save the company a large sum on the £100m issue.' Do you agree with the trainee's logic?

3 In what circumstances would you recommend borrowing from a bank rather than a capital market bond issue?

4 What are the fundamental considerations to which you would advise a firm to give thought if it were contemplating borrowing from a bank? What are the essential differences between an overdraft and a term loan?

5 What do banks take into account when considering the granting of an overdraft or loan?

6 'Taking a long time to pay suppliers' invoices is always a cheap form of finance.' Consider this statement.

7 What is hire purchase and what are the advantages of this form of finance?

8 Explain the terms 'operating lease' and 'finance lease'.

9 Why does convertible debt carry a lower coupon than straight debt?

10 What is a syndicated loan and why do banks join so many syndicates?

11 What are the differences between a domestic bond, a Eurobond and a foreign bond?

12 What is the credit rating on a bond and what factors determine it?

13 Why do bond issuers accept restrictive covenants?

14 What are high-yield bonds? What is their role in financing firms?

15 What are the main considerations when deciding whether to borrow long or short?

Quick numerical questions

1 Imagine that the market yield to maturity for three-year bonds in a particular risk class is 12 per cent. You buy a bond in that risk class which offers an annual coupon of 10 per cent for the next three years, with the first payment in one year. The bond will be redeemed at par (£100) in three years.

   a How much would you pay for the bond?
   b If you paid £105 what yield to maturity would you obtain?

2 A £100 bond with two years to maturity and an annual coupon of 9 per cent is available. (The next coupon is payable in one year.)

   a If the market requires a yield to maturity of 9 per cent for a bond of this risk class what will be its market price?
   b If the market price is £98, what yield to maturity does it offer?
   c If the required yield to maturity on this type of bond changes to 7 per cent, what will the market price change to?

3 a If the government sold a 10-year gilt with a par value of £100 and an (annual) coupon of 9 per cent, what price can be charged if investors require a 9.5 per cent yield to maturity on such bonds?
   b If yields to maturity on bonds of this risk class fall to 8.5 per cent, what could the bonds be sold for?
   c If it were sold for £105, what yield to maturity is the bond offering?
   d What is the income yield on this bond if it is selling at £105?

AN EXCEL SPREADSHEET VERSION OF THESE CALCULATIONS IS AVAILABLE AT
www.pearsoned.co.uk/arnold

4 The price of a bond issued by C&M plc is 85.5 per cent of par value. The bond will pay an annual 8.5 per cent coupon until maturity (the next coupon will be paid in one year). The bond matures in seven years.

(i)   What will be the market price of the bond if yields to maturity for this risk class fall to 7.5 per cent?
(ii) What will be the market price of the bond if yields to maturity for this risk class rise to 18 per cent?

5 If the yield to maturity on a two-year zero coupon bond is 13 per cent and the yield to maturity on a one-year zero coupon bond is 10 per cent what is the expected spot rate of one-year bonds in one year's time assuming the expectations hypothesis is applicable?

6 If the yield to maturity on a one-year bond is 8 per cent and the expected spot rate on a one-year bond, beginning in one year's time, is 7 per cent what will be the yield to maturity on a two-year bond under the expectations hypothesis of the term structure of interest rates?

7 Lummer plc has issued £60m 15-year 8.5 per cent coupon bonds with a par value of £100. Each bond is convertible into 40 shares of Lummer ordinary shares, which are currently trading at £1.90. What is the conversion price? What is the conversion premium?

Questions and problems

For questions marked with an asterisk answers are given in the Lecturer's Guide

1* You are considering three alternative investments in bonds. The bonds have different times to maturity, but carry the same default risk. You would like to gain an impression of the extent of price volatility for each given alternative change in future interest rates. The investments are:

(i)   A two-year bond with an annual coupon of 6 per cent, par value of £100 and the next coupon payment in one year. The current yield to maturity on this bond is 6.5 per cent.
(ii) A ten-year bond with an annual coupon of 6 per cent, a par value of £100 and the next coupon payable in one year. The current yield to maturity on this bond is 7.2 per cent.
(iii) A 20-year bond with an annual coupon of 6 per cent, a par value of £100 and the next coupon due in one year. The current yield to maturity on this bond is 7.7 per cent.

a Draw an approximate yield curve.
b Calculate the market price of each of the bonds.
c Calculate the market price of the bonds on the assumption that yields to maturity rise by 200 basis points for all bonds.
d Now calculate the market price of the bonds on the assumption that yields to maturity fall by 200 basis points.
e Which bond price is the most volatile in circumstances of changing yields to maturity?
f Explain the liquidity-preference theory of the term structure of yields to maturity.

> **AN EXCEL SPREADSHEET VERSION OF THESE CALCULATIONS IS AVAILABLE AT**
> www.pearsoned.co.uk/arnold

2 Find the current yield to maturity on government securities with maturities of one year, five years and ten years in the *Financial Times*. How has the yield curve changed since 2004 as shown in the chapter? What might account for this shift?

3 Iris plc borrows £50m at 9.5 per cent from Westlloyds bank for five years. What cash flows will the firm have to find if the interest and principal are paid in the following ways?

a All interest and capital is paid at the end of the period.
b Interest only is paid for each of the years (at the year-ends); all principal is paid at the end.
c £10m of the capital plus annual interest is paid on each anniversary date.

4 'Convertibles are great because they offer a lower return than straight debt and we just dish out shares rather than having to find cash to redeem the bonds' – executive at Myopic plc. Comment on this statement as though you were a shareholder in Myopic.

5 (*Examination level*) Flying High plc plans to expand rapidly over the next five years and is considering the following forms of finance to support that expansion.

  a A five-year £10m floating-rate term loan from MidBarc Bank plc at an initial annual interest of 9 per cent.
  b A five-year Eurodollar bond fixed at 8 per cent with a nominal value of US$15m.
  c A £10m convertible bond offering a yield to redemption of 6 per cent and a conversion premium of 15 per cent.

As the financial adviser to the board you have been asked to explain each of these forms of finance and point out the relative advantages and drawbacks. Do this in report form.

6 'We avoid debt finance because of the unacceptable constraint placed on managerial actions.' Explain what this executive means and suggest forms of long-term borrowing which have few constraints.

7 Ronsons plc, the jewellery retailer, has a highly seasonal business with peaks in revenue in December and June. One of Ronsons' banks has offered the firm a £200,000 overdraft with interest charged at 10% p.a. (APR) on the daily outstanding balance, with £3,000 payable as an arrangement fee. Another bank has offered a £200,000 loan with a fixed interest rate of 10% p.a. (APR) and no arrangement fee. Any surplus cash can be deposited to earn 4% APR. The borrowing requirement for the forthcoming year is as follows:

Month	J	F	M	A	M	J	J	A	S	O	N	D
£000s	0	180	150	180	200	0	150	150	180	200	200	0

Which offer should the firm accept?

8 Snowhite plc has taken delivery of 50,000 units of Dwarf moulds for use in its garden ornament business. The supplier has sent an invoice which states the following:

'£50,000 is payable if the purchaser pays in 30 days. However, if payment is within 10 days, a 1 per cent discount may be applied.'

Snowhite has an unused overdraft facility in place, on which interest is payable at 12 per cent annual percentage rate on the daily outstanding balance. If Snowhite paid after 10 days the overdraft facility would have to be used for the entire payment.

  a Calculate whether to pay on the 30th day or on the 10th day, on the basis of the information provided.
  b Despite the 30-day credit limit on the contract Snowhite is aware that it is quite normal in this industry to pay on the 60th day without incurring a penalty legally, financially or in terms of reputation and credit standing. How does this alter your analysis?

9 (*Examination level*) Gordons plc has an annual turnover of £3m and a pre-tax profit of £400,000. It is not quoted on a stock exchange and the family owning all the shares have no intention of permitting the sale of shares to outsiders or providing more finance themselves. Like many small and medium-sized firms, Gordons has used retained earnings and a rolled-over overdraft facility to finance expansion. This is no longer seen as adequate, especially now that the bank manager is pushing the firm to move to a term loan as its main source of external finance.

You, as the recently hired finance director, have been in contact with some financial institutions. The Matey hire purchase company is willing to supply the £1m of additional equipment the firm needs. Gordons will have to pay for this over 25 months at a rate of £50,000 per month with no initial deposit.

The Helpful leasing company is willing to buy the equipment and rent it to Gordons on a finance lease stretching over the four-year useful life of the equipment, with a nominal rent thereafter. The cost of this finance is virtually identical to that for the term loan, that is, 13 per cent annual percentage rate.

Required:

Write a report for the board of directors explaining the nature of the four forms of finance which may be used to purchase the new equipment: hire purchase, leasing, bank term loan and overdraft. Point out their relative advantages and disadvantages.

10 The Cable Company sells its goods on six months' credit which until now it has financed through term loans and overdrafts. Recently factoring firms have been pestering the managing director, saying that they can offer him immediate cash and the chance to get rid of the hassle of collecting debts. He is very unsure of factoring and has requested a report from you outlining the main features and pointing out the advantages and hazards. Write this report.

11 A small firm is considering the purchase of a photocopier. This will cost £2,000. An alternative to purchase is to enter into a leasing agreement known as an operating lease, in which the agreement can be terminated with only one month's notice. This will cost £60 per month. The firm is charged interest of 12 per cent on its overdraft.

Required:

Consider the advantages and disadvantages of each method of obtaining the use of a photocopier.

12 (*Examination level*) A factoring company has offered a one-year agreement with Glub Ltd to both manage its debtors and advance 80 per cent of the value of all its invoices immediately a sale is invoiced. Existing invoices will be eligible for an immediate 80 per cent cash payment.

The annual sales on credit of Glub are £6m spread evenly through the year, and the average delay in payment from the invoice date is at present 80 days. The factoring company is confident of reducing this delay to only 60 days and will pay the remaining 20 per cent of invoice value to Glub immediately on receipt from the customer.

The charge for debtor management will be 1.7 per cent of annual credit turnover payable at the year-end. For the advance payment on the invoices a commission of 1 per cent will be charged plus interest applied at 10 per cent per annum on the gross funds advanced.

Glub will be able to save £80,000 during this year in administration costs if the factoring company takes on the debtor management. At the moment it finances the trade credit it offers customers through an overdraft facility with an interest rate of 11 per cent.

Required:

Advise Glub on whether to enter into the agreement. Discuss the relative advantages and disadvantages of overdraft, factoring and term loan financing.

Assignments

1 Consider some of the items of equipment that your firm uses and investigate the possibility of alternative methods of financing/obtaining the use of those assets. Write a report outlining the options with their advantages and disadvantages, fully costed (if possible) and make recommendations.

2 If a firm familiar to you is at present heavily reliant on bank finance, consider the relative merits of shifting the current balance from overdraft to term loans. Also consider the greater use of alternative forms of short-term or medium-term finance.

3 Obtain a representative sample of recently paid invoices. Examine the terms and conditions, calculate the benefit of paying early and recommend changes in policy if this seems appropriate.

4 Review the long-term debt instruments used by a company familiar to you. Consider the merits and drawbacks of these and explain alternative long-term debt strategies.

Visit www.pearsoned.co.uk/arnold to get access to Gradetracker diagnostic tests, Podcasts, Excel Spreadsheet Solutions, FT articles, a Flashcard revision tool, Weblinks, a searchable Glossary and more.

CHAPTER 8

The cost of capital

LEARNING OUTCOMES

By the end of this chapter the reader should be able to:

- calculate and explain the cost of debt capital, both before and after tax considerations;

- describe the difficulties in estimating the equity cost of capital and explain the key elements that require informed judgement;

- calculate the weighted average cost of capital (WACC) for a company and explain the meaning of the number produced;

- describe the evidence concerning how UK companies actually calculate the WACC;

- explain the outstanding difficulties in this area of finance.

Introduction

Until this point a cost of capital (required rate of return) has been assumed for, say, a project, but we have not gone into much detail about how an appropriate cost of capital is calculated. This vital issue is now addressed.

The objective set for management is the maximisation of long-term shareholder wealth. This means achieving a return on invested money that is greater than shareholders could obtain elsewhere for the same level of risk. Shareholders (and other finance providers) have an opportunity cost associated with putting money into your firm. They could withdraw the money placed with you and invest it in a comparable company's securities. If, for the same risk, the alternative investment offers a higher return than your firm's shares, then as a management team you are destroying shareholder wealth.

The cost of capital is the rate of return that a company has to offer finance providers to induce them to buy and hold a financial security. This rate is determined by the returns offered on alternative securities with the same risk.

Using the correct cost of capital as a discount rate is important. If it is too high, investment will be constrained, firms will not grow as they should and shareholders will miss out on value-enhancing opportunities. There can be a knock-on effect to the macroeconomy and this causes worry for politicians. For example, the one-time President of the Board of Trade, Michael Heseltine, complained:

> Businesses are not investing enough because of their excessive expectations of investment returns . . . The CBI tells me that the majority of firms continue to require rates of return above 20 per cent. A senior banker last week told me his bank habitually asked for 30 per cent returns on capital.[1]

This chapter focuses on the question of how to measure the returns available on a variety of financial securities at different risk levels. This will provide the base for estimating the required rate of return for a particular enterprise.

A word of warning

Too often, academics and consultants give the impression of scientific preciseness in calculating a firm's cost of capital. The reality is that behind any final number generated lies an enormous amount of subjective assessment or, worse, opinion. Choices have to be made between competing judgements on a range of issues, including the appropriate risk premium, financial gearing level and risk measure. Good decision making comes from knowing the limitations of the input variables to the decision. Knowing where informed judgement has been employed in the cost of capital calculation is required to make value-enhancing decisions and thus assist the art of management. In short, the final number for the required rate of return is less important than knowledge of the factors behind the calculation and the likely size of the margin of error. Precision is less important than knowledge of what is a reasonable range.

The required rate of return

The capital provided to large firms comes in many forms. The main forms are equity and debt capital, but there are a number of hybrids, such as convertible bonds. When a finance provider chooses to supply funds in the form of debt finance, there is a deliberate attempt to reduce risk, e.g. by imposing covenants or requiring collateral. However, a lender to a corporation cannot expect to eliminate all risk and so the required rate of return is going to be above that of lending to a reputable state such as the USA or the UK. Placing your savings with the UK government by buying its bonds in return for the promise of regular interest and the payment of a capital sum in a future year is the closest you are going to get to risk-free lending. The rate of return offered on government bonds and Treasury bills is the bedrock rate that is used to benchmark other interest rates. It is called the risk-free rate of return, given the symbol r_f.

---

[1] Quoted in Philip Coggan and Paul Cheeseright, *Financial Times*, 8 November 1994.

A stable well-established company with a relatively low level of borrowing and low-risk operations might have to pay a slightly higher rate of return on debt capital than the UK government. Such a company, if it issued a corporate bond with a fairly high credit rating, would pay, say, an extra 100 basis points per year. This is described as the risk premium (RP) on top of the risk-free rate:

Then, the cost of debt capital, k_D, is:

$$k_D = r_f + RP$$

If the current risk free rate is 6 per cent, then k_D = 7 per cent.

If the firm has a high level of debt it may need to offer, say, 300 basis points above the risk-free rate. So the required return might be 9 per cent.

$$k_D = r_f + RP = 6 + 3 = 9\%$$

If the form of finance provided is equity capital then the investor is accepting a fairly high probability of receiving no return at all on the investment. On the other hand, if the firm performs well very high returns can be expected. It is the expectation of high returns that causes ordinary shareholders to accept high risk.

Different equities have different levels of risk, and therefore returns. A shareholder in Marks & Spencer is likely to be content with a lower return than a shareholder in, say, an internet start-up, or a company quoted on the Russian stock exchange. Thus we have a range of financial securities with a variety of risk and associated return – *see* Exhibit 8.1.

Exhibit 8.1 **Risk–return hypothetical examples**

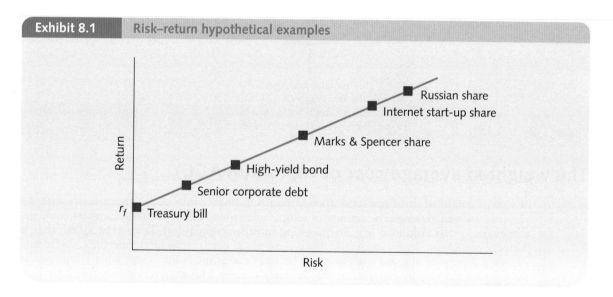

Two sides of the same coin

The issues of the cost of capital for managerial use within the business and the value placed on a share (or other financial security) are two sides of the same coin. They both depend on the level of return – *see* Exhibit 8.2. The holders of shares make a valuation on the basis of the returns they estimate they will receive. Likewise, from the firm's perspective, it estimates the cost of raising money through selling shares (or retaining earnings) as the return that the firm will have to pay to shareholders to induce them to buy and hold the shares. The same considerations apply to bondholders, preference shareholders and so on. If the future cash flowing from the form of finance is anticipated to fall from a previously assumed level then the selling price of the share, bond, etc. goes down until the return is at the level dictated by the returns on financial securities of a similar type and risk. If a company fails to achieve returns that at least compensate finance providers for their opportunity cost it is unlikely to survive for long.

Exhibit 8.2	Two sides of the same coin

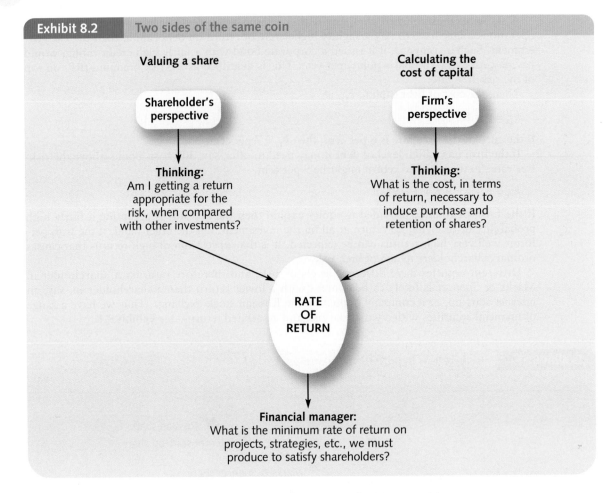

The weighted average cost of capital (WACC)

We have established that firms need to offer returns to finance providers commensurate with the risk they are undertaking. The amount of return is determined by what those investors could get elsewhere at that risk level (e.g. by investing in other companies). If we take a firm that is financed entirely by share capital (and this is the optimal capital structure), then the required rate of return to be used in value analysis, e.g. a project or strategic business unit (SBU)[2] appraisal, is the return demanded by investors on the company's shares. However, this is only true if the new project (or division) has the same level of risk as the existing set of projects.

The stock market prices shares on the basis of the current risk of the firm. This is determined by the activities it undertakes. A company can be seen as merely a bundle of projects from the perspective of ordinary shareholders. If these projects are, on average, of high risk then the required return will be high. If the proposed project (or division) under examination has the same risk as the weighted average of the current set then the required return on the company's equity capital is the rate appropriate for this project (if the company received all its capital from shareholders and none from lenders). If the new project has a lower risk, the company-wide cost of capital needs to be adjusted down for application to this project.

If we are dealing with a company that has some finance in the form of debt and some in the form of equity the situation becomes a little more complicated. Imagine that a corporation is to be established by obtaining one-half of its £1,000 million of capital from lenders, who require an 8 per cent rate of return for an investment of this risk class, and one-half from shareholders, who require a 12 per cent rate of return for the risk they are accepting. Thus we have the following facts:

---

[2] See the next chapter for a description of strategic business units.

Cost of debt			$k_D = 8\%$
Cost of equity			$k_E = 12\%$
Weight of debt	$\dfrac{V_D}{V_D + V_E}$	£500 million / £1 billion	$W_D = 0.5$
Weight of equity	$\dfrac{V_E}{V_D + V_E}$	£500 million / £1 billion	$W_E = 0.5$

Where V_D = Market value of debt, V_E = Market value of equity

We need to calculate the weighted average cost of capital (WACC) to establish the minimum return needed on an investment within the firm, that will produce enough to satisfy the lenders and leave just enough to give shareholders their 12 per cent return. Anything less than this WACC and the shareholders will receive less than 12 per cent. They will recognise that 12 per cent is available elsewhere for that level of risk and remove money from the firm.

Weighted average cost of capital, $\text{WACC} = k_E\,W_E + k_D\,W_D$

$$\text{WACC} = (12 \times 0.5) + (8 \times 0.5) = 10\%$$

Illustration

Imagine the firm invested £100,000 in a project that produced a net cash flow per year of £10,000 to infinity (assuming a perpetuity makes the example simple); the first call on that cash flow is from the debt holders, who effectively supplied £50,000 of the funds. They require £4,000 per annum. That leaves £6,000 for equity holders – an annual return of 12 per cent on the £50,000 they provided. Thus an overall return of 10 per cent (the WACC) provides an 8 per cent return on the capital supplied by lenders and 12 per cent on the capital supplied by shareholders.

If things go well and a return of £11,000 (i.e. 11 per cent) is generated then debt holders still receive the contracted amount of £4,000, but the equity holders get a return significantly above the minimum they require, at 14 per cent return: £7,000 is left to pay out to shareholders on their £50,000 capital input to this project.

Of course, this example assumes that all new projects use the same proportions of debt and equity finance as the firm as a whole, that is 50 per cent of its capital comes from debt. The issue of whether you should use different types (or weights) of finance for different projects (say, borrow all the £100,000 for this particular project at 8 per cent) rather than use the 50 : 50 mixture is discussed later.

Lowering the WACC and increasing shareholder returns

Examining the WACC formula we see an apparently simple way of reducing the required rate of return, and thus raising the value of a project, division or the entire firm: change the weights in the formula in favour of debt. In other words, alter the capital structure of the firm by having a higher proportion of its capital in the form of cheaper debt.

For example, if the company is expected to produce £100 million cash flow per year (to infinity), and its WACC is 10 per cent, its total corporate value ('enterprise value', that is, the value of the debt and equity) is:

£100 million/0.10 = £1,000 million

Let us try to lower the WACC.

Imagine that instead of the firm being established with 50 per cent debt in its overall capital it is set up with 70 per cent debt. The proportion of total capital in the form of equity is therefore 30 per cent. If (a big if) the equity holders remain content with a 12 per cent return while the debt holders accept an 8 per cent annual return the WACC will fall, and the value of the firm will rise.

$$\text{WACC} = k_E \, W_E + k_D \, W_D$$

$$\text{WACC} = (12 \times 0.3) + (8 \times 0.7) = 9.2\%$$

Firm value = £100 million/0.092 = £1,086.96 million

Why don't all management teams increase the proportion of debt in the capital structure and 'magic up' some shareholder value? The fly in the ointment for many firms is that equity investors are unlikely to be content with 12 per cent returns when their shares have become more risky due to the additional financial leverage. The key question is: how much extra return do they demand? The financial economists and Nobel laureates Franco Modigliani and Merton Miller (MM) presented the case that in a perfect capital market (in which all participants such as shareholders and managers have all relevant information, all can borrow at the same rate of interest, etc.) the increase in k_E would exactly offset the benefit from the increase in the debt proportion; this would leave the WACC constant, so increasing the debt proportion does not add to shareholder value; the only factor that can add value is the improvement in the underlying performance of the business, i.e. its cash flows. According to this view (that there is no optimal capital structure that will maximise shareholder wealth) there is no point in adjusting the debt or equity proportions.

In this stylised world k_D remains at 8 per cent, but k_E moves to 14.67 per cent, leaving the WACC, firm value and shareholder value constant.

$$\text{WACC} = k_E \, W_E + k_D \, W_D$$

$$\text{WACC} = (14.67 \times 0.3) + (8 \times 0.7) = 10\%$$

However, there is hope for managers trying to improve shareholder wealth by adjusting the capital structure because in constructing a perfect world Modigliani and Miller left out at least two important factors: tax and financial distress.[3]

The benefit of tax

The first consideration is tax. A benefit of financing through debt is that the annual interest can be used to reduce taxable profit thus lowering the cash that flows out to the tax authorities. In contrast, the annual payout on equity (dividends) cannot be used to reduce the amount of profit that is taxed. The benefits gained from being able to lower the tax burden through financing through debt reduces the effective cost of this form of finance.[4]

To illustrate: Firm A is a company in a country that does not permit interest to be deducted from taxable profit. Firm B is in a country that does permit interest to be deducted. In both companies the interest is 8 per cent on £500m. Observe the effect on the amount of profit left for distribution to shareholders in the table below.

	Firm A £m	Firm B £m
Profits before interest and tax	100	100
Interest		−40
Taxable profit	100	60
Amount taxed @ 30%	−30	−18
Interest	−40	
Amount available for distribution shareholders	30	42

---

[3] Modigliani and Miller did not ignore tax and financial distress in their work, but did downplay them in the formulation of their early model.

[4] Note this reduction is only valid if the company is profitable and paying corporation tax.

The extra £12 million for Firm B reduces the effective cost of debt from 8 per cent to only 8 $(1 - T)$, where T = the corporation tax rate, 30 per cent. The cost of debt capital falls to $8(1 - 0.3) = 5.6$, or £28 million on £500 million of debt. The taxman, by taking £12m less from the company purely because the tax rules allow the deductibility of interest from taxable profit, lowers the effective cost of the debt.

So including the 'tax shield' effect, we find a reduction in the WACC that leads to an increase in the amount available for shareholders. In our example, if we assume tax on corporate profits at 30 per cent then the effective cost of debt falls to 5.6 per cent. This results in the WACC becoming 8.8 per cent.

k_{DBT} = Cost of debt before tax benefit = 8%

k_{DAT} = Cost of debt after tax benefit = $8(1 - T) = 8(1 - 0.30) = 5.6\%$

If we assume a 50 : 50 capital structure the WACC is:

$$WACC = k_E \, W_E + k_{DAT} \, W_D$$

$$WACC = (12 \times 0.5) + (5.6 \times 0.5) = 8.8\%$$

Investment project cash flows discounted at this lower rate will have a higher present value than if discounted at 10 per cent. Given that the debt holders receive only their contractual interest and no more, this extra value flows to shareholders.

Financial distress constrains gearing

The introduction of the tax benefit strongly pushes the bias towards very high gearing levels to obtain a lower WACC and higher value. However, we do not observe such extreme gearing very often in real-world companies. There are a number of reasons for this, the most important of which is the increasing risk to the finance providers (particularly equity capital holders) of financial distress and, ultimately, liquidation. (*See* Chapter 11 for more reasons and a more detailed discussion of capital structure.)

As gearing rises so does the probability of equity investors receiving a poor (no) return. So they demand higher expected returns to compensate. At first, the risk premium rises slowly, but at high gearing levels it rises so fast that it more than offsets the benefit of increasing debt in the capital structure. This is demonstrated in **Exhibit 8.3**, in which the WACC at lower levels of debt is primarily influenced by the increasing debt proportion in the capital structure, and at higher levels by the rising cost of equity (and eventually debt).

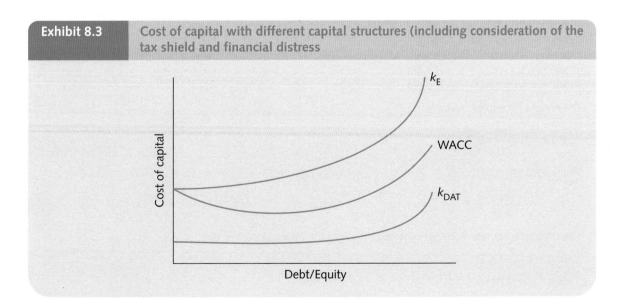

Exhibit 8.3   Cost of capital with different capital structures (including consideration of the tax shield and financial distress

The conclusion drawn from the capital structure literature is that there is an optimal gearing level that achieves the lowest WACC and highest firm value. When companies are calculating their WACC they should use this target gearing ratio and not a gearing ratio they happen to have at the time of calculation.

So, if in our example the required return on equity rises from 12 per cent to 13 per cent when the proportion of the debt in the capital structure rises to 65 per cent from 50 per cent, and the effective rate of return payable on debt is 5.6 per cent after the tax shield benefit (i.e. remaining at 8 per cent before the tax benefit) then the WACC falls and the value available for shareholders rises.

$$\text{WACC} = k_E\, W_E + k_{DAT}\, W_D$$

$$\text{WACC} = (13 \times 0.35) + (5.6 \times 0.65) = 8.19\%$$

Taking financial gearing too far

For this particular company we will assume that 65 per cent gearing is the optimum debt/equity ratio. If we go to 80 per cent debt we find this reduces shareholder wealth because the firm's projects (in aggregate) are now discounted at a higher rate of return (WACC), reducing their present value. The main reason the discount rate rises significantly is that the required return on shares rises to, say, 30 per cent as investors fear massive potential loss due to the large commitment of the firm to pay out interest whether or not the firm is doing well. The debt holders are also worried about increased financial distress risk – i.e. they might not receive their capital or interest – and so they increase their required rate of return to 10 per cent before the tax shield benefit, which is an effective cost to the firm of 7 per cent after allowing for the tax shield benefit.

$$\text{WACC} = k_E\, W_E + k_{DAT}\, W_D$$

$$\text{WACC} = (30 \times 0.2) + (7 \times 0.8) = 11.6\%$$

Worked example 8.1   **Poise plc**

The rate of return offered to debt holders of Poise plc before considering the benefit to shareholders of the tax shield, k_{DBT}, is 10 per cent, whereas the required return on equity is 20 per cent. The total amount of capital in use (equity + debt), V, is £2m. Of that, £1.4m represents the market value of its equity, V_E, and £600,000 equals the market value of its debt, V_D. These are the optimum proportions of debt and equity.
    Thus:

k_{DBT}	= 10%
k_E	= 20%
V	= £2m
V_E	= £1.4m
V_D	= £0.6m

The weight for equity capital is:

$$W_E = \frac{V_E}{V} = \frac{1.4}{2.0} = 0.7$$

The weight for debt is:

$$W_D = \frac{V_D}{V} = \frac{0.6}{2.0} = 0.3$$

The corporate tax rate is 30 per cent and therefore the after-tax cost of debt is:

$$k_{DAT} = k_{DBT}\,(1 - T)$$

$$k_{DAT} = 10\,(1 - 0.30) = 7\%$$

| Worked example 8.1 | Continued |

The weighted average cost of capital for Poise is:

$$WACC = k_E W_E + k_{DAT} W_D$$
$$= 20\% \times 0.7 + 7\% \times 0.3 = 16.1\%$$

This is the rate of return Poise needs to achieve on new business projects if they are of the same risk as the average risk of the current set of projects. If the new projects are of higher or lower risk an adjustment needs to be made to the discount rate used – this is discussed in more detail later in the chapter.

If Poise is considering a project that requires an investment of £1m at Time 0 and then produces after-tax annual cash flows before interest payments of £161,000 as a perpetuity (i.e. it achieves a 16.1 per cent rate of return) then the net cost of satisfying the debt holders after the tax shield benefit is £21,000. (The debt holders supplied 30 per cent of the £1m invested, i.e. £300,000; and the cost to the firm of satisfying them is £300,000 × 7% = £21,000.)

The remainder of the annual cash flows go to the shareholders; so they receive £140,000 per year, which is a 20 per cent return on the £700,000 they supplied.

If the project produces a much lower annual cash flow of £100,000 (a rate of return of 10 per cent) then the debt holders still need a net £21,000 (after allowing for the tax shield benefit to the company), leaving only £79,000 for the shareholders. These investors could have achieved a return of 20 per cent by investing in other companies at this level of risk. An annual return of £79,000 represents a mere 11.3 per cent return (£79,000/£700,000). Thus shareholders suffer a loss of wealth relative to the forgone opportunity.

AN EXCEL SPREADSHEET VERSION OF THESE CALCULATIONS IS AVAILABLE AT www.pearsoned.co.uk/arnold

The cost of equity capital

A shareholder has in mind a minimum rate of return determined by the returns available on other shares of the same risk class. Managers, in order to maximise shareholder wealth, must obtain this level of return for shareholders from the firm's activities. If a company does not achieve the rate of return to match the investor's opportunity cost it will find it difficult to attract new funds and will become vulnerable to takeover or liquidation.

With debt finance there is generally a specific rate payable for the use of capital. In contrast, ordinary shareholders are not explicitly offered payments. However, there is an implicit rate of return that has to be offered to attract investors. It is the expectation of high returns that causes ordinary shareholders to accept high risk.

Investors in shares require a return that provides for two elements. First, they need a return equal to the risk-free rate (usually taken to be that on government securities). Second, there is the risk premium, which rises with the degree of systematic risk:

Rate of return on shares = Risk-free rate + Risk premium

$$k_E = r_f + RP$$

The risk-free rate gives a return sufficient to compensate for both impatience to consume and inflation (*see* Chapter 2).[5] To estimate the relevant risk premium on a firm's equity we generally take two steps.

- Stage one is to estimate the average extra return demanded by investors above the risk-free return to induce them to buy a portfolio of average-risk-level shares. We usually look back

---

[5] This is assuming that future inflation is included in the projected cash flows. That is, we are using nominal cash flows and a nominal interest rate. An alternative method is to use real cash flows and a real discount rate (i.e. with inflation removed).

at the returns shareholders have *actually* received on average-risk shares above the risk-free return in the past and make the assumption that this is what they also demanded before the event, *ex ante* in the jargon, and then make the further assumption that this is the extra rate that they demand on shares today.[6] The average annual risk premium actually obtained by shareholders can only be calculated over an extended period of time (many decades) as short-term returns on shares can be distorted (they are often negative for a year, for example). The risk premium is expressed as the difference between the market return, r_m, and the risk-free return, r_f, that is $(r_m - r_f)$.

● The second stage is to adjust the risk premium for a typical (average-risk-level) share to suit the risk level for the particular company's shares under consideration. If the share is more risky than the average then $(r_m - r_f)$ is multiplied by a systematic risk factor greater than 1. If it is less risky it may be multiplied by a systematic risk factor of less than 1, say 0.8, to reduce the premium.

The capital-asset pricing model (CAPM)

In the forty years following the development of the CAPM, in practical cost of capital calculations, the risk premium has generally been adjusted by a beta based on the extent to which a share had moved when a market index moved (its co-variance with the market), say over a five-year period:

$$k_E = r_f + \beta(r_m - r_f)$$

There are some fairly obvious problems with this approach; for example, does historical co-movement with the market index reflect future risk accurately? (*See* Chapter 5 for more problems.) But at least we have some anchor points for equity cost calculations. We have general acceptance that it is only systematic risk that is compensated for in the required returns. We also have an approximate figure for the historical risk premium on the average-risk share (around 4–5 per cent per year) and thus, given a certain risk-free rate, we know roughly what rate of return is required for an average share – with rates on government securities at 5 per cent this would be around 9–10 per cent. We could also probably agree that the relative volatility of a share against the market index is some indicator of riskiness, and that therefore more variable shares should bear a higher risk premium. Despite this progress we are still left with some uncertainty over how to adjust the average risk premium for specific shares – beta is less than perfect.

The Gordon growth model method for estimating the cost of equity capital

The most influential model for calculating the cost of equity in the early 1960s (and one which is still used today in some companies) was created by Gordon and Shapiro (1956), and further developed by Gordon (1962). Suppose a company's shares priced at P produce earnings of E per share and pay a dividend of d per share. The company has a policy of retaining a fraction, b, of its earnings each year to use for internal investments. If the rate of return (discount or capitalisation rate) required on shares of this risk class is k_E then, under certain restrictive conditions, it can be shown that earnings, dividends and reinvestment will all grow continuously, at a rate of $g = br$, where r is the rate of return on the reinvestment of earnings, and we have:

$$P = \frac{d_1}{k_E - g}$$

(There is more on this formula in Chapter 10.)

---

[6] An alternative is the 'forward looking approach' in which the analyst tries to obtain estimates of what extra future annual return investors require at this time for investing in an averagely risky share. There are some serious doubts about the subjective nature of the inputs to these calculations.

Solving for k_E we have:

$$k_E = \frac{d_1}{P} + g$$

where d_1 is the dividend to be received next year.

That is, the rate of return investors require on a share is equal to the prospective dividend yield (d_1/P) *plus* the rate at which the dividend stream is expected to grow (g).

Gordon and Shapiro said that there are other approaches to the estimation of future dividends than the extrapolation of the current dividend on the basis of the growth rate explicit in b and r, so we can derive g in other ways and still the k_E formula remains valid.

A major problem in the practical employment of this model is obtaining a trustworthy estimate of the future growth rate of dividends to an infinite horizon. Gordon and Shapiro (1956) told us to derive this figure from known data in an objective manner, using common sense and with reference to the past rate of growth in a corporation's dividend. In other words, a large dose of judgement is required. The cost of equity capital under this model is very sensitive to the figure put in for g, and yet there is no reliable method of estimating it for the *future*; all we can do is make reasoned estimates and so the resulting k_E is based merely on an informed guess. Using past growth rates is one approach, but it means that it is assumed that the future growth of the company's earnings and dividends will be exactly the same as in the past – often an erroneous supposition. Professional analysts' forecasts could be examined, but their record of predicting the future is generally a poor one – especially for more than two years ahead (this model requires us to estimate g for all future years, to an infinite horizon).

The cost of retained earnings

The most important source of long-term finance for most corporations is retained earnings. There are many companies that rarely, if ever, go to their shareholders to raise new money, but rely on previous years' profits. There is a temptation to regard retained earnings as 'costless' because it was not necessary for the management to go out and persuade investors to invest by offering a rate of return.

However, retained earnings should be seen as belonging to the shareholders. They are part of the equity of the firm. Shareholders could make good use of these funds by investing in other firms and obtaining a return. These funds therefore have an opportunity cost. We should regard the cost of retained earnings as equal to the expected returns required by shareholders buying new shares in a firm. There is a slight modification to this principle in practice because new share issues involve costs of issuance and therefore are required to give a marginally higher return to cover the costs of selling the shares.

The cost of debt capital

The cost of debt is generally determined by the following factors:

- The prevailing interest rates.
- The risk of default (and expected rate of recovery of money lent in the event of default).
- The benefit derived from interest being tax deductible.

There are two types of debt capital. The first is debt that is traded, that is, bought and sold in a security market. The second is debt that is not traded.

Traded debt

In the UK bonds are normally issued by companies to lenders with a nominal value of £100. Vanilla bonds carry an annual coupon rate until the bonds reach maturity when the nominal or par value of £100 is paid to the lender (*see* Chapter 7 for more details). The rate of return required by the firm's creditors, k_D, is represented by the interest rate in the following equation which causes the future discounted cash flows payable to the lenders to equal the current market price of the bond P_D. We know the current price P_D of the bond in the market, the annual cash flow that will go to the lenders in the form of interest, i, and we know the cash to be received, R_n, when the bond is redeemed at the end of its life. The only number we don't yet have is the rate of return, k_D. This is found in the same way as the internal rate of return is found:

$$P_D = \sum_{t=1}^{t=n} \frac{i}{(1 + k_D)^t} + \frac{R_n}{(1 + k_D)^n}$$

where:

i = annual nominal interest (coupon payment) receivable from year 1 to year n;

R_n = amount payable upon redemption;

k_D = cost of debt capital (pre-tax benefit).

$\sum_{t=1}^{t=n}$ means add up the results of all the $\frac{i}{(1 + k_D)^t}$ from next year (year 1) to the t number of years of the bond's life.

For example, Elm plc issued £100m of bonds six years ago carrying an annual coupon rate of 8 per cent. They are due to be redeemed in four years for the nominal value of £100 each. The next coupon is payable in one year and the current market price of a bond is £93. The cost of this redeemable debt can be calculated by obtaining the internal rate of return, imagining that a new identical set of cash flows is being offered to the lenders from a new (four-year) bond being issued today. The lenders would pay £93 for such a bond (in the same risk class) and receive £8 per year for four years plus £100 at the end of the bond's life. Thus, the cash flows from the firm's perspective are:

Year	0	1	2	3	4
Cash flow	+£93	–£8	–£8	–£8	–£108

Thus the rate of return being offered is calculated from:

$$93 = \frac{8}{1 + k_D} + \frac{8}{(1 + k_D)^2} + \frac{8}{(1 + k_D)^3} + \frac{108}{(1 + k_D)^4}$$

With k_D at 11 per cent the discounted cash flow on the right hand side = 90.69.
With k_D at 10 per cent the discounted cash flow on the right hand side = 93.66.
Using linear interpolation the IRR can be found:

$$k_D = 10\% + \frac{93.66 - 93.00}{93.66 - 90.69} (11 - 10) = 10.22\%$$

Even though the bonds were once worth a total of £100m (assuming they sold for £100) in the market, this is no longer their value because they are now selling at £93 each. The total market value of the bonds today, V_D, is calculated as follows:

$$V_D = £100m \times \frac{£93}{£100} = £93m$$

We are concerned with finding the cost to a company of the various types of capital it might use to finance its investment projects, strategic plans, etc. It would be wrong to use the coupon rate of 8 per cent on the bond for the cost of debt. This was the required rate of return six years ago (assuming the bond was sold for £100). A rate of 10.22 per cent is appropriate because this is the rate of return bond investors are demanding in the market today. The cost of capital is the best available return elsewhere for the bondholders for the same level of risk. Managers are charged with using the money under their command to produce a return at least equal to the opportunity cost. If the cash flows attributable to these lenders for a project or SBU are discounted at 8 per cent then a comparison of the resulting net present value of the investment with the return available by taking the alternative of investing the cash in the capital markets at the same risk is not being made. However, by using 10.22 per cent for the bond cost of capital we can compare the alternatives available to the lenders in the financial markets.

In the calculation for Elm plc taxation has been ignored and so the above result of 10.22 per cent should be properly defined as the cost of debt before tax, k_{DBT}. An adjustment is necessary to establish the true cost of the bond capital to the firm. If T is the rate of corporate tax, 30 per cent, then the cost of debt after tax, k_{DAT}, is:

$$k_{DAT} = k_{DBT} (1 - T) \quad k_{DAT} = 10.22 (1 - 0.30) = 7.15\%$$

A short cut

We have calculated the yield to redemption on a very simple bond from first principles, to illustrate the key elements. In reality, most bonds offer coupon payments every six months – this complicates the type of analysis shown above. However, yields to redemption on bonds of different risk classes are available commercially, which avoids effort. The *Financial Times* displays the yields ('bid yield' or 'GRY' – gross redemption yield) offered on a range of frequently traded bonds of various risk classes (*see* the tables, 'Global Investment Grade', 'High Yield and Emerging Market Bonds' in weekday editions and 'Sterling bond prices' in Saturday editions). Two useful websites for bond yields are *Investors Chronicle*: www.ic-community.co.uk/bonds and the Bondsonline Group, Inc.: www.bondsonline.com. These sources may not be able to provide the yield to redemption for the particular bond that interests you, but you can discover the rates payable for bonds of different credit ratings. So if you know or can estimate the credit rating of the company under examination you can obtain an approximate rate of return (before the tax shield benefit, k_{DBT}).

Untraded debt

Most debt capital, such as bank loans, is not traded and repriced regularly on a financial market. We need to find the rate of interest that is the opportunity cost of lenders' funds – the current 'going rate' of interest for the risk class. The easiest way to achieve this is to look at the rate being offered on similar tradable debt securities.

Floating-rate debt

Most companies have variable-rate debt in the form of either bonds or bank loans. Usually the interest payable is set at a margin over a benchmark rate such as bank base rate or LIBOR. For practical purposes the current interest payable can be taken as the before-tax rate of return (k_{DBT}) because these rates are the market rates. There is a rational argument against this simple approach based on the difference between short- and long-term interest rates. For example, it may be that a firm rolls over a series of short-term loans and so in effect will be using this as long-term finance. In this case the theoretically correct approach is to use the long-term interest rate and not the current short-term rate because the former more accurately reflects what is likely to be required to be paid over the life of the loan.

The cost of preference share capital

Preference shares have some characteristics in common with debt capital (e.g. a specified annual payout of higher ranking than ordinary share dividends) and some characteristics in common with equity (dividends may be missed in some circumstances, and the dividend is not tax deductible) – *see* Chapter 6 for more details. If the holders of preference shares receive a fixed annual dividend and the shares are irredeemable the perpetuity formula may be used to value the security:

$$P_p = \frac{d_1}{k_p}$$

where P_p is the price of preference shares, d_1 is the annual preference dividend, k_p is the investors' required rate of return.

Therefore, the cost of this type of preference share is given by:

$$k_p = \frac{d_1}{P_p}$$

Hybrid securities

Hybrid securities can have a wide variety of features – e.g. a convertible bond is a combination of a straight bond offering regular coupons and an option to convert the bond to shares in the company. It is usually necessary to calculate the cost of capital for each of the component elements separately. This can be complex and is beyond the scope of this chapter.

Calculating the weights

Book (balance sheet) values for debt, equity and hybrid securities should not be used in calculating the weighted average cost of capital. Market values should be used. For example, a company might have raised £100m by selling £100 perpetual bonds, which promised annual coupons of £5 each without a definite cease date, when interest rates were 5 per cent. However, if general interest rates rise to, say, 10 per cent for this risk, class bonds offering £5 per year will not be attractive at £100 each, therefore the price will fall to £50; that is, they keep falling until they yield the required 10 per cent return. It is the £50m current market value figure that should be used in the weightings. The rationale for using market values is that we need to generate a return for the finance providers on the basis of their current contribution to the capital of the firm and in relation to the current opportunity cost – accounting values have little relevance to this. Investors in bonds right now are facing an opportunity cost of £50m (i.e. they could sell the bonds and release £50m of cash) so this is the figure that managers should see as the amount sacrificed by these finance providers, not the £100m that the bonds once traded at.

With equity capital it is correct to use the market capitalisation figure (current share price multiplied by number of shares issued to investors). This is the amount that current investors are sacrificing to invest in this company today – the shares could be sold in the marketplace at that value. The balance sheet value for equity shareholders' funds is not relevant. This is likely to be very different from the market capitalisation. Balance sheets consist of a series of historical accounting entries that bear little relation to the value placed on the shares by investors. Market capitalisation figures are available in Monday editions of the *Financial Times* for quoted companies. Most financial websites provide market capitalisation, e.g. www.london-stockexchange.com.

The WACC with three or more types of finance

The formula becomes longer, but not fundamentally more difficult, when there are three (or more) types of finance. For example, if a firm has preference share capital as well as debt and equity the formula becomes:

$$\text{WACC} = k_E\, W_E + k_{DAT}\, W_D + k_p\, W_p$$

where W_p is the weight for preference shares and

$$W_E = \frac{V_E}{V_E + V_D + V_P} \qquad W_D = \frac{V_D}{V_E + V_D + V_P} \qquad W_P = \frac{V_P}{V_E + V_D + V_P}$$

The weight for each type of capital is proportional to market values – and, of course, $W_E + W_D + W_p$ totals to 1.0.

Classic error

Managers are sometimes tempted to use the cost of the latest capital raised to discount projects, SBUs, etc. This is wrong. Also they must not use the cost of the capital they might be about to raise to finance the project.

The latest capital raised by a company might have been equity at, say, 12 per cent, or debt at a cost of, say, 8 per cent. If the firm is trying to decide whether to go ahead with a project that will produce an IRR of 10.5 per cent the project will be rejected if the latest capital-raising exercise was for equity and the discount rate used was 12 per cent. On the other hand, the project will be accepted if, by chance, the latest funds raised happen to be debt with a cost of 8 per cent. The WACC should be used for all projects – at least, for all those of the same risk class as the existing set of projects. The reason is that a firm cannot move too far away from its optimum debt-to-equity ratio level. If it does its WACC will rise. So, although it may seem attractive for a subsidiary manager to promote a favoured project by saying that it can be financed with borrowed funds and therefore it needs only to achieve a rate of return in low single figures it must be borne in mind that the next capital-raising exercise after that will have to be for equity to maintain an appropriate financial gearing level.

What about short-term debt?

Short-term debt should be included as part of the overall debt of the firm when calculating the WACC. The lenders of this money will require a return. However, to the extent that this debt is temporary or offset by cash and marketable securities held by the firm it may be excluded.

Finance and operating leases usually require fixed regular payments over lengthy periods of time incorporating an interest rate. These commitments are similar to bank loan obligations and so the capitalised value of the leases should be regarded as adding to the debt of the firm.

Applying the WACC to projects and SBUs

The overall return generated on the finance provided to a firm is determined by the portfolio of current projects. Likewise the risk (systematic) of the firm is determined by the collection of projects to which it is currently committed. If a firm made an additional capital investment that has a much higher degree of risk than the average in the existing set then it is intuitively obvious that a higher return than the normal rate for this company will be required. On the other hand, if an extraordinarily low-risk activity is contemplated this should require a lower rate of return than usual.

Some multidivisional firms make the mistake of demanding that all divisions achieve the same rate of return. This results in low-risk projects being rejected when they should be accepted and high-risk projects being accepted when they should be rejected.

Just how high the discount rate has to be is as much a matter for managerial judgement as one based on the measures of risk and return developed by theorists. The CAPM provides a starting point, a framework for thinking about risk premiums, but judging the viability of a project or division is still largely an art which requires experience and perceptive thought, not least because it is very difficult to quantify the likely risk of, say, an internet business. It may be possible to classify projects into broad categories, say, high, medium and low, but precise categorisation is difficult. What is clear is that the firm should not use a single discount rate for all its activities.

Empirical evidence of corporate practice

Academic literature promotes forcefully the use of the WACC. But to what extent have UK firms adopted the recommended methods? In 1983 Richard Pike expressed a poor opinion of the techniques used by business people to select the cost of capital: 'the methods commonly applied in setting hurdle rates are a strange mixture of folk-lore, experience, theory and intuition'. In 1976 Westwick and Shohet reported that less than 10 per cent of the firms they studied used a WACC. The position has changed significantly; Arnold and Hatzopoulos (2000), in a study of 96 UK firms, found that the majority now calculate a WACC – *see* Exhibit 8.4.

Exhibit 8.4	Replies to the question: How does your company derive the discount rate used in the appraisal of major capital investments? (percentage of respondents)			
	Category of company			
Method used	**Small (%)**	**Medium (%)**	**Large (%)**	**Composite (%)**
WACC	41	63	61	54
The cost of equity derived from the capital asset pricing model is used	0	8	16	8
Interest payable on debt capital is used	23	8	1	11
An arbitrarily chosen figure	12	4	3	6
Dividend yield on shares plus estimated growth in capital value of share	0	0	3	1
Earnings yield on shares	3	0	0	1
Other	12	8	11	10
Blank	9	8	5	7

Source: Arnold and Hatzopoulos (2000).

Despite years of academic expounding on the virtues of the WACC and extensive managerial education, a significant minority of firms do not calculate a WACC for use in capital investment appraisal.[7] Furthermore, as Exhibits 8.5 and 8.6 show, many firms that calculate a WACC do not follow the prescribed methods. Further evidence of a light grasp of textbook procedure was demonstrated in some of the statements made by respondents: 'Above is a minimum [WACC]. A hurdle rate is also used which is the mid-point of the above [WACC] and

Exhibit 8.5	Method of calculating the weighted average cost of capital (percentage of respondents that use the WACC)			
	Category of company			
Method	**Small (%)**	**Medium (%)**	**Large (%)**	**Composite (%)**
Using the capital asset pricing model for equity and the market rate of return on debt capital	50	68	79	70
Cost of the equity calculated other than through the capital asset pricing model with the cost of debt derived from current market interest rates	50	32	18	29
Other	0	0	31	

Source: Arnold and Hatzopoulos (2000).

---

[7] Another 1997 survey, by McLaney *et al.* (2004) found 53.4% of survey responders (UK listed companies) used WACC.

Exhibit 8.6	If the weighted average cost of capital is used, then how are the weights defined? (percentage of respondents)			
	Category of company			
Method of defining weights	**Small (%)**	**Medium (%)**	**Large (%)**	**Composite (%)**
A long-term target debt and equity ratio	19	26	39	30
The present market values of debt and equity	44	47	42	44
Balance sheet ratios of debt and equity	37	26	19	26

Source: Arnold and Hatzopoulos (2000).

the lowest rate of return required by venture capitalists.' 'WACC + safety margin', 'Weighted average cost of capital plus inflation'.

Gregory and Rutterford (1999) and Rutterford (2000) carried out a series of in-depth interviews with 18 FTSE 100 company finance directors or heads of corporate finance in 1996. All 18 estimate their weighted average cost of capital. They found that 14 of the companies made use of the capital asset pricing model to estimate the equity cost of capital, five used the dividend yield plus growth method (Gordon's growth model), four used the historic real rate of return on equity and five used more than one method.

Risk-free rate and betas used

In terms of the risk-free rate most firms (12 out of 14 using the CAPM) used the yield on UK government bonds – they generally chose a bond with a maturity of between 7 and 20 years. The remainder used a real (excluding inflation) rate of interest. None used the Treasury bill rate.

Betas were sourced from financial databases, such as that of the London Business School, or from financial advisers – most firms used more than one source. Many interviewees felt that any fine-tuning of the beta estimate would have less impact on the k_E estimate than would the choice of the equity risk premium.

Risk premiums used

Two out of the 13 firms which estimated an equity risk premium chose a figure from a mid-1990s Barclays Capital Equity Gilt Study. This was based on a different time period from that of the study of Dimson, Marsh and Staunton described in Chapter 6. The Barclays studies published in the mid-1990s tracked returns from 1918 only rather than from January 1900 (the more recent Equity Gilt studies go back to 1900). The risk premium figures picked up by companies from these reports, at around 7.5 per cent, are much higher than that used earlier in this book. The other 11 firms chose a number in a narrow range of 4.5 per cent to 6 per cent. The firms concerned admitted that their estimates were a 'gut feel' choice 'that came from our planning manager. He's an MBA and a lot of his MBA work was on the cost of capital. 5 per cent is a figure he's plucked out of the air based on his experience and knowledge' (Company O: Gregory and Rutterford, 1999, p. 43). Alternatively, managers tended to rely on advice from their bankers that the current equity risk premium was lower than at any time in the past – this had the effect of reducing the WACC estimate by almost two percentage points (compared with using a risk premium of 7.5 per cent) in most cases. This intuitive approach has subsequently been borne out by the downward revision of historical risk premiums in empirical studies.

Cost of debt

All 11 firms that explicitly consider the cost of debt allow for the corporate tax rate to reduce the effective cost. All the companies used the cost of long-term debt. The majority chose to base the cost of debt on the cost of government debt and either take this as the cost of debt or add a credit risk premium. Three companies took the yield on their own outstanding bonds and the remainder chose a long-term bond yield 'based on experience'. 'We do not put in our real cost of debt. There are certain, for example tax driven, vehicles which give us actually quite a low cost of debt . . . So we tend to ignore those. That does build up a nice margin of safety within the target (cost of capital) of course' (Company C: Gregory and Rutterford, 1999, p. 46).

Debt/equity ratios

Ten out of 15 firms that calculated a WACC used a long-run target debt/equity ratio, five used the actual debt/equity ratio and one used both. For firms using a target ratio, this was taken as 20 per cent, 25 per cent or 30 per cent, and was at least as high as the current actual debt/equity ratio, in some cases substantially higher – one firm with a cash surplus nevertheless chose a ratio of 20 per cent.

Ten companies chose to estimate a nominal (including inflation) WACC (average value of 11.67 per cent). Five used a real (excluding inflation) WACC (average value of 8.79 per cent) and three used both a nominal and a real WACC. Rutterford (2000) comments: 'differences in data inputs for the equity risk premium (from 4 per cent to 7.5 per cent) and the choice of debt/equity ratio (from 0 per cent to 50 per cent) meant that the final WACC estimate was a fairly subjective estimate for each firm.'

Hurdle rates

Corporations seem to make a distinction between the WACC and the hurdle rate. Gregory and Rutterford found that the average *base* hurdle rate was 0.93 per cent higher than the average WACC. The base hurdle rate is defined as the rate for standard projects, before any adjustments for divisional differences in operating risk, financial risk or currency risk. Most of the firms had a range of hurdle rates, depending on project or the risk factors.

However, there was no consensus among the firms on how to adjust the differential project risk. Fourteen out of 18 made some adjustment for different levels of risk, with nine of those 14 making some adjustment for country risk or foreign exchange risk as well as for systematic risk. Note however that in 17 out of 18 cases the adjustment was made to the base hurdle rate and not to the more theoretically appropriate WACC. There was a general impression of sophistication in attaining the WACC in the first place, followed by a rule-of-thumb-type approach when making risk adjustments: 'The comment I make in terms of the hurdle rates for investment purposes is that we do it relatively simplistically in terms of low risk, high risk, country-specific risk' (Company P: Gregory and Rutterford, 1999, p. 53). Methods range from adding two percentage point increments, to having two possible hurdle rates, say, 15 per cent and 20 per cent. Fifteen firms had premiums of 0 per cent to 8 per cent over the base hurdle rate, while three firms added more than 10 percentage points for the highest-risk projects.

Some way to go yet

Even when the textbook model is accepted a range of WACCs can be estimated for the same firm: 'for example, altering the choice of target debt/equity ratio or equity risk premium can have an impact of 2 per cent or more on the resulting WACC figure. Furthermore, little work has yet been done to extend the complex analysis for the firm's WACC to the divisional level' (Rutterford, 2000, p. 149). This lack of sophistication was confirmed in another study, carried out by Francis and Minchington (2000), that discovered 24 per cent of firms (of varied sizes) used a divisional cost of capital that reflects the cost of debt capital only, thus significantly underestimating the cost of capital. Furthermore, 69 per cent did not use a different rate for different divisions to reflect levels of risk.

Implementation issues

How large is the equity risk premium?

To understand the controversy over the equity risk premium we need to appreciate that it can only ever be a subjective estimate. The reason for this is that we are trying to figure out how much additional annual return investors in an averagely risky share require above the risk-free rate today. When deciding this, investors are looking at the future, not the past. Each investor is likely to have a different assessment of the appropriate extra return compared with the risk-free investment. We need to assess the weighted average of investors' attitudes.

Using historical returns to see the size of the premium actually received may be a good starting point, but we must be aware that we are making a leap of faith to then assume that the past equity risk premium is relevant for today's analysis with its future focus. In using historic data we are making at least two implicit assumptions:

● There has been no systematic change in the risk aversion of investors over time.

● The index being used as a benchmark has had an average riskiness that has not altered in a systematic way over time.

Differing views

Some City analysts believe that things have changed so radically in terms of the risk of ordinary shares for a fully diversified investor that the risk premium is now very small – some plump for 2 per cent while extremists say that over the long run shares are no more risky than gilts, and therefore say that the premium is zero. To justify their beliefs they point to the conquest of inflation, the lengthening of economic cycles, the increased internationalisation of investment opportunities reducing portfolio volatility, the long bull market (an argument weakened recently) and the increasing supply of risk capital as ageing industrial societies start to save more for retirement.

Barclays Capital, by undertaking a more thorough analysis of historical return data on shares and government bonds, have recently dramatically revised the equity risk premium in their Equity Gilt studies, from over seven percentage points greater than gilts to around 4 per cent. The Competition Commission tends to take a range of between 3.5 and 5 per cent. Ofcom uses 5 per cent as an input to the cost of capital calculation for regulated telecom and media companies. Ofwat (the UK water industry regulator) uses a range of between 4 and 5 per cent, but adds a premium of 0.2 per cent to 0.7 per cent if the company is small (this relates to the evidence that small companies share returns outperform large companies – some researchers put this down to additional risk carried by small firms resulting in investors demanding a higher return, rather than pricing inefficiency). Ofgem (the UK gas and electricity regulator) uses a range of 2.5 per cent to 4.5 per cent. The regulators calculate the amount of capital these firms are using and then allow prices charged to the consumer to be at a level which targets an appropriate rate of return (WACC) on the money invested in the business.[8]

An opinion

Equities have not become as safe as gilts. For equities the last two decades of the twentieth century were a charmed period. If long-term history is a guide shareholders will eventually learn the hard way that one can lose a great deal of money in stock markets. It is possible for returns to be negative for an entire decade or more. Turbulence and volatility will be as present in the twenty-first century as in the last. The prudent investor needs to examine a long period of time, in which rare, but extreme, events have disrupted the financial system (wars, depressions, manias and panics) to gain an impression of the risk of shares.

What is clear is that obtaining the risk premium is not as scientific as some would pretend. The range of plausible estimates is wide and the choosing of 2 per cent rather than 4.4 per cent, or even 7.5 per cent, can have a significant effect on the acceptance or rejection of capital investment projects within the firm, or the calculation of value performance metrics. One of

---

[8] The regulators' websites and publications often include a detailed discussion of the theory and practical difficulties of the calculation of the WACC as well as a justification of the rate they choose.

the respondents to the Arnold and Hatzopoulos survey expressed the frustration of practitioners by pointing out that precision in the WACC method is less important than to have reliable basic data: 'The real issue is one of risk premium on equity. Is it 2% or 8%?!'

Which risk-free rate?

The risk-free rate is a completely certain return. For complete certainty two conditions are needed:

- The risk of default is zero.
- When intermediate cash flows are earned on a multi-year investment there is no uncertainty about reinvestment rates.

The return available on a zero coupon government bond which has a time horizon equal to the cash flow (of a project, an SBU, etc.) being analysed is the closest we are going to get to the theoretically correct risk-free rate of return.

Business projects usually involve cash flows arising at intervals, rather than all at the end of an investment. Theoretically, each of these separate cash flows should be discounted using different risk-free rates. So, for the cash flows arising after one year on a multi-year project, the rate on a one-year zero coupon government bond should be used as part of the calculation of the cost of capital. The cash flows arising in year five should be discounted on the basis of a cost of capital calculated using the five-year zero coupon rate and so on. However, this approach is cumbersome, and there is a practical alternative that gives a reasonable approximation to the theoretical optimum. It is considered acceptable to use a long-term government rate on all the cash flows of a project that has a long-term horizon. Furthermore, the return on a government bond with coupons, rather than a zero coupon bond, is generally taken to be acceptable. The rule of thumb seems to be to use the return available on a reputable government security having the same time horizon as the project under consideration – so for a short-term project one should use the discount rate which incorporates the short-term government security rate, for a 20-year project use the 20-year government bond yield to maturity.

Note that the risk-free rate used depends on whether the future cash flows are expressed in nominal or real terms. If they are in nominal (money) terms then the risk-free rate should also include the inflation element. If the cash flows are in real terms then the r_f should exclude an allowance for inflation.[9]

How reliable is CAPM's beta?

There are many problems with the use of the capital asset pricing model's beta in the cost of equity capital calculation. We will consider two of them here.

The use of historical betas for future analysis

The mathematics involved in obtaining a historical beta are straightforward enough; however, it is not clear whether using weekly data is more appropriate than monthly, or whether the historical data on the returns on the market and the return on a particular share should be recorded over a one-, three-, five- or ten-year period. Each is likely to provide a different estimate of beta. Even if this is resolved the difficulty of using an historic measure for estimating a future relationship is very doubtful. Betas tend to be unstable over time. If the requirement is to compensate investors for the risk class of the share they hold surely we need a measure of

---

[9] Lockett (2002) describes the increasingly popular approach of using the rate of return offered on a UK government index-linked gilt in a WACC calculation that is based on real rates of return and real cash flows. That is, with inflation removed from both. This would appear to be a method used by regulators such as Ofgem, Ofwat and the Competition Commission. This generally provides a figure of around 2 per cent as the required return in the absence of inflation or risk (although at the time of writing it has strangely fallen to less than 1%). If you are conducting an analysis with actual projected cash flows (i.e. with inflation built into the assumptions) then you need to add an estimated inflation rate, which will take you back (approximately) to the rate on the conventional government bond of the same time to maturity,

risk that is not volatile, otherwise managers will be rejecting projects in one year that they accept in another purely because of the different time period over which beta was measured (and whether weekly or monthly data are used). Exhibit 8.7 gives an impression of the variability of the betas for some randomly selected UK firms – some have been stable, while others have changed significantly.

Exhibit 8.7	Betas as measured for the five years to 1997, 2000 and 2005		
	1997	**2000**	**2005**
BOC	0.65	0.59	0.88
Barclays Bank	1.22	1.55	1.01
BT	0.91	0.94	1.58
GUS	0.59	0.39	1.20
Marks & Spencer	0.95	0.44	0.48
J. Sainsbury	0.60	0.19	0.93

Source: Thomson Financial Datastream.

One potential explanation for the shifting betas is that the risk of the security changes – firms change the way they operate and the markets they serve. A company that was relatively insensitive to general market change two years ago may now be highly responsive – but have the companies in Exhibit 8.7 really changed the nature (risk) of their businesses very much over these periods? I doubt it. Alternatively, the explanation may lie in measurement error – large random errors cause problems in producing comparable betas from one period to another. To add to this problem we have a wide variety of market indices (such as the FTSE 100, or the FTSE All-Share) to choose from when calculating the historical co-variability of a share with the market (its beta).

The breakdown in the relationship between beta and return

The fundamental point about the CAPM is that investors demand higher returns on shares that are more volatile relative to the market index. Investors require that a share with a beta of 1.5 should provide a higher return than a share with a beta of 1. Recent evidence has cast doubt on the strength of the relationship between CAPM's beta and return – *see* Chapter 5.

Fundamental beta

Instead of using historical betas calculated through a regression of the firm's returns against a proxy for the market portfolio (e.g. the FTSE 100) some analysts calculate a 'fundamental beta'. This is based on the intuitive underpinning of the risk-return relationship: if the firm (or project) cash flows are subject to more (systematic) variability then the required return should be higher. What causes greater systematic variability? Three factors have been advanced.

1 **The type of business that the company (SBU or project) is engaged in** Some businesses are more sensitive to market conditions than others. The turnover and profits of cyclical industries change a great deal with macroeconomic fluctuations. So, for example, the sale of yachts, cars or designer clothes rises in a boom and crashes in declines. On the other hand, non-cyclical industries, such as food retailing or tobacco, experience less variability with the economic cycle. Thus, in a fundamental beta framework cyclical businesses would be allocated a higher beta than non-cyclical businesses – if the variability is systematic rather than specific to the firm. If the purchase of the product can be delayed for months, years or even indefinitely (i.e. it is discretionary) then the industry is more likely to be vulnerable to an economic downturn.

2 **Degree of operating gearing** If the firm has high fixed costs compared with variable costs of production its profits are highly sensitive to output (turnover) levels. A small percentage fall in sales can result in a large percentage change in profits. The higher variability in profit means that a higher beta should be allocated. (Chapter 11 discusses operating gearing.)

3 **Degree of financial gearing** If the company has high borrowings, with a concomitant requirement to pay interest regularly, then profits attributable to shareholders are likely to be more vulnerable to shocks. So the beta will rise if the company has higher financial gearing (or leverage). The obligation to meet interest payments increases the variability of after-interest profits. In a recession profits can more easily turn into losses. Financial gearing exacerbates the underlying business risk.

The obvious problem with using the fundamental beta approach is the difficulty of deriving the exact extent to which beta should be adjusted up or down depending on the strength of the three factors.

Some thoughts on the cost of capital

Progress

There have been a number of significant advances in theory and in practice over the last forty years. No longer do most firms simply use the current interest rate, or adjust for risk in an entirely arbitrary manner. There is now a theoretical base to build on, both to determine a cost of capital for a firm, and to understand the limitations (or qualities) of the input data and economic modelling.

It is generally accepted that a weighted average of the costs of all the sources of finance is to be used. It is also accepted that the weights are to be based on market values (rather than book values), as market values relate more closely to the opportunity cost of the finance providers. Furthermore, it is possible that the WACC may be lowered and shareholder value raised by shifting the debt/equity ratio.

Even before the development of modern finance it was obvious that projects (or collections of projects, as firms are) that had a risk higher than that of investing in government securities require a higher rate of return. A risk premium must be added to the risk-free rate to determine the required return. However, modern portfolio theory has refined the definition of risk, so the analyst need only consider compensation (additional return) for systematic risk.

Outstanding issues

Despite the progress, considerable difficulties remain. Practitioners need to be aware of both the triumphs of modern financial theory as well as its gaps. The area of greatest controversy is the calculation of the cost of equity capital. In determining the cost of equity capital we start with the following facts.

- The current risk-free rate is the bedrock. It is acceptable to use the rate on a government bond with the same maturity as the project, SBU, etc.
- The return should be increased to allow for the risk of a share with average systematic risk. (Add a risk premium to the risk-free rate return.) As a guide, investors have received a risk premium of around 4–5 per cent for accepting the risk level equivalent to that on the average ordinary share over the past 100 years.
- A particular company's shares do not carry average equity risk, therefore the risk premium should be increased or decreased depending on the company's systematic risk level.

So, if the project or SBU under examination has a systematic risk which is lower than that on the average share it would seem sensible that the returns attributable to shareholders on this project should be somewhere between the risk-free rate and the risk-free rate plus, say, 5 per cent. If the project has a systematic risk greater than that exhibited by shares generally then the returns required for shareholders will be more than the risk-free rate plus, say, 5 per cent.

There is a major difficulty calculating the systematic risk level. In the heyday of the CAPM this was simple: beta was all you needed. Today we have to allow for the possibility that investors want compensation for a multiplicity of systematic risk factors. Not unnaturally many business people are unwilling to adopt such a burdensome approach and fall back on their 'judgement' to adjust for the risk of a project. In practice it is extremely difficult to state precisely the risk of a project – we are dealing with future uncertainties about cash flows from day-to-day business operations subject to sudden and unforeseen shocks. The pragmatic approach is to avoid precision and simply place each proposed project into one of three risk categories: low, medium or high. This neatly bypasses the complexities laid out by the theorists and also reflects the fact that decisions made in the real world are made with less than complete knowledge. Mechanical decision making within the firm based on over-simplistic academic models is often a poor substitute for judgement that recognises the imperfections of reality.

One thing is certain: if anyone ever tells you that they can unequivocally state a firm's cost of capital to within a tenth of a percentage point, you know you are talking to someone who has not quite grasped the complexity of the issue.

Concluding comments

A firm that asks an unreasonably high rate of return will be denying its shareholders wealth-enhancing opportunities and ceding valuable markets to competitors. One that employs an irrationally low cost of capital will be wasting resources, setting managers targets that are unduly easy to reach and destroying wealth.

This chapter has described the academic foundations for calculating a company's cost of capital. It has also pointed out the practical difficulties of calculating real-world discount rates. The difficulties are severe, but please don't throw your hands up and conclude that the economists and finance theorists have taken us on a long, arduous road back to where we started. We are not at square one. We have a set of rules to provide a key management number. We now know that judgement is required at many stages in the process and where those particular points are. This allows us to view any number produced by our own calculations, or those of the finance team, with the required amount of reasoned scepticism. And, in making decisions on whether to invest in that new factory or close down a division, we have some grasp of the degree to which there is room for error in the value calculation. This chapter reinforces again that in this uncertain world we should think in terms of a range of possible outcomes, with all too imprecise subjective probabilities, not in terms of cut-and-dried pinpoint precision. The arguments in this chapter should, I hope, allow you to estimate the boundaries for the range values you feel comfortable with. Returns falling below the acceptable range can be easily rejected; those with a good margin above are simple to make a decision about. Management at these extremes is survivable even for the humdrum executive. It is those projects that give returns lying in the middle that require insightful judgement that is the art of management: they call for leaders.

Key points and concepts

- **The cost of capital** is the rate of return that a company has to offer finance providers to induce them to buy and hold a financial security.

- The **weighted average cost of capital (WACC)** is calculated by weighting the cost of debt and equity in proportion to their contribution to the total capital of the firm:

$$\text{WACC} = k_E W_E + k_{DAT} W_D$$

- **The WACC can be lowered** (or raised) by altering the proportion of debt in the capital structure. The **weights in the WACC are based on market values**, not balance sheet values.

- **Investors in shares** require a return, k_E, which provides for two elements: (i) a return equal to the risk-free rate; plus (ii) a risk premium. The most popular method for calculating the risk premium has two stages: (i) estimate the average risk premium for shares $(r_m - r_f)$; and (ii) adjust the average premium to suit the risk on a particular share. The CAPM, using a beta based on

Key points and concepts continued

the relative co-movement of a share with the market, has been used for the second stage but other risk factors appear to be relevant.

- An alternative method for calculating the required rate of return on equity is to use the **Gordon growth model**:

$$k_E = \frac{d_1}{P} + g$$

- The **cost of retained earnings** is equal to the expected returns required by shareholders buying new shares in a firm.

- The **cost of debt capital**, k_D, is the current market rate of return for a risk class of debt. The cost to the firm is reduced to the extent that interest can be deducted from taxable profits:

$$k_{DAT} = k_{DBT}(1 - T)$$

- The **cost of irredeemable constant dividend preference share capital** is: $k_p = \dfrac{d_1}{P_p}$

- For projects, etc. with similar risk to that of the existing set, use the WACC, which is based on the target debt to equity ratio. **Do not use the cost of the latest capital raised.**

- For projects, SBUs, etc. of a **different systematic from that of the firm**, raise or lower the discount rate in proportion to the risk.

- **Companies use** a mixture of theoretically correct techniques with rules of thumb to calculate hurdle rates of return.

- **Calculating a cost of capital relies a great deal on judgement** rather than scientific precision. But there is a theoretical framework to guide that judgement.

- **Some of the difficulties remaining**: (i) estimating the equity risk premium; (ii) obtaining the risk-free rate; (iii) unreliability of the CAPM's beta.

- **Fundamental beta** is based on factors thought to be related to systematic risk: (i) type of business; (ii) operating gearing; (iii) financial gearing.

Further reading

Surveys of corporate practice: Al-Ali, J. and T. Arkwright (2000), Arnold, G.C. and Hatzopoulos, P.D. (2000), Francis, G. and Minchington, C. (2000), Graham, J.R. and Harvey, C.R. (2001), Gregory, A. and Rutterford, J. (1999), Lockett, M. (2001), Lockett, M. (2002), McLaney *et al.* (2004), Pike, R.H. (1983), Rutterford, J. (2000), Westwick, C.A. and Shohet, P.S.D. (1976).

Data and discussion on historical return to shares etc.: Barclays Capital, *Equity Gilt Studies* (annual), Dimson, E., Marsh, P. and Staunton, M. (2001), Dimson, E., Marsh, P. and Staunton, M. (2002).

Books containing further discussion of the theoretical and/or practical issues in WACC calculation: Damodaran, A. (1999), Damodaran, A. (2002), Ogier, T., Rugman, J. and Spicer, L. (2004), Solomon, E. (1963) (WACC presented for the first time).

Dividend growth model: Gordon, M.J. (1962), Gordon, M.J. and Shapiro, E. (1956).

Websites

Bondsonline Group, Inc. www.bondsonline.com
Investors Chronicle www.ic-community.co.uk/bonds
London Stock Exchange www.londonstockexchange.com

Self-review questions

1 Explain the term 'the cost of capital'.

2 Explain how you might calculate the cost of equity capital.

3 Why can we not always take the coupon rate on a bond issued years ago as the cost of bond capital?

4 Describe the weighted average cost of capital and explain why a project, SBU or product line should not be evaluated using the cost of finance associated with the latest portion of capital raised.

5 Should the WACC be used in all circumstances?

6 Explain two of the practical difficulties in calculating a firm's cost of capital.

Quick numerical questions

1 A company obtains 65% of its capital from equity and 35% from debt. This is the optimum capital structure. The equity holders require a return of 9% per year given their opportunity cost of capital. The debt holders require 5.5% return. The corporate tax rate is currently 30% of profits. Calculate the weighted average cost of capital.

2 The projected cash flows for a company to be established are £1m per year forever. The company will require £9m in capital to be viable and produce the £1m annual cash flows. The prospective directors suggest that they raise £2m by borrowing from a bank at a fixed rate of 6% per year. The remaining £7m will come from an issue of shares. Shares with a similar systematic risk are currently offering an expected return of 11%. This cautious level of borrowing suits the directors because their livelihood depends on the survival of the firm. The corporation tax rate is 30%.

a Calculate the WACC and the value of the enterprise (debt + equity value).
b If a higher level of financial gearing is targeted such that £5m of the capital comes from lenders and £4m comes from shareholders the required rates of return change. The debt holders now require 7% per annum, whereas the equity holders expect a return of 16% per year. Does this capital structure raise or lower the WACC and value of the firm?

> **AN EXCEL SPREADSHEET VERSION OF THESE CALCULATIONS IS AVAILABLE AT**
> **www.pearsoned.co.uk/arnold**

3 Triglass plc has three types of capital. The market capitalisation of its equity is £20m. These ordinary shares have a beta of 0.9, as measured over the past five years of monthly returns. The current risk-free rate on government bonds is 4.5%. The historical equity risk premium is 5% per year. The market value of its irredeemable non-participating non-convertible preference shares is £5m and the rate of return being offered is 7.5% per year. The debt of the firm amounts to £15m and costs 6.5% per year before allowing for tax shield benefits. The corporation tax rate is 30%. Calculate the WACC for Triglass plc.

> **AN EXCEL SPREADSHEET VERSION OF THESE CALCULATIONS IS AVAILABLE AT**
> **www.pearsoned.co.uk/arnold**

Questions and problems

For those questions marked with an asterisk* the answers are given in the lecturer's guide.

1 (*Examination level*) The managers of Petalt plc do not yet know the cost of capital but do have the following information. The capital is in three forms:

i   A floating-rate bank loan for £1m at 2 per cent over bank base rate. Base rates are currently 9 per cent.
ii A 25-year vanilla bond issued 20 years ago at par (£100) raising £1m. The bond has an annual coupon of 5 per cent and is currently trading at £80. The next coupon is due in one year.
iii Equity capital with a market value of £2m.

The tax rate on corporate profits is 31 per cent. The rate of return available by purchasing long-term government securities is currently 6 per cent and the average risk premium for shares over the risk-free rate has averaged 5 per cent. Petalt's shares have an above-average risk and its historic beta as measured by the co-movement of its shares and the market index correctly reflects the risk adjustment necessary to the average risk premium – this is 1.3.

Required

a Calculate the cost of bond finance.
b Calculate the cost of equity finance.
c Calculate the weighted average cost of capital.
d Compare and contrast the Gordon growth model for estimating the equity cost of capital with the capital asset pricing model method.

AN EXCEL SPREADSHEET VERSION OF THESE CALCULATIONS IS AVAILABLE AT
www.pearsoned.co.uk/arnold

2 (*Examination level*) Diversified plc is trying to introduce an improved method of assessing investment projects using discounted cash flow techniques. For this it has to obtain a cost of capital to use as a discount rate.

The finance department has assembled the following information:

– The company has an equity beta of 1.50, which may be taken as the appropriate adjustment to the average risk premium. The yield on risk-free government securities is 7 per cent and the historical premium above the risk-free rate is estimated at 5 per cent for shares.
– The market value of the firm's equity is twice the value of its debt.
– The cost of borrowed money to the company is estimated at 12 per cent (before tax shield benefits).
– Corporation tax is 30 per cent.

Required

a Estimate the equity cost of capital using the capital asset pricing model (CAPM). Create an estimate of the weighted average cost of capital (WACC).
b Comment on the appropriateness of using this technique for estimating the cost of capital for project appraisal purposes for a company with many subsidiaries in different markets.
c Given the difficulties in the calculation of WACC are companies justified in using rules of thumb rather than theoretically precise methods? Explain the difficulties and describe the approximations used by business people.

3* (*Examination level*) Burgundy plc is financed through bonds and ordinary shares. The bonds were issued five years ago at a par value of £100 (total funds raised £5m). They carry an annual coupon of 10 per cent, are due to be redeemed in four years and are currently trading at £105.
   The company's shares have a market value of £4m, the return on risk-free government securities is 8 per cent and the risk premium for an average-risk share has been 5 per cent. Burgundy's shares have a lower than average risk and its historic beta as measured by the co-movement of its shares and the market index correctly reflects the risk adjustment necessary to the average risk premium – this is 0.85. The corporate tax rate is 30 per cent. Burgundy has a net asset figure of £3.5m showing in its balance sheet.

Required

a Calculate the cost of debt capital.
b Calculate the cost of equity capital.
c Calculate the weighted average cost of capital.
d Should Burgundy use the WACC for all future projects and SBUs? Explain your answer.
e Describe the two difficulties in obtaining good input data for the equity cost of capital.

Assignments

Calculate the weighted average cost of capital for a company or SBU of a company you know well. Explain those areas where you have made difficult judgements in deciding which numbers to use.

Visit www.pearsoned.co.uk/arnold to get access to Gradetracker diagnostic tests, Podcasts, Excel Spreadsheet Solutions, FT articles, a Flashcard revision tool, Weblinks, a searchable Glossary and more.

CHAPTER 9

Value-based management

LEARNING OUTCOMES

This chapter demonstrates the rationale behind value-based management techniques. By the end of it the reader should be able to:

■ explain the failure of accounts-based management (e.g. profits, balance sheet assets, earnings per share and accounting rate of returns) to guide value-maximising decisions in many circumstances;

■ describe the four key drivers of value and the five actions to increasing value;

■ outline the extent of the ramifications of value-based management;

■ describe the four main tasks for the corporate centre (head office);

■ describe and explain the use of discounted cash flow, shareholder value analysis and economic profit, and be able to provide a brief outline of economic value added;

■ explain the value metrics entitled total shareholder return and market value added, pointing out their advantages and the problems in practical use.

Introduction

The first few chapters of this book linked together the objective of shareholder wealth maximisation and acceptance or otherwise of proposed projects. This required knowledge of the concepts of the time value of money and the opportunity cost of investors' funds placed into new investments. If managers are unable to achieve returns at least as high as those available elsewhere for the same level of risk then, as agents for investors, they are failing in their duty. If a group of investors place £1m in the hands of managers who subsequently generate annual returns of 10 per cent, those managers would in effect be destroying value for those investors if, for the same level of risk, a 14 per cent return is available elsewhere. With a future project the extent of this value destruction is summarised in the projected negative NPV figure.

This technique, and the underlying concepts, are well entrenched throughout modern corporations. However, the full potential of their application is only now dawning on a few particularly progressive organisations. Applying the notion of opportunity cost of capital and focusing on the cash flow rather than profit figures of *new projects* is merely skimming the surface. Since the mid-1980s a growing band of corporations, ranging from Pepsi in the USA to Lloyds TSB bank in the UK, have examined their businesses, or parts of their businesses, in terms of the following questions:

● How much money has been (or will be) placed in this business by investors?
● What rate of return is being (or will be) generated for those investors?
● Is this sufficient given the opportunity cost of capital?

These questions can be asked about past performance or about future plans. They may be asked about the entire organisation or about a particular division, strategic business unit or product line. If a line of business does not create value on the capital invested by generating a return greater than the minimum required then managerial attention can be directed to remedying the situation. Ultimately every unit should be contributing to the well-being of shareholders.

The pervasiveness of the value approach

The examination of an organisation to identify the sources of value may not seem particularly remarkable to someone who has absorbed the concepts discussed in Chapters 1 to 8, but to many managers steeped in the traditions of accounting-based performance measures such as profits, return on investment and earnings per share, they have revolutionary consequences.

The ideas themselves are not revolutionary or even particularly new. It is the far-reaching application of them to create a true shareholder-value-oriented company that can revolutionise almost everything managers do.

● Instead of working with *plans* drawn up in terms of accounting budgets, with their associated distorted and manipulable view of 'profit' and 'capital investment', managers are encouraged to think through the extent to which their new strategies or operational initiatives will produce what shareholders are interested in: a discounted inflow of cash greater than the cash injected.

● Instead of being *rewarded* for meeting objectives set in terms of accounting rates of return (and other 'non-value' performance measures, such as earnings per share and turnover) achieved in the short term, they are rewarded by the extent to which they contribute to shareholder value over a long time horizon. This can radically alter the incentive systems in most firms.

● Instead of directors accepting a low *cash flow return on the value of assets tied up* in a poorly performing subsidiary because the accounting profits look satisfactory, they are forced to consider whether greater wealth would be generated by either closure and selling off the subsidiary's assets or selling the operation to another firm which can make a more satisfactory return.

● There then follows a second decision: should the **cash** released be invested in other activities or be **given back to shareholders** to invest elsewhere in the stock market? The answers, when genuinely sought, can sometimes be uncomfortable for executives who prefer to expand rather than contract the organisation.

Dealing with such matters is only the beginning once an organisation becomes value based. Mergers must be motivated and evaluated on the criterion of the extent to which a margin above the cost of capital can be achieved given the purchase price. Strategic analysis does not stop at the point of often vague and woolly qualitative analysis; it goes on to a second phase of valuation of the strategies and quantitative sensitivity analysis. The decisions on the most appropriate debt levels and the dividend payout ratios have as their core consideration the impact on shareholder wealth. In the field of human resources, it is accepted that all organisations need a committed workforce. But committed to what? Shareholder value-based management provides an answer but also places an onus on managers to communicate, educate and convert everyone else to the process of value creation. This may require a shift in culture, in systems and procedures as well as a major teaching and learning effort. Value-based management is much more than a technique employed by a few individuals 'good with numbers'. The principles behind it must pervade the organisation; it touches almost all aspects of organisational life.

> Value-based management is a managerial approach in which the primary purpose is long-run shareholder wealth maximisation. The objective of the firm, its systems, strategy, processes, analytical techniques, performance measurements and culture have as their guiding objective shareholder wealth maximisation.

Confusing objectives

Some managers claim that there are measures of performance that are synonymous with, or good proxies for, shareholder wealth – such as customer satisfaction, market share leadership or lowest-cost producer. These proxies are then set as 'strategic objectives'. In many cases achieving these goals does go hand in hand with shareholder returns but, as Exhibit 9.1 shows, the pursuit of these objectives can be taken too far. There is frequently a trade-off between shareholder value and these proxy goals. Taking market share as an example: it is apparent that for many firms increasing market share will bring greater economies of scale, create barriers to entry for potential competitors and help establish brand loyalty, among other benefits. This sort of situation is demonstrated by moving from A to Z in Exhibit 9.1. High market share is clearly an important factor in many industries but some firms seem to become trapped in an obsessive quest for market share.

The car industry is notorious for its very poor returns to shareholders combined with addiction to market share data. For example, the Detroit car makers averaged returns on capital of 3 per cent per year in the 1990s.[1] Perhaps some in the industry have taken matters too far and ended up at point B in Exhibit 9.1. Enormous investment in plant capacity, marketing and price promotions has created a situation where the risk-adjusted returns on the investment are lower than the optimum.

Exhibit 9.1	Market share as a strategic objective can be taken too far

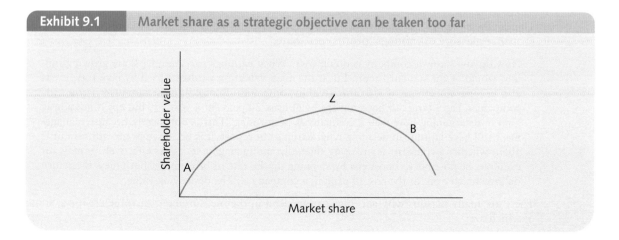

[1] *The Economist*, 23 February 2002, p. 100.

Three steps of value

There are three steps to creating shareholder value – *see* Exhibit 9.2. First, create awareness of, and a genuine commitment to, a shareholder wealth-enhancing mission throughout the organisation. Second, put in place techniques for measuring whether value is being created at various organisational levels. And make sure everyone understands and respects the measures adopted. Third, ensure that every aspect of management is suffused with the shareholder value objective, from human resource management to research and development.

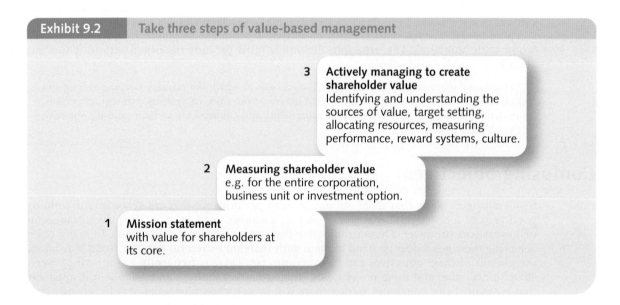

Exhibit 9.2	Take three steps of value-based management

3 Actively managing to create shareholder value
Identifying and understanding the sources of value, target setting, allocating resources, measuring performance, reward systems, culture.

2 Measuring shareholder value
e.g. for the entire corporation, business unit or investment option.

1 Mission statement
with value for shareholders at its core.

It is clearly important to have a management team that both understand and are fully committed to shareholder value. To implement true shareholder wealth maximisation managers need to know how to measure the wealth-creating potential of their actions. Before turning to appropriate methods of evaluating value creation we will examine some of the more popular and increasingly dated measurement techniques used to guide (or misguide) a business.

Earnings-based management

The *Financial Times*'s Lex column expressed a view on the traditional accounting-based performance measure of earnings (profits) per share:

> How do you know a company is doing well? When earnings per share (eps) are growing rapidly, would be the standard reply. Eps is the main valuation yardstick used by investors; it has also become something of a fixation within companies. Rentokil, most famously among UK companies, has a target of boosting eps by at least 20 per cent a year . . . But eps is not a holy grail in determining how well a company is performing. This is not merely because management still have latitude in deciding what earnings to report; it is because eps growth says little about whether a company is investing shrewdly and managing its assets effectively. It may, for example, be possible to boost eps by stepping up the rate of investment. But unless the return on investment exceeds the cost of capital, a company will be destroying value.[2]

There are many reasons why earnings can mislead in the measurement of value creation, some of which are:

---

[2] *Financial Times*, 7 May 1996, 'Lex column: Return on Investment'.

- accounting is subject to distortions and manipulations;
- the investment made is often inadequately represented;
- the time value of money is excluded from the calculation;
- risk is not considered.

Accounting numbers

In drawing up profit and loss accounts and balance sheets accountants have to make judgements and choose a basis for their calculations. They try to match costs and revenues. Unfortunately for the users of the resulting 'bottom line' figures, there can be many alternative approaches, which give completely different results and yet all follow accounting body guidelines.

Take the example of the identical companies X and Y. These have just started up and in the first three years annual profits before deducting depreciation of £3m are expected. Both companies invested their entire initial capital of £10m in plant and machinery. The accountant at X takes the view that the machinery has a useful life of ten years and that a 25 per cent declining balance depreciation is appropriate. The accountant at Y, after reviewing the information on the plant and machinery, is more pessimistic and judges that a seven-year life with straight-line depreciation more truly reflects the future reality. The first three years' profits are shown in Exhibit 9.3.

Exhibit 9.3	Companies X and Y: Profits for the first three years		
	Years (£000s)		
	1	2	3
Company X			
Pre-depreciation profit	3,000	3,000	3,000
Depreciation	2,500	1,875	1,406
Earnings	500	1,125	1,594
Company Y			
Pre-depreciation profit	3,000	3,000	3,000
Depreciation	1,429	1,429	1,429
Earnings	1,571	1,571	1,571

The underlying economic position is the same for both company X and company Y, but in the first two years company X appears to be less profitable. Outside observers and management comparing the two companies may gain a distorted view of quality of stewardship and the potential of the firm. Investment decisions and incentive schemes based on profit figures can lead to sub-optimal decisions and behaviour. They may also lead to deliberate manipulation.

Ignoring the investment money sacrificed

Examining earnings per share growth as an indicator of success fails to take account of the investment needed to generate that growth. Take the case of companies A and B (see Exhibit 9.4), both of which have projected growth in earnings of 10 per cent per year and are therefore equally attractive to an earnings-based analyst or manager.

To a value-oriented analyst A is much more interesting than B if we allow for the possibility that less additional investment is needed for A to create this improving profits pattern. For example, both firms need to offer credit terms to their customers: however, B has to offer much more generous terms than A to gain sales; therefore it has to invest cash in supporting

Exhibit 9.4	Companies A and B: Earnings			

		Year (£000s)		
		1	**2**	**3**
Earnings of A		1,000	1,100	1,210
Earnings of B		1,000	1,100	1,210

higher debtor balances. B is also less efficient in its production process and has to invest larger amounts in inventory for every unit increase in sales.

When B's accounts are drawn up the additional debtors and inventory are included as an asset in the balance sheet and do not appear as a cost element in the profit and loss account. This results in the costs shown in the profit and loss account understating the cash outflow during a period.

If we examine the cash flow associated with A and B (**Exhibit 9.5**) we can see immediately that A is generating more shareholder value (assuming the pattern continues and all other factors are the same).

Exhibit 9.5	Companies A and B: Earnings and cash flow						

	Company A (£000s)			Company B (£000s)		
Year	**1**	**2**	**3**	**1**	**2**	**3**
Profit (earnings)	1,000	1,100	1,210	1,000	1,100	1,210
Increase in debtors	0	20	42	0	60	126
Increase in inventory	0	30	63	0	50	105
Cash flow before tax	1,000	1,050	1,105	1,000	990	979
Percentage change		+5%	+5.2%		–1%	–1.1%

If B also has to invest larger amounts than A in vehicles, plant, machinery and property for each unit increase in sales and profit, the difference in the relative quality of the earnings growth will be even more marked.

Time value

It is possible for growth in earnings to destroy value if the rate of return earned on the additional investment is less than the required rate. Take the case of a team of managers trying to decide whether to make a dividend payment of £10m. If they retained the money within the business both earnings and cash flow would rise by £1,113,288 for each of the next ten years. Managers motivated by earnings growth might be tempted to omit the dividend payment. Future earnings would rise and therefore the share price would also rise on the announcement that the dividend would not be paid. Right? Wrong! Investors in this firm are likely to have a higher annual required rate of return on their £10m than the 2 per cent offered by this plan.[3] The share price will fall and shareholder value will be destroyed. What the managers forgot was that money has a time value and investors value shares on the basis of *discounted* future cash flows.

---

[3] A ten-year annuity of £1,113,288 per year for a £10m investment at time 0 has an effective annual rate of return of about 2 per cent.

It seems so obvious that a 2 per cent rate of return on invested money is serving shareholders badly. Yet how many companies do you know holding tens or hundreds of millions of pounds in cash rather than giving it back to shareholders to invest elsewhere? Certainly, it gives managers a greater sense of security to have all that cash around – how can the company be liquidated and they lose their jobs? – but shareholders would rather this money was used more effectively and any money that cannot be used to generate good returns should be handed back to shareholders. If earnings per share are rising what have the shareholders got to complain about, retort the managers? The thundering reply is: it is easy to increase earnings per share just by holding on to ever-larger quantities of money; what shareholders want is a return greater than the opportunity cost of capital (the time value of money) – the return available elsewhere for the same level of risk.

Ignoring risk

Focusing purely on the growth in earnings fails to take account of another aspect of the quality of earnings: risk. Increased profits that are also subject to higher levels of risk require a higher discount rate. Imagine a firm is contemplating two alternative growth options with the same expected earnings, of £100,000 per year to infinity. Each strategy is subject to risk but S has a wider dispersion of possible outcomes than T (*see* Exhibit 9.6). Investors are likely to value strategy T more highly than strategy S. Examining crude profit figures, either historical or projected, often means a failure to allow adequately for risk. In a value-based approach it is possible to raise the discount rate in circumstances of greater uncertainty, as we saw in Chapters 4 and 8.

Exhibit 9.6	Probabilities of annual returns on strategies S and T			
	Strategy S		**Strategy T**	
	Outcome earnings (profits) £	**Probability**	**Outcome earnings (profits) £**	**Probability**
	−100,000	0.10	80,000	0.10
	0	0.20	90,000	0.15
	100,000	0.40	100,000	0.50
	200,000	0.20	110,000	0.15
	300,000	0.10	120,000	0.10
Expected outcome	£100,000		£100,000	

Worked example 9.1　　Earnings growth and value

Earnings and earnings per share growth can lead to higher shareholder value in some circumstances. In others it can lead to value destruction. Shareholder value will rise if the return obtainable on new investment is at least as great as the required rate of return for the risk class. Consider EPSOS plc, financed entirely with equity capital and with a required rate of return on that capital of 15 per cent (assume for simplicity that this is the optimal financial gearing level). To make the example simple we assume that EPSOS does not need to invest in higher levels of working capital if sales expand. EPSOS pays shareholders its entire earnings after tax every year and is expected to continue doing this indefinitely. Earnings and cash flow amount to £100m per year. (The amount charged as depreciation is just sufficient to pay for investment to maintain sales and profits.) The value of the company given the opportunity cost of shareholders' money of 15 per cent is £100m/0.15 = £666.67m.

▶

Worked example 9.1　　**Continued**

	£m
Sales	300.00
Operating expenses	157.14
Pre-tax profit	142.86
Taxes @ 30 per cent	42.86
Profits and cash flow after tax	100.00

Now imagine that EPSOS takes the decision to omit this year's dividend. Shareholders are made poorer by £100m now. However, as a result of the additional £100m investment in its operations for the next year and every subsequent year sales, earnings, eps and cash flows after tax will rise by 20 per cent. This is shown below.

	£m
Sales	360.00
Operating expenses	188.57
Pre-tax profit	171.43
Taxes @ 30 per cent	51.43
Profits and cash flow after tax	120.00

Earnings have grown by an impressive 20 per cent. Also value has been created. The extra £20m cash flow per annum stretching into the future is worth £20m/0.15 = £133.33m. This is achieved with a £100m sacrifice now. Here a growth in earnings has coincided with an increase in value: £33.33m of value is created.

Now consider a scenario in which sales growth of 20 per cent is achieved by using the £100m to expand the business, but this time the managers, in going for sales growth, push up operating expenses by 32 per cent. Earnings and cash flow increase by a respectable 6.81 per cent, but, crucially, value falls.

	£m
Sales	360.00
Operating expenses (157.14 × 1.32)	207.42
Pre-tax profit	152.58
Taxes @ 30 per cent	45.77
Profits and cash flow after tax	106.81

The incremental perpetual cash flow is worth a present value of £6.81m/0.15 = £45.4m. But the 'cost' of achieving this is the sacrifice of £100m of income now. Therefore overall shareholder value has been destroyed despite earnings and eps growth. It is surprising how often senior managers make this basic error.

For an example of a real company growing earnings (profits carefully defined as before the deduction of interest, tax, depreciation and amortisation) but producing poor returns on invested capital we turn to Vodafone – *see* **Exhibit 9.7**. Perhaps we should not focus exclusively on income over a few recent years. Perhaps this near-term sacrifice is worth it. Perhaps net cash flows will rocket once the basic infrastructure is in place. Perhaps.

Exhibit 9.7

Big feet, shrinking values, surreal numbers

John Plender

There was something faintly surreal about the accounts of telecom companies in the 1990s bubble, with their multiple definitions of profit and their customary invitation to ignore the bottom line loss. Now that the bubble has burst there is still a hint of surrealism about, as I found when thumbing through Vodafone's figures last week.

Vodafone is now the 13th largest company in the world measured by stock market capitalisation. The obvious pertinent question is whether, when Vodafone's managers talk of 'enlarging our footprint', they are employing a euphemism for size for size's sake or whether they are creating real value.

The preliminary announcement contains a welter of figures, including a loss for the year of £9.8bn. ('Once again we have delivered excellent results,' says Lord MacLaurin, the chairman.) Then you have operating profit before goodwill amortisation and exceptional items; adjusted earnings per share; earnings before interest, tax, depreciation and amortisation (ebitda); and free cash flow.

These numbers are more flattering. Understandably enough, they are also the ones on which Sir Christopher Gent, Vodafone's outgoing chief executive, chooses to dwell.

I emphasise that this is no criticism of Sir Christopher or Vodafone, which observes the normal reporting conventions, but of the conventions themselves. Despite the shareholder value movement, traditional disclosure is hopelessly deficient in explaining the efficiency with which companies deploy capital.

Ebitda, earnings per share, free cash flow and the rest mean nothing without adequate information on the capital used to generate them.

Yet nobody has had the wit to ask the quoted companies to report routinely their weighted average cost of capital along with some sensible measure of return on capital.

For that you have to turn to a securities analyst like Mustapha Omar at brokers Collins Stewart. His figures will tell you that Vodafone's cash flow return on investment stopped covering its cost of capital in 2000. Given the wholesale destruction of value since then, he worries that Arun Sarin, the incoming chief executive, is already talking about those damned footprints again . . .

Forcing companies, analysts and investors to focus on whether a surplus is being earned over the cost of capital could do wonders for value creation.

Source: Financial Times, 2 June 2003, p. 22. Reprinted with permission.

Return on capital employed (ROCE) has failings

It is becoming clear that simply examining profit figures is not enough for good decision making and performance evaluation. Obviously the amount of capital invested has to be considered alongside the income earned. This was recognised long before the development of value-based management, as signified by the widespread use of a ratio of profits to assets employed. There are many variations on this theme: return on capital employed (ROCE), return on investment (ROI), return on equity (ROE) and accounting rate of return (ARR), but they all have the same root. They provide a measure of return as a percentage of resources devoted. The major problem with using these metrics of performance is that they are still based on accounting data. The profit figure calculations are difficult enough, but when they are combined with balance sheet asset figures we have a recipe for unacceptable distortion. The *Financial Times* puts it this way:

> Unfortunately, the crude figures for return on capital employed – operating profit/capital employed – that can be derived from a company's accounts are virtually useless. Here the biggest problem is not so much the reported operating profit as the figures for capital employed contained in the balance sheet. Not only are assets typically booked at historic cost, meaning they can be grossly undervalued if inflation has been high since they were acquired; the capital employed is also often deflated by goodwill write-offs. Once balance sheets have been shrunk, pedestrian profits translate into fabulous returns.[4]

---

[4] *Financial Times*, 7 May 1996, 'Lex column: Return on investment'.

Added to the list of problems is the issue of capitalisation. That is, the extent to which an item of expenditure is written off against profits as an expense or taken on to the balance sheet and capitalised as an asset. For example, firms differ in their treatment of research and development; companies that spend significant sums on R&D and then have a policy of writing it off immediately are likely to have lower asset value than those that do not write it off against profits in the year of expenditure. Cross-company comparisons of profits/assets can therefore be very misleading.

Focusing on accounting rates of return can lead to short-termism. Managers who are judged on this basis may be reluctant to invest in new equipment, as this will raise the denominator in the ratio, producing a poor ARR in the short term. This can destroy value in the long run. Fast-growing companies needing extensive investment in the near term with the expectation of reaping rich rewards in the long term should not be compared with slow-growth and low-investing firms on the basis of ARR.

The superficial highlighting of eps and ARR

One of the most pervasive myths of our time is: 'But our shareholders do focus on eps and ARR, don't they?' – and it is easy to see why. Senior executives when talking with institutional shareholders and analysts often find the conversation reverting to a discussion of short-term earnings forecasts. If a merger is announced directors feel the need to point out in press releases that the result will not be 'earnings dilutive' in the forthcoming year.

This surface noise is deceiving. Intelligent shareholders and analysts are primarily interested in the long-term cash flow returns on shares. The earnings attributable to the next couple of years are usually an insignificant part of the value of a share. Over two-thirds of the value of a typical share is determined by income to be received five or more years hence (*see* Chapter 10 for these calculations). Knowledge of this or next year's earnings is not particularly interesting in itself. It is sought because it sheds light on the medium- and long-term cash flows.

There are hundreds of quoted companies that do not expect to produce any positive earnings at all in the next two to five years and yet these shares are frequently among the most highly valued in the market. There are dozens of biotechnology companies that have tapped shareholders for funds through rights issues and the like for years. Some have become massive concerns and yet have never made a profit or paid a dividend. The same applies to internet companies, and, in the past it was true of satellite television operators (for example BSkyB) which have now reached the phase of high cash generation. **Exhibit 9.8** describes what investors are looking for.

Exhibit 9.8

Investment community piles on pressure for better returns

Companies need increasingly to develop medium-term corporate strategies which will enable them to meet the rising expectations of those who provide their equity capital

Tapping into the booming liquidity of global capital markets is the corporate ideal – but the gatekeepers of that liquidity, the global investor and analyst communities, are basing their investment strategies on increasingly focused information. In this environment, the historical reporting model is living on borrowed time – investors, who typically base share price valuations on their forecasts of future cash flows, demand forward-looking information to feed into their valuation models.

Management is increasingly sensitive to the stark fact that the use of equity capital is not 'free' – it has been invested in the hope of earning a return. It is this required

Exhibit 9.8 continued

return . . . that defines the company's cost of equity capital. Management can only create value for shareholders if the company consistently generates a return on capital greater than its cost of capital . . .

For companies, the challenge must be to use this escalating value focus in their strategic planning, and in measuring performance. Once the internal systems are in place, the priority is to establish effective communication into the marketplace . . .

'Historical cost accounting measures are becoming less relevant, with more companies using value-based information and non-financial indicators to judge performance internally. Greater disclosure in these areas will allow investors to make more informed decisions on the potential future of companies.'

The international investment community is well aware of the limitations of annual reports, which provide emphasis on accounting profit – itself no real indicator of the creation of economic value . . .

Analysts and institutional investors focus much of their research on company strategy and the 'value platforms' underlying that strategy and recent surveys of investors' demand for, and use of, information confirm their desire for more forward-looking information, as well as the importance of drivers of future performance to their investment decisions.

Source: Nigel Page, *Financial Times*, 10 December 1999, FT Director (special section), p. VIII. Reprinted with permission.

How a business creates value

Value is created when investment produces a rate of return greater than that required for the risk class of the investment. Shareholder value is driven by the four factors shown in Exhibit 9.9.

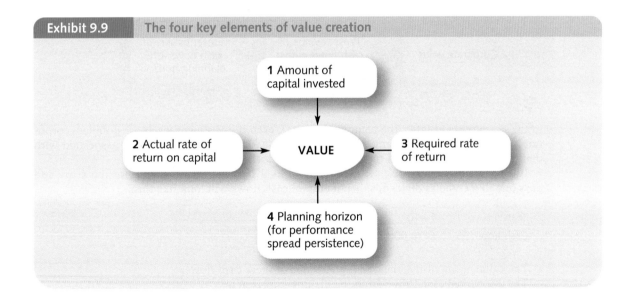

Exhibit 9.9   The four key elements of value creation

The difference between the second and third elements in Exhibit 9.9 creates the *performance spread*. The performance spread is measured as a percentage spread above or below the required rate of return, given the finance provider's opportunity cost of capital. Value is destroyed if 3 is greater than 2, and is created when 2 is greater than 3.

The absolute amount of value generated is determined by the quantity of capital invested multiplied by the performance spread. So, for example, if Black plc has a required rate of return of 14 per cent per annum and actually produces 17 per cent on an investment base of £1,000,000 it will create £30,000 of value per year:

Annual value creation = Investment × (Actual return − Required return)

= I $(r - k)$

= £1,000,000 × (0.17 − 0.14) = £30,000

The fourth element in Exhibit 9.9 needs more explanation. It would be unreasonable to assume that positive or negative return spreads will be maintained forever. If return spreads are negative, presumably managers will (eventually) take the necessary action to prevent continued losses. If they fail to respond then shareholders will take the required steps through, say, sackings or the acceptance of a merger offer. Positive spreads arise as a result of a combination of the attractiveness of the industry and the competitive strength of a firm within that industry. High returns can be earned because of market imperfections. For example, a firm may be able to prevent competitors entering its market segment because of economies of scale, brand strength or legal exclusion through patents. However, most firms will sooner or later experience increased competition and reduced margins. The higher the initial performance spread the more attractive market entry seems to potential competitors (or substitute product developers). Examples of industries that were at one time extremely profitable and which were penetrated to the point where they have become highly competitive include personal computers and mobile phone manufacture.

In shareholder value calculations it is usually assumed that returns will, over time, be driven towards the required rate of return. Beyond some point in the future (the planning horizon) any new investment will, on average, earn only the minimum acceptable rate of return. Having said this, I do acknowledge that there are some remarkable businesses that seem to be able to maintain positive performance spreads for decades. Their economic franchises are protected by powerful barriers preventing serious competitive attack, e.g. Coca-Cola, Gillette. Warren Buffett calls such companies 'Inevitables' because there is every reason to believe they will be dominating their industries decades from now – see Arnold (2002). If we leave Inevitables to one side, we see that for the majority of businesses corporate value consists of two components:

Corporate value	=	Present value of cash flows within planning horizon	+	Present value of cash flows after planning horizon

In the second period (after the planning horizon), even if investment levels are doubled, corporate value will remain constant, as the discounted cash inflows (to time zero) associated with that investment exactly equal the discounted cash outflows (to time zero).

If it is assumed that Black plc can maintain its 3 per cent return spread for ten years and pays out all income as dividends then its future cash flows will look like this:

Years:	1→10	11→infinity
Cash flow:	£170,000	£140,000

The value of the firm is the discounted value of these cash flows.
The discounted cash flow within the planning horizon is:

£170,000 × Annuity factor (10 years, 14 per cent) = £170,000 × 5.2161 = £886,737

plus the discounted cash flow after the planning horizon:
First discounted to time 10: £140,000/0.14 = £1,000,000.

This is then discounted back 10 years to time zero: $\dfrac{1,000,000}{(1 + 0.14)^{10}}$ =   £269,744

Value of the firm	£1,156,481
Less initial investment	(£1,000,000)
Value created	£156,481

An alternative approach: The value of the firm is equal to the initial investment in the firm (£1,000,000) plus the present value of all the values created annually.

Investment	+	Value created within planning horizon	+	Value created after planning horizon
£1,000,000	+	$\dfrac{£30,000 \times 5.2161}{£30,000 \times \text{Annuity factor (10 years, 14\%)}}$	+	£1,000,000 (0.14 – 0.14)
£1,000,000	+	£156,481	+	0 = £1,156,481

The five actions for creating value

Good growth occurs when a business unit or an entire corporation obtains a positive spread on the new investment capital. Bad growth, the bane of shareholders, occurs when managers invest in strategies that produce negative return spreads. This can so easily happen if the focus of attention is on sales and earnings growth. To managers encouraged to believe that their job is to expand the business and improve the bottom line, acceptance of the notion of bad growth in profits is a problem. But, as we have seen, it is perfectly possible to show growing profits on a larger investment base producing an incremental return less than the incremental cost of capital.

Exhibit 9.10 shows the options open to managers. This model can be applied at the corporate, business unit or product line level.

Exhibit 9.10	To expand or not to expand?

	Grow	Shrink
Positive performance spread	Value creation	Value opportunity forgone
Negative performance spread	Value destruction	Value creation

It has already been demonstrated that overall Black plc produces a more than satisfactory return on investment. Now assume that the firm consists of two divisions: a clothing factory and a toy import business. Each business is making use of £500,000 of assets (at market value). The clothing division is expected to produce an 11 per cent return per annum over the next ten years whereas the toy division will produce a 23 per cent per annum return over the same period. After the ten-year planning horizon both divisions will produce returns equal to their risk-adjusted required return: for the clothing division this is 13 per cent and for the more risky toy division this is 15 per cent.

The cash flows are:

Year	1→10	11→infinity
Clothing	£55,000	£65,000
Toys	£115,000	£75,000

The annual value creation within the planning horizon is:

$$I \times (r - k)$$

Clothing   £500,000 × (0.11 − 0.13) = −£10,000

Toys   £500,000 × (0.23 − 0.15) = +£40,000

Despite the higher return required in the toy division, it creates value. For the next ten years a 15 per cent return is achieved plus a shareholder bonus of £40,000. This division could fit into the top left box of Exhibit 9.10. The management team may want to consider further investment in this unit so long as the marginal investment can generate a return greater than 15 per cent. To pass up positive return spread investments would be to sacrifice valuable opportunities and enter the top right box of Exhibit 9.10.

The clothing operation does not produce returns sufficient to justify its present level of investment. Growth in this unit would only be recommended if such a strategy would enable the division to somehow transform itself so as to achieve a positive spread. If this seems unlikely then the best option is probably a scaling down or withdrawal from the market. This will release resources to be more productively employed elsewhere, either within or outside the firm. Such shrinkage would create value by reducing the drag this activity has on the rest of the firm.

This line of thought can assist managers at all levels to allocate resources. At the corporate level knowledge of potential good-growth and bad-growth investments will help the selection of a portfolio of businesses. At the business unit level, product and customer groups can be analysed to assess the potential for value contribution. Lower down, particular products and customers can be ranked in terms of value. A simplified example of corporate level value analysis is shown in **Exhibit 9.11**.

In Exhibit 9.11, strategic business unit A (SBU_A) is a value destroyer due to its negative return spread. Perhaps there is over-investment here and shareholders would be better served if resources were transferred to other operations. SBU_B produces a small positive spread. However, it is only just managing this, and, in the uncertain world of business it may falter, so a managerial watchful eye will be trained on it to ensure that it continues to produce positive performance spreads. SBU_C produces a lower return spread than SBU_E, but manages to create more value because of its higher future investment levels. Some businesses have greater potential than others for growth while maintaining a positive spread. For example, SBU_E might be a niche market player in fine china where greatly expanded activity would reduce the premium paid by customers for the exclusivity of the product – quickly producing negative spread on

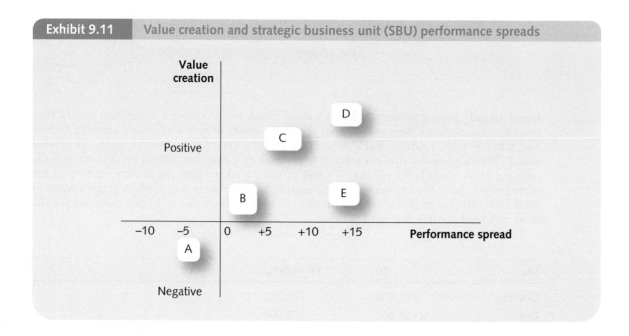

Exhibit 9.11   Value creation and strategic business unit (SBU) performance spreads

the marginal production. Strategic business unit C might be in mid-priced tableware competing on design where investment in the design and marketing teams might produce positive spread growth. Strategic business unit D is capable of high spreads over a long period producing the largest overall gain in value. Drugs with lengthy patent rights often produce high positive spreads for many years leading to high value creation over their lifetimes.

There are five actions available to managers to increase value. These are shown in the value action pentagon (**Exhibit 9.12**).

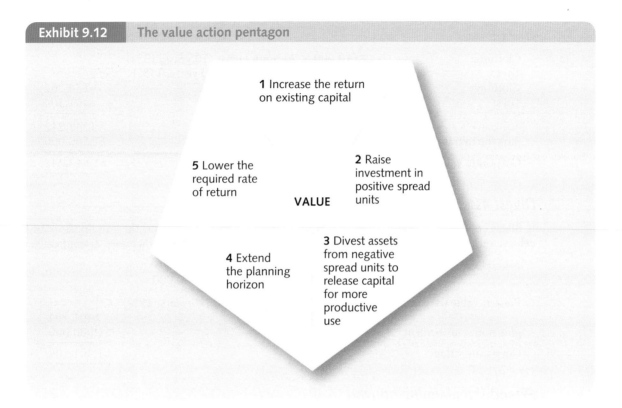

Exhibit 9.12   The value action pentagon

1 Increase the return on existing capital

5 Lower the required rate of return

VALUE

2 Raise investment in positive spread units

4 Extend the planning horizon

3 Divest assets from negative spread units to release capital for more productive use

The five actions in the value action pentagon could be applied to Black plc.

Increase the return on existing capital

The value of Black of £1,000,000 + £156,481 could be increased if the management implemented a plan to improve the efficiency of their existing operations. If the rate of return on investment for the firm as a whole over the next ten years is raised to 18 per cent then the firm's value rises to £1,208,644, viz:

Annual value creation	$= I \times (r - k)$
	$= £1,000,000 \times (0.18 - 0.14)$
	$= £40,000$
Present value over ten years	$= £40,000 \times$ annuity factor (10 years, 14%)
	$= £40,000 \times 5.2161 =$ £208,644
plus initial investment	£1,000,000
Corporate value	£1,208,644

An increase of £52,163 (£1,208,644 – £1,156,481) in value is available for every 1 per cent improvement in return spread.

Raise investment in positive spread units

If Black could obtain a further £500,000 from investors with a required rate of return of 15 per cent to invest in the toy division to produce a 23 per cent return the value of the firm would rise to £1,847,242 (of this £500,000 is the new capital invested).

Annual value creation on clothing	=	–£10,000
Annual value creation on toys = £40,000 × 2	=	£80,000
		£70,000

Over ten years

Clothing:	–£10,000 × Annuity factor (10 years, 13%)		
Toys:	£80,000 × Annuity factor (10 years, 15%)		
Clothing:	–£10,000 × 5.4262	=	–£54,262
Toys:	£80,000 × 5.0188	=	£401,504
			£347,242
plus the initial investment			£1,500,000
Corporate value			£1,847,242

Divest assets

If Black could close its clothing division, release £500,000 to expand the toy division and achieve returns of 23 per cent on the transferred investment then value increases dramatically:

Annual value creation	$= I \times (r - k)$	
	= £1,000,000 × (0.23–0.15) = £80,000	
Present value over ten years	= £80,000 × Annuity factor (10 years, 15%)	
	= £80,000 × 5.0188	£401,504
plus initial investment		£1,000,000
Corporate value		£1,401,504

Extend the planning horizon

Sometimes there are steps that can be taken to exploit a competitive advantage over a longer period than originally expected. For example, perhaps the toy division could negotiate a long-term exclusive import licence with the supplier of an established premium-priced product, thus closing the door on the entry of competitors. If we suppose that the toy division will now produce a return spread of 23 per cent for a 15-year period rather than ten years the value of the company rises to £1,179,634, viz:

Annual value creation on clothing	= –£10,000		
Annual value creation on toys	= –£40,000		
Present value over 10 years (clothing)	= –£10,000 × Annuity factor (10 years, 13%)		
	= –£10,000 × 5.4262 = –£54,262		
Present value over 15 years (toys)	= £40,000 × Annuity factor (15 years, 15%)		
	= £40,000 × 5.8474 = £233,896		
Total value creation	= £233,896 – £54,262	=	£179,634
plus initial investment		=	£1,000,000
Corporate value			£1,179,634

Lower the required rate of return

It may be possible to lower the required rate of return (the WACC) by adjusting the proportion of debt to equity in the capital structure or by reducing business risk.[5] Suppose that Black can lower its required rate of return by shifting to a higher proportion of debt, so that the overall rate falls to 12 per cent. Then the value of the firm rises to £1,282,510.

Annual value creation

$$= I \times (r - k)$$
$$= 1,000,000 \times (0.17 - 0.12)$$
$$= £50,000$$

Present value over ten years $= £50,000 \times$ Annuity factor (10 years, 12%)

Total value creation	$= £50,000 \times 5.6502$	$=$	£282,510
plus initial investment			£1,000,000
Corporate value			£1,282,510

(Many companies tend to borrow little. They finance their businesses almost entirely through equity money. The motivation is often to reduce the risk of financial distress. This may be due to a desire to serve the interests of shareholders, but more often it is because managers want to avoid financial distress for their own safety. They can become too cautious and forgo the opportunity of reducing the overall cost of capital (discount rate) by not using a higher proportion of cheaper debt finance.)

Using value principles in strategic business unit management

A strategic business unit (SBU) is a business unit within the overall corporate entity which is distinguishable from other business units because it serves a defined external market in which management can conduct strategic planning in relation to products and markets.

Large corporations often have a number of SBUs which each require strategic thought and planning. Strategy means selecting which product or market areas to enter/exit and how to ensure a good competitive position in those markets/products. Establishing a good competitive position requires a consideration of issues such as price, service level, quality, product features, methods of distribution, etc., but these issues are secondary to deciding which products to produce and which markets to enter or exit.

It is the managers of an SBU that are the individuals who come into regular contact with customers in the competitive market environment and it is important that SBU strategy be developed largely by those managers who will be responsible for its execution. By doing this, by harnessing these managers' knowledge and encouraging their commitment through a sense of 'ownership' of a strategy, the firm is more likely to prosper.

Before the creation of new strategic options it is advisable to carry out a review of the value creation of the present strategy. This can be a complex task, but an example will demonstrate one approach. Imagine that the plastic products division of Red plc is a defined strategic business unit with a separable strategic planning ability servicing markets distinct from Red's other SBUs. This division sells three categories of product, A, B and C, to five types of customer, (a) UK consumers, (b) UK industrial users, (c) UK government, (d) European Union consumers and (e) other overseas consumers. Information has been provided showing the value expected to be created from each of the product/market categories based on current strategy. These are shown in Exhibits 9.13 and 9.14.

---

[5] Business risk can be reduced by, for example, reducing operating gearing (that is, reducing the proportion of costs that are fixed, thus lowering the break-even point – see Chapter 11); or by encouraging customers (e.g. through advertising) to regard your products as essential rather than discretionary; or by matching assets and liabilities better, in terms of maturity and currency.

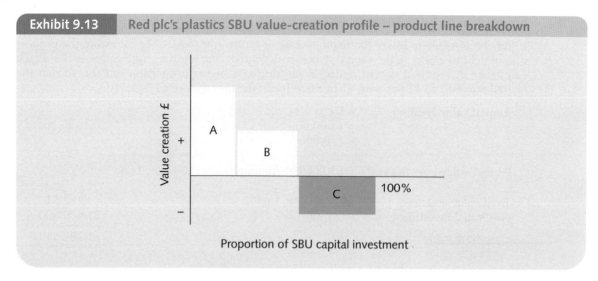

Exhibit 9.13   Red plc's plastics SBU value-creation profile – product line breakdown

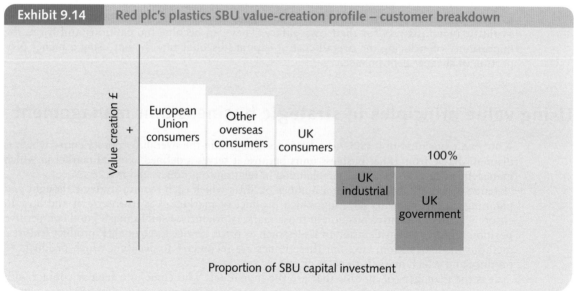

Exhibit 9.14   Red plc's plastics SBU value-creation profile – customer breakdown

Product line C is expected to destroy shareholder value while absorbing a substantial share of the SBU's resources. Likewise this analysis has identified sales to UK industry and government as detrimental to the firm's wealth. This sort of finding is not unusual: many businesses have acceptable returns at the aggregate level but hidden behind these figures are value-destructive areas of activity. The analysis could be made even more revealing by showing the returns available for each product and market category; for example, product A in the UK consumer market can be compared with product A in the European market.

Warren Buffett, the financier, has made some pithy comments on the tendency for firms to fail to identify and root out value-destructive activities:

> Many corporations that consistently show good returns both on equity and on overall incremental capital have, indeed, employed a large portion of their retained earnings on an economically unattractive, even disastrous, basis. Their marvellous core businesses, however, whose earnings grow year after year, camouflage repeated failures in capital allocation elsewhere (usually involving high-priced acquisitions of businesses that have inherently mediocre economics). The managers at fault periodically report on the lessons they have learned from the latest disappointment. They then usually seek out future lessons. (Failure seems to go to their heads.)

Source: Berkshire Hathaway 1984 Annual Report.© Warren Buffett. Reproduced with the permission of the author.

To get a clear line of sight from the customer to the shareholder many businesses need to build an entirely new fact base showing the full economic cost and cash flows associated with customers and product markets. Recognising that some activities are far more valuable than others prepares the ground for a shift of strategic resources. Attention can be directed at restructuring or eliminating value-destructive operations, while building up value-creative aspects of the business.

The impact of value principles on corporate strategy

So far the firm has been described as consisting of a group of strategic business units. So where does the head office fit into this picture if each of these units has a separately identifiable market and is capable of independent strategic action?

We know that companies need to apply value-based principles to all their activities and so this must include the centre. Everything the head office does must create value for shareholders. This means there must be awareness of the quantity of assets used in each task and the return generated by those assets in that task. Many companies fail to think this through; head office costs spiral as new activities are taken to the centre to add to those traditionally carried out, without thought as to whether these tasks are (a) necessary, or (b) if necessary, most efficiently executed by the centre.

In a value-based company the role of the corporate centre (head office) has four main aspects:

1 *Portfolio planning* – allocating resources to those SBUs and product and/or customer areas offering the greatest value creation while withdrawing capital from those destroying value. **Exhibit 9.15** discusses this kind of action at Shell.

2 *Managing strategic value drivers shared by two or more SBUs* – these crucial extraordinary resources, giving the firm competitive advantage, may need to be centrally managed or at least coordinated by the centre to achieve the maximum benefit. An example here could be strong brand management or technological knowledge. The head office needs to ensure adequate funding of these and to achieve full, but not over-exploitation.

3 *Provide the pervading philosophy and governing objective* – training, goal setting, employee rewards and the engendering of commitment are all focused on shareholder value. A strong lead from the centre is needed to avoid conflict, drift and vagueness.

4 *The overall structure of the organisation* needs to be appropriate for the market environment and designed to build value. Roles and responsibilities are clearly defined with clear accountability for value creation.

Exhibit 9.15

Shell all but withdraws from Angola

By Carola Hoyos

Royal Dutch/Shell, Europe's second-largest listed energy group, has all but bowed out of one of the world's biggest new oil regions, selling its stake in a key field in the waters off Angola for $600m (£327m).

The company said: 'We don't have critical mass in Angola. The funds will be reinvested in other parts of the business where we believe higher returns for our shareholders can be achieved.'

Source: Financial Times, 10 April 2004, p. M5. Reprinted with permission.

| Case study 9.1 | Strategy, planning and budgeting at Lloyds TSB |

Although business units are responsible for their own strategy development, the Lloyds TSB group provides guidelines on how strategy should be developed . . . These unit plans are then consolidated into an aggregate plan for the value centre. The process undertaken is then subjected to scrutiny by the centre. The strategic planning process consists of five stages:

1 *Position assessment*. Business units are required to perform a value-based assessment of the economics of the market in which the business operates and of the relative competitive position of the business within that market. Market attractiveness and competitive position must include a numerical rather than a purely qualitative assessment.

2 *Generate alternative strategies*. Business units are required to develop a number of realistic and viable alternatives.

3 *Evaluate alternative strategies*. Business units are required to perform shareholder value calculations in order to prioritise alternatives. Even if a potential strategy has a high positive net present value, this does not necessarily mean that it will be accepted. An assessment of project risk or do-ability is overlaid across the net present value calculations.

4 *Agree chosen strategy with the centre*. While it is perceived to be vital that the managers who best understand their business are given sufficient authority to develop strategies which they consider to be most appropriate, it is nevertheless considered equally important that there is a challenge mechanism at the centre to ensure that appropriate analyses have been performed and assumptions made are credible.

5 *The chosen strategy becomes a contract*. Once the preferred strategy has been agreed with the centre, resource allocation and milestones are agreed. Budgetary performance targets are derived from the projections included within the strategic plan. Beyond this, however, business unit managers are free to choose whatever structures and performance indicators are considered to be relevant and appropriate.

Source: M. Davies (2000), 'Lessons from practice: VBM at Lloyds TSB', in G. Arnold and M. Davies (eds), *Value-Based Management*, Chichester: Wiley.

Value-creation metrics

The remainder of this chapter describes some of the popular techniques used to measure whether value is created. We have space to look at only the most well known:

● Cash flow.
● Shareholder value analysis.
● Economic profit.
● Economic value added (trade marked by consultants Stern Stewart).
● Total shareholder return.
● Market value added.

Managers at all levels need to establish plans for future actions. In drawing up these plans they need reliable measures of value to choose between alternative paths. Then, as strategic moves at both the corporate level and the business unit level unfold, managers need to monitor progress to see if they are still on track to create value. Targets can be set, and, as milestones are passed, incentive schemes can bestow a share of the value created on those responsible. The aim is to make sure every member of staff understands what value is, and each person becomes fully committed to creating it.

At each level of responsibility there should be knowledge of how much of the finance provider's cash has been used in an SBU, product line or project and the required rate of return on that capital. Everyone should know that extra rewards flow to those who help achieve returns above the required rate of return. The metrics we now discuss quantify the plan, targets and incentives to encourage high performance from the boardroom to the shopfloor. They can be used to judge the entire firm or just a small part of it.

Using cash flow to measure value

There are many measures of value promoted by different consultants. There is hot debate between rival consultants as to which is the best for guiding managers seeking to create value. However, they all agree that the measure that lies at the theoretical heart of all the others is discounted cash flow.

In Chapter 2 the value of an investment is described as the sum of the discounted cash flows (NPV). This principle was applied to the assessment of a new project: if the investment produced a rate of return greater than the finance provider's opportunity cost of capital it is wealth enhancing. The same logic can be applied to a range of different categories of business decisions, including: resource allocation; business unit strategies; corporate-level strategy. Consider the figures for Gold plc in **Exhibit 9.16**. These could refer to the entire company. Alternatively the figures could be for business unit returns predicated on the assumption of a particular strategy being pursued. Or they could be for a product line.

Exhibit 9.16	Gold plc forecast cash flows

Required rate of return = 12% per annum

Year	1	2	3	4	5	6	7	8 and subsequent years
	£	£	£	£	£	£	£	£
Forecast profits	1,000	1,100	1,100	1,200	1,300	1,450	1,600	1,600
Add book depreciation and other non-cash items (e.g. amortisation of goodwill)	500	600	800	800	800	800	800	800
Less fixed capital investment	−500	−3,000	−600	−600	−300	−600	−800	−800
Less additional investment in working capital*								
Inventory	50	−100	−70	−80	−50	−50	−50	0
Debtors	−20	−20	−20	−20	−20	−20	−20	0
Creditors	10	20	10	10	20	20	30	0
Cash	−10	−10	−10	−10	−10	−10	−10	0
Add interest previously charged to profit and loss account	100	150	200	200	200	200	200	200
Taxes	−300	−310	−310	−420	−450	−470	−550	−550
Cash flow	830	−1,570	1,100	1,080	1,490	1,320	1,200	1,250
Discounted cash flow	$\dfrac{830}{1.12}$	$-\dfrac{1,570}{(1.12)^2}$	$+\dfrac{1,100}{(1.12)^3}$	$+\dfrac{1,080}{(1.12)^4}$	$+\dfrac{1,490}{(1.12)^5}$	$+\dfrac{1,320}{(1.12)^6}$	$+\dfrac{1,200}{(1.12)^7}$	$+\dfrac{1,250}{0.12} \times \dfrac{1}{(1.12)^7}$
	741	−1,252	783	686	845	669	543	4,712

Note: *A positive figure for inventory, debtors and cash floats indicates cash released from these forms of investment. A negative figure indicates additional cash devoted to these areas. For creditors a positive figure indicates higher credit granted by suppliers and therefore a boost to cash flows.

We start with forecasted profit figures and then make a number of adjustments to arrive at cash flow figures. This method is valuable because it reflects the corporate reality that forward estimates for business units are usually in the form of accounting budgets rather than cash flows, and managers need to know how to work from these numbers toward cash flow rather than starting from scratch to obtain reliable cash flow projections.

Profit figures are created after a number of deductions, such as depreciation, that do not affect the company's cash flow for the year. To move toward cash flow we therefore add depreciation and other non-cash items that were deducted in calculating the future profit figures. Instead of depreciation we take away the amount that actually flows out each year for investment in fixed capital equipment such as factories, machinery and vehicles (fixed capital investment).

In drawing up the profit figures the accountant does not recognise the using up of shareholder's cash when inventory (e.g. raw materials stock) or debtors (granting credit to customers) are increased. The accountant observes one asset (cash in hand) being replaced by another (inventory, money owed by customers) and so there is no expense to deduct. However, the cash flow analyst sees cash being used for these items as the business grows and so makes an adjustment to the profit figures when deriving the cash flow numbers. If shareholders had to supply extra cash floats in a period this is deducted from the profit numbers when trying to get at cash flow. Increases in the creditors mean that the full amount of the expense recorded in the profit and loss account may not yet have flowed out in cash. We need to recognise that the profit and loss account has overstated the outflow of cash. We need then to add back the extent to which the creditor amount outstanding has increased from the beginning of the year to the end to arrive at the cash flow figure. We also add back the interest charged to profit because the 12 per cent discount rate already includes an allowance for the required return to lenders.

The cash flow figures at the bottom of the columns are sometimes referred to as 'free cash flow'. That is, they represent the amount that is free to be paid out to the firm's investors (shareholders and debt holders). These amounts could be paid out without affecting future operating cash flows because the necessary investment for future growth in the form of fixed capital items and working capital (inventory, debtors, cash floats less trade credit) is already allowed for.

The total of the discounted cash flows provides us with a value of the SBU (or firm, etc.) after taking into account all the cash inflows/outflows and reducing those distant cash flows by the required rate of return – the WACC.

By examining the discounted cash flow the SBU management and the firm's managing director can assess the value contribution of the SBU. The management team putting forward these projected cash flows could then be judged and rewarded on the basis of performance targets expressed in cash flow terms. On the other hand, the cash flows may refer to a particular product line or specific customer(s). At each of these levels of management a contribution to overall corporate value is expected.

The planning horizon is seven years and so the present value of the future cash flows is:

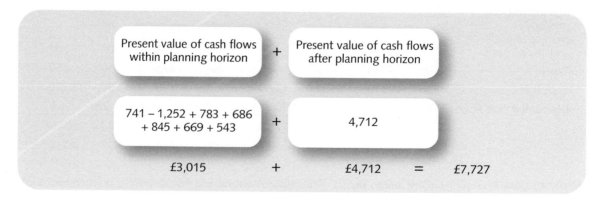

Present value of cash flows within planning horizon	+	Present value of cash flows after planning horizon
741 – 1,252 + 783 + 686 + 845 + 669 + 543	+	4,712
£3,015	+	£4,712 = £7,727

In analysis of this kind it is not unusual to find that most of the value arises after the planning horizon. However, bear in mind that it is the actions (strategic positioning, etc.) and the investments made within the planning horizon that creates the platform for these high post-planning-horizon free cash flows.

Note that in the case of Gold we have not shown a large initial cash outflow, unlike with the NPV calculations described in the first part of the book. This is to illustrate how you can use discounted cash flow analysis to analyse the present value of the future cash flows (not net present value) of an SBU, etc. that was established years before, and you do not have the start-up costs to consider – this type of analysis only considers the future cash inflows and outflows, not the bygone (sunk?) costs.

The value shown in the calculation based on one particular strategic direction (say, the result from Exhibit 9.16) can be compared with alternatives to see which is likely to provide the highest value. You could also conduct sensitivity and scenario analysis to highlight areas of concern in order that managerial attention may be directed to reduce the probability of a poor outcome.

Corporate value

If the SBU that we are valuing has other assets that are not used in the creation of operational free cash flow and those assets have a market value then we add this to the total of the discounted operational cash flow to arrive at the total firm value. For example, many firms hold portfolios of shares or bonds as investments with no connection to the firm's operations. The market value of these adds to the value of the firm derived from the operational free cash flow. Likewise, if a company owns an empty and unused factory which could be sold its value can be added to the total.

| Corporate value (Enterprise value) | = | Present value of free cash flow from operations | + | Value of non-operating assets |

Shareholder value from operations and total shareholder value

If the value of debt is deducted from the total present value from operations we derive the value belonging to shareholders from operations. So, if we assume that this SBU has £3,000 of debt the shareholder value before taking account of non-operating assets is £4,727.

| Shareholder value from operations | = | Present value of free cash flow from operations | – | Debt |

| £4,727 | = | £7,727 | – | £3,000 |

If we now assume that this SBU has £800 of government bonds held as investments separate from operations and £600 of equity investment, total shareholder value amounts to £6,127:

| Total shareholder value | = | Shareholder value from operations | + | Value of non-operating assets |

| £6,127 | = | £4,727 | + | £1,400 |

The figure of £4,727 is the shareholder value of all the future operating cash flows. An alternative course of action is to sell off the SBU's assets, either piecemeal or as a whole. We should compare these alternatives with the present value of continuing to own and run the business. The opportunity cost of following the strategy is the value of the best forgone alternative.

Real management is not about precise numbers – it's about what lies behind the numbers

By embarking on cash-flow-based analysis (or shareholder value analysis or economic profit or economic value added) the decision maker is forced to investigate and understand the underlying business. Only by thorough examination is he/she going to put reasonably realistic numbers into the future projection table. This means a knowledge of the competitive environment and the extraordinary resources that the firm possesses to produce high returns in its chosen industry(ies). In other words, the decision maker needs to investigate the key 'value drivers' in the company and the industry.

However, there is a trap here for the unwary and ill-informed. A manager lacking the intellectual tools, theoretical frameworks and facts to carry out high-quality strategic analysis will produce simplistic and misleading input numbers to the cash flow forecasts: GIGO – garbage in/garbage out.

Value-based management is not a mechanical discipline. It is not about inputting a few numbers to a computer program and then waiting until *the* answer pops out. It is a process requiring judgement every step of the way; it requires careful reflection on the results and their sensitivity to the input numbers. Deep thought is required to appreciate the impact of making slightly (or greatly) different judgements on the input variables; and in assessing the probabilities of variations occurring. Value-based management is a decision-making-in-a-haze-of-uncertainty discipline. How can it be otherwise if it is to be useful in the real world of unpredictability and vagueness? But it gives us a framework and the tools for navigating the best-judged route given these circumstances.

A premium is put on people who can exercise good judgement despite the imprecision – they are not paralysed by uncertainty. These people search for more data to try to see through the haze of the future. More data leads to thought and action designed to reduce the range of probable outcomes.

Investment after the planning horizon

After the planning horizon annual cash flows may well differ from the figure of £1,250 due to additional investment in fixed and working capital items but this will make no difference to present value as any new investment made (when discounted) will be the same as the discounted value of the future cash inflows from that investment. In other words, the company is able to earn merely the required rate of return from Year 8 onwards so no new investment can create value. For example, suppose that Gold raised additional funds of £1,000 and at time 9 (nine years from the present time) invested this in a project generating a perpetual annual net cash inflow of £120 starting at time 10. When these figures are discounted to time 0 the NPV is zero:

Present value of cash outflow $\dfrac{-£1,000}{(1.12)^9} = -360.61$

Present value of cash inflows $\dfrac{£120/0.12}{(1.12)^9} = +360.61$

Thus incremental investment beyond the planning horizon generates no incremental value and so can be ignored for value calculations.

Shareholder value analysis

Alfred Rappaport (1998) has taken the basic concept of cash flow discounting and developed a simplified method of analysis. In the example of Gold plc (see Exhibit 9.16) the component elements of the cash flow did not change in a regular pattern. For example, fixed capital investment was ten times as great in Year 2 as in Year 5. Rappaport's shareholder value analysis assumes relatively smooth change in the various cash flow elements from one year to the next as they are all taken to be related to the sales level.

Rappaport's seven key factors that determine value are:

1 Sales growth rate
2 Operating profit margin
3 Tax rate
4 Fixed capital investment
5 Working capital investment
6 The planning horizon (forecast period)
7 The required rate of return

Rappaport calls the seven key factors value drivers, and this can be confusing given that other writers describe a value driver as a factor that enables some degree of competitive advantage. To distinguish the two types of value driver the quantitative seven listed will be referred to as Rappaport's value drivers. To estimate future cash flows Rappaport assumes a constant percentage rate of growth in sales. The operating profit margin is a constant percentage of sales. Profit here is defined as profit before deduction of interest and tax, PBIT. The tax rate is a constant percentage of the operating profit. Fixed capital and working capital investment are related to the *increase* in sales.

So, if sales for the most recent year amount to £1,000,000 and are expected to continue to rise by 12 per cent per year, the operating profit margin on sales[6] is 9 per cent, taxes are 31 per cent of operating profit, the incremental investment in fixed capital items is 14 per cent of the *change* in sales, and the incremental working capital investment is 10 per cent of the *change* in sales, the cash flow for the next year will be as set out in Exhibit 9.17.

Exhibit 9.17	Silver plc: Sales, operating profit and cash outflows for next year	
Sales in year 1		
= Sales in prior year × (1 + Sales growth rate)	= 1,000,000 × 1.12	1,120,000
Operating profit		
= Sales × Operating profit margin	= 1,120,000 × 0.09	100,800
Taxes		
= Operating profit × 31%	= 100,800 × 0.31	–31,248
Incremental investment in fixed capital		
= Increase in sales × Incremental fixed capital investment rate	= 120,000 × 0.14	–16,800
Incremental investment in working capital		
= Increase in sales × Working capital investment rate	= 120,000 × 0.10	–12,000
Operating free cash flow		£40,752

---

[6] Operating profit margin on sales is sales revenue less cost of sales and all selling and administrative expenses before deduction of tax and interest.

Rappaport's corporate value has three elements, due to his separation of the discounted cash flow value of marketable securities from the cash flows from operations (*see* **Exhibit 9.18**). The value of the marketable securities is expressed as their current market price.

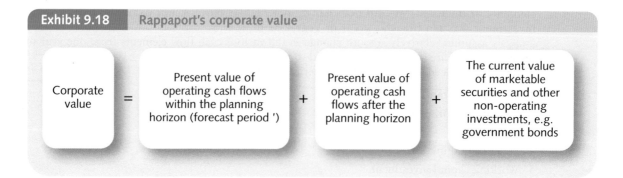

Exhibit 9.18   Rappaport's corporate value

A closer look at depreciation and investment in fixed capital

Investment in plant, machinery, vehicles, buildings, etc. consists of two parts:

- Type 1. Annual investment to replace worn-out equipment and so on, leaving the overall level of assets constant.
- Type 2. Investment that adds to the stock of assets, presumably with the intention of permitting growth in productive capacity. This is called incremental fixed-capital investment.

A simplifying assumption often employed in shareholder value analysis is that the 'depreciation' figure in the profit and loss account is equal to the type 1 investment. This avoids the necessity of first adding back depreciation to operating profit figures and then deducting type 1 capital investment. It is only necessary to account for that extra cash outflow associated with incremental fixed-capital investment. Thus, **free cash flow** is the operating cash flow after incremental fixed and working capital investment.

Illustration

We can calculate the shareholder value of Silver plc by using Rappaport's seven value drivers if we assume a planning horizon of eight years and a required rate of return of 15 per cent (*see* **Exhibit 9.19**).

The company also has £60,000 of investments in foreign and domestic shares and £50,000 in long-term fixed interest rate securities. These are assets not required to produce operating profit and can be sold off with the proceeds given to their owners, i.e. the shareholders. Corporate value is as set out in **Exhibit 9.20**.

The required rate of return used in shareholder value analysis is the weighted average required return on debt and equity capital (the WACC), allowing for a return demanded by the debt holders and shareholders in proportion to their provision of finance. This explains why cash flows before deduction of interest are discounted rather than just those attributable to shareholders: some of those cash flows will go to debt holders. The discounted cash flows derived in this way are then summed to give corporate value (sometimes called enterprise value). When debt, in this case £200,000, is deducted, shareholder value is obtained.

Shareholder value = Corporate value – Debt

Shareholder value = £705,000 – £200,000 = £505,000

Again, this kind of analysis can be used at a number of different levels: whole business; division/SBU; operating unit; project; product line or customer.

Exhibit 9.19	An example of shareholder value analysis – Silver plc

1 Sales growth   12% per year
2 Operating profit margin   9% of sales
3 Taxes   31% of operating profit
4 Incremental fixed capital investment   14% of the change in sales
5 Incremental working capital investment   10% of the change in sales
6 The planning horizon (forecast period)   8 years
7 The required rate of return   15% per year

Year	0	1	2	3	4	5	6	7	8	9 and subsequent years
£000s Sales	1,000	1,120	1,254	1,405	1,574	1,762	1,974	2,210	2,476	2,476
Operating profits		101	113	126	142	159	178	199	223	223
Less taxes		–31	–35	–39	–44	–49	–55	–62	–69	–69
Less incremental investment in fixed capital		–17	–19	–21	–24	–26	–30	–33	–37	0
Less incremental working capital investment		–12	–13	–15	–17	–19	–21	–24	–27	0
Operating free cash flow		41	46	51	57	65	72	80	90	154

Note: All figures are rounded to whole numbers. There is no additional investment in fixed assets and working capital after year 8 shown. This indicates that the perpetual cash flow of £154,000 can be produced without expanding the physical capacity of the firm (no new factories, etc.). However, investment in the form of replacement of existing facilities subject to wear and tear is taking place, equal to the depreciation amount deducted before the figure for operating profits is input to the analysis. Investment above and beyond this replacement investment may take place, but it has no impact on the value calculation because investment after the planning horizon generates a return equal to the required rate of return, i.e. there is no performance spread for these assets, and so such investment is ignored for the calculation of firm value.

AN EXCEL SPREADSHEET SHOWING THE CALCULATIONS FROM EXHIBITS 9.19 AND 9.20 IS AVAILABLE AT www.pearsoned.co.uk/arnold

Problems with shareholder value analysis

There are some disadvantages to the use of shareholder value analysis:

● Constant percentage increases in value drivers lack realism in some circumstances; in others it is a reasonable simplification.

● It can be misused in target setting, for example if managers are given a specific cash flow objective for a 12-month period they may be dissuaded from necessary value-enhancing investment (i.e. using cash) in order to achieve the short-term cash flow target. Alleviate this problem by setting both short- and long-term targets. The short-term ones may show negative cash flows.

● Data availability – many firms' accounting systems are not equipped to provide the necessary input data. The installation of a new cash flow-oriented system may be costly.

Exhibit 9.20	Corporate value, Silver plc.

Present value of operating cash flows within the planning horizon (forecast period)

$$\frac{41}{1.15} + \frac{46}{(1.15)^2} + \frac{51}{(1.15)^3} + \frac{57}{(1.15)^4}$$

$$+ \frac{65}{(1.15)^5} + \frac{72}{(1.15)^6} + \frac{80}{(1.15)^7} + \frac{90}{(1.15)^8} = 259$$

+

Present value of operating cash flows after the planning horizon

$$\frac{154}{0.15} = 1,027 \text{ then discount result by 8 years } \frac{1,027}{(1.15)^8} = 336$$

+

The current value of marketable securities and other non-operating investments

$$60 + 50 = 110$$

Corporate value

$$= 705$$

or £705,000

Economic profit

Economic profit, EP (also called residual income), has an advantage over shareholder value analysis because it uses the existing accounting and reporting systems of firms by focusing on profit rather than cash flow information. This not only reduces the need to implement an overhaul of the data-collecting and reporting procedures but also provides evaluatory and performance measurement tools which use the familiar concept of profit. Thus, managers used to 'bottom line' figures are more likely to understand and accept this metric than one based on cash flow information.

> Economic profit for a period is the amount earned by a business after deducting all operating expenses and a charge for the opportunity cost of the capital employed.

There are two versions of economic profit.

1 The entity approach to EP

One version of EP is based on profit after tax is deducted but before interest is deducted. There are two ways to calculate this entity EP.

(a) *The profit less capital charge method* Here a charge for the use of capital equal to the invested capital multiplied by the return required by the share and debt holders (the WACC) is deducted from the operating profits after tax:

Economic profit (Entity approach)	=	Operating profit before interest deduction and after tax deduction	−	Capital charge

Economic profit (Entity approach)	=	Operating profit before interest deduction and after tax deduction	−	Invested capital × WACC

(b) The *'performance spread' method* The difference between the return achieved on invested capital and the weighted average cost of capital (WACC), i.e. the required rate of return, is the performance spread. This percentage figure is then multiplied by the quantity of invested capital to obtain EP:

As can be seen from the following illustration both methods lead to the same EP.

Illustration

EoPs plc has a weighted average cost of capital (required rate of return) of 12 per cent and has used £1,000,000 of invested capital (share and debt) to produce an operating profit before interest and after tax of £180,000 during the past year.

Profit less capital charge approach

EP = Operating profits before interest and after tax – (Invested capital × WACC)
   = £180,000 – (£1,000,000 × 0.12)
   = £60,000

Performance spread approach

EP = (Return on captial – WACC) × Invested capital
   = (18% – 12%) × £1,000,000
   = £60,000

2 The equity approach to EP

The entity EP approach described above, based on operating profit before the deduction of interest, calculates the surplus above the return to all the finance providers to the business entity including the debt holders. The alternative is the 'equity approach'. With this, interest is deducted from the profit figure so we obtain the profit that belongs to the shareholders. Also the required return is the return demanded on the equity capital only. So, EP is the profit attributable to shareholders after a deduction for the implicit cost of employing shareholders' capital.

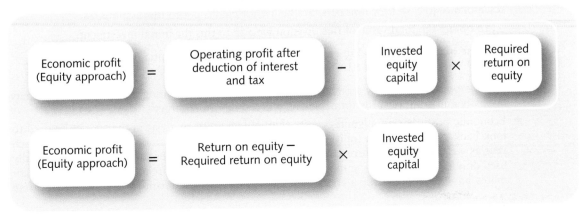

Illustration

In the case of EoPs let us assume that one-half the £1,000,000 of capital is equity and the other half debt. The equity required rate of return is 15 per cent and the debt required rate of return is 9 per cent (i.e. £45,000 per year), therefore the weighted average cost of capital is 12 per cent (that is, $(15\% \times 0.5) + (9\% \times 0.5) = 12\%$).

Profit less capital charge approach

Deducting £45,000 of interest from the operating profit after tax figure we have £135,000.

$$
\begin{aligned}
\text{EP (equity)} &= \text{Operating profits after interest and tax} - (\text{Invested equity capital} \times \text{Required} \\
&\quad \text{return on equity}) \\
&= £135,000 - (£500,000 \times 0.15) \\
&= £60,000
\end{aligned}
$$

Performance spread approach:

$$
\begin{aligned}
\text{EP (equity)} &= (\text{Return on equity} - \text{Required return on equity}) \times \text{Invested equity capital} \\
&= (27\% - 15\%) \times £500,000 \\
&= £60,000
\end{aligned}
$$

The return on equity is 27 per cent (£135,000/£500,000).

Usefulness of economic profit

- A focus on EP rather than the traditional accounting profit has the advantage that every manager down the line is encouraged (rewarded) for paying close attention to the cost associated with using capital in a business unit, project, product line or the entire corporation. The introduction of EP targets has resulted in some dramatic reductions in money tied up wastefully in assets such as raw material stocks, and to significant reductions in requests for major fixed capital expenditure. Managers who are judged on profits may not be as keen to reduce capital employed as those judged on EP.

- Economic profit can be used to evaluate strategic options that produce returns over a number of years. For example, Spoe plc is considering the investment of £2,000,000 in a new division that is expected to produce a consistent operating profit before interest after tax of £300,000 per year to infinity without the need for any further investment in fixed capital or working capital in subsequent years. The company has a required rate of return on capital of 13 per cent. The extra 'value' created on top of the initial investment of £2m is:

$$
\begin{aligned}
\text{Economic profit (entity) per year} &= (\text{Return on capital} - \text{WACC}) \times \text{Invested capital} \\
&= (15\% - 13\%) \times £2,000,000 \\
&= £40,000
\end{aligned}
$$

The present value of this perpetuity is: £40,000/0.13 = £307,692

This £307,692 is the additional value, in present terms, of economic profit. Of course, we can only call this value if we make the bold assumption that profit numbers bear a close resemblance to cash flow numbers. See below for challenges to this assumption.

To obtain the total value of this division we add to this the initial investment:

$$
\begin{aligned}
\text{Value of new division} &= \text{Present value of economic profit} + \text{Initial investment} \\
&= £307,692 + £2,000,000 = £2,307,692
\end{aligned}
$$

Having expressed the new strategy in terms of EP, in implementing it we can set EP targets annually and grant rewards for achieving (exceeding) those targets.

- Economic profit has an advantage over shareholder value analysis in that it can be used to look back at how the firm (unit) has performed relative to the amount of capital used each year as well as creating future targets in terms of EP. Shareholder value analysis is generally used only in forward-looking mode. (Nevertheless, once the shareholder value analysis estimates have been made for a strategy it is possible to set interim targets, which, as time passes, are examined for deviation. So, in this sense it can be used in backward-looking mode, i.e. within a plan.) With EP it is possible to go to a firm and examine past performance from scratch, without the need for established EP targets within a plan.

● Economic profit per unit can be calculated: for example, economic profit per square foot or economic profit per unit of output. Economic profit sends a more powerful signal because it is expressed in absolute amounts of money generated for shareholders above the minimum required, e.g. £1.20 EP per unit sold, rather than a percentage, e.g. a profit margin of 14 per cent. Profit margins fail to allow for the size of the capital commitment.

Difficulties with economic profit

There are, however, some difficulties to be borne in mind when using economic profit.

1 *The balance sheet does not reflect invested capital* Balance sheets are not designed to provide information on the present economic value of assets being used in a business. Assets are generally recorded at original cost less depreciation, amortisation (reduction in intangibles) and depletion (e.g reduction in oil reserves). With or without inflation it does not take many years for these balance sheet values to deviate dramatically from the theoretically correct capital employed figures for most firms. Generally balance sheets significantly understate the amount of capital employed, and this understatement therefore causes EP to appear high. Moreover, many businesses invest in assets that never find their way to a balance sheet. For example, some firms pour vast sums into building up brand images and do so with the belief, often correct, that shareholders' money is being well invested, with the pay-off arising years later. Nevertheless, accounting convention insists on such expenditures being written off against profits rather than being taken into the balance sheet. The same problem applies to other investments such as business reputation and management training. The early theorists in value measurement suggested using current values of assets. Following them I would be tempted, depending on the circumstances, to use either (a) the sum of the resale value of individual assets, or (b) the replacement cost. Much depends on the objective of the analysis:

● If the objective is to monitor past performance in terms of examining the efficiency with which money was invested, the historical amount invested seems somewhat relevant as the 'capital' figure. However, there will be many circumstances where a distinctly unsatisfactory capital figure is derived from a balance sheet, e.g. when assets were acquired decades before the current period.

● If you are monitoring current (this year) performance perhaps the current replacement value or the sum of the resale value of individual assets may be most useful. Sometimes the resale value is very low when the assets are highly specific with little secondary market. In such a case relying on the resale value alone would give an artificially low asset value. In other circumstances the replacement value is clearly way above the level at which any manager would actually replace and so a more informed decision can be made by using the sum of resale values as this figure represents the opportunity cost of using the assets this year.

● If the asset value is needed to make future-oriented decisions about where to apply assets at present owned by the firm then the sum of the resale value of the individual assets would be most useful because this would capture the opportunity cost – the firm could sell off these assets as an alternative. The sunk costs associated with past investment are not relevant in such a decision and so balance sheet values are not very useful.

● If the decision concerns the obtaining of new assets to implement a project/strategy then the cost of obtaining them is relevant.

Note that we use the 'sum of the resale value of individual assets' rather than the current market value of all-the-assets-when-welded-together-as-a-coherent-whole for the corporation/SBU because to use the latter would eliminate any value by definition. For example, if a firm starts up with £1m of capital and a brilliant idea, immediately the strategy is put in place to exploit the idea the resale value of the firm as an operating entity rises to, say, £10m. That is, the resale value of the firm is equal to the initial capital plus the present value of the future cash flows or EPs. The £10m current market value of all-the-assets-when-welded-together-as-a-coherent-whole includes £9m of value, but the value of the sum of the individual assets is in the region of £1m.

2 *Manipulation and arbitrariness* The difficulties caused by relying on accounting data are exacerbated by the freedom available to manipulate such figures as well as the degree of subjectivity involved in arriving at some of the figures in the first place.

3 *High economic profit and negative NPV can go together* There is a danger of over-reliance on EP. For example, imagine a firm has become a convert to economic profit and divisional managers are judged on annual economic profit. Their bonuses and promotion prospects rest on good performance spreads over the next 12 months. This may prompt a manager to accept a project with an impressive EP over the short term whether or not it has a positive NPV over its entire life. Projects that produce poor or negative EPs in the first few years, for example biotechnology investments, will be rejected even if they will enhance shareholder wealth in the long term.

Also, during the life of a project managers may be given specific EP targets for a particular year. They may be tempted to ensure the profit target is met by cutting down on certain expenditures such as training, marketing and maintenance. The target will be achieved but long-term damage may be inflicted.

A third value-destroying use of EP occurs when managers are demotivated by being set EP targets. For example, if managers have no control over the capital employed in their part of the business, they may become resentful of and cynical about value-based management if they are told nevertheless to achieve certain EP targets.

Care must be taken by external observers when examining the EP (or EVA – see next section) to judge performance, particularly in annual league tables. Misleading impressions are frequent over periods as short as one year because some firms that are on a high value-creating path often have years where EP is low (or nil). Then there are firms on a value-destructive path which report high current-year EP. It is only possible to judge performance over a number of years. When EP is used internally, however, it frequently does make sense to produce annual (or even six-monthly) EP figures to compare with a plan to see if the value-creation strategy is on target. Within the plan there will probably be periods of negative EP (e.g. in the start-up phase), as well as periods of high surpluses over the cost of capital.

4 *Difficult to allocate revenues, costs and capital to business units, products, etc.* To carry out EP analysis at the sub-firm level it is necessary to measure profit and capital invested separately for each area of the business. Many costs and capital assets are shared between business units, product lines and customers. It is very difficult in some situations to identify the proportion of the cost, debt or asset that is attributable to each activity. It can also be expensive.

Economic value added (EVA®)

Economic value added, developed and trademarked by the US consultants Stern Stewart and Co., is a variant of EP that attempts to overcome some of the problems outlined above. Great energy has been put into its marketing and it is probably the most widely talked about value metric.

EVA = Adjusted invested capital × (Adjusted return on capital – WACC)

or

EVA = Adjusted operating profits after tax – (Adjusted invested capital × WACC)

The adjustments to profit and capital figures are meant to refine the basic EP.[7] Stern Stewart suggest that up to 164 adjustments to the accounting data may be needed. For example, spending on marketing and R&D helps build value and so if expenditure on these has been deducted in past years it is added back to the balance sheet as an asset (and amortised over the period expected to benefit from the expenditure). Goodwill on acquisitions previously written off is also returned and is expressed as an asset, thus boosting both profits and the balance sheet.

---

[7] Notice that EVA is analogous to the entity EP rather than equity EP because the WACC contains an allowance for a return to all finance providers including debt holders. Therefore, the 'adjusted invested capital' is equity plus debt capital.

There are a number of difficulties with these adjustments – for example, over what period should these reconstituted 'assets' be amortised? After all they are not expected to be valuable forever; they often gradually (or suddenly) fail to maintain their contributions to the firm. Should you add back 'assets' for, say, R&D expenditure that took place five years ago, ten years ago, or over the whole life of the firm?

EVA, like the generic EP, has the virtue of being based on familiar accounting concepts and it is arguably more accurate than taking ordinary accounting figures. However, critics have pointed out that the adjustments can be time consuming and costly, and many are based on decisions that are as subjective as the original accountant's numbers. There also remains the problem of poorly, if enthusiastically, implemented EVA reward systems producing results that satisfy targets for EVA but which produce poor decisions with regard to NPV. Furthermore, the problem of allocating revenue, costs and capital to particular business units and products is not solved through the use of EVA. Also the Stern Stewart definition of capital is 'the sum of all the cash that has been invested in a company's net assets over its life' (Stewart, 1991, p. 86). Imagine the difficulties in establishing this given that most invested 'cash' put in will be in the form of many years of retained earnings, which leads us back to the difficulties of accounting numbers and the dubiousness of making 'adjustments' to the raw numbers. Added to this problem is the issue of accepting this capital figure as relevant for many decisions. For example, in judging future strategic plans perhaps the opportunity cost of those assets (the sum of the individual resale values) would be more relevant than what was paid for them, much of which may have become a sunk cost years ago (see Chapter 3). Likewise if you are monitoring managers' performance this year the historical cost of assets they are using may be totally irrelevant to the analysis of their efficiency, whereas the money that they could have raised through the alternative of selling off the assets rather than operating them might be of enormous interest, as this may be the best alternative use.

Total shareholder return (TSR)

Shareholders are interested in the total return earned on their investment relative to general inflation, a peer group of firms, and the market as a whole. Total return includes dividend returns and share price changes over a specified period. For one-period TSR:

$$\text{TSR} = \frac{\text{Dividend per share} + (\text{Share price at end of period} - \text{Initial share price})}{\text{Initial share price}} \times 100$$

When dealing with multi-period TSRs we need to account for the dividends received in the interim years as well as the final dividend. The TSR can be expressed either as a total return over the period or as an annualised rate.

So, for example, if a share had a beginning price of £1, paid annual dividends at the end of each of the next three years of 9p, 10p and 11p and had a closing price of £1.30, the total average annual return (assuming dividends are reinvested in the company's shares immediately on receipt) is calculated via the internal rate of return:

$$-100 + \frac{9}{1+r} + \frac{10}{(1+r)^2} + \frac{141}{(1+r)^3} = 0$$

At: $r = 19\%$: -1.7037, $r = 18\%$: 0.6259

$$\text{The internal rate of return} = 18 + \frac{0.6259}{0.6259 + 1.7037} = 18.27\%$$

The annualised TSR is 18.27 per cent.

The total shareholder return over the three years = $(1 + 0.1827)^3 - 1 = 65.4\%$

TSRs for a number of periods are available from financial data organisations, such as Datastream and on most financial websites.

Thoughtful use of the TSR

There are three issues to be borne in mind when making use of the TSR:

1 *Relate return to risk class* Two firms may have identical TSRs and yet one may be subject to more risk due to the greater volatility of earnings as a result, say, of the economic cycle. The risk differential must be allowed for in any comparison. This may be particularly relevant in the setting of incentive schemes for executives. Managers may be tempted to try to achieve higher TSRs by taking greater risk.

2 *TSR assumes efficient share pricing* It is difficult to assess the extent to which share return outperformance is due to management quality and how much is due to exaggerated (or pessimistic) expectations of investors at the start and end of the period being measured. If the market is not efficient in pricing shares and is capable of being swayed by irrational optimism and pessimism then TSRs can be an unreliable guide to managerial performance.

3 *TSR is dependent on the time period chosen* A TSR over a three-year period can look very different from a TSR measured over a one-year or ten-year period (relative to other firms).

4 *Useless in the case of companies not quoted on a stock market (over 99% of firms)*

Market value added (MVA)

Stern Stewart and Co. also developed the concept of **market value added (MVA)**. This looks at the difference between the total amount of capital put into the business by finance providers (debt and equity) and the current market value of the company's shares and debt. It provides a measure of how executives have performed with the capital entrusted to them. A positive MVA indicates value has been created. A negative MVA indicates value has been destroyed.

MVA = Market value – Invested capital

where:

Market value   = Current value of debt, preference shares and ordinary shares.
Invested capital = All the cash raised from finance providers or retained from earnings to finance new investment in the business, since the company was founded. In practice, balance asset values (with a few adjustments) are used.

Managers are able to push up the conventional yardstick, total market value of the business, simply by investing more capital. The MVA, by subtracting capital injected or retained from the calculation, measures net value generated for shareholders.

Points to consider when using MVA

There are a number of issues to be borne in mind when using MVA.

- **Estimating the amount of cash invested** Measuring the amount of capital put into and retained within a business after it has been trading for a few years is fraught with problems. Stern Stewart make use of a proxy measure called 'economic book value'. This is based on the balance sheet capital employed figure, subject to a number of adjustments. Critics have pointed out that these adjustments are rather arbitrary and complex, making it difficult to claim that economic book value equals the theoretically correct 'capital' in most cases.

- **When was the value created?** The fact that a positive MVA is produced is often of limited use when it comes to evaluating the quality of the current managers. For a company that is a few decades old the value drivers may have been put in place by a previous generation of directors and senior managers. The MVA measure can be considered crude in that it measures value created over the entire life of the firm but fails to pinpoint when it was created. Nor does it indicate whether value creation has stopped and the firm is living off accumulated fat in terms of strong market positions, patents, etc. Ideally we need to know whether new value-creating positions are being constructed rather than old ones being eroded.

Worked example 9.2	Illustration of the MVA

MerVA plc was founded 20 years ago with £15m of equity finance. It has no debt or preference shares. All earnings have been paid out as dividends. The shares in the company are now valued at £40m. The MVA of MerVA is therefore £25m:

MVA = Market value – Capital
MVA = £40m – £15m = £25m

If the company now has a rights issue raising £5m from shareholders the market value of the firm must rise to at least £45m in order for shareholder wealth to be maintained. If the market value of the shares rose to only £44m because shareholders are doubtful about the returns to be earned when the rights issue money is applied within the business (that is, a negative NPV project) shareholders will lose £1m of value. This is summarised in the table below.

	Before rights issue	After rights issue
Market value	£40m	£44m
Capital	£15m	£20m
MVA	£25m	£24m

- **Is the rate of return high enough?** It is difficult to know whether the amount of MVA generated is sufficiently in excess of capital used to provide a satisfactory return relative to the risk-adjusted time value of money. Positive MVA companies can produce poor rates of return. For example, a company founded 50 years ago with £1m now has a market value of £2m and has produced a positive MVA, but a very poor annual rate of return.

- **Inflation distorts the MVA** If the capital element in the equation is based on a balance sheet figure then during times of inflation the value of capital employed may be understated. If capital is artificially lowered by inflation *vis-à-vis* current market value for companies where investment took place a long time ago then the MVA will appear to be superior to that for a similar firm with recently purchased assets.

- **Trusting that the stock market prices shares correctly at all times** This is a very dubious assumption.

- **The MVA is an absolute measure** Judging companies on the basis of absolute amounts of pounds means that companies with larger capital bases will tend to be at the top (and bottom) of the league tables of MVA performance. Size can have a more significant impact on the MVA than efficiency. This makes comparison between firms of different sizes difficult.

- **Useless in the case of companies not quoted on a stock market**

Concluding comments

The switch from management by accounting numbers to management using financial concepts such as value, the time value of money and opportunity cost is only just beginning. Some highly successful firms are leading the way in insisting that each department, business unit and project add value to shareholders' investment. This has required a re-examination of virtually all aspects of management, ranging from performance measurement systems and strategic planning to motivational schemes and training programmes.

A commercial organisation that adopts value principles is one that has an important additional source of strength. The rigorous thought process involved in the robust application of these principles will force managers to review existing systems and product/market strategies, and to bring an insistence on a contribution to shareholder value from all parts of the company. A firm that has failed to ask the right questions of its operating units or to use the correct metrics in measuring performance will find its position deteriorating *vis-à-vis* its competitors.

Key points and concepts

- **Value-based management** is a managerial approach in which the primacy of purpose is long-run shareholder-wealth maximisation. The objective of the firm, its systems, strategy, processes, analytical techniques, performance measurement and culture have as their guiding objective shareholder-wealth maximisation.

- **Earnings-based management is flawed**. Profit figures are drawn up following numerous subjective allocations and calculations relying on judgement rather than science, they are therefore open to manipulation and distortion; the investment required to produce earnings growth is not made explicit; the time value of money is ignored; the riskiness of earnings is ignored.

- **Bad growth** is when the return on the marginal investment is less than the required rate of return, given the finance providers' opportunity cost of funds. This can occur even when earnings-based figures are favourable.

- **Using accounting rates of return** (ROCE, ROI, ROE, etc.) is an attempt to solve some of the problems associated with earnings or earnings per share metrics, especially with regard to the investment levels used to generate the earnings figures. However, balance sheet figures are often too crude to reflect capital employed. Using ARRs can also lead to short-termism.

- **Value is created** when investment produces a rate of return greater than that required for the risk class of investment.

- **Shareholder value is driven by four key elements**: (i) Amount of capital invested; (ii) Required rate of return; (iii) Actual rate of return on capital; (iv) Planning horizon (for performance spread persistence).

- **Performance spread** = Actual rate of return on capital – required return.

- **Corporate value from operations** = Present value of cash flows within planning horizon + Present value of cash flows after planning horizon.

- **To expand or not to expand?**

	Grow	Shrink
Positive performance spread	Value creation	Value opportunity forgone
Negative performance spread	Value destruction	Value creation

- **The value action pentagon** indicates five ways of increasing value: (i) Increase the return on existing capital; (ii) Raise investment in positive spread units; (iii) Divest assets from negative spread units to release capital for more productive use; (iv) Extend the planning horizon; (v) Lower the required rate of return.

- **A review of current SBU** activities using **value-creation profile charts** may reveal particular product or customer categories that destroy wealth.

Key points and concepts continued

- The **corporate centre** has four main roles in a value-based firm: (i) portfolio planning; (ii) managing strategic value drivers shared by SBUs; (iii) providing and inculcating the pervading philosophy and governing objective; (iv) structuring the organisation so that rules and responsibilities are clearly defined, with clear accountability for value creation.

- **Discounted cash flow** is the bedrock method underlying value management metrics. It requires the calculation of future annual free cash flows attributable to both shareholders and debt holders, then discounting these cash flows at the weighted average cost of capital.

- **Corporate value (Enterprise value)** equals present value of free cash flows from operations plus the value of non-operating assets. **Shareholder value from operations** equals present value of free cash flows from operations minus debt. **Total shareholder value** equals shareholder value of free cash flows from operations plus the value of non-operating assets.

- **Investment after the planning horizon does not increase value.**

- **Shareholder value analysis** simplifies discounted cash flow analysis by employing **(Rappaport's) seven value drivers**, the first five of which change in a consistent fashion from one year to the next.

- **Economic profit (EP)** is the amount earned after deducting all operating expenses and a charge for the opportunity cost of the capital employed. A major advantage over shareholder value analysis is that it uses accounting data.

- **The entity approach to EP**

    (a) The profit less capital charge method

    (b) The 'performance spread' method

Key points and concepts continued

- **The equity approach to EP**

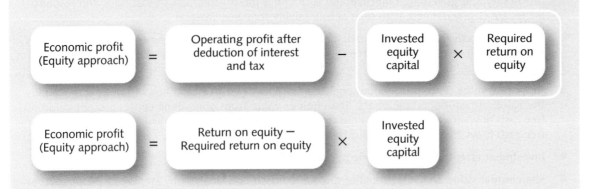

- **Usefulness of economic profit:** (i) Managers become aware of the amount of the investment in an SBU, product line or entire business. (ii) Can be used to evaluate strategic options. (iii) Can be used to look back at past performance. (iv) Economic profit per unit can be calculated.

- **Difficulties in using EP:** (i) The balance sheet does not reflect invested capital; (ii) open to manipulation and arbitrariness; (iii) high economic profit and negative NPV can go together; (iv) problem with allocating revenues, costs and capital to business units.

- **Economic value added (EVA®)** is an attempt to overcome some of the accounting problems of standard EP. EVA = Adjusted invested capital × (Adjusted return on capital – WACC) or EVA = Adjusted operating profit after tax – (Adjusted invested capital × WACC)

- **Total shareholder returns (TSR)**

  Single period: $\text{TSR} = \dfrac{\text{Dividend per share} + (\text{Share price at end of period} - \text{initial share price})}{\text{Initial share price}}$

  Multi-period: Allow for intermediate dividends in an internal rate of return calculation.

- **Market value added (MVA)**

  MVA = Market value – Invested capital

Further reading

A more detailed discussion of Value-based management is in Arnold, G. (2005).

The following are books/chapters written by consultants on VBM: McKinsey & Co. (Koller, Goedhart and Wessels) (2005), McTaggart, J.M., Kontes, P.W. and Mankins, M.C. (1994), Rappaport, A. (1998), Stern, J.M., Stewart, G.B. and Chew, D.H. (2001), 'The EVA® Financial Management System', in Chew, D.H. (ed.), Stewart, G.B. (1991), Young, S.D. and O'Byrne, S.F. (2001).

Arnold, G.C. and Davies, M. (eds) (2000) contains a collection of research monographs, including Davies, M. (2000) 'Lessons from Practice: VBM at Lloyds TSB'.

Arnold, G. (2000) presents a method for analysing the competition strength of a firm.

Website

Stern Stewart www.stern.stewart.com Some useful additional literature.

Self-review questions

1 In what ways are accounting-based performance measures inadequate for guiding managerial decisions?

2 Define value-based management.

3 What are the four key drivers of shareholder value creation?

4 What are the five actions available to increase value?

5 What is 'good growth' and what is 'bad growth'?

6 In what circumstances would you reduce investment in a strategic business unit even if its profits are on a rising trend?

7 Briefly describe the main roles of the corporate centre in a value-led organisation.

8 What is shareholder value analysis and what are the seven value drivers as described by Rappaport?

9 What is economic profit (EP)? Describe the alternative ways of measuring it.

10 Describe the relative merits and problems of shareholder value analysis and EP.

11 What is the total shareholder return (TSR) and what are its advantages and problems as a metric of shareholder wealth creation?

12 Describe the metric market value added (MVA) and note the problems in its practical use.

Quick numerical questions

1 What is the annual value creation of Sheaf plc which has an investment level of £300,000 and produces a rate of return of 19 per cent per annum compared with a required rate of return of 13 per cent? What is the performance spread? Assuming that the planning horizon for Sheaf plc is 12 years, calculate the value of the firm. (Assume the investment level is constant throughout.)

2 Last year Tops plc (a firm financed entirely by equity) produced an accounting operating profit after tax of £5m. Its equity cost of capital is 14 per cent and the firm has £50m of capital. What was the economic profit?

3 a Tear plc has not paid a dividend for 20 years. The current share price is 580p and the current index level is 3,100. Calculate total shareholder returns for the past three years, the past five years and the past ten years, given the following data:

Time before present	Share price (pence)	Share index
1 year	560	3,000
2 years	550	2,400
3 years	600	2,500
4 years	500	2,000
5 years	450	1,850
6 years	400	1,700
7 years	250	1,300
8 years	170	1,500
9 years	130	1,300
10 years	125	1,000

b Comment on the problems of total shareholders' returns as a metric for judging managerial performance.

4 Sity plc has paid out all earnings as dividends since it was founded with £15m of equity finance 25 years ago. Today its shares are valued on the stock market at £90m and its long-term debt has a market value and book value of £20m.

 a How much market value added (MVA) has Sity produced?
 b Given that another company, Pity plc, was founded with £15m of equity capital five years ago and has paid out all earnings since its foundation and is now worth (equity and debt) £110m (£90m equity, £20m debt), discuss the problems of using the MVA for inter-firm comparison.

Questions and problems

For those questions marked with an asterisk* the answers are provided in the lecturer's guide only.

1 (*Examination level*) 'Thirty years ago we measured the success of our divisional managers on the basis of market share growth, sales and profits. In the late 1970s we switched to return on capital employed because the old system did not take account of the amount of capital invested to achieve growth targets. Now you are telling me that we have to change again to value-based performance metrics. Why?' Explain in the form of an essay to this chief executive what advantages value-based management has over other approaches.

2 'EPS (earnings per share) is not a holy grail in determining how well a company is performing': Lex column of the *Financial Times*, 7 May 1996. Describe and explain the reasons for dissatisfaction with eps for target setting and increasing performance.

3* Which of the following two companies creates more value, assuming that they are making the same initial investment?

Company A's projected profits		Company B's projected profits	
Year	Profit (£000s)	Year	Profit (£000s)
Last year	1,000	Last year	1,000
1 (forthcoming year)	1,000	1 (forthcoming year)	1,000
2	1,100	2	1,080
3	1,200	3	1,160
4	1,400	4	1,350
5	1,600	5	1,500
6 and all subsequent years	1,800	6 and all subsequent years	1,700

Profits for both companies are 20 per cent of sales in each year. With company A, for every £1 increase in sales 7p has to be devoted to additional debtors because of the generous credit terms granted to customers. For B, only 1p is needed for additional investment in debtors for every £1 increase in sales. Higher sales also mean greater inventory levels at each firm. This is 6p and 2p for every extra £1 in sales for A and B respectively.

Apart from the debtor and inventory adjustments the profit figures of both firms reflect their cash flows. The cost of capital for both firms is 14 per cent.

4 Ready plc is financed entirely by equity capital with a required return of 13 per cent. Ready's business is such that, as sales increase, working capital does not change. Ready currently has £10m in cash not needed for business operations that could be used to pay a dividend immediately. Under current policy, post-tax earnings (and free cash flow) of £10m per year are expected to continue indefinitely. All earnings in future years are expected to be paid out as dividends in the year of occurrence.

Calculate

 a The value of the company before the current dividend is paid from the £10m of cash.
 b The value of the company if the current dividend (time 0) is missed and the retained earnings are put into investments (with the same risk as current set of projects) yielding an extra £2m per year to infinity in addition to the current policy's earnings. What happens to earnings and cash flow? Is this good or bad investment?

c The value of the company if half of the current dividend is missed and the retained earnings are put into investment yielding £0.5m per year to infinity. What happens to earnings and cash flows? Is this good or bad investment?

5* Busy plc, an all-equity-financed firm, has three strategic business units. The polythene division has capital of £8m and is expected to produce returns of 11 per cent for the next five years. Thereafter it will produce returns equal to the required rate of return for this risk level of 14 per cent. The paper division has an investment level of £12m and a planning horizon of 10 years. During the planning horizon it will produce a return of 22 per cent compared with a risk-adjusted required rate of return of 15 per cent. The cotton division uses £2m of capital, has a planning horizon of seven years and a required rate of return of 16 per cent compared with the anticipated actual rate of 17 per cent over the first seven years.

a Calculate the value of the firm.
b Draw a value-creation and strategic business unit performance spread chart.
c Develop five ideas for increasing the value of the firm. State your assumptions.

6 Blue plc is a relatively small company with only one SBU. It manufactures wire grilles for the consumer market for cooker manufacturers and for export. Following a thorough investigation by the finance department and the heads of the customer lines some facts emerged about the returns expected in each of the customer sectors. The consumer sector uses £1m of the firm's capital and is expected to produce a return of 18 per cent on this capital, for the next five years, after which it will return the same as its risk-adjusted cost of capital (WACC), 15 per cent.

The cooker sales sector uses £2m of capital and will return 14 per cent per annum for seven years when its planning horizon ends. Its WACC is 16 per cent.

The export sector has a positive performance spread of 2 per cent over WACC for the next six years. The required rate of return is 17 per cent. From Year 7 the performance spread becomes zero. This division uses £1.5m of capital.

Required

a Calculate the annual (entity version) economic profit of each sector.
b What is the total value creation from each if you assume profit numbers equate to cash flow numbers?
c Display a value-creation profile chart and suggest possible action.

7* Apply shareholder value analysis to an all-equity firm with the following Rappaport value drivers, assuming that the last reported annual sales were £25m.

Sales growth rate	13%
Operating profit margin before tax	10%
Tax rate	31%
Incremental fixed capital investment (IFCI)	11% of the change in sales
Incremental working capital investment (IWCI)	8% of the change in sales
Planning horizon	4 years
Required rate of return	15%

Marketable securities amount to £5m and depreciation can be taken to be equal to the investment needed to replace worn-out equipment.

> **AN EXCEL SPREADSHEET VERSION OF THE ANSWERS TO THIS QUESTION IS AVAILABLE AT www.pearsoned.co.uk/arnold**

8 Buit plc is trying to estimate its value under the current strategy. The managerial team have forecast the following profits for the next five years:

Year	1	2	3	4	5
Forecast profit (£m)	12	14	15	16	16

Depreciation of fixed capital items in each of the first two years is £2m. In each of the following three years it is £3m. This has been deducted before arriving at the profit figures shown above. In years 1, 2 and 3 capital expenditure will be £5m per year which both replaces worn-out assets and pays for fresh investment to grow the business. In the fourth and fifth year capital expenditure will be £3m.

The planning horizon is four years. Additional working capital will be needed in each of the next four years. This will be £1m in year 1, £1.2m in year 2, £1.5m in year 3 and £1.8m in year 4.

The company is partially financed by debt – it owes £20m – and partially by equity capital. The required rate of return (WACC) is 10 per cent.

The forecast profit figures include a deduction for interest of £1.2m per year, but do not include a deduction for tax, which is levied at 30 per cent of forecasted profits, payable in the year profits are made.

The company also owns a number of empty factories that are not required for business operations. The current market value of these is £16m.

Required

a Calculate the future cash flows for the company to an infinite horizon – assume year 5 cash flows apply to each year thereafter. Discount the cash flows and calculate the present value of all the cash flows.
b Calculate corporate value and shareholder value.

9 Mythier plc, in its first year, produced profits after deduction of tax but before deduction of interest of £1m. The amount invested by debt holders was £4m. Equity holders also invested £4m. Interest paid during the year was £0.24m and the weighted average cost of capital is 8 per cent, while the cost of equity capital is 10 per cent.

a Calculate economic profit using the entity approach.
b Calculate economic profit using the equity approach.
c Describe the advantages of using economic profit in the modern corporation.
d Explain the difficulties with economic profit.

Assignments

1 Apply the four key elements of value creation, the 'expand or not to expand?' model and the value action pentagon to a firm you are familiar with. Write a report for senior executives.

2 Conduct a value-based analysis and write a report for a company you know well. Show the current position and your recommendations for change. Include in the analysis value-creation profile charts, sources of competitive advantage (value drivers), cash flow analysis, shareholder value analysis, EP, TSR and MVA.

Visit www.pearsoned.co.uk/arnold to get access to Gradetracker diagnostic tests, Podcasts, Excel Spreadsheet Solutions, FT articles, a Flashcard revision tool, Weblinks, a searchable Glossary and more.

CHAPTER 10

Valuing shares and companies

LEARNING OUTCOMES

By the end of this chapter the reader should be able to:

■ describe the principal determinants of share prices and be able to estimate share value using a variety of approaches;

■ demonstrate awareness of the most important input factors and appreciate that they are difficult to quantify;

■ use valuation models to estimate the value of shares when managerial control is achieved.

Introduction

Knowledge of the main influences on share prices is important from the perspective of two groups. The first group is managers, who, if they are to be given the responsibility of maximising the wealth of shareholders, need to know the factors influencing that wealth, as reflected in the share price of their own company. Without this understanding they will be unable to determine the most important consequence of their actions – the impact on share value. Managers need to appreciate share price derivation because their company's share price is one of the key factors by which they are judged. It is also useful for them to know how share prices are set if the firm plans to gain a flotation on a stock exchange, or when it is selling a division to another firm. In mergers an acquirer needs good valuation skills so as not to pay more than necessary, and a seller needs to ensure that the price is fair.

The second constituency for whom the ideas and models presented in this chapter will be of practical use is investors, who risk their savings by buying shares.

This chapter describes the main methods of valuing shares: net asset value, dividend valuation models, price-earnings ratio models and cash flow models. There is an important subsection in the chapter which shows that the valuation of shares when the size of the shareholding is large enough to give managerial control over the firm is somewhat different from the valuation when there is only a small holding providing only a small minority stake.

The two skills

Two skills are needed to be able to value shares. The first is analytical ability, to be able to understand and use mathematical valuation models. Second, and most importantly, good judgement is needed, because most of the inputs to the mathematical calculations are factors, the precise nature of which cannot be defined with absolute certainty, so great skill is required to produce reasonably accurate results. The main problem is that the determinants of value occur in the future, for example future cash flows, dividends or earnings.

The monetary value of an asset is what someone is prepared to pay for it. Assets such as cars and houses are difficult enough to value with any degree of accuracy. At least corporate bonds generally have a regular cash flow (coupon) and an anticipated capital repayment. This contrasts with the uncertainties associated with shares, for which there is no guaranteed annual payment and no promise of capital repayment.

The difficulties of share valuation are amply represented by the case of Amazon.com – *see* **Case study 10.1**.

Case study 10.1	Amazon.com

Amazon, the internet retailer, did not make a profit in its first six years. For example, it lost over $700m in 1999 and offered little prospect of profits in the near term. So, if you were an investor in early 2000 what value would you give to a company of this calibre? Anything at all? Amazingly, investors valued Amazon at over $30 billion in early 2000 (more than all the traditional book retailers put together). The brand was well established and the numbers joining the online community rose by thousands every day. Investors were confident that Amazon would continue to attract customers and produce a rapid rate of growth in revenue. Eventually, it was thought, this revenue growth would translate into profits and high dividends. When investors had calmed down after taking account of the potential for rivalrous competition in this business and the fact that by 2001 Amazon was still not producing profits they reassessed the value of Amazon's likely future dividends. In mid-2001, they judged the company to be worth only $4bn – it had run up losses of $1.4bn in 2000, indicating that profits and dividends were still a long way off. However, by 2006 the company was starting to report some profits and its future prospects were thought to be sufficiently good to accord the company a valuation of $18 billion.

Valuation using net asset value (NAV)

The balance sheet seems an obvious place to start when faced with the task of valuation. In this method the company is viewed as being worth the sum of the value of its net assets. The balance sheet is regarded as providing objective facts concerning the company's ownership of assets and obligations to creditors. Here fixed assets are recorded along with stocks, debtors, cash and other liquid assets. With the deduction of long-term and short-term creditors from the total asset figure we arrive at the net asset value (NAV).

An example of this type of calculation is shown in Exhibit 10.1 for the publisher Pearson.

Exhibit 10.1	Pearson plc abridged balance sheet at 31 December 2004	
		£m
Fixed assets		3,428
Current assets		2,558
Creditors: Amounts falling due within one year		(1,275)
Creditors: Amounts falling due after more than one year		(1,772)
Provisions for liabilities and charges		(123)
Net assets		2,816
Equity shareholders' funds		2,603
Equity minority interests		213
		2,816

Source: Pearson plc, Annual Review 2004.

The NAV after deduction of equity minority interests of £2,603m[1] of Pearson compares with a market value placed on all Pearson's shares when totalled of £5,000m (market capitalisation figures are available in Monday editions of the *Financial Times* and on most financial websites). This great difference makes it clear that the shareholders of Pearson are not rating the firm on the basis of balance sheet net asset figures. This point is reinforced by an examination of Exhibit 10.2.

Some of the firms listed in Exhibit 10.2 have a very small balance sheet value in comparison with their total market capitalisation. BSkyB has a negative net asset value! For most companies, investors look to the income flow to be derived from a holding. This flow is generated

Exhibit 10.2	Net asset values (after deducting minority interests) and total capitalisation of some firms	
Company (Accounts year)	NAV £m	Total capitalisation (market value of company's shares) £m
BP (2004)	76,656	130,450
BSkyB (2005)	−34	9,759
Cadbury Schweppes (2004)	2,859	11,465
GlaxoSmithKline (2004)	5,924	85,389

Source: Annual reports and accounts; *Financial Times*, 10 October 2005.

---

[1] i.e. the net assets available to Pearson's shareholders rather than the total net assets available to both Pearson's shareholders and those that hold some of the shares in subsidiaries of Pearson.

when the balance sheet assets are combined with assets impossible to quantify: these include the unique skills of the workforce, the relationships with customers and suppliers, the value of brands, the reservoir of experience within the management team, and the competitive positioning of the firm's products. Thus assets, in the crude sense of balance sheet values, are only one dimension of overall value – *see* **Exhibit 10.3**. Investors in the market generally value intangible, unmeasurable assets more highly than those which can be identified and recorded by accountants.

Exhibit 10.3	What creates value for shareholders?

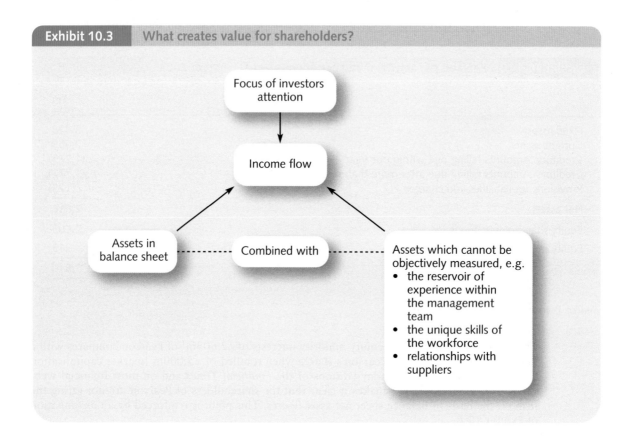

Criticising accountants for not producing balance sheets which reflect the true value of a business is unfair. Accounts are not usually designed to record up-to-date market values. Land and buildings are frequently shown at cost rather than market value; thus the balance sheet can provide a significant over- or under-valuation of the assets' current value. Plant and machinery is shown at the purchase price less a depreciation amount. Stock is valued at the lower of cost or net realisable value – this can lead to a significant underestimate, as the market value can appreciate to a figure far higher than either of these. The list of balance sheet entries vulnerable to subjective estimation, arbitrary method and even cynical manipulation is a long one: goodwill, provisions, merger accounting, debtors, intangible brand values and so on.

The slippery concept of balance sheet value is demonstrated in the article about Hanson reproduced in **Exhibit 10.4**.

When asset values are particularly useful

The accounts-based approach to share value is fraught with problems but there are circumstances in which asset backing is given more attention:

Exhibit 10.4

Hanson cuts asset value by £3.2bn

Hanson, the industrial conglomerate, yesterday marked the latest stage of its four-way demerger by announcing a £3.2bn reduction in assets following accounting changes and write-downs in the value of its US mineral reserves.

The write-downs at Peabody, the largest coal producer in the US, and Hanson's Cornerstone aggregates subsidiary will bring the company into line with US accounting standards on the treatment of 'long lived assets'.

Mr Derek Bonham, chief executive, said the move would have no impact on operational cash flow and added: 'It in no way reflects on the accuracy of previous accounts.'

Some industry analysts, however, suggested Hanson might have overvalued the assets of both Peabody and Cornerstone in the past – a charge rejected by the company.

In total, the book value of mineral reserves at Cornerstone have been reduced by £2.3bn to £1.3bn and by £600m at Peabody to £1.5bn. A further £300m charge is being made against Peabody's reserves to cover accounting changes over industry liabilities.

As part of the accounting changes, Hanson has removed £1.2bn of its £1.5bn provisions from Peabody's balance sheet and plans to charge £300m of previous payments to profit and loss reserves. Mr Bonham said this move would cut the carrying value of Peabody's coal reserves by £1.5bn.

Source: Tim Burt, *Financial Times*, 9 July 1996, p. 17. Reprinted with permission.

Firms in financial difficulty

The shareholders of firms in financial difficulty may pay a great deal of attention to the asset backing of the firm. They may weigh up the potential for asset sales or asset-backed borrowing. In extreme circumstances they may try to assess the break-up value.

Takeover bids

In a takeover bid shareholders will be reluctant to sell at less than NAV even if the prospect for income growth is poor. A standard defensive tactic in a takeover battle is to revalue balance sheet assets to encourage a higher price.

When discounted income flow techniques are difficult to apply

For some types of company there is no straightforward way of employing income-flow-based methods:

1 *Property investment companies* are primarily valued on the basis of their assets. It is generally possible to put a fairly realistic up-to-date price on the buildings owned by such a company. These market values have a close link to future cash flows. That is, the future rents payable by tenants, when discounted, determine the value of property assets and thus the company. If higher rent levels are expected than were previously anticipated, chartered surveyors will place a higher value on the asset, and the NAV in the balance sheet will rise, forcing up the share price. For such companies, future income, asset values and share values are all closely linked. However, the value of a property investment company may be less than its NAV. **Exhibit 10.5** describes two reasons for a discount to NAV: the capital gains tax the company would incur on the sale of its assets; and the cost of paying off high interest rate debt. Analysts also deduct the costs of remaining as a going concern (the present value of management costs and general overheads).

2 *Investment trusts* The future income of investment trusts comes from the individual shareholdings. The shareholder in a trust would find it extremely difficult to calculate the future income to be received from each of the dozens or hundreds of shares held. An easier approach is simply to take the current share price of each holding as representing the future

discounted income. The share values are aggregated to derive the trusts' NAV and this has a strong bearing on the price at which the trust shares are traded.

3 *Resource-based companies* For oil companies, mineral extractors, mining houses and so on, the proven or probable reserves have a significant influence on the share price.

Exhibit 10.5

Canary Wharf reflects change of sentiment to unloved sector

Juliana Ratner

This week's angry outburst from Canary Wharf shareholders – attacking the board for selling the development group too cheaply – shows how far sentiment has changed to the unloved property sector.

A year ago, UK property companies traded at an average 40 per cent discount to net asset value (NAV), a key measure of performance for UK property groups . . .

The discount has narrowed from 19 per cent to 16 per cent this year . . .

The shrinking discount has made obsolete triple-net asset value – a relatively new measure of what a buyer would have to pay to take a UK property company private. Now, investors are more confident of the value of their businesses as the market picks up and discounts narrow.

Triple-net asset value was first used as a valuation tool in 2000

when GE Real Estate and Hermes took MEPC private. It was, in effect, a way to drive down the price.

Triple-net is a liquidation value. It takes the company's net asset value as estimated by chartered surveyors, and deducts its investment portfolio's unbooked capital gains tax (CGT) liability. It also subtracts the cost of refinancing existing debt at current interest rates.

While investors, four years ago, were happy to sell at discounts to triple-net, they are no longer inclined to give that value away. The mood has changed because triple-net was probably not the most appropriate measure of MEPC's worth.

The buyers paid £1.9bn for MEPC. But the price had been reduced to allow the new owners to repay outstanding bonds. In fact, they retained the bonds and

kept the difference in cost. Fancy footwork in asset disposals cut the expected CGT liability, enhancing further the returns for MEPC's new owners . . .

Increasingly, Canary Wharf's shareholders are concerned the board is asking them to sell at the wrong price and at the wrong time.

Morgan Stanley this month raised its offer to 292p, or £1.7bn, trumping a rival £1.6bn bid from Brascan, the Canadian group. Yet Morgan's offer is still well below the group's NAV of 344p as of June 31 and below 299p, which the company last autumn indicated was its triple-net. In addition, Canary Wharf in December sold two buildings, which it said would have increased the June NAV to 350p . . .

Source: Financial Times, 26 March 2004, p. 28. Reprinted with permission.

Valuation using income-flow methods

The value of a share is usually determined by the income flows that investors expect to receive in the future from its ownership. Information about the past is only of relevance to the extent that it contributes to an understanding of expected future performance. Income flows will occur at different points in the future and so they have to be discounted. There are three classes of income valuation model:

● dividend-based models;
● earnings-based models;
● cash-flow-based models.

The dividend valuation models

The dividend valuation models (DVMs) are based on the premise that *the market value of ordinary shares represents the sum of the expected future dividend flows, to infinity, discounted to present value.*

The only cash flows that investors ever receive from a company are dividends. This holds true if we include a 'liquidation dividend' upon the sale of the firm or on formal liquidation, and any share repurchases can be treated as dividends. Of course, an individual shareholder is not planning to hold a share forever to gain the dividend returns to an infinite horizon. An individual holder of shares will expect two types of return:

(a) income from dividends; and

(b) a capital gain resulting from the appreciation of the share and its sale to another investor.

The fact that the individual investor is looking for capital gains as well as dividends to give a return does not invalidate the model. The reason for this is that, when a share is sold, the purchaser is buying a future stream of dividends; therefore, the price paid is determined by future dividend expectations.

To illustrate this, consider the following: A shareholder intends to hold a share for one year. A single dividend will be paid at the end of the holding period, d_1, and the share will be sold at price P_1 in one year.

To derive the value of a share at time 0 to this investor (P_0), the future cash flows, d_1 and P_1, need to be discounted at a rate that includes an allowance for the risk class of the share, k_E.

$$P_0 = \frac{d_1}{1 + k_E} + \frac{P_1}{1 + k_E}$$

Worked example 10.1

An investor is considering the purchase of some shares in Willow plc. At the end of one year a dividend of 22p will be paid and the shares are expected to be sold for £2.43. How much should be paid if the investor judges that the rate of return required on a financial security of this risk class is 20 per cent?

Answer

$$P_0 = \frac{d_1}{1 + k_E} + \frac{P_1}{1 + k_E}$$

$$P_0 = \frac{22}{1 + 0.2} + \frac{243}{1 + 0.2} = 221p$$

The dividend valuation model to infinity

The relevant question to ask in order to understand DVMs is: Where does P_1 come from? The buyer at time 1 estimates the value of the share based on the present value of future income given the required rate of return for the risk class. So if the second investor expects to hold the share for a further year and sell at time 2 for P_2, the price P_1 will be:

$$P_1 = \frac{d_2}{1 + k_E} + \frac{P_2}{1 + k_E}$$

Returning to the P_0 equation we are able to substitute discounted d_2 and P_2 for P_1. Thus:

$$P_0 = \frac{d_1}{1 + k_E} + \frac{P_1}{1 + k_E}$$

$$P_0 = \frac{d_1}{1 + k_E} + \frac{d_2}{(1 + k_E)^2} + \frac{P_2}{(1 + k_E)^2}$$

If a series of one-year investors bought this share, and we in turn solved for P_2, P_3, P_4, etc., we would find:

$$P_0 = \frac{d_1}{1 + k_E} + \frac{d_2}{(1 + k_E)^2} + \frac{d_3}{(1 + k_E)^3} + \dots + \frac{d_n}{(1 + k_E)^n}$$

Even a short-term investor has to consider events beyond his or her time horizon because the selling price is determined by the willingness of a buyer to purchase a future dividend stream. If this year's dividends are boosted by short-termist policies such as cutting out R&D and brand-support marketing the investor may well lose more on capital value changes (as other investors push down the share price when their forecasts for future dividends are lowered) than the gains in dividend income.

Worked example 10.2

If a firm is expected to pay dividends of 20p per year to infinity and the rate of return required on a share of this risk class is 12 per cent then:

$$P_0 = \frac{20}{1 + 0.12} + \frac{20}{(1 + 0.12)^2} + \frac{20}{(1 + 0.12)^3} + \dots + \frac{20}{(1 + 0.12)^n}$$

$$P_0 = 17.86 + 15.94 + 14.24 + \dots + \dots +$$

Given this is a perpetuity there is a simpler approach:

$$P_0 = \frac{d_1}{k_E} = \frac{20}{0.12} = 166.67p$$

The dividend growth model

In contrast to the situation in the above example, for most companies dividends are expected to grow from one year to the next. To make DVM analysis manageable simplifying assumptions are usually made about the patterns of growth in dividends. Most managers attempt to make dividends grow more or less in line with the firm's long-term earnings growth rate. They often bend over backwards to smooth out fluctuations, maintaining a high dividend even in years of poor profits or losses. In years of very high profits they are often reluctant to increase the dividend by a large percentage for fear that it might have to be cut back in a downturn.[2] So, given management propensity to make dividend payments grow in an incremental or stepped fashion it seems that a reasonable model could be based on the assumption of a constant growth rate. (Year to year deviations around this expected growth path will not materially alter the analysis.) *See* Worked examples 10.3 and 10.4 for the use of the constant dividend growth model.

---

[2] For a discussion on the propensity for directors to keep to a steadily rising dividend policy, see Chapter 12.

Worked example 10.3   A constant dividend growth valuation: Shhh plc

If the last dividend paid was d_0 and the next is due in one year, d_1, then this will amount to $d_0 (1 + g)$ where g is the growth rate of dividends.

For example, if Shhh plc has just paid a dividend of 10p and the growth rate is 7 per cent then:

d_1 will equal $d_0 (1 + g) = 10 (1 + 0.07) = 10.7$p

and

d_2 will be $d_0(1 + g)^2 = 10(1 + 0.07)^2 = 11.45$p

The value of a share in Shhh will be all the future dividends discounted at the risk-adjusted discount rate of 11 per cent:

$$P_0 = \frac{d_0 (1 + g)}{(1 + k_E)} + \frac{d_0 (1 + g)^2}{(1 + k_E)^2} + \frac{d_0 (1 + g)^3}{(1 + k_E)^3} + ... + \frac{d_0 (1 + g)^n}{(1 + k_E)^n}$$

$$P_0 = \frac{10(1 + 0.07)}{(1 + 0.11)} + \frac{10(1 + 0.07)^2}{(1 + 0.11)^2} + \frac{10 (1 + 0.07)^3}{(1 + 0.11)^3} + ... + \frac{10 (1 + 0.07)^n}{(1 + 0.11)^n}$$

Using the above formula could require a lot of time. Fortunately it is mathematically equivalent to the following formula (if the dividends continue to grow at the rate g in perpetuity), which is much easier to employ. This is called the Gordon growth model.

$$P_0 = \frac{d_1}{k_E - g} = \frac{d_0 (1 + g)}{k_E - g} = \frac{10.7}{0.11 - 0.07} = 267.50\text{p}$$

Note that, even though the shortened formula only includes next year's dividend, all the future dividends are represented.

A further illustration is provided by the example of Pearson plc.

Worked example 10.4   Pearson plc

Pearson plc has the following dividend history.

Year	Dividends per share (p)
1996	16.1
1997	17.4
1998	18.8
1999	20.1
2000	21.4
2001	22.3
2002	23.4
2003	24.2
2004	25.4

The average annual growth rate, g, over this period has been:

$$g = \sqrt[8]{\frac{25.4}{16.1}} - 1 = 0.059 \text{ or } 5.9\%$$

If it is assumed that this historical growth rate will continue into the future (a big if) and 10 per cent is taken as the required rate of return, the value of a share can be calculated.

▶

Worked example 10.4   Continued

$$P_0 = \frac{d_1}{k_E - g} = \frac{25.4(1 + 0.059)}{0.10 - 0.059} = 656p$$

Over 2005 Pearson's shares ranged as high as 694p and as low as 590p. So there were times when investors were more optimistic than we have been in the above analysis: perhaps they were anticipating a faster rate of growth in future than in the past, or judged the risk to be less, thus lowering k_E. On other occasions investors were more pessimistic, perhaps seeing Pearson's shares as sufficiently risky to require a rate of return higher than 10 per cent per year or anticipating lower future profit and dividend growth.

AN EXCEL SPREADSHEET VERSION OF THIS CALCULATION FOR PEARSON IS AVAILABLE AT www.pearsoned.co.uk/arnold

Non-constant growth

Firms tend to go through different phases of growth. If they have a strong competitive advantage in an attractive market they might enjoy super-normal growth for a while. Eventually, however, most firms come under competitive pressure and growth becomes normal. Ultimately, many firms fail to keep pace with the market environmental change in which they operate and growth falls to below that for the average company.

To analyse companies which will go through different phases of growth a two-, three- or four-stage model may be used. In the simplest case of two-stage growth the share price calculation requires the following:

1 Calculate each of the forecast annual dividends in the first period.

2 Estimate the share price at the point at which the dividend growth shifts to the new permanent rate.

3 Discount each of the dividends in the first period and the share price given in 2. Add all the discounted numbers to obtain the current value.

Worked example 10.5   Two-stage growth of dividends : Noruce plc

You are given the following information about Noruce plc.

The company has just paid an annual dividend of 15p per share and the next is due in one year. For the next three years dividends are expected to grow at 12 per cent per year. This rapid rate is caused by a number of favourable factors: for example an economic upturn, the fast acceleration stage of newly developed products and a large contract with a government department. After the third year the dividend will grow at only 7 per cent per annum, because the main boosts to growth will, by then, be absent.

Shares in other companies with a similar level of systematic risk to Noruce produce an expected return of 16 per cent per annum.

What is the value of one share in Noruce plc?

Answer

Stage 1 Calculate dividends for the super-normal growth phase

$d_1 = 15 (1 + 0.12) = 16.8$
$d_2 = 15 (1 + 0.12)^2 = 18.8$
$d_3 = 15 (1 + 0.12)^3 = 21.1$

Worked example 10.5	Continued

Stage 2 Calculate share price at time 3 when the dividend growth rate shifts to the new permanent rate

$$P_3 = \frac{d_4}{k_E - g} = \frac{d_3(1 + g)}{k_E - g} = \frac{21.1(1+0.07)}{0.16 - 0.07} = 250.9$$

Stage 3 Discount and sum the amounts calculated in Stages 1 and 2

$$\frac{d_1}{1 + k_E} \qquad = \frac{16.8}{1 + 0.16} \qquad = \quad 14.5$$

$$+ \frac{d_2}{(1 + k_E)^2} \qquad = \frac{18.8}{(1 + 0.16)^2} \qquad = \quad 14.0$$

$$+ \frac{d_3}{(1 + k_E)^3} \qquad = \frac{21.1}{(1 + 0.16)^3} \qquad = \quad 13.5$$

$$+ \frac{P_3}{(1 + k_E)^3} \qquad = \frac{250.9}{(1 + 0.16)^3} \qquad = \quad \underline{160.7}$$

$$\underline{202.7\text{p}}$$

AN EXCEL SPREADSHEET VERSION OF THIS CALCULATION FOR NORUCE IS AVAILABLE AT
www.pearsoned.co.uk/arnold

What is a normal growth rate?

Growth rates will be different for each company but for corporations taken as a whole dividend growth will not be significantly different from the growth in nominal gross national product (real GNP plus inflation) over the long run. If dividends did grow in a long-term trend above this rate then they would take an increasing proportion of national income – ultimately squeezing out the consumption and government sectors. This is, of course, ridiculous. Thus in an economy with inflation of 2 per cent per annum and economic growth of 2.5 per cent we might expect the long-term growth in dividends to be about 4.5 per cent. Also, it is unreasonable to suppose that a firm can grow its earnings and dividends forever at a rate significantly greater than that for the economy as a whole. To do so is to assume that the firm eventually becomes larger than the economy. There will be years, even decades, when average corporate dividends do grow faster than the economy as a whole and there will always be companies with much higher projected growth rates than the average for periods of time. Nevertheless, the real GNP + inflation growth relationship provides a useful benchmark.

Companies that do not pay dividends

Some companies, for example Warren Buffett's Berkshire Hathaway, do not pay dividends. This is a deliberate policy as there is often a well-founded belief that the funds are better used within the firms than they would be if the money is given to shareholders. This presents an apparent problem for the DVMs, but the formulae can still be applied because it is reasonable to suppose that one day these companies will start to pay dividends. Perhaps this will take the form of a final break-up payment, or perhaps when the founder is approaching retirement he/she will start to distribute the accumulated resources. At some point dividends must be paid, otherwise there would be no attraction in holding the shares. Microsoft is an example of a company that did not pay a dividend for 28 years. However, in 2003 it decided it would start the process of paying out some of its enormous cash pile and paid a dividend. In 2004 it decided to pay a 'special dividend' on top of its now regular dividend, amounting to a massive $32bn. Furthermore it made a commitment to share at least $43bn with shareholders over the next four years in the form of share repurchases and its regular dividend.

Some companies do not pay dividends for many years due to regular losses. Often what gives value to this type of share is the optimism that the company will recover and that dividends will be paid in the distant future.

Problems with dividend valuation models

Dividend valuation models present the following problems.

1 They are highly sensitive to the assumptions. Take the case of Pearson above. If we change the growth assumption to 8 per cent and reduce the required rate of return to 9.5 per cent, the value of the share leaps to 1,828p.

$$P_0 = \frac{d_1}{k_E - g} = \frac{25.4(1 + 0.08)}{0.095 - 0.08} = 1828.8p$$

As the growth rate converges on the required rate of return the value goes to infinity.

2 The quality of input data is often poor. The problems of calculating an appropriate required rate of return on equity were discussed in Chapters 5 and 8. Added to this is great uncertainty about the future growth rate.

3 If g exceeds k_E a nonsensical result occurs. This problem is dealt with if the short-term super-normal growth rate is replaced with a g which is some weighted average growth rate reflecting the return expected over the long run. However, this is unlikely to result in a g more than one or two percentage points greater than the growth rate for the economy as a whole (because the largest weight will be given to the near term supernormal growth period, we may allow a growth rate slightly higher than the economy). Alternatively, for those periods when g is greater than k, you may calculate the specific dividend amounts and discount them as in the non-constant growth model. For the years after the super-normal growth occurs, the usual growth formula may be used (as in the case of Noruce in worked example 10.5).

The difficulties of using the DVMs are real and yet they are to be favoured, less for the derivation of a single number than for the understanding of the principles behind the value of financial assets that the exercise provides. They demand a disciplined thought process that makes the analyst's assumptions about key variables explicit.

Forecasting dividend growth rates – *g*

The most influential variable, and the one subject to most uncertainty, on the value of shares is the growth rate expected in dividends. Accuracy here is a much sought-after virtue. While this book cannot provide readers with perfect crystal balls for seeing future dividend growth rates, it can provide a few pointers.

Determinants of growth

There are three factors which influence the rate of dividend growth.

1 *The quantity of resources retained and reinvested within the business* This relates to the percentage of earnings not paid out as dividends. The more a firm invests, the greater its potential for growth.

2 *The rate of return earned on those retained resources* The efficiency with which retained earnings are used will influence value.

3 *Rate of return earned on existing assets* This concerns the amount earned on the existing baseline set of assets, that is, those assets available before reinvestment of profits. This cate-

gory may be affected by a sudden increase or decrease in profitability. If the firm, for example, is engaged in oil exploration and production, and there is a worldwide increase in the price of oil, profitability will rise on existing assets. Another example would be if a major competitor is liquidated, enabling increased returns on the same asset base due to higher margins because of an improved market position.

There is a vast range of influences on the future return from shares. One way of dealing with the myriad variables is to group them into two categories: at the firm and the economy level.

Focus on the firm

A dedicated analyst would want to examine numerous aspects of the firm, and its management, to help develop an informed estimate of its growth potential. These will include the following.

1 *Strategic analysis* The most important factor in assessing the value of a firm is its strategic position. The analyst needs to consider the attractiveness of the industry and the competitive position of the firm within the industry to appreciate the potential for increased dividends (*see* Arnold (2002) or Arnold (2004) for a fuller discussion).

2 *Evaluation of management* Running a close second in importance for the determination of a firm's value is the quality of its management. A starting point for analysis might be to collect factual information such as the age of the key managers and their level of experience (particularly longevity with the company) and of education. But this has to be combined with far more important evaluatory variables which are unquantifiable, such as judgement, and even gut feeling about issues such as competence, integrity, intelligence and so on. Having honest managers with a focus on increasing the wealth of shareholders is at least as important for valuing shares as the factor of managerial competence. Investors downgrade the shares of companies run by the most brilliant managers if there is any doubt about their integrity – highly competent crooks can destroy shareholder wealth far more quickly than any competitive action: just ask the shareholders in WorldCom, Enron and Parmalat. (For a fuller discussion of the impact of managerial competence and integrity on share values *see* Arnold (2002).)

3 *Using the historical growth rate of dividends* For some firms past growth may be extrapolated to estimate future dividends. If a company demonstrated a growth rate of 6 per cent over the past ten years it might be reasonable to use this as a starting point for evaluating its future potential. This figure may have to be adjusted for new information such as new strategies, management or products – that is the tricky part.

4 *Financial statement evaluation and ratio analysis* An assessment of the firm's profitability, efficiency and risk through an analysis of accounting data can be enlightening. However, adjustments to the published figures are likely to be necessary to view the past clearly, let alone provide a guide to the future. Accounts are valuable sources of information but they have three drawbacks: (a) they are based in the past when it is the future which is of interest, (b) the fundamental value-creating processes within the firm are not identified and measured in conventional accounts, and (c) they are frequently based on guesses, estimates and judgements, and are open to arbitrary methods and manipulation. Armed with a questioning frame of mind the analyst can adjust accounts to provide a truer and fairer view of a company. The analyst may wish to calculate three groups of ratios to enable comparisons:

   (a) Internal liquidity ratios permit some judgement about the ability of the firm to cope with short-term financial obligations – quick ratios, current ratios, etc.

   (b) Operating performance ratios may indicate the efficiency of the management in the operations of the business – asset turnover ratio, profit margins, debtor turnover, etc.

   (c) Risk analysis concerns the uncertainty of income flows – sales variability over the economic cycle, operational gearing (fixed costs as a proportion of total), financial gearing (ratio of debt to equity), cash flow ratios, etc.

Ratios examined in isolation are meaningless. It is usually necessary to compare with the industry, or the industry sub-group comprising the firm's competitors. Knowledge of changes in ratios over time can also be useful.

Focus on the economy

All firms, to a greater or lesser extent, are influenced by macroeconomic changes. The prospects for a particular firm can be greatly affected by sudden changes in government fiscal policy, the central bank's monetary policy, changes in exchange rates, etc. Forecasts of macroeconomic variables such as GNP are easy to find (for example, *The Economist* publishes a table of forecasts every week). Finding a forecaster who is reliable over the long term is much more difficult. Perhaps the best approach is to obtain a number of projections and through informed judgement develop a view about the medium-term future. Alternatively, the analyst could recognise that there are many different potential futures and then develop analyses based on a range of possible scenarios – probabilities could be assigned and sensitivity analysis used to provide a broader picture.

It is notable that many of the most respected investors (e.g. Benjamin Graham, Philip Fisher, Warren Buffett and Charles Munger) pay little attention to macroeconomic forecasts when valuing companies. The reason for this is that value is determined by income flows to the shareholder over many economic cycles stretching over decades, so the economists' projection (even if accurate) for this or that economic number for the next year is of little significance.

The price-earnings ratio (PER) model

The most popular approach to valuing a share is to use the price-to-earnings ratio (PER). The historical PER compares a firm's share price with its latest earnings (profits) per share. Investors estimate a share's value as the amount they are willing to pay for each unit of earnings. If a company produced earnings per share of 10p in its latest accounts and investors are prepared to pay 20 times historical earnings for this type of share it will be valued at £2.00. The historical PER is calculated as follows:

$$\text{Historical PER} = \frac{\text{Current market price of share}}{\text{Last year's earnings per share}} = \frac{200\text{p}}{10\text{p}} = 20$$

So, the retailer Boots, which reported earnings per share of 45.7p for the year to March 2005, with a share price of 631p in October 2005, had a PER of 13.8 (631/45.7). PERs of other retailers are shown in **Exhibit 10.6**.

Exhibit 10.6

PERs for retailers   **FT**

Retailer	PER
Blacks	11.6
Body Shop	13.0
Boots	13.8
Burberry	17.6
DSG (Dixons etc.)	12.2
JJB Sports	8.2
Kingfisher	11.6
Marks & Spencer	17.6
Next	10.8

Source: Financial Times, 11 October 2005. Reprinted with permission.

Investors are willing to buy Burberry shares at 17.6 times last year's earnings compared with only 8.2 times last year's earnings for JJB Sports. One explanation for the difference in PERs is that companies with higher PERs are expected to show faster growth in earnings in the future. Burberry may appear expensive relative to JJB Sports based on historical profit figures but the differential may be justified when forecasts of earnings are made. If a PER is high, investors expect profits to rise. This does not necessarily mean that all companies with high PERs are expected to perform to a high standard, merely that they are expected to do significantly better than in the past. Few people would argue that Marks & Spencer has performed, or will perform, well in comparison with Burberry and yet it stands on the same historical PER, reflecting the market's belief that Marks & Spencer has equal growth potential from its low base as Burberry (or has lower risk). So, using the historical PER can be confusing because a company can have a high PER because it is usually a high-growth company or because it has recently had a reduction of profits from which it is expected soon to recover.

PERs are also influenced by the uncertainty of the future earnings growth. So, perhaps, Next and Kingfisher might have the same expected growth rate but the growth at Next is subject to more risk and therefore the market assigns a lower earnings multiple.

PERs over time

There have been great changes over the years in the market's view of what is a reasonable multiple of earnings to place on share prices. What is excessive in one year is acceptable in another. This is illustrated in **Exhibit 10.7**.

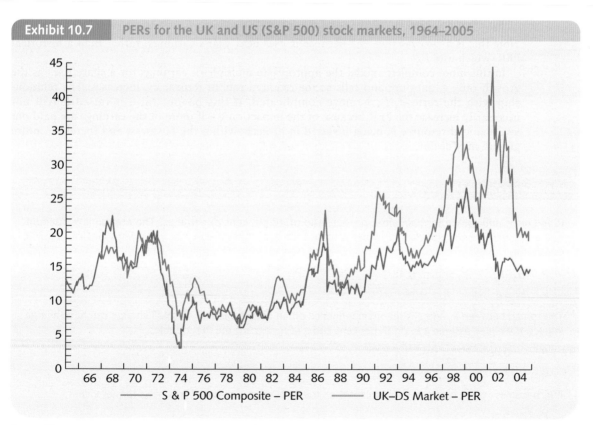

Exhibit 10.7 PERs for the UK and US (S&P 500) stock markets, 1964–2005

Source: Datastream.

The crude and the sophisticated use of the PER model

Some analysts use the historical PER (P_0/E_0), to make comparisons between firms without making explicit the considerations hidden in the analysis. They have a view of an appropriate

PER based on current prevailing PERs for other firms in the same industry. So, for example, in 2005 Barclays with a PER of 9.8 may be judged to be priced correctly relative to similar firms – HSBC had a PER of 12.9, Lloyds TSB 8.9 and Royal Bank of Scotland 10.2. Analysing through comparisons lacks intellectual rigour. First, the assumption that the 'comparable' companies are correctly priced is a bold one. It is easy to see how the market could be pulled up (or down) by its own bootstraps and lose touch with fundamental considerations by this kind of thinking. A good example of this is the rise of telecommunication shares in the 1998–2000 bubble. Second, it fails to provide a framework for the analyst to test the important implicit input assumptions – for example, the growth rate expected in earnings in each of the companies, or the difference in required rate of return given the different risk level of each. These elements are probably in the mind of the analyst, but there are benefits in making these more explicit. This can be done with the more complete PER model, which is forward looking and recognises both risk levels and growth projections.

The infinite dividend growth model can be used to develop the more complete PER model because they are both dependent on the key variables of growth, g (in dividends or earnings), and the required rate of return, k_E. The dividend growth model is:

$$P_0 = \frac{d_1}{k_E - g}$$

If both sides of the dividend growth model are divided by the expected earnings for the next year, E_1, then:

$$\frac{P_0}{E_1} = \frac{d_1/E_1}{k_E - g}$$

Note this is a *prospective PER* because it uses next year's earnings, rather than a historical PER, which uses E_0.

In this more complete model the appropriate multiple of earnings for a share rises as the growth rate, g, goes up; and falls as the required rate of return, k_E, increases. The relationship with the ratio d_1/E_1 is more complicated. If this payout ratio is raised it will not necessarily increase the PER because of the impact on g – if more of the earnings are paid out less financial resource is being invested in projects within the business, and therefore future growth may decline.

Worked example 10.6   Ridge plc

Ridge plc is anticipated to maintain a payout ratio of 48 per cent of earnings. The appropriate discount rate for a share for this risk class is 14 per cent and the expected growth rate in earnings and dividends is 6 per cent.

$$\frac{P_0}{E_1} = \frac{d_1/E_1}{k_E - g} \qquad \frac{P_0}{E_1} = \frac{0.48}{0.14 - 0.06} = 6$$

The spread between k_E and g is the main influence on an acceptable PER. A small change can have a large impact. If we now assume a k_E of 12 per cent and g of 8 per cent the PER doubles.

$$\frac{P_0}{E_1} = \frac{0.48}{0.12 - 0.08} = 12$$

If k_E becomes 16 per cent and g 4 per cent then the PER reduces to two-thirds of its former value:

$$\frac{P_0}{E_1} = \frac{0.48}{0.16 - 0.04} = 4$$

Worked example 10.7	Whizz plc

You are interested in purchasing shares in Whizz plc. This company produces high-technology products and has shown strong earnings growth for a number of years. For the past five years earnings per share have grown, on average, by 10 per cent per annum.

Despite this performance and analysts' assurances that this growth rate will continue for the foreseeable future you are put off by the exceptionally high prospective price-earnings ratio (PER) of 25.

In the light of the more complete forward-looking PER method, should you buy the shares or place your money elsewhere?

Whizz has a beta of 1.8 which may be taken as the most appropriate systematic risk adjustment to the risk premium for the average share. The risk premium for equities over government bonds has been 5 per cent over the past few decades, and the current risk-free rate of return is 7 per cent.

Whizz pays out 50 per cent of its earnings as dividends.

Answer

Stage 1 Calculate the appropriate cost of equity

$$k_E = r_f + \beta(r_m - r_f)$$
$$k_E = 7 + 1.8(5) = 16\%$$

Stage 2 Use the more complete PER model

$$\frac{P_0}{E_1} = \frac{d_1/E_1}{k_E - g} = \frac{0.5}{0.16 - 0.10} = 8.33$$

The maximum multiple of next year's earnings you would be willing to pay is 8.33. This is a third of the amount you are being asked to pay, therefore you will refuse to buy the share.

Prospective PER varies with g and k_E

If an assumption is made concerning the payout ratio, then a table can be drawn up to show how PERs vary with k_E and g – *see* Exhibit 10.8.

Exhibit 10.8	Prospective PER for various risk classes and dividend growth rates

Assumed payout ratio $= \dfrac{d_1}{E_1} = 0.5$

		Discount rate, k_E			
		8	**9**	**10**	**12**
Growth rate, g	0	6.3	5.6	5.0	4.2
	4	12.5	10.0	8.3	6.3
	5	16.7	12.5	10.0	7.1
	6	25.0	16.7	12.5	8.3
	8	–	50.0	25.0	12.5

A payout ratio of 40–50 per cent of after-tax earnings is normal for UK shares.

Exhibit 10.9	The more complete PER model makes explicit key elements hidden in the crude PER model

Crude PER P_0/E_1

The assumptions here are implicit, e.g:

1 Valuation (P_0) consists of two parts:
   (a) value of earnings assuming no growth;
   (b) value of growth in earnings.
2 No explicit recognition of the need for different required rates of return (k_E) for shares in different risk classes.
   More complete PER, P_0/E_1.

$$\frac{P_0}{E_1} = \frac{d_1/E_1}{k_E - g}$$

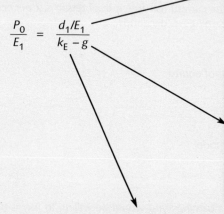

Payout ratio
Superficially P_0 relative to E_1 could be raised by increasing payout ratio. However, a lower retention ratio may reduce g to leave the overall value lower.

Growth rate, g
A complex composite of myriad influences on a firm's future growth of earnings and dividends, e.g.:
- proportion of profit retained;
- efficient use of resources;
- market opportunities;
- quality of management;
- strategy.

Required return for risk class, k_E, related to risk class of share

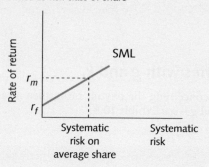

Rate of return

r_m

r_f

SML

Systematic risk on average share

Systematic risk

Note the influences on k_E: e.g. if prospective inflation rises, interest rates (probably) rise and SML shifts upwards thus increasing k_E (g will probably also rise). Also the risk profile of the firm may change with a new strategy, therefore altering k_E.

With the market propensity to focus on the future it can appear to provide strange valuations if historical relationships are examined. Take the case of Jefferson Smurfit, the Irish paper and packaging company which announced a fivefold jump in interim profits in August 1995 to IR£200.6m. The company was optimistic about its prospects, yet the consensus view on the stock exchange was that Jefferson Smurfit should be valued at a PER which was one-third of that for the average quoted firm, 6 compared with 18. The market was concerned about future earnings and was far less sanguine than the company. The Lex column of the *Financial Times* summed up the market view (*see* **Exhibit 10.10**).

The pessimism of the *Financial Times* proved to be correct as over-capacity hit the industry again by 2003 – *see* **Exhibit 10.11**.

The more complete model can help explain the apparently perverse behaviour of stock markets. If there is 'good' economic news such as a rise in industrial output or a fall in unemployment the stock market often falls. The market likes the increase in earnings that such news implies, but this effect is often outweighed by the effects of the next stage. An economy growing at a fast pace is vulnerable to rises in inflation and the market will anticipate rises in interest rates to reflect this. Thus the r_f and the rest of the SML are pushed upward. The return required on shares, k_E, will rise, and this will have a depressing effect on share prices. The article reproduced in **Exhibit 10.12** expresses this well.

Exhibit 10.10

Jefferson Smurfit

The world's paper companies have a reputation for being like the Bible's Gadarene swine which, in a fit of madness, charged down a cliff. Paper groups are enjoying sharp increases in profitability, as shown by Jefferson Smurfit's interim results yesterday; but shareholders believe the industry will bring disaster on itself through over-investment in new capacity just as demand turns down. Hence, the sector's lowly ratings: Smurfit trades on little over six times next year's projected earnings; its US and European rivals trade on multiples of about seven or eight.

But, according to Smurfit, the industry is not about to repeat the destructive behaviour of previous cycles. New capacity is coming on stream less quickly than demand is growing. Some groups, notably Smurfit itself, have put plans for new plants on the back-burner. Instead, the industry has embarked on a wave of takeovers, since it is cheaper to buy old capacity than build new plants.

Such consolidation is healthy since it should lead to a more dis-ciplined market. A further healthy development is the trend, joined by Smurfit yesterday, for share buy-backs and large dividend increases. The more cash chan-nelled into buy-backs, dividend increases and takeovers, the less will be left over for new capacity. While it is hard to believe that the industry's suicidal tendencies are permanently in check, current moves towards self-control are positive.

Source: Lex column, *Financial Times*, 24 August 1995. Reprinted with permission.

Exhibit 10.11

Paper groups see few signs of upturn

By Nicholas George in Stockholm

Stora Enso and UPM-Kymmene, two of the world's largest paper producers, yesterday reported a sharp drop in third-quarter oper-ating profits and said they saw only weak signs of economic recovery in Europe and North America.

Although the Finnish compa-nies reckoned product prices were stabilising at low levels, overca-pacity meant huge paper machines were being left to stand idle and the market was slow to accept price increases . . .

Source: *Financial Times*, 24 October 2003, p. 29. Reprinted with permission.

Exhibit 10.12

Why policymakers should take note

One issue which always mystifies the novice investor is why the financial markets always react so joyously to bad economic news. A rise in unemployment or a fall in industrial production seems to be worth a point on bonds and a jump in the stock market index.

Experienced global investors explain patiently that the key determinant of short term finan-cial market performance is interest rates. Slower growth prompts monetary authorities to lower rates; this in turn reduces corpo-rate costs, reduces the appeal of holding cash, and in the case of falling long term yields, by lower-ing the rate at which future income streams are discounted, increases the present value of shares.

Conversely, of course, faster economic growth causes govern-ments and central banks to fear higher inflation, prompting them to increase interest rates, with consequent adverse effects on share prices.

Source: Philip Coggan, 'Global Investors', *Financial Times*, 5 February 1996, p. 20. Reprinted with permission.

Valuation using cash flow

The third and most important income-based valuation method is cash flow. In business it is often said that 'cash is king'. From the shareholders' perspective the cash flow relating to a share is crucial – they hand over cash and are interested in the ability of the business to return cash to them. John Allday, head of valuation at Ernst & Young, says that discounted cash flow 'is the purest way. I would prefer to adopt it if the information is there.'[3]

The interest in cash flow is promoted by the limited usefulness of published accounts. Scepticism about the accuracy of earnings figures, given the flexibility available in their construction, prompts attempts to find a purer valuation method than PER.

The cash flow approach involves the discounting of future cash flows, that is, the cash generated by the business after investment in fixed assets and working capital to fully maintain its

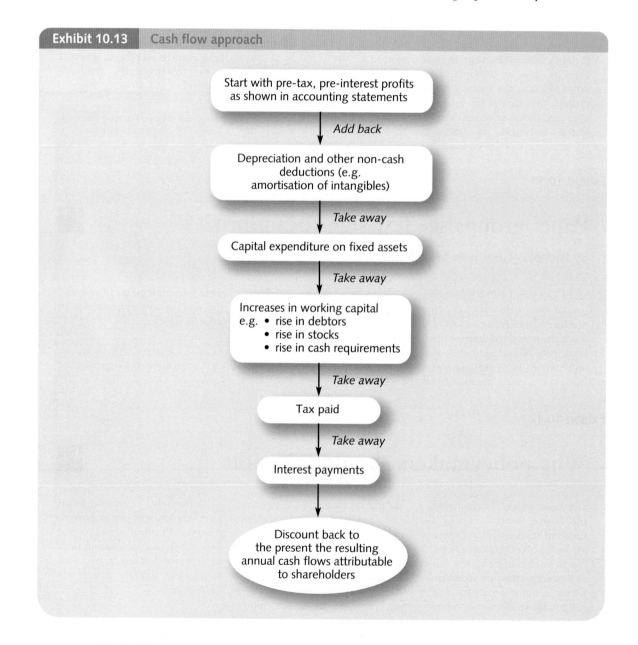

Exhibit 10.13   Cash flow approach

Start with pre-tax, pre-interest profits as shown in accounting statements

Add back

Depreciation and other non-cash deductions (e.g. amortisation of intangibles)

Take away

Capital expenditure on fixed assets

Take away

Increases in working capital
e.g. • rise in debtors
      • rise in stocks
      • rise in cash requirements

Take away

Tax paid

Take away

Interest payments

Discount back to the present the resulting annual cash flows attributable to shareholders

---

[3] Quoted by Robert Outram (1997), p. 70.

long-term competitive position and its unit volume, and to make investment in all new value-creating projects. To derive the cash flow attributable to shareholders, any interest paid in a particular period is deducted. The process of the derivation of cash flow from profit figures is shown in Exhibit 10.13.

An example of a cash flow calculation is shown in Exhibit 10.14. Note that the earnings figures for 2007 are very different from the cash flow because of the large capital investment in fixed assets – earnings are positive because only a small proportion of the cost of the new fixed assets is depreciated in that year.

Exhibit 10.14	Cash flow-based share valuation					
£m	2006	2007	2008	2009	2010	Estimated average annual cash flow for period beyond planning horizon 2011 to infinity
Forecast pre-tax, pre-interest profits	+11.0	+15.0	+15.0	+16.0	+17.0	
Add depreciation, amortisation, etc.	+1.0	+2.5	+5.5	+4.5	+4.0	
Working capital increase (–) decrease (+)	+1.0	–0.5	0.0	+1.0	+1.0	
Tax (paid in year)	–3.3	–5.0	–5.0	–5.4	–5.8	
Interest on debt capital	–0.5	–0.5	–0.5	–0.6	–0.7	
Fixed capital investment	–1.0	–16.0	0.0	–1.2	–1.8	
Cash flow	+8.2	–4.5	+15.0	+14.3	+13.7	+14.0
Cash flow per share (assuming 100m shares in issue)	8.2p	–4.5p	15p	14.3p	13.7p	14p
Discounted cash flow	$\dfrac{8.2}{1.14}$	$-\dfrac{4.5}{(1.14)^2}$	$+\dfrac{15}{(1.14)^3}$	$+\dfrac{14.3}{(1.14)^4}$	$+\dfrac{13.7}{(1.14)^5}$	$+\dfrac{14}{0.14}\times\dfrac{1}{(1.14)^5}$
$k_E = 14\%$						
Share value =	7.20	–3.5	+10.1	+8.5	+7.1	+ 51.9
						= 81.3p

AN EXCEL SPREADSHEET VERSION OF THIS CALCULATION IS AVAILABLE AT
www.pearsoned.co.uk/arnold

There is a subtle assumption in this type of analysis. This is that all annual cash flows are paid out to shareholders rather than reinvested. If all positive NPV projects have been accepted using the money allocated to additional capital expenditures on fixed assets and working capital, then to withhold further money from shareholders would be value destructive because any other projects would have negative NPVs. An alternative assumption, which amounts to the same effect in terms of share value, is that any cash flows that are retained and reinvested generate a return that merely equals the required rate of return for that risk class; thus no additional value is created. Of course, if the company knows of other positive-value projects, either at the outset or comes across them in future years, it should take them up. This will alter the numbers in the table and so a new valuation is needed.

The definition of cash flow used here (which includes a deduction of expenditure on investment in fixed and working capital to maintain long-term competitive position, unit volume, and to make investment in all new value-creating projects) is significantly different from many accountants' and analysts' definitions of cash flow. They often neglect to allow for one or more of these factors. Be careful if you are presented with alternative cash flow numbers based on a different definition of cash flow.

Valuation using owner earnings

A simplified version of cash flow analysis is owner earnings. For shares, intrinsic value is the discounted value of the owner earnings that can be taken out of a business during its remaining life. These correspond with standard cash flow analysis shown in the last section except that we calculate a sustainable level of owner earnings for a typical year (probably subject to a steady growth) rather than lumpy cash flows for the future years. Future owner earnings are determined by the strength and durability of the economic franchise (attractiveness of the industry plus competitive position of the firm in the industry), the quality of management and the financial strength of the business. In the following analysis we make use of Warren Buffett's definition of owner earnings, but with the additional factor in (c) and (d) of 'investment in all new value-creating projects'.[3] Owner earnings are defined as:

(a) reported earnings after tax; *plus*

(b) depreciation, depletion, amortisation and certain other non-cash charges; *less*

(c) the amount of expenditures for plant and machinery, etc. that a business requires to fully maintain its long-term competitive position and its unit volume and to make investment in all new value-creating projects; *less*

(d) any extra amount for working capital that is needed to maintain the firm's long-term competitive position and unit volume and to make investment in all new value-creating projects.

Thus, there are two types of investment. First, that which is needed to permit the firm to continue to maintain its existing competitive position at the current level of output. Second, investment in value-creating growth opportunities beyond the current position.

So, for example, Cotillo plc has reported earnings after tax for the most recent year of £16.3 million. In drawing up the income (profit and loss) account deductions of £7.4 million were made for depreciation and £152,000 for the amortisation of intangible assets, and £713,000 of goodwill was written off. It is estimated that an annual expenditure of £8.6 million on plant, machinery, etc. will be required for the company to maintain its long-term competitive position and unit volume. For the sake of simplicity we will assume that no further monies will be needed for extra working capital to maintain long-term competitive position and unit volume. Also, Cotillo has no new value-creating projects.

The trading record of Cotillo plc has been remarkably stable in the past and is unlikely to alter in the future. It is therefore reasonable to use the above figures for all the future years. This would result in estimated annual owner earnings of £15.965 million (*see* **Exhibit 10.15**).

Intrinsic value is determined by the owner earnings that can be taken out of the business during its remaining life. Logically the management of Cotillo should pay out the full £15.965m each year to shareholders if the managers do not have investment projects within the firm that will generate returns of 10 per cent or more because shareholders can get 10 per cent return elsewhere for the same level of risk as holding a share in Cotillo. If the managers come across another project that promises a return of exactly 10 per cent, shareholder wealth will be unchanged whether the company invests in this or chooses to ignore the project and continues with the payment of all owner earnings each year. If the management discover, in a future year, a value-creating project that will produce, say, a 15 per cent rate of return (for the same level of risk as the existing projects) then shareholders will welcome a reduction in dividends during the

---

[3] This form of analysis is set out in Arnold (2002).

Exhibit 10.15   Cotillo plc, owner earnings

		£000s
(a)	Reported earnings after tax	16,300
	Plus	
(b)	Depreciation, depletion, amortisation and other non-cash charges (7,400 + 152 + 713)	8,265
		24,565
	less	
(c) and (d)	Expenditure on plant, equipment, working capital, etc. required to maintain long-term competitive position, unit volume and investment in new projects	8,600
		15,965

The discounted value of this perpetuity = £159.65m, if we take the discount rate to be 10 per cent:

$$\text{Intrinsic value} = \frac{£15.965m}{0.10} = £159.65m$$

years of additional investment. The total value of discounted future owner earnings will rise and intrinsic value will be greater than £159.65m if such a project is undertaken.

Now let us assume that Cotillo has a series of new value-creating projects (i.e. generating returns greater than 10 per cent) in which it can invest. By investing in these projects owner earnings will rise by 5 per cent year on year (on the one hand, owner earnings are decreased by the need for additional investment under (c) and (d), but, on the other hand, reported earnings are boosted under (a), to produce a net 5 per cent growth). The intrinsic value becomes £335.26m, viz:

Next year's owner earnings = £15.965m (1 + g) = £15.965m (1 + 0.05) = £16.763m

$$\text{Intrinsic value} = \text{next year's owners earnings}/(k_E - g) = \frac{16.763}{0.10 - 0.05} = £335.26m$$

It is legitimate to discount owner earnings because they amount to that which can be paid out to shareholders after all value-creating projects are financed and payments have been made for the investment to maintain the firm's competitive position and unit volume. It would not be legitimate to discount conventional accounting earnings. These are much larger than dividends because part of these earnings is ploughed back into the business for capital items and working capital. Owner earnings are usually much smaller than conventional earnings, and are in general closer to the dividend level than the conventional earnings figure, much of which could not be paid out to shareholders without jeopardising the future income flows of the business.

Valuing unquoted shares

The principles of valuation are the same for companies with a quoted share price on an exchange and for unquoted firms. The methods of valuation discussed above in relation to shares quoted on an exchange may be employed, but there may be some additional factors to consider in relation to unquoted firms' shares.

1 *There may be a lower quality and quantity of information* The reporting statements tend to be less revealing for unquoted firms. There may also be a managerial reluctance to release information – or managers may release information selectively so as to influence price, for example, in merger discussions.

2 *These shares may be subject to more risk* Firms at an early stage in their life cycle are often more susceptible to failure than are established firms.

3 *The absence of a quotation usually means the shares are less liquid,* that is, there is a reduced ability to sell quickly without moving the price. This lack of marketability can be a severe drawback and often investors in unquoted firms, such as venture capitalists, insist on there being a plan to provide an exit route within, say, five years, perhaps through a stock market float. But that still leaves a problem for the investor within the five years, should a sale be required.

4 *Cost of tying in management* When a substantial stake is purchased in an unquoted firm, in order for the existing key managers to be encouraged to stay they may be offered financial incentives such as 'golden hand-cuffs' which may influence value. Or the previous owner-managers may agree an 'earn-out' clause in which they receive a return over the years following a sale of their shares (the returns paid to these individuals will be dependent on performance over a specified future period).

Unquoted firms' shares tend to sell at significantly lower prices than those of quoted firms. Philip Marsden, deputy managing director of corporate finance at 3i, discounts the price by anything from one-third to one-half[4] and the BDO Stoy Hayward/Acquisitions Monthly Private Company Price Index (www.bdo.co.uk) shows unquoted firms being sold at an average PER of under two-thirds that for quoted shares.

Managerial control and valuation

The value of a share can change depending on whether the purchaser gains a controlling interest in the firm. The purchase of a single share brings a stream of future dividends without any real influence over the level of those dividends. However, control of a firm by, say, purchasing 50 per cent or more of the shares, permits the possibility of changing the future operations of the firm and thus enhancing returns. A merger may allow economies of scale and other synergies, or future earnings may be boosted by the application of superior management skills. The difference in value between a share without management control and one with it helps to explain why we often witness a share price rise of 30–50 per cent in a takeover bid battle. There are two appraisals of the value of the firm, both of which may be valid depending on the assumption concerning managerial control.

The takeover of Abbey National by Santander Central Hispanó (SCH) in 2004 will provide a framework for illustrating possible use of the income flow model when managerial control is obtained. SCH claimed that it could reduce costs at Abbey National by £307m per year and add to its revenue by £75m, a total of £382m, largely as a result of the application of new technology. In the absence of a takeover the value of a share in either company is:

$$P_0 = \frac{d_1}{k_E - g}$$

This is where d_1 and g are generated by the existing structure and strategy.

Alternatively, we could examine the entire cash flow of the company (available to be paid out to shareholders after maintaining the firm's competitive position and unit volume and investing in all value-generating projects) rather than a single share.

$$V_E = \frac{C_1}{k_E - g_c}$$

where:

V_E = value of the entire share capital of the firm;
C_1 = total net cash flows at time 1 expected to continue growing at a constant rate of g_c in future years.

---

[4] *Source*: Robert Outram (1997), p. 71.

If there is a new strategy the values in the equations change:

$$P_0 = \frac{d_1^*}{k_E - g^*}$$

or, for the entire cash flow:

$$V_E = \frac{C_1^*}{k_E - g_c^*}$$

d_1^*, C_1^*, g^*, g_c^* allow for the following: synergy; cutting out costs; tax benefits; superior management; other benefits (for example, lower finance costs, greater public profile, market power) less any additional costs.

Alternatively, a marginal approach could be adopted in which C_1^*, d_1^*, g^* and g_c^* are redefined as the *additional* cash flows and growth in cash flows due to changes in ownership, and V_E is the additional equity value. For example, let us assume that the annual earnings gain of £382m is obtained in Year 1 but does not increase thereafter. Therefore $g = 0$. Let us further assume that the required rate of return on an investment of this risk class is 10 per cent. Thus the present value of the efficiency gains is:

$$V_E = \frac{C_1^*}{k_E - g_c^*} = \frac{£382m}{0.10 - 0} = £3,820m$$

We could change the assumption to gain insight into the sensitivity of the added value figure. For example, if it is anticipated that the benefits will rise each year by 2 per cent (so they are £390m in Year 2 and £397m in Year 3, etc.) then the maximum bid premium will rise:

$$V_E = \frac{C_1^*}{k_E - g_c^*} = \frac{£382m}{0.10 - 0.02} = £4,775m$$

On the other hand, the management of SCH might have been carried away with the excitement of the bid battle and the £382m quoted might have come from hype or hubris, and, in fact, the difficulties of integration produce negative incremental cash flows.

Concluding comments

There are two points about valuation worth noting. First, going through a rigorous process of valuation is more important than arriving at an answer. It is the understanding of the assumptions and an appreciation of the nature of the inputs to the process which give insight, not a single number at the end. It is the recognition of the qualitative, and even subjective, nature of key variables in a superficially quantitative analysis that leads to knowledge about values. We cannot escape the uncertainty inherent in the valuation of a share – what someone is willing to pay depends on what will happen in the future – and yet this is no excuse for rejecting the models as unrealistic and impractical. They are better than the alternatives: guessing, or merely comparing one share with another with no theoretical base to anchor either valuation. At least the models presented in this chapter have the virtue of forcing the analyst to make explicit the fundamental considerations concerning the value of a share. As the sage of finance, Warren Buffett, says, 'Valuing a business is part art and part science'.[5]

The second point leads on from the first. It makes sense to treat the various valuation methods as complementary rather than rivals. Obtain a range of values in full knowledge of the weaknesses of each approach and apply informed judgement to provide an idea of the value region.

---

[5] Quoted by Adam Smith, ' The modest billionaire', *Esquire*, October 1988, p. 103. Reprinted in Janet Lowe (1997), p. 100.

Key points and concepts

- **Knowledge of the influences on share value** is needed by: (a) managers seeking actions to increase that value; and (b) investors interested in allocating savings.

- **Share valuation requires a combination of two skills**: analytical ability using mathematical models; and good judgement.

- **The net asset value (NAV)** approach to valuation focuses on balance sheet values. These may be adjusted to reflect current market or replacement values. Advantage: 'objectivity'. Disadvantages: (a) excludes many non-quantifiable assets; (b) less objective than is often supposed.

- **Asset values are given more attention in some situations**: (a) firms in financial difficulty; (b) takeover bids; (c) when discounted income flow techniques are difficult to apply, for example in property investment companies, investment trusts, resource-based firms.

- **Income flow valuation methods** focus on the future flows attributable to the shareholder. The past is only useful to the extent that it sheds light on the future.

- **The dividend valuation models (DVM)** are based on the premise that the market value of ordinary shares represents the sum of the expected future dividend flows to infinity, discounted to a present value.

- **A constant dividend valuation model**: $P_0 = \dfrac{d_1}{k_E}$

- **The dividend growth model**: $P_0 = \dfrac{d_1}{k_E - g}$ This assumes constant growth in future dividends to infinity.

- **Problems with dividend valuation models**: (a) highly sensitive to the assumptions; (b) the quality of input data is often poor; (c) g cannot be greater than k_E, but then, on a long-term view, it would not be.

- **Factors determining the growth rate of dividends**: (a) the quantity of resources retained and reinvested; (b) the rate of return earned on retained resources; (c) the rate of return earned on existing assets.

- **How to calculate g, some pointers**: (a) Focus on the firm: (i) evaluate strategy; (ii) evaluate the management; (iii) extrapolate historical dividend growth; (iv) financial statement evaluation and ratio analysis. (b) Focus on the economy.

- **The historical price-earnings ratio (PER)** compared with PERs of peer firms is a crude method of valuation (it is also very popular):

$$\text{Historical PER} = \frac{\text{Current market price of share}}{\text{Last year's earnings per share}}$$

- **Historical PERs may be high for two reasons**: (a) the company is fast growing; (b) the company has been performing poorly, has low historic earnings, but is expected to improve. Risk is also reflected in differences between PERs.

- **The more complete PER model**: $\dfrac{P_0}{E_1} = \dfrac{d_1/E_1}{k_E - g}$

This is a prospective PER model because it focuses on next year's dividend and earnings.

- The **discounted cash flow method**:

$$P_0 = \sum_{t=1}^{t=n} \left(C/(1 + k_E)^t \right) \text{ For constant growth in cash flow: } P_0 = \frac{C_1}{k_E - g_c}$$

Key points and concepts continued

- *The owner earnings model* requires the discounting of the company's future owner earnings which are standard reported earnings after tax plus non-cash charges less the amount of expenditure on plant, machinery and working capital needed for the firm to maintain its long-term competitive position and its unit volume and to make investment in all new value-creating projects.

- Additional factors to consider when *valuing unquoted shares*: (a) lower quality and quantity of information; (b) more risk; (c) less marketable; (d) may involve 'golden hand-cuffs' or 'earn-outs'.

- *Control over a firm* permits the possibility of changing the future cash flows. Therefore a share may be more highly valued if control is achieved. *A target company could be valued on the basis of its discounted future cash flows*, e.g.:

$$V_E = \frac{C_1{}^*}{k_E - g_c{}^*}$$

- Alternatively the *incremental flows* expected to flow from the company under new management could be discounted to estimate the bid premium ($d_1{}^*$, $C_1{}^*$ and g^* are redefined to be incremental factors only):

$$P_0 = \frac{d_1{}^*}{k_E - g^*} \text{ or } V_E = \frac{C_1{}^*}{k_E - g_c{}^*}$$

Further reading

More details on the qualitative issues of valuation (e.g. management quality and strategic position) are provided in Arnold, G. (2002) and Arnold, G. (2004).

Easy to read introductions to valuation models: Lofthouse, S. (2001), Sharpe, W.F., Alexander, G.J. and Bailey, J.V. (1999).

A more mathematical approach is taken in the following: Blake, D. (2000), Damodaran, A. (1999), Damodaran, A. (2002), McKinsey and Company (Koller, Goedhart and Wessels) (2005).

Dividend growth model: Gordon, M.J. (1962), Gordon, M.J. and Shapiro, E. (1956), Solomon, E. (1963).

Lundholm and Sloan (2004) describe a valuation method with a heavy emphasis on accounting data leading to cash flow analysis.

Self-review questions

1 What are the problems of relying on NAV as a valuation method? In what circumstances is it particularly useful?

2 Why do analysts obtain historical information on a company for valuation purposes?

3 Explain why the dividend valuation model discounts all dividends to infinity and yet individual investors hold shares for a shorter period, making capital gains (and losses).

4 The dividend growth model takes the form:

$$P_0 = \frac{d_1}{k_E - g}$$

Does this mean that we are only valuing next year's dividend? Explain your answer.

5 What are the main investigatory routes you would pursue to try to establish the likely range of future growth rates for a firm?

6 What are the differences between the crude PER model and the more complete PER model?

7 Why do PERs vary over time, and between firms in the same industry?

8 What additional factors might you consider when valuing an unquoted share rather than one listed on a stock exchange?

9 Why might a share have a different value to someone who was able to exercise control over the organisation from to someone who had a small, almost powerless, stake?

Quick numerical questions

1 ElecWat is a regulated supplier of electricity and water. It is expected to pay a dividend of 24p per share per year for ever. Calculate the value of one share if a company of this risk class is required to return 10 per cent per year.

2 Shades plc has the following dividend history:

Year	Dividend per share
Recently paid	21p
Last year	19p
Two years ago	18p
Three years ago	16p
Four years ago	14p
Five years ago	12p

The rate of return required on a share of this risk class is 13 per cent. Assuming that this dividend growth rate is unsustainable and Shades will halve its historical rate in the future, what is the value of one share?

3 Tented plc has developed a new tent which has had rave reviews in the camping press. The company paid a dividend of 11p per share recently and the next is due in one year. Dividends are expected to rise by 25 per cent per year for the next five years while the company exploits its technological and marketing lead. After this period, however, the growth rate will revert to only 5 per cent per year.

The rate of return on risk-free securities is 7 per cent and the risk premium on the average share has been 5 per cent. Tented is in a systematic risk class which means that the average risk premium should be adjusted by a beta factor of 1.5.

Calculate the value of one share in Tented plc.

Questions and problems

For questions marked with an asterisk* the answers are provided in the lecturer's guide only.

1 'Valuing shares is either a simple exercise of plugging numbers into mathematical formulae or making comparisons with shares in the same sector.' Explain the problems with this statement.

2 (*Examination level*) The current share price of Blueberry plc is 205p. It recently reported earnings per share of 14p and has a policy of paying out 50 per cent of earnings in dividends each year. The earnings history of the firm is as follows:

Last reported	14p
One year ago	13p
Two years ago	12p
Three years ago	11p
Four years ago	10p
Five years ago	9p

The rate of growth in earnings and dividends shown in the past is expected to continue into the future. The risk-free rate of return is 6.5 per cent and the risk premium on the average share has been 5 per cent for decades. Blueberry is in a higher systematic risk class than the average share and therefore the risk premium needs to be adjusted by a beta factor of 1.2.

Required

a   Calculate the historical price-earnings ratio.
b   Calculate the future growth rate of dividends and earnings.
c   Calculate the required rate of return on a share of this risk class.
d   Use the more complete PER model to decide if the shares at 205p are over- or under-priced.
e   Describe and explain the problems of using the crude historic PER as an analytical tool.
f   What additional factors would you need to allow for when valuing an unquoted share rather than one listed on a stock exchange?

3 (*Examination level*) The following figures are extracted from Tes plc's Annual Report and Accounts.

Balance sheet	£m
Fixed assets	
Tangible assets	5,466
Investments	19
	5,485
Current assets	
Stocks	559
Debtors	80
Investments	54
Cash at bank and in hand	38
	731
Creditors: falling due within one year	(2,002)
Creditors: falling due after more than one year	(598)
Provisions for liabilities and charges	(22)
	3,594
Capital and reserves	
Called-up share capital	108
Share premium account	1,383
Other reserves	40
Profit and loss account	2,063
Equity shareholders' funds	3,594

Dividend and earnings history	Dividends per share	Earnings per share
16 years ago	0.82p	3.51p
Most recent	9.60p	21.9p

The average risk premium over risk-free securities is 5 per cent. The risk-free rate of return is 6.25 per cent and Tes's beta of 0.77 represents the appropriate adjustment to the average risk premium.

Required

a Calculate a revised net asset value (NAV) for the Tes group assuming the following:
   - buildings are overvalued in the balance sheet by £100m;
   - 20 per cent of the debtors figure will never be collected;
   - the stock figure includes £30m of unsaleable stock;
   - 'Current investments' now have a market value of £205m.
b The total market capitalisation of Tes at the present time is £8bn. Provide some possible reasons for the great difference between the value that the market placed on Tes and the NAV.
c For what type of company and in what circumstances does NAV provide a good estimate of value?
d If you assume that the dividend growth rate over the past 16 years is unsustainable, and that in the future the rate of growth will average half the rate of the past, at what would you value one share using the dividend growth model?
e Give some potential explanatory reasons for the difference between the value given in (d) and the value placed on a share in the London Stock Market of 355p.
f Given the answer in (d) for share price, what is the prospective price-earnings ratio (PER) if future earnings grow at the same rate as future dividends?
g What would be the PER if, (i) $k = 14$, $g = 12$; (ii) $k = 15$, $g = 11$ and next year's dividend and earnings are the same as calculated in (d) and (f) and the payout ratio is the same for all future years?
h If you assumed for the sake of simplicity that all the long-term debt in the balance sheet is a debenture issued six years ago which is due for redemption three years from now at par value of £100, what is the weighted average cost of capital for this firm?

Other information

- The debenture pays a coupon of 9 per cent on par value.
- The coupons are payable annually – the next is due in 12 months.
- The debenture is currently trading at 105.50.
- The balance sheet shows the nominal value, not the market value.
- Tax is payable at 30 per cent (relevant to question (h) only).
- Use the capitalisation figure given in (b) for the equity weight.
- You can ignore short-term debt.

4* (*Examination level*) You have been asked to carry out a valuation of Dela plc, a listed company on the main London market.

At the last year-end Dela's summarised balance sheet is as shown in Table 1.

Table 1 Dela, 1 May 2006

		£m
Fixed assets		300
Current assets		
Stocks	70	
Debtors	120	
Cash at bank	90	
		280
Liabilities		
Creditors: trade creditors falling due within one year		(400)
Creditors falling due after more than one year		(50)
Shareholders' funds (Net assets)		130

Table 2 Dela plc trading history

Year-end	Earnings per share (pence)	Dividend per share (pence)
2006	20	10
2005	18	9.5
2004	17	9
2003	16	8
2002	13	7
2001	12	6
2000	10	5.5
1999	10	5

Datastream has calculated a beta for Dela of 1.2 and this may be used as the appropriate adjustment to the risk premium on the average share. The risk-free rate of return on UK Treasury bills is 6.5 per cent and the latest study shows an annual equity risk premium over the yield on UK government bonds of 5 per cent for the period 1900–2005.

The impressive average annual growth in Dela's earnings and dividends over the last few years is likely to persist.

Additional information

– You have obtained an independent valuation of Dela's fixed assets at £350m.
– You believe that Dela has overstated the value of stocks by £30m and one-quarter of its debtors are likely to be uncollectable.
– There have been no new issues of shares in the past eight years.
– Dela has 1,000 million shares in issue.

Required

a Value Dela using the net asset value (NAV) method.
b Briefly explain why balance sheets generally have limited usefulness for estimating the value of a firm.
c Briefly describe two circumstances where balance sheet net asset values become very important for corporate valuation.
d Value one of Dela's shares using the dividend valuation model. (Assume the dividend of 10p has just been paid and the next dividend is due in one year.)
e What is the prospective price to earnings ratio (P/E ratio) given the share price in (d)?
f Calculate a weighted average cost of capital given that the balance sheet entry 'Creditors falling due after more than one year' consists entirely of the nominal value of a debenture issue and this is the only form of debt you need to consider for a WACC calculation. The debenture will be redeemed at par in three years, it carries an annual coupon of 8 per cent (the next payment will be in one year) and it is presently trading in the market at 96.50 per £100 nominal. The total nominal value is £50m.

    Assume for the purpose of (f) that the shares are valued at your valuation in (d) and that Dela is taxed at a rate of 30 per cent.

Assignments

1 Estimate the value of a share in your company (or one you know well) using the following approaches: (i) net asset value; (ii) dividend valuation model; (iii) crude price-earnings ratio – comparing with peer firms; (iv) more complete price-earnings ratio model; (v) cash flow model; (vi) owner earnings model. In a report make clear your awareness of the sensitivity of the results to your assumptions.

2 If your company has recently acquired a business or is considering such a purchase obtain as much data as you can to calculate a possible bargain range. The upper boundary of this is fixed by the value of the business to your firm, given the implementation of a plan to change the future cash flows. The lower boundary is fixed by the value to the present owner.

Visit www.pearsoned.co.uk/arnold to get access to Gradetracker diagnostic tests, Podcasts, Excel Spreadsheet Solutions, FT articles, a Flashcard revision tool, Weblinks, a searchable Glossary and more.

CHAPTER 11

Capital structure

LEARNING OUTCOMES

The level of debt relative to ordinary share capital is, for most firms, of secondary consideration behind strategic and operational decisions. However, if wealth can be increased by getting this decision right, managers need to understand the key influences. By the end of the chapter the reader should be able to:

■ discuss the effect of gearing, and differentiate business and financial risk;

■ describe the underlying assumptions, rationale and conclusions of Modigliani and Miller's models, in worlds with and without tax;

■ explain the relevance of some important, but often non-quantifiable, influences on the optimal gearing level question.

Introduction

Someone has to decide what is an appropriate level of borrowing for a firm given its equity capital base. The fundamental question of this chapter is: if future cash flows generated by the business are assumed to be constant, can managers simply by altering the proportion of debt in the total capital structure increase shareholder value? If this is possible then surely managers have a duty to move the firm towards the optimal debt proportion.

The traditional view was that it would be beneficial to increase gearing from a low (or zero) level because the firm would then be financed to a greater extent by cheaper borrowed funds, therefore the weighted average cost of capital (WACC) would fall. The discounting of future cash flows at this lower WACC produces a higher present value and so shareholder wealth is enhanced. However, as debt levels rise the firm's earnings attributable to shareholders become increasingly volatile due to the requirement to pay large amounts of interest prior to dividends. Eventually the burden of a large annual interest bill can lead the firm to become financially distressed and, in extreme circumstances, to be liquidated. So the traditional answer to the question of whether there was an optimal gearing level was 'yes'. If the gearing level is too low, shareholder value opportunities are forgone by not substituting 'cheap' debt for equity. If it is too high the additional risk leads to a loss in shareholder value through a higher discount rate being applied to the future cash flows attributable to ordinary shareholders. This is because of the higher risk and, at very high gearing, the penalty of complete business failure becomes much more of a possibility.

Then, in the 1950s, a theory was developed by Franco Modigliani and Merton Miller (1958) which said that it did not matter whether the firm had a gearing level of 90 per cent debt or 2 per cent debt – the overall value of the firm is constant and shareholder wealth cannot be enhanced by altering the debt to equity ratio. This conclusion was based on some major assumptions and required the firm to operate in a perfect world of perfect knowledge, a world in which individual shareholders can borrow and lend at the same rate as giant corporations, and in which taxation and cost of financial distress do not exist.

Later Modigliani and Miller (MM) modified the no-taxation assumption. This led to a different conclusion: the best gearing level for a firm interested in shareholder wealth maximisation is, generally, as high as possible. This was an astonishing result; it means that a company financed with £99m of debt and £1m of equity serves its shareholders better than one funded by £50m of debt and £50m of equity. Within academic circles thousands of hours of thinking and research time have been spent over the past four decades building on the MM foundations, and millions of hours of undergraduates' and postgraduates' precious time have been spent learning the intricacies of the algebraic proofs lying behind MM conclusions. Going through this process has its virtues: the models provide a systematic framework for evaluating the capital structure question and can lead to some rigorous thought within the confines of the models.

However, this chapter will not dwell on algebra (the interested reader is referred to some more advanced reading at the end of the chapter). Emphasis will be given to explanations which have been advanced to explain actual gearing levels. A conclusion will be drawn which fits neither the MM first conclusion, that there is not an optimal gearing level, nor their modified theory with taxes, in which there is an optimum at the most extreme level of debt.

A fundamental question for any chapter of this book is: does this subject have any relevance to the real world? Perhaps **Case Study 11.1** will help. As the case study shows, senior managers frequently consider the balance between debt and ordinary share capital in a company's financial make-up.

Case study 11.1   The balance between debt and ordinary share capital

Philip Green, the retail billionaire, instructed Arcadia (Topshop, Wallis, Burton, etc.) to pay the biggest single dividend payment ever in the UK in 2005. The company paid £1.2bn to Tina, Philip Green's wife who owns 92% of the shares. The payment was 'merely an efficient use of the balance sheet' according to Mr Green.[1]

---

[1] Quoted in Sophy Buckley, 'Marriage pays dividends for Mrs Green', *Financial Times*, 21 October 2005, p. 1.

Whitbread (Beefeater, Pizza Hut, Premier Travel Inn, etc.) had already returned £400m to shareholders after disposing of Marriott UK when in 2005 it considered increasing its debt burden 'as part of a review of its capital structure'. According to the *FT* it was exploring ways of making its balance sheet more efficient: 'We've had a fairly conservative approach to the balance sheet', said Alan Parker, chief executive. 'We will be looking at a range of options to increase shareholder value'.[2] Similarly, David Finch, Chief Financial Officer of O$_2$, conceded that the company was 'not optimally financed at the moment' which could result in more cash being returned to shareholders.[3]

In 2001 BT management was in serious trouble. The company had accumulated debt of over £30bn following a worldwide acquisition spree and infrastructure investment. The net assets of the company were roughly half the debt level, at £14bn. City institutions were desperately concerned by the high level of debt. Sir Peter Bonfield, the chief executive, recognised that he had allowed the debt to rise too high. 'We identified the need to introduce new equity capital into the business to support the reduction in the unsustainable level of group debt'.[4] The company raised £5.9bn through a rights issue, sold off property, slashed investment and sold stakes in telecom businesses around the world. It also stopped paying a dividend.

In 2004 Marks & Spencer finally got around to implementing its long-talked-about buy-back plans. It bought 28 per cent of its share capital for £2.3 billion from shareholders, in 'a move to re-engineer the balance sheet after years of underperformance'. The retailer said: 'We think we are getting a more efficient balance sheet by increasing debt and reducing equity'.[5]

Clearly there is a perception among directors, analysts and financial commentators that there is an optimal gearing level, or at least a range of gearing levels which help to maximise shareholder wealth and this lies at neither extreme of the spectrum.

Debt finance is cheaper and riskier (for the company)

Financing a business through borrowing is cheaper than using equity. This is, first, because lenders require a lower rate of return than ordinary shareholders. Debt financial securities present a lower risk than shares for the finance providers because they have prior claims on annual income and in liquidation. In addition, security is often provided and covenants imposed.

A profitable business effectively pays less for debt capital than equity for another reason: the debt interest can be offset against pre-tax profits before the calculation of the corporation tax bill, thus reducing the tax paid.

Third, issuing and transaction costs associated with raising and servicing debt are generally less than for ordinary shares.

There are some valuable benefits from financing a firm with debt. So why do firms tend to avoid very high gearing levels? One reason is financial distress risk. This could be induced by the requirement to pay interest regardless of the cash flow of the business. If the firm hits a rough patch in its business activities it may have trouble paying its bondholders, bankers and other creditors their entitlement. **Exhibit 11.1** shows that, as gearing increases, the risk of financial failure grows.

Note the crucial assumption in Exhibit 11.1 – if the returns to equity are constant, or do not rise much, the overall cost of finance declines. This is obviously unrealistic because as the risk of financial distress rises ordinary shareholders are likely to demand higher returns. This is an important issue and we will return to it after a discussion of some basic concepts about gearing.

[2] Quoted in Matthew Garrahan, 'Whitbread looks to extend debt', *Financial Times*, 15 June 2005.
[3] Quoted in Mark Odell, 'O$_2$ review could return more cash to investors', *Financial Times*, 21 July 2005, p. 21.
[4] BT Annual Report 2001.
[5] 'M&S gives details of cash return', by Susanna Voyle, *Financial Times*, 24 January 2002.

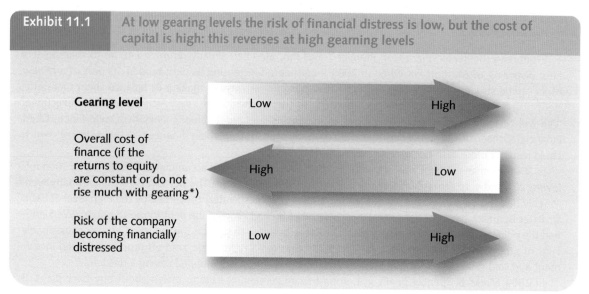

| Exhibit 11.1 | At low gearing levels the risk of financial distress is low, but the cost of capital is high: this reverses at high gearing levels |

Note: *This assumption is considered in the text.

What do we mean by 'gearing'?

We need to avoid some confusion which is possible when using the word 'gearing'. First, we should make a distinction between operating gearing and financial gearing.

Operating gearing refers to the extent to which the firm's total costs are fixed. The profits of firms with high operating gearing, such as car or steel manufacturers, are very sensitive to changes in the sales level. They have high break-even points (the turnover level at which profits are achieved) but when this level is breached a large proportion of any additional sales revenue turns into profit because of the relatively low variable costs.

Financial gearing is the focus of this chapter and concerns the proportion of debt in the capital structure. Net income to shareholders in firms with high financial gearing is more sensitive to changes in operating profits.

Secondly, the terms gearing and leverage are used interchangeably by most practitioners, although leverage is used more in America.

Thirdly, there are many different ways of calculating financial gearing (to be called simply 'gearing' throughout this chapter). Financial analysts, the press and corporate managers usually measure gearing by reference to balance sheet (book) figures, but it is important to recognise that much of finance theory concentrates on the market values of debt and equity. Both book and market approaches are useful, depending on the purpose of the analysis.

There are two ways of putting into perspective the levels of debt that a firm carries. *Capital gearing* focuses on the extent to which a firm's total capital is in the form of debt. *Income gearing* is concerned with the proportion of the annual income stream (that is, the pre-interest profits) which is devoted to the prior claims of debtholders, in other words, what proportion of profits is taken by interest charges.

Capital gearing

There are alternative measures of the extent to which the capital structure consists of debt. One popular approach is the ratio of long-term debt to shareholders' funds (the debt to equity ratio). The long-term debt is usually taken as the balance sheet item 'amounts falling due after more than one year', and shareholders' funds is the net asset (or net worth) figure in the balance sheet.

$$\text{Capital gearing (1)} = \frac{\text{Long-term debt}}{\text{Shareholders' funds}}$$

This ratio is of interest because it may give some indication of the firm's ability to sell assets to repay debts. For example, if the ratio stood at 0.3, or 30 per cent, lenders and shareholders might feel relatively comfortable as there would be, apparently, over three times as many net (that is after paying off liabilities) assets as long-term debt. So, if the worst came to the worst, the company could sell assets to satisfy its long-term lenders.

There is a major problem with relying on this measure of gearing. The book value of assets can be quite different from the saleable value. This may be because the assets have been recorded at historical purchase value (perhaps less depreciation) and have not been revalued over time. It may also be due to the fact that companies forced to sell assets to satisfy creditors often have to do so at greatly reduced prices if they are in a hurry.[6]

Second, this measure of gearing can have a range of values from zero to infinity and this makes inter-firm comparisons difficult. The measure shown below puts gearing within a range of zero to 100 per cent as debt is expressed as a fraction of all long-term capital.[7]

$$\text{Capital gearing (2)} = \frac{\text{Long-term debt}}{\text{Long-term debt + Shareholders' funds}}$$

These ratios could be further modified by the inclusion of 'provisions', that is, sums set aside in the accounts for anticipated loss or expenditure, for example a bad debt or costs of merger integration. Deferred tax, likewise, may be included as an expected future liability.

The third capital gearing measure, in addition to allowing for long-term debt, includes short-term borrowing.

$$\text{Capital gearing (3)} = \frac{\text{All borrowing}}{\text{All borrowing + Shareholders' funds}}$$

Many firms rely on overdraft facilities and other short-term borrowing, for example commercial bills. Technically these are classified as short term. In reality many firms use the overdraft and other short-term borrowing as a long-term source of funds. Furthermore, if we are concerned about the potential for financial distress, then we must recognise that an inability to repay an overdraft can be just as serious as an inability to service a long-term bond.

To add sophistication to capital gearing analysis it is often necessary to take into account any cash (or marketable securities) holdings in the firm. These can be used to offset the threat that debt poses.

A measure of gearing which is gaining prominence is the ratio of debt to the total market value of the firm's equity.

$$\text{Capital gearing (4)} = \frac{\text{Long-term debt}}{\text{Total market capitalisation}}$$

This has the advantage of being closer to the market-value-based gearing measures (assuming book long-term debt is similar to the market value of the debt). It gives some indication of the relative share of the company's total value belonging to debtholders and shareholders.

It is plain that there is a rich variety of capital gearing measures and it is important to know which measure people are using – it can be very easy to find yourself talking at cross-purposes.

Income gearing

The capital gearing measures rely on the appropriate valuation of net assets either in the balance sheet or in a revaluation exercise. This is a notoriously difficult task to complete with any great certainty. Try valuing a machine on a factory floor, or a crate of raw material. Also the capital gearing measures focus on a worst-case scenario: 'What could we sell the business assets for if we had to, in order to pay creditors?'

It may be wrong to focus exclusively on assets when trying to judge a company's ability to repay debts. Take the example of a successful advertising agency. It may not have any saleable

---

[6] These problems also apply to capital gearing measures (2) and (3)

[7] To make this discussion easier to follow it will be assumed that there are only two types of finance: debt and ordinary shares. However, the introduction of other types of finance does not fundamentally alter the analysis.

assets at all, apart from a few desks and chairs, and yet it may be able to borrow hundreds of millions of pounds because it has the ability to generate cash to make interest payments. Thus, quite often, a more appropriate measure of gearing is one concerned with the level of a firm's income relative to its interest commitments:

$$\text{Interest cover} = \frac{\text{Profit before interest and tax}}{\text{Interest charges}}$$

The lower the interest cover ratio the greater the chance of interest payment default and liquidation. The inverse of interest cover measures the proportion of profits paid out in interest – this is called income gearing.

The Lex column of the *Financial Times* commented on the most appropriate measures of gearing for modern industry (*see* Exhibit 11.2).

Exhibit 11.2

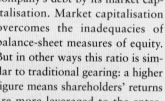

Goodbye gearing

Investors have long used balance-sheet gearing as the main yardstick of a company's indebtedness. In the past, this was appropriate as the balance sheet offered a reasonable guide to a company's value. But balance sheets are now scarcely relevant as a measure of corporate worth. As the world economy shifts from manufacturing to services, value is increasingly the product of human brains. Companies like Microsoft, Disney and Marks & Spencer owe their success to intellectual property, media creations and brands. Unlike physical property or machines, such products of the mind do not typically appear on balance sheets. Even in manufacturing, inflation and arbitrary depreciation policies make balance sheets a misleading guide to value.

If balance-sheet gearing is no longer useful, what yardsticks should be employed instead? One option is to look at interest cover – either operating profit or operating cash flow divided by interest payments. Such ratios measure how easy it is for companies to service their debts. Different levels of interest cover are appropriate for different types of company; clearly, cyclicals need higher ratios than utilities.

Another option is to divide a company's debt by its market capitalisation. Market capitalisation overcomes the inadequacies of balance-sheet measures of equity. But in other ways this ratio is similar to traditional gearing: a higher figure means shareholders' returns are more leveraged to the enterprise's underlying performance and so more risky. In future, debt/market capitalisation and interest cover will be Lex's preferred yardsticks.

Source: *Financial Times*, 9 October 1995. Reprinted with permission.

The effect of gearing

The introduction of interest-bearing debt 'gears up' the returns to shareholders. Compared with those of the ungeared firm, the geared firm's returns to its owners are subject to greater variation than underlying earnings. If operating profits are high, the geared firm's shareholders will experience a more than proportional boost in their returns compared with the ungeared firm's shareholders. On the other hand, if operating profits turn out to be low, the geared firm's shareholders will find their returns declining to an exaggerated extent.

The effect of gearing can best be explained through an example. Harby plc is shortly to be established. The prospective directors are considering three different capital structures, which will all result in £10m of capital being raised.

1 All equity – 10 million shares sold at a nominal value of £1.

2 £3m debt (carrying 10 per cent interest) and £7m equity.

3 £5m debt (carrying 10 per cent interest) and £5m equity.

To simplify their analysis the directors have assigned probabilities to three potential future performance levels (*see* Exhibit 11.3).

Exhibit 11.3   Probabilities of performance levels and the effect of gearing

Customer response to firm's products	Income before interest*	Probability (%)
Modest success	£0.5m	20
Good response	£3.0m	60
Run-away success	£4.0m	20

*Taxes are to be ignored.

The effect of gearing

Customer response	Modest	Good	Run-away
Earnings before interest	£0.5m	£3.0m	£4.0m
All-equity structure			
Debt interest at 10%	0.0	0.0	0.0
Earnings available for shareholders	£0.5m	£3.0m	£4.0m
Return on shares	$\dfrac{£0.5m}{£10m}=5\%$	$\dfrac{£3.0m}{£10m}=30\%$	$\dfrac{£4.0m}{£10m}=40\%$
30% gearing (£3m debt, £7m equity)			
Debt interest at 10%	£0.3m	£0.3m	£0.3m
Earnings available for shareholders	£0.2m	£2.7m	£3.7m
Return on shares	$\dfrac{£0.5m}{£10m}=5\%$	$\dfrac{£3.0m}{£10m}=30\%$	$\dfrac{£4.0m}{£10m}=40\%$
50% gearing (£5m debt, £5m equity)			
Debt interest at 10%	£0.5m	£0.5m	£0.5m
Earnings available for shareholders	0.0	£2.5m	£3.5m
Return on shares	$\dfrac{£0.0m}{£5m}=0\%$	$\dfrac{£2.5m}{£5m}=50\%$	$\dfrac{£3.5m}{£5m}=70\%$

We can now examine what will happen to shareholder returns for each of the gearing levels.

Note, in Exhibit 11.3, what happens as gearing increases: the changes in earnings attributable to shareholders is magnified. For example, when earnings before interest rise by 500 per cent from £0.5m to £3.0m the returns on the 30 per cent geared structure rises by 1,200 per cent from 3 per cent to 39 per cent. This magnification effect works in both positive and negative directions – if earnings before interest are only £0.5m the all-equity structure gives shareholders some return, but with the 50 per cent geared firm they will receive nothing. Harby's shareholders would be taking a substantial risk that they would have no profits if they opted for a high level of gearing.

The data for the ungeared and the 50 per cent geared capital structure are displayed in Exhibit 11.4. The direction of the effect of gearing depends on the level of earnings before interest. If this is greater than £1m, the return to shareholders is increased by gearing. If it is less than £1m, the return is reduced by gearing. Note that the return on the firm's overall assets at this pivot point is 10 per cent (£1m/£10m). If a return of more than 10 per cent on assets is achieved, shareholders' returns are enhanced by gearing.

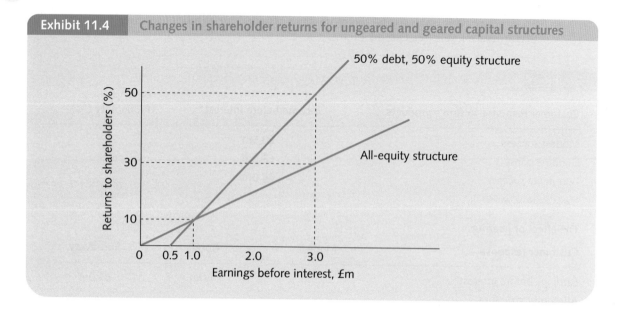

Exhibit 11.4 Changes in shareholder returns for ungeared and geared capital structures

Expected returns and standard deviations for Harby plc

It makes intuitive sense to say that year-to-year variations in income will be greater for a more highly geared firm as it experiences good and bad trading years. We can be more precise for Harby if we calculate the standard deviation of the return to shareholders under the three gearing levels (*see* Exhibit 11.5).

As Exhibit 11.5 indicates, as the gearing levels rise for Harby, the expected return for shareholders also rises (from 27 per cent to 34.6 per cent to 44 per cent), but this is accompanied by a rising level of risk. Management need to weigh up the relative importance of the 'good' resulting from the increase in expected returns and the 'bad' from the wider dispersion of returns attributable to shareholders.

Business risk and financial risk

Business risk is the variability of the firm's operating income, that is, the income before interest. In the case of Harby this is found by examining the dispersion of returns for the all-equity capital structure. This dispersion is caused purely by business-related factors, such as the characteristics of the industry and the competitive advantage possessed by the firm within that industry. This risk will be influenced by factors such as the variability of sales volumes or prices over the business cycle, the variability of input costs, the degree of market power and the level of growth.

The business risk of a monopoly supplier of electricity, gas or water is likely to be significantly less than that for, say, an entrepreneurial company trying to gain a toehold in the internet optical switch market. The range of possible demand levels and prices is likely to be less for the utilities than for the high-tech firm. Business risk is determined by general business and economic conditions and is not related to the firm's financial structure.

Financial risk is the additional variability in returns to shareholders that arises because the financial structure contains debt. An increasing proportion of debt raises the firm's fixed financial costs and the standard deviation of returns to shareholders. At high gearing levels there is an increased probability of the firm not only failing to make a return to shareholders, but also failing to meet the interest cost obligation, and thus raising the likelihood of insolvency.

Firms with low business risk are in a position to take on higher levels of financial risk (more debt) than those with high business risk. The increased expected return more than compensates for the higher variability resulting in climbing share prices.

Exhibit 11.5	Expected returns and standard deviations of return to shareholders in Harby plc

All equity

Return, R (%)	Probability, p_i	Return × probability	
5	0.2	1	
30	0.6	18	
40	0.2	8	
		27	Expected return, $\bar{R}$ = 27%

Return, R (%)	Expected return, $\bar{R}$	Probability	$(\bar{R} - R)^2 p_i$
5	27	0.2	96.8
30	27	0.6	5.4
40	27	0.2	33.8
			Variance σ^2 = 136.0
			Standard deviation σ = 11.7%

30% gearing

Return, R (%)	Probability, p_i	Return × probability	
3	0.2	0.6	
39	0.6	23.4	
53	0.2	10.6	
		34.6	Expected return, $\bar{R}$ = 34.6%

Return, R (%)	Expected return, $\bar{R}$	Probability	$(\bar{R} - R)^2 p_i$
3	34.6	0.2	199.71
39	34.6	0.6	11.62
53	34.6	0.2	67.71
			Variance σ^2 = 279.04
			Standard deviation σ = 16.7%

50% gearing

Return, R (%)	Probability, p_i	Return × probability	
0	0.2	0	
50	0.6	30	
70	0.2	14	
		44	Expected return, $\bar{R}$ = 44%

Return, R (%)	Expected return, $\bar{R}$	Probability	$(\bar{R} - R)^2 p_i$
0	44	0.2	387.2
50	44	0.6	21.6
70	44	0.2	135.2
			Variance σ^2 = 544.0
			Standard deviation σ = 23.3%

It is appropriate at this point to remember that, until now, we have focused primarily on accounting values for debt and equity – book debt, net assets in the balance sheet, etc. In the models which follow the correct bases of analysis are the market values of debt and equity. This is because we are interested in the effect of the capital structure decision on share values in the marketplace, not on accounting entries.

The value of the firm and the cost of capital

Recall from Chapters 8 and 10 that the value of the firm is calculated by estimating its future cash flows and then discounting these at the cost of capital. For the sake of simplification we will assume, in the following theoretical discussion, that the future cash flows are constant and perpetual (at annual intervals to an infinite horizon) and thus the value of the firm is:

$$V = \frac{C_1}{\text{WACC}}$$

where:

V = value of the firm
C_1 = cash flows to be received one year hence
WACC = the weighted average cost of capital

The same logic can be applied to cash flows which are increasing at a constant rate, or which vary in an irregular fashion. The crucial point is this: if the cash flows are assumed to be at a set level then the value of the firm depends on the rate used to discount those cash flows. If the cost of capital is lowered the value of the firm is raised.

What is meant by the value of the firm, V, is the combination of the market value of equity capital, V_E (total capitalisation of ordinary shares), plus the market value of debt capital, V_D.

$$V = V_E + V_D$$

Does the cost of capital (WACC) decrease with higher debt levels?

The question of whether the cost of capital decreases with higher debt levels is obviously crucial to the capital structure debate. If the WACC is diminished by increasing the proportion of debt in the financial structure of the firm then company value will rise and shareholders' wealth will increase.

The firm's cost of capital depends on both the return needed to satisfy the ordinary shareholders given their opportunity cost of capital, k_E, and the return needed to satisfy lenders given their opportunity cost of capital k_D. (We will ignore taxes for now.)

$$\text{WACC} = k_E W_E + k_D W_D$$

where:

W_E = proportion of equity finance to total finance;
W_D = proportion of debt finance to total finance.

If some numbers are now put into this equation, conclusions might be possible about the optimal debt level and therefore the value of the firm. If it is assumed that the cost of equity capital is 20 per cent, the cost of debt capital is 10 per cent, and the equity and debt weights are both 50 per cent, the overall cost of capital is 15 per cent.

$$\text{WACC} = (20\% \times 0.5) + (10\% \times 0.5) = 15\%$$

If it is further assumed that the firm is expected to generate a perpetual annual cash flow of £1m, then the total value of the firm is:

$$V = \frac{C_1}{\text{WACC}} = \frac{£1m}{0.15} = £6.667m$$

This whole area of finance revolves around what happens next, that is, when the proportion of debt is increased. So, let us assume that the debt ratio is increased to 70 per cent through the substitution of debt for equity. We will consider four possible consequences.

Scenario 1: The cost of equity capital remains at 20 per cent

If shareholders remain content with a 20 per cent return, the WACC decreases:

$$\text{WACC} = k_E \, W_E + k_D \, W_D$$
$$\text{WACC} = (20\% \times 0.3) + (10\% \times 0.7) = 13\%$$

If the cost of capital decreases, the value of the firm (and shareholder wealth) increases:

$$V = \frac{C_1}{\text{WACC}} - \frac{£1m}{0.13} = £7.69m$$

Under this scenario the debt proportion could be increased until it was virtually 100 per cent of the capital. The WACC would then approach 10 per cent (assuming that the cost of debt capital remains at 10 per cent).

Scenario 2: The cost of equity capital rises due to the increased financial risk to exactly offset the effect of the lower cost of debt

In this case the WACC and the firm's value remain constant.

$$\text{WACC} = k_E \, W_E + k_D \, W_D$$
$$\text{WACC} = (26.67\% \times 0.3) + (10\% \times 0.7) = 15\%$$

Scenario 3: The cost of equity capital rises, but this does not completely offset all the benefits of the lower cost of debt capital

Let us assume that equity holders demand a return of 22 per cent at a 70 per cent gearing level:

$$\text{WACC} = k_E \, W_E + k_D \, W_D$$
$$\text{WACC} = (22\% \times 0.3) + (10\% \times 0.7) = 13.6\%$$

In this case the firm, by increasing the proportion of its finance which is in the form of debt, manages to reduce the overall cost of capital and thus to increase the value of the firm and shareholder wealth.

$$V = \frac{C_1}{\text{WACC}} = \frac{£1m}{0.136} = £7.35m$$

Scenario 4: The cost of equity rises to more than offset the effect of the lower cost of debt

Here the equity holders are demanding much higher returns as compensation for the additional volatility and risk of liquidation. Let us assume that shareholders require a return of 40 per cent.

$$\text{WACC} = k_E \, W_E + k_D \, W_D$$
$$\text{WACC} = (40\% \times 0.3) + (10\% \times 0.7) = 19\%$$

$$V = \frac{C_1}{\text{WACC}} = \frac{£1\text{m}}{0.19} = £5.26\text{m}$$

The first of the four scenarios is pretty unrealistic. If the amount of debt that a firm has to service is increased, the riskiness of the shares will presumably rise and therefore the shareholders will demand a higher return. Thus, we are left with the three other scenarios. It is around these three possibilities that the capital structure debate rumbles.

Modigliani and Miller's argument in a world with no taxes

The capital structure decision was first tackled in a rigorous theoretical analysis by the financial economists Modigliani and Miller in 1958. MM created a simplified model of the world by making some assumptions. Given these assumptions they concluded that the value of a firm remains constant regardless of the debt level. As the proportion of debt is increased, the cost of equity will rise just enough to leave the WACC constant. If the WACC is constant then the only factor which can influence the value of the firm is its cash flow generated from operations. Capital structure is irrelevant. Thus, according to MM, firms can only increase the wealth of shareholders by making good investment decisions. This brings us to MM's first proposition.

Proposition 1

The total market value of any company is independent of its capital structure

The total market value of the firm is the net present value of the income stream. For a firm with a constant perpetual income stream:

$$V = \frac{C_1}{\text{WACC}}$$

The WACC is constant because the cost of equity capital rises to exactly offset the effect of cheaper debt and therefore shareholder wealth is neither enhanced nor destroyed by changing the gearing level.

The assumptions

Before going any further, some of the assumptions upon which this conclusion is reached need to be mentioned.

1 There is no taxation.
2 There are perfect capital markets, with perfect information available to all economic agents and no transaction costs.
3 There are no costs of financial distress and liquidation (if a firm is liquidated, shareholders will receive the same as the market value of their shares prior to liquidation).
4 Firms can be classified into distinct risk classes.
5 Individuals can borrow as cheaply as corporations.

Clearly, there are problems relating some of these assumptions to the world in which we live. For now, it is necessary to suspend disbelief so that the consequences of the MM model can be demonstrated. Many of the assumptions will be modified later in the chapter.

An example to illustrate the MM no-tax capital structure argument

In the following example it is assumed that the WACC remains constant at 15 per cent regardless of the debt to equity ratio.

A company is shortly to be formed, called Pivot plc. It needs £1m capital to buy machines, plant and buildings. The business generated by the investment has a given systematic risk and the required return on that level of systematic risk for an all-equity firm is 15 per cent.

The expected annual cash flow is a constant £150,000 in perpetuity. This cash flow will be paid out each year to the suppliers of capital. The prospective directors are considering three different finance structures.

- **Structure 1** All-equity (1,000,000 shares selling at £1 each).
- **Structure 2** £500,000 of debt capital giving a return of 10 per cent per annum. Plus £500,000 of equity capital (500,000 shares at £1 each).
- **Structure 3** £700,000 of debt capital giving a return of 10 per cent per annum. Plus £300,000 of equity capital (300,000 shares at £1 each).

Exhibit 11.6 shows that the returns to equity holders, in this MM world with no tax, rise as gearing increases so as to leave the WACC and the total value of the company constant. Investors purchasing a share receive higher returns per share for a more highly geared firm but the discount rate also rises because of the greater risk, to leave the value of each share at £1.

Exhibit 11.6	Pivot plc capital structure and returns to shareholders		
	Structure 1 **£**	**Structure 2** **£**	**Structure 3** **£**
Annual cash flows	150,000	150,000	150,000
less interest payments	0	50,000	70,000
Dividend payments	150,000	100,000	80,000
Return on debt, k_D	0	50,000/500,000 = 10%	70,000/700,000 = 10%
Return on equity, k_E	150,000/1m = 15%	100,000/500,000 = 20%	80,000/300,000 = 26.7%
Price of each share, $\dfrac{d_1}{k_E}$	$\dfrac{15p}{0.15} = 100p$	$\dfrac{20p}{0.20} = 100p$	$\dfrac{26.7p}{0.267} = 100p$
WACC $(k_E W_E + k_D W_D)$	(15 × 1.0) + 0 = 15%	(20 × 0.5) + (10 × 0.5) = 15%	(26.7 × 0.3) + (10 × 0.7) = 15%
Total market value of debt, V_D	0	500,000	700,000
Total market value of equity, V_E	$\dfrac{150,000}{0.15} = 1m$	$\dfrac{100,000}{0.2} = 0.5m$	$\dfrac{80,000}{0.267} = 0.3m$
Total value of the firm, $V = V_D + V_E$	£1,000,000	£1,000,000	£1,000,000

The relationship given in the tabulation in Exhibit 11.6 can be plotted as a graph (*see* **Exhibit 11.7**). Under the MM model the cost of debt remains constant at 10 per cent,[8] and the cost of equity capital rises just enough to leave the overall cost of capital constant.

---

[8] An alternative scenario is also discussed in the MM 1958 paper in which the cost of debt rises at high gearing levels.

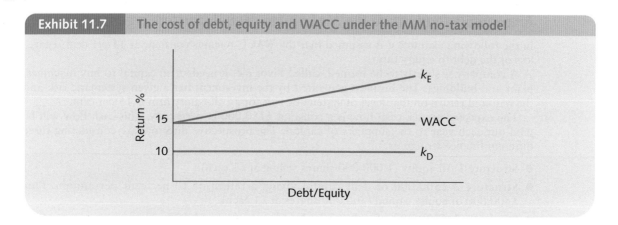

Exhibit 11.7   The cost of debt, equity and WACC under the MM no-tax model

If the WACC is constant and cash flows do not change, then the total value of the firm is constant:

$$V = V_E + V_D = £1m$$

$$V = \frac{C_1}{\text{WACC}} = \frac{£150,000}{0.15} = £1m$$

This is presented in **Exhibit 11.8**.

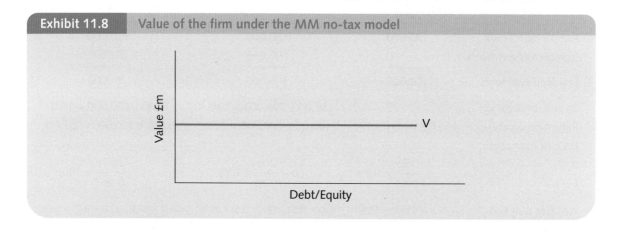

Exhibit 11.8   Value of the firm under the MM no-tax model

Pivot also illustrates the second and third propositions put forward by MM.

Proposition 2

The expected rate of return on equity increases proportionately with the gearing ratio

As shareholders see the risk of their investment increase because the firm is taking on increasing debt levels, they demand a higher level of return. The geared firm pays a risk premium for financial risk. The increase in the cost of equity exactly offsets the benefit to the WACC of 'cheaper' debt.

Proposition 3

The cut-off rate of return for new projects is equal to the weighted average cost of capital – which is constant regardless of gearing

---

Worked example 11.1	Cost of equity capital for a geared firm that becomes an all-equity financed firm in a world with no taxes

Assume that the world is as described by MM, with no taxes, to answer the following.

What would the cost of equity capital be if the firm described below is transformed into being all-equity financed rather than geared?

Perpetual future cash flow of £2.5m

$$\frac{\text{Market value of debt}}{\text{Market value of debt} + \text{Market value of equity}} = 0.4$$

$k_D = 9\%$ regardless of gearing ratio. At a gearing level of 40%, $k_E = 22\%$.

Answer

Calculate the weighted average cost of capital at the gearing level of 40 per cent.

$$\text{WACC} = k_E W_E + k_D W_D$$
$$\text{WACC} = (22 \times 0.6) + (9 \times 0.4) = 16.8\%$$

Under the MM no-tax model the WACC is constant at all gearing levels; therefore, at zero debt the return to equity holders will be 16.8 per cent.

The capital structure decision in a world with tax

The real world is somewhat different from that created for the purposes of MM's original 1958 model. One of the most significant differences is that individuals and companies do have to pay taxes. MM corrected for this assumption in their 1963 version of the model – this changes the analysis dramatically.

Most tax regimes permit companies to offset the interest paid on debt against taxable profit. The effect of this is a tax saving which reduces the effective cost of debt capital[9] (*see* Chapter 8 for a discussion of this).

In the previous no-tax analysis the advantage of gearing up (a lower cost of debt capital) was exactly matched by the disadvantage (the increased risk for equity holders and therefore an increased k_E). The introduction of taxation brings an additional advantage to using debt capital: it reduces the tax bill. Now value rises as debt is substituted for equity in the capital structure because of the tax benefits (or tax shield). The WACC declines for each unit increase in debt so long as the firm has taxable profits. This argument can be taken to its logical extreme, such that the WACC is at its lowest and corporate value at its highest when the capital of the company is almost entirely made up of debt.

In **Exhibit 11.9** the cost of equity rises but the extent of the rise is insufficient to exactly offset the cheaper debt. Thus the overall cost of capital falls throughout the range of gearing. In a 30 per cent corporate tax environment a profitable firm's cost of debt falls from a pre-tax 10 per cent to only 7 per cent after the tax benefit:

$$10\% (1 - T) = 10\% (1 - 0.30) = 7\%$$

---

[9] Note that the required rate of return on debt is not lowered; rather, the cash outflow to the tax authorities is less, resulting in more being available for equity investors, thus the *effective* cost of debt is less.

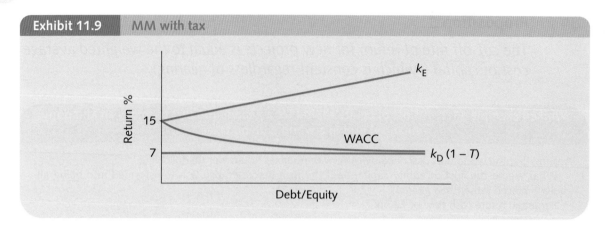

Exhibit 11.9   MM with tax

For a perpetual income firm, the value is $V = C_1/\text{WACC}$. As the WACC falls, the value of the company rises, benefiting ordinary shareholders. *See* **Exhibit 11.10**.

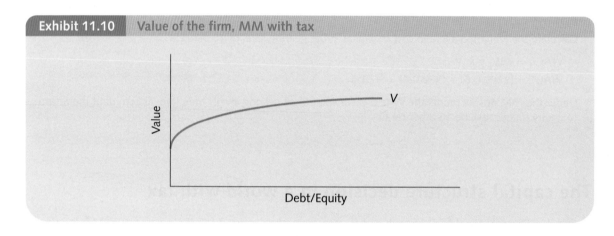

Exhibit 11.10   Value of the firm, MM with tax

The conclusion from this stage of the analysis, after adjusting for one real-world factor, is that companies should be as highly geared as possible. The article reproduced in **Exhibit 11.11** shows a company that has structured itself so that it can take on an extreme capital structure – Glas Cymru is financed entirely by debt. Note that this is possible only because the risk of financial distress has been substantially reduced and it remains profitable enough to take advantage of the tax deductibility of interest at high gearing levels. The bond offerings were eagerly taken up by lenders.

Exhibit 11.11

Glas Cymru launches bond campaign

Water marketing drive in plan to raise £2bn for purchase of Dwr Cymru

by Aline van Duyn and Andrew Taylor

Glas Cymru, the self-styled 'Welsh people's company' which has agreed to buy the principality's water supplier, will today launch a £2bn bond marketing campaign to turn the company into the UK's first fully debt-financed water utility...

The bond issues, if successful, will reduce Glas Cymru's cost of

Exhibit 11.11 continued

capital to between 4 and 4.5 per cent, compared with a 6.5 per cent industry threshold set by the regulator.

Glas Cymru, a non-profit making company, will buy Dwr Cymru (Welsh Water) in return for taking on debts of £1.8bn. It will be fully debt financed and switch from shareholder ownership ...

Bond investors in the water sector have seen prices on their holdings fall after rating downgrades following the regulatory price cuts and concern over diversification strategies.

The Glas Cymru deal aims to address these concerns by giving bondholders full control and ensuring that they are exposed purely to the water sector, which is a monopoly business with stable cash flows.

Most of the bonds will be denominated in sterling, although euro and dollar tranches are also being considered. About £1bn worth of bonds will have a Triple A rating, the highest rating category, due to a guarantee from an insurance company.

Just under £700m worth will be rated A minus. About £250m is

rated Triple B, with £100m worth of unrated bonds also sold.

The Glas Cymru structure is possible because the assets are bought for less than their regulatory asset value, giving a £150m cushion. Between now and the next regulatory price review in 2004–2005, Glas Cymru can lock in a lower cost of capital and accumulate the excess, boosting its reserves to £350m. It expects to tap the markets for £100m–£150m a year.

Source: Financial Times, 9 April 2001, p. 26. Reprinted with permission.

Additional considerations

In the real world companies do not, generally, raise their debt-to-equity ratios to very high levels. This suggests that the models described so far are not yet complete. There are some important influences on capital structure not yet taken into account. As Stewart Myers[10] wrote, 'Our theories don't seem to explain actual financing behaviour, and it seems presumptuous to advise firms on optimal structure when we are so far from explaining actual decisions.'

We now turn to some additional factors which have a bearing on the gearing level.

Financial distress

A major disadvantage for a firm taking on higher levels of debt is that it increases the risk of financial distress, and ultimately liquidation. This may have a detrimental effect on both the equity holders and the debt holders.

Financial distress: where obligations to creditors are not met or are met with difficulty.

The risk of incurring the costs of financial distress has a negative effect on a firm's value which offsets the value of tax relief of increasing debt levels. These costs become considerable with very high gearing. Even if a firm manages to avoid liquidation its relationships with suppliers, customers, employees and creditors may be seriously damaged.

Suppliers providing goods and services on credit are likely to reduce the generosity of their terms, or even stop supplying altogether, if they believe that there is an increased chance of the firm not being in existence in a few months' time. Rover's collapse in 2005 was made difficult by supplier nervousness – *see* **Exhibit 11.12**.

The situation may be similar with customers. Many customers expect to develop close relationships with their suppliers, and plan their own production on the assumption of a continuance of that relationship. If there is any doubt about the longevity of a firm it will not be able to secure high-quality contracts. In the consumer markets customers often need assurance that firms are sufficiently stable to deliver on promises, for example package holiday companies taking bookings six months in advance. **Exhibit 11.13** discusses the case of NTL which lost 800 customers each day. Furthermore, the cash shortage meant a cut in advertising to win new customers.

---

[10] Myers (1984), p. 575.

Exhibit 11.12

Rover's suppliers tighten terms

■ Extended credit and late payment not available as companies guard against collapse ■ Carmaker keen to settle on time to keep goodwill

By James Mackintosh, Motor Industry Editor

Suppliers to MG Rover have tightened the terms under which they provide components and services to the troubled Birmingham carmaker to protect themselves against its possible collapse.

Six large suppliers contacted by the Financial Times said they had shortened payment periods or were enforcing payment more strictly, reducing their exposure to the possible failure of a rescue deal with Shanghai Automotive Industry Corp, China's largest carmaker.

The stricter payment terms have left Rover without the benefit of late payment and extended credit available to more stable manufacturers. 'We are providing no leeway at all,' one of Rover's largest suppliers said.

However, none of the suppliers contacted was demanding cash upfront, a move which one said could force the company into liquidation by hurting its cashflow.

'We all recognise that at some point down the road the business becomes unviable (without the rescue deal),' said a small supplier. 'But no one wants to be seen as the one who made it go bang.'

Rover declined to comment but insiders confirmed suppliers had changed their terms in the past year, although no one was demanding cash on delivery.

Both the UK government and SAIC are keen to ensure Rover does not collapse before a deal can be completed. People close to the talks said the two sides were aiming to complete next month, perhaps in time for the Shanghai motor show.

Garel Rhys, director of the centre for automotive industry research at Cardiff University Business School, said it was 'unusual' for a vehicle manufacturer to have suppliers enforce prompt payment. But he said Rover was keen to pay on time in order to keep the goodwill of suppliers ahead of the Chinese deal.

Rover and SAIC jointly wrote to suppliers recently to say the discussions on the deal were 'well advanced' and promised more details in the coming weeks.

SAIC has already handed over £67m in return for intellectual property rights, money which will help keep Rover on its feet. The

government has also given the company a partial tax holiday, deferring payment of up to £40m of VAT, national insurance and income tax.

Suppliers in the Midlands are expected to suffer badly if Rover's rescue deal fails, with some estimates suggesting 18,000 supplier jobs – three times the 6,100 at Rover's Longbridge factory – could be at risk.

But Nick Matthews, a principal fellow at Warwick Unviersity and member of the Warwick Manufacturing Group, said Rover's production had fallen so far that the 'ripple effect' of Longbridge's closure might hit only another 6,000 jobs.

'The emotional and cultural impact would be very big but the economic impact very small,' he said. 'The regional economy is very robust and much more diverse than it has ever been.'

No supplier was willing to be named.

Source: Financial Times, 21 March 2005. Reprinted with permission.

Employees may become demotivated in a struggling firm as they sense increased job insecurity and few prospects for advancement. The best staff will start to move to posts in safer companies.

Bankers and other lenders will tend to look upon a request for further finance from a financially distressed company with a prejudiced eye – taking a safety-first approach – and this can continue for many years after the crisis has passed. They may also insist that managerial freedom to act be constrained. In 2003, for example, Waterford Wedgwood was told by its banks to reduce stock levels, to undertake no further capital expenditure other than what was already under way, to issue a high-yield bond to replace some of the bank debt, and not to pay an interim dividend.

Exhibit 11.13

NTL lost 73,400 customers during rescue talks

Falls in its three largest residential services underline fears over impact of restructuring

by Carlos Grande

NTL shed a net 73,400 UK customers in the three months to March 31 while it slashed spending and held urgent talks on the rescue_plan forecast to cost it about $95m in advisers' fees and other charges to execute.

The falls were in its three largest residential services – telephony, cable television and dial-up internet – and in dual users . . .

The trend towards a shrinking UK-customer base is expected to continue since it has taken an axe to advertising, some capital expenditure and other funding on winning new customers.

Barclay Knapp, chief executive, said: 'We remain on track to improve the state of our balance sheet.' . . .

Source: Financial Times, 12 June 2002, p. 21. Reprinted with permission.

Management find that much of their time is spent 'firefighting' – dealing with day-to-day liquidity problems – and focusing on short-term cash flow rather than long-term shareholder wealth. Companies are often forced to sell off their most profitable operations in an attempt to raise cash. For instance, in 2003 Fiat put up for sale its most valuable businessess (e.g. Fiat Avio) to raise enough cash to allow it to continue producing cars.

The indirect costs associated with financial distress can be much more significant than the more obvious direct costs such as paying for lawyers and accountants and for refinancing programmes. Some of these indirect and direct costs are shown in **Exhibit 11.14**.

Exhibit 11.14   Costs of financial distress

Indirect examples

- Uncertainties in customers' minds about dealing with this firm – lost sales, lost profits, lost goodwill.
- Uncertainties in suppliers' minds about dealing with this firm – lost inputs, more expensive trading terms.
- If assets have to be sold quickly the price may be very low.
- Delays, legal impositions, and the tangles of financial reorganisation may place restrictions on management action, interfering with the efficient running of the business.
- Management may give excessive emphasis to short-term liquidity, e.g. cut R&D and training, lower credit terms are offered to customers, which impacts on the marketing effort.
- Temptation to sell healthy businesses as this will raise the most cash.
- Loss of staff morale, tendency to examine possible alternative employment, difficulty in recruiting talented people.

Direct examples

- Lawyers' fees.
- Accountants' fees.
- Court fees.
- Management time.

As the risk of financial distress rises with the gearing ratio shareholders (and lenders) demand an increasing return in compensation. The important issue is at what point does the probability of financial distress so increase the cost of equity and debt that it outweighs the benefit of the tax relief on debt? **Exhibit 11.15** shows that there is an optimal level of gearing. At low levels of debt the major influence on the overall cost of capital is the cheaper after-tax cost of debt. As gearing rises investors become more concerned about the risk of financial distress and therefore the required rates of return rise. The fear of loss factor becomes of overriding importance at high gearing levels.

In the capital structure literature the balancing of the benefits of debt, such as the tax shield, with the costs of debt, such as distress costs, to achieve an optimal debt to equity ratio is known as the trade-off model.

Exhibit 11.15	The cost of capital and the value of the firm with taxes and financial distress as gearing increases

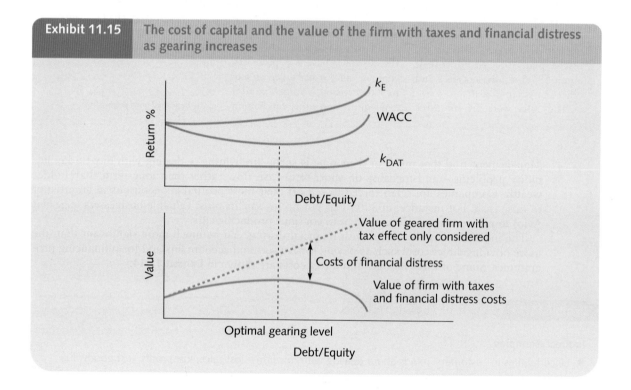

Some factors influencing the risk of financial distress costs

The susceptibility to financial distress varies from company to company. Here are some influences:

1 *The sensitivity of the company's revenues to the general level of economic activity* If a company's revenues are highly responsive to the ups and downs in the economy, shareholders and lenders may perceive a greater risk of liquidation and/or distress and demand a higher return in compensation for gearing compared with that demanded for a firm which is less sensitive to economic events.

2 *The proportion of fixed to variable costs* A firm that is highly operationally geared, and which also takes on high borrowing, may find that equity and debt holders demand a high return for the increased risk.

3 *The liquidity and marketability of the firm's assets* Some firms invest in a type of asset which can be easily sold at a reasonably high and certain value should they become distressed and go into liquidation. This is of benefit to the financial security holders and so they may not demand such a high risk premium. A hotel chain, for example, should it suffer a decline in profitability, can usually sell hotels in a reasonably active property market. On the other hand, investors in an advertising agency, with few saleable assets, would be less sanguine about rises in gearing.

4 *The cash-generative ability of the business* Some firms produce a high regular flow of cash and so can reasonably accept a higher gearing level than a firm with lumpy, highly uncertain and delayed cash inflows.

Exhibit 11.16 illustrates that the optimal gearing level for two example firms shifts depending on key characteristics of the underlying business.

Exhibit 11.16	The characteristics of the underlying business influence the risk of liquidation/distress, and therefore WACC, and the optimal gearing level	
Characteristic	**Food retailer**	**Steel producer**
Sensitivity to economic activity	Relatively insensitive to economic fluctuations	Dependent on general economic prosperity
Operational gearing	Most costs are variable	Most costs are fixed
Asset liquidity	Shops, stock, etc., easily sold	Assets have few/no alternative uses
		Thin second-hand market
Cash-generative ability	High or stable cash flow	Irregular cash flow
Likely acceptable gearing ratio	**HIGH**	**LOW**

Agency costs

Another restraining influence on the decision to take on high debt is the agency cost of doing so. Agency costs arise out of what is known as the 'principal–agent' problem. In most large firms the finance providers (principals) are not able to actively manage the firm. They employ 'agents' (managers) and it is possible for these agents to act in ways that are not always in the best interests of the equity or debt holders.

> Agency costs are the direct and indirect costs of attempting to ensure that agents act in the best interest of principals as well as the loss resulting from failure to get them to act this way.

If management are acting for the maximisation of shareholder wealth, debt holders may have reason to fear agency problems because there may be actions which potentially benefit the owners at the expense of lenders. It is possible for lenders to be fooled or misled by managers. For example, management might raise money from bondholders, saying that this is low-risk lending (and therefore paying a low interest rate) because the firm has low gearing and the funds will be used for a low-risk project. In the event the managers invest in high-risk ventures, and the firm becomes more highly geared by borrowing more. As a result the original lenders do not receive a return sufficient for the level of risk and the firm has the benefit of low-interest financing.

Alternatively, consider a firm already in financial distress. From the shareholders' point of view there is little to lose from taking an enormous gamble by accepting very high risk projects. If the gamble pays off, the shareholders will win but the debt holders will gain no more than the obligatory fixed interest. If it fails, the shareholders are no worse off but the lenders experience default on their securities. Another temptation is for the shareholders to take large amounts out of a business through the payment of dividends when the managers become aware of a high chance of liquidation, leaving the debt holders with little to salvage.

The problem boils down to one of *information asymmetry* – that is, the managers are in possession of knowledge unavailable to the debt providers. One of the solutions is to spend money on monitoring. The lenders will require a premium on the debt interest to compensate for this additional cost. Also restrictions (covenants) are usually built into a lending agreement. For example, there may be limits on the level of dividends so that shareholders do not strip the company of cash. There may be limits placed on the overall level of indebtedness, with precise capital and income-gearing ratios. Managers may be restricted in the disposal of major assets or constrained in the type of activity they may engage in.

Extensive covenants imposed by lenders can be costly for shareholders because they reduce the firm's operating freedom and investment flexibility. Projects with a high NPV may be forgone because of the cautiousness of lenders. The opportunity costs can be especially frustrating for firms with high growth potential.

Thus agency costs include monitoring costs passed on as higher interest rates and the loss of value caused by the inhibition of managerial freedom to act. These increase with gearing, raising the implicit cost of debt and lowering the firm's value.[11]

There may also be a psychological element related to agency costs; managers generally do not like restrictions placed on their freedom of action. They try to limit constraints by not raising a large proportion of capital from lenders. This may help to explain why, in practice, we find companies generally have modest gearing levels.

Borrowing capacity

Borrowing capacity has a close connection with agency costs. Lenders prefer secured lending, and this often sets an upper limit on gearing. They like to have the assurance that if the worst happened and the firm was unable to meet its interest obligations they could seize assets to sell off in order that loans could be repaid. Thus, high levels of gearing are unusual because companies run out of suitable assets to offer as security against loans. So, the gearing level may not be determined by a theoretical, informed and considered management decision, but by the limits to total borrowing imposed by lenders.

Firms with assets which have an active second-hand market, and which do not tend to depreciate, such as property, are likely to have a higher borrowing capacity than firms that invest in assets with few alternative uses.

Managerial preferences

This is another agency cost. Liquidation affects not only shareholders, but managers and other employees. Indeed, the impact on these people can be far greater than the impact on well-diversified investors. It may be argued that managers have a natural tendency to be cautious about borrowing.

Pecking order

There is a 'pecking order' for financing. Firms prefer to finance with internally generated funds. If a firm has potentially profitable investments it will first of all try to finance the investments by using the store of previous years' profits, that is, retained earnings. If still more funds are needed, firms will go to the capital markets. However, the debt market is called on first, and only as a last resort will companies raise equity finance. The pecking order of financing is in sharp contrast to the MM plus financial distress analysis, in which an optimal capital structure is targeted. Myers (1984, p. 581) puts it this way: 'In this story, there is no well-defined target debt–equity mix, because there are two kinds of equity, internal and external, one at the top of the pecking order and one at the bottom.'

One reason for placing new issues of equity at the bottom is supposedly that the stock markets perceive an equity issue as a sign of problems – an act of desperation. Myers and Majluf (1984) provide a theoretical explanation of why an equity issue might be bad news – managers will only issue shares when they believe the firm's shares are overpriced. In the capital structure literature the term 'adverse selection problem' is used to convey the idea that managers are likely to act on their informational advantage over investors and so there is an extra

---

[11] On the other hand, Jensen (1986) has argued that if managers have less free cash flow they are less likely to invest in negative NPV projects, and this restraint is better for shareholders.

degree of risk for equity investors because usually only those managers observing overpricing of their shares relative to the company's prospects would elect for a new share issue. Companies with underpriced shares would generally raise debt capital. This means that equity has 'an adverse selection premium' – a raised level of return required – making newly raised equity an expensive form of finance. Thus managers prefer to raise debt finance rather than external equity finance.[12] Bennett Stewart (1990, p. 391) puts it differently: 'Raising equity conveys doubt. Investors suspect that management is attempting to shore up the firm's financial resources for rough times ahead by selling over-valued shares.'

There is an argument that firms do not try to reach the 'correct' capital structure as dictated by theory, because managers are following a line of least resistance. Internal funds are the first choice because using retained earnings does not involve contact with outside investors. This avoids the discipline involved in trying to extract investors' money. For example, the communication process required to raise equity finance is usually time consuming and onerous, with a formal prospectus, etc., and investors will scrutinise the detailed justifications advanced for the need to raise additional finance. It seems reasonable to suppose that managers will feel more comfortable using funds they already have in their hands. However, if they do have to obtain external financing then debt is next in the line of least resistance. This is because the degree of questioning and publicity associated with a bank loan or bond issue is usually significantly less than that associated with a share issue.

Another reason for a pecking order is that ordinary shares are more expensive to issue (in terms of administrative costs) than debt capital, which in turn is more expensive than simply applying previously generated profits. The costs of new issues and rights issues of shares can be very expensive, whereas retained earnings are available without transaction costs.

The pecking order idea helps to explain why the most profitable companies often borrow very little. It is not that they have a low target debt ratio, but because they do not need outside finance. If they are highly profitable they will use these profits for growth opportunities and so end up with very little debt and no need to issue shares. Less profitable firms with many positive NPV projects to fund issue debt because they do not have internal funds sufficient for their capital investment programme and because debt is first in the pecking order of externally raised finance.

Exhibit 11.17 shows that rights issues (particularly 'rescue' rights issues designed to save the company from the danger of liquidation) can be viewed in a very negative light by financial markets.

Exhibit 11.17

Companies go back to basics in search for cash

Rights issues are a trusted route to funds

says Arkady Ostrovsky

Two French groups yesterday joined the lengthening queue of cash-hungry European companies lining up to raise money from shareholders through rights issues.

Scor, the reinsurer, plans a capital increase of €400m (£251.2m) – equivalent to its market capitalisation – but the move was poorly received and the company's shares tumbled by a third. Meanwhile, Bouygues Telecom said it was looking to launch a rights issue to pay for its €619m licence to operate a third-generation mobile phone network.

Rights issues – offerings of new shares to existing shareholders on a pro-rata basis to their holdings – have been the most popular way for companies to raise money this

---

[12] Some theorists have taken the argument a step further: managers will want to issue debt even if their shares are currently over-valued. The logic is as follows: investors are aware that managers have an incentive to sell shares when they are over-priced and therefore take an equity issue as a bad signal. So, if management go ahead with the share sale the equity price will fall. To avoid this, managers choose to issue debt.

Exhibit 11.17 continued

year. Shareholders can either subscribe to a rights issue or reject it, depending on their view of the company's future. But when stock markets are tumbling and other sources of financing have dried up, it can be a life-and-death choice for a company.

'For a number of highly geared companies, bond markets have been, in effect, shut this year, the IPO market is dry and banks are reluctant to lend long-term money to indebted companies, so companies have no choice but to ask shareholders for money,' says

James Renwick, European head of equity capital markets at UBS Warburg . . .

'Rights issues are the most basic way of raising money, which companies undertook before capital markets were properly developed. But when times get tough, companies go back to basics,' says Dante Roscini, global co-head of equity capital markets at Merrill Lynch . . .

'European companies are facing up to reality. Volatility is at record high levels and a rescue rights issue is likely to be the only

way of restructuring balance sheets in the short to medium term,' says Mr Renwick . . .

There is little doubt that a rising level of rights issues is a sign of desperation on the part of many companies. But it is also the first step towards balance sheet restructurings and the reducing of debt, which, ultimately, should lead to the revival of equity capital markets.

Source: Financial Times, 1 October 2002, p. 23. Reprinted with permission.

Financial slack

Operating and strategic decisions are generally the prime determinants of company value, not the financing decision. Being able to respond to opportunities as they fleetingly appear in business is important. If a firm is already highly geared it may find it difficult to gain access to more funds quickly as the need arises. Financial slack means having cash (or near-cash) and/or spare debt capacity. This slack can be extremely valuable and firms may restrict debt levels below that of the 'optimal' gearing level in order that the risk of missing profitable investments is reduced. Graham and Harvey (2001) show that 59 per cent of US companies deliberately restrict debt 'so we have enough internal funds available to pursue new projects when they come along'. This was the most important factor determining the debt levels of these firms, out-ranking tax deductibility of debt and risk of distress.

Financial slack is also valuable for meeting unforeseen circumstances. Managers may wish to be cautious and have a reserve of cash or spare borrowing capacity to cope with a 'rainy day'. An interesting example of this is described by the treasurer of Pfizer, Richard Passov, who argued in a Harvard Business Review article (2003) that the reason Pfizer, Intel and other firms with high levels of investment in intangible assets have cash on their balance sheets and no borrowing is because they are subject to high business risk through their risky R&D programmes. This means that they cannot take the chance of having any financial risk at all. They have billions in cash as cushions to meet unforeseen shocks and allow the continuance of investment in potential winners, many of which may not be providing cash inflows for five years or more. They are concerned about the potential for financial distress either to halt promising investment or to force the hurried sale of expensive equity (i.e. selling a chunk of the company too cheaply) at a time of crisis.

Signalling

Managers and other employees often have a very powerful incentive to ensure the continuance of the business. They are usually the people who suffer most should it become insolvent. Because of this, it is argued, managers will generally increase the gearing level only if they are confident about the future. Shareholders are interested in obtaining information about the company's prospects, and changes in financing can become a signal representing management's assessment of future returns. Ross (1977) suggests that an increase in gearing should lead to a rise in share price as managers are signalling their increased optimism. Managers, therefore, need to consider the signal transmitted to the market concerning future income whenever it announces major gearing changes.

Control

The source of finance chosen may be determined by the effect on the control of the organisation. For example, if a shareholder with 50 per cent of a company's shares is unable to pay for more shares in a rights issue, he or she may be reluctant to allow the company to raise funds in this way, especially if shares are sold to a rival. This limits the range of sources of finance and may lead to a rise in debt levels.

Tax exhaustion

Many companies do not have extremely high debt levels because their profits are not high enough to benefit from the benefit of the tax shield.

Industry group gearing

Suppose you are a financial manager trying to decide on an appropriate gearing ratio and have absorbed all the above theories, ideas and models. You might have concluded that there is no precise formula which can be employed to establish the best debt to equity ratio for firms in all circumstances. It depends on so many specific, and often difficult to measure, factors. One must consider the tax position of the firm, the likelihood of financial distress, the type of business the firm is in, the saleability of its assets, the level of business risk and the 'psychology' of the market. (For example, are rights issues perceived as bad signals, and debt issues a sign of confidence, or not?)

Given all these difficulties about establishing the theoretically 'correct' gearing level that will maximise shareholder wealth, managers may be tempted simply to follow the crowd, to look at what similar firms are doing, to find out what the financial markets seem to regard as a reasonable level of gearing, and to follow suit.

Some further thoughts on debt finance

There are some intriguing ideas advanced to promote the greater use of debt in firms' capital structure. Three of them are considered here.

Motivation

High debt will motivate managers to perform better and in the interests of shareholders. Consider this thought: if an entrepreneur (an owner-manager) wishes to raise finance for expansion purposes, debt finance is regarded as the better choice from the perspective of entrepreneurs and society. The logic works like this: if new shares are sold to outside investors, this will dilute the entrepreneur's control and thus the level of interest of the entrepreneur in the success of the business. The manager would now be more inclined to take rewards in the form of salary, perks and leisure, rather than concentrating purely on returns to shareholders. The firm will be run less efficiently because less effort is provided by the key person.

Or consider this argument: Bennett Stewart believes that, in firms without a dominant shareholder and with a diffuse shareholder base, a recapitalisation which substitutes debt for equity can result in the concentration of the shares in the hands of a smaller, more proactive group. These shareholders have a greater incentive to monitor the firm. (If managers are made part of this shareholder owning group there is likely to be a greater alignment of shareholders' and managers' interests.) Large quoted firms often have tens of thousands of shareholders, any one of whom has little incentive to go to the expense of opposing managerial action detrimental to shareholders' interests – the costs of rallying and coordinating investors often outweigh the benefits to the individuals involved. However, if the shareholder base is shrunk through the substitution of debt for equity, the remaining shareholders would have greater incentive to act against mismanagement. An extreme form of this switch to concentration is when a management team purchases a company through a leveraged buy-out or buy-in. Here a dispersed, divided and effectively powerless group of shareholders is replaced with a focused and knowledgeable small team, capable of rapid action and highly motivated to ensure the firm's success.

Reinvestment risk

High debt forces the firm to make regular payments to debt holders, thereby denying 'spare' cash to the managers. In this way the firm avoids placing a temptation in the manager's path, which might lead to investment in negative NPV projects and to making destructive acquisitions. Deliberately keeping managers short of cash avoids the problem that shareholders' funds may be applied to projects with little thought to returns. If funds are needed, instead of drawing on a large pot held within the firm, managers have to ask debt and equity finance providers. This will help to ensure that their plans are subject to the scrutiny and discipline of the market.

The problem of managers over-supplied with money, given the limited profitable investment opportunities open to them, seems to be widespread, but specific examples are only clearly seen with hindsight. For example, in the 1990s GEC was a cash-rich company under Arnold Weinstock. New managers changed the name to Marconi and spent billions buying high-technology communication infrastructure companies working at the cutting edge, but with little in the way of certainty over the likely future demand for the services/goods they offered. Hope of a glorious future was all that was needed for the spending of the large pot of money (as well as additional borrowings). When demand projections were shown to be absurdly optimistic the company barely survived – shareholder value was destroyed on a massive scale.

The danger of poor investment decisions is at its worst in firms that are highly profitable but which have few growth opportunities. The annual surplus cash flow is often squandered on increasingly marginal projects within existing SBUs or wasted in a diversification effort looking to buy growth opportunities. It is far better, say Stewart (1990), Hart (1995), Jensen (1986) and others, that managers are forced to justify the use of funds by having to ask for it at regular intervals. This process can be assisted by having high debt levels which absorb surplus cash through interest and principal payments and deposit it out of the reach of empire-building, perk-promoting, lazy managers.

Operating and strategic efficiency

'Equity is soft; debt is hard. Equity is forgiving; debt is insistent. Equity is a pillow; debt is a dagger.' This statement by Bennett Stewart (1990, p. 580) emphasises that operating and strategic problems and inefficiencies are less likely to be attended to and corrected with a capital base which is primarily equity. However, the managers of a highly geared company are more likely to be attuned to the threat posed by falling efficiency and profitability. The failing is the same under both a high equity and a high debt structure: it just seems more of a crisis when there is a large interest bill each month. The geared firm, it is argued, simply cannot afford to have any value-destructive activities (SBUs or product lines). Managers are spurred on by the pressing need to make regular payments, to reform, dispose or close – and quickly.

These are some of the arguments put forward, particularly in America in the era of massive leveraged buy-outs (LBOs), junk bonds and share repurchase programmes (in the 1980s and 1990s), in support of high debt. They seem to make some sense, but the downside of excessive debt must be balanced against these forcefully advanced ideas. Turning back to Exhibit 11.14, which shows the costs of financial distress, can help to give some perspective. In addition, many firms have found themselves crippled and at a competitive disadvantage because of the burden of high debt. For example, Marconi is a shadow of its former self, as are Cable & Wireless and Vivendi Universal.

Concluding comments

The proportion of debt in the total capital of a firm can influence the overall cost of capital and therefore the value of the firm and the wealth of shareholders. If, as a result of increasing the gearing ratio, it is possible to lower the weighted average cost of capital, then all the future net cash flows will be discounted at a lower rate. It is generally observed that as gearing increases the WACC declines because of the lower cost of debt. This is further enhanced by the tax relief available on debt capital.

But as gearing increases the risk of financial distress causes shareholders (and eventually debt holders) to demand a greater return. This eventually rises to such an extent that it outweighs the benefit of the lower cost of debt, and the WACC starts to rise. This risk factor is difficult, if not impossible, to quantify and therefore the exact position and shape of the WACC curve for each firm remains largely unknown. Nevertheless, it seems reasonable to postulate there is a U-shaped relationship like that shown in **Exhibit 11.18**.

Exhibit 11.18 The WACC is U-shaped and value can be altered by changing the gearing level

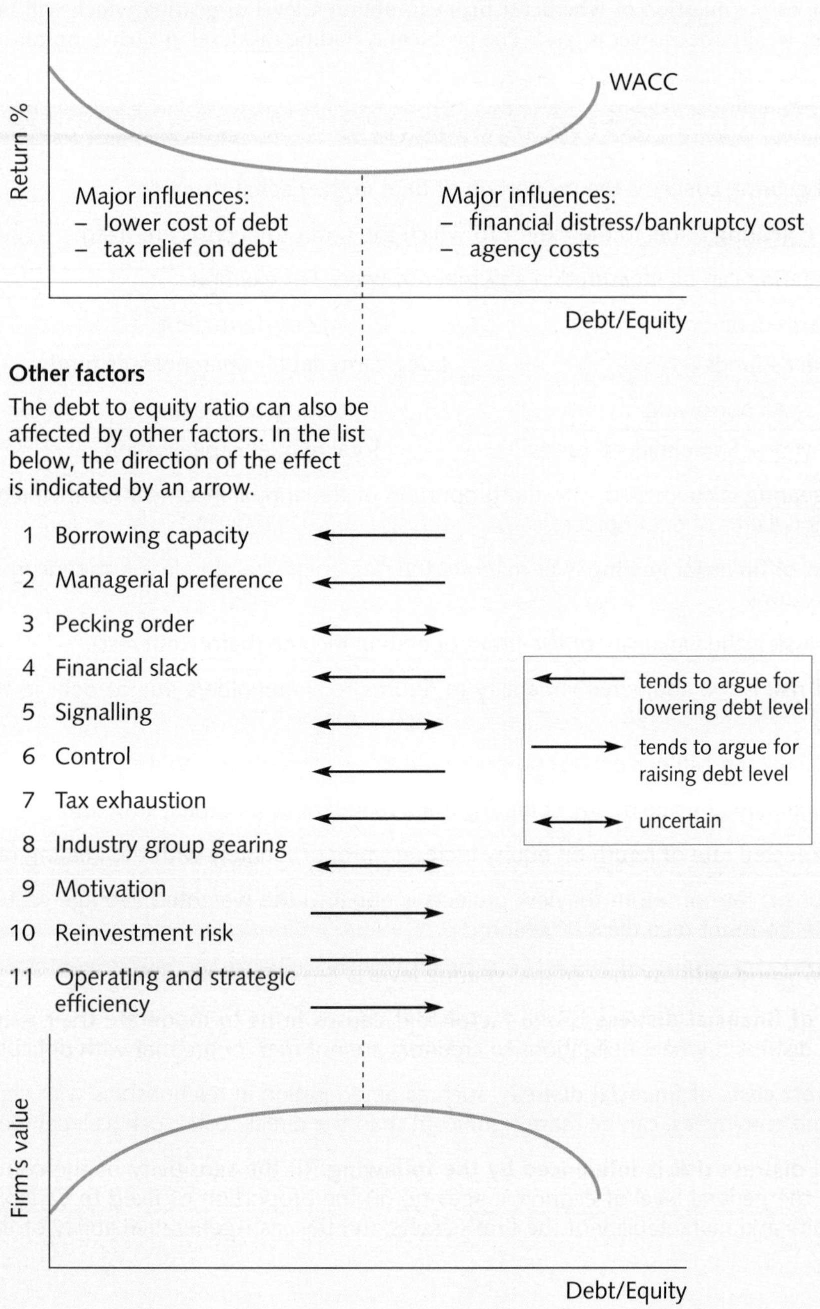
Return %
WACC
Major influences:
– lower cost of debt
– tax relief on debt
Major influences:
– financial distress/bankruptcy cost
– agency costs
Debt/Equity
Other factors
The debt to equity ratio can also be affected by other factors. In the list below, the direction of the effect is indicated by an arrow.
1 Borrowing capacity
2 Managerial preference
3 Pecking order
4 Financial slack
5 Signalling
6 Control
7 Tax exhaustion
8 Industry group gearing
9 Motivation
10 Reinvestment risk
11 Operating and strategic efficiency
tends to argue for lowering debt level
tends to argue for raising debt level
uncertain
Firm's value
Debt/Equity

We cannot scientifically establish a best debt to equity ratio. There are many complicating factors which determine the actual gearing levels adopted by firms. These cloud the picture sufficiently for us to say that, while we accept that the WACC is probably U-shaped for firms generally, we cannot precisely calculate a best gearing level.

This explains why there is such a variation in gearing levels. Some firms are under the influence of particular factors to a greater extent than other firms: some may have very low borrowing capacity, and others may have management keen on signalling confidence in the future; some may have very cautious management unwilling to borrow and a diffuse unco-ordinated shareholder body; some may be in very volatile product markets with high liquidation probabilities and others in stable industries with marketable tangible assets; other companies may be dominated by leaders steeped in the high gearing thinking of the 1980s and 1990s, believing that managers are better motivated and less likely to waste resources if the firm is highly indebted.

So, to the question of whether a firm can obtain a level of gearing which will maximise shareholder wealth the answer is 'yes'. The problem is finding this level in such a multifaceted analysis.

Key points and concepts

- **Financial gearing** concerns the proportion of debt in the capital structure.

- **Operating gearing** refers to the extent to which the firm's total costs are fixed.

- **Capital gearing** can be measured in a number of ways. For example:

$$\frac{\text{Long-term debt}}{\text{Shareholder's funds}} \qquad \frac{\text{Long-term debt}}{\text{Long-term debt + Shareholder's funds}}$$

$$\frac{\text{All borrowing}}{\text{All borrowing + Shareholders' funds}} \qquad \frac{\text{Long-term debt}}{\text{Total market capitalisation}}$$

- **Income gearing** is concerned with the proportion of the annual income stream which is devoted to the prior claims of debt holders.

- The **effect of financial gearing** is to magnify the degree of variation in a firm's income for shareholders' returns.

- **Business risk** is the variability of the firm's operating income (before interest).

- **Financial risk** is the additional variability in returns to shareholders due to debt in the financial structure.

- In **Modigliani and Miller's perfect no-tax world** three propositions hold true:

  1 The total market value of any company is independent of its capital structure.

  2 The expected rate of return on equity increases proportionately with the gearing ratio.

  3 The cut-off rate of return for new projects is equal to the weighted average cost of capital – which is constant regardless of gearing.

- In an **MM world with tax** the optimal gearing level is the highest possible.

- The **risk of financial distress** is one factor that causes firms to moderate their gearing levels. Financial distress is where obligations to creditors are not met, or are met with difficulty.

- The **indirect costs of financial distress**, such as deterioration in relationships with suppliers, customers and employees, can be more significant than the direct costs, such as legal fees.

- **Financial distress risk is influenced by the following:** (i) the sensitivity of the company's revenues to the general level of economic activity; (ii) the proportion of fixed to variable costs; (iii) the liquidity and marketability of the firm's assets; (iv) the cash-generative ability of the business.

Key points and concepts continued

- **Agency costs** are the direct and indirect costs of ensuring that agents (e.g. managers) act in the best interests of principals (e.g. shareholders, lenders), for example monitoring costs, restrictive covenants, loss of managerial freedom of action and opportunities forgone.

- **Financial distress and agency costs eventually outweigh the lower cost of debt** as gearing rises causing the WACC to rise and the firm's value to fall.

- **Borrowing capacity** is determined by the assets available as collateral – this restricts borrowing.

- There is often a **managerial preference** for a lower risk stance on gearing.

- **The pecking order:** (1) internally generated funds; (2) borrowings; (3) new issue of equity.

- The reasons for the pecking order: (i) equity issue perceived as 'bad news' by the markets; (ii) line of least resistance; (iii) transaction costs.

- **Financial slack** means having cash (or near-cash) and/or spare debt capacity so that opportunities can be exploited quickly (and trouble avoided) as they arise in an unpredictable world and to provide a contingency reserve – it tends to reduce borrowing levels.

- **Signalling** An increased gearing level is taken as a positive sign by the financial markets because managers would only take the risk of financial distress if they were confident about future cash flows.

- The source of finance chosen may be determined by the effect on the **control** of the organisation.

- **Tax exhaustion** (profit insufficient to take advantage of debt's tax shield benefit) may be a factor limiting debt levels

- Managers may be tempted to adopt the **industry group gearing** level.

- It is suggested that high gearing **motivates** managers to perform if they have a stake in the business, or if a smaller group of shareholders are given the incentive to monitor and control managers.

- **Reinvestment risk** is diminished by high gearing.

- It is argued that **operating and strategic efficiency** can be pushed further by high gearing.

Further reading

Books giving a more detailed treatment of theoretical material: Brealey, R.H., Myers, S.C. and Allen, F. (2006), Damodaran, A. (1999), Ross, S.A., Westerfield, R.W. and Jaffe, J. (2002).

Early theoretical papers: Miller, M.H. (1977), Miller, M.H. (1988), Miller, M.H. (1991), Modigliani, F. and Miller, M.H. (1958), Modigliani, F. and Miller, M.H. (1963), Modigliani, F. and Miller, M.H. (1969), Solomon, E. (1963).

Agency factors are considered in the following: Anderson, R.C, Mansi, S.A. and Reeb, D.M. (2003), Hart, O. (1995a and 1995b), Jensen, M.C. (1986), Jensen, M.C. (1989), Jensen and Meckling (1976), Stern, J. (1998).

Pecking order considered: Baker, A. and Wurgler, J. (2002), Booth, L., Aivazian, V., Demirgue-Kunt, A. and Maksimovic, V. (2001), Donaldson, G. (1961), Frank, M.Z. and Goyal, V.K. (2003), Myers, S.C. (1984), Myers, S. and Majluf, N. (1984), Shyam-Sunder, L. and Myers, S.C. (1999).

Empirical evidence of practice: Bunn P. and G. Young (2004), Graham, J.R. and Harvey, C.R. (2001), Watson, R. and Wilson, N. (2002).

Other papers on capital structure: Korajczyk, R.A. and Levy, A. (2003), Marsh, P. (1982), Myers (2001), Passov, R. (2003).

A sceptical approach to the over-elaborate algebraic examination of financial structure: Lowenstein, L. (1991).

Signalling: Ross, S. (1977).

Merton, R. (2005) argues that through the use of modern derivatives a company can reduce risk which has an impact on the optimum debt level.

In praise of high gearing: Stewart, G.B. (1990).

Self-review questions

1 Explain the terms operating gearing, financial gearing, capital gearing, income gearing.

2 What are business risk and financial risk?

3 Modigliani and Miller's original model resulted in three propositions. Describe them. Also, what are the major assumptions on which the model was built?

4 Describe how MM analysis changes if taxes are allowed into the model.

5 What is financial distress and how does it affect the gearing decision?

6 What are agency costs and how do they affect the gearing decision?

7 Describe the following ideas which are advanced to explain the low levels of gearing in some companies: (a) borrowing capacity, (b) managerial preferences, (c) pecking order, (d) financial slack, (e) control.

8 Some writers advocate the increased use of debt because of its beneficial effect on (a) managerial motivation, (b) reinvestment risk and (c) operating and strategic efficiency. Explain these ideas.

Quick numerical questions

1 Hickling plc has estimated the cost of debt and equity for various financial gearing levels:

Proportion of debt	Required rate of return	
$\dfrac{V_D}{(V_D + V_E)}$	Debt, k_{DAT} %	Equity, k_E %
0.80	9.0	35.0
0.70	7.5	28.0
0.60	6.8	21.0
0.50	6.4	17.0
0.40	6.1	14.5
0.30	6.0	13.5
0.20	6.0	13.2
0.10	6.0	13.1
0.00	–	13.0

What is the optimal capital structure?

2 Given the following facts about Company X, what would the equity cost of capital be if it was transformed from its current gearing to having no debt, if Modigliani and Miller's model with no tax applied?

$k_E = 30\%,$
$k_D = 9\%$

$$\frac{V_D}{V_D + V_E} = 0.6$$

Questions and problems

1 (*Examination level*) Eastwell plc is to be established shortly. The founders are considering their options with regard to capital structure. A total of £1m will be needed to establish the business and the three ways of raising these funds being considered are:

a Selling 500,000 shares at £2.00.
b Selling 300,000 shares at £2.00 and borrowing £400,000 with an interest rate of 12 per cent.
c Selling 100,000 shares at £2.00 and borrowing £800,000 at an interest rate of 13 per cent.

There are three possible outcomes for the future annual cash flows before interest:

Success of product	Cash flow before interest	Probability
Poor	£60,000	0.25
Good	£160,000	0.50
Excellent	£300,000	0.25

Note: Taxes may be ignored.

Required

a Calculate the expected annual return to shareholders under each of the capital structures.
b Calculate the standard deviation of the expected annual return under each of the capital structures.
c Explain the terms business risk and financial risk.
d Some writers have advocated the high use of debt because of the positive effect on managerial actions. Describe these ideas and consider some counter-arguments.

2 (*Examination level*) (a) Hose plc presently has a capital structure that is 30 per cent debt and 70 per cent equity. The cost of debt before tax shield benefits is 9 per cent and that for equity is 15 per cent. The firm's future cash flows, after tax but before interest, are expected to be a perpetuity of £750,000. The tax rate is 30 per cent.

Calculate the WACC and the value of the firm.

b The directors are considering the partial replacement of equity finance with borrowings so that the borrowings make up 60 per cent of the total capital. Director A believes that the cost of equity capital will remain constant at 15 per cent; Director B believes that shareholders will demand a rate of return of 23.7 per cent; Director C believes that shareholders will demand a rate of return of 17 per cent and Director D believes the equity rate of return will shift to 28 per cent. Assuming that the cost of borrowings before income taxes remains at 9 per cent, what will the WACC and the value of the firm be under each of the directors' estimates?
c Relate the results in question 2(b) to the capital structure debate. In particular draw on Modigliani and Miller's theory, financial distress and agency theory.

3 (*Examination level*) 'It is in management's interest to keep the financial gearing level as low as possible, while it is in shareholders' interests to keep it at a high level.' Discuss this statement.

4 (*Examination level*) In 1984 Stewart Myers wrote, 'our theories do not seem to explain actual financing behaviour', when referring to the capital structure debate. In what ways do the main MM economic models of gearing fail? Discuss some alternative explanations for the actual gearing levels of companies.

5 (*Examination level*) The managing director of your firm is thinking aloud about an appropriate gearing level for the company:

'The consultants I spoke to yesterday explained that some academic theorists advance the idea that, if your objective is the maximisation of shareholder wealth, the debt to equity ratio does not matter. However, they did comment that this conclusion held in a world of no taxes. Even more strangely, these theorists say that in a world with tax it is best to 'gear-up' a company as high as possible. Now I may not know much about academic theories but I do know that there are limits to the debt level which is desirable. After listening to these consultants I am more confused than ever.'

You step forward and offer to write a report for the managing director, both outlining the theoretical arguments and explaining the real-world influences on the gearing levels of firms.

Assignments

1 Obtain accounting and other information on a company of interest to you and calculate gearing ratios. Point out in a report the difficulties involved in this process.

2 Analyse a company you know well in the light of the various ideas, theories and models regarding capital structure. Write up your findings in a report, and include implications and recommendations for action.

Visit www.pearsoned.co.uk/arnold to get access to Gradetracker diagnostic tests, Podcasts, Excel Spreadsheet Solutions, FT articles, a Flashcard revision tool, Weblinks, a searchable Glossary and more.

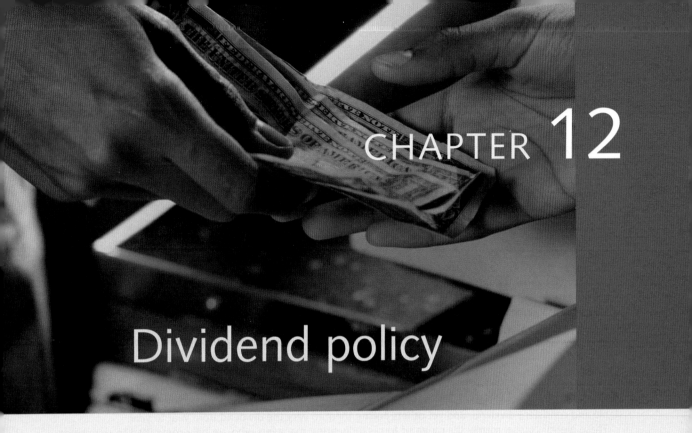

CHAPTER 12

Dividend policy

LEARNING OUTCOMES

This area of finance has no neat overarching theoretical model to provide a simple answer. However, there are some important arguments that should inform the debate within firms. By the end of this chapter the reader should be able to:

- explain the rationale and conclusion of the ideas of Miller and Modigliani's dividend irrelevancy hypothesis, as well as the concept of dividends as a residual;

- describe the influence of particular dividend policies attracting different 'clients' as shareholders, the effect of taxation and the importance of dividends as a signalling device;

- outline the hypothesis that dividends received now, or in the near future, have much more value than those in the far future because of the resolution of uncertainty and the exceptionally high discount rate applied to more distant dividends;

- discuss the impact of agency theory on the dividend decision;

- discuss the role of scrip dividends and share repurchases (buy-backs).

Introduction

Dividend policy is often reported to shareholders, but seldom explained. A company will say something like, 'Our goal is to pay out 40% to 50% of earnings and to increase dividends at a rate at least equal to the rise in the CPI.'[1] And that's it – no analysis will be supplied as to why that particular policy is best for the owners of the business. Yet, allocation of capital is crucial to business and investment management. Because it is, we believe managers and owners should think hard about the circumstances under which earnings should be retained and under which they should be distributed.

Source: Warren Buffett, a letter to shareholders attached to the *Annual Report of Berkshire Hathaway Inc* (1984). Reprinted with kind permission of Warren Buffett. © Warren Buffett.

After fifty years of observing managers Warren Buffett's comments may be viewed as a sad indictment of the quality of managerial thought. On the central issue of whether to retain profits, or distribute them to shareholders to use elsewhere, there appears to be vagueness and confusion. He has suggested that the issue is addressed at a superficial level with the employment of simple rules of thumb and no analysis. This conclusion may or may not be unfair – this chapter is not designed to highlight managerial failings in terms of depth of thought. What it can do, however, is point out the major influences on the level of the dividend decision in any one year. Some of these are fully 'rational' in the sense of the economist's model; others are less quantifiable and stem more from the field of psychology.

The conclusion reached is that managers have to weigh up a range of forces – some pulling them in the direction of paying out either a high proportion of earnings or a low one; other forces pulling them to provide a stable and consistent dividend, and yet others pulling them to vary the dividend from year to year.

These are, of course, merely the range of forces influencing managers who are fully committed to shareholder wealth maximisation and thinking 'hard about the circumstances under which earnings should be retained'. If we admit the possibility that managers have other goals, or that they make little intellectual effort, the possible outcomes of the annual or semi-annual boardroom discussion on the dividend level can range widely.

Defining the problem

Dividend policy is the determination of the proportion of profits paid out to shareholders – usually periodically. The issue to be addressed is whether shareholder wealth can be enhanced by altering the *pattern* of dividends not the *size* of dividends overall. Naturally, if dividends over the lifetime of a firm are larger, value will be greater. So in the forthcoming analysis we will assume that:

(a) the underlying investment opportunities and returns on business investment are constant; and

(b) the extra value that may be created by changing the capital structure (the debt to equity ratio) is constant.

Therefore, only the pattern of dividend payments may add or subtract value. For example, perhaps a pattern of high payouts in the immediate future, with a consequential reduction in dividend growth thereafter, may be superior to a policy of zero or small dividends now followed by more rapid growth over time.

Another aspect of the pattern question is whether a steady, stable dividend growth rate is better than a volatile one which varies from year to year depending on the firm's internal need for funds.

Some background

UK-quoted companies usually pay dividends every six months. In each financial year there is an *interim dividend* related to the first half-year's trading, followed by the *final dividend* after

---

[1] The CPI, consumer price index, is the main US measure of inflation.

the financial year-end. The board of directors are empowered to recommend the final dividend level but it is a right of shareholders as a body to vote at the annual general meeting whether or not it should be paid. Not all companies follow the typical cycle of two dividends per year: a few pay dividends quarterly and others choose not to pay a dividend at all.

Dividends may only be paid out of accumulated profits and not out of capital. This means that companies which have loss-making years may still pay dividends, but only up to the point that they have retained profits from previous years. This rule is designed to provide some protection to creditors by putting a barrier in the way of shareholders looking to remove funds from the firm, and thereby withdrawing the cushion of capital originally provided by shareholders. Further restrictions may be placed on the firm's freedom of action with regard to dividend levels by constraints contained in bond, preference share and bank-loan agreements.

The proportion of after tax earnings paid as a dividend varies greatly between firms, from zero to more than 100 per cent. The average for companies listed on the London Stock Exchange is usually around 40–50 per cent. However, recently the payout ratio rose to about 70 per cent – see **Exhibit 12.1**.

Exhibit 12.1

Dividend payouts surge to new record

By Henry Tricks

Dividend payments by listed UK companies surged 16 per cent last year to a record £52.3bn.
Morgan Stanley estimates the payout ratio has risen to about 70 per cent, its highest level since 1993.

Source: Financial Times, 2 April 2005. Reprinted with permission.

Miller and Modigliani's dividend irrelevancy proposition

According to an important 1961 paper by Miller and Modigliani (MM), if a few assumptions can be made, dividend policy is irrelevant to share value. The determinant of value is the availability of projects with positive NPVs; and the pattern of dividends makes no difference to the acceptance of these. The share price would not move if the firm declared either a zero dividend policy or a policy of high near-term dividends. The conditions under which this was held to be true included:

1 There are no taxes.

2 There are no transaction costs; for example:

   (a) investors face no brokerage costs when buying or selling shares;

   (b) companies can issue shares with no transaction costs.

3 All investors can borrow and lend at the same interest rate.

4 All investors have free access to all relevant information.

5 Investors are indifferent between dividends and capital gains.

Given these assumptions, dividend policy can become irrelevant. For example, a firm which has plenty of positive NPV projects but nevertheless paid all profits each year as dividends would not necessarily be destroying shareholder wealth because in this ideal world any money paid out could quickly be replaced by having a new issue of shares.[2] The investors in these shares would willingly pay a fair price because of their access to all relevant information. The shares can be issued by the firm without costs of underwriting or investment banks' fees, etc.,

---

[2] The complicating effect of capital structure on firms' value is usually eliminated by concentrating on all-equity firms.

and bought by the shareholders without brokers' fees or costs associated with the time spent filling in forms, etc. That is, there are no transaction costs.

If a company chose not to pay a dividend and shareholders required an income then this could be achieved while leaving the firm's value intact. 'Homemade dividends' can be created by shareholders selling a portion of their shares to other investors – again, as there are no costs of transactions and no taxation the effect is identical to the receipt of cash in the form of an ordinary dividend from the firm.

Take the example of Belvoir plc, an all-equity company which has a policy of paying out all annual net cash flow as dividend. The company is expected to generate a net cash flow of £1m to an infinite horizon. Given the cost of equity capital is 12 per cent we can calculate the value of this firm using the dividend valuation model (with zero growth – *see* Chapter 10 for details).

$$P_0 = d_0 + \frac{d_1}{k_E} = \text{£1m} + \frac{\text{£1m}}{0.12} = \text{£9.333m}$$

This includes £1m of dividend due to be paid immediately, plus the £1m perpetuity.

Now suppose that the management have identified a new investment opportunity. This will produce additional cash flows of £180,000 per year starting in one year. However, the company will be required to invest £1m now. There are two ways in which this money for investment could be found. First, the managers could skip the present dividend and retain £1m. Second, the company could maintain its dividend policy for this year and pay out £1m, but simultaneously launch a new issue of shares, say a rights issue, to gain the necessary £1m.

It will now be demonstrated that in this perfect world, with no transaction costs, shareholder value will be the same whichever dividend policy is adopted.

What *will* increase shareholder value is the NPV of the project.

$$\text{NPV} = -\text{£1m} + \frac{\text{£180,000}}{0.12} = \text{£500,000}$$

The value of the firm is raised by £500,000, by the acceptance of the project and not because of the dividend policy. If the project is financed through the sacrifice of the present dividend the effect on shareholder wealth is:

Year	0	1	2	3, etc.
Cash flow to shareholders	0	1,180,000	1,180,000	1,180,000

$$\text{Shareholder's wealth} = \frac{1,180,000}{0.12} = \text{£9.833m}$$

Thus shareholders' wealth is increased by £500,000.

If the project is financed through a rights issue while leaving the dividend pattern intact the effect on shareholder wealth is the same – an increase of £500,000.

Year	0	1	2	3, etc.
Cash flow to shareholders:				
Receipt of dividend	+ £1,000,000			
Rights issue	– £1,000,000			
	0	1,180,000	1,180,000	1,180,000

$$\text{Shareholders' wealth} = \frac{1,180,000}{0.12} = \text{£9.833m}$$

Shareholders' wealth is enhanced because £1m of shareholders' money is invested in a project which yields more than 12 per cent. If the incremental cash inflows amounted to only

£100,000 then the wealth of shareholders would fall, because a 10 per cent return is insufficient given the opportunity cost of shareholders' money:

$$\frac{£1,100,000}{0.12} = £9.167m$$

If the new investment produces a 12 per cent return shareholders will experience no loss or gain in wealth. The critical point is that in this hypothetical, perfect world the pattern of dividend makes no difference to shareholders' wealth. This is determined purely by the investment returns. If a firm chose to miss a dividend for a year, because it had numerous high-yielding projects to invest in, this would not decrease share values, because the perfectly well-informed investors are aware that any cash retained will be going into positive NPV projects which will generate future dividend increases for shareholders.

If a shareholder needs income this year he/she can sell a proportion of shares held to create a 'homemade dividend' confident in the knowledge that a fair price would be obtained in this perfect world, which takes into account the additional value from the project.

Dividends as a residual

Now we take another extreme position. Imagine that the raising of external finance (for example rights issues) is so expensive that to all intents and purposes it is impossible. The only source of finance for additional investment is earnings. Returning to the example of Belvoir, it is obvious that, under these circumstances, to pay this year's dividend will reduce potential shareholder value by £500,000 because the new project will have to be abandoned.

In this world dividends should only be paid when the firm has financed all its positive NPV projects. Once the firm has provided funds for all the projects which more than cover the minimum required return, investors should be given the residual. They should receive this cash because they can use it to invest in other firms of the same risk class which provide an expected return at least as great as the required return on equity capital, k_E. If the firm kept all the cash flows and continued adding to its range of projects the marginal returns would be likely to decrease, because the project with the highest return would be undertaken first, followed by the one with the next highest return, and so on, until returns became very low.

In these circumstances dividend policy becomes an important determinant of shareholder wealth:

1 If cash flow is retained and invested within the firm at less than k_E, shareholder wealth is destroyed; therefore it is better to raise the dividend payout rate.

2 If retained earnings are insufficient to fund all positive NPV projects, shareholder value is lost, and it would be beneficial to lower the dividend.

What about the world in which we live?

We have discussed two extreme positions so far and have reached opposing conclusions. In a perfect world the dividend pattern is irrelevant because the firm can always fund itself costlessly if it has positive NPV projects, and shareholders can costlessly generate 'homemade dividends' by selling some of their shares. In a world with no external finance the pattern of dividends becomes crucial to shareholder wealth, as an excessive payout reduces the take-up of positive NPV projects; and an unduly low payout means value destruction because investors miss out on investment opportunities elsewhere in the financial securities market.

In our world there are transaction costs to contend with. If a firm pays a dividend in order to keep to its avowed dividend pattern and then, in order to fund projects, takes money from shareholders through a rights issue, this is not frictionless: there are costs. The expense for the firm includes the legal and administrative cost of organising a rights issue or some other issue of shares; it may be necessary to prepare a prospectus and to incur advertising costs; underwriting fees alone can be as much as 2 per cent of the amount raised. The expense for the shareholder of receiving money with one hand only to give it back with the other might include brokerage costs and the time and hassle involved. Taxes further complicate the issue by imposing additional costs.

It is plain that there is a powerful reason why dividend policy might make some difference to shareholder wealth: the investment opportunities within the firm obviously have some effect. This may help to explain why we witness many young rapidly growing firms with a need for investment finance having a very low dividend (or zero) payouts, whereas mature 'cash cow' type firms choose a high payout rate.

The relationship between investment opportunity and dividend policy is a far from perfect one and there are a number of other forces pulling on management to select a particular policy. These will be considered after some more down-to-earth arguments from Warren Buffett (*see* Exhibit 12.2).

Exhibit 12.2   Buffett on dividends

Berkshire Hathaway Inc

'Earnings should be retained only when there is a reasonable prospect – backed preferably by historical evidence or, when appropriate, by a thoughtful analysis of the future – *that for every dollar retained by the corporation, at least one dollar of market value will be created for owners.* This will happen only if the capital retained produces incremental earnings equal to, or above, those generally available to investors.'

Warren Buffett says that many managers think like owners when it comes to demanding high returns from subordinates but fail to apply the same principles to the dividend payout decision:

'The CEO of multi-divisional company will instruct Subsidiary A, whose earnings on incremental capital may be expected to average 5%, to distribute all available earnings in order that they may be invested in Subsidiary B, whose earnings on incremental capital are expected to be 15%. The CEO's business school oath will allow no lesser behaviour. But if his own long-term record with incremental capital is 5% – and market rates are 10% – he is likely to impose a dividend policy on shareholders of the parent company that merely follows some historic or industry-wide payout pattern. Furthermore, he will expect managers of subsidiaries to give him a full account as to why it makes sense for earnings to be retained in their operations rather than distributed to the parent-owner. But seldom will he supply his owners with a similar analysis pertaining to the whole company . . . shareholders would be far better off if earnings were retained only to expand the high-return business, with the balance paid in dividends or used to repurchase stock.'

Source: Warren Buffett, a letter to shareholders attached to the *Annual Report of Berkshire Hathaway Inc.* (1984). Reprinted with kind permission of Warren Buffett. © Warren Buffett.

HMV (*see* Exhibit 12.3) is handing cash back to shareholders when it has cash surplus to requirements, as that is 'the responsible thing to do'. Arc, on the other hand, has been criticised for holding on to cash that it cannot use for value-creating investments (*see* Exhibit 12.4).

Clientele effects

Some shareholders prefer a dividend pattern which matches their desired consumption pattern. There may be natural clienteles for shares which pay out a high proportion of earnings, and another clientele for shares which have a low payout rate. For example, retired people, living off their private investments, may prefer a high and steady income, so they would tend to be attracted to firms with a high and stable dividend yield.

Exhibit 12.3

Double boost for HMV shareholders

By Sophy Buckley

HMV, the music, book and film retailer, is increasing the return to its shareholders with a 31 per cent jump in its interim dividend and a 12-month share buy-back programme that could be worth about £50m.

The group, which includes the Waterstone's book chain, said the moves reflected its confidence despite showing a degree of caution about slowing sales growth.

Alan Giles, chief executive, said: 'We are very comfortable with the level of gearing in the business – if you talk to analysts most think we will be debt free by the end of the financial year.'

'We can very comfortably fund £60m–£65m on our ongoing organic expansion and still have £50m plus left over. Obviously the responsible thing to do with that is to return it to shareholders.'

Source: Financial Times, 19 January 2005, p. 2. Reprinted with permission.

Exhibit 12.4

Arc agrees to hand back £50m

by Astrid Wendlandt

Arc International has agreed to hand back £50m excess cash after arm-twisting by some of its largest shareholders.

The lossmaking chip designer yesterday announced plans to return to investors 17p a share in the first half of next year.

The move came after at least one institutional shareholder threatened to call an extraordinary meeting to remove management if their demands for a return of the cash were not heeded.

Mike Gulett, Arc chief executive, said: 'We decided that we had more cash than we needed and decided to give some of it back to increase shareholder value.'

However, some shareholders had been hoping to see Arc, which has £100m of cash, return at least £75m, or 25p a share. Yesterday, the shares closed up $^3/_4$p at 21p.

One of the company's largest shareholders said: 'It's been a battle to get 17p but they have not gone far enough. The board does not understand that shareholders would rather have the cash in their hands than sitting on the company's balance sheet.' . . .

Source: Financial Times, 23/24 November 2002, p. 13. Reprinted with permission.

Shareholders who need a steady flow of income could, of course, generate a cash flow stream by selling off a proportion of their shares on a regular basis as an alternative to investing in firms with a high payout ratio. But this approach will result in transaction costs (brokerage, market makers' spread and loss of interest while waiting for cash after sale). Also it is time consuming and inconvenient regularly to sell off blocks of shares; it is much easier to receive a series of dividend cheques through the post. Furthermore, people often acknowledge self-control problems and so make rules for themselves, such as 'we will live off the income but never touch the capital' (Shefrin and Statman, 1984). They are afraid of starting down a slippery slope of selling off a proportion of shares each year in case they are tempted to overindulge. Thus shares with high dividends are attractive because they give income without the need to dig into capital.

Another type of clientele is people who are not interested in receiving high dividends in the near term. These people prefer to invest in companies with good growth potential – companies which pay low dividends and use the retained money to invest in projects with positive NPVs within the firm. The idea behind such practices is that capital gains (a rising share price) will be the main way in which the shareholder receives a return. An example of such a clientele group might be wealthy middle-aged people who have more than enough income from their paid employment for their consumption needs. If these people did receive large amounts of cash in dividends now they would probably only reinvest it in the stock market. A cycle of receiving dividends followed by reinvestment is very inefficient.

Thus, it seems reasonable to argue that a proportion of shareholders choose to purchase particular shares at least partially because the dividend policy suits them. This may place pressure on the management to produce a stable and consistent dividend policy because investors need to know that a particular investment is going to continue to suit their preferences. Inconsistency would result in a lack of popularity with any client group and would depress the share price. Management therefore, to some extent, target a particular clientele.[3]

The clientele force acting on dividend policy at first glance seems to be the opposite of the residual approach. With the clientele argument, stability and consistency are required to attract a particular type of clientele, whereas with the residual argument, dividends depend on the opportunities for reinvestment – the volume of which may vary from year to year, resulting in fluctuating retentions and dividends. Most firms seem to 'square this circle' by having a consistent dividend policy based on a medium- or long-term view of earnings and investment capital needs. The shortfalls and surpluses in particular years are adjusted through other sources of finance: for example, borrowing or raising equity through a rights issue in years when retained earnings are insufficient; paying off debt or storing up cash when retentions are greater than investment needs. There are costs associated with such a policy, for example the costs of rights issues, and these have to be weighed against the benefit of stability.

The clientele effect is often reinforced by the next factor we will examine, taxation. The consistent dividend pattern is encouraged by the information aspect of dividends – discussed after that.

Taxation

The taxation of dividends and capital gains on shares is likely to influence the preference of shareholders for receiving cash either in the form of a regular payment from the company (a dividend) or by selling shares. If shareholders are taxed more heavily on dividends than on capital gains they are more likely to favour shares which pay lower dividends. In the past, UK and US dividends were taxed at a higher rate than that which applied to the capital gains made on the sale of shares for those shareholders subject to these taxes. However, in recent years, the difference has been narrowed significantly. In the UK, for example, capital gains are now taxed at the individual's marginal tax rate. Capital gains still, however, have tax advantages. Investors are allowed to make annual capital gains of £8,000 (in 2006–7) tax free. Furthermore, they only pay tax on realised gains (when the shares are sold). Therefore, they can delay payment by continuing to hold the shares until they can, say, take advantage of a future year's capital allowance of £8,000. In addition, if shares are held for a few years the tax falls significantly.[4]

Elton and Gruber (1970) found evidence that there was a statistical relationship between the dividend policy of firms and the tax bracket of their shareholders – shareholders with higher income tax rates were associated with low-dividend shares and those with lower income tax rates with high-dividend shares.

Gordon Brown, the Chancellor, changed the tax system explicitly to encourage lower dividends and raise investment by firms (the tax that was paid on dividends was deducted by the company and sent to the tax authorities before the dividend was sent to shareholders, then the pension funds got the tax back via a tax credit). He said:

---

[3] The following researchers present evidence on the clientele effect: Elton and Gruber (1970), Pettit (1977), Lewellen, Stanley, Lease and Schlarbaum (1978), Litzenberger and Ramaswamy (1982), Shefrin and Statman (1984), Crossland, Dempsey and Moizer (1991).

[4] On the other hand, basic rate taxpayers only pay 10% tax on dividends (higher rate taxpayers are charged 32.5%).

The present system of tax credits encourages companies to pay out dividends rather than rein- vest their profits. This cannot be the best way of encouraging investment for the long term ... Many pension funds are in substantial surplus and at present many companies are enjoying pension holidays [not paying into employee pension funds], so this is the right time to under- take long-needed reform. So, with immediate effect, I propose to abolish tax credits paid to pension funds and companies.[5]

Dividends as conveyors of information

Dividends appear to act as important conveyors of information about companies. An unex- pected change in the dividend is regarded as a sign of how the directors view the future prospects of the firm. An unusually large increase in the dividend is often taken to indicate an optimistic view about future profitability. A declining dividend often signals that the directors view the future with some pessimism.

The importance of the dividend as an information-transferring device occurs because of a significant market imperfection – information asymmetry. That is, managers know far more about the firm's prospects than do the finance providers. Investors are continually trying to piece together scraps of information about a firm. Dividends are one source that the investor can draw upon. They are used as an indicator of a firm's sustainable level of income. It would seem that managers choose a target dividend payout ratio based on a long-term earnings trend.[6] It is risky for managers' career prospects for them to increase the dividend above the regular growth pattern if they are not expecting improved business prospects. This sends a false signal and eventually they will be found out when the income growth does not take place.

It is the increase or decrease over the *expected* level of dividends that leads to a rise or fall in share price. This phenomenon can be illustrated from the article on Hanson reproduced in Exhibit 12.5. Here Hanson reported falling profits and yet the share price rose because man- agement signalled its optimism by raising the dividend.

Exhibit 12.5

Higher pay-out welcomed at Hanson

by Lucy Smy

Shares in Hanson, the aggregates group, rose more than 6 per cent yesterday as investors chose to ignore falling full-year profits, focusing instead on a 10 per cent increase in the dividend.

Jonathan Nicholls, finance director, said: 'It is a visible state- ment of our confidence. We have listened to our shareholders who say we have the cashflow there to support it.'

However, Mr Nicholls admitted that such a level of dividend increase could not last forever. 'We will look at it year by year,' he said . . .

Source: Financial Times, 21 February 2003, p. 22. Reprinted with permission.

Generally company earnings fluctuate to a far greater extent than dividends. This smoothing of the dividend flow is illustrated in Exhibit 12.6 where Cadbury Schweppes has shown a rise and a fall in earnings per share but a steadily rising dividend.

---

[5] Gordon Brown, Chancellor of the Exchequer, Budget Speech, 2 July 1997.
[6] Lintner (1956) observed this. It was also recorded in a 3i (1993) survey, in which 93 per cent of finance directors agreed with the statement that 'dividend policy should follow a long-term trend in earnings'. Baker, Powell and Veit (2002) found more than 90% of Nasdaq company managers surveyed agreed that a firm should avoid increasing its regular dividend if it expects to reverse the decision in a year or so and the firm should strive to maintain an uninter- rupted record of dividend payments.

Exhibit 12.6	Cadbury Schweppes' earnings and dividend, twelve-year record (pence per share)	

Year	Earnings	Dividends
1994	16.1	7.5
1995	16.2	8.0
1996	16.9	8.5
1997	34.0	9.0
1998	17.1	9.5
1999	32.0	10.0
2000	24.8	10.5
2001	27.0	11.0
2002	27.4	11.5
2003	18.2	12.0
2004	23.3	12.5
2005	33.4	13.0

Source: Cadbury Schweppes, *Report and Accounts 2003 and 2005*.

A reduction in earnings is usually not followed by a reduction in dividends, unless the earnings fall is perceived as likely to persist for a long time. Researchers, ever since Lintner's (1956) survey on managers' attitudes to dividend policy, have shown that directors are aware that the market reacts badly to dividend downturns and they make strenuous efforts to avoid a decline. Almost every day the financial press reports firms making losses and yet still paying a dividend. By continuing the income stream to shareholders the management signal that the decline in earnings is temporary and that positive earnings are expected in the future.

When times are good and profits are bounding ahead directors tend to be cautious about large dividend rises. To double or treble dividends in good years increases the risk of having to reduce dividends should the profit growth tail off and losing the virtue of predictability and stability cherished by shareholders.

Signals are funny things. A number of the large US technology companies started paying dividends for the first time in the years 2000–5. In many cases the share price fell. The reason: investors took the dividends as a signal that the companies had run out of growth opportunities.

Resolution of uncertainty

Myron Gordon (1963) argued that investors perceive that a company, by retaining and reinvesting a part of its current cash flow, is replacing a certain dividend flow to shareholders now with an uncertain more distant flow in the future. Because the returns from any reinvested funds will occur in the far future they are therefore subject to more risk and investors apply a higher discount rate than they would to near-term dividends. Thus the market places a greater value on shares offering higher near-term dividends. Investors are showing a preference for the early resolution of uncertainty. Under this model investors use a set of discount rates that rise through time to calculate share values; therefore the dividend valuation model becomes:

$$P_0 = \frac{d_1}{1 + k_{E1}} + \frac{d_2}{(1 + k_{E2})^2} + \dots + \frac{d_n}{(1 + k_{En})^n} + \dots$$

where:

$$k_{E1} < k_{E2} < k_{E3} \dots$$

The dividends received in Years 2, 3 or 4 are of lower risk than those received seven, eight or nine years hence.

The crucial factor here may not be actual differences in risk between the near and far future, but *perceived* risk. It may be that immediate dividends are valued more highly because the investors' perception of risk is not perfect. They overestimate the risk of distant dividends and thus undervalue them. However, whether the extra risk attached to more distant dividends is real or not, the effect is the same – investors prefer a higher dividend in the near term than they otherwise would and shareholder value can be raised by altering the dividend policy to suit this preference – or so the argument goes.

There have been some impressive counter-attacks on what is described as the 'bird-in-the-hand fallacy'. The riskiness of a firm's dividend derives from the risk associated with the underlying business and this risk is already allowed for through the risk-adjusted discount rate, k_E. To discount future income even further would be excessive. Take a company expected to produce a dividend per share of £1 in two years and £2 in ten years. The discount rate of, say, 15 per cent ensures that the £2 dividend is worth, in present value terms, less than the dividend received in two years, and much of this discount rate is a compensation for risk.

$$\text{Present value of £1 dividend} = \frac{£1}{(1.15)^2} = 75.6\text{p}$$

$$\text{Present value of £2 dividend} = \frac{£2}{(1.15)^{10}} = 49.4\text{p}$$

Alternatively, take a company that pays out all its earnings in the hope of raising its share price because shareholders have supposedly had resolution of uncertainty. Now, what is the next move? We have a company in need of investment finance and shareholders wishing to invest in company shares – as most do with dividend income. The firm has a rights issue. In the prospectus the firm explains what will happen to the funds raised: they will be used to generate dividends in the future. Thus shareholders buy shares on the promise of future dividends; they discount these dividends at a risk-adjusted discount rate determined by the rate of return available on alternative, equally risky investments, say, 15 per cent (applicable to *all* the future years). To discount at a higher rate would be to undervalue the shares and pass up an opportunity of a good investment.

Owner control (agency theory)

Many people take the view that firms pay out an excessive proportion of their earnings as dividends. The argument then runs that this stifles investment because of the lower retention rate.

However, set alongside this concern should go the observation that many firms seem to have a policy of paying high dividends, and then, shortly afterwards, issuing new shares to raise cash for investment. This is a perplexing phenomenon. The cost of issuing shares can be burdensome and shareholders generally pay tax on the receipt of dividends. One possible answer is that it is the signalling (information) value of dividends that drives this policy. But the costs are so high that it cannot always be explained by this. A second potential explanation lies with agency cost.

Managers (the agents) may not always act in the best interests of the owners. One way for the owners to regain some control over the use of their money is to insist on relatively high payout ratios. Then, if managers need funds for investment they have to ask. A firm that wishes to raise external capital will have its plans for investment scrutinised by a number of experts, including:

● investment bankers who advise on the issue;
● underwriters who, like investment bankers, will wish to examine the firm and its plans as they are attaching their good name to the issue;
● analysts at credit-rating agencies;
● analysts at stockbroking houses who advise shareholders and potential shareholders;
● shareholders.

In ordinary circumstances the firm's investors can only influence managerial action by voting at a general meeting (which is usually ineffective due to apathy and the use of proxy votes by the board), or by selling their shares. When a company has to ask for fresh capital investors can tease out more information and can examine managerial action and proposed actions. They can exercise some control over their savings by refusing to buy the firm's securities if they are at all suspicious of managerial behaviour. Of particular concern might be the problem of investment in projects with negative NPV for the sake of building a larger managerial empire (Easterbrook, 1984; Jensen, 1986). A more generous view, from the field of behavioural finance, is that managers are merely overoptimistic and overconfident about their ability to invest the money wisely, rather than deliberately acting in their own interests.

From the viewpoint of lenders there is also an agency problem. Managers may pay out excessive dividends to shareholders to keep the money out of the reach of the lenders – particularly in the case of a company likely to fail. Thus lenders' agreements often restrict dividend payments.

Exhibit 12.7 discusses an implicit bargain in which companies return to investors capital they do not need, on the understanding that it will be returned to the company when it is needed.

Exhibit 12.7

Lurid acquisitions lose their edge as the retro dividend makes a comeback   **FT**

Shareholders are pushing companies to return surplus cash instead of pursuing the vagaries of capital appreciation

writes Henry Tricks

There was a fashion statement buried deep in French Connection's interim results yesterday that had nothing to do with fcuk, and everything to do with the dowdy world of dividends.

In an era of bare midriffs, the UK corporate sector is revisiting a fashion that dates back to a time when City gents wore bowler hats and bow ties.

After a long spell in the cold, the dividend is making a comeback. Bankers say there is such pressure on companies to hand back cash to shareholders that some are forsaking the lurid world of acquisitions as a result.

Yesterday, French Connection, the fashion retailer, showed its commitment to the dividend with a 20 per cent half-year increase – double the rate of earnings growth – in spite of headwinds in the UK high streets. Redrow, the house-

builder, also raised its dividend 20 per cent, pledging to do the same for the next three years even if the housing market cooled.

Merrill Lynch, meanwhile, said yesterday that for the second month running its monthly survey of 290 global fund managers showed more preferred companies to return cash than increase capital spending or improve balance sheets.

This represented a significant change from 2002 and 2003, which is as far back as Merrill's survey goes.

'It's a story that's still gathering momentum,' said David Bowers, Merrill's chief global investment strategist. 'The economy isn't strong enough to justify increased capex, but it isn't really weak enough to persuade companies to rebuild their balance sheets.'

The watershed for dividend payments started across the Atlantic

this summer when Microsoft risked its established rating as a growth company by agreeing to pay $32bn (£17.8bn) in a special dividend this year, and $44bn in buy-backs and an enhanced dividend over the next four years . . .

Michael Tory, head of UK investment banking at Morgan Stanley, said the UK was far ahead of its continental European counterparts in getting the message.

The backdrop, he said, was the period of balance sheet repair that went on after the dotcom collapse, which had put much of corporate Britain on a sounder fiscal footing. However, the uncertain economic outlook, together with a more disciplined and selective approach towards mergers and acquisitions, meant companies had more surplus cash. This combination had intensified investor pressure to return cash, he said.

Exhibit 12.7 continued

'The implicit bargain is that companies that are well managed and return capital they don't immediately need will be supplied if they do change their minds and need the capital back,' Mr Tory said.

In boardrooms, the debate about what to do with cash on the balance sheet is often tense. Returning it to shareholders is not the virile growth sport executives are used to. Often, non-executive directors will have to fight the shareholders' corner.

Paul Gibbs, a banker at JP Morgan, said it was unclear how much cash UK companies were returning to shareholders, and he believed it should be more – especially as they were not spending it on takeovers.

'UK companies are accumulating a lot of cash and we can't tell

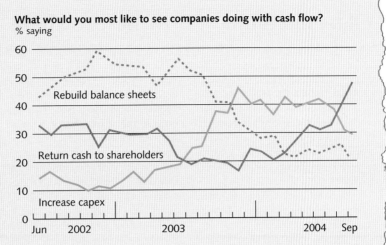

What would you most like to see companies doing with cash flow?
% saying

where it's going. It's sitting on the balance sheet, which is why investors, quite rightly, are asking for it back,' he said.

It is also feared that returning too much cash to shareholders can carry risks, however. Companies

should not liquidate their cash balances to please investors if that jeopardises their ability to compete on the global stage . . .

Source: *Financial Times*, 15 September 2004, p. 25. Reprinted with permission.

Scrip dividends

A scrip dividend gives shareholders an opportunity to receive additional shares in proportion to their existing holding instead of the normal cash dividend. The shareholders can then either keep the shares or sell them for cash. From the company's point of view scrip dividends have the advantage that *cash does not leave the company*. This may be important for companies going through difficult trading periods or as a way of adjusting the gearing (debt to equity) ratio. Shareholders may welcome a scrip dividend because they can increase their holdings without brokerage costs and other dealing costs.

An enhanced scrip dividend is one where the shares offered are worth substantially more than the alternative cash payout. Such an offer is designed to encourage the take-up of shares and is like a mini-rights issue.

Share buy-backs and special dividends

An alternative way to return money, held within the company, to the owners is to repurchase issued shares. In 2004 Marks & Spencer paid out £2.3bn by buying back shares. This was to raise the level of borrowings on its balance sheet – *see* **Exhibit 12.8** for a discussion of this and alternative ways of handing cash to shareholders.

Buy-backs are also useful when the company is unsure about the sustainability of a possible increase in the normal cash dividend. A stable policy may be pursued on dividends, then, as and when surplus cash arises, shares are repurchased. This two-track approach avoids sending an overoptimistic signal about future growth through underlying dividend levels.

A second possible approach to returning funds without signalling that all future dividends will be raised abnormally is to pay a *special dividend*. This is the same as a normal dividend but usually bigger and paid on a one-off basis.

Exhibit 12.8

The dilemma of how best to share the wealth

Maggie Urry

Amid the blizzard of announcements from Marks and Spencer this week was the apparently welcome news that it was 'giving' £2.3bn to shareholders, reported widely as being 'worth' £1 per share . . .

But before M&S shareholders start spending, they need to read the detail.

Rather than paying a special dividend to all shareholders, investors will be invited to tender shares they would like to sell back to M&S and can specify the price they want to sell at, within a range set by the company.

M&S will work out the lowest possible price at which it can spend the full £2.3bn, and then cancel the shares it buys in the process.

Shareholders can benefit in two ways: either by selling some or all of their shares in the tender, or because the value of the shares they continue to hold should rise afterwards since the M&S pie will then be divided into fewer, bigger, slices.

The retailer is the latest in an increasing number of companies seeking to return cash to investors, mostly through share buybacks.

Graham Secker, equity strategist at Morgan Stanley, says this trend reflects the current strength of company balance sheets and their free cashflow generation . . .

But do shareholders really benefit from buybacks? In theory, yes. Buying in and cancelling shares – at the right price – enhances earnings per share. If the market then applies the same price/earnings ratio to the shares, investors will see the value of their stake rise.

In practice, though, it is not at all certain that the amount of money the company puts into the market through a buyback is equal to the increase in value shareholders enjoy. That is the sort of question academics can debate for hours. At the least, the expected share price gain can take months or even longer to materialise, and can never be disentangled from other market moving factors.

Further, not all investors want to receive their returns in the form of a higher share price, which can be reaped only on the sale of shares.

Some, such as pension funds, like a capital gain since they do not pay gains tax. Others prefer their return in the form of income, and would, given the choice, plump for a special dividend.

There is likely to be conflict between the interests of different types of shareholders, which companies must try to resolve.

J Sainsbury, which is returning 35p a share to its investors after selling its US grocery chain, thinks it has come up with a scheme that offers its shareholders a choice. It was approved by investors this week.

Investors could opt to take the 35p as a dividend – to be taxed as income – or a capital gain. If they pick the capital gain, they can then choose to take the money now or defer some or all of the gain to later tax years to make use of their annual gains tax exemptions.

The supermarket group thinks that is the fairest way to give the £680m to shareholders, and worth paying the extra administration costs involved. Critics say that the one choice shareholders do not have is not to participate at all.

Meanwhile Centrica, the gas and telephone group, which has agreed the sale of its AA business for £1.75bn, plans to return £1.5bn of that money to shareholders. It has decided to pay a £1bn special dividend, and use £500m to buy shares in the market.

Centrica argues that its shareholders' preference is for immediate income. Hence the special dividend, which is also the cheapest route for the company. The buy-back element gives the company some flexibility.

Investors in Vodafone, the mobile phone group, are being rewarded by 20 per cent dividend increases and a rolling buyback programme planned to total £3bn this year.

As more companies face the dilemma of how to return cash to shareholders, the debate of the best way of doing it is likely to grow. There does not yet seem to be a perfect, one-size-fits-all, solution that makes all investors happy. But then, as M&S knows, shareholders come in as many shapes and sizes as its customers do.

Source: Financial Times, 17/18 July 2004, p. M21. Reprinted with permission.

Share repurchases are permitted under UK law, subject to the requirement that the firm gain the permission of shareholders as well as warrant holders, option holders or convertible holders. The rules of the London Stock Exchange (and especially the Takeover Panel) must also be obeyed. These are generally aimed at avoiding the creation of an artificial market in the company's shares.

A special dividend has to be offered to all shareholders. However, a share repurchase may not always be open to all shareholders as it can be accomplished in one of three ways:

(a) purchasing shares in the stock market;

(b) all shareholders are invited to tender some or all of their shares;

(c) an arrangement with particular shareholders.

An alternative method of returning money to shareholders is via a 'B share scheme' – *see* the example of William Hill in **Exhibit 12.9**. Some shareholders pay lower tax if the B shares are taxed as a capital gain rather than income.

Exhibit 12.9

William Hill hands back £453m to investors

by Matthew Garrahan, Leisure Industries Correspondent

The government's moves to scale back its controversial gambling bill has prompted bookmaker William Hill to give shareholders a £453m windfall, which is equivalent to 115p a share or 20 per cent of the group's market capitalisation.

With William Hill having a strong cash position and not anticipating any big acquisitions the company said it could support a 'significantly higher amount of debt'.

It has secured a new £1.2bn facility and will have increased its net debt to about £900m once the capital has been returned to investors. David Harding, chief executive, said the company would be left with about £300m for acquisitions, should any arise.

Funds will be returned to investors via a B share scheme. Shareholders will be able to choose how they take the benefit, either by redeeming the new B shares for 115p, receiving an immediate 115p dividend or deferring redemption.

The amount returned to investors by William Hill since its float in 2002 will rise to £752m following the return of capital.

Tom Singer, Hill's finance director, said the group had chosen the B share scheme instead of a more conventional special dividend because it was fair and gave investors more choice. 'Shareholders, when offered a choice, would usually be split 50-50 between taking the money as income or as a capital receipt,' he said.

'If you only offer a special dividend, you're going to upset the remaining 50 per cent.'

Source: Financial Times, 3 March 2005, p. 25. Reprinted with permission.

Buy-backs and special dividends are growing in popularity. Some companies are giving the impression that they are regular events and so signals about the persistence of payouts to shareholders are becoming jumbled – *see* **Exhibit 12.10**.

Exhibit 12.10

The 'quasi-dividend' of a buy-back programme

Henry Tricks finds no long-term commitment to this corporate tool

According to a joke doing the rounds in the City, dividends are like marriage and share buy-backs are like affairs, requiring no long-term commitment.

So why has there been such commiseration when companies such as Royal Dutch/Shell, Barclays and Boots cast a veil of uncertainty over their share repurchase programmes?

The answer, according to Rolf Elgeti, strategist at ABN Amro, is that investors are viewing buy-backs as 'quasi-dividends' instead of the flexible way of returning cash to shareholders they are meant to be.

'We have been seeing a shift here since the beginning of this year where more and more

Exhibit 12.10 continued

investors have incorporated share buy-backs into their dividend yield forecasts,' he said. 'It may be that playing around with the buy-back programme will come to have the same potential impact as a dividend cut.'

This month, shareholders have been disappointed by the impact a $45bn (£25bn) capital spending programme over the next three years will have on Shell's buy-back programme. When Barclays announced it was in talks to buy South Africa's Absa, it indicated it might be forced to suspend its buy-back programme if it makes a cash purchase. Meanwhile, Boots has left open the possibility of suspending the second tranche of its £700m share repurchase programme.

Bankers and analysts say it is perfectly legitimate for companies to adjust their buy-back programmes if they can increase returns by investing the money in improving the business rather than handing it back to shareholders. The trouble comes when companies use the cash for mis-adventures, or shareholders lack the confidence that management will spend their surplus cash wisely. However, shareholders should not become complacent, they say.

'The market has got used to a continuous stream of buy-backs but it has to recognise buy-backs are driven by management's view of what constitutes genuine surplus,' warns a senior London investment banker. 'They should not be counted on.'

According to Graham Secker, of Morgan Stanley, share buy-backs are running at a record rate of £14bn this year, equating to what he calls a 'buy-back yield' of 1.2 per cent. Adding this to UK companies' dividend yield of 3.4 per cent provides a combined yield of 4.6 per cent – slightly lower than the return on 10-year gilts.

That combined yield, he says, is at a nine-year high.

It is easy to exaggerate the inherent value of buy-backs. According to analysts, in the UK there are few meaningful tax advantages to buy-backs over dividends.

JP Morgan notes that share repurchases do not create value unless the cash payment is big enough to permanently increase leverage, or if the stock is undervalued and subsequently re-rates. Sometimes, share repurchases signal a lack of management vision. There is little evidence to prove over the long-term that buy-backs provide a lasting boost to shareholder returns.

However, in times of uncertainty, it is heartening for shareholders to know that management believes its own growth story. Moreover, buy-backs enhance earnings per share, even if that is merely cosmetic.

That, perhaps, is why managers are in love with them. But buy-backs, like love, are a fickle thing.

Source: Financial Times, 2 October 2004, p. M3. Reprinted with permission.

A round-up of the arguments

There are two questions at the core of the dividend policy debate.

- *Question 1* Can shareholder wealth be increased by changing the pattern of dividends over a period of years?
- *Question 2* Is a steady, stable dividend growth rate better than one which varies from year to year depending on the firm's internal need for funds?

The answer to the first question is 'yes'. The accumulated evidence suggests that shareholders for one reason or another value particular patterns of dividends across time. But there is no neat, simple, straightforward formula into which we can plug numbers in order to calculate the best pattern. It depends on numerous factors, many of which are unquantifiable, ranging from the type of clientele shareholder the firm is trying to attract to changes in the taxation system.

Taking the residual theory alone the answer to Question 2 is that the dividend will vary from year to year because it is what is left over after the firm has retained funds for investment in all available projects with positive NPV. Dividends will be larger in years of high cash flow and few investment opportunities, and will be reduced when the need for reinvestment is high relative to internally generated cash flow. However, in practice, shareholders appear to prefer stable, consistent dividend growth rates. Many of them rely on a predictable stream of dividends to meet (or contribute to) their consumption needs. They would find an erratic dividend flow inconvenient. Investors also use dividend policy changes as an indication of a firm's prospects. A reduced dividend could send an incorrect signal and depress the share price.

There are so many factors influencing dividend policy that it is very difficult to imagine that someone could develop a universally applicable model which would allow firms to identify an optimal payout ratio. Exhibit 12.11 shows the range of forces pulling managers towards a high payout rate, and other forces pulling towards a low payout rate. Simultaneously, there are forces encouraging a fluctuating dividend and other factors promoting a stable dividend.

Most of the factors in Exhibit 12.11 have already been explained, but there are two which need a comment here: liquidity and credit standing. Dividends require an outflow of cash from firms; therefore, companies with plenty of liquid assets, such as cash and marketable securities, are more able to pay a dividend. Other firms, despite being highly profitable, may have very few liquid assets. For example, a rapidly growing firm may have a large proportion of its funds absorbed by fixed assets, inventory and debtors. Thus some firms may have greater difficulty paying cash dividends than others.

Exhibit 12.11   The forces pulling management in the dividend decision

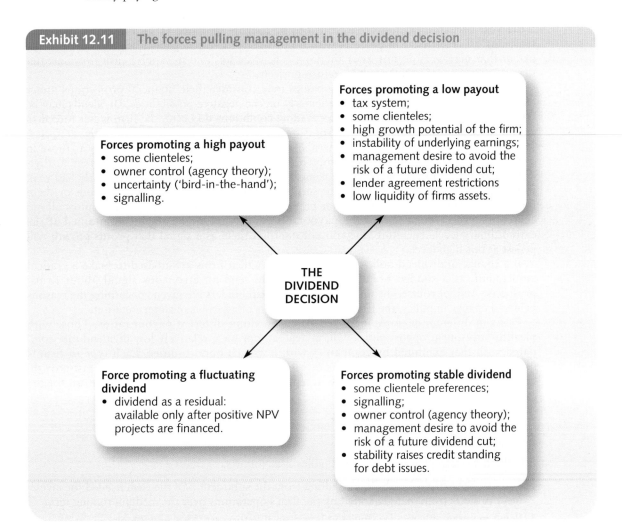

Lenders generally prefer to entrust their money to stable firms rather than ones that are erratic, as this reduces risk. Therefore, it could be speculated that a consistent dividend flow helps to raise the credit standing of the firm and lowers the interest rates payable. Creditors suffer from information asymmetry as much as shareholders and may therefore look to this dividend decision for an indication of managerial confidence about the firm's prospects.

Concluding comments

This section considers a possible practical dividend policy, taking into account the various arguments presented in the chapter.

Most large firms forecast their financial position for a few years ahead. Their forecasts will include projections for fixed capital expenditure and additional investment in working capital as well as sales, profits, etc. This information, combined with a specified target debt to equity ratio, allows an estimation of medium- to long-term cash flows.

These companies can then determine a dividend level that will leave sufficient retained earnings to meet the financing needs of their investment projects without having to resort to selling shares. (Not only does issuing shares involve costs of issue but, as described in Chapter 11, investors sometimes view share issues as a negative omen.) Thus a *maintainable regular dividend* on a growth path is generally established. This has the virtue of providing some certainty to a particular clientele group and provides a stable background, to avoid sending misleading signals. At the same time the residual theory conclusions have been recognised, and (over, say, a five-year period) dividends are intended to be roughly the same as surplus cash flows after financing all investment in projects with a positive NPV. Agency costs are alleviated to the extent that managers do not, over the long run, store up (and misapply) cash flows greater than those necessary to finance high-return projects.

The future is uncertain and so companies may consider their financial projections under various scenarios. They may focus particularly on the negative possibilities. Dividends may be set at a level low enough that, if poorer trading conditions do occur, the firm is not forced to cut the dividend. Thus a margin for error is introduced by lowering the payout rate.

Companies that are especially vulnerable to macroeconomic vicissitudes, such as those in cyclical industries, are likely to be tempted to set a relatively low maintainable regular dividend so as to avoid the dreaded consequences of a reduced dividend in a particularly bad year. In years of plenty directors can pay out surplus cash in the form of special dividends or share repurchases. This policy of low regular payouts supplemented with irregular bonuses allows shareholders to recognise that the payouts in good years might not be maintained at the extraordinary level. Therefore, they do not interpret them as a signal that profits growth will persist at this high level.

If a change in dividend policy becomes necessary then firms are advised to make a gradual adjustment, as a sudden break with a trend can send an erroneous signal about firms' prospects. And, of course, the more information shareholders are given concerning the reasons behind a change in policy, the less likelihood there is of a serious misinterpretation.

Firms in different circumstances are likely to exhibit different payout ratios. Those with plentiful investment opportunities will, in general, opt for a relatively low dividend rate compared with that exhibited by companies with few such opportunities. Each type of firm is likely to attract a clientele favouring its dividend policy. For example, investors in fast-growth, high-investment firms are prepared to accept low (no) near-term dividends in return for the prospect of higher capital gains.

A suggested action plan

A suggested action plan for a dividend policy is as follows.

1 Forecast the 'surplus' cash flow resulting from the subtraction of the cash needed for investment projects from that generated by the firm's operations over the medium to long term.

2 Pay a maintainable regular dividend based on this forecast. This may be biased on the conservative side to allow for uncertainty about future cash flows.

3 If cash flows are greater than projected for a particular year, keep the maintainable regular dividend fairly constant (hopefully with stable growth), but pay a special dividend or initiate a share repurchase programme. If the change in cash flows is permanent, gradually shift the maintainable regular dividend while providing as much information to investors as possible about the reasons for the change in policy.

Key points and concepts

- **Dividend policy** concerns the pattern of dividends over time and the extent to which they fluctuate from year to year.

- UK-quoted companies generally pay dividends every six months – an **interim** and a **final**. They may only be paid out of accumulated profits.

- **Miller and Modigliani** proposed that, in a perfect world, the policy on dividends is irrelevant to shareholder wealth. Firms are able to **finance investments** from retained earnings or new share sales at the same cost (with no transaction costs). Investors are able to manufacture '**homemade dividends**' by selling a portion of their shareholding.

- In a world with **no external finance, dividend policy should be residual**.

- In a world with some transaction costs associated with issuing dividends and obtaining investment finance through the sale of new shares, dividend policy will be **influenced by**, but not exclusively determined by, the '**dividends as a residual approach**' to dividend policy.

- The **clientele effect** is the concept that shareholders are attracted to firms that follow dividend policies consistent with their objectives. It encourages stability in dividend policy.

- **Taxation** can influence the investors' preference for the receipt of high dividends or capital gains from their shares.

- **Dividends can act as conveyors of information**. An unexpected change in dividends is regarded as a **signal** of how directors view the future prospects of the firm.

- It has been argued (e.g. by Myron Gordon) that **investors perceive more distant dividends as subject to more risk**, therefore they prefer a higher near-term dividend – a 'bird in the hand'. This '**resolution of uncertainty**' argument has been attacked on the grounds that it implies an extra risk premium on the rate used to discount cash flows.

- The **owner control** argument says that firms are encouraged to distribute a high proportion of earnings so that investors can reduce the **principal–agent problem** and achieve greater goal congruence. Managers have to ask for investment funds; this subjects their plans to scrutiny.

- A **scrip dividend** gives the shareholders an opportunity to receive additional shares in proportion to their existing holding instead of the normal cash dividend.

- A **share repurchase** is when the company buys a proportion of its own shares from investors.

- A **special dividend** is similar to a normal dividend but is usually bigger and paid on a one-off basis.

Further reading

Books giving more technical detail: Damodaran, A. (1999), Solomon, E. (1963).

On the clientele effect: Baker, M. and Wurgler, J. (2004), Crossland, M., Dempsey, M. and Moizer, P. (1991), Elton, E.J. and Gruber, M.J. (1970), Lewellen, W.G., Stanley, K.L., Lease, R.C. and Schlarbaum, G.G. (1978), Litzenberger, R. and Ramaswamy, K. (1982), Pettit, R.R. (1977), Shefrin, H.M. and Statman, M. (1984).

On MM theory: Brealey, R.H. (1986), Brennan, M. (1971), Miller, M.II. and Modigliani, F. (1961).

On share buy-backs: Grullon, G. and Michaely, R. (2002), Jagannathan, M., C.P. Stephens and M.S. Weisbach (2000).

On the early resolution of uncertainty: Gordon, M.J. (1963), Keane, S. (1974).

On signalling: Baker, H.K., G.E. Powell and E.T. Veit (2002), Mougoué, M. and Rao, R.P. (2003), Nissim, D. and Ziv, A. (2001), Rozeff, M. (1986).

Agency considerations: Easterbrook, F. H. (1984), Gustavo, G. and Roni, M. (2004), Jensen M.C. (1986), Jensen M.C. and Meckling, W.H. (1976).

Tax as a factor: Elton, E.J. and Gruber, M.J. (1970).

Empirical evidence of practice: Baker, H.K., G.E. Powell and E.T. Veit (2002), Julio, B. and D.L. Ikenberry (2004), Lintner, J. (1956), 3i (1993).

Other important papers: Black, F. (1976), Fama, E.F. and K.R. French (2001), Gordon, M.J. (1959), Gustavo, G., M. Roni and B. Swaminathan (2002).

Self-review questions

1   What are the two fundamental questions in dividend policy?

2   Explain the main elements of MM's dividend irrelevancy hypothesis.

3   Explain the idea that dividends should be treated as a residual.

4   How might clientele effects influence dividend policy?

5   What is the effect of taxation on dividend payout rates?

6   What is meant by 'asymmetry of information' and 'dividends as signals'?

7   Explain the 'resolution of uncertainty' argument supporting high dividend payout rates. What is the counter-argument?

8   In what ways does agency theory influence the dividend debate?

9   When are share repurchases and special dividends particularly useful?

10 Outline a dividend policy for a typical fast-growth and high-investment firm.

Questions and problems

1   (*Examination level*) 'These days we discuss the dividend level for about an hour a year at board meetings. It changes very little from one year to the next – and it is just as well if you consider what happened to some of the other firms on the stock exchange which reduced their dividend' – director of a large company.

Explain, with reference to dividend theory, how this firm may have settled into this comfortable routine. Describe any problems that might arise with this approach.

2   (*Examination level*) 'We believe managers and owners should think hard about the circumstances under which earnings should be retained and under which they should be distributed.'

Use the above sentence together with the following one written in the same letter to shareholders by Warren Buffett (1984), plus dividend policy theory, to explain why this is an important issue: 'Nothing in this discussion is intended to argue for dividends that bounce around from quarter to quarter with each wiggle in earnings or in investment opportunities.'

3   (*Examination level*) Sendine plc has maintained a growth path for dividends per share of 5 per cent per year for the past seven years. This was considered to be the maintainable regular dividend. However, the company has developed a new product range which will require major investment in the next 12 months. The amount needed is roughly equivalent to the proposed dividend for this year. The project will not provide a positive net cash flow for three to four years but will give a positive NPV overall.

Required

Consider the argument for and against a dividend cut this year and suggest a course of action.

4   (*Examination level*) Vale plc has the following profit-after-tax history and dividend-per-share history shown in the table below:

Two years ago the number of issued ordinary shares was increased by 30 per cent (at the beginning of financial year $t - 1$). Four years ago a rights issue doubled the number of shares (at the beginning of financial year $t - 3$). Today there are 100 million ordinary shares in issue with a total market value of £190m. Vale is quoted on the Alternative Investment Market. Vale's directors are committed to shareholder wealth maximisation.

Year		Profit after tax £	Dividend per share
This year	(t_0)	10,800,000	5.4
Last year	$(t-1)$	8,900,000	4.92
2 years ago	$(t-2)$	6,300,000	4.48
3 years ago	$(t-3)$	5,500,000	4.083
4 years ago	$(t-4)$	3,500,000	3.71
5 years ago	$(t-5)$	2,600,000	3.38

Required

a Explain the following dividend theories and models and relate them to Vale's policy:
   i   dividends as a residual;
   ii signalling;
   iii clientele preferences.
b The risk-free return on government securities is currently 6.5 per cent, the risk premium for shares above the risk-free rate of return has been 5 per cent per annum and Vale is in a risk class of shares which suggests that the average risk premium of 5 should be adjusted by a factor of 0.9. The company's profits after tax per share are expected to continue their historic growth path, and dividends will remain at the same proportion of earnings as this year.
   Use the dividend valuation model and state whether Vale's shares are a good buying opportunity for a stock market investor.

5 (*Examination level*) Tesford plc has estimated net cash flows from operations (after interest and taxation) for the next five years as follows:

Year	Net cash flows £
1	3,000,000
2	12,000,000
3	5,000,000
4	6,000,000
5	5,000,000

The cash flows have been calculated before the deduction of additional investment in fixed capital and working capital. This amounts to £2m in each of the first two years and £3m for each year thereafter. The firm currently has a cash balance of £500,000 which it intends to maintain to cope with unexpected events. There are 24 million shares in issue. The directors are committed to shareholder wealth maximisation.

Required

a Calculate the annual cash flows available for dividend payments and the dividend per share if the residual dividend policy was strictly adhered to.
b If the directors chose to have a smooth dividend policy based on the maintainable regular dividend what would you suggest the dividends in each year should be? Include in your consideration the possibility of a special dividend or share repurchase.
c Explain why companies tend to follow the policy in (b) rather than (a).

6 (*Examination level*) The retailers Elec Co. and Lighting are competitors in the electrical goods market. They are similar firms in many respects: profits per share have been very similar over the past 10 years, and are projected to be the same in the future; they both have (and have had) a 50 per cent debt to equity ratio; and they have similar investment needs, now and in the future. However, they do differ in their dividend policies. Elec Co. pays out 50 per cent of earnings as dividends, whereas Lighting has adopted a stable dividend policy. This is demonstrated in the table.

The managing director of Elec Co. has asked you to conduct a thorough review of dividend policy and to try to explain why it is that Lighting has a market value much greater than Elec Co. (Both companies have, and have had, the same number of shares in issue.)

Write a report detailing the factors that influence dividend policy and recommend a dividend policy for Elec Co. based on your arguments.

Year	Elec Co.		Lighting	
	Earnings per share	Dividend per share	Earnings per share	Dividend per share
x1	11p	5.5p	11p	5.5p
x2	16p	8.0p	17p	6.25p
x3	13p	6.5p	11p	7.11p
x4	20p	10.0p	21p	8.1p
x5	10p	5.0p	9p	9.2p
x6	0	0	0	10.5p
x7	15p	7.5p	17p	11.9p
x8	25p	12.5p	24p	13.5p
x9	30p	15.0p	31p	15.4p
x10	35p	17.5p	35p	17.5p

7 (*Examination level*) Guff plc, an all-equity firm, has the following earnings per share and dividend history (paid annually).

Year	Earnings per share	Dividend per share
This year	21p	8p
Last year	18p	7.5p
2 years ago	16p	7p
3 years ago	13p	6.5p
4 years ago	14p	6p

This year's dividend has just been paid and the next is due in one year. Guff has an opportunity to invest in a new product, Stuff, during the next two years. The directors are considering cutting the dividend to 4p for each of the next two years to fund the project. However, the dividend in three years can be raised to 10p and will grow by 9 per cent per annum thereafter due to the benefits from the investment. The company is focused on shareholder wealth maximisation and requires a rate of return of 13 per cent for its owners.

Required

a If the directors chose to ignore the investment opportunity and dividends continued to grow at the historical rate, what would be the value of one share using the dividend valuation model?
b If the investment is accepted, and therefore dividends are cut for the next two years, what will be the value of one share?
c What are the dangers associated with dividend cuts and how might the firm alleviate them?

Assignment

1 Consider the dividend policy of your firm or one you know well. Write a report detailing the factors contributing to the selection of this particular policy. Make recommendations on the decision-making process, range of influences considered and how a change in policy could be executed.

Visit www.pearsoned.co.uk/arnold to get access to Gradetracker diagnostic tests, Podcasts, Excel Spreadsheet Solutions, FT articles, a Flashcard revision tool, Weblinks, a searchable Glossary and more.

Appendices

Appendix I

Future value of £1 at compound interest

Interest rate

Periods	1	2	3	4	5	6	7	8	9	10	11	12	13	14	15	
1	1.0100	1.0200	1.0300	1.0400	1.0500	1.0600	1.0700	1.0800	1.0900	1.1000	1.1100	1.1200	1.1300	1.1400	1.1500	1
2	1.0201	1.0404	1.0609	1.0816	1.1025	1.1236	1.1449	1.1664	1.1881	1.2100	1.2321	1.2544	1.2769	1.2996	1.3225	2
3	1.0303	1.0612	1.0927	1.1249	1.1576	1.1910	1.2250	1.2597	1.2950	1.3310	1.3676	1.4049	1.4429	1.4815	1.5209	3
4	1.0406	1.0824	1.1255	1.1699	1.2155	1.2625	1.3108	1.3605	1.4116	1.4641	1.5181	1.5735	1.6305	1.6890	1.7490	4
5	1.0510	1.1041	1.1593	1.2167	1.2763	1.3382	1.4026	1.4693	1.5386	1.6105	1.6851	1.7623	1.8424	1.9254	2.0114	5
6	1.0615	1.1262	1.1941	1.2653	1.3401	1.4185	1.5007	1.5869	1.6771	1.7716	1.8704	1.9738	2.0820	2.1950	2.3131	6
7	1.0721	1.1487	1.2299	1.3159	1.4071	1.5036	1.6058	1.7138	1.8280	1.9487	2.0762	2.2107	2.3526	2.5023	2.6600	7
8	1.0829	1.1717	1.2668	1.3686	1.4775	1.5938	1.7182	1.8509	1.9926	2.1436	2.3045	2.4760	2.6584	2.8526	3.0590	8
9	1.0937	1.1951	1.3048	1.4233	1.5513	1.6895	1.8385	1.9990	2.1719	2.3579	2.5580	2.7731	3.0040	3.2519	3.5179	9
10	1.1046	1.2190	1.3439	1.4802	1.6289	1.7908	1.9672	2.1589	2.3674	2.5937	2.8394	3.1058	3.3946	3.7072	4.0456	10
11	1.1157	1.2434	1.3842	1.5395	1.7103	1.8983	2.1049	2.3316	2.5804	2.8531	3.1518	3.4785	3.8359	4.2262	4.6524	11
12	1.1268	1.2682	1.4258	1.6010	1.7959	2.0122	2.2522	2.5182	2.8127	3.1384	3.4985	3.8906	4.3345	4.8179	5.3503	12
13	1.1381	1.2936	1.4685	1.6651	1.8856	2.1329	2.4098	2.7196	3.0658	3.4523	3.8833	4.3635	4.8980	5.4924	6.1528	13
14	1.1495	1.3195	1.5126	1.7317	1.9799	2.2609	2.5785	2.9372	3.3417	3.7975	4.3104	4.8871	5.5348	6.2613	7.0757	14
15	1.1610	1.3459	1.5580	1.8009	2.0789	2.3966	2.7590	3.1722	3.6425	4.1772	4.7846	5.4736	6.2543	7.1379	8.1371	15
16	1.1726	1.3728	1.6047	1.8730	2.1829	2.5404	2.9522	3.4259	3.9703	4.5950	5.3109	6.1304	7.0673	8.1372	9.3576	16
17	1.1843	1.4002	1.6528	1.9479	2.2920	2.6928	3.1588	3.7000	4.3276	5.0545	5.8951	6.8660	7.9861	9.2765	10.7613	17
18	1.1961	1.4282	1.7024	2.0258	2.4066	2.8543	3.3799	3.9960	4.7171	5.5599	6.5436	7.6900	9.0243	10.5752	12.3755	18
19	1.2081	1.4568	1.7535	2.1068	2.5270	3.0256	3.6165	4.3157	5.1417	6.1159	7.2633	8.6128	10.1974	12.0557	14.2318	19
20	1.2202	1.4859	1.8061	2.1911	2.6533	3.2071	3.8697	4.6610	5.6044	6.7275	8.0623	9.6463	11.5231	13.7435	16.3665	20
25	1.2824	1.6406	2.0938	2.6658	3.3864	4.2919	5.4274	6.8485	8.6231	10.8347	13.5855	17.0001	21.2305	26.4619	32.9190	25

Periods	16	17	18	19	20	21	22	23	24	25	26	27	28	29	30	
1	1.1600	1.1700	1.1800	1.1900	1.2000	1.2100	1.2200	1.2300	1.2400	1.2500	1.2600	1.2700	1.2800	1.2900	1.3000	1
2	1.3456	1.3689	1.3924	1.4161	1.4400	1.4641	1.4884	1.5129	1.5376	1.5625	1.5876	1.6129	1.6384	1.6641	1.6900	2
3	1.5609	1.6016	1.6430	1.6852	1.7280	1.7716	1.8158	1.8609	1.9066	1.9531	2.0004	2.0484	2.0972	2.1467	2.1970	3
4	1.8106	1.8739	1.9388	2.0053	2.0736	2.1436	2.2153	2.2889	2.3642	2.4414	2.5205	2.6014	2.6844	2.7692	2.8561	4
5	2.1003	2.1924	2.2878	2.3864	2.4883	2.5937	2.7027	2.8153	2.9316	3.0518	3.1758	3.3038	3.4360	3.5723	3.7129	5
6	2.4364	2.5652	2.6996	2.8398	2.9860	3.1384	3.2973	3.4628	3.6352	3.8147	4.0015	4.1959	4.3980	4.6083	4.8268	6
7	2.8262	3.0012	3.1855	3.3793	3.5832	3.7975	4.0227	4.2593	4.5077	4.7684	5.0419	5.3288	5.6295	5.9447	6.2749	7
8	3.2784	3.5115	3.7589	4.0214	4.2998	4.5950	4.9077	5.2389	5.5895	5.9605	6.3528	6.7675	7.2058	7.6686	8.1573	8
9	3.8030	4.1084	4.4355	4.7854	5.1598	5.5599	5.9874	6.4439	6.9310	7.4506	8.0045	8.5946	9.2234	9.8925	10.6045	9
10	4.4114	4.8068	5.2338	5.6947	6.1917	6.7275	7.3046	7.9259	8.5944	9.3132	10.0857	10.9153	11.8059	12.7614	13.7858	10
11	5.1173	5.6240	6.1759	6.7767	7.4301	8.1403	8.9117	9.7489	10.6571	11.6415	12.7080	13.8625	15.1116	16.4622	17.9216	11
12	5.9360	6.5801	7.2876	8.0642	8.9161	9.8497	10.8722	11.9912	13.2148	14.5519	16.0120	17.6053	19.3428	21.2362	23.2981	12
13	6.8858	7.6987	8.5994	9.5964	10.6993	11.9182	13.2641	14.7491	16.3863	18.1899	20.1752	22.3588	24.7588	27.3947	30.2875	13
14	7.9875	9.0075	10.1472	11.4198	12.8392	14.4210	16.1822	18.1414	20.3191	22.7374	25.4207	28.3957	31.6913	35.3391	39.3738	14
15	9.2655	10.5387	11.9737	13.5895	15.4070	17.4494	19.7423	22.3140	25.1956	28.4217	32.0301	36.0625	40.5648	45.5875	51.1859	15
16	10.7480	12.3303	14.1290	16.1715	18.4884	21.1138	24.0856	27.4462	31.2426	35.5271	40.3579	45.7994	51.9230	58.8079	66.5417	16
17	12.4677	14.4265	16.6722	19.2441	22.1861	25.5477	29.3844	33.7588	38.7408	44.4089	50.8510	58.1652	66.4614	75.8621	86.5042	17
18	14.4625	16.8790	19.6733	22.9005	26.6233	30.9127	35.8490	41.5233	48.0386	55.5112	64.0722	73.8698	85.0706	97.8622	112.4554	18
19	16.7765	19.7484	23.2144	27.2516	31.9480	37.4043	43.7358	51.0737	59.5679	69.3889	80.7310	93.8147	108.8904	126.2422	146.1920	19
20	19.4608	23.1056	27.3930	32.4294	38.3376	45.2593	53.3576	62.8206	73.8641	86.7362	101.7211	119.1446	139.3797	162.8524	190.0496	20
25	40.8742	50.6578	62.6686	77.3881	95.3962	117.3909	144.2101	176.8593	216.5420	264.6978	323.0454	393.6344	478.9049	581.7585	705.6410	25

Appendix II

Present value of £1 at compound interest

Interest rate

Periods	1	2	3	4	5	6	7	8	9	10	11	12	13	14	15
1	0.9901	0.9804	0.9709	0.9615	0.9524	0.9434	0.9346	0.9259	0.9174	0.9091	0.9009	0.8929	0.8850	0.8772	0.8696
2	0.9803	0.9612	0.9426	0.9246	0.9070	0.8900	0.8734	0.8573	0.8417	0.8264	0.8116	0.7972	0.7831	0.7695	0.7561
3	0.9706	0.9423	0.9151	0.8890	0.8638	0.8396	0.8163	0.7938	0.7722	0.7513	0.7312	0.7118	0.6931	0.6750	0.6575
4	0.9610	0.9238	0.8885	0.8548	0.8227	0.7921	0.7629	0.7350	0.7084	0.6830	0.6587	0.6355	0.6133	0.5921	0.5718
5	0.9515	0.9057	0.8626	0.8219	0.7835	0.7473	0.7130	0.6806	0.6499	0.6209	0.5935	0.5674	0.5428	0.5194	0.4972
6	0.9420	0.8880	0.8375	0.7903	0.7462	0.7050	0.6663	0.6302	0.5963	0.5645	0.5346	0.5066	0.4803	0.4556	0.4323
7	0.9327	0.8706	0.8131	0.7599	0.7107	0.6651	0.6227	0.5835	0.5470	0.5132	0.4817	0.4523	0.4251	0.3996	0.3759
8	0.9235	0.8535	0.7894	0.7307	0.6768	0.6274	0.5820	0.5403	0.5019	0.4665	0.4339	0.4039	0.3762	0.3506	0.3269
9	0.9143	0.8368	0.7664	0.7026	0.6446	0.5919	0.5439	0.5002	0.4604	0.4241	0.3909	0.3606	0.3329	0.3075	0.2843
10	0.9053	0.8203	0.7441	0.6756	0.6139	0.5584	0.5083	0.4632	0.4224	0.3855	0.3522	0.3220	0.2946	0.2697	0.2472
11	0.8963	0.8043	0.7224	0.6496	0.5847	0.5268	0.4751	0.4289	0.3875	0.3505	0.3173	0.2875	0.2607	0.2366	0.2149
12	0.8874	0.7885	0.7014	0.6246	0.5568	0.4970	0.4440	0.3971	0.3555	0.3186	0.2858	0.2567	0.2307	0.2076	0.1869
13	0.8787	0.7730	0.6810	0.6006	0.5303	0.4688	0.4150	0.3677	0.3262	0.2897	0.2575	0.2292	0.2042	0.1821	0.1625
14	0.8700	0.7579	0.6611	0.5775	0.5051	0.4423	0.3878	0.3405	0.2992	0.2633	0.2320	0.2046	0.1807	0.1597	0.1413
15	0.8613	0.7430	0.6419	0.5553	0.4810	0.4173	0.3624	0.3152	0.2745	0.2394	0.2090	0.1827	0.1599	0.1401	0.1229
16	0.8528	0.7284	0.6232	0.5339	0.4581	0.3936	0.3387	0.2919	0.2519	0.2176	0.1883	0.1631	0.1415	0.1229	0.1069
17	0.8444	0.7142	0.6050	0.5134	0.4363	0.3714	0.3166	0.2703	0.2311	0.1978	0.1696	0.1456	0.1252	0.1078	0.0929
18	0.8360	0.7002	0.5874	0.4936	0.4155	0.3503	0.2959	0.2502	0.2120	0.1799	0.1528	0.1300	0.1108	0.0946	0.0808
19	0.8277	0.6864	0.5703	0.4746	0.3957	0.3305	0.2765	0.2317	0.1945	0.1635	0.1377	0.1161	0.0981	0.0829	0.0703
20	0.8195	0.6730	0.5537	0.4564	0.3769	0.3118	0.2584	0.2145	0.1784	0.1486	0.1240	0.1037	0.0868	0.0728	0.0611
25	0.7798	0.6095	0.4776	0.3751	0.2953	0.2330	0.1842	0.1460	0.1160	0.0923	0.0736	0.0588	0.0471	0.0378	0.0304
30	0.7419	0.5521	0.4120	0.3083	0.2314	0.1741	0.1314	0.0994	0.0754	0.0573	0.0437	0.0334	0.0256	0.0196	0.0151
35	0.7059	0.5000	0.3554	0.2534	0.1813	0.1301	0.0937	0.0676	0.0490	0.0356	0.0259	0.0189	0.0139	0.0102	0.0075
40	0.6717	0.4529	0.3066	0.2083	0.1420	0.0972	0.0668	0.0460	0.0318	0.0221	0.0154	0.0107	0.0075	0.0053	0.0037
45	0.6391	0.4102	0.2644	0.1712	0.1113	0.0727	0.0476	0.0313	0.0207	0.0137	0.0091	0.0061	0.0041	0.0027	0.0019
50	0.6080	0.3715	0.2281	0.1407	0.0872	0.0543	0.0339	0.0213	0.0134	0.0085	0.0054	0.0035	0.0022	0.0014	0.0009

Periods	16	17	18	19	20	21	22	23	24	25	26	27	28	29	30
1	0.8621	0.8547	0.8475	0.8403	0.8333	0.8264	0.8197	0.8130	0.8065	0.8000	0.7937	0.7874	0.7812	0.7752	0.7692
2	0.7432	0.7305	0.7182	0.7062	0.6944	0.6830	0.6719	0.6610	0.6504	0.6400	0.6299	0.6200	0.6104	0.6009	0.5917
3	0.6407	0.6244	0.6086	0.5934	0.5787	0.5645	0.5507	0.5374	0.5245	0.5120	0.4999	0.4882	0.4768	0.4658	0.4552
4	0.5523	0.5337	0.5158	0.4987	0.4823	0.4665	0.4514	0.4369	0.4230	0.4096	0.3968	0.3844	0.3725	0.3611	0.3501
5	0.4761	0.4561	0.4371	0.4190	0.4019	0.3855	0.3700	0.3552	0.3411	0.3277	0.3149	0.3027	0.2910	0.2799	0.2693
6	0.4104	0.3898	0.3704	0.3521	0.3349	0.3186	0.3033	0.2888	0.2751	0.2621	0.2499	0.2383	0.2274	0.2170	0.2072
7	0.3538	0.3332	0.3139	0.2959	0.2791	0.2633	0.2486	0.2348	0.2218	0.2097	0.1983	0.1877	0.1776	0.1682	0.1594
8	0.3050	0.2848	0.2660	0.2487	0.2326	0.2176	0.2038	0.1909	0.1789	0.1678	0.1574	0.1478	0.1388	0.1304	0.1226
9	0.2630	0.2434	0.2255	0.2090	0.1938	0.1799	0.1670	0.1552	0.1443	0.1342	0.1249	0.1164	0.1084	0.1011	0.0943
10	0.2267	0.2080	0.1911	0.1756	0.1615	0.1486	0.1369	0.1262	0.1164	0.1074	0.0992	0.0916	0.0847	0.0784	0.0725
11	0.1954	0.1778	0.1619	0.1476	0.1346	0.1228	0.1122	0.1026	0.0938	0.0859	0.0787	0.0721	0.0662	0.0607	0.0558
12	0.1685	0.1520	0.1372	0.1240	0.1122	0.1015	0.0920	0.0834	0.0757	0.0687	0.0625	0.0568	0.0517	0.0471	0.0429
13	0.1452	0.1299	0.1163	0.1042	0.0935	0.0839	0.0754	0.0678	0.0610	0.0550	0.0496	0.0447	0.0404	0.0365	0.0330
14	0.1252	0.1110	0.0985	0.0876	0.0779	0.0693	0.0618	0.0551	0.0492	0.0440	0.0393	0.0352	0.0316	0.0283	0.0254
15	0.1079	0.0949	0.0835	0.0736	0.0649	0.0573	0.0507	0.0448	0.0397	0.0352	0.0312	0.0277	0.0247	0.0219	0.0195
16	0.0930	0.0811	0.0708	0.0618	0.0541	0.0474	0.0415	0.0364	0.0320	0.0281	0.0248	0.0218	0.0193	0.0170	0.0150
17	0.0802	0.0693	0.0600	0.0520	0.0451	0.0391	0.0340	0.0296	0.0258	0.0225	0.0197	0.0172	0.0150	0.0132	0.0116
18	0.0691	0.0592	0.0508	0.0437	0.0376	0.0323	0.0279	0.0241	0.0208	0.0180	0.0156	0.0135	0.0118	0.0102	0.0089
19	0.0596	0.0506	0.0431	0.0367	0.0313	0.0267	0.0229	0.0196	0.0168	0.0144	0.0124	0.0107	0.0092	0.0079	0.0068
20	0.0514	0.0433	0.0365	0.0308	0.0261	0.0221	0.0187	0.0159	0.0135	0.0115	0.0098	0.0084	0.0072	0.0061	0.0053
25	0.0245	0.0197	0.0160	0.0129	0.0105	0.0085	0.0069	0.0057	0.0046	0.0038	0.0031	0.0025	0.0021	0.0017	0.0014
30	0.0116	0.0090	0.0070	0.0054	0.0042	0.0033	0.0026	0.0020	0.0016	0.0012	0.0010	0.0008	0.0006	0.0005	0.0004
35	0.0055	0.0041	0.0030	0.0023	0.0017	0.0013	0.0009	0.0007	0.0005	0.0004	0.0003	0.0002	0.0002	0.0001	0.0001
40	0.0026	0.0019	0.0013	0.0010	0.0007	0.0005	0.0004	0.0003	0.0002	0.0001	0.0001	0.0001	0.0001	0.0000	0.0000
45	0.0013	0.0009	0.0006	0.0004	0.0003	0.0002	0.0001	0.0001	0.0001	0.0000	0.0000	0.0000	0.0000	0.0000	0.0000
50	0.0006	0.0004	0.0003	0.0002	0.0001	0.0001	0.0000	0.0000	0.0000	0.0000	0.0000	0.0000	0.0000	0.0000	0.0000

Appendix III

Present value of an annuity of £1 at compound interest

$$\frac{1 - 1/(1+i)^n}{i} \times A$$

Interest rate

Periods	1	2	3	4	5	6	7	8	9	10	11	12	13	14	15
1	0.9901	0.9804	0.9709	0.9615	0.9524	0.9434	0.9346	0.9259	0.9174	0.9091	0.9009	0.8929	0.8850	0.8772	0.8696
2	1.9704	1.9416	1.9135	1.8861	1.8594	1.8334	1.8080	1.7833	1.7591	1.7355	1.7125	1.6901	1.6681	1.6467	1.6257
3	2.9410	2.8839	2.8286	2.7751	2.7232	2.6730	2.6243	2.5771	2.5313	2.4869	2.4437	2.4018	2.3612	2.3216	2.2832
4	3.9020	3.8077	3.7171	3.6299	3.5460	3.4651	3.3872	3.3121	3.2397	3.1699	3.1024	3.0373	2.9745	2.9137	2.8550
5	4.8534	4.7135	4.5797	4.4518	4.3295	4.2124	4.1002	3.9927	3.8897	3.7908	3.6959	3.6048	3.5172	3.4331	3.3522
6	5.7955	5.6014	5.4172	5.2421	5.0757	4.9173	4.7665	4.6229	4.4859	4.3553	4.2305	4.1114	3.9975	3.8887	3.7845
7	6.7282	6.4720	6.2303	6.0021	5.7864	5.5824	5.3893	5.2064	5.0330	4.8684	4.7122	4.5638	4.4226	4.2883	4.1604
8	7.6517	7.3255	7.0197	6.7327	6.4632	6.2098	5.9713	5.7466	5.5348	5.3349	5.1461	4.9676	4.7988	4.6389	4.4873
9	8.5660	8.1622	7.7861	7.4353	7.1078	6.8017	6.5152	6.2469	5.9952	5.7590	5.5370	5.3282	5.1317	4.9464	4.7716
10	9.4713	8.9826	8.5302	8.1109	7.7217	7.3601	7.0236	6.7101	6.4177	6.1446	5.8892	5.6502	5.4262	5.2161	5.0188
11	10.3676	9.7868	9.2526	8.7605	8.3064	7.8869	7.4987	7.1390	6.8052	6.4951	6.2065	5.9377	5.6869	5.4527	5.2337
12	11.2551	10.5753	9.9540	9.3851	8.8633	8.3838	7.9427	7.5361	7.1607	6.8137	6.4924	6.1944	5.9176	5.6603	5.4206
13	12.1337	11.3484	10.6350	9.9856	9.3936	8.8527	8.3577	7.9038	7.4869	7.1034	6.7499	6.4235	6.1218	5.8424	5.5831
14	13.0037	12.1062	11.2961	10.5631	9.8986	9.2950	8.7455	8.2442	7.7862	7.3667	6.9819	6.6282	6.3025	6.0021	5.7245
15	13.8651	12.8493	11.9379	11.1184	10.3797	9.7122	9.1079	8.5595	8.0607	7.6061	7.1909	6.8109	6.4624	6.1422	5.8474
16	14.7179	13.5777	12.5611	11.6523	10.8378	10.1059	9.4466	8.8514	8.3126	7.8237	7.3792	6.9740	6.6039	6.2651	5.9542
17	15.5623	14.2919	13.1661	12.1657	11.2741	10.4773	9.7632	9.1216	8.5436	8.0216	7.5488	7.1196	6.7291	6.3729	6.0472
18	16.3983	14.9920	13.7535	12.6593	11.6896	10.8276	10.0591	9.3719	8.7556	8.2014	7.7016	7.2497	6.8399	6.4674	6.1280
19	17.2260	15.6785	14.3238	13.1339	12.0853	11.1581	10.3356	9.6036	8.9501	8.3649	7.8393	7.3658	6.9380	6.5504	6.1982
20	18.0456	16.3514	14.8775	13.5903	12.4622	11.4699	10.5940	9.8181	9.1285	8.5136	7.9633	7.4694	7.0248	6.6231	6.2593
25	22.0232	19.5235	17.4131	15.6221	14.0939	12.7834	11.6536	10.6748	9.8226	9.0770	8.4217	7.8431	7.3300	6.8729	6.4641
30	25.8077	22.3965	19.6004	17.2920	15.3725	13.7648	12.4090	11.2578	10.2737	9.4269	8.6938	8.0552	7.4957	7.0027	6.5660
35	29.4086	24.9986	21.4872	18.6646	16.3742	14.4982	12.9477	11.6546	10.5668	9.6442	8.8552	8.1755	7.5856	7.0700	6.6166
40	32.8347	27.3555	23.1148	19.7928	17.1591	15.0463	13.3317	11.9246	10.7574	9.7791	8.9511	8.2438	7.6344	7.1050	6.6418
45	36.0945	29.4902	24.5187	20.7200	17.7741	15.4558	13.6055	12.1084	10.8812	9.8628	9.0079	8.2825	7.6609	7.1232	6.6543
50	39.1961	31.4236	25.7298	21.4822	18.2559	15.7619	13.8007	12.2335	10.9617	9.9148	9.0417	8.3045	7.6752	7.1327	6.6605

Periods	16	17	18	19	20	21	22	23	24	25	26	27	28	29	30
1	0.8621	0.8547	0.8475	0.8403	0.8333	0.8264	0.8197	0.8130	0.8065	0.8000	0.7937	0.7874	0.7812	0.7752	0.7692
2	1.6052	1.5852	1.5656	1.5465	1.5278	1.5095	1.4915	1.4740	1.4568	1.4400	1.4235	1.4074	1.3916	1.3761	1.3609
3	2.2459	2.2096	2.1743	2.1399	2.1065	2.0739	2.0422	2.0114	1.9813	1.9520	1.9234	1.8956	1.8684	1.8420	1.8161
4	2.7982	2.7432	2.6901	2.6386	2.5887	2.5404	2.4936	2.4483	2.4043	2.3616	2.3202	2.2800	2.2410	2.2031	2.1662
5	3.2743	3.1993	3.1272	3.0576	2.9906	2.9260	2.8636	2.8035	2.7454	2.6893	2.6351	2.5827	2.5320	2.4830	2.4356
6	3.6847	3.5892	3.4976	3.4098	3.3255	3.2446	3.1669	3.0923	3.0205	2.9514	2.8850	2.8210	2.7594	2.7000	2.6427
7	4.0386	3.9224	3.8115	3.7057	3.6046	3.5079	3.4155	3.3270	3.2423	3.1611	3.0833	3.0087	2.9370	2.8682	2.8021
8	4.3436	4.2072	4.0776	3.9544	3.8372	3.7256	3.6193	3.5179	3.4212	3.3289	3.2407	3.1564	3.0758	2.9986	2.9247
9	4.6065	4.4506	4.3030	4.1633	4.0310	3.9054	3.7863	3.6731	3.5655	3.4631	3.3657	3.2728	3.1842	3.0997	3.0190
10	4.8332	4.6586	4.4941	4.3389	4.1925	4.0541	3.9232	3.7993	3.6819	3.5705	3.4648	3.3644	3.2689	3.1781	3.0915
11	5.0286	4.8364	4.6560	4.4865	4.3271	4.1769	4.0354	3.9018	3.7757	3.6564	3.5435	3.4365	3.3351	3.2388	3.1473
12	5.1971	4.9884	4.7932	4.6105	4.4392	4.2784	4.1274	3.9852	3.8514	3.7251	3.6059	3.4933	3.3868	3.2859	3.1903
13	5.3423	5.1183	4.9095	4.7147	4.5327	4.3624	4.2028	4.0530	3.9124	3.7801	3.6555	3.5381	3.4272	3.3224	3.2233
14	5.4675	5.2293	5.0081	4.8023	4.6106	4.4317	4.2646	4.1082	3.9616	3.8241	3.6949	3.5733	3.4587	3.3507	3.2487
15	5.5755	5.3242	5.0916	4.8759	4.6755	4.4890	4.3152	4.1530	4.0013	3.8593	3.7261	3.6010	3.4834	3.3726	3.2682
16	5.6685	5.4053	5.1624	4.9377	4.7296	4.5364	4.3567	4.1894	4.0333	3.8874	3.7509	3.6228	3.5026	3.3896	3.2832
17	5.7487	5.4746	5.2223	4.9897	4.7746	4.5755	4.3908	4.2190	4.0591	3.9099	3.7705	3.6400	3.5177	3.4028	3.2948
18	5.8178	5.5339	5.2732	5.0333	4.8122	4.6079	4.4187	4.2431	4.0799	3.9279	3.7861	3.6536	3.5294	3.4130	3.3037
19	5.8775	5.5845	5.3162	5.0700	4.8435	4.6346	4.4415	4.2627	4.0967	3.9424	3.7985	3.6642	3.5386	3.4210	3.3105
20	5.9288	5.6278	5.3527	5.1009	4.8696	4.6567	4.4603	4.2786	4.1103	3.9539	3.8083	3.6726	3.5458	3.4271	3.3158
25	6.0971	5.7662	5.4669	5.1951	4.9476	4.7213	4.5139	4.3232	4.1474	3.9849	3.8342	3.6943	3.5640	3.4423	3.3286
30	6.1772	5.8294	5.5168	5.2347	4.9789	4.7463	4.5338	4.3391	4.1601	3.9950	3.8424	3.7009	3.5693	3.4466	3.3321
35	6.2153	5.8582	5.5386	5.2512	4.9915	4.7559	4.5411	4.3447	4.1644	3.9984	3.8450	3.7028	3.5708	3.4478	3.3330
40	6.2335	5.8713	5.5482	5.2582	4.9966	4.7596	4.5439	4.3467	4.1659	3.9995	3.8458	3.7034	3.5712	3.4481	3.3332
45	6.2421	5.8773	5.5523	5.2611	4.9986	4.7610	4.5449	4.3474	4.1664	3.9998	3.8460	3.7036	3.5714	3.4482	3.3333
50	6.2463	5.8801	5.5541	5.2623	4.9995	4.7616	4.5452	4.3477	4.1666	3.9999	3.8461	3.7037	3.5714	3.4483	3.3333

Appendix IV

Future value of an annuity of £1 at compound interest $A\left[\dfrac{(1+i)^n - 1}{i}\right]$

Interest rate

Periods	1	2	3	4	5	6	7	8	9	10	12	14	16	18	20	25	30	35	40	45	50
1	1.0000	1.0000	1.0000	1.0000	1.0000	1.0000	1.0000	1.0000	1.0000	1.0000	1.0000	1.0000	1.0000	1.0000	1.0000	1.0000	1.0000	1.0000	1.0000	1.0000	1.0000
2	2.0100	2.0200	2.0300	2.0400	2.0500	2.0600	2.0700	2.0800	2.0900	2.1000	2.1200	2.1400	2.1600	2.1800	2.2000	2.2500	2.3000	2.3500	2.400	2.4500	2.5000
3	3.0301	3.0604	3.0909	3.1216	3.1525	3.1836	3.2149	3.2464	3.2781	3.3100	3.3744	3.4396	3.5056	3.5724	3.6400	3.8125	3.9900	4.1725	4.3600	4.5525	4.7500
4	4.0604	4.1216	4.1836	4.2465	4.3101	4.3746	4.4399	4.5061	4.5731	4.6410	4.7793	4.9211	5.0665	5.2154	5.3680	5.7656	6.1870	6.6329	7.1040	7.6011	8.1250
5	5.1010	5.2040	5.3091	5.4163	5.5256	5.6371	5.7507	5.8666	5.9847	6.1051	6.3528	6.6101	6.8771	7.1542	7.4416	8.2070	9.0431	9.9544	10.9456	12.0216	13.1875
6	6.1520	6.3081	6.4684	6.6330	6.8019	6.9753	7.1533	7.3359	7.5233	7.7156	8.1152	8.5355	8.9775	9.4420	9.9299	11.2588	12.7560	14.4834	16.3238	18.4314	20.7813
7	7.2135	7.4343	7.6625	7.8983	8.1420	8.3938	8.6540	8.9228	9.2004	9.4872	10.0890	10.7305	11.4139	12.1415	12.9159	15.0735	17.5828	20.4919	23.8534	27.7255	32.1719
8	8.2857	8.5830	8.8923	9.2142	9.5491	9.8975	10.2598	10.6366	11.0285	11.4359	12.2997	13.2328	14.2401	15.3270	16.4991	19.8419	23.8577	28.6640	34.3947	41.2019	49.2578
9	9.3685	9.7546	10.1591	10.5828	11.0266	11.4913	11.9780	12.4876	13.0210	13.5795	14.7757	16.0853	17.5185	19.0859	20.7989	25.8023	32.0150	39.6964	49.1526	60.7428	74.8867
10	10.4622	10.9497	11.4639	12.0061	12.5779	13.1808	13.8164	14.4866	15.1929	15.9374	17.5487	19.3373	21.3215	23.5213	25.9587	33.2529	42.6195	54.5902	69.8137	89.0771	113.330
11	11.5668	12.1687	12.8078	13.4864	14.2068	14.9716	15.7836	16.6455	17.5603	18.5312	20.6546	23.0445	25.7329	28.7551	32.1504	42.5661	56.4053	74.6967	98.7391	130.162	170.995
12	12.6825	13.4121	14.1920	15.0258	15.9171	16.8699	17.8885	18.9771	20.1407	21.3843	24.1331	27.2707	30.8502	34.9311	39.5805	54.2077	74.3270	101.841	139.235	189.735	257.493
13	13.8093	14.6803	15.6178	16.6268	17.7130	18.8821	20.1406	21.4953	22.9534	24.5227	28.0291	32.0887	36.7862	42.2187	48.4966	68.7596	97.6250	138.485	195.929	276.115	387.239
14	14.9474	15.9739	17.0863	18.2919	19.5986	21.0151	22.5505	24.2149	26.0192	27.9750	32.3926	37.5811	43.6720	50.8180	59.1959	86.9495	127.913	187.954	275.300	401.367	581.859
15	16.0969	17.2934	18.5989	20.0236	21.5786	23.2760	25.1290	27.1521	29.3609	31.7725	37.2797	43.8424	51.6595	60.9653	72.0351	109.687	167.286	254.738	386.420	582.982	873.788
16	17.2579	18.6393	20.1569	21.8245	23.6575	25.6725	27.8881	30.3243	33.0034	35.9497	42.7533	50.9804	60.9250	72.9390	87.4421	138.109	218.472	344.897	541.988	846.324	1311.68
17	18.4304	20.0121	21.7616	23.6975	25.8404	28.2129	30.8402	33.7502	36.9737	40.5447	48.8837	59.1176	71.6730	87.0680	105.931	175.636	285.014	466.611	759.784	1228.17	1968.52
18	19.6147	21.4123	23.4144	25.6454	28.1324	30.9057	33.9990	37.4502	41.3013	45.5992	55.7497	68.3941	84.1407	103.740	128.117	218.045	371.518	630.925	1064.70	1781.85	2953.78
19	20.8109	22.8406	25.1169	27.6712	30.5390	33.7600	37.3790	41.4463	46.0185	51.1591	63.4397	78.9692	98.6032	123.414	154.740	273.556	483.973	852.748	1491.58	2584.68	4431.68
20	22.0190	24.2974	26.8704	29.7781	33.0660	36.7856	40.9955	45.7620	51.1601	57.2750	72.0524	91.0249	115.380	146.628	186.688	342.945	630.165	1152.21	2089.21	3748.78	6648.51
25	28.2432	32.0303	36.4593	41.6459	47.7271	54.8645	63.2490	73.1059	84.7009	98.3471	133.334	181.871	249.214	342.603	471.981	1054.79	2348.80	5176.50	11247.1990	24040.7	50500.3
30	34.7849	40.5681	47.5754	56.0849	66.4388	79.0582	94.4608	113.283	136.308	164.494	241.333	356.787	530.312	790.948	1181.88	3227.17	8729.99	23221.6	60501.1	154107	383500
35	41.6603	49.9945	60.4621	73.6522	90.3203	111.435	138.237	172.317	215.711	271.024	431.663	693.573	1120.71	1816.65	2948.34	9856.76	32422.9	104136	325400	987794	2912217
40	48.8864	60.4020	75.4013	95.0255	120.800	154.762	199.635	259.057	337.882	442.593	767.091	1342.03	2360.76	4163.21	7343.86	30088.7	120393	466960	1750092	6331512	22114663
45	56.4811	71.8927	92.7199	121.029	159.700	212.744	285.749	386.506	525.859	718.905	1358.23	2590.56	4965.27	9531.58	18281.3	91831.5	447019	2093876	9412424	40583319	167933233
50	64.4632	84.5794	112.797	152.667	209.348	290.336	406.529	573.770	815.084	1163.91	2400.02	4994.52	10435.6	21813.1	45497.2	280256	1659761	9389020	50622288	260128295	1275242998

Appendix V
Areas under the standardised normal distribution

z	0.00	0.01	0.02	0.03	0.04	0.05	0.06	0.07	0.08	0.09
0.0	0.0000	0.0040	0.0080	0.0120	0.0160	0.0199	0.0239	0.0279	0.0319	0.0359
0.1	0.0398	0.0438	0.0478	0.0517	0.0557	0.0596	0.0636	0.0675	0.0714	0.0753
0.2	0.0793	0.0832	0.0871	0.0910	0.0948	0.0987	0.1026	0.1064	0.1103	0.1141
0.3	0.1179	0.1217	0.1255	0.1293	0.1331	0.1368	0.1406	0.1443	0.1480	0.1517
0.4	0.1554	0.1591	0.1628	0.1664	0.1700	0.1736	0.1772	0.1808	0.1844	0.1879
0.5	0.1915	0.1950	0.1985	0.2019	0.2054	0.2088	0.2123	0.2157	0.2190	0.2224
0.6	0.2257	0.2291	0.2324	0.2357	0.2389	0.2422	0.2454	0.2486	0.2517	0.2549
0.7	0.2580	0.2611	0.2642	0.2673	0.2704	0.2734	0.2764	0.2794	0.2823	0.2852
0.8	0.2881	0.2910	0.2939	0.2967	0.2995	0.3023	0.3051	0.3078	0.3106	0.3133
0.9	0.3159	0.3186	0.3212	0.3238	0.3264	0.3289	0.3315	0.3340	0.3365	0.3389
1.0	0.3413	0.3438	0.3461	0.3485	0.3508	0.3531	0.3554	0.3577	0.3599	0.3621
1.1	0.3643	0.3665	0.3686	0.3708	0.3729	0.3749	0.3770	0.3790	0.3810	0.3830
1.2	0.3849	0.3869	0.3888	0.3907	0.3925	0.3944	0.3962	0.3980	0.3997	0.4015
1.3	0.4032	0.4049	0.4066	0.4082	0.4099	0.4115	0.4131	0.4147	0.4162	0.4177
1.4	0.4192	0.4207	0.4222	0.4236	0.4251	0.4265	0.4279	0.4292	0.4306	0.4319
1.5	0.4332	0.4345	0.4357	0.4370	0.4382	0.4394	0.4406	0.4418	0.4429	0.4441
1.6	0.4452	0.4463	0.4474	0.4484	0.4495	0.4505	0.4515	0.4525	0.4535	0.4545
1.7	0.4554	0.4564	0.4573	0.4582	0.4591	0.4599	0.4608	0.4616	0.4625	0.4633
1.8	0.4641	0.4649	0.4656	0.4664	0.4671	0.4678	0.4686	0.4693	0.4699	0.4706
1.9	0.4713	0.4719	0.4726	0.4732	0.4738	0.4744	0.4750	0.4756	0.4761	0.4767
2.0	0.4772	0.4778	0.4783	0.4788	0.4793	0.4798	0.4803	0.4808	0.4812	0.4817
2.1	0.4821	0.4826	0.4830	0.4834	0.4838	0.4842	0.4846	0.4850	0.4854	0.4857
2.2	0.4861	0.4864	0.4868	0.4871	0.4875	0.4878	0.4881	0.4884	0.4887	0.4890
2.3	0.4893	0.4896	0.4898	0.4901	0.4904	0.4906	0.4909	0.4911	0.4913	0.4916
2.4	0.4918	0.4920	0.4922	0.4925	0.4927	0.4929	0.4931	0.4932	0.4934	0.4936
2.5	0.4938	0.4940	0.4941	0.4943	0.4945	0.4946	0.4948	0.4949	0.4951	0.4952
2.6	0.4953	0.4955	0.4956	0.4957	0.4959	0.4960	0.4961	0.4962	0.4963	0.4964
2.7	0.4965	0.4966	0.4967	0.4968	0.4969	0.4970	0.4971	0.4972	0.4973	0.4974
2.8	0.4974	0.4975	0.4976	0.4977	0.4977	0.4978	0.4979	0.4979	0.4980	0.4981
2.9	0.4981	0.4982	0.4982	0.4983	0.4984	0.4984	0.4985	0.4985	0.4986	0.4986
3.0	0.4987	0.4987	0.4987	0.4988	0.4988	0.4989	0.4989	0.4989	0.4990	0.4990

1 (a) £124   (b) £125.97

2 (a) £26,533   (b) £163,665

3 (a) 14.2 years   (b) 4.96 years

4 Present values of the four options:
    (a) £1,000,000   (c) £1,500,000
    (b) £1,104,883   (d) £1,283,540
    Given the time value of money of 9 per cent per annum and certainty about the future
    (e.g. that you will live to enjoy the perpetuity) then the official answer is (c). You may like
    to question whether this is what you would really go for. If you prefer another option, try
    to explain what that option says about your time value of money.

5 6%

6 £675

7 14.93%

8 (a) £32.20   (b) £31.18

9 £4,731

10 £6,217, 8.24%

11 Present value of a ten-year £800 annuity = £4,711. Therefore, you could invest £4,711 @
    11% and receive £800 per year for ten years. Reject Supersalesman's offer.

12 £6,468

Appendix VII
Solutions to selected questions and problems

This Appendix provides suggested solutions to those end-of-chapter numerical questions and problems not marked with an asterisk*. Answers to questions and problems marked * are given in the *Lecturer's Guide*. Answers to discussion questions, essays and reports questions can be found by reading the text.

Chapter 1

No numerical questions; answers to all questions may be found by reading the text.

Chapter 2

1 Proast plc

(a) Project A

Point in time (yearly intervals)	Cash flow	Discount factor	Discounted cash flow
0	−120	1.0	−120.00
1	60	0.8696	52.176
2	45	0.7561	34.025
3	42	0.6575	27.615
4	18	0.5718	10.292
		NPV	4.108
			£4,108

Project B

Cash flow	Discount factor	Discounted cash flow
−120	1.0	−120.00
15	0.8696	13.044
45	0.7561	34.025
55	0.6575	36.163
60	0.5718	34.308
	NPV	−2.460
		−£2,460

Advice: Accept project A and reject project B, because A generates a return greater than that required by the firm on projects of this risk class, but B does not.

(b) The figure of £4,108 for the NPV of project A can be interpreted as the surplus (in present value terms) above and beyond the required 15 per cent return. Therefore, Proast would be prepared to put up to £120,000 + £4,108 into this project at time zero, because it could thereby obtain the required rate of return of 15 per cent. If Proast put in any more than this, it would generate less than the opportunity cost of the finance providers. Likewise, the maximum cash outflow at time zero (0) for project B which permits the generation of a 15 per cent return is £120,000 − £2,460 = £117,540.

2 Highflyer plc

(a) First, recognise that annuities are present (to save a lot of time).

Project A: Try 15% −420,000 + 150,000 × 2.855 = +£8,250.
              Try 16% −420,000 + 150,000 × 2.7982 = −£270.

$$\text{IRR} = 15 + \frac{8{,}250}{8{,}250 + 270} \times (16 - 15) = 15.97\%$$

Project B: Try 31% and 32%.

Point in time (yearly intervals)	Cash flow	Discounted cash flow @ 31%	Discounted cash flow @ 32%
0	−100,000	−100,000	−100,000
1	75,000	57,252	56,818
2	75,000	43,704	43,044
		+956	−138

$$\text{IRR} = 31 + \frac{956}{956 + 138} \times (32 - 31) = 31.87\%$$

(b) NPV: *Project A*
     −420,000 + 150,000 × 3.0373 = + £35,595

     Project B
     −100,000 + 75,000 × 1.6901 = + £26,758

(c) Comparison:

	IRR	NPV
Project A	15.97%	+£35,595
Project B	31.87%	+£26,758

If the projects were not mutually exclusive, Highflyer would be advised to accept both. If the firm has to choose between them, on the basis of the IRR calculation it would select B, but, if NPV is used, project A is the preferred choice. In mutually exclusive situations with projects generating more than the required rate of return, NPV is the superior decision-making tool. It measures in absolute amounts of money rather than in percentages and does not have the theoretical doubts about the reinvestment rate of return on intra-project cash inflows.

4 Point in time (yearly intervals)	0	1	2	3
Cash flow	−300	+260	−200	+600
Discount factor	1.0	0.885	0.7831	0.6931
Discounted cash flow	−300	+230.1	−156.62	+415.86

NPV = +£189.34

There is more than one IRR calculated for this project; therefore, it is difficult to compare with required rate of return.

Chapter 3

Quick numerical questions

1 Tenby-Saundersfoot Dock Company

(a) London head office cost allocation is irrelevant as this is non-incremental.

Point in time (yearly intervals)	0 £000	1 → ∞ £000
Fees		255
Repairs	−250	
Employees		−70
Administration, etc.		−85
Electricity		−40
Other docks		−20
Cash flow	−250	+40

Additional overhead costs are included, but those which would have occurred, whether or not the dock project proceeded, are excluded. The loss of trade to other profit centres (docks) is included in the assessment of this project because this is an incidental effect which only occurs because of this new project.

(b) $\text{NPV} = -250 + \dfrac{40}{0.17} = -14.706$ or £14,706.

2 Railcam

Point in time (yearly intervals)	20X2 £m	20X3 £m	20X4 £m
Sales	+22	+24	+21
Debtor adjustments			
Opening debtors	5.00	5.50	6.00
Closing debtors	5.50	6.00	5.25
	−0.50	−0.50	+0.75
Wages	−6.00	−6.00	−6.00
Materials	−11.00	−12.00	−10.50
Creditor adjustments			
Opening creditors	2.50	2.75	3.00
Closing creditors	2.75	3.00	2.625
	+0.25	+0.25	−0.375
Overhead	−5.00	−5.00	−5.00
	−0.25	+0.75	−0.125

3 Payback: A: 6 years B: 3 years C: 4 years D: 4 years E: 5 years

Discounted payback

A	£	Cumulative
500 × 0.893	446.5	446.5
500 × 0.797	398.5	845
500 × 0.712	356	1,201
500 × 0.636	318	1,519
500 × 0.567	283.5	1,802.5
500 × 0.507	253.5	2,056
500 × 0.452	226	2,282

Discounted payback is not achieved (also shareholder wealth-destroying project).

B	£	Cumulative
2,000 × 0.893	1,786	1,786
5,000 × 0.797	3,985	5,771
3,000 × 0.712	2,136	7,907
2,000 × 0.636	1,272	9,179

Discounted payback is not achieved (also shareholder wealth-destroying project).

C	£	Cumulative
5,000 × 0.893	4,465	4,465
4,000 × 0.797	3,188	7,653
4,000 × 0.712	2,848	10,501
5,000 × 0.636	3,180	13,681
10,000 × 0.567	5,670	19,351

Discounted payback at year 5.

D	£	Cumulative
1,000 × 3.0373	3,037	3,037
7,000 × 0.5674	3,972	7,008

Discounted payback at year 5.

E	£	Cumulative
500 × 2.4018	1,201	1,201
2,000 × 0.6355	1,271	2,472
5,000 × 0.5674	2,837	5,309
10,000 × 0.5066	5,066	10,375

Discounted payback at year 6.

4 Payback: 3 years in both cases. Yet the first project is clearly superior to the second. The ignoring of cash flow beyond the payback cut-off is a drawback of the payback method.

5 $(1 + m) = (1+h)(1+i)$

$(1+0.09) = (1+h)(1+0.05)$

$(1+h) = \dfrac{1.09}{1.05} - 1$

$h = 3.81\%$

6 Premiums: £25,194.

PV $= 25{,}194/(1.17)^3 = £15{,}730$

Questions and problems

1 Pine Ltd

(a) Recognition of sunk cost: £20,000 research.

Recognition of irrelevant data: depreciation.

£000s	20X1 start	20X1 end	20X2	20X3	20X4	20X5	20X6
Sales		+400	+400	+400	+320	+200	
Equipment	−240					+40	
Stock	−30					+30	
Working capital	−20					+20	
Overheads		−8	−8	−9.6	−9.6	−9.6	
Materials		−240	−240	−240	−192	−120	
Variable costs		−40	−40	−40	−32	−20	
Debtors adjustment							
Opening debtors		0	400	400	400	320	200
Closing debtors		400	400	400	320	200	0
		−400	0	0	+80	+120	+200
Cash flow	−290	−288	+112	+110.4	+166.4	+260.4	+200
Discount factor	1.0	0.8929	0.7972	0.7118	0.6355	0.5674	0.5066
Discounted cash flow	−290	−257.2	+89.3	+78.6	+105.7	+147.8	+101.3

NPV $= -£24{,}500$

A negative NPV indicates that the project produces less than the opportunity cost of capital of the finance providers. This firm would serve its shareholders best by not proceeding with this project.

(b) The answer should explain, with a minimal use of technical language, the following: The time value of money; discounting cash flows to a common point in time; opportunity cost of investors' funds; minimum rate of return required on a project; NPV = shareholder wealth increase; NPV decision rule; the significance of being cash flow based rather than profit based; only incremental cash flows are considered.

6 Maple plc

A possible solution

Project A	Year 1	2	3	4	5
Profit before depr.	800	800	800	800	800
Depreciation	400	400	400	400	400
Profit after depr.	400	400	400	400	400
Assets at start of year	2300	1900	1500	1100	700
ARR	17.4%	21.1%	26.7%	36.4%	57.1%

Average ARR = 31.7%

Project B	Year 1	2	3	4	5
Profit before depr.	250	250	250	250	250
Depreciation	120	120	120	120	120
Profit after depr.	130	130	130	130	130
Assets at start of year	660	540	420	300	180
ARR	19.7%	24.1%	31%	43.3%	72.2%

Average ARR = 38.1%

NPV: A: +£530,920, B: +£207,882; Project A has the higher NPV and therefore generates most shareholder value.

10 Plumber plc

(a) *Project A*:
NPV = −1.5 + 0.5 × 0.8929 + 0.5 × 0.7972 + 1 × 0.7118 + 1 × 0.6355 = +0.69235

Project B:
NPV = −2.0 + 4 × 0.6355 = +0.542.

Project C:
NPV = −1.8 + 1.2 × 0.7118 + 1.2 × 0.6355 = −0.1832

Project D:
NPV = −3.0 + 1.2 × 3.0373 = +0.64476

Project E:
NPV = −0.5 + 0.3 × 3.0373 = +0.41119

Project	Investment £m	NPV £m	NPV/investment	Ranking
A	1.5	0.69235	0.4616	2
B	2.0	0.542	0.271	3
D	3.0	0.64476	0.215	4
E	0.5	0.41119	0.822	1

Allocation of £5m:

Project	Investment £m	NPV
E	0.5	0.41119
A	1.5	0.69235
B	2.0	0.54200
$D \times {}^1/_3$	1.0	0.21492
	5.0	1.86046

Maximum NPV available = £1.86046m.

(b) £2,290,300.

(c) Project	NPV
A	0.69235
D	0.64476
E	0.41119
	1.74830

Chapter 4

Quick numerical questions

1 +£348.7K   (a) +£269.7K   (b) +£198.8K

2 **Project W**

Return	p_i	$R \times p_i$	Expected return	$(R_i - \bar{R})^2 p_i$
2	0.3	0.6	3.4	0.588
4	0.7	2.8	3.4	0.252
		3.4		0.840

Standard deviation £0.917m.

Project X

Return	p_i	$R \times p_i$	Expected return	$(R_i - \bar{R})^2 p_i$
−2	0.3	−0.6	5.0	14.7
8	0.7	5.6	5.0	6.3
		5.0		21.0

Standard deviation £4.58m.

Observation: W has a lower return and a much lower standard deviation than X.
            X has a higher return than Y, but also a higher risk.

$$3 \quad \frac{-80,000 - 220,000}{160,000} = 1.875 \text{ Probability of insolvency} = 50\% - 46.96\% = 3.04\%$$

4

	Outcome	Probability	$R_i \times p_i$	$(R_i - \bar{R})^2 p_i$
a	272,321	0.10	27,232	12,125,368,620
b	−46,556	0.10	−4,656	86,071,824
c	−75,255	0.56	−42,143	228,660
d	−234,694	0.24	−56,327	6,052,185,600
		Expected return, $\bar{R}$	−75,894	18,263,854,710

Standard deviation £135,144.

Questions and problems

3 (a) *Annual cash flows:*

		£
Sales	22,000 × 21	462,000
Variable direct costs	22,000 × 16	−352,000
		110,000

$$-400,000 + 110,000 \times af = 0 \quad af = \frac{400,000}{110,000} = 3.6364$$

$$\text{From annuity tables: } 24 + \frac{3.6819 - 3.6364}{3.6819 - 3.5705}(25\text{-}24) = 24.4\%$$

IRR = 24.4%

(b) *Sales volume:*

		£
Sales	20,900 × 21	438,900
VDC	20,900 × 16	−334,400
		104,500

$$af = \frac{400,000}{104,500} = 3.8278 \quad 22 + \frac{3.9232 - 3.8278}{3.9232 - 3.7993}(23-22) = 22.8$$

IRR = 22.8%

Sales price:		£
Sales	22,000 × 19.95	438,900
Variable direct costs		−352,000
		86,900

$$af = \frac{400,000}{86,900} = 4.6030 \quad 17 + \frac{4.6586 - 4.6030}{4.6586 - 4.4941}(18 - 17) = 17.3$$

IRR = 17.3%

Variable direct costs:		£
Sales	22,000 × 21	462,000
Variable direct costs	22,000 × 16.8	−369,600
		92,400

$$af = \frac{400,000}{92,400} = 4.3290 \quad 19 + \frac{4.3389 - 4.3290}{4.3389 - 4.1925}(19 - 18) = 19.1\%$$

(c) Consult the chapter for details.

4	NPV (£000s)	Prob.	NPV × p_i	$(NPV_i - \overline{NPV})^2 p_i$
Recession	−178.8	0.3	−53.6	30,912
Growth	177.8	0.5	88.9	634
Boom	534.5	0.2	106.9	30,780
		Expected NPV	142.2	62,326

Standard deviation = $\sqrt{62,326}$ = 250

Chapter 5

Quick numerical questions

1 32%

2 4.17%

3 22.74%; 84.9%

4 14.5%

5 7.33

Questions and problems

1 (a) and (b)

	Expected returns (%)			Standard deviations (%)	
	S		T	S	T
	0.15 × 45 = 6.75		0.15 × 18 = 2.7	99.5	0.15
	0.70 × 20 = 14.0		0.70 × 17 = 11.9	0.4	0.00
	0.15 × −10 = −1.5		0.15 × 16 = 2.4	128.3	0.15
		19.25	17.0	σ^2 228.2	σ^2 0.30
		Standard deviations		15.11	0.548

(c) *Covariances*

	Returns		Expected returns		Deviations		
Prob.	S	T	S	T	S	T	
0.15	45	18	19.25	17	25.75	1	$25.75 \times 1 \times 0.15 = 3.86$
0.70	20	17	19.25	17	0.75	0	$0.75 \times 0 \times 0.7 = 0.00$
0.15	–10	16	19.25	17	–29.25	–1	$-29.25 \times -1 \times 0.15 = \underline{4.39}$
							Covariance = $\underline{8.25}$

(d)   Expected return = 18.5%, Standard deviation = 10.25%

4 (a) Ihser: 21%; 429; 20.7%
Resque: 15%; 15; 3.87%

Covariance

$R_I - \bar{R}_I$	$R_R - \bar{R}_R$	p_i	$(R_I - \bar{R}_I)(R_R - \bar{R}_R)p_i$
19	–5	0.3	–28.5
9	0	0.4	0.0
–31	+5	0.3	$\underline{-46.5}$
			$\underline{-75.0}$

(b) (i) Expected return: 18%
Variance: 73.5
Standard deviation: 8.57%
(ii) Expected return   15.6%
Variance: 2.94
Standard deviation: 1.71%

(d) A: 17%, B: 9.5%, C: 12%

6 (a) $r_f = 10\%$; risk premium = 8%.

(b) P is above SML, offering a high return for risk level. The price will rise until the return offered is 23.6%.

(c) Q is below SML, offering a low return for its risk level. The price will fall until the return offered is 16.4%.

8 Threshold rate for discussion is $10 + 1.4(5) = 17\%$.

9 (a) False   (b) False
(c) True   (d) False
(e) True

Chapter 6

7 £1.82; 8p.

Chapter 7

Quick numerical questions

1 (a) £95.20   (b) 8.06%

2 (a) £100   (b) 10.15%   (c) £103.62

3 (a) $9 \times 6.278 + 100/(1.095)^{10} = £96.86$
   (b) $9 \times 6.561 + 100/(1.085)^{10} = £103.28$
   (c) 8.25%
   (d) 8.57%

4 (i) £105.30   (ii) £63.79

5 16.08%

6 7.5%

7 (a) $100/40 = £2.50$,   (b) $(2.50 - 1.90)/1.90 = 31.6\%$

Questions and problems

3 (a) £78.71m

(b)

Year	1	2	3	4	5
Payments (£m)	4.75	4.75	4.75	4.75	54.75

(c)

Year	1	2	3	4	5
Payments (£m)	14.75	13.80	12.85	11.90	10.95
Outstanding at the beginning of the year		40.00	30.00	20.00	10.00

7 **Ronsons**

1 *Interest on overdraft*   £

$180,000 \times {}^{3}/_{12} \times 0.1$	4,500
$150,000 \times {}^{3}/_{12} \times 0.1$	3,750
$200,000 \times {}^{3}/_{12} \times 0.1$	5,000
	13,250
Arrangement fee	3,000
	16,250

Interest on loan
$200,000 \times 0.1$ 20,000

Less Interest receivable

$200,000 \times {}^{3}/_{12} \times 0.04$	2,000
$20,000 \times {}^{3}/_{12} \times 0.04$	200
$50,000 \times {}^{3}/_{12} \times 0.04$	500
	£17,300

The loan is significantly more expensive. If cost is the only consideration, then the overdraft should be selected.

8 Snowhite

(a) Payment on the 10th day: saving = £50,000 × 0.01 = £500
Saving on overdraft interest if payment is on 30th day:

$$d = \sqrt[365]{1 + 0.12} - 1 = 0.0003105$$

Twenty days' interest: $(1+0.0003105)^{20} - 1 = 0.006229$
49,500 × 0.006229 = £308.34
Conclusion: pay on the 10th day

(b) Pay on the 10th day, saving £500
Pay on the 60th day: $49,500[(1 + 0.0003105)^{50} - 1] = £774$
Conclusion: pay on the 60th day

12 Benefits: Daily credit granted = £6,000,000/365 = £16,438
Immediate cash boost: £16,438 × 80 × 0.8 = £1,052,055

Annual interest saving £1,052,055 × 0.11 =	£115,726
Plus interest saving on earlier settlement:	
£16,438 × 20 × 0.2 × 0.11 =	£7,233
plus administration saving =	£80,000
	£202,959
Costs:	
0.017 × 6,000,000	£102,000.0
1,052,055 × 0.1	£105,205.5
6,000,000 × 0.8 × 0.01	£48,000.0
	£255,205.5

On a strict interpretation of the data, Glub should favour continuing without the help of the factoring company because the charges are higher than the savings (even with the assumption of immediate reduction if the credit period is taken from 80 days to 60 days). However, there are at least three other considerations that may affect the decision. First, real businesses often feel the pressure of cash flow shortages (the capital markets are not perfect). Therefore, the managers may value the cash flow boost more highly than allowed for. Second, senior management time devoted to the problem of debtors may not have been included in 'administration costs'. Third, customer relationships may be damaged by the actions of a factor keen on reducing the average debtor period.

Chapter 8

Quick numerical questions

1 7.2%

2 (a) WACC = $11\% \times \dfrac{7}{9} + 6\%\ (1{-}0.3) \times \dfrac{2}{9} = 9.49\%$

Enterprise value: $\dfrac{£1m}{0.0949} = £10.54m$

2 (b) WACC = $16\% \times \dfrac{4}{9} + 7\%\ (1{-}0.3) \times \dfrac{5}{9} = 9.83\%$

Enterprise value: $\dfrac{£1m}{0.0983} = £10.17m$

WACC rises and value of the firm falls

3 $K_E = 4.5\% + 0.9\ (5\%) = 9\%$

$$\text{WACC} = 9\% \times \frac{20}{40} + 7.5 \times \frac{5}{40} + 6.5\ (1\text{--}0.3)\frac{15}{40} = 7.14\%$$

4 (a) $\quad -80 + \dfrac{5}{1 + k_{DBT}} + \dfrac{5}{(1 + k_{DBT})^2} + \dfrac{5}{(1 + k_{DBT})^3} + \dfrac{5}{(1 + k_{DBT})^4} + \dfrac{105}{(1 + k_{DBT})^5} = 0$

Try 10%: +1.05
Try 11%: −2.178
$K_{DBT} = 10.32\%$
$K_{DAT} = 10.32(1 - 0.31) = 7.12\%$

(b) $K_E = r_f + \beta\ (r_m - r_f)$
$\quad = 6 + 1.3(5) = 12.5\%$

(c) $K_{BANK} = (9 + 2)(1 - 0.31) = 7.59\%$
$\quad\text{WACC} = K_E W_E + K_{DAT} W_D + K_{BANK} W_{BANK}$
$\qquad\qquad = 12.5 \times 0.526 + 7.13 \times 0.211 + 7.59 \times 0.263$
$\qquad\qquad = 10.08\%$

Market values	£	Weight
Equity	2m	0.526
Loan	1m	0.263
Bond	0.8m	0.211
	3.8m	1.000

5 Diversified

(a) $K_E \quad = r_f + \beta\ (r_m - r_f)$
$\qquad\quad = 7 + 1.5(5) = 14.5\%$
$\quad K_{DAT} \quad = K_{DBT}\ (1-T) = 12(1 - 0.3) = 8.4$
$\quad \text{WACC} = K_E W_E + K_{DAT} W_D$
$\qquad\qquad\ = 14.5 \times 0.6667 + 8.4 \times 0.333 = 12.47$

(b) *See* Chapter 8.

(c) *See* Chapter 8.

Chapter 9

Quick numerical questions

1 Annual value creation: £300,000 × (0.19 − 0.13) = + £18,000
Performance spread = 0.19 − 0.13 = 0.06 or 6%
Value of the firm: 300,000 + 18,000 × 5.9176 = £406,517

2 Tops plc EP= operating profit − invested capital × WACC
$\qquad\qquad\quad = £5\text{m} - £50 \times 0.14 = -£2\text{m}$

3 $\dfrac{580 - 600}{600} \times 100 = -3.3\ \%$

$\dfrac{580 - 450}{450} \times 100 = 28.9\%$

$\dfrac{580 - 125}{125} \times 100 = 364\%$

(b) To put additional meaning to TSR calculations, it is often useful to compare them with a benchmark:

Share index returns		
	3 years	24%
	5 years	68%
	10 years	210%

On the basis of these calculations, we observe that Tear has performed relatively well over a ten-year period but relatively poorly over three-year and five-year periods. This leads to a problem with TSR: it is highly dependent on the time period chosen.

Additional issues: It is important to relate relative returns to risk class; it measures in percentage terms rather than absolute terms.

4 Sity and Pity: $90 - 15 = £75m$

Questions and problems

4 (a) Value: $10m + \dfrac{10m}{0.13} = £86.92$

(b) Value: $\dfrac{12m}{0.13} = £92.31m$

Earnings rise to £12m each year.
This is good investment, as the present value of the additional cash inflows ($2/0.13 = £15.4m$) is greater than the sacrifice (£10m). Here a rise in earnings coincides with a rise in value.

(c) Value: $5m + \dfrac{10.5m}{0.13} = £85.77m$

Earnings rise to £10.5m each year.
This is bad investment, as the present value of the additional cash inflows ($0.5/0.13 = £3.8m$) is less than the sacrifice at time 0 (£5m). Here a rise in earnings is achieved but value is lost.

6 Blue plc:
(a)
Consumer: £1m × (0.18 −0.15)	=	+£30,000
Cooker: £2m × (0.14 − 0.16)	=	−£40,000
Export: £1.5m × 0.02	=	+£30,000

(b)
Consumer: £30,000 × 3.3522	=	+£100,566
Cooker: −£40,000 × 4.0386	=	−£161,544
Export: £30,000 × 3.5892	=	+£107,676

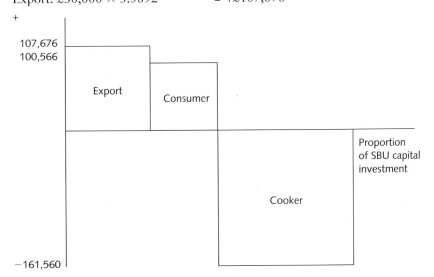

8 Buit plc

Point in time	1 £m	2 £m	3 £m	4 £m	5 → infinity £m
Forecast profits	12	14	15	16	16
Add depreciation	2	2	3	3	3
Less Fixed capital investment	−5	−5	−5	−3	−3
Less Working capital investment	−1	−1.2	−1.5	−1.8	0
Add Interest	1.2	1.2	1.2	1.2	1.2
Tax	−3.6	−4.2	−4.5	−4.8	−4.8
Cash flow	5.6	6.8	8.2	10.6	12.4
Discounted cash flow	$\dfrac{5.6}{1.1}$	$\dfrac{6.8}{(1.1)^2}$	$\dfrac{8.2}{(1.1)^3}$	$\dfrac{10.6}{(1.1)^4}$	$\dfrac{12.4}{0.1} \times \dfrac{1}{(1.1)^4}$
	5.09	+5.62	+6.16	+7.24	+84.69 = 108.8m

(b) Corporate value = £108.8m + £16m = £124.8m
     Shareholder value = £124.8m − £20m = £104.8m

9 Mythier plc

(a) £1m − (£8m × 0.08) = £0.36m

(b) (£1m − £0.24) − (£4m × 0.1) = £0.36m

Chapter 10

Quick numerical questions

1 240p

2 $g = \sqrt[5]{\dfrac{21}{12}} - 1 = 11.8$

$P_0 = \dfrac{21(1 + 0.059)}{0.13 - 0.059} = 313\text{p}$

3 Tented

$K_E = 7 + 1.5(5) = 14.5$

Year	Pence per share	Discounted dividends		
1	13.75	13.75/1.145	=	12.01
2	17.19	17.19/(1.145)²	=	13.11
3	21.48	21.48/(1.145)³	=	14.31
4	26.86	26.86/(1.145)⁴	=	15.63
5	33.57	33.57/(1.145)⁵	=	17.06

Price at year 5 = $P_5 = \dfrac{d_6}{k_E - g} = \dfrac{33.57(1.05)}{0.145 - 0.05} \div (1.145)^5$ = 188.54

Value of one share   260.66p

Questions and problems

2 Blueberry plc

(a) $\dfrac{P_0}{E_0} = \dfrac{205}{14} = 14.6$

(b) $\sqrt[5]{\dfrac{14}{9}} - 1 = 0.0923$ or 9.23%

(c) $6.5 + 1.2(5) = 12.5\%$

(d) $\dfrac{P_0}{E_1} = \dfrac{d_1/E_1}{k_E - g}$

$\dfrac{P_O}{14(1.0923)} = \dfrac{0.5}{0.125 - 0.0923} = 15.3$

$P_0 = 15.3 \times 14(1.0923) = 234$p; shares are underpriced

3 Tes plc

(a)
NAV in BS	3,594
Building	−100
Debtors	−16
Stock	−30
Investments	151
	£3,599m

(d) $\sqrt[16]{\dfrac{9.60}{0.82}} - 1 = 16.62\%$ $16.62 \times 0.5 = 8.31$

$k_E = 6.25 + 0.77(5) = 10.1\%$

$P_0 = \dfrac{d_1}{k_E - g} = \dfrac{9.6(1 + 0.0831)}{0.101 - 0.0831} = 580.90$ p

(e) Some ideas:
The assumed g could be inaccurate
The market might be undervaluing
The constant growth assumption could be wrong
k_E could be wrong, especially given the doubts about the CAPM

(f) $\dfrac{P_0}{E_1} = \dfrac{580.90}{21.9(1 + 0.0831)} = 24.5$

(g) 21.9, 10.96

(h) $k_{DBT} = 6.91\%$, $k_{DAT} = 6.91(1 - 0.30) = 4.84\%$

Market value of equity: £8,000m, of debt: $598(105.50/100) = £631$m
Total capital £8,631m
Weights: Equity = 0.93, Debt = 0.07

WACC $= k_{DAT}W_D + k_E W_E = 4.84 \times 0.07 + 10.1 \times 0.93 = 9.73\%$

Chapter 11

Quick numerical questions

1 (a) $6.1 \times 0.4 + 14.5 \times 0.6 = 11.14$
40% debt, 60% equity

2 WACC $= 30 \times 0.4 + 9 \times 0.6$
$= 17.4\%$

Questions and problems

1 Eastwell plc

(a)

	£	£	£
Cash flow	60,000	160,000	300,000
All-equity structure			
Return on equity	$\dfrac{60,000}{1,000,000} = 6\%$	$\dfrac{160,000}{1,000,000} = 16\%$	$\dfrac{300,000}{1,000,000} = 30\%$
40% gearing			
Debt interest @ 12%	48,000	48,000	48,000
Earnings available for shareholders	12,000	112,000	252,000
Return on equity	$\dfrac{12,000}{600,000} = 2\%$	$\dfrac{112,000}{600,000} = 18.67\%$	$\dfrac{252,000}{600,000} = 42\%$
80% gearing			
Debt interest @ 13%	104,000	104,000	104,000
Earnings available for shareholders	−44,000	56,000	196,000
Return on equity	$\dfrac{-44,000}{200,000} = -22\%$	$\dfrac{56,000}{200,000} = 28\%$	$\dfrac{196,000}{200,000} = 98\%$

(a) and (b) Expected returns and standard deviations

Return $R_i\%$	Probability	Return $\times$ probability	$(R_i - \bar{R})^2 p$
All equity			
6	0.25	1.50	30.25
16	0.50	8.00	0.50
30	0.25	7.50	42.25
Expected return, $\bar{R}$		17.00%	σ^2 73.00
Standard deviation, σ			8.54%
40% gearing			
2	0.25	0.5	84.04
18.67	0.50	9.335	1.39
42	0.25	10.50	117.34
Expected return, $\bar{R}$		20.335%	σ^2 202.77
Standard deviation, σ			14.24%
80% gearing			
–22	0.25	–5.5	756.25
28	0.50	14.0	12.50
98	0.25	24.5	1,056.25
Expected return, $\bar{R}$		33.0%	σ^2 1,825.00
Standard deviation, σ			42.72%

2 Hose plc

(a) WACC = $k_E W_E + k_{DAT} W_D$

WACC = $15 \times 0.7 + 9(1 - 0.30) \times 0.3 = 12.39\%$

Value of the firm:

$$\frac{750,000}{0.1239} = £6,053,268$$

(b) *Director A*

WACC = $15 \times 0.4 + 9(1 - 0.30) \times 0.6 = 9.78\%$

Value of the firm $= \dfrac{750,000}{0.0978} = £7,668,712$

Director B
WACC = $23.7 \times 0.4 + 9(1 - 0.30) \times 0.6 = 13.26\%$

Value of the firm $= \dfrac{750,000}{0.1326} = £5,656,109$

Director C
WACC = $17 \times 0.4 + 9(1 - 0.30) \times 0.6 = 10.58\%$

Value of the firm $= \dfrac{750,000}{0.1058} = £7,088,847$

Director D
WACC = $28 \times 0.4 + 9(1 - 0.30) \times 0.6 = 14.98\%$

Value of the firm $= \dfrac{750,000}{0.1498} = £5,006,676$

Chapter 12

Questions and problems

4 Vale plc

(a)

	No. of shares (million)	Profit per share
This year	100.000	10.8p
t − 1	100.000	8.9p
t − 2	76.923	8.19p
t − 3	76.923	7.15p
t − 4	38.4615	9.10p
t − 5	38.4615	6.76p

(b) $g = \sqrt[5]{\dfrac{5.4}{3.38}} - 1 = 9.82\%$

$k_E = 6.5 + 0.9(5) = 11\%$

$P = \dfrac{5.4(1.0982)}{0.11 - 0.0982} = 502.6p$

The current market price is below the value given by the dividend valuation model and therefore the shares are a good buy.

5 Tesford plc

(a)

Year	Net cash flows	Investment	Cash flows after investment (for dividends)	Dividend per share
	£m	£m	£m	(p)
1	3	2	1	4.17
2	12	2	10	41.67
3	5	3	2	8.33
4	6	3	3	12.50
5	5	3	2	8.33

(b)

Year	Cash flows paid out as regular dividends	Maintainable regular dividends per share	Cash flows available for special dividends or share repurchase	Special dividends or share repurchase per share
	£m	(p)	£m	(p)
1	1.000	4.17	0	0
2	1.189	4.95	8.811	36.71
3	1.414	5.89	0.586	2.44
4	1.682	7.01	1.318	5.49
5	2.000	8.33	0	0

In practice a special dividend or share repurchase in consecutive years is unlikely. Perhaps Tesford directors will choose to have one or two special payouts to distribute the surplus cash.

7 (a) $g = 7.46$
$P_0 = 155p$

(b)

	Discounted
$d_1 = 4p$	3.54
$d_2 = 4p$	3.13
$d_3 = 10p$	6.93
$P_3 = \dfrac{d_4}{K_E - g} = \dfrac{10(1.09)}{0.13 - 0.09} = 272.5$	188.86

Answer 202p.
Therefore, the sacrifice of short-term dividends is worthwhile.

(c) Issues to be discussed: signalling, information asymmetry, clientele effects and residual theory.

GLOSSARY

Abnormal return (residual return) A return greater than the market return after adjusting for differences in risk.

Accounting rate of return (ARR) A measure of profitability based on accounting numbers. Profit divided by assets devoted to the activity (e.g. project, entire business) as a percentage.

Accumulated profits Profits that have accumulated from all the previous years of the company's history not yet paid out in dividends.

Acid test *See* Quick ratio.

Additivity Able to add up.

Adverse selection problem When there is an opportunity or incentive for some firms/individuals to act to take advantage of their informational edge over others then the firms/individuals doing that activity will be disproportionately those taking advantage rather than being truly representative of the population as a whole.

Affirmative covenants Loan agreement conditions that require positive action on the part of the borrower, e.g. a statement that a bond will pay regular dividends, or that the borrower will distribute information regularly.

Agency Acting for or in the place of another with his/her/their authority.

Agency costs Costs of preventing agents (e.g. managers) pursuing their own interests at the expense of their principals (e.g. shareholders). Examples include contracting costs and costs of monitoring. In addition there is the agency cost of the loss of wealth caused by the extent to which prevention measures have not worked and managers continue to pursue non-shareholder wealth goals.

Agent A person who acts for or in the place of another with that other person's authority (the 'principal').

AGM *See* Annual general meeting.

AIM admission document The document needed for a company to be quoted on the Alternative Investment Market. It is similar to a prospectus.

Allocation of capital The mechanism for selecting competing investment projects leading to the production of a mixture of goods and services by a society. This can be influenced by the forces of supply and demand; and by central authority direction. The term may also be used for selection of securities (e.g. shares) by investors or business units and activities by managers.

Allocational efficiency of markets Efficiency in the process of allocating society's scarce resources between competing real investments.

Allotment In a new issue of shares, if more shares are demanded at the price than are available, they may be apportioned (allotted) between the applicants.

Alpha (Alpha coefficient, α) A measure of market outperformance (underperformance) after allowing for beta in the capital asset pricing model (q.v.). That portion of a share's return that cannot be explained by its responsiveness to moves in the market as a whole. Sometimes called stock-specific return.

Alternative Investment Market (AIM) The lightly regulated share market operated by the London Stock Exchange, focused particularly on smaller, less well-established companies.

Amortisation The repayment of a debt by a series of instalments.

Amortisation of assets The reduction in book value of an intangible asset such as goodwill.

Angel *See* Business angel.

Angel network events Meetings of business angels at which entrepreneurs can ask for investment capital.

Annual equivalent annuity (AEA) A regular annual amount which is equivalent, in present value terms, to another set of cash flows.

Annual equivalent rate (AER) *See* Annual percentage rate.

Annual general meeting (AGM) A limited company must hold in each calendar year an annual general meeting. It is an opportunity for shareholders to meet and talk with each other and with those who run the company on their behalf. The managers give an account of their stewardship. All shareholders are entitled to attend and vote. Election of directors may take place.

Annual percentage rate (APR) The true annual interest rate charged by a lender. It takes full account of the timing of payments of interest and principal.

Annual results Annual company accounts. This term is often used for the preliminary results.

Annuity An even stream of payments (the same amount each time) over a given period of time with a fixed frequency of payments.

Annuity due An annuity where the cash flows occur at the start of each period rather than at the end – the first payment is due now, not in one year's time.

Arbitrage The act of exploiting price differences on the same instrument or similar securities by simultaneously selling the overpriced security and buying the underpriced security.

Arbitrage pricing theory (APT) A type of multi-factor model which relates return on securities to various non-diversifiable risk factors. The expected return on any risky security is a linear combination of these factors.

Arithmetic mean or average The average of a set of numbers equals the sum of the observations divided by the number of observations.

Asset In the financial markets an asset is anything that can be traded as a security, e.g. share, option, commodity, bond.

Asset backing The value of the assets held in the business – often measured on a per share basis.

Asset class Asset types, e.g. bonds, shares.

Asset liquidity The extent to which assets can be converted to cash quickly and at a low transaction cost.

Asset transformers Intermediaries who, by creating a completely new security – the intermediate security – mobilise savings and encourage investment. The primary security is issued by the ultimate borrower to the intermediary, who offers intermediate securities to the primary investors.

Asymmetric information One party in a negotiation or relationship is not in the same position as other parties, being ignorant of, or unable to observe, some information which is essential to the contracting and decision-making process.

Authorised but unissued ordinary share capital Shares that have not yet been sold by the company to investors. However, they have been created (authorised by the shareholders) and may be sold or given to existing shareholders or sold to new shareholders.

Authorised share capital The maximum amount of share capital that a company can issue. The limit can be changed by a shareholder vote.

Bad growth When a company increases investment in an area of business that generates returns less than the opportunity cost of capital.

Balance sheet Provides a picture of what a company owned, what it owes and is owed on a particular day in the past. It summarises assets, liabilities and net worth (capital).

Balloon repayment on a loan The majority of the repayment of a loan is made at or near the maturity date, with the final payment substantially larger than the earlier payments.

Ballot In a new issue of shares when a company floats on a stock exchange if the demand is greater than the supply, the shares are allocated to some applicants but not others, selected at random.

Bank covenants *See* Covenant.

Bank of England The central bank of the United Kingdom, responsible for monetary policy. It oversees the affairs of other financial institutions, issues banknotes and coins, manages the national debt and exchange rate, and is lender of last resort.

Bankruptcy Commonly used to describe an individual or company that cannot meet its fixed commitments on borrowing which leads to legal action. However, technically, in the UK individuals become bankrupt whereas firms become insolvent.

Base rate The reference rate of interest that forms the basis for interest rates on bank loans, overdrafts and deposit rates.

Basis point (bp) One-hundredth of 1 per cent, usually applied to interest rates.

Bearer bond The ownership of a bond is not recorded on a register. Possession of the bond is sufficient to receive interest, etc.

Benefit–cost ratio A measure of present value per £ invested. Benefit–cost ratio = Net present value (NPV) (q.v.) divided by Initial outlay.

Beta A measure of the systematic risk of a financial security. In the capital asset pricing model (q.v.) it is a measure of the sensitivity to market movements of a financial security's return, as measured by the covariance between returns on the asset and returns on the market portfolio divided by the variance of the market portfolio. In practice a proxy (e.g. FTSE 100 index) is used for the market portfolio.

Bid price The price at which a market maker will buy shares or a dealer in other markets will buy a security or commodity.

Bid–offer spread ('Bid–ask spread' in USA) The difference between the market maker's buy and sell prices.

Bid yield The yield to maturity on a bond given the market price at which market makers will buy from investors.

Bird-in-the-hand fallacy The belief that dividends received earlier are discounted at a lower annual rate than those received in more distant years.

Blue chip A company regarded as of the highest quality – little risk of a sharp decline in profits or market value.

Board of directors People elected by shareholders to run a company.

Bond A debt obligation with a long-term maturity (more than one year), usually issued by firms and governments.

Bond covenant *See* Covenant.

Bonus issue *See* Scrip issue.

Book value Balance sheet value. Can be expressed on a per share basis.

Book-building A bookrunner (lead manager) invites major institutional investors to suggest how many shares (or other financial securities) they would be interested in purchasing and at what price in a new issue or secondary issue of shares (or other financial securities). This helps to establish the price and allocate shares.

Book-to-market equity ratio The ratio of a firm's balance sheet value to the total market value of its shares.

Bookrunner The manager who is in charge of managing a new issue, especially allocation of the securities to investors.

Borrowing capacity Limits to total borrowing levels imposed by lenders, often determined by available collateral.

Bottom line Profit attributable to the shareholders.

Bought deal An investment bank (the 'lead manager', perhaps together with co-managers of the issue), buys an entire security issue (e.g. shares) from a client corporation raising finance. The investment bank usually intends to then sell it out to institutional clients within hours.

Break-even analysis Analysing the level of sales at which a project, division or business produces a zero profit (accounting emphasis).

Break-even NPV The extent to which a single variable can change before the net present value (NPV) (q.v.) of a proposed project switches from positive to negative (or vice versa).

Broker Assists in the buying and selling of financial securities by acting as a 'go-between', helping to reduce search transaction and information costs.

Bubble An explosive upward movement in financial security prices not based on fundamentally rational factors, followed by a crash.

Building society A UK financial institution, the primary role of which is the provision of mortgages. Building societies are non-profit-making mutual organisations. Funding is mostly through small deposits by individuals.

Bulldog A foreign bond issued in the UK.

Bullet bond A bond where all the principal on a loan is repaid at maturity.

Business angels Wealthy individuals prepared to invest between £10,000 and £250,000 in a start-up, early-stage or developing firm. They often have managerial and/or technical experience to offer the management team as well as equity and debt finance. Medium- to long-term investment in high-risk situation.

Business risk The risk associated with the underlying operations of a business. The variability of the firm's operating income, before interest income: this dispersion is caused purely by business-related factors and not by the debt burden.

CAC-40 (Compagnie des Agents de Change 40 Index) A stock market index of French shares quoted in Paris.

Cadbury report The Committee on the Financial Aspects of Corporate Governance chaired by Sir Adrian Cadbury made recommendations on the role of directors and auditors, published in 1992.

Called-up (issued) share capital The total value of shares sold by a company when expressed at par or nominal value.

Capex *See* Capital expenditure

Capital (1) Funding for a business – can be equity only or equity plus debt. (2) Another term for net worth – total assets minus total liabilities.

Capital Asset Pricing Model (CAPM) An asset (e.g. share) pricing theory which assumes that financial assets, in equilibrium, will be priced to produce rates of return which compensate investors for systematic risk as measured by the covariance of the assets' return with the market portfolio return (i.e. beta).

Capital budgeting The process of analysing and selecting long-term capital investments.

Capital expenditure (capex) The purchase of long-lived (more than one year) assets (that is, fixed assets).

Capital gearing The extent to which the firm's total capital is in the form of debt.

Capital lease *See* Finance lease and Leasing.

Capital market Where those raising finance can do so by selling financial investments to investors, e.g. bonds, shares.

Capital rationing When funds are not available to finance all wealth-enhancing (positive NPV) projects.

Capital reconstruction (restructuring) Altering the shape of the firm's liabilities, e.g. increases/decreases in the amount of equity; increases/decreases in debt; lengthening/shortening debt maturities.

Capital structure The proportion of the firm's capital which is equity or debt.

Capitalisation (1) An item of expenditure is taken on to the balance sheet and capitalised as an asset rather than written off against profits. (2) Short for market capitalisation (q.v.).

Capitalisation factor A discount rate.

Capitalisation issue *See* Scrip issue.

Capitalisation rate Required rate of return for the class of risk.

Captives A venture capital organisation that raises its capital from one institution (or a small group of institutions)

Cash cow A company with low growth and stable market conditions with low investment needs. The company's competitive strength enables it to produce surplus cash.

Cash dividend A normal dividend by a company, paid in cash rather than a scrip dividend.

Central bank A bankers' bank and lender of last resort, which controls the credit system of an economy, e.g. controls note issue, acts as the government's bank, controls interest rates and regulates the country's banking system.

Characteristic line The line that best relates the return on a share to the return on a broad market index.

Chartism Investment analysis that relies on historical price charts (and/or trading volumes) to predict future movements.

City Code on Takeovers and Mergers Provides the main governing rules for UK-based companies engaged in merger activity. Self-regulated and administered by the Takeover Panel.

City of London A collective term for the financial institutions located in the financial district to the east of St Paul's Cathedral in London (also called the Square Mile). However, the term is also used to refer to all UK-based financial institutions, wherever they are located.

Clawback Existing shareholders often have the right to reclaim shares sold under a placing as though they were entitled to them under a rights issue.

Clean price On a bond the prices are generally quoted 'clean'; that is, without taking account of the accrued interest since the last coupon payment.

Clearing bank Member of the London Bankers' Clearing House, which clears cheques, settling indebtedness between two parties.

Clearing house An institution which registers, monitors, matches and settles mutual indebtedness between a number of individuals or organisations. The clearing house may also act as a counterparty.

Clientele effect In dividend theory the level of dividend may be influenced by shareholders preferring a dividend pattern which matches their consumption pattern and/or tax position.

Closed-end funds Collective investment vehicles (e.g. investment trusts) that do not create or redeem shares on a daily basis in response to increases and decreases in demand. They have a fixed number of shares for lengthy periods.

Coefficient of determination, R-squared For single linear regression this is the proportion of variation in the dependent variable that is related to the variation in the independent variable. A measure of the 'goodness of fit' in a regression equation.

Co-lead manager The title given to an underwriter who has joint lead manager status and may sometimes be engaged in structuring the transaction. Usually part of the selling group. Usually does not act as a bookrunner.

Collateral Property pledged by a borrower to protect the interests of the lender.

Collective funds See Pooled funds.

Combined Code A set of guidelines for best practice corporate governance. The latest alterations were made by Sir Ronald Hampel's committee (see Hampel report). The United Kingdom Listing Authority (q.v.) requires compliance or an explanation.

Commercial banking A range of banking services undertaken, including taking deposits and making loans, chequing facilities, trustee services, securities advisory services.

Commercial bill (bank bill or trade bill) A document expressing the commitment of a borrowing firm to repay a short-term debt at a fixed date in the future.

Commercial paper (CP) An unsecured note promising the holder (lender) a sum of money to be paid in a few days – average maturity of 40 days. If they are denominated in a foreign currency and placed outside the jurisdiction of the authorities of that currency then the notes are Eurocommercial paper.

Commitment fee A fee payable in return for a commitment by a bank to lend money at some future date. In some cases the fee is only payable on the undrawn portion of the loan; in others the fee also applies to funds already drawn down under the arrangement.

Common stock The term used in the USA to describe ordinary shares in a company.

Companies Acts The series of laws enacted by Parliament governing the establishment and conduct of incorporated business enterprises. The Companies Act 1985 consolidated the Acts that preceded it.

Companies House The place where records are kept of every UK company. These accounts, etc. are then made available to the general public.

Company registrar See Registrar.

Competition Commission The Commission may obtain any information needed to investigate possible monopoly anti-competitive situations referred to it. It may then block anti-competitive action.

Competitive advantage (edge) The possession of extraordinary resources that allow a firm to rise above the others in its industry to generate exceptional long-run rates of return on capital employed.

Competitive position The competitive strength of the firm vis-à-vis rivals in a product market.

Compound interest Interest is paid on the sum which accumulates, whether or not that sum comes from principal or from interest received at intermediate dates.

Compound return The income received on an investment is reinvested in the investment and future returns are gained on both the original capital and the ploughed-back income.

Conditional trading The buying and selling (of, say, shares during a new issue on the stock market) is conditional on some other event to be effective (with new share issues it will be the receipt of the shares from the company).

Conflict of preferences There is a conflict of preferences between the primary investors wanting low-cost liquidity and low risk on invested funds, and the ultimate borrowers wanting long-term risk-bearing capital.

Conglomerate A holding company with subsidiaries with operations in different business areas.

Conglomerate bank A bank with a wide range of activities, products and markets.

Consideration The price paid for something.

Consolidated accounts All the income costs, assets and all the liabilities of all group companies, whether wholly or partially owned, are brought together in the consolidated accounts. Consolidation must take place if 50 per cent or more of a subsidiary's shares are held by the parent. If less than 50 per cent of the shares are held consolidation may still be required.

Consolidation of shares The number of shares is reduced and the nominal value of each remaining share rises.

Consumer price index (CPI) The main US measure of general inflation.

Continuing obligations Standards of behaviour and actions required of firms listed on the London Stock Exchange, enforced by the United Kingdom Listing Authority (q.v.).

Contractual theory Views the firm as a network of contracts, actual and implicit, which specify the roles to be played by various participants. Most participants bargain for low risk and a satisfactory return. Shareholders accept high risk in anticipation of any surplus returns after all other parties have been satisfied.

Controlling shareholder Any shareholder able to control the composition of the board of directors and therefore the direction of the company. Strictly speaking this is 50 per cent, but even a 30 per cent shareholder can exercise this degree of power, and therefore 30 per cent is used as the cut-off point for some purposes.

Conventional cash flows Where an outflow is followed by a series of inflows, or a cash inflow is followed by a series of cash outflows.

Conversion premium The difference between the current share price and the conversion price, expressed as a percentage of the current share price for convertible bonds.

Conversion price The share price at which convertible bonds may be converted.

Conversion ratio The nominal (par) value of a convertible bond divided by the conversion price. The number of shares available per bond.

Conversion value The value of a convertible bond if it were converted into ordinary shares at the current share price.

Convertible bonds Bonds which carry a rate of interest and give the owner the right to exchange the bonds at some stage in the future into ordinary shares according to a prearranged formula.

Convertible loan stock Same definition as Convertible bond.

Convertible preferred stock A preferred share that can be changed into another type of security, e.g. an ordinary share, at the holder's option.

Conveyers of information Dividend levels and patterns over time send signals to shareholders regarding the director's views of the firm's prospects.

Corporate adviser One who gives advice to companies.

Corporate acquisition One company acquires another by purchasing all (or the majority) of the shares.

Corporate bond A bond issued by a company.

Corporate broker Stockbrokers that act on behalf of companies quoted on an exchange. For example, they may provide advice on market conditions or may represent the company to the market. Corporate brokers are knowledgeable about the share and other financial markets. They advise companies on fund raising (e.g. new issues). They try to generate interest among investors for the company's securities. They stand prepared to buy and sell companies' shares.

Corporate governance The system of management and control of the corporation.

Corporate value The present value of cash flows for the entire corporation within the planning horizon plus the present value of cash flows after the planning horizon plus the saleable value of assets not required for cash flow generation. Includes cash flows attributable to equity and debt holders.

Corporate venturing Large companies fostering the development of smaller enterprises through, say, joint capital development or equity capital provision.

Corporation tax A tax levied on the profits of companies.

Correlation coefficient A measure of the extent to which two variables show a relationship, expressed on a scale of -1 to $+1$.

Correlation scale A scale between -1 and $+1$ showing the degree of co-movement of two variables, e.g. the returns on two shares. A value of -1 indicates exact opposite movement, a value of $+1$ indicates perfect movement in the same direction.

Cost of capital The rate of return that a company has to offer finance providers to induce them to buy and hold a financial security.

Counterparty The buyer for a seller or the seller for a buyer.

Counterparty risk The risk that a counterparty to a contract defaults and does not fulfil its obligations.

Country risk Risk to transactions overseas or assets held abroad due to political, legal, regulatory or settlement changes or difficulties, e.g. nationalisation or law forbidding repatriation of profits.

Coupons An attachment to bond or loan note documents which may be separated and serve as evidence of entitlement to interest. Nowadays it refers to the interest itself: the nominal annual rate of interest expressed as a percentage of the principal value.

Covariance The extent to which two variables move together.

Covenant A solemn agreement.

Creative accounting The drawing up of accounts which obey the letter of the law and accounting body rules but which involve the manipulation of accounts to show the most favourable profit and balance sheet.

Credit facility or Credit line A short-term borrowing arrangement with a bank or other lender under which borrowing may fluctuate at the behest of the borrower up to a fixed total amount, e.g. overdraft, revolving facility.

Credit insurance An insurance policy that pays out on trade debts held by the firm when customers fail to meet their obligations.

Credit rating An estimate of the quality of a debt from the lender's viewpoint in terms of the likelihood of interest and capital not being paid and of the extent to which the lender is protected in the event of default. Credit-rating agencies are paid fees by companies, governments, etc. wishing to attract lenders.

Credit risk The risk that a counterparty to a financial transaction will fail to fulfil its obligation.

Credit risk premium or credit spread The additional yield (over, say, reputable government bonds) on a debt instrument due to the borrower's additional perceived probability of default.

Creditor One to whom a debt is owed.

CREST An electronic means of settlement and registration of shares following a sale on the London Stock Exchange operated by CRESTCo.

Cum-dividend (1) When an investor buys a government bond (q.v.) when it is still designated cum-dividend or cum-coupon he/she is entitled to the accrued interest since the last coupon was paid. (2) A share (q.v.) designated cum-dividend indicates that the buyer will be entitled to a dividend recently announced by the company.

Cum-rights Shares bought on the stock market prior to the ex-rights day are designated cum-rights and carry to the new owner the right to subscribe for the new shares in the rights issue.

Cumulative If a payment (interest or dividend) on a bond (q.v.) or share (q.v.) is missed in one period those securities are given priority when the next payment is made. These arrears must be cleared up before shareholders received dividends.

Current assets Cash and other assets that can be rapidly turned into cash. Includes stocks of raw materials, partially finished goods and finished goods, debtors and investments expected to be sold within one year.

Current liabilities Amounts owed that the company expects to have to pay within the next year.

Current ratio The ratio of current assets to the current liabilities of a business.

Current yield (Flat yield, income yield or running yield) The ratio of the coupon (q.v.) on a bond (q.v.) to its current market price.

Cyclical companies (industries, shares) Those companies in which profits are particularly sensitive to the growth level in the economy, which may be cyclical.

Dax 30 (Deutsche Aktienindex) A stock market index of German shares quoted on Deutsche Börse (q.v.).

Debentures Bonds issued with redemption dates a number of years into the future or irredeemable. Usually secured against specific assets (mortgage debentures) or through a floating charge on the firm's assets (floating debentures). In the USA debenture means an unsecured debt with a fixed coupon.

Debt An obligation to pay.

Debt capital Capital raised with (usually) a fixed obligation in terms of interest and principal payments.

Debt maturity The length of time left until the repayment on a debt becomes due.

Debt-to-equity ratio The ratio of a company's long-term debt to shareholders' funds.

Debtors Those who owe a debt.

Declining (reducing) balance method of depreciation The amount by which an asset is depreciated declines from one year to the next as it is determined by a constant percentage of the asset's depreciated value at the start of each year.

Deep discounted bonds Bonds sold well below par value, usually because they have little or no coupon.

Deep discounted rights issue A rights issue price is much less than the present market price of the old shares.

Default A failure to make agreed payments of interest or principal, or failure to comply with some other provision.

Defensive shares Having a beta value of less than 1.

Demerger The separation of companies or business units that are currently under one corporate umbrella. It applies particularly to the unravelling of a merger.

Depletion A reduction in the value of a natural resource, e.g. oil in the ground, owned by a company.

Depository receipts Certificates, representing evidence of ownership of a company's shares (or other securities) held by a depository. Depository Receipts (DRs) are negotiable (can be traded) certificates which represent ownership of a given number of a company's shares which can be listed and traded independently from the underlying shares. There are a number of forms of DRs including American Depository Receipts (ADRs), Global Depository Receipts (GDRs), Euro Depository Receipts (EDRs) and Retail Depository Receipts (RDRs).

Derivative A financial asset (instrument), the performance of which is based on (derived from) the behaviour of the value of an underlying asset.

Development capital Second-stage finance (following seed finance – see Seedcorn capital or money *and* Early-stage capital) to permit business expansion.

Differentiated product One that is slightly different in significant ways from those supplied by other companies. The unique nature of the product/service offered allows for a premium price to be charged.

Dilution The effect on the earnings and voting power per ordinary share from an increase in the number of shares issued without a corresponding increase in the firm's earnings.

Diminishing marginal utility Successive equal increments in quantity of a good (money) yield smaller and smaller increases in utility.

Directors' dealings The purchase or sale of shares in their own company. This is legal (except at certain times of the company's year). Some investors examine directors' dealings to decide whether to buy or sell.

Dirty price On a bond a buyer pays a total of the clean price and the accrued interest since the last coupon payment.

Discount (1) The amount below face value at which a financial claim sells, e.g. bill of exchange or zero coupon bond. (2) The extent to which an investment trust's shares sell below the net asset value. (3) The amount by which a future value of a currency is less than its spot value. (4) The action of purchasing financial instruments, e.g. bills, at a discount. (5) The degree to which a security sells below its issue price in the secondary market. (6) The process of equating a cash flow at some future date with today's value using the time value of money.

Discount rate (1) The rate of return used to discount cash flows received in future years. It is the opportunity cost of capital given the risk class of the future cash flows. (2) The rate of interest at which some central banks lend money to the banking system.

Discounted cash flow Future cash flows are converted into the common denominator of time zero money by adjusting for the time value of money.

Discounted payback The period of time required to recover initial cash outflow when the cash inflows are discounted at the opportunity cost of capital.

Discounting The process of reducing future cash flows to a present value using an appropriate discount rate.

Disintermediation Borrowing firms bypassing financial institutions and obtaining debt finance directly from the market.

Disinvest To sell an investment.

Diversifiable risk *See* Unsystematic risk.

Diversification To invest in varied projects, enterprises, financial securities, products, markets, etc.

Divestiture (Divestment) The selling off of assets or subsidiary businesses by a company or individual.

Dividend That part of profit paid to ordinary shareholders, usually on a regular basis.

Dividend cover The number of times net profits available for distribution exceed the dividend actually paid or declared. Earnings per share divided by gross dividend per share *or* Total post-tax profits divided by total dividend payout.

Dividend discount model – *See* Dividend valuation models.

Dividend payout ratio The percentage of a company's earnings paid out as dividends.

Dividend per share The total amount paid or due to be paid in dividends for the year (interim and final) divided by the number of shares in issue.

Dividend policy The determination of the proportion of profits paid out to shareholders over the longer term.

Dividend valuation models (DVMs) These methods of share valuation are based on the premise that the market value of ordinary shares represents the sum of the expected future dividend flows, to infinity, discounted to present value.

Dividend yield The amount of dividend paid on each share as a percentage of the share price.

Divisible projects It is possible to undertake a fraction of a project.

Divorce of ownership and control In large corporations shareholders own the firm but may not be able to exercise control. Managers often have control because of a diffuse and divided shareholder body, proxy votes and apathy.

Dominance When one (investment) possibility is clearly preferable to a risk-averse investor because it possesses a better expected return than another possibility for the same level of risk.

Dow or Dow Jones Industrial Average The best known index of movements in the price of US stocks and shares. There are 30 shares in the index.

Drawdown arrangement A loan facility is established and the borrower uses it (takes the money available) in stages as the funds are required.

Early-settlement discount The reduction of a debt owed if it is paid at an early date.

Early-stage capital Funds for initial manufacturing and sales for a newly formed company. High-risk capital available from entrepreneurs, business angels and venture capital funds.

Earn-out The purchase price of a company is linked to the future profits performance. Future instalments of the purchase price may be adjusted if the company performs better or worse than expected.

Earning power The earning (profit) capacity of a business in a normal year. What the company might be expected to earn year after year if the business conditions continue unchanged.

Earnings Profits, usually after deduction of tax.

Earnings multiple Price–earnings ratio.

Earnings per share (EPS) Profit after tax and interest divided by number of shares in issue.

Earnings yield Earnings per share divided by current market price of share.

EBIT A company's earnings (profits) before interest and taxes are deducted

EBITDA Earnings before interest, taxation, depreciation and amortisation. Or as cynics have it: Earnings Before I Tricked The Dumb Auditor.

Economic book value A term used by Stern Stewart & Co. It is based on the balance sheet capital employed figure subject to a number of adjustments.

Economic franchise Pricing power combined with strong barriers to entry. The strength and durability of an economic franchise are determined by (1) the structure of the industry; and (2) the ability of the firm to rise above its rivals in its industry and generate exceptional long-run rates of return on capital employed.

Economic profit (EP) For a period the economic profit is the amount earned by a business after deducting all operating expenses and a charge for the opportunity cost of the capital employed.

Economic value added (EVA) Developed by Stern Stewart & Co. A value-based metric of corporate performance which multiplies the invested capital (after adjustments) by the spread between the (adjusted) actual return on capital and the weighted cost of capital (q.v.). The adjustments are to the profit figures to obtain the actual return and to the balance sheet to obtain the invested capital figure.

Economies of scale Larger size of output often leads to lower cost per unit of output.

Economies of scope The ability to reduce the unit costs of an item by sharing some costs between a number of product lines, e.g. using the same truck to deliver both ketchup and beans to a store.

Effective annual rate *See* Annual percentage rate.

Efficient market hypothesis (EMH) The EMH implies that new information is incorporated into a share (or other security) price (1) rapidly and (2) rationally. *See also* Efficient stock market.

Efficient portfolio A portfolio that offers the highest expected return for a given level of risk (standard deviation) and the lowest risk for its expected return.

Efficient stock market Share prices rationally reflect available information. In an efficient market no trader will be presented with an opportunity for making an abnormal return, except by chance. *See also* Efficient market hypothesis.

EGM *See* Extraordinary general meeting.

Emerging markets Security markets in newly industrialising countries and/or capital markets at an early stage of development.

Endowment policies (savings schemes) Insurance policies in which a lump sum is payable, either at the end of the term of the policy or on death during the term of the policy.

Enterprise investment scheme (EIS) Tax relief is available to investors in qualifying company shares (unquoted firms not involved in financial investment and property).

Enterprise value The sum of a company's total equity market capitalisation and borrowings.

Entrepreneur Defined by economists as the owner-manager of a firm. Usually supplies capital, organises production, decides on strategic direction and bears risk.

Equities An ownership share of a business, each equity share representing an equal stake in the business. The risk capital of a business.

Equity approach An economic profit approach to value measurement that deducts interest from operating profit as well as tax. From this is deducted the required return on equity funds devoted to the activity only (i.e. does not include required return for debt capital).

Equity indices Baskets of shares indicating the movement of the equity market as a whole or sub-sets of the market.

Equity kicker (sweetener) The attachment to a bond or other debt finance of some rights to participate in and benefit from a good performance (e.g. to exercise an option to purchase shares). Often used with mezzanine finance (q.v.) and high-yield bonds.

Equity-linked bonds *See* Convertible bonds.

Equity shareholders' funds *See* Shareholders' funds.

Equity warrants A security issued by a company that gives to the owners the right but not the obligation to purchase shares in the company from the company at a fixed price during or at the end of a specified time period.

Euribor Short-term interest rates in the interbank market (highly stable banks lending to each other) in the currency of euros.

Euro medium-term notes (EMTN) *See* Medium-term note.

Eurobond Bond sold outside the jurisdiction of the country in whose currency the bond is denominated. For example, a bond issued in yen outside Japan.

Eurocommercial paper *See* Commercial paper.

Eurocredit A market in credit outside the jurisdiction of the country in whose currency the loan is denominated. (Borrowers can gain access to medium-term bank lending, for 1–15 years.)

Eurocurrency Currency held outside its country of origin, for example, Australian dollars held outside Australia. Note: this market existed long before the creation of the currency in the eurozone. It has no connection with the euro.

Eurocurrency banking Transactions in a currency other than the host country's currency. For example, transactions in Canadian dollars in London. No connection with the currency in the eurozone.

Eurocurrency deposits Short-term wholesale money market deposits made in the eurocurrency market.

Eurodeposit account Short-term wholesale money market deposits are made into an account set up for that purpose made in the eurocurrency market.

Eurodollar A deposit or credit of dollars held outside the regulation of the US authorities, say in Tokyo, London or Paris. No connection with the currency in the eurozone.

Euromarkets Informal (unregulated) markets in money held outside the jurisdiction of the country of origin, e.g. Swiss francs lending outside the control of the Swiss authorities – perhaps the francs are in London. No connection with the euro, the currency in use in the eurozone. Euromarkets began in the late 1950s and now encompass the eurocurrency, eurocredit and eurobond markets as well as over-the-counter derivatives and commodity markets.

Euronext The combined financial stock market comprising the French, Dutch, Belgian and Portuguese bourses.

Euronext.liffe Euronext, the organisation combining the French, Dutch, Belgian and Portuguese stock markets, bought LIFFE (q.v.) and renamed it Euronext.liffe.

Euronotes A short-term debt security. These are normally issued at a discount to face value for periods of one, three and six months' maturity. They are tradable once issued and are bearer securities. They are issued outside the jurisdiction of the currency stated on the note. They are backed up by a revolving underwriting facility which ensures that the issuer will be able to raise funds.

Eurosecurities Financial securities such as bonds, commercial paper, ordinary shares, convertibles, floating rate notes, medium-term notes, and promissory notes offered on or traded in the euromarkets.

Eurosterling Sterling traded in the eurocurrency market.

Euro Swiss francs Swiss francs traded in the eurocurrency market.

Euroyen Japanese yen traded in the eurocurrency market.

Eurozone Those countries that joined together in adopting the euro as their currency in 1999.

Event risk The risk that some future event may increase the risk on a financial investment, e.g. an earthquake event affects returns on Japanese bonds.

Ex ante Intended, desired or expected before the event.

Ex-coupon A bond sold without the right to the next interest payment.

Ex-dividend When a share or bond is designated ex-dividend a purchaser will not be entitled to a recently announced dividend or the accrued interest on the bond since the last coupon – the old owner will receive the dividend (coupon).

Ex post The value of some variable after the event.

Ex-rights When a share goes 'ex-rights' any purchaser of a share after that date will not have a right to subscribe for new shares in the rights issue.

Ex-rights price of a share The theoretical market price following a rights issue.

Excess return (ER) The return above the level expected given the level of risk taken.

Exchange rate The price of one currency expressed in terms of another.

Exchangeable bond A bond that entitles the owner to choose at a later date whether to exchange the bond for shares in a company. The shares are in a company other than the one that issued the bonds.

Exclusive franchise *See* Economic franchise.

Exit (1) The term used to describe the point at which a venture capitalist can recoup some or all of the investment made. (2) The closing of a position created by a transaction.

Exit barrier A factor preventing firms from stopping production in a particular industry.

Expansion capital Capital needed by companies at a fast-development phase to increase production capacity or to increase working capital for the further development of the product or market. Venture capital is often used.

Expectation hypothesis of the term structure of interest rates (yield curve) Long-term interest rates reflect the market consensus on the changes in short-term interest rates.

Expected return The mean or average outcome calculated by weighting each of the possible outcomes by the probability of occurrence and then summing the result.

External finance Outside finance raised by a firm, i.e. finance that it did not generate internally, for example through profits retention.

External metrics Measures of corporate performance which are accessible to individuals outside the firm and concern the performance of the firm as a whole.

extraMARK An attribute market for investment companies and products on the Official List (q.v.) of the London Stock Exchange.

Extraordinary general meeting (EGM) A meeting of the company (shareholders and directors) other than the annual general meeting (q.v.). It may be convened when the directors think fit. However, shareholders holding more than 10 per cent of the paid-up share capital carrying voting rights can requisition a meeting.

Extraordinary resources Those that give the firm a competitive edge. A resource which when combined with other (ordinary) resources enables the firm to outperform competitors and create new value-generating opportunities. Critical extraordinary resources determine what a firm can do successfully.

Face value *See* Par value.

Factor model A model which relates the returns on a security to that security's sensitivity to the movements of various factors (e.g. GDP growth, inflation) common to all shares.

Factor risk/Non-factor risk A factor risk is a systematic risk in multi-factor models describing the relationship between risk and return for fully diversified investors. Non-factor risk is unsystematic risk in multi-factor models.

Factoring To borrow against the security of trade debtors. Factoring companies also provide additional services such as sales ledger administration and credit insurance.

Fair game In the context of a stock market this is where some investors and fund raisers are not able to benefit at the expense of other participants. The market is regulated to avoid abuse, negligence and fraud. It is cheap to carry out transactions and the market provides high liquidity.

Fair value (Fair-market value) The amount an asset could be exchanged for in an arm's-length transaction between informed and willing parties.

Fallen angel Debt which used to rate as investment grade but which is now regarded as junk, mezzanine finance (q.v.) or high-yield finance.

Final dividend The dividend announced with the annual accounts. The final dividend plus the interim dividend make the total dividend for the year for a company that reports results every six months.

Finance house A financial institution offering to supply finance in the form of hire purchase, leasing and other forms of instalment credit.

Finance lease (also called **capital lease, financial lease** or **full payout lease**) The lessor expects to recover the full cost (or almost the full cost) of the asset plus interest, over the period of the lease.

Financial assets (securities, instruments) or **Financial claim.** Contracts that state agreement about the exchange of money in the future, e.g. shares, bonds, bank loans, derivatives.

Financial distress Obligations to creditors are not met or are met with difficulty.

Financial gearing (leverage) *See* Gearing.

Financial institutions Organisations that exist to provide services in the financial markets. They might also trade with their own money to try to make a profit.

Financial risk The additional variability in a firm's returns to shareholders which arises because the financial structure contains debt.

Financial Services and Markets Act The 2000 Act (and orders made under it) form the bedrock of financial regulations in the UK.

Financial Services Authority (FSA) The chief financial services regulator in the UK.

Financial slack Having cash (or near-cash) and/or spare debt capacity available to take up opportunities as they appear.

Financing gap The gap in the provision of finance for medium-sized, fast-growing firms. Often these firms are too large or fast growing to ask the individual shareholders for more funds or to obtain sufficient bank finance. Also they are not ready to launch on the stock market.

Financing-type decision In an investment project the initial cash flow is positive

Fisher's equation The money rate of return m is related to the real rate of return h and the expected inflation rate i through the following equation: $(1 + m) = (1 + h) (1 + i)$.

Fixed assets Those not held for resale, but for use in the business.

Fixed charge (e.g. **fixed charged debenture or loan**) A specific asset(s) assigned as collateral security for a debt.

Fixed cost A cost that does not vary according to the amount of goods or services that are produced. Those business costs that have to be paid regardless of the firm's turnover and activity.

Fixed interest (Fixed rate) Interest on a debt security is constant over its life.

Fixed-interest securities Strictly, the term applies to securities, such as bonds, on which the holder receives a predetermined interest pattern on the par value (e.g. gilts, corporate bonds, Eurobonds). However, the term is also used for debt securities even when there is no regular interest, e.g. zero-coupon bonds (q.v.), and when the interest varies, as with floating rate notes (q.v.), for example.

Flat rate The rate of interest quoted by a hire purchase company (or other lender) to a hiree which fails to reflect properly the true interest rate being charged as measured by the annual percentage rate (APR) (q.v.).

Flat yield *See* Yield.

Float (1) The difference between the cash balance shown on a firm's chequebook and the bank account. Caused by delays in the transfer of funds between bank accounts. (2) An exchange rate that is permitted to vary against other currencies. (3) An issuance of shares to the public by a company joining a stock market. (4) For insurance companies it is the pool of money held in the firm in readiness to pay claims.

Floating charge The total assets of the company or an individual are used as collateral security for a debt. There is no specific asset assigned as collateral.

Floating-rate notes (FRNs) Notes issued in which the coupon fluctuates according to a benchmark interest rate charge (e.g. LIBOR – q.v.). Issued in the euromarkets generally with maturities of 7 to 15 years. **Reverse floaters** Those on which the interest rate declines as LIBOR rises.

Floating-rate borrowing (floating interest) The rate of interest on a loan varies with a standard reference rate, e.g. LIBOR.

Flotation The issue of shares in a company for the first time on a stock exchange.

'Footsie' Nickname for FTSE 100 index. Trademarked.

Foreign banking Transactions in the home currency with non-residents.

Foreign bond A bond denominated in the currency of the country where it is issued when the issuer is a non-resident.

Foreign exchange markets (Forex or FX) Markets that facilitate the exchange of one currency into another.

Forex A contraction of 'foreign exchange'.

Forward A contract between two parties to undertake an exchange at an agreed future date at a price agreed now.

Free cash flow Cash generated by a business not required for operations or for reinvestment. Profit before depreciation, amortisation and provisions, but after interest, tax, capital expenditure on long-lived items and increases in working capital necessary to maintain the company's competitive position and accept all value-generating investments.

Free float (Free capital) The proportion of a quoted company's shares not held by those closest (e.g. directors, founding families) to the company who may be unlikely to sell their shares.

Frequency function (probability or frequency distribution) The organisation of data to show the probabilities of certain values occurring.

FTSE 100 share index An index representing the UK's 100 largest listed shares. Arithmetic average weighted by market capitalisation.

FTSE Actuaries All-Share Index (the 'All-Share') The most representative index of UK shares, reflecting about 700 companies' shares.

FTSE Global All Cap An index of share price movements around the world.

FTSE Eurofirst300 An index of European shares.

Full-payout lease *See* Leasing.

Fund management Investment of and administering a quantity of money, e.g. pension fund, insurance fund, on behalf of the fund's owners.

Fund raising Companies can raise money through rights issues, etc.

Fundamental beta An adjustment to the risk premium on the average share, developed by Barr Rosenburg and others, which amalgamates a number of operating and financial characteristics of the specific company being examined.

Fungible Interchangeable securities; can be exchanged for each other on identical terms.

Future A contract between two parties to undertake a transaction at an agreed price on a specified future date.

GAAP Generally accepted accounting principles. United States accounting rules for reporting results. However, the term has come to mean any widely accepted set of accounting conventions.

Gearing (financial gearing) The proportion of debt capital in the overall capital structure. Also called leverage. High gearing can lead to exaggeratedly high returns if things go well or exaggerated losses if things do not go well.

Gearing (operating) The extent to which the firm's total costs are fixed. This influences the break-even point and the sensitivity of profits to changes in sales level.

General inflation The process of steadily rising prices resulting in the diminishing purchasing power of a given nominal sum of money. Measured by an overall price index which follows the price changes of a 'basket' of goods and services through time.

General insurance Insurance against specific contingencies, e.g. fire, theft and accident.

Geometric mean The geometric mean of a set of n positive numbers is the nth root of their product, e.g. the geometric mean of 2 and 5 is $\sqrt{2 \times 5} = \sqrt{10} = 3.16$. The compound rate of return.

Gilts (gilt-edged securities) Fixed-interest UK government securities (bonds) traded on the London Stock Exchange. A means for the UK government to raise finance from savers. They usually offer regular interest and a redemption amount paid years in the future.

Globalisation The increasing internationalisation of trade, particularly financial product transactions. The integration of economic and capital markets throughout the world.

Goal congruence The aligning of the actions of senior management with the interests of shareholders.

Going long Buying a financial security (e.g. a share) in the hope that its price will rise.

Going public Market jargon used when a company becomes quoted on a stock exchange (the company may have been a public limited company, plc, for years before this).

Going short *See* Short selling.

Golden handcuffs Financial inducements to remain working for a firm.

Golden shares Shares with extraordinary special powers over the company, e.g. power of veto over a merger.

Good growth When a firm grows by investment in positive-performance-spread activities.

Goodwill An accounting term for the difference between the amount that a company pays for another company and the sum of the fair value of that company's individual assets (after deducting all liabilities). Goodwill is thus an intangible asset representing things like the value of the company's brand names and the skills of its employees.

Grace period A lender grants the borrower a delay in the repayment of interest and/or principal at the outset of a lending agreement.

Greenbury Committee report Recommendations on corporate governance (1995).

Greenshoe An option that permits an issuing house, when assisting a corporation in a new issue, to sell more shares than originally planned. They may do this if demand is particularly strong.

Grey market A market in shares where the shares have not yet come into existence, e.g. in the period between investors being told they will receive shares in a new issue and the actual receipt they may sell on the expectation of obtaining them later.

Gross present value The total present value of all the cash flows, excluding the initial investment.

Gross redemption yield (Gross yield to redemption) A calculation of the redemption yield (*see* Yield) before tax.

Guaranteed loan stock (bond) An organisation other than the borrower guarantees to the lender the repayment of the principal plus the interest payment.

Hampel report A follow-up to the Cadbury (1992) and Greenbury (1995) reports on corporate governance. Chaired by Sir Ronald Hampel and published in 1998.

Hang Seng The main index for shares in Hong Kong.

Hard capital rationing Agencies external to the firm will not supply unlimited amounts of investment capital, even though positive NPV projects are identified.

Hedge or Hedging Reducing or eliminating risk by undertaking a countervailing transaction.

Hedge fund A collective investment vehicle that operates free from regulation allowing it to take steps in managing a portfolio that other fund managers are unable to take, e.g. borrowing to invest, shorting the market.

Higgs Committee report Recommendations on corporate governance published in 2003.

High-yield debt *See* Mezzanine finance or Junk bonds.

High-yield shares (yield stocks, high yielder) Shares offering a high current dividend yield because the share price is low due to the expectation of low growth in profits and dividends or because of perceived high risk. Sometimes labelled value shares.

Hire purchase (HP) The user (hiree) of goods pays regular instalments of interest and principal to the hire-purchase company over a period of months. Full ownership passes to the hiree at the end of the period (the hiree is able to use the goods from the outset).

Historical PER (P_0/E_0) Current share price divided by the most recent annual earnings per share.

Holding company *See* Parent company.

Holding period returns Total holding period returns on a financial asset consist of (1) income, e.g. dividend paid; and (2) capital gain – a rise in the value of the asset.

Homemade dividends Shareholders creating an income from shareholdings by selling a portion of their shareholding.

Hurdle rate The required rate of return. The opportunity cost of the finance provider's money. The minimum return required from a position, making an investment or undertaking a project.

Hybrid finance A debt issue or security that combines the features of two or more instruments, e.g. a convertible bond is a package of a bond with an option to convert. Also used to indicate that a form of finance has both debt risk/return features (e.g. regular interest and a right to receive principal at a fixed date) and equity risk/return features (e.g. the returns depend to a large extent on the profitability of the firm).

Idiosyncratic risk An alternative name for unsystematic risk.

Impact day The day during the launch of a new issue of shares when the price is announced, the prospectus published and offers to purchase are solicited.

Impatience to consume People are naturally keen on consuming goods and services sooner rather than later.

Income gearing The proportion of the annual income streams (i.e. pre-interest profits) devoted to the prior claims of debt holders. The reciprocal of income gearing is the interest cover.

Income statement Alternative title for profit and loss account.

Income yield *See* Yield.

Incorporation The forming of a company (usually offering limited liability to the shareholders), including the necessary legal formalities.

Incremental cash flow The new cash flows that occur as a result of going ahead with a project.

Incremental effects Those cash flows indirectly associated with a project, e.g. the cash flows on an existing project are boosted if the new project under consideration goes ahead.

Incremental fixed-capital investment Investment in fixed assets which adds to the stock of assets and does not merely replace worn-out assets.

Incubators Organisations established to assist fast-growing young firms. They may provide finance, accounting services, legal services, offices, etc.

Independent director One that is not beholden to the dominant executive directors. Customers, suppliers or friends of the founding family are not usually regarded as independent.

Independent variables The two variables are completely unrelated; there is no co-movement.

Independents A venture capital organisation that raises its capital from the financial markets – it is not owned by one institution.

Index *See* Market index.

Index funds (trackers) Collective investment funds (e.g. unit trusts) which try to replicate a stock market index rather than to pick winners in an actively managed fund.

Index-linked gilts (stocks) The redemption value and the coupons rise with inflation over the life of the UK government bond.

Indices *See* Market index.

Industry attractiveness The economics of the market for the product(s), part of which is determined by the industry structure.

Industry structure The combination of the degree of rivalry within the industry among existing firms; the bargaining strength of industry firms with suppliers and customers; and the potential for new firms to enter and for substitute products to take customers. The industry structure determines the long-run rate of return on capital employed within the industry.

Inevitables Companies that are likely to be dominating their field for many decades due to their competitive strength.

Inflation The process of prices rising resulting in the fall of the purchasing power of one currency unit.

Informal venture capitalist An alternative name for business angel (q.v.).

Information asymmetry One party to a transaction (e.g. loan agreement) has more information on risk and return relating to the transaction than the other party.

Information costs The cost of gathering and analysing information, e.g. in the context of deciding whether to lend money to a firm.

Initial public offering (IPO) (new issue) The offering of shares in the equity of a company to the public for the first time.

Insider trading (dealing) Trading shares, etc. on the basis of information not in the public domain.

Insolvent A company unable to pay debts as they become due.

Instalment credit A form of finance to pay for goods or services over a period through the payment of principal and interest in regular instalments.

Institutional neglect Share analysts, particularly at the major institutions, may fail to spend enough time studying small firms, preferring to concentrate on the larger 100 or so.

Institutionalisation The increasing tendency for organisational investing, as opposed to individuals investing money in securities (e.g. pension funds and investment trusts collect the savings of individuals to invest in shares).

Insurable risk Risk that can be transferred through the payment of premiums to insurance companies.

Intangible assets Those that you cannot touch – they are non-physical, e.g. goodwill.

Interbank market The wholesale market in short-term money and foreign exchange in which banks borrow and lend among themselves. It is now extended to include large companies and other organisations.

Interest cover The number of times the income of a business exceeds the interest payments made to service its loan capital.

Interest rate risk The risk that changes in interest rates will have an adverse impact.

Interest yield *See* Yield.

Interim dividend A dividend related to the first half-year's (or quarter's) trading.

Interim profit reports A statement giving unaudited profit figures for the first half of the financial year, shortly after the end of the first half-year.

Intermediaries offer A method of selling shares in the new issue market. Shares are offered to financial institutions such as stockbrokers. Clients of these intermediaries can then apply to buy shares from them.

Intermediate debt *See* Mezzanine finance or Junk bonds.

Intermediate security A financial asset created by a financial institution designed to attract funds from the savers in society.

Internal finance Funds generated by the firm's activities, and available for investment within the firm after meeting contractual obligations.

Internal metrics Measures of corporate performance available to those inside the company. They can be used at the corporate, SBU (q.v.) or product-line level.

Internal rate of return (IRR) The discount rate that makes the present value of a future stream of cash flows equal to the initial investment(s).

International banking Banking transactions outside the jurisdiction of the authorities of the currency in which the transaction takes place.

International bonds Some people use the term to mean the same as Eurobonds; others extend the definition to encompass foreign bonds as well.

International Capital Market Association (ICMA) A self-regulatory organisation designed to promote orderly trading and the general development of the euromarkets.

Interpolation Estimating intermediate data points on a set of data where observed points are at intervals.

Intrinsic value (company) The discounted value of the cash that can be taken out of a business during its remaining life.

Introduction A company with shares already quoted on another stock exchange, or where there is already a wide spread of shareholders, may be introduced to the market. This allows a secondary market in the shares even though no new shares are issued.

Inventory *See* Stock.

Investing-type decision In an investment project the initial cash flow is negative.

Investment bank or Merchant bank Banks that carry out a variety of financial services, usually excluding high street banking. Their services are usually fee based, e.g. fees for merger advice to companies.

Investment grade debt Debt with a sufficiently high credit rating (BBB– or Baa and above) to be regarded as safe enough for institutional investors that are restricted to holding only safe debt.

Investment trusts (investment companies) Collective investment vehicles set up as companies selling shares. The money raised is invested in assets such as shares, gilts, corporate bonds and property.

Invoice An itemised list of goods shipped, usually specifying the terms of sale and price.

Invoice discounting Invoices sent to trade debtors are pledged to a finance house in return for an immediate payment of up to 80 per cent of the face value.

Invoice finance A method of receiving finance secured by receivables (trade debtors). A finance house advances funds to a firm. When a customer pays on the invoice the company pays the finance house with interest.

IOU A colloquialism intended to mean 'I owe you'. The acknowledgement of a debt.

Irredeemable Financial securities with no fixed maturity date at which the principal is repaid.

Issued share capital That part of a company's share capital that has been subscribed by shareholders, either paid up or partially paid up.

Issuing house *See* Sponsor.

Joint stock enterprise The ownership (share) capital is divided into small units, permitting a number of investors to contribute varying amounts to the total. Profits are divided between stockholders in proportion to the number of shares they own.

Junior debt (junior security) *See* Subordinated debt.

Junk bonds Low-quality, low credit-rated company bonds. Rated below investment grade (less than BBB– or Baa). Risky and with a high yield.

Kicker *See* Equity kicker.

landMARK Groups of London Stock Exchange's Official List companies from particular UK regions.

Lead manager In a new issue of securities (e.g. shares, bonds, syndicated loans) the lead manager controls and organises the issue. There may be joint lead managers, co-managers and regional lead managers.

Leasing The owner of an asset (lessor) grants the use of the asset to another party (lessee) for a specified period in return for regular rental payments. The asset does not become the property of the lessee at the end of the specified period. *See also* Finance lease and Operating lease.

Lessee The user of an asset under a lease.

Lessor The provider of an asset under a lease.

Leverage *See* Gearing.

Leveraged buy-out (LBO) The acquisition of a company, subsidiary or unit by another, financed mainly by borrowings.

Leveraged recapitalisation The financial structure of the firm is altered in such a way that it becomes highly geared.

LIBOR (London Interbank Offered Rate) The rate of interest offered on loans to highly rated (low-risk) banks in the London interbank market for a specific period (e.g. three months). Used as a reference rate for other loans.

Life assurance An insurer guarantees to pay sums of money to a beneficiary(ies) in the event of the death of the insured in return for premiums.

LIFFE (London International Financial Futures and Options Exchange) The main derivatives exchange in London – now called Euronext.liffe (q.v.).

Limit bid In a book-building exercise a potential institutional investor states that it will buy a given number of shares at a particular price.

Limited companies (Ltd) 'Private' companies with no minimum amount of share capital, but with restrictions on the range of investors who can be offered shares. The owners of shares in a business have a limit on their loss, set as the amount they have committed to invest in shares. These companies cannot be quoted on the London Stock Exchange.

Limited liability The owners of a business have a limit to their loss should the business fail. This is the amount of capital they have agreed to invest in it by buying shares.

Line of credit *See* Credit facility.

Line of least resistance Taking the path with the least hassle.

Liquidation of a company The winding-up of the affairs of a company when it ceases business. This could be forced by an inability to make a payment when due or it could be voluntary when shareholders choose to end the company. Assets are sold, liabilities paid (if sufficient funds) and the surplus (if any) is distributed to shareholders.

Liquidity The degree to which an asset can be sold quickly and easily without loss in value.

Liquidity-preference hypothesis of the term structure of interest rates The yield curve is predominantly upward sloping because investors require an extra return for lending on a long-term basis.

Liquidity risk The risk that an organisation may not have, or may not be able to raise, cash funds when needed.

Listed companies Those on the Official List (q.v.) of the London Stock Exchange.

Listing agreement The UK Listing Authority (q.v.) insists that a company signs a listing agreement committing the directors to certain standards of behaviour and levels of reporting to shareholders.

Listing particulars *See* Prospectus.

Listing Rules The regulations concerning the initial flotation of a company on the London Stock Exchange and the continuing requirements the company must meet.

Lloyds Insurance Market A medium-sized insurance business in London founded over two centuries ago. 'Names' supply the capital to back insurance policies. Names can now be limited liability companies rather than individuals with unlimited liability to pay up on an insurance policy.

Loan stock A fixed-interest debt financial security. May be unsecured.

London Stock Exchange The marketplace for the trading of various financial instruments located in London and regulated under UK law.

Long bond Often defined as bonds with a time to maturity greater than 15 years, but there is some flexibility in this, so a 10-year bond is often described as being long.

Long position A positive exposure to a quantity – if the market rises, the position improves. Owning a security or commodity; the opposite of a short position (selling).

Low-grade debt *See* Mezzanine finance or Junk bonds.

Ltd Private limited company.

Macroeconomic changes Changes in large economic aggregates such as national income and aggregate saving.

Main market The Official List of the London Stock Exchange, as opposed to the Alternative Investment Market (qq.v.).

Management buy-in (MBI) A new team of managers makes an offer to a company to buy the whole company, a subsidiary or a section of the company, with the intention of taking over the running of it themselves. Venture capital often provides the major part of the finance.

Management buy-out (MBO) A team of managers makes an offer to its employers to buy a whole business, a subsidiary or a section so that the managers own and run it themselves. Venture capital is often used to finance the majority of the purchase price.

Managementism/Managerialism Management not acting in shareholders' best interests by pursuing objectives attractive to the management team. There are three levels: (1) dishonest managers; (2) honest but incompetent managers; (3) honest and competent but as humans are subject to the influence of conflicts of interest.

Market capitalisation The total value at market prices of the shares in issue for a company (or a stock market, or a sector of the stock market).

Market entry Firms that previously did not supply goods or services to this industry now do so.

Market in managerial control Teams of managers compete for control of corporate assets, e.g. through merger activity.

Market index A sample of shares is used to represent a share (or other) market's level and movements.

Market makers Organisations that stand ready to buy and sell shares from investors on their own behalf at the centre of the London Stock Exchange's quote-driven system of share trading.

Market portfolio A portfolio which contains all assets. Each asset is held in proportion to the asset's share of the total market value of all the assets. A proxy for this is often employed, e.g. the FTSE 100 index.

Market power The ability to exercise some control over the price of the product.

Market risk *See* Systematic risk.

Market segmentation hypothesis of the term structure of interest rates The yield curve is created (or at least influenced) by the supply and demand conditions in a number of sub-markets defined by maturity range.

Market-to-book ratio (MBR) The market value of a firm divided by capital invested.

Market value added The difference between the total amount of capital put into a business by finance providers (debt and equity) and the current market value of the company's shares and debts.

Matching principle The maturity structure of debt matches the maturity of projects or assets held by the firm. Short-term assets are financed by short-term debt and long-term assets are financed by long-term debt.

Maturity, Maturity date or Final maturity (Redemption date) The time when a financial security (e.g. a bond) is due to be redeemed and the par value is paid to the lender.

Maturity structure The profile of the length of time to the redemption and repayment of a company's various debts.

Maturity transformation Intermediaries offer securities with liquid characteristics to induce primary investors to purchase or deposit funds. The money raised is made available to the ultimate borrowers on a long-term, illiquid basis.

Maximisation of long-term shareholder wealth The assumed objective of the firm in finance. It takes into account the time value of money and risk.

Mean (1) arithmetic mean: a set of numbers are summed, and the answer is divided by the number of numbers; (2) geometric mean: calculated as the nth root of the product of n number, e.g. the geometric mean of 2 and 5 is $\sqrt{2 \times 5} = \sqrt{10} = 3.16$.

Mean reversion *See* Reversion to the mean.

Mean-variance rule If the expected return on two projects is the same but the second has a higher variance (or standard deviation) (qq.v.), then the first will be preferred. Also, if the variance on the two projects is the same but the second has a higher expected return, the second will be preferred.

Medium-term note (MTN) A document setting out a promise from a borrower to pay the holders a specified sum on the maturity date and, in many cases, a coupon interest in the meantime. Maturity can range from nine months to 30 years (usually one to five years). If denominated in a foreign currency they are called euro medium-term notes.

Merchant bank *See* Investment bank.

Metric Method of measurement.

Mezzanine finance Unsecured debt or preference shares offering a high return with a high risk. Ranked behind secured debt but ahead of equity. It may carry an equity kicker (q.v.).

Minority shareholder A shareholder who owns less than 50 per cent of a company.

Mobilisation of savings The flow of savings primarily from the household sector to the ultimate borrowers to invest in real assets. This process is encouraged by financial intermediaries.

Model Code for Director Dealings London Stock Exchange rules for directors dealing in shares of their own company.

Money cash flow All future cash flows are expressed in the prices expected to rule when the cash flow occurs.

Money markets Wholesale financial markets (i.e. those dealing with large amounts) in which lending and borrowing on a short-term basis takes place (less than 1 year). Examples of instruments: commercial paper, Treasury bills.

Money rate of return The rate of return which includes a return to compensate for inflation.

Moral hazard The presence of a safety net (e.g. an insurance policy) encourages adverse behaviour (e.g. carelessness). An incentive to take extraordinary risks (risks that tend to fall on others) aimed at rectifying a desperate position. The risk that a party to a transaction is not acting in good faith by providing misleading or inadequate information.

Mortgage debentures Bonds secured using property as collateral.

Mortgage-style repayment schedule A regular monthly amount is paid to a lender which covers both interest and some capital repayment. At first most of the monthly payment goes towards interest. As the outstanding debt is reduced, the monthly payment pays off a larger and larger amount of the capital.

Mutual funds A collective investment vehicle the shares of which are sold to investors – a very important method of investing in shares in the USA.

NASDAQ (National Association of Securities Dealers Automated Quotation system) A series of computer-based information services and an order execution system for the US over-the-counter securities (e.g. share) market.

Natural clientele An investor whose requirement from an investment matches the dividend paying pattern selected by the firm.

Near-cash (near-money, quasi-money) Highly liquid financial assets but which are generally not usable for transactions and therefore cannot be fully regarded as cash, e.g. Treasury bills.

Negative covenants Loan agreements conditions that restrict the actions and rights of the borrower until the debt has been repaid in full.

Negotiability (1) Transferable to another – free to be traded in financial markets. (2) Capable of being settled by agreement between the parties involved in a transaction.

Net assets (Net worth), Net asset value (NAV) Total assets minus all the liabilities. Fixed assets, plus stocks, debtors, cash and other liquid assets, minus long-and short-term creditors.

Net operating cash flow Profit plus depreciation plus or minus the change in working capital.

Net present value (NPV) The present value of the expected cash flows associated with a project after discounting at a rate which reflects the value of the alternative use of the funds.

Net profit (Net income) Profit after interest, tax and extraordinary charges and receipts.

Net realisable value What someone might reasonably be expected to pay less the costs of the sale.

Net worth Total assets minus total liabilities.

Neuer Markt German stock exchange for smaller young companies. Now closed due to financial scandals and loss of confidence among investors.

New issue The sale of securities, e.g. debentures or shares, to raise additional finance or to float existing securities of a company on a stock exchange for the first time.

Nikkei The Nikkei 225 index is a price average index of the largest 225 companies quoted on the Tokyo Stock Exchange.

Nil paid rights Shareholders may sell the rights to purchase shares in a rights issue without having paid anything for these rights.

Nominal return (or interest rate) The return on an investment including inflation. If the return necessary to compensate for the decline in the purchasing power of money (inflation) is deducted from the nominal return we have the real rate of return.

Nominal value *See* Par value.

Nominated adviser (Nomad) Each company on the AIM (q.v.) has to retain a nomad. They act as quality controllers, confirming to the London Stock Exchange that the company has complied with the rules. They also act as consultants to the company.

Nominated brokers Each company on the AIM (q.v.) has to retain a nominated broker, who helps to bring buyers and sellers together and comments on the firm's prospects.

Non-executive director (Outside director) A director without day-to-day operational responsibility for the firm.

Non-recourse A lending arrangement, say in project finance, where the lenders have no right to insist that the parent company(s) pay the due interest and capital should the project company be unable to do so.

Non-voting shares A company may issue two or more classes of ordinary shares, one of which may be of shares that do not carry any votes.

Normal rate of return A rate of return that is just sufficient to induce shareholders to put money into the firm and hold it there.

Note (promissory note) A financial security with the promise to pay a specific sum of money by a given date, e.g. commercial paper, floating rate notes. Usually unsecured.

Note issuance facility (Note purchase facility) A medium-term arrangement allowing borrowers to issue a series of short-term promissory notes (usually 3–6 month maturity). A group of banks guarantees the availability of funds by agreeing to purchase any unsold notes at each issue date while the facility is in place.

NYSE The New York Stock Exchange.

Objective probability A probability that can be established theoretically or from historical data.

Objectives maximised To have one's objectives maximised is to receive all the surplus from, say, a business enterprise after all other parties have received just enough to satisfy them, encouraging them to make their contribution.

Oblique way Achieving an objective by approaching it in an indirect way.

OFEX The farmer name for PLUS An unregulated share market offering a secondary market trading facility.

Off-balance-sheet finance Assets are acquired in such a way that liabilities do not appear on the balance sheet, e.g. some lease agreements permit the exclusion of the liability in the accounts.

Offer document (1) A formal document sent by a company attempting to buy all the shares in a target firm to all the shareholders of the target setting out the offer. (2) The legal document for an offer for sale in a new issue.

Offer for sale A method of selling shares in a new issue. The company sponsor offers shares to the public by inviting subscriptions from investors. (1) Offer for sale by fixed price – the sponsor fixes the price prior to the offer. (2) Offer for sale by tender – investors state the price they are willing to pay. A strike price is established by the sponsors after receiving all the bids. All investors pay the strike price.

Offer for subscription A method of selling shares in a new issue. The issue is aborted if the offer does not raise sufficient interest from investors.

Offer price (1) The price at which a market maker in shares will sell a share, or a dealer in other markets will sell a security or asset. (2) The price of a new issue of securities, e.g. a new issue of shares.

Office of Fair Trading (OFT) The Director-General of Fair Trading has wide powers to monitor and investigate trading activities, and take action against anti-competitive behaviour. He can also refer monopoly situations to the Competition Commission (q.v.).

Official List (OL) The daily list of securities admitted for trading on the London Stock Exchange. It does not include securities traded on the Alternative Investment Market (AIM) (q.v.).

Open-ended funds The size of the fund and the number of units depends on the amount investors wish to put into the fund, e.g. unit trusts. The manager adds to or liquidates part of the assets of the fund depending on the level of purchases or sales of the units in the fund.

Open-ended investment companies (OEICs) Collective investment vehicles with one price for investors. OEICs are able to issue more shares if demand increases from investors, unlike investment trusts. OEICs invest the finance raised in securities, primarily shares.

Open offer New shares are sold to a wide range of external investors (not existing shareholders). However, and under clawback provisions, existing shareholders can buy the shares at the offer price if they wish.

Open outcry Where trading is through oral calling of buy and sell offers and hand signals by market members.

Operating gearing *See* Gearing.

Operating lease The lease period is significantly less than the expected useful life of the asset and the agreed lease payments do not amount to a present value of more than 90 per cent of the value of the asset.

Operating profit (operating income) The accounting income remaining after paying all costs other than interest.

Operating profit margin (operating margin, trading margin) Operating profit as a percentage of sales.

Operational efficiency of a market Relates to how the market minimises the cost to buyers and sellers of transactions in securities on the exchange.

Operational risks The risks that come from the business activity itself rather than from, say, financial risks such as interest rates changing.

Opportunity cost The value forgone by opting for one course of action; the next best use of, say, financial resources.

Opportunity cost of capital The return that is sacrificed by investing finance in one way rather than investing in an alternative of the same risk class, e.g. a financial security.

Option A contract giving one party the right, but not the obligation, to buy or sell a financial instrument, commodity or some other underlying asset at a given price, at or before a specified date.

Ordinary shares The equity capital of the firm. The holders of ordinary shares are the owners and are therefore entitled to all distributed profits after the holders of preference shares, debentures and other debt have had their claims met. They are also entitled to control the direction of the company through the power of their votes – usually one vote per share.

Organic growth Growth from within the firm rather than through mergers.

Over-allotment issue Same as Greenshoe (q.v.).

Overdraft A permit to overdraw on an account (e.g. a bank account) up to a stated limit; to take more out of a bank account than it contains. This arrangement is usually offered for a period, say six months or one year, but most banks retain the right to call in the loan (demand repayment) at any time.

Overheads Costs that do not vary with output.

Over-subscription In a new issue of securities investors offer to buy more securities (e.g. shares) than are made available.

Over-the-counter trade (OTC) Securities trading carried on outside regulated exchanges. These bilateral deals allow tailor-made transactions.

Owner earnings Reported earnings plus depreciation, depletion, amortisation and certain other non-cash charges less the amount of expenditure for plant and machinery and working capital, etc. that a business requires to fully maintain its long-term competitive position, its unit volume and to invest in value-generating opportunities.

Paid-up capital The amount of the authorised share capital that has been paid for or subscribed for by shareholders.

Paper A term for some securities, e.g. certificates of deposit, commercial paper.

Par value (nominal, principal or face value) A stated nominal value of a share or bond. Not related to market value.

Parent company (Holding company) The one that partially or wholly owns other companies.

Partnership An unincorporated business formed by the association of two or more persons who share the risk and profits.

Pathfinder prospectus In a new issue of shares a detailed report on the company is prepared and made available to potential investors a few days before the issue price is announced.

Payback The period of time it takes to recover the initial cash put into a project.

Payout ratio The percentage of after-tax profit paid to shareholders in dividends.

Pecking order theory of financial gearing Firms exhibit preferences in terms of sources of finance. The most acceptable source of finance is retained earnings, followed by borrowing and then by new equity issues.

Pension funds Financial institutions that invest and administer money on behalf of those saving for retirement or those drawing a pension from previously saved funds.

Perfect competition (perfect market) Entry to the industry is free and the existing firms have no bargaining power over suppliers or customers. Rivalry between existing firms is fierce because products are identical. The following assumptions hold: (1) There is a large number of buyers. (2) There is a large number of sellers. (3) The quantity of goods bought by any individual transaction is so small relative to the total quantity traded that individual trades leave the market price unaffected. (4) The units of goods sold by different sellers are the same – the product is homogeneous. (5) There is perfect information – all buyers and all sellers have complete information on the prices being asked and offered in other parts of the market. (6) There is perfect freedom of exit from the market.

Perfect negative correlation When two variables (e.g. returns on two shares) always move in exactly opposite directions.

Perfect positive correlation When two variables (e.g. returns on two shares) always move in the same direction by the same proportional amount.

Performance spread The percentage difference between the actual rate of return on an investment and the required rate given its risk class.

Perpetuity A regular sum of money received at intervals forever.

Personal guarantee An individual associated with a company, e.g. director, personally guarantees that a debt will be repaid.

Placing, place or placement A method of selling shares and other financial securities in the primary market. Securities are offered to the sponsors' or brokers' private clients and/or a narrow group of institutions.

Plain vanilla A bond that lacks any special features such as a call or put provision.

Planning horizon The point in the future after which an investment will earn only the minimum acceptable rate of return.

plc Public limited company.

PLUS-Markets Group plc This is a provider of primary and secondary equity market services independent of the London Stock Exchange. It operates and regulates the PLUS service.

Political risk Changes in government or government policies impacting on returns and volatility of returns.

Pooled funds Organisations (e.g. unit trusts) that gather together numerous small quantities of money from investors and then invest in a wide range of financial securities.

Portfolio A collection of investments.

Portfolio investment (1) Investment in a variety of instruments; (2) (in national accounting) investment made by firms and individuals in bonds and shares issued in another country. An alternative form of foreign investment is direct investment, buying commercial assets such as factory premises and industrial plant.

Portfolio planning Allocating resources within the company to those SBUs (q.v.) and product/customer areas offering the greatest value creation, while withdrawing capital from those destroying value.

Portfolio theory Formal mathematical model for calculating risk-returns trade-offs as securities are combined in a portfolio.

Post-completion audit The monitoring and evaluation of the progress of a capital investment project through a comparison of the actual cash flows and other benefits with those forecast at the time of authorisation.

Pre-emption rights The strong right of shareholders of UK companies to have first refusal to subscribe for further issues of shares. *See* Rights issue.

Preference shares These normally entitle the holder to a fixed rate of dividend but this is not guaranteed. Holders of preference shares precede the holders of ordinary shares, but follow bond holders and other lenders, in payment of dividends and return of principal. *Participating preference share*: share in residual profits. *Cumulative preference share*: share carries forward the right to preferential dividends. *Redeemable preference share*: a preference share with a finite life. *Convertible preference share*: may be converted into ordinary shares.

Preliminary annual results (Preliminary profit announcements, prelims) After the year-end and before the full reports and accounts are published, a statement on the profit for the year and other information is provided by companies quoted on the London Stock Exchange.

Premium (1) (On an option) The amount paid to an option writer to obtain the right to buy or sell the underlying. (2) (Foreign exchange) The forward rate of exchange stands at a higher level than the current spot rate. (3) (Investment trusts) By how much the share price exceeds the net asset value per share.

Prescribed market A market, such as PLUS, in which the participants have to following certain rules designed to encourage fairness and follow minimum standards laid down in law. However, these markets are not as tightly regulated as those run by the London Stock Exchange. A market which has been prescribed by the Treasury in the Prescribed Markets and qualifying Investments Order.

Present value The current worth of future cash flows when discounted.

Pre-tax profit Profit on ordinary activities before deducting taxation.

Pre-tax profit margin (pre-tax margin) Profit after all expenses including interest expressed as a percentage of sales.

Price discovery The process of forming prices through the interaction of numerous buy and sell orders in an exchange.

Price-earnings ratio (PER, Price-earnings multiple, PE multiple, PE ratio, P/E ratio) Share price divided by earnings per share over the latest twelve months. *Historical*: Share price divided by most recently reported annual earnings per share. *Forward* (prospective): share price divided by anticipated annual earnings per share.

Price-sensitive information That which may influence the share price or trading in the shares.

Price-to-book ratio (market to book) The price of a share as a multiple of PER share book (balance sheet) value.

Pricing power An ability to raise prices even when product demand is flat without the danger of losing significant volume or market share.

Primary investors The household sector contains the savers in society who are the main providers of funds used for investment in the business sector.

Primary market A market in which securities are initially issued to investors rather than a secondary market in which investors buy and sell to each other.

Primary security A security (e.g. bond or share) issued by an organisation raising finance, rather than by a financial intermediary.

Principal (1) The capital amount of a debt, excluding any interest. (2) A person acting for their own purposes accepting risk in financial transactions, rather than someone acting as an agent for another. (3) The amount invested.

Principal–agent problem In which an agent, e.g. a manager, does not act in the best interests of the principal, e.g. the shareholder.

Private equity Share capital invested in companies not quoted on an exchange.

Private limited company (Ltd) A company which is unable to offer its shares to the wider public.

Privatisation The sale to private investors of government-owned equity (shares) in state-owned industries or other commercial enterprises.

Pro forma earnings Projected or forecast earnings. These are not audited and may be unreliable.

Profit and loss account Records whether a company's sales revenue was greater than its costs.

Profit margin Profits as a percentage of sales.

Profitability index A measure of present value per pound invested.

Project An investment within the business requiring medium- to long-term commitment of resources.

Project appraisal The assessment of the viability of proposed long-term investments in real assets within the firm.

Project finance Finance assembled for a specific project. The loan and equity returns are tied to the cash flows and fortunes of the project rather than being dependent on the parent company/companies.

Promissory note A debtor promises to pay on demand or at a fixed date or a date to be determined by circumstances. A note is created stating this obligation.

Proprietary transactions (Proprietary trading) A financial institution, as well as acting as an agent for a client, may trade on the financial markets with a view to generating profits for itself, e.g. speculation on Forex (q.v.).

Prospective PER Current share price divided by next year's anticipated earnings per share.

Prospectus A document containing information about a company (or unit trust/OEIC – q.v.), to assist with a new issue (initial public offering) by supplying detail about the company and how it operates.

Provision (1) Sum set aside in accounts for anticipated loss or expenditure. (2) A clause or stipulation in a legal agreement giving one party a right.

Proxy votes Shareholders unable to attend a shareholders' meeting may authorise another person, e.g. a director or the chairman, to vote on their behalf, either as instructed or as that person sees fit.

Public limited company (plc) A company which may have an unlimited number of shareholders and offer its shares to the wider public (unlike a limited company – q.v.). Must have a minimum share value of £50,000. Some plcs are listed on the London Stock Exchange.

Pure rate of interest The rate of interest required by a lender in the absence of inflation and risk.

Put option This gives the purchaser the right, but not the obligation, to sell a financial instrument, commodity or some other underlying asset at a given price, at or before a specified date.

Quick asset value (net) Current assets minus stock minus current liabilities (qq.v.).

Quick ratio (acid test) The ratio of current assets, less stock, to total current liabilities (qq.v).

Quoted Those shares with a price quoted on a recognised investment exchange (RIE) (e.g. the Official List of the London Stock Exchange (qq.v.)).

Random walk theory The movements in (share) prices are independent of one another; one day's price change cannot be predicted by looking at the previous day's price change.

Ranking (debt) Order of precedence for payment of obligations. Senior debt receives annual interest and redemption payments ahead of junior (or subordinated) debt. So, if the company has insufficient resources to pay its obligation the junior debt holders may receive little or nothing.

Rappaport's shareholder value analysis A value-based method of analysis that uses seven key factors to determine value. Rappaport's value drivers: (1) Sales growth rate. (2) Operating profit margin. (3) Tax rate. (4) Incremental fixed capital investment. (5) Incremental working capital investment. (6) The planning horizon. (7) The required rate of return.

Rating *See* Credit rating.

Real assets Assets used to carry on a business. These assets can be tangible (e.g. buildings) or intangible (e.g. a brand) as opposed to financial assets.

Real cash flows Future cash flows are expressed in terms of constant purchasing power.

Real option An option to undertake different courses of action in the real asset market (strategic and operational options), as opposed to a tradable option on financial securities or commodities.

Real rate of return The rate that would be required (obtained) in the absence of inflation. The nominal return minus inflation.

Recapitalisation A change in the financial structure, e.g. in debt to equity ratio.

Receivable (Accounts receivable) A sum due from a customer for goods delivered: trade credit.

Receiver A receiver takes control of a business if a creditor successfully files a bankruptcy petition. The receiver may then sell the company's assets and distribute the proceeds among the creditors.

Recognised investment exchange (RIE) A body authorised to regulate securities trading in the UK, e.g. the London Stock Exchange.

Recourse If a financial asset is sold (such as a trade debt), the purchaser could return to the vendor for payment in the event of non-payment by the borrower.

Redemption The repayment of the principal amount, or the par value, of a security (e.g. bond) at the maturity date resulting in the retirement and cancellation of the bond.

Redemption yield *See* Yield.

Registrar An organisation that maintains a record of share (and other securities) ownership for a company. It also communicates with shareholders on behalf of the company.

Regulated exchange market A market where there is a degree of supervision concerning market behaviour or other control on the freedom of participants.

Reinvestment rate The rate of return on the periodic cash flows generated by a project when invested.

Repayment holiday *See* Grace period.

Reporting accountant A company planning to float on the London Stock Exchange employs a reporting accountant to prepare a detailed report on the firm's financial controls, track record, financing and forecasts.

Required return The minimum rate of return given the opportunity cost of capital.

Rescheduling Rearranging the payments made by a borrower to a lender – usually over a long period.

Rescue rights issue A company in dire trouble, in danger of failure, carries out a rights issue to raise capital.

Residual income An alternative term for economic profit.

Residual theory of dividends Dividends should only be paid when the firm has financed all its positive NPV projects.

Resolution A proposal put to the vote at a shareholders' meeting.

Resolution of uncertainty theory of dividends The theory that the market places a greater value on shares offering higher near-term dividends because these are more certain than more distant dividends.

Retail banks Offer banking for individual customers or small firms, normally for small amounts. High-volume, low-value banking.

Retained earnings That part of a company's profits not paid as dividends.

Retention ratio Retained profits for the year as a proportion of profits after tax attributable to ordinary shareholders for the year.

Return on capital employed (ROCE); return on investment (ROI) Traditional measures of profitability. Profit return divided by the volume of resources devoted to the activity. Resources usually include shareholders funds, net debt and provisions. Cumulative goodwill, previously written off, may be added back to the resources total. *See also* Accounting rate of return.

Return on equity (ROE) Profit attributable to shareholders as a percentage of equity shareholders' funds.

Revaluation reserve A balance sheet entry that records accumulated revaluations of fixed assets.

Reverse floating-rate notes *See* Floating-rate notes.

Reverse takeover The acquiring company is smaller than the target in terms of market capitalisation and offers newly created shares in itself as consideration for the purchase of the shares in the acquirer. So many new shares are created that the former shareholders in the target become the dominant shareholders in the combined entity.

Reversion to the mean The behaviour of financial markets is often characterised as reverting to the mean, in which an otherwise random process of price changes or returns tends over the medium to long term to move towards the average.

Revolving credit An arrangement whereby a borrower can draw down short-term loans as the need arises, to a maximum over a period of years.

Revolving underwriting facility (RUF) A bank(s) underwrites the borrower's access to funds at a specified rate in the short-term financial markets (e.g. by issuing euronotes) throughout an agreed period. If the notes are not bought in the market the underwriter(s) is obliged to purchase them.

Rights issue An invitation to existing shareholders to purchase additional shares in the company in proportion to their existing holdings.

Risk A future return has a variety of possible values. Sometimes measured by standard deviation (q.v.).

Risk arbitrage Taking a position (purchase or sale) in a security, commodity, etc. because it is judged to be mispriced relative to other securities with similar characteristics. The comparator securities are not identical (e.g. shares in Unilever and in Procter & Gamble) and therefore there is an element of risk that the valuation gap will widen rather than contract. An extreme form of risk arbitrage is to take a position hoping to make a profit if an event occurs (e.g. a takeover). If the event does not occur there may be a loss. The word 'arbitrage' has been stretched beyond breaking point, as true arbitrage should be risk free.

Risk averter Someone who prefers a more certain return to an alternative with an equal expected return but which is more risky.

Risk lover (seeker) Someone who prefers a more uncertain alternative to an alternative with an equal but less risky outcome.

Risk management The selection of those risks a business should take and those which should be avoided or mitigated, followed by action to avoid or reduce risk.

Risk premium The extra return, above the risk-free rate, for accepting risk.

Risk transformation Intermediaries offer low-risk securities to primary investors to attract funds, which are then used to purchase higher-risk securities issued by the ultimate borrowers.

Risk-free rate of return (RFR) The rate earned on riskless investment, denoted r_f. A reasonable proxy is the rate on lending to a reputable government.

Risk-return line A line on a two-dimensional graph showing all the possible expected returns, i.e. standard deviation combinations, available from the construction of portfolios from two assets. This can also be called the two-asset opportunity set or feasibility set.

Roadshow Companies and their advisers make a series of presentations to potential investors, usually to entice them into buying a new issue of securities.

Rolled-over overdraft Short-term loan facilities are perpetuated into the medium and long term by the renewal of the overdraft facility.

RPI (retail price index) The main UK measure of general inflation.

R-squared, R^2 *See* Coefficient of determination.

Running yield *See* Yield.

Samurai A foreign bond, yen-denominated, issued by a non-Japanese entity in the domestic Japanese market.

Satisficed When a contributor to an organisation is given just enough of a return to make their contribution, e.g. banks are given contracted interest and principal, and no more.

Scaledown In a new issue, when a company floats on a stock exchange, if demand is greater than supply at the offer price the applicants receive less than they applied for, according to a prearranged formula.

Scenario analysis An analysis of the change in NPV (q.v.) brought about by the simultaneous change in a number of key inputs to an NPV analysis. Typically a 'worst case scenario', when all the changes in variables are worsening, and a 'best case scenario', when all variable changes are positive, are calculated.

Scrip dividends Shareholders are offered the alternative of additional shares rather than a cash dividend.

Scrip issue The issue of more shares to existing shareholders according to their current holdings. Shareholders do not pay for these new shares. Company reserves are converted into issued capital.

Search costs The cost of finding another person or organisation with which to transact business/investment.

Secondary buy-out A company that has been backed by private equity finance is then sold to another private equity firm(s).

Seasoned Equity Offerings (SEOs) Companies that have been on a stock exchange for some time selling new shares, e.g. via a rights issue.

Secondary market Securities already issued are traded between investors.

Securities and Exchange Commission (SEC) The US federal body responsible for the regulation of securities markets (exchanges, brokers, investment advisers, etc.).

Securities house This may mean simply an issuing house. However, the term is sometimes used more broadly for an institution concerned with buying and selling securities or acting as agent in the buying and selling of securities.

Securitisation Financial payments (e.g. a claim to a number of mortgage payments) which are not tradable can be repackaged into other securities (e.g. bonds) and then sold. These are called asset-backed securities.

Security (1) A financial asset, e.g. a share or bond. (2) Asset pledged to be surrendered in the event of a loan default.

Security Market Line (SML) A linear (straight) line showing the relationship between systematic risk and expected rates of return for individual assets (securities). According to the capital asset pricing model (q.v.) the return above the risk-free rate of return (q.v.) for a risky asset is equal to the risk premium for the market portfolio multiplied by the beta coefficient.

Seedcorn capital or money (Seed capital or money) The financing of the development of a business concept. High risk; usually provided by venture capitalists, entrepreneurs or business angels.

Self-amortising A reduction in the amount outstanding on a loan by regular payments to the lender.

Self-regulation Much of the regulation of financial services in the UK is carried out by self-regulatory organisations (SROs), i.e. industry participants regulate themselves within a light-touch legislated framework.

Selling the rights nil paid In a rights issue those entitled to new shares (existing shareholders) are entitled to sell the rights to the new shares without the need to purchase the new shares.

Semi-annual Twice a year at regular intervals.

Semi-captives A venture capital organisation that raises its capital from the financial markets, but is dominated by the participation of an organising institution.

Semi-strong efficiency Share prices fully reflect all the relevant, publicly available information.

Senior debt *See* Subordinated debt.

Sensitivity analysis An analysis of the effect on project NPV of changes in the assumed values of key variables, e.g. sales level, labour costs. Variables are changed one at a time. It is a 'what-if' analysis, e.g. what if raw material costs rise by 20 per cent?

Separate legal person A company is a legal entity under the law. It is entitled to make contracts and be sued, for example, separately from the owners of the company.

Separation principle The decision on asset allocation can be split into (1) selecting the optimum market portfolio on the efficiency frontier, and (2) allocating wealth between the optimum portfolio and the risk-free asset.

Serious Fraud Office (SFO) Investigates and prosecutes crimes of serious fraud in the UK.

Settlement The completion of a transaction, e.g. upon the sale of a share in the secondary market cash is transferred as payment, in return ownership is transferred.

Share Companies divide the ownership of the company into ordinary shares. An owner of a share usually has the same rights to vote and receive dividends as another owner of a share. Also called equity (q.v.).

Share buy-back The company buys back a proportion of its shares from shareholders.

Share certificate A document showing ownership of part of the share capital of a company.

Share market Institutions which facilitate the regulated sale and purchase of shares; includes the primary and secondary markets.

Share option scheme Employees are offered the right to buy shares in their company at a pre-set price some time in the future.

Share premium account A balance sheet entry represented by the difference between the price received by a company when it sells shares and the par value of those shares.

Share repurchase The company buys back its own shares.

Share split (stock split) Shareholders receive additional shares from the company without payment. The nominal (par) value of each share is reduced in proportion to the increase in the number of shares, so the total book value of shares remains the same.

Shareholder value analysis A technique developed by Rappaport (q.v.) for establishing value creation. It equals the present value of operating cash flows within the planning horizon *plus* the present value of operating cash flows after the planning horizon *plus* the current value of marketable securities and other non-operating investments *less* corporate debt.

Shareholder wealth maximisation The maximising of shareholders' purchasing power. In a pricing efficient market, it is the maximisation of the current share price.

Shareholders' funds (Equity) The net assets of the business (after deduction of all short- and long-term liabilities and minority interests) shown in the balance sheet.

Short position In a derivative contract the counterparty in a short position is the one that has agreed to deliver the underlying (q.v.).

Short selling The selling of financial securities (e.g. shares) not yet owned, in the anticipation of being able to buy at a later date at a lower price.

Short-termism A charge levelled at the financial institutions in their expectations of the companies to which they provide finance. It is argued that long-term benefits are lost because of pressure for short-term performance.

Shorting Same as short selling.

Shorts UK government bonds (gilts) with less than five years to maturity.

Sight bank account (current account) One where deposits can be withdrawn without notice.

Sigma A measure of dispersion of returns, standard deviation (q.v.).

Signalling Some financial decisions are taken to be signals from the managers to the financial markets, e.g. an increase in gearing, or a change in dividend policy.

Simple interest Interest is paid on the original principal; no interest is paid on the accumulated interest payments.

Sinking fund Money is accumulated in a fund through regular payments in order eventually to repay a debt.

Soft capital rationing Internal management-imposed limits on investment expenditure.

Solvency The ability to pay legal debts.

Special dividend An exceptionally large dividend paid on a one-off basis.

Special purpose entity Companies set these up as separate organisations (companies) for a particular purpose. They are designed so that their accounts are not consolidated with those of the rest of the group.

Special resolution A company's shareholders vote at an AGM or EGM with a majority of 75 per cent of those voting. Normally special resolutions are reserved for important changes in the constitution of the company. Other matters are dealt with by way of an ordinary resolution (50 per cent or more of the votes required).

Specific inflation The price changes in an individual good or service.

Specific risk *See* Unsystematic risk.

Speculative grade Bonds with a credit rating below investment grade.

Speculators Those that take a position in financial instruments and other assets with a view to obtaining a profit on changes in their value.

Sponsor Lends its reputation to a new issue of securities, advises the client company (along with the issuing broker) and coordinates the new issue process. Sponsors are usually merchant banks or stockbrokers. Also called an issuing house.

Spot market A market for immediate transactions (e.g. spot Forex market, spot interest market), as opposed to an agreement to make a transaction some time in the future (e.g. forward, option, future).

Spot rate of interest The interest rate fixed today on a loan that is made today.

Spread The difference between the price to buy and the price to sell a financial security. Market makers quote a bid–offer spread for shares. The lower price (bid) is the price an investor receives if selling to the market maker. The higher (offer) price is the price if the investor wishes to buy from the market maker.

Stakeholder A party with an interest (financial or otherwise) in an organisation, e.g. employees, customers, suppliers, the local community.

Standard deviation A statistical measure of the dispersion around an average. A measure of volatility. The standard deviation is the square root of the variance. A fund or a share return can be expected to fall within one standard deviation of its average two-thirds of the time if the future is like the past.

Standard and Poor's 500 An index of leading (largest) 500 US shares listed on the New York Stock Exchange. Companies are weighted by market capitalisation. Represents 80 per cent of the capitalisation of the NYSE.

Start-up capital Finance for young companies that have not yet sold their product commercially. High risk; usually provided by venture capitalists, entrepreneurs or business angels.

Statistically independent shares The movement of two variables is completely unrelated (e.g. the returns on two shares are unrelated).

Statutory Established, regulated or imposed by or in conformity with laws passed by a legislative body, e.g. Parliament.

Sterling bonds Corporate bonds that pay interest and principal in sterling.

Stock Another term for inventory of raw materials, work-in-progress and finished items.

Stock exchange A market in which securities are bought and sold. In continental Europe the term bourse may be used.

Stock market *See* Stock exchange.

Stocks and shares There is some lack of clarity in the distinction between stocks and shares. Shares are equities in companies. Stocks are financial instruments that pay interest, e.g. bonds. However, in the USA shares are also called 'common stocks' and the shareholders are sometimes referred to as the stockholders. So when some people use the term stocks they could be referring to either bonds or shares.

Straight bond One with a regular fixed rate of interest and without the right of conversion (to, say, shares) or any other unusual rights.

Strategic analysis The analysis of industries served by the firm and the company's competitive position within the industry.

Strategic business unit (SBU) A business unit within the overall corporate entity which is distinguishable from other business units because it serves a defined external market where management can conduct strategic planning in relation to products and markets.

Strategic objectives These goals are used as the criteria to guide the firm, e.g. market share targets. However, they may not always be good indicators of whether shareholder wealth is being maximised.

Strategic position A firm's competitive position within an industry and the attractiveness of the industry.

Strategy planes chart Maps a firm's, SBU's or product line's position in terms of industry attractiveness, competitive advantage and life-cycle stage of value potential.

Strike bid In a book-building exercise a potential institutional investor states that it will buy a given number of shares within the initial price range.

Strong-form efficiency All relevant information, including that which is privately held, is reflected in the share price.

Subjective probability Probabilities are devised based on personal judgement of the range of outcomes along with the likelihood of their occurrence.

Subordinated debt A debt that ranks below another liability in order of priority for payment of interest or principal. Senior debt ranks above junior (subordinated) debt for payment.

Subscription rights A right to subscribe for some shares.

Subsidiary A company is a subsidiary of another company if the parent company holds the majority of the voting rights (more than 50%), or has a minority of the shares but has the right to appoint or remove directors holding a majority of the voting rights at meetings of the board on all, or substantially all, matters or it has the right to exercise a dominant influence.

Sunk cost A cost the firm has incurred or to which it is committed that cannot be altered. This cost does not influence subsequent decisions and can be ignored in, for example, project appraisal.

Super normal returns A rate of return above the normal rate of return.

Syndicated loan A loan made by one or more banks to one borrower.

Synergies A combined entity (e.g. two companies merging) will have a value greater than the sum of the parts.

Systematic (undiversifiable or **market** or **residual) risk** That element of return variability from an asset which cannot be eliminated through diversification (q.v.). Measured by beta (q.v.). It comprises the risk factors common to all firms.

Systemic risk The risk of failure within the financial system causing a domino-type effect bringing down large parts of the system.

Take-out Market expression of bid made to a seller to 'takeout' his position – e.g. venture capital backed companies are bought allowing the venture capitalist to exit from the investment.

Takeover Panel The committee responsible for supervising compliance with the (UK) City Code on Takeovers and Mergers (q.v.).

Tangible assets Those that have a physical presence.

Tax allowance An amount of income or capital gain that is not taxed.

Tax shield The benefit for a company that comes from having some of its capital in debt form, the interest on which is tax deductible, resulting in a lower outflow from the company to the tax authorities.

Taxable profit That element of profit subject to taxation. This frequently differs from reported profit.

techMARK The London Stock Exchange launched techMARK in 1999. It is a subsection of the shares within the Official List (q.v.). It is a grouping of technology companies.

Technical analysis Analysis of share price movements and trading volume to forecast future movements from past movements.

Tender offer A public offer to purchase securities.

Term assurance Life assurance taken out for less than the whole life – the insured sum is paid only in the event of the insured person dying within the term.

Term loan A loan of a fixed amount for an agreed time and on specified terms, usually with regular periodic payments. Most frequently provided by banks.

Term structure of interest rates The pattern of interest rates on bonds with differing lengths of time to maturity but with the same risk. Strictly it is the zero coupon implied interest rate for different lengths of time. *See also* Yield curve.

Terminal value The forecast future value of sums of money compounded to the end of a common time horizon.

'Time adjusted' measures of profitability The time value of money is taken into account.

Time value of money A pound received in the future is worth less than a pound received today – the present value of a sum of money depends on the date of its receipt.

Total shareholder return (TSR) or **Total return** The total return earned on a share over a period of time: dividend per share plus capital gain divided by initial share price.

Trade credit Where goods and services are delivered to a firm for use in its production and are not paid for immediately.

Trade debtor A customer of a firm who has not yet paid for goods and services delivered.

Trade sale A company buys another company in the same line of business.

Treasury UK government department responsible for financial and economic policy.

Treasury bill A short-term money market instrument issued (sold) by the central bank, mainly in the UK and the USA, usually to supply the government's short-term financing needs.

Treasury management To plan, organise and control cash and borrowings of a firm so as to optimise interest and currency flows, and minimise the cost of funds. Also to plan and execute communications programmes to enhance investors' confidence in the firm.

Trust deed A document specifying the regulation of the management of assets on behalf of beneficiaries of the trust.

Trustees Those that are charged with the responsibility for ensuring compliance with the trust deed.

Turnover (revenue or sales) (1) Money received or to be received by the company from goods and services sold during the year. (2) In portfolio management, the amount of trading relative to the value of the portfolio.

Ultimate borrowers Firms investing in real assets need finance which ultimately comes from the primary investors.

Uncertainty Strictly (in economists' terms), uncertainty is when there is more than one possible outcome to a course of action; the form of each possible outcome is known, but the probability of getting any one outcome is not known. However, the distinction between risk (the ability to assign probabilities) and uncertainty has largely been ignored for the purposes of this text.

Unconventional cash flows A series of cash flows in which there is more than one change in sign.

Underwriters These (usually large financial institutions) guarantee to buy the proportion of a new issue of securities (e.g. shares) not taken up by the market, in return for a fee.

Undiversifiable risk *See* Systematic risk.

Unique risk *See* Unsystematic risk.

Unit trust An investment organisation that attracts funds from individual investors by issuing units to invest in a range of securities, e.g. shares or bonds. It is open ended, the number of units expanding to meet demand.

United Kingdom Listing Authority (UKLA) This organisation is part of the Financial Services Authority (q.v.) and rigorously enforces a set of demanding rules on companies at the time when they join the stock market and in subsequent years.

Universal banks Financial institutions involved in many different aspects of finance including retail banking and wholesale banking.

Unlisted Shares and other securities not on the Official List of the London Stock Exchange (qq.v.) are described as unlisted.

Unquoted Those shares with a price not quoted on a recognised investment exchange, RIE (e.g. the Official List or AIM of the London Stock Exchange – qq.v.).

Unsecured A financial claim with no collateral or any charge over the assets of the borrower.

Unsystematic (unique or diversifiable or specific) risk That element of an asset's variability in returns which can be eliminated by holding a well-diversified portfolio.

Utility (1) The satisfaction, pleasure or fulfilment of needs derived from consuming some quantity of a good or service. (2) A business involved in basic goods and services, e.g. water, electricity.

Value action pentagon This displays the five actions for creating value: (1) Increase the return on existing capital. (2) Raise investment in positive spread units. (3) Divest assets from negative spread units to release capital for more productive use. (4) Extend the planning horizon. (5) Lower the required rate of return.

Value creation The four key elements are: (1) Amount of capital invested. (2) Actual rate of return on capital. (3) Required rate of return. (4) Planning horizon (for performance-spread persistence).

Value-creation profile An analysis of the sources of value creation within the firm from its products and market segments, which maps value creation against the proportion of capital invested.

Value drivers Crucial organisational capabilities, giving the firm competitive advantage. Different from Rappaport's value drivers (q.v.).

Value-based management A managerial approach in which the primary purpose is long-term shareholder wealth maximisation. The objective of the firm, its systems, strategy, processes, analytical techniques, performance measurements and culture have as their guiding objective long-term shareholder wealth maximisation.

Vanilla bond *See* Straight bond.

Variable costs Costs that rise or fall with product output and sales.

Variable rate bond (loan) The interest rate payable varies with short-term rates (e.g. LIBOR six months).

Variance A measure of volatility around an average value. It is the square of the standard deviation.

Vendor placing Shares issued to a company to pay for assets, or issued to shareholders to pay for an entire company in a takeover are placed with investors keen on holding the shares in return for cash. The vendors can then receive the cash.

Venture and development capital investment trusts (VDCITs) Standard investment trusts (without tax breaks) with a focus on more risky developing companies.

Venture capital (VC) Finance provided to unquoted firms by specialised financial institutions. This may be backing for an entrepreneur, financing a start-up or developing business, or assisting a management buy-out or buy-in. Usually it is provided by a mixture of equity, loans and mezzanine finance. It is used for medium-term to long-term investment in high-risk situations.

Venture capital trusts (VCTs) An investment vehicle introduced to the UK in 1995 to encourage investment in small and fast-growing companies. The VCT invests in a range of small businesses. The providers of finance to the VCT are given important tax breaks.

Volatility The speed and magnitude of price movements over time, often measured by standard deviation or variance (qq.v.).

Volume transformation Intermediaries gather small quantities of money from numerous savers and repackage these sums into larger bundles for investment in the business sector or elsewhere.

Warrant A financial instrument that gives the holder the right to subscribe for a specified number of shares or bonds at a fixed price at some time in the future.

Weak-form efficiency Share prices fully reflect all information contained in past price movements.

Weighted average cost of capital (WACC) The weighted average cost of capital (the discount rate) is calculated by weighting the cost of debt and equity in proportion to their contributions to the total capital of the firm.

Whole-of-life policies Life assurance that pays out to beneficiaries when the insured dies (not limited to, say, the next 10 years).

Wholesale bank One that lends, arranges lending or supplies services on a large scale to corporations and within the interbank market. As opposed to retail banks dealing in relatively small sums for depositors and borrowers.

Wholesale financial markets Markets available only to those dealing in large quantities. Dominated by interbank transactions.

Winding-up The process of ending a company, selling its assets, paying its creditors and distributing the remaining cash among shareholders.

Withholding tax Taxation deducted from income by the payer of that income (e.g. company paying interest or dividends) and then sent to tax authorities.

Working capital The difference between current assets and current liabilities – net current assets or net current liabilities (qq.v.).

Write down (Write off) Companies change the recorded value of assets when they are no longer worth the previously stated value.

Writing-down allowance (WDA) (Capital allowance) Reductions in taxable profit related to a firm's capital expenditure (e.g. plant, machinery, vehicles).

Yankees A foreign bond, US dollar-denominated, issued by a non-US entity in the domestic US market.

Yield The income from a security as a proportion of its market price. The flat yield (interest yield, running yield and income yield) on a fixed interest security is the gross interest amount, divided by the current market price, expressed as a percentage. The redemption yield or yield to maturity of a bond is the discount rate such that the present value of all cash inflows from the bond (interest plus principal) is equal to the bond's current market price.

Yield curve A graph showing the relationship between the length of time to the maturity of a bond and the interest rate.

Yield stock *See* High-yield shares.

Yield to maturity *See* Yield

Zero coupon bond (or zero coupon preference share) A bond that does not pay regular interest (dividend) but instead is issued at a discount (i.e. below par value) and is redeemable at par, thus offering a capital gain.

Z statistic A measure of the number of standard deviations away from the mean (average) value a point (say an NPV outcome) is.

For a much wider range of definitions and descriptions, consult: Moles, P. and Terry, N. (1997) *The Handbook of International Financial Terms* (Oxford: Oxford University Press).

Bibliography

3i (1993) 'Dividend Policy'. Reported in *Bank of England Quarterly Review* (1993), August, p. 367.

Adedeji, A. (1997) 'A test of the CAPM and the Three Factor Model on the London Stock Exchange', paper presented to the British Accounting Association Northern Accounting Group 1997 Annual Conference, 10 Sept. 1997, Loughborough University.

Amran, M. and Kulatilaka, N. (1999) *Real Options: Managing Strategic Investment in an Uncertain World*. Boston, MA: Harvard Business School Press.

Anderson, R.C, Mansi, S.A. and Reeb, D.M. (2003) 'Founding family ownership and the agency cost of debt', *Journal of Financial Economics*, 68, pp. 263–85.

Al-Ali, J. and Arkwright, T. (2000) 'An investigation of UK companies practices in the determination, interpretation and usage of cost of capital', *Journal of Interdisciplinary Economics*, 11, pp. 303–19.

Armitage, S. (2000) 'The direct costs of UK rights issues and open offers', *European Financial Management*, March.

Arnold, G.C. (2002) *Valuegrowth Investing*. London: Financial Times Prentice Hall.

Arnold, G.C. (2004) *The Financial Times Guide to Investing*. Harlow: Financial Times Prentice Hall.

Arnold, G.C. (2005) *Corporate Financial Management*, 3rd edition. Harlow: Financial Times Prentice Hall.

Arnold, G.C. and Davies, M. (eds) (2000) *Value-Based Management*. London: Wiley.

Arnold, G.C. and Davis, P. (1995) 'Profitability trends in West Midlands industries'. A study for Lloyds Bowmaker. Edinburgh: Lloyds Bowmaker.

Arnold, G.C. and Hatzopoulos, P.D. (2000) 'The theory practice gap in capital budgeting: evidence from the United Kingdom', *Journal of Business Finance and Accounting*, 27(5) and (6), June/July, pp. 603–26.

Arnold, G.C. and Smith, M. (1999) *The European High Yield Bond Market: Drivers and Impediments*. London: Financial Times Finance Management Report.

Arnott, R. and Bernstein, P. (2002) 'What risk premium is normal?' *Financial Analysts Journal*, March/April.

Association of Corporate Treasurers. *The Treasurer's Handbook*.

Baker, H.K., G.E. Powell and E.T. Veit (2002) 'Revisiting managerial perspectives on dividend policy', *Journal of Economics and Finance*, 26(3), pp. 267–83.

Baker, A. and Wurgler, J. (2002) 'Market timing and capital structure', *Journal of Finance*, 62(1), February, pp. 1–32.

Baker, M. and Wurgler, J. (2004) 'A catering theory of dividends', *Journal of Finance*, 59(3), June, pp. 1125–65.

Bank for International Settlements Quarterly Review. Available online – free (www.bis.org).

Bank of England Quarterly Bulletins.

Bank of England, www.bankofengland.co.uk.

Barclays Capital (annual) *Equity Gilt Study*. London: Barclays Capital.

Barry, C.B., Peavy J.W. III and Rodriguez, M. (1998) 'Performance characteristics of emerging capital markets', *Financial Analysts Journal*, January/February, pp. 72–80.

Berry, A. *et al.* (1990) 'Leasing and the smaller firm', The Chartered Association of Certified Accountants, Occasional Research Paper No. 3.

Black, F. (1972) 'Capital market equilibrium with restricted borrowing', *Journal of Business* (July), pp. 444–55.

Black, F. (1976) 'The dividend puzzle', *Journal of Portfolio Management*, 2, pp. 5–8.

Black, F. (1993) 'Beta and return', *Journal of Portfolio Management*, 20, Fall, pp. 8–18.

Black, F., Jensen, M.C. and Scholes, M. (1972) 'The Capital Asset Pricing Model: some empirical tests', in M. Jensen (ed.), *Studies in the Theory of Capital Markets*. New York: Praeger.

Blake, D. (2000) *Financial Market Analysis*. 2nd edn. London: Wiley.

Blume, M.E. (1971) 'On the assessment of risk', *Journal of Finance*, 26(1), March, pp. 1–10.

Blume, M.E. (1975) 'Betas and their regression tendencies', *Journal of Finance*, 30(3), June, pp. 785–95.

Blume, M. and Friend, I. (1973) 'A new look at the Capital Asset Pricing Model', *Journal of Finance*, March, pp. 19–33.

Booth, L., Aivazian, V., Demirgue-Kunt, A. and Maksimovic, V. (2001) 'Capital Structures in Developing Countries', *Journal of Finance*, 61(1) February, pp. 87–130.

Brealey, R.H. (1986) 'Does dividend policy matter?' in J.M. Stern and D.H. Chew (eds), *The Revolution in Corporate Finance*, Oxford: Basil Blackwell.

Brealey, R.M., S.C. Myers, and F. Allen (2006) *Principles of Corporate Finance*. 8th edn. New York: McGraw-Hill.

Brennan, M. (1971) 'A note on dividend irrelevance and the Gordon valuation model', *Journal of Finance*, December, pp. 1115–21.

Brennan, M.J. and Schwartz, E.S. (1985) 'Evaluating Natural Resource Investments', *Journal of Business*, 58, pp. 135–57.

Brennan, M.J. and Trigeorgis, L. (eds) (2000) *Project Flexibility, Agency, and Competition: New Developments in the Theory and Application of Real Options*. Oxford, New York: Oxford University Press. 5th edn. London: Random House.

Brett, M. (2000) *How to Read the Financial Pages*, 5th edn. London: Random House Business Books.

British Venture Capital Association, London (www.bvca.co.uk).

Buckle, M. and Thompson, J. (2004) *The UK Financial System: Theory and Practice*, 4th edn. Manchester: Manchester University Press.

Buckley, A. (2004) *Multinational Finance*, 5th edn. Harlow: FT Prentice Hall.

Buffett, W. (1982) Letter to shareholders accompanying the *Berkshire Hathaway Annual Report*. Omaha, Neb. www.berkshirehathaway.com.

Buffett, W. (1984) *Berkshire Hathaway Annual Report*. Omaha, Nebraska: Berkshire Hathaway.

Buffett, W. (1993) Letter to shareholders accompanying the *Berkshire Hathaway Annual Report*. Omaha, Neb. www.berkshirehathaway.com.

Bunn, P. and G. Young (2004) 'Corporate capital structure in the United Kingdom: determinants and adjustment'. Bank of England Working Paper No. 26 (www.bankofengland.co.uk/wp/index.html).

'The Cadbury Report' (1992) Report of the Committee on the Financial Aspects of Corporate Governance. London: Gee.

Campbell, K. (2003) *Smarter ventures: A survivor's guide to venture capital through the new cycle*. Harlow: Financial Times Prentice Hall.

Carsberg, B.V. and Hope, A. (1976) *Business Investment Decisions Under Inflation: Theory and Practice*. London: Institute of Chartered Accountants in England and Wales.

Chan, A. and Chui, A.P.L. (1996) 'An empirical re-examination of the cross-section of expected returns: UK evidence', *Journal of Business Finance and Accounting*, 23, pp. 1435–52.

Chan, L.K.C., Hamao, Y. and Lakonishok, J. (1991) 'Fundamentals and stock returns in Japan', *Journal of Finance*, 46, pp. 1739–64.

Chan, L.K.C. and Lakonishok, J. (1993) 'Are the reports of beta's death premature?' *Journal of Portfolio Management*, 19, Summer, pp. 51–62. Reproduced in S. Lofthouse (ed.), *Readings in Investment*. Chichester: Wiley (1994).

Chew, D.H. (ed.) (2001) *The New Corporate Finance*, 3rd edn. New York: McGraw Hill Irwin.

Childs, P.D., Ott, S.M. and Triantis, A.J. (1998) 'Capital Budgeting for Interrelated Projects: A Real Options Approach', *Journal of Financial and Quantitative Analysis*, 33(3), pp. 305–34.

Chi-Hsiou Hung, D., M. Shackleton and X. Xu (2004) 'CAPM, higher co-movement and factor models of UK stock returns', *Journal of Business Finance and Accounting*, 31(1) & (2), January/March, pp. 87–112.

Cochrane, J.H. (2001) *Asset Pricing*. Princeton, NJ, and Oxford: Princeton University Press.

Cooper, I. and Kaplanis, E. (1994) 'Home bias in equity portfolios, inflation hedging and international capital market equilibrium', *Review of Financial Studies*, 7(1), pp. 45–60.

Copeland, T. and Antikarov, V. (2001) *Real Options: A Practitioner's Guide*. New York: Texere.

Copeland, T. and P. Tufano (2004) 'A real-world way to manage real options', *Harvard Business Review*, March, pp. 1–11.

Corhay, A., Hawawini, G. and Michel, P. (1987) 'Seasonality in the risk-return relationship: some international evidence', *Journal of Finance*, 42, pp. 49–68.

Corporate Finance Magazine. London: Euromoney.

Coulthurst, N.J. (1986) 'Accounting for inflation in capital investment: state of the art and science', *Accounting and Business Research*, Winter, pp. 33–42.

Coulthurst, N.J. (1986) 'The application of the incremental principle in capital investment project evaluation', *Accounting and Business Research*, Autumn.

Crossland, M., Dempsey, M. and Moizer, P. (1991) 'The effect of cum- to ex-dividend changes on UK share prices', *Accounting and Business Research*, 22(85), pp. 47–50.

Damodaran, A. (1999) *Applied Corporate Finance: A User's Manual*. New York: Wiley.

Damodaran, A. (2002) *Investment Valuation*, 2nd edn. New York: Wiley.

Davies, M. (2000) 'Lessons from Practice: VBM at Lloyds TSB', in G.C. Arnold and M. Davies (eds) *Value-Based Management*. London: Wiley.

Davies, M., Arnold, G.C., Cornelius, I. and Walmsley, S. (2001) *Managing For Shareholder Value*. London: Informa Publishing Group.

DeAngelo, H., DeAngelo, L. and Skinner, D.J. (2004) *Are dividends disappearing?*

Dhrymes, P.J., Friend, I. and Gultekim, N.B. (1984) 'A critical reexamination of the empirical evidence on the arbitrage pricing theory', *Journal of Finance*, 39, June, pp. 323–46.

Dimson, E., Marsh, P. and Staunton, M. (2001) *The Millennium Book II: 101 Years of Investment Returns*. London: London Business School and ABN Amro.

Dimson, E., Marsh, P.R. and Staunton, M. (2002) *The Triumph of the Optimists: 101 years of global investment returns*. Princeton, NJ: Princeton University Press.

Divecha, A.B., Drach, J. and Stefek, D. (1992) 'Emerging markets: a quantitative perspective', *Journal of Portfolio Management*, Fall, pp. 41–50.

Dixit, A. and Pindyck, R. (1994) *Investment Under Uncertainty*. Princeton, NJ: Princeton University Press.

Dixit, A.K. and Pindyck, R.S. (1995) 'The Options Approach to Capital Investment', *Harvard*

Business Review, May–June. (Also reproduced in J. Rutterford (ed.) *Financial Strategy*. New York: John Wiley, 1998.)

Donaldson, G. (1961) *Corporate debt policy and the determination of corporate debt capacity*. Boston: Harvard Graduate School of Business Administration.

Donaldson, G. (1963) 'Financial goals: management vs. stockholders', *Harvard Business Review*, May–June, pp. 116–29.

Doyle, P. (1994) 'Setting business objectives and measuring performance', *Journal of General Management*, Winter, pp. 1–19.

Dreman, D. (1998) *Contrarian Investment Strategies: The Next Generation*. New York: Wiley.

Easterbrook, F.H. (1984) 'Two agency-cost explanations of dividends', *American Economic Review*, Sept., 74(4) pp. 650–60.

Eiteman, D.K., Stonehill, A.I. and Moffett, M.H. (2003) *Multinational Business Finance: International Edition*, 10th edn. Reading, MA: Addison Wesley.

Elton, E.J. and Gruber, M.J. (1970) 'Marginal stockholder tax rates and the clientele effect', *Review of Economics and Statistics*, February, pp. 68–74.

Elton, E.J., Gruber, M.J., Brown, S.J. and Goetzmann, W.N. (2003) *Modern Portfolio Theory and Investment Analysis*, 6th edn. Chichester: Wiley.

Fabozzi, F.J. (2003) *Bond Markets, Analysis and Strategies*, 5th edn. Harlow: Financial Times Prentice Hall.

Fama, E.F. (1970) 'Efficient capital markets: A review of theory and empirical work', *Journal of Finance*, May, pp. 383–417.

Fama, E.F. and French, K.R. (1992) 'The cross-section of expected stock returns', *Journal of Finance*, 47, pp. 427–65.

Fama, E.F. and French, K.R. (1993) 'Common risk factors in the returns on stocks and bonds', *Journal of Financial Economics*, 33, pp. 3–56.

Fama, E.F. and French, K.R. (1995) 'Size and book-to-market factors in earnings and returns', *Journal of Finance*, 50(1), March, pp. 131–55.

Fama, E.F. and French, K.R. (1996) 'Multifactor explanations of asset pricing anomalies', *Journal of Finance*, 50(1), March, pp. 55–84.

Fama, E.F. and French, K.R. (2001) 'Disappearing dividends: changing firm characteristics or lower propensity to pay?' *Journal of Financial Economics*, 60(1), April, pp. 3–43.

Fama E.F. and French, K.R. (2002) 'The Equity Premium', *Journal of Finance*, 57(2), April, pp. 637–59.

Fama, E.F. and MacBeth, J. (1973) 'Risk, return and equilibrium: empirical test', *Journal of Political Economy*, May/June, pp. 607–36.

Fama, E.F. and Miller, M.H. (1972) *The Theory of Finance*. Orlando, FL: Holt, Rinehart & Winston.

Finance and Leasing Association (FLA) Annual Report. London: FLA.

Financial Times.

Fisher, I. (1930) *The Theory of Interest*. Reprinted in 1977 by Porcupine Press.

Francis, G. and Minchington, C. (2000) 'Value-based Metrics as Divisional Performance Measures', in G.C. Arnold and M. Davies (eds) *Value-Based Management*. London: Wiley.

Frank, M.Z. and Goyal, V.K. (2003) 'Testing the pecking order theory of capital structure', *Journal of Financial Economics*, 67, pp. 217–48.

Friedman, M. (1970) 'The social responsibility of business is to increase its profits', *New York Times Magazine*, 30 Sept.

Friend, I. and Blume, M. (1970) 'Measurement of portfolio performance under uncertainty', *American Economic Review*, September, pp. 561–75.

Friend, I., Westerfield, R. and Granito, M. (1978) 'New evidence on the Capital Asset Pricing model', *Journal of Finance*, 33, June, pp. 903–20.

Frost, P.A. and Savarino, J.E. (1986) 'Portfolio size and estimation risk', *Journal of Portfolio Management*, 12, Summer, pp. 60–4.

Fuller, R.J. and Wong, G.W. (1988) 'Traditional versus theoretical risk measures', *Financial Analysts Journal*, 44, March–April, pp. 52–7. Reproduced in S. Lofthouse (ed.), *Readings in Investment*. Chichester: Wiley (1994).

Gadella, J.W. (1992), 'Post-project appraisal', *Management Accounting*, March, pp. 52 and 58.

Galbraith, J. (1967) 'The goals of an industrial system' (excerpt from *The new industrial state*). Reproduced in H.I. Ansoff, *Business Strategy*. London: Penguin, 1969.

Gordon, M.J. (1959) 'Dividends, earnings and stock prices', *Review of Economics and Statistics*, 41, May, pp. 99–105.

Gordon, M.J. (1962) *The Investment, Financing and Valuation of the Corporation*. Homewood, IL: Irwin.

Gordon, M.J. (1963) 'Optimal investment and financing policy', *Journal of Finance*, May.

Gordon, M.J. and Shapiro, E. (1956) 'Capital equipment analysis: the required rate of profit', *Management Science*, III, pp. 102–10.

Graham, B. (1973) *The Intelligent Investor*, revised 4th edn. New York: Harper Business (reprinted 1997).

Graham, B. (2003) *The Intelligent Investor*, revised edition, updated by Jason Zweig. New York: Harper Business Essentials.

Graham, B. and Dodd, D. (1934) *Security Analysis*. New York: McGraw-Hill.

Graham, J.R. and Harvey, C.R. (2001) 'The theory and practice of corporate finance: evidence from the field', *Journal of Financial Economics*, 60(2–3), May, pp. 187–243.

'The Greenbury Report' (1995) Directors' remuneration: report of a Study Group chaired by Sir Richard Greenbury. London: Gee.

Gregory, A. and Rutterford, J. (1999) 'The cost of capital in the UK: a comparison of industry and the city'. CIMA monograph, May. Evidence on UK practice.

Grullon, G. and Michaely, R. (2002) 'Dividends, share repurchases, and the substitution hypothesis', *Journal of Finance*, 57(4), pp. 1649–84.

Gustavo, G. and M. Roni (2004) 'The information content of share repurchase programs', *Journal of Finance*, April, 59(2), pp. 651–80.

Gustavo, G., M. Roni and B. Swaminathan (2002) 'Are dividends a sign of firm maturity?' *Journal of Business*, July, 75(3), pp. 387-424.

'The Hampel Report' (1998) The Committee on Corporate Governance, Final report. London: Gee.

Hart, O.D. (1995a) *Firms, Contracts and Financial Structure*. Oxford: Clarendon Press.

Hart, O.D. (1995b) 'Corporate governance: some theory and implications', *Economic Journal*, 105, pp. 678–9.

Haugen, R.A. (2001) *Modern Investment Theory*, 5th edn. Upper Saddle River, NJ: Prentice-Hall.

Hayek, F.A. (1969) 'The corporation in a democratic society: in whose interests ought it and will it be run?' Reprinted in H.I. Ansoff, *Business Strategy*. London: Penguin, 1969.

Hertz, D.B. (1964) 'Risk analysis in capital investment', *Harvard Business Review*, January/February, pp. 95–106.

Hertz, D.B. and Thomas, H. (1984) *Practical Risk Analysis: An Approach Through Case Histories*. Chichester: Wiley.

Hickman, B.G. (1958) 'Corporate bond quality and investor experience', *National Bureau of Economic Research*, 14, Princeton.

Hicks, J.R. (1946) *Value and Capital: An Inquiry into some Fundamental Principles of Economic Theory*, 2nd edn. Oxford: Oxford University Press.

Higgs Report (2003) *Review of the Role and Effectiveness of Non-Executive Directors*, January.

Ho, S. and Pike, R.H. (1991) 'Risk analysis in capital budgeting contexts: simple or sophisticated', *Accounting and Business Research*, 21(83), Summer, pp. 227–38.

Howell, S., Stark, A., Newton, D., Paxson, D., Cavus, M. and Pereira, J. (2001) *Real Options: Evaluating Corporate Investment Opportunities in a Dynamic World*. Harlow: Financial Times Prentice Hall.

Howells, P. and Bain, K. (2004) *Financial Markets and Institutions*, 4th edn. Harlow: Financial Times Prentice Hall.

Hsia, C-C., B.R. Fuller and B.Y.J. Chen (2000) 'Is beta dead or alive?' *Journal of Business Finance and Accounting*, 27(3) & (4), April/May, pp. 283–311.

Hung, D. C-H., M. Shackleton and X. Xu (2004) 'CAPM, higher co-movement and factor models of UK stock returns', *Journal of Business Finance and Accounting*, 31(1) & (2), January/March, pp. 87–112.

Jagannathan, M., C.P. Stephens and M.S. Weisbach (2000) 'Financial flexibility and the choice between dividends and stock repurchases', *Journal of Financial Economics*, 57(3), September, pp. 355-84.

Jenkinson, T. and Ljungquist, A. (2001) *Going Public: The Theory and Evidence on How Companies Raise Equity Finance*, 2nd edn. Oxford: Clarendon.

Jensen, M.C. (1986) 'Agency costs of free cash flow, corporate finance and takeovers', *American Economic Review*, 76, pp. 323–9.

Jensen, M.C. (1989) 'Eclipse of the public corporation', *Harvard Business Review*, September–October, pp. 61–74.

Jensen, M.C. (2001) 'Value Maximisation, Stakeholder Theory, and the Corporate Objective Function', *Journal of Applied Corporate Finance*, 14(3), Fall.

Jensen, M.C. and Meckling, W.H. (1976) 'Theory of the firm: managerial behavior, agency costs and ownership structure', *Journal of Financial Economics*, 3, Oct., pp. 305–60.

Jorion, P. (1992) 'Portfolio optimisation in practice', *Financial Analysts Journal*, 48, January/February, pp. 68–74.

Julio, B., and D.L. Ikenberry (2004) 'Reappearing dividends', *Journal of Applied Corporate Finance*, 16(4), Fall, pp. 89–100.

Kaplan, R. and Norton, D.P. (1996) *The Balanced Scorecard*. Boston, MA: Harvard Business School Press.

Kaplanis, E. and Schaefer, S. (1991) 'Exchange risk and international diversification in bond and equity portfolios', *Journal of Economics and Business*, 43, pp. 287–307.

Kay, J. (2004) 'Forget how the crow flies', *Financial Times Magazine*, 17–18 January, pp. 17–21.

Keane, S. (1974) 'Dividends and the resolution of uncertainty', *Journal of Business Finance and Accountancy*, Autumn.

Korajeczyk, R.A. and Levy, A. (2003) 'Capital structure choice: macroeconomic conditions and financial constraints', *Journal of Financial Economics*, 68, pp. 75–109.

Lakonishok, J. and Shapiro, A.C. (1984) 'Stock returns, beta, variance and size: an empirical analysis', *Financial Analysts Journal*, 40, July–August, pp. 36–41.

Lakonishok, J. and Shapiro, A.C. (1986) 'Systematic risk, total risk and size as determinants of stock market returns', *Journal of Banking and Finance*, 10, pp. 115–32.

Levinson, M. (2002) *Guide to Financial Markets*, 3rd edn. London: The Economist Books.

Levy, H. (1978) 'Equilibrium in an imperfect market: a constraint on the number of securities in the portfolio', *American Economic Review*, September, pp. 643–58.

Levy, R.A. (1971) 'On the short-term stationarity of beta coefficients', *Financial Analysts Journal*, Nov–Dec, pp. 55–62.

Lewellen, W.G., Stanley, K.L., Lease, R.C. and Schlarbaum, G.G. (1978) 'Some direct evidence of the dividend clientele phenomenon', *Journal of Finance*, December, pp. 1385–99.

Lewis, K. (1996) 'Consumption, stock returns, and the gains from international risk-sharing', *NBER Working Paper*, No. 5410, January.

Lintner, J. (1956) 'Distribution of income of corporations among dividends, retained earnings and taxes', *American Economic Review*, 46, May, pp. 97–113.

Lintner, J. (1965) 'The valuation of risky assets and the selection of risky investments in stock portfolios and capital budgets', *Review of Economics and Statistics*, 47, February, pp. 13–37.

Litzenberger, R. and Ramaswamy, K. (1982) 'The effects of dividends on common stock prices: tax effects or information effects?' *Journal of Finance*, May, pp. 429–43.

Lockett, M. (2001) 'Calculating the Cost of Capital for the Regulated Electricity Distribution Companies', Aston University MBA Project.

Lockett, M. (2002) 'Calculating the cost of capital for the regulated electricity distribution companies', *Power Engineering Journal*, October, pp. 251–63.

Lofthouse, S. (2001) *Investment Management*, 2nd edn. Chichester: Wiley.

London, S. (2003) 'The Long View: Lunch with the FT, Milton Friedman', *Financial Times Magazine*, 7–8 June, pp. 12–13.

London Stock Exchange (2004) *A Practical Guide to Listing on the London Stock Exchange*.

Lowe, J. (1997) *Warren Buffett Speaks*. New York: Wiley.

Lowenstein, L. (1991) *Sense and Nonsense in Corporate Finance*. Reading, MA: Addison Wesley.

Lundholm, R. and Sloan, R. (2004) *Equity Valuation and Analysis*. New York: Irwin McGraw Hill.

Luehrman, T.A. (1998a) 'Investment opportunities as real options: getting started on the numbers', *Harvard Business Review*, July–August, pp. 3–15.

Luehrman, T.A. (1998b) 'Strategy as a portfolio of real options', *Harvard Business Review*, September–October, pp. 89–99.

Lutz, F.A. and Lutz, V.C. (1951) *The Theory of Investment in the Firm*. Princeton, NJ: Princeton University Press.

Macqueen, J. (1986) 'Beta is dead! Long live Beta!' in J.M. Stern and D.H. Chen (eds), *The Revolution in Corporate Finance*. Oxford: Basil Blackwell.

Malkiel, B.G. (1999) *A Random Walk Down Wall Street*. New York: W.W. Norton & Co.

Markowitz, H.M. (1952) 'Portfolio selection', *Journal of Finance*, 7, pp. 77–91.

Markowitz, H.M. (1959) *Portfolio Selection: Efficient Diversification of Investments*. New York: Wiley (1991); 2nd edn. Cambridge, MA: Basil Blackwell.

Markowitz, H.M. (1991) 'Foundations of portfolio theory', *Journal of Finance*, June.

Marsh, P. (1982) 'The choice between equity and debt: An empirical study', *Journal of Finance*, 37, March, pp. 121–44.

McIntyre, A.D. and Coulthurst, N.J. (1986) *Capital Budgeting Practices in Medium-Sized Businesses – A Survey*. London: Institute of Cost and Management Accountants.

McKinsey: T. Koller, M. Goedhart, D. Wessels (2005) *Valuation: Measuring and managing the value of companies*, University Edition, 4th edn. J. Wiley and Sons.

McLaney, E., J. Pointon, M. Thomas and J. Tucker (2004) 'Practitioners' perspectives on the UK cost of capital', *The European Journal of Finance*, 10, April, pp. 123–38.

McTaggart, J.M., Kontes, P.W. and Mankins, M.C. (1994) *The Value Imperative*. New York: Free Press.

Mehra, R. (2003) 'The equity premium puzzle?' NBER Working Paper. Available at www.nber.org/papers/w9512.

Mehra, R. and Prescott, E.C. (1985) 'The equity premium: A puzzle', *Journal of Monetary Economics*, 15, pp. 145–161.

Merton, R.C. (1998) 'Application of Option-Pricing Theory: Twenty-Five Years Later', *American Economic Review*, June, No. 3, pp. 323–49.

Merton, R.C. (2005) 'You have more capital than you think', *Harvard Business Review*, November, pp. 1–10.

Michaud, R.O. (1989) 'The Markowitz optimization enigma: Is "optimized" optimal?' *Financial Analysts Journal*, 45, January–February, pp. 31–42.

Michaud, R.O., Bergstorm, G.L., Frashure, R.D. and Wolahan, B.K. (1996) 'Twenty years of international equity investment', *Journal of Portfolio Management*, Fall, pp. 9–22.

Miles, D. and Timmermann, A. (1996) 'Variations in expected stock returns: evidence on the pricing of equities from a cross-section of UK companies', *Economica*, 63, pp. 369–82.

Miller, M.H. (1977) 'Debt and taxes', *Journal of Finance*, 32, May, pp. 261–75.

Miller, M.H. (1988) 'The Modigliani–Miller propositions after thirty years', *Journal of Economic Perspectives*, (Fall). Also reproduced in D.H. Chew (ed.) (2001) *The New Corporate Finance*. New York: McGraw-Hill. 3rd edn.

Miller, M.H. (1991) 'Leverage', *Journal of Finance*, 46, pp. 479–88.

Miller, M.H. and Modigliani, F. (1961) 'Dividend policy, growth and the valuation of shares', *Journal of Business*, 34, October, pp. 411–33.

Modigliani, F. and Miller, M.H. (1958) 'The cost of capital, corporation finance and the theory of investment', *American Economic Review*, 48, June, pp. 261–97.

Modigliani, F. and Miller, M.H. (1963) 'Corporate income taxes and the cost of capital: A correction', *American Economic Review*, 53, June, pp. 433–43.

Modigliani, F. and Miller, M.H. (1969) 'Reply to Heins and Sprenkle', *American Economic Review*, 59, September, pp. 592–5.

Moel, A. and Tufano, P. (2002) 'When Are Real Options Exercised? An Empirical Study of Mine Closings', *The Review of Financial Studies*, Spring, 15(1), pp. 35–64.

Montier, J. (2002) *Behavioural Finance: Insights into irrational minds and markets*. London: J. Wiley.

Mossin, J. (1966) 'Equilibrium in a capital asset market', *Econometrica*, 34, October, pp. 768–83.

Mougoué, M. and Rao, R.P. (2003) 'The information signalling hypothesis of dividends: Evidence from cointegration and causality tests', *Journal of Business Finance and Accounting*, 30(3) and (4), April/May, pp. 441–78.

Myers, S.C. (1984) 'The capital structure puzzle', *Journal of Finance*, 39, July, pp. 575–82.

Myers, S.C. (1996) 'Fischer Black's contributions to corporate finance', *Financial Management*, 25(4), Winter, pp. 95–103.

Myers, S.C. (2001) 'Capital Structure', *Journal of Economic Perspectives*, 15(2), Spring, pp. 81–102.

Myers, S. and Majluf, N. (1984). 'Corporate financing and investment decisions when firms have information investors do not have', *Journal of Financial Economics*, June, pp. 187–221.

Nissim, D. and Ziv, A. (2001) 'Dividend changes and future profitability', *Journal of Finance*, 56(6), pp. 2111–33.

Office for National Statistics (2004) *Share Ownership: A report on ownership of shares as at 31st December 2003*. Norwich: HMSO.

Ogier, T., Rugman, J. and Spicer, L. (2004) *The real cost of capital*. London: FT Prentice Hall.

Outram, R. (1997) 'For what it's worth', *Management Today*, May, pp. 70–1.

Passov, R. (2003) 'How much cash does your company need?' *Harvard Business Review*, November, pp. 1–9.

Pettit, R.R. (1977) 'Taxes, transaction costs and clientele effects of dividends', *Journal of Financial Economics*, December.

Pike, R.H. (1982) *Capital Budgeting in the 1980s*. London: Chartered Institute of Management Accountants.

Pike, R.H. (1983) 'A review of recent trends in formal capital budgeting processes', *Accounting and Business Research*, Summer, pp. 201–8.

Pike, R.H. (1983) 'The capital budgeting behaviour and corporate characteristics of capital-constrained firms', *Journal of Business Finance and Accounting*, 10(4), Winter, pp. 663–71.

Pike, R.H. (1985) 'Owner-manager conflict and the role of payback', *Accounting and Business Research*, Winter, pp. 47–51.

Pike, R.H. (1988) 'An empirical study of the adoption of sophisticated capital budgeting practices and decision-making effectiveness', *Accounting and Business Research*, 18(72), Autumn, pp. 341–51.

Pike, R.H. (1996) 'A longitudinal survey of capital budgeting practices', *Journal of Business Finance and Accounting*, 23(1), January.

Pike, R.H. and Wolfe, M. (1988) *Capital Budgeting in the 1990s*. London: Chartered Institute of Management Accountants.

Quigg, L. (1993) 'Empirical testing of Real Option Pricing Models', *Journal of Finance*, 48(2), pp. 621–40.

Rappaport, A. (1998) *Creating Shareholder Value*. (Revised and updated version.) New York: Free Press.

Reinganum, M.R. (1982) 'A direct test of Roll's conjecture on the firm size effect', *Journal of Finance*, 37, pp. 27–35.

Roberts, R. (2004) *The City: A Guide to London's Global Financial Centre*. London: The Economist Newspaper/Profile books.

Roberts, M.J. and L. Barley (2004) 'How venture capitalists evaluate potential venture opportunities', *Harvard Business Review*, December, pp. 1–19.

Roll, R. (1977) A critique of the Asset Pricing Theory's tests: Part 1: On past and potential testability of the theory, *Journal of Financial Economics*, 4, March, p. 126–76.

Roll, R. and Ross, S.A. (1980) 'An empirical investigation of the Arbitrage Pricing Theory', *Journal of Finance*, 35, December, pp. 1073–103.

Rosenberg, B. and Rudd, A. (1986) The Corporate Uses of Beta' in J.M. Stern and D.H. Chew (eds) *The Revolution in Corporate Finance*. Oxford: Blackwell.

Ross, S.A. (1974) 'Return, risk and arbitrage', in I. Friend and J.L. Bicksler (eds), *Risk and Return in Finance*. New York: Heath Lexington.

Ross, S.A. (1976) 'The arbitrage theory of capital asset pricing', *Journal of Economic Theory*, 13, December, pp. 341–60.

Ross, S.A. (1977) 'The determination of financial structure: The incentive-signalling approach', *Bell Journal of Economics*, 8, pp. 23–40.

Ross, S.A., Westerfield, R.W. and Jaffe, J. (2002) *Corporate Finance*, 6th edn. New York: McGraw-Hill.

Rouwenhorst, K.G. (1999) 'Local return factors and turnover in emerging stock markets', *Journal of Finance*, 54, August, pp. 1439–64.

Rouwenhorst, K.G., Heston, S. and Wessels, R.E. (1999) 'The role of beta and size in the cross-section of European stock returns', *European Financial Management*, 4.

Rozeff, M. (1986) 'How companies set their dividend payout ratios'. Reprinted in J.M. Stern and D.H. Chew (eds) *The Revolution in Corporate Finance*. Oxford: Basil Blackwell.

Rutterford, J. (2000) 'The cost of capital and shareholder value', in G.C. Arnold and M. Davies (eds) *Value-Based Management*. London: Wiley.

Sangster, A. (1993) 'Capital investment appraisal techniques: a survey of current usage', *Journal of Business Finance and Accounting*, 20(3), April, pp. 307–33.

Schwartz, E.S. and Trigeorgis, L. (eds) (2001) *Real Options and Investment Under Uncertainty: Classical Readings and Recent Contributions*. Cambridge, MA and London: MIT Press.

Sharpe, W.F. (1963) 'A simplified model for portfolio analysis', *Management Science*, 9, pp. 277–93.

Sharpe, W.F. (1964) 'Capital asset prices: a theory of market equilibrium under conditions of risk', *Journal of Finance*, 19, Sept., pp. 425–42.

Sharpe, W.F., Alexander, G.J. and Bailey, J.V. (1999) *Investments*, 6th edn. Upper Saddle River, NJ: Prentice-Hall.

Shefrin, H. (2000) *Beyond Greed and Fear*. Boston, MA: Harvard Business School Press.

Shefrin, H.M. and Statman, M. (1984) 'Explaining investor preference for cash dividends', *Journal of Financial Economics*, 13, pp. 253–82.

Shiller, R.J. (2000) *Irrational Exuberance*. Princeton, NJ: Princeton University Press.

Shleifer, A. (2000) *Inefficient Markets: An Introduction to Behavioural Finance*. Oxford: Oxford University Press.

Shyam-Sunder, L. and Myers, S.C. (1999) 'Testing static trade off against pecking order models of capital structure', *Journal of Financial Economics*, 51, pp. 219–44.

Simon, H.A. (1959) 'Theories of decision making in economics and behavioural science', *American Economic Review*, June.

Smith, A. (1776) *The Wealth of Nations*. Reproduced in 1910 in two volumes by J.M. Dent, London.

Solnik, B.H. (1974) 'Why not diversify internationally rather than domestically?' *Financial Analysts Journal*, July–August, pp. 48–54.

Solnik, B.H. and McLeavey, D. (2003) *International Investments*, 5th edn. Boston, MA: Pearson Education.

Solomon, E. (1963) *The Theory of Financial Management*. New York: Columbia University Press.

Spiedell, L.S. and Sappenfield, R. (1992) 'Global diversification in a shrinking world', *Journal of Portfolio Management*, Fall, pp. 57–67.

Stern, J. (1998) 'The capital structure puzzle', *Journal of Applied Corporate Finance*, II(I), Spring, pp. 8–23.

Stern, J.M., Stewart, G.B. and Chew, D.H. (2001) 'The EVA® Financial Management System', in Chew, D.H. (ed.) *The New Corporate Finance*. New York: McGraw-Hill/Irwin.

Stern Stewart's website provides some additional literature: www/sternstewart.com.

Stewart, G.B. (1990) *The Quest for Value*, New York: Harper Business.

Stewart, G.B. (2001) 'Market Myths', in *The New Corporate Finance*, 3rd edn. Edited by Donald H. Chew. New York: McGraw-Hill/Irwin.

Strong, N. and Xu, X.G. (1997) 'Explaining the cross-section of UK expected stock returns', *British Accounting Review*, 29(1), pp. 1–23.

Thaler, R. (ed.) (1993) *Advances in Behavioral Finance*. New York: Russell Sage Foundation.

Thaler R. (ed.) (2005) *Advances in Behavioral Finance*, Vol. II, Princeton University Press.

Tobin, J. (1958) 'Liquidity preference as behaviour toward risk', *Review of Economic Studies*, February, 26, pp. 65–86.

The Treasurer (a monthly journal). London: Euromoney.

The Treasurers Handbook. London: Association of Corporate Treasurers.

Treynor, J. (1965) 'How to rate management of investment funds', *Harvard Business Review*, Jan–Feb.

Triantis, A.J. and Barisan, A. (2001) 'Real Options: State of the Practice', *Journal of Applied Corporate Finance*, 14, Summer, pp. 8–24.

Triantis, A.J. and Hodder, J.E. (1990) 'Valuing Flexibility as a Complex Option', *Journal of Finance*, 45, pp. 545–66.

Trigeorgis, L. (1996) *Real Options: Managerial Flexibility and Strategy in Resource Allocation*. Cambridge, MA: MIT Press.

Vaitilingam, R. (2001) *The Financial Times Guide to Using the Financial Pages*, 4th edn. London: FT Prentice Hall.

Valdez, S. and Wood, J. (2003) *An Introduction to Global Financial Markets*, 4th edn. Basingstoke: Palgrave Macmillan.

Van Putten, A.B. and I.C. MacMillan (2004) 'Making real options really work', *Harvard Business Review*, December, pp. 1–7.

Wagner, W.H. and Lau, S. (1971) 'The effects of diversification on risk', *Financial Analysts Journal*, November–December.

Watson, R. and Wilson, N. (2002) 'Small and medium size enterprise financing: A note of some empirical implications of a pecking order', *Journal of Business Finance and Accounting*, 29(3) and (4), April/May, pp. 557–78.

Westwick, C.A. and Shohet, P.S.D. (1976) 'Investment Appraisal and Inflation', ICAEW Research Committee, Occasional Paper, No. 7.

Williamson, O. (1963) 'Managerial discretion and business behaviour', *American Economic Review*, 53, pp. 1033–57.

Young, D.S. and O'Byrne, S.F. (2001) *EVA and value-based management: a practical guide to implementation*. New York: McGraw-Hill.

Zider, B. (1998) 'How venture capital works', *Harvard Business Review*, November–December, pp. 131–9.

Index